COHANE, Tim. Great college football coaches of the twenties and
    thirties. Arlington House, 1973. 329p il tab 73-7543. 11.95.
    ISBN 0-87000-152-3.   C.I.P.
This outstanding book portrays the lives of 43 coaching greats of the
1920s and '30s. It is complete with 325 oversized pages, over 100 photo-
graphs, and an index with approximately 1,500 entries. Cohane, one
of the country's great football writers and now a university professor
of journalism, captures the golden years when college football was the
country's number-one attraction and gives a biographical profile of
each great coach of that era. The reader will find this an abounding
source of hard-to-find facts; game-by-game records of the 43 coaches
and many significant records of all the other coaching notables of the
period. He will also meet the great players of yesterday and see them
from a different perspective — through the eyes of the coaches who
made them great. This is the first book of its kind to be published and
is very readable. Highly recommended for all libraries, public or
academic.

GREAT COLLEGE FOOTBALL COACHES OF THE TWENTIES AND THIRTIES

Tim Cohane, born in 1912 in New Haven, started his sportswriting career as Director of Sports Information at his alma mater, Fordham University, in 1935. Later he was on the sports staff of the New York *World-Telegram* and for over twenty years was Sports Editor of *Look*. A longtime friend of Grantland Rice, Mr. Cohane took over Granny's College Football Forecast when the dean of sportswriters died. Cohane subse-

quently originated the Grantland Rice Award, annually presented to the national collegiate football champion. Besides hundreds of articles for *Look* and other national periodicals, he has written four other books: *Gridiron Grenadiers, The Yale Football Story, You Have to Pay the Price* (with Earl [Red] Blaik), and *Bypaths of Glory*. Mr. Cohane is a frequent speaker at groups ranging from businessmen's organizations to varsity clubs. He is often a guest on TV and had his own show in New York. Now a professor of journalism at Boston University, Mr. Cohane lives in Brighton, Mass., with his wife Margaret. They have seven children.

Books by Tim Cohane

BYPATHS OF GLORY: A Sportswriter Looks Back
YOU HAVE TO PAY THE PRICE (with Col. Earl H. "Red" Blaik)
THE YALE FOOTBALL STORY
GRIDIRON GRENADIERS: The Story of West Point Football

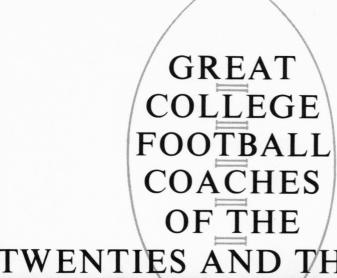

GREAT COLLEGE FOOTBALL COACHES OF THE TWENTIES AND THIRTIES

Tim Cohane

Arlington House   *New Rochelle, New York*

Library of Congress Cataloging in Publication Data

Cohane, Tim.
    Great college football coaches of the twenties and
thirties.

    1. Football coaching—History.   2. Football
coaches.   I. Title.   II. Title: College football
coaches.
GV956.6.C63   796.33'2077   73-7543
ISBN 0-87000-152-3

Manufactured in the United States of America

TO

all who have had the privilege of coaching young Americans

CONTENTS

FOREWORD

Great College Football Coaches of the Twenties and Thirties brings to colorful life not only the coaches of that era but also its outstanding teams, players, games and human interest anecdotes.

It will appeal not only to those who lived and followed football from 1920 to '40, but also to all those who cherish the history and tradition of the great collegiate game.

Nobody is better qualified to tell this story than the author. As a New York newspaper man, as sports editor of *Look* for 21 years, as author of four books and of syndicated columns, Tim Cohane has been closely identified with college football for over 35 years. He is recognized nationally as a superior craftsman and an authentic, articulate student of the game. Currently he serves as a professor of writing in Boston University's School of Public Communication, Journalism Division.

Great College Football Coaches of the Twenties and Thirties is certain to become a major addition to the bibliography of football. And coaches, players, and fans of all ages will find it fascinating reading.

BUD WILKINSON

January 1973

PREFACE

From 1920 through 1939—the Golden Twenties and the Testy Thirties—college football first began to challenge baseball as America's favorite spectator sport. Large stadia sprang up across the country. The Orange, Cotton, Sugar, and Sun Bowls, and the East-West Shriners game were instituted to join the daddy Bowl, the Rose. In-season intersectional games achieved wide popularity.

More and more people were picking All-America teams. The Heisman Trophy, to the most valuable player, came into being, as did the Coach of the Year Award. Wire services began listing the top twenty teams each week to increase national championship consciousness.

It was the day of the Warner single and double wing and the Notre Dame box formations. Teams in all areas, encouraged mainly by the Southwest, learned to use the forward pass as an integral part of offense and not as a last-ditch tactic. The East, where the game had been born and brought up, had to move over to make room for the Midwest, South, Far West, and Southwest.

Led by Grantland Rice, romanticism permeated the press boxes, and stories flashed on the wires about the Four Horsemen, the Galloping Ghost, the Seven Blocks of Granite, the Dream Backfield, and the Seven Iron Dukes.

But most of all it was the time of the colorful coaching personality—Amos Alonzo Stagg, Knute Rockne, Pop Warner, Bob Zuppke, Fielding H. Yost, Dan McGugin, and many more.

TIM COHANE

November 1972

ACKNOWLEDGMENTS

The author was aided considerably by the available books on college football in the twenties and thirties, and is especially grateful to Colonel Alexander M. Weyand and David M. Nelson for use of their personal libraries on the sport, to Allison Danzig for his monumental volume, *The History of American Football,* and to Edwin Pope for his fascinating *Football's Greatest Coaches.* The following bibliography also was researched:

The Modern Notre Dame Formation by Charles W. Bachman.

Don't Bring That Up by Bob Broeg and Bob Burrill.

Alexander of Georgia Tech by Edwin Camp.

Sports' Golden Age edited by Allison Danzig and Peter Brandwein.

Ten Top Trojan Football Thrillers by Braven Dyer.

War Eagle by James Stewart Edson.

Fifty Years of Football at Syracuse by Arthur Evans.

The Southwest Conference Record Book by Wilbur Evans and Bill Morgan.

The Fighting Tigers by Peter Finney.

Football—Greatest Moments in the Southwest Conference by Will Grimsley.

From T to T at UT by Ed Harris.

Rockne—Idol of American Football by Robert Harron.

Athletics at Boston College by Nat Hasenfus.

The Football Thesaurus by Deke Houlgate.

How to Coach and Play Football by Howard Jones.

The American Sporting Scene by John Kieran.

75 Years with the Fighting Hawkeyes by Dick Lamb and Bert McGrane.

It Was a Different Game by Elmer Layden with Ed Snyder.

The Color of Life Is Red by Don Liebendorfer.

The Wearers of the 'T' by Tom Little.

A Hand in Sport by Willard Mullin and Dave Camerer.

Going Back by Arch Murray.

College Football—All-Time Galaxy—National Collegiate Sports Services.

College Football—All-Time Record Book—National Collegiate Sports Services.

The Impact of Southern Football by Zipp Newman.

The Power and the Glory by Harold W. Ratliff.

The Tumult and the Shouting by Grantland Rice.

The Big Nine by Howard Roberts.

Football, Today and Tomorrow by Bill Roper.

Bury Me in an Old Press Box by Fred Russell.

The Golden Hurricane by Robert Rutland.

The Rose Bowl Game by Rube Samuelson.

Famous Football Players by Robert H. Shoemaker.

Tennessee—Football's Greatest Dynasty by Tom Siler.

Pittsburgh and Western Pennsylvania Sports and Hall of Fame by Chet Smith.

Coach Tommy of the Crimson Tide by Naylor Stone.

Knute Rockne—Man Builder by Harry Stuhldreher.

Football—Texas Style by Kern Tips.

College Football and All-America Review by Christy Walsh.

Football Immortals by Alexander M. Weyand.

The Big Ten by Kenneth L. (Tug) Wilson and Jerry Brondfield.

Paper Tiger by Stanley Woodward.

The Second 'H' Book of Harvard Athletics.

I also wish to thank for their assistance William D. Barfield, Jay Barry, Dr. R. H. Baxter, Joe Bedenk, Josh Billings, Eugene Carson Blake, Judge Amos Blandin, Hod Blaney, Dr. A. F. Brandstatter, Bob Broeg, Royal Brougham, Don Bryant, Asa Bushnell, Jim Butler, Robert Calihan, Frank Carver, Nola Cattabriga, Dan Caulkins, Michael Cohen, Jeff Coleman, Tony Constantine, Hal Cowan, Dick Cullum.

Also Joe Davis, Jack DeGange, Ted Drews, Tippy Dye, Braven Dyer, Wilbur Evans, Forest Evashevski, Til Ferdenzi, Jim Flynn, William Flynn, Dick Friendlich, Karey Fuqua, Jim Garner, Frank Garrity, Jerry Gentzen, Max Gerber, Mike Gonring, Dr. John A. Hannah, Bob Hartley, Bill Hartman, Mel Hein, Dean Hill, Jr., Marian E. Hines, Dan Hinman, Stuart Hockenbury, Al Horwits, Frank Howard, Dick Hyland.

Also Robert Jackson, Nordy Jensen, Bob Johnson, Charlie Johnson, Lester Jordan, Charlie Justice, Hugh Kahler, Charles E. Kaufman, Harold Keith, Johnny Keith, Vic Kelley, Larry Kimball, Mary Jo Lauchle, Lester Lautenschlaeger, Richard Lewis, Donald Lourie, Dave Lucey, Ben Lusk, Hubert McDonough, Jimmie McDowell, H. B. McElroy, Bob McFarland, John P. McGowan, Mike McLure, Ed McMillan, Kirk McNair, Paul Manasseh, Bob Millie, Bishop Jeremiah Minihan, Ben Mintz, John Morris, Paul Morrison, Bill Morton, Bob Murphy, E. E. Myers, Frank L. Myers.

Also Dick Nash, Robert Noble, Hugh Ortman, Frank Patrick, Walter Paulison, Jimmy Peacock, Will Perry, Joseph Prendergast, David Price, Bruce Ramey, Col. Red Reeder, Jack Riley, Gene Rose, Seymour Rothman, Fred Russell, Frank E. Rutan, Jr., Al Santoro, Bill Schroeder, Rea Schuessler, Paul Severin, Ken Smith, Fred Stabley, Gene Stauber, Naylor Stone, George Strickler, Bill Stryker.

Also Ken Tilley, Mike Tranghesi, John Troan, Roger Valdiserri, Jac Weller, Al Wesson, Ned West, Dave Wohlhueter, W. H. Yeckley, Steve Zaks, Paul Zimmerman, Dr. Howard C. Zindel.

I'm also indebted to Mrs. Frances Bostick, Mrs. Ellen Russell, and Mrs. Al Smith, for their help in typing the manuscript, and to my wife, Margaret, for her help on the appendices.

GREAT
COLLEGE
FOOTBALL
COACHES
OF THE
TWENTIES AND THIRTIES

Bill Alexander

THE BATTLEMENTS WHITE AND GOLD

For stark dramatic madness nothing in the twenties, the thirties, or any other decade of football has matched it. The setting was the Rose Bowl on New Year's Day, 1929, the second quarter, the score Georgia Tech and California 0–0, the ball in Tech's possession on its 23-yard line near the sideline. Now let Frank Waddey, Georgia Tech end, a principal in the crazy play, tell what happened:

"We had a play that faked toward the sideline and came back with Stumpy Thomason carrying. He fumbled the ball and Roy Riegels, California center, grabbed it while it was still in the air. It had been my business to block Benny Lom, Cal halfback, but now it was his business to block me.

"Riegels took two steps in the right direction, toward our goal, but I was bearing down on him, so he turned, lost his sense of direction, and took off for his own goal. Lom was caught short, and we both set off after the ball carrier.

"We ran like a team, with me one stride behind Lom, who finally caught Riegels at the 1. He grabbed Riegels by the right shoulder with his left hand and spun him around. Then I hit him high and spilled him in the end zone, where he lost the ball and we recovered. I've never been able to understand why we didn't get a touchdown, but they gave the ball to Cal on the 1."

On the next play, Lom tried to punt out of the end zone and Vance Maree, Tech's star tackle, blocked the kick for a safety and two points. The two points proved decisive as Tech won the game, 8–7. Roy Riegels was henceforth known as Roy (Wrong Way) Riegels, but the identification enhanced rather than impeded him through life.

But back to those seconds of delirium. Ninety thousand had witnessed them. One of the few calm people, perhaps the calmest person, in the Bowl was the Georgia Tech coach, William Anderson Alexander.

"Sit down, sit down," Alex counseled his excited players. "He's just running the wrong way. Every step he takes is to our advantage."

Not that Alex was always calm. In fact, if you didn't know him, you might be inclined at times to write him off as a kind of grumpy boor. Bobby Dodd, who succeeded him, first as head coach, later as athletic director, says of him:

"Alex could growl and snap and carry on something awful. He would chase a visiting photographer off the field. Then he'd try to get a local photographer to help out the fellow he chased. When it came down to an emergency, he was your guy.

"He engineered the purchase of the house I've lived in for over 20 years—a neat financial deal, if

Bill Alexander of Georgia Tech

there ever was one. And he did the same for our Negro trainer, Porto Rico. The Old Man was a clearinghouse for every personal matter for every player, coach, or employee of the Tech athletic department, from toothaches to funerals to household quarrels.

"He had the football know-how of Knute Rockne, the sense of humor and storytelling ability of Mark Twain, the storehouse of miscellaneous information of a John Kieran or Oscar Levant, and the sympathetic understanding of Dorothy Dix."

The tactical know-how and applied psychology that Alex had on call was emphasized in Tech's victory over Alabama en route to the Rose Bowl in 1928. At halftime, Tech was lucky to have a 13–13 tie. Both of its touchdowns came after breaks, while the Crimson Tidemen had earned theirs through the effectiveness on spinner plays of a little halfback named Monk Campbell, mixed with plunges by fullback Tony Holm.

Alex felt that the situation traced ultimately to some swollen heads, and at halftime in the dressing room he gave them the worst dressing down any of them had ever undergone. And he did it, as usual, without profanity. After he had called them false alarms and everything worse he could think of, he turned to the blackboard and thundered, "If anything can penetrate your thick skulls, look at this." Then he diagramed Campbell's spinner play and showed how it could be defensed.

The pace of the game was sustained in the third period, but nobody scored. In the final quarter, Tech quarterback Ron Durant finally got his attack going. Thomason scored twice behind crisp blocking, and Durant returned an interception 75 yards for another. To be beaten 33–13 was a new experience for an Alabama team coached by Wallace Wade.

Most of Bill Alexander's big coaching years came from 1920 through '28 and from 1939 through '44. In the ten years from 1929 through '38, his record was 36–55–8, and included only one winning season, 6–3–1 in '37. Except for Lou Little at Columbia, nobody has been able to survive negative scoreboards that long.

But Alex, from childhood, had been conditioned to sustained adversity. He was born in Mud River, Kentucky, June 6, 1889. Mud River, which you'll not find on any map, had its short day, a few mountainside farms near a coal mine. Penrod, nearest railroad station, was ten miles away.

Alex's father, Luther Alexander, son of a Presbyterian minister, met his bride, the beautiful Gertrude Anderson, at Sunday school, and they planned to go to China as missionaries. But Luther agreed to help his father-in-law manage the Mud River coal mine, in which he'd invested most of his capital. They had two children, William and Elizabeth.

Adversity struck the family with one punch after another. Their home was burned to the ground, all their belongings lost. The mine had to be abandoned. And Luther Alexander died of a lung ailment when Bill was only six. But the mother, who had been well educated, became a successful teacher, first at Peabody College in Macon, and then at Cox College, part of the State Normal School in Athens.

Young Bill had wanted to be a doctor, but rejected it because of the expense of four years of college and four more of medical school. Since his high school background was lacking, he had to enter Georgia Tech in 1906 as an apprentice student, and it took him six years to graduate, 1912, with a Bachelor of Science Degree in engineering.

It is ironic that Alex should have become both an instructor of mathematics after his graduation and, later in France, as a young officer, an instructor in the mathematics of field artillery. For it took him the second time around at Tech to get passing grades in algebra, trigonometry, calculus, and physics.

If his academic career was filled with roadblocks, so was his athletic experience. He was one of the lowliest of scrubs, putting himself on the chopping block but always coming back. In 1908, at the suggestion of L. R. (Chip) Roberts, captain of the team, John Heisman, the Georgia Tech coach, appointed Alex captain of the scrubs, a position he held for four seasons, 1908 through '11. In 1911, he got in the Georgia and Clemson games long enough to win a letter.

John Heisman, whose name lives on the trophy presented to the outstanding back or end in intercollegiate football each year, was a restless soul, who in the off-season played the heavy role in touring stock companies. His performances as a villain evoked mainly amusement. Although he had delivered several outstanding seasons at Tech, including the undefeated 1917 Golden Tornado team, he left to become coach at his alma mater, Pennsylvania. After some debate the Tech job was turned over to the young returning graduate, Bill Alexander.

Presiding over a practice session

Thirty years later Alex could survey many tangible evidences of his sure stewardship. Grant Field, which had held only a few thousand, had become a concrete horseshoe accommodating 40,000. Tech had built up the best intersectional rivalries of any Southern school. There were also the Naval Armory, the gymnasium, the swimming pool, Rose Bowl Field (used for practice), tennis courts, a new baseball field, and new athletic offices.

It was not until the middle of his fifth season, the fifth game of 1924, that a Tech team coached by Alex lost to a Southern school, to Alabama, 14–0. Through his friendship with Rockne, he arranged a series with Notre Dame that is still alive today and was unbroken from 1922 through '29.

"They will beat us nine times out of ten," Alex reasoned, "but in losing we will learn a lot of football. We will gain a lot of prestige nationally. And when we win, it will be a mighty sweet victory. It means something to beat Notre Dame."

He was right on all counts, including the wins and losses. Of the first eight games, Tech won only in 1928, 13–0.

Alex's first Tech team, 1920, lost only to Pittsburgh, 10–3; 1921 lost only to Penn State, 28–7; and 1922 only to Navy, 13–0, and Notre Dame, 13–3, back to back.

One of Tech's big victories came in 1920 against Centre College's Praying Colonels and their celebrated quarterback, Alvin (Bo) McMillin. Mike Thompson, the well-known referee, who worked the game, told about it eleven years later.

The day before the game, Thompson noted dozens of flashily dressed strangers around the hotel lobby. The Chicago "Black Sox" scandal in the 1919 World Series with the Cincinnati Reds had left a cloud over all sports. Thompson knew that a $10,000 bribe wouldn't be much to a gambler who might have $100,000 bet on a game.

That night at a dinner he met a grand-jury foreman and apprised him of the situation. As a result the foreman investigated the strangers, found out they were New York mobsters, and had them placed under surveillance.

Two of Tech's most famous backs, Bucky Flowers and Red Barron, proved too much for Centre. Flowers kicked a 35-yard field goal, Barron scored on a 55-yard run from scrimmage, and Frank Ferst tallied on a 55-yard return of an interception. Judy Harlan scored another touchdown and the final was 24–0.

In 1927, Tech enjoyed an 8–1–1 season and a victory over previously undefeated Georgia, 12–0, that probably cost the Bulldogs a trip to the Rose Bowl. Two sophomore backs gave Alex much hope going into '27: Jack (Stumpy) Thomason, who succeeded Red Barron as a breakaway runner, and Warner Mizell, who could run, pass, and kick.

The Jackets won their first four games, including a 13–0 victory over Alabama, before suffering their only loss, to Notre Dame, 26–7. Ahead lay five games: Vanderbilt, Louisiana State, Oglethorpe, Auburn, and Georgia.

After the defeat by Notre Dame, with the season half over, Alexander made a decision probably unique in coaching annals. But he did not announce it until the Monday after the 0–0 tie at Vanderbilt. Then he took a piece of paper out of his pocket and announced what became known as The Plan:

"These men will report to me on the field: Crowley and Waddey; Drennon and Martin; Pund and Durant; Mizell and Thomason; Read and Randolph; Speer and Watkins. These twelve men will be the team that will play Georgia on December 3."

Alex then read off eighteen other names and said: "These men will make up the team that will play LSU, Oglethorpe, and Auburn. They will

report to Coach Fincher. He will be in full charge of them. This team will win these three games. It is capable of doing so. It will do so.

"The rest of the squad will make up a team which we will call 'Georgia.' They will report to Coach Don Miller. Coach Miller, as you all know, was one of the Four Horsemen. He knows every play Notre Dame has used for seven years.

"Georgia employs the Rockne system. Coach Miller has scouted every game Georgia has played. He knows every play Georgia has used. Coach Clay has also scouted Georgia, and we know as much as anyone knows about their offense and defense, their personnel, the thinking of their coaches and their quarterbacks. We will continue to scout them in every game from now on.

"Coach Miller will teach his team Georgia's offense and defense. He will call the plays for his team and my team will scrimmage against his team for the next four weeks. Our attention will not be diverted to the other games. They are the business of Coach Fincher's team.

"Coach Miller's team will not be as good as Georgia, and its plays won't go as well. But my team will learn what to expect, and it will learn to run its plays correctly against Georgia's defense. This plan will be carried out. It cannot fail. Everybody out."

The Plan proceeded in detail and on schedule. Then the day before the game it began to rain. By kickoff time, Grant Field resembled an antediluvian marsh.

"Now about this mud ... ," said Alex. "The better team will win in the mud but not by as wide a margin as on a dry field. You are the better team."

Georgia had won all nine of its games, had scored 248 points to 26, and had been pressed only by Yale, 14–10, Yale's only defeat. Victories included a 20–6 win over Alabama the week before.

Georgia took the opening kickoff and drove down to Tech's 8-yard line. There the Bulldogs tried a screen pass over the line, but Joe Westbrook, who had been moved up to guard and had been schooled against just such a pass, batted it down and fell on his nose trying to intercept it. On fourth down and needing a yard for first down, Herdis McCrary, the powerful, quick fullback, was thrown back by Drennon and most of the Tech line.

An unexpected pass from Mizell to Durant, slowest of Tech's backs, caught Georgia napping for one touchdown, and Thomason's 50-yard run set up another. The final was 12–0. The Plan had worked, indeed.

Although Tech knew lean years between 1929 and '38, there never were many calls to replace Alex, and those that rose didn't get very far. Most Tech fans agreed with Rockne's appraisal that Alex got more out of a little than any other coach he knew.

Alex's prestige was so high in 1930 that he was offered the job at Alabama, to replace Wallace Wade, who was going to Duke. At Alabama, he would have received twice what Tech was paying him and would have had more material.

"I wouldn't consider the offer," he said. "I'm not sure I would be a good coach at Alabama. . . . Come to think of it, I'm not sure I'm a good coach here. We lost six games last fall, and won only three. That's a comedown from the Rose Bowl, and it looks as though it might be as bad this fall."

He was right. In 1930 the Jackets finished 2–6–1. The 55–7 loss to Florida was the worst defeat for Tech since the 73–0 affair with Clemson back in 1903. The going-over by the Gators had one merit. It provided the hook for a story that Alex liked to tell on himself.

That spring the lacrosse team, coached by a well-loved professor, Dr. J. B. Crenshaw, had lost at Georgia, and Alex teased Doc Crenshaw about it.

"How was the game?"

"It was a fine game," said Crenshaw. "The players enjoyed it."

"But what," Alex persisted, "was the score?"

"Only 8–1," Doc replied.

"Only 8–1," Alex yelled. "What do you mean *only*? Why that's the equivalent of 56–7 in football, and I don't see anything fine about that."

The doctor stomped out of Alex's office. But with the Florida debacle came his day of revenge. He shook his head at the dejected Alex, laughed joyously, and said, "Ha! Ha! Only 55–7. That's like 8–1 in lacrosse. It was a fine game and everybody had a good time. Ha! Ha!"

Before and through the World War II years, Alex had good times again. The 1939 team, with a razzle-dazzle hidden-ball series, enjoyed a 7–2 season, losing only to Notre Dame, 17–14, and Duke, 7–6. The principal magicians were quarterback Howard Ector, halfback Johnny Bosch, and end Bob Ison.

They dazzled the late Paul Christman and Missouri in the Orange Bowl, 21–7. Later, Tech

Bill (*left*) with his successor, another great, Bobby Dodd, ca. 1948

under Alex would become the first team to play in all four major Bowls, Rose, Sugar, Orange, and Cotton.

The 1942 team featured an Atlantan from Boys High, Clint Castleberry, who soon after would lose his life in military service. The Jackets beat Frank Leahy's team that had quarterback Angelo Bertelli, 13–6, beat Alabama in a defensive duel, 7–0, and were undefeated and untied going into the Georgia game. Georgia, undefeated until upset by Auburn, which had Frankie Sinkwich and Charlie Trippi, would eventually go to the Rose Bowl and beat UCLA.

Following Tech's victory over Duke, Alex was bedded by a heart attack and a gall bladder ailment, and placed the team in Bobby Dodd's capable hands. On the day before the Georgia game, Alex told Ed Camp, Tech football historian:

"We are in for a bad day, and there's nothing Dodd can do about it. The team is 'shot.' It showed that in the Florida game. Dodd has done everything a coach can do, but in this day and time, a small, frail team with inadequate replacements cannot reach four peaks in one season.

"We reached a peak for Notre Dame in early October. We reached another for Navy in late October and held it a week for Duke. We reached a third for Alabama in mid-November, and exhaustion has set in."

He hit it right on the nose. Georgia, with Sinkwich and Trippi, won 34–0.

That night Alex received a phone call.

"Aleck, this is D. X. Bible calling from Austin." Bible, head coach of Texas, had served many years on the rules committee with Alexander. "We've been named for the Cotton Bowl and want to play you and Georgia Tech. Will you accept?"

"D. X.," said Alex, "have you heard what the score was today? It was 34–0—the worst licking Georgia has given us in 40 years."

"I know the score," said Bible, "and I know you and your team. It has been one of the best in the country this year and will be again on January 1. Our people out here want to see Georgia Tech and I want to play you. The Cotton Bowl will be filled."

Alex compromised with his doctors. In return for his promising to cut back his work schedule and to diet, they let him return to coaching. He was on the bench at Dallas when a rested Tech team put on a good show before losing to Texas, 14–7.

His coaching peers voted Alex Coach of the Year, and other honors rolled in on him. The Georgia Tech alumni bestowed on him their Distinguished Service Award, and the Chamber of Commerce of Atlanta presented him its Certificate of Achievement as a first citizen.

In the custom of his lifetime, he wore his honors lightly.

The late Walter Stewart, gifted sports editor of the Memphis *Commercial Appeal*, wrote of Bill Alexander's passing:

"Old Alex was a sort of synonym for Georgia Tech—the very texture of the school's personality—tough cement between the stones of battlements brave with White and Gold.

"Death called gently to him in the first gray light of Sunday—broke another link to a gracious and gallant past. For he had been the core of Georgia Tech's athletic destiny through 25 years of harsh combat. He had symbolized the dignity and honor of Southern football and a great emptiness surges behind him.

"He led without fear and asked no quarter. He leaves a memorial builded in the lives of those who served him."

Dr. Eddie Anderson

FOOTBALL DOCTOR

Dr. Edward N. Anderson, who prescribed some fine football at Holy Cross and Iowa in the thirties, liked to tell how he arrived at Notre Dame in 1918 as a 17-year-old freshman weighing 149 pounds. Knute Rockne, in his first year as head coach, looked at Eddie Anderson and asked, "How big are you, son?"

"Five-ten and 149 pounds, sir," Anderson replied.

"What position do you play?"

"End, sir."

"Hmm, I've got 16 right ends and 14 left ends," the coach growled.

"I guess I'm a left end, then," said Anderson.

Rockne laughed and threw Anderson a pair of football pants far too large for him and well tattered.

"These are lucky pants, son," said Rockne. "Don't lose them. Take them to a tailor and have them sewed up."

"Only a skinny kid like me could have worn those pants after all the tears in them had been mended," Anderson recalled. "Rock again told me they were lucky pants, but I also knew they were the only pair left at Notre Dame."

Lucky pants or not, Anderson made the traveling squad for the opening game, with Case Tech at Cleveland. Rockne started the second team, but when Case scored first on a fumble, he sent in the regulars, including the fabulous George Gipp and Anderson. (The freshman rule was suspended because of the war.)

Rockne looked down to the end of the bench and hollered, "What say, Eddie? Ready?"

"Sure am, sir," Anderson said.

For four years, 1918 through '21, Eddie Anderson played right end. "I never saw him knocked off his feet," Rockne said. In Anderson's sophomore and junior years, Notre Dame made 9–0 records, and in his senior year, Anderson captained the '21 team. In that period, the Irish enjoyed a defeatless string of 22 games before bowing at Iowa in 1921, 10–7, to the Hawkeye team of Duke Slater, Aubrey Devine, and Gordon Locke. The defeat had a special sourness for Anderson, an Iowan born in Oskaloosa and brought up in Mason City, but he made All-America that year.

The name Dr. Eddie Anderson is favorably recalled as a coach by fans who go back to the thirties. Only six coaches have won 200 or more games; Dr. Anderson, with 201, is one of them.

He gave Holy Cross its most healthful football times; from 1933 through '38 the Crusaders won 47, lost 7, and tied 4. The 1935 and '37 teams gave the school its only full-season undefeated records.

After the 1938 season, Anderson signed a three-year contract at $10,000 a year to return to his home state and coach the University of Iowa. He inherited a situation decidedly down. In the previous nine seasons the Hawkeyes had won only 22 of 72 games; in Western Conference competition they had won only five. Following the 14–0 loss to Colgate in 1938, one Iowa paper commented,

"Iowa's football hopes, such as they were, painfully passed away yesterday afternoon. . . . Interment services will be held on any Iowa City street corner. . . . The sooner the better."

Anderson was expected gradually to build Iowa into a Big Ten contender. Nobody expected him to accomplish it within one year. Bill Osmanski, Anderson's great fullback and later a star with the Chicago Bears, helped out in spring practice at Iowa City, and on his return to Worcester was quoted:

"Among 5,000 male students at the University of Iowa, there are only five real football players. Right now Iowa would love to have next fall's Holy Cross team face any Big Ten opponent, and would not fear one of them."

As a prophet, Osmanski maintained his reputation as a fullback. Anderson and his top assistants, line coach Jim Harris and backfield coach Frank Carideo, faced the season with enthusiasm and quiet optimism, however. For they had inherited some 15 good football players. Many of them would play 60 minutes in several games to earn the appellation "Iron Men." One of them, Nile Kinnick, would become a legend, not only in Iowa but in Big Ten and national football as well.

Kinnick, a strongly built five-nine 170-pounder, had come to Iowa from Benson High School in Omaha, Nebraska. As a sophomore in 1937, he had made All–Big Ten quarterback. In 1938, as a

junior, he was handicapped by a bad ankle and Iowa won only one game, from anemic Chicago, 27–14.

Other returning lettermen, who would provide Kinnick solid support, were ends Erwin Prasse, Ken Pettit, and Dick (Whitey) Evans; tackles Jim Walker and Mike Enich; guards Mike Hawkins and Charlie Tollefson; centers Bill Diehl and Bruno Andruska; quarterback Al Coupee; halfback Floyd (Buzz) Dean, and fullback Bill Green.

Team esprit and lack of depth were underlined by left tackle Wally Bergstrom. He had never played football in high school, or in college until his senior year. But when Walker was injured, Bergstrom started against Wisconsin, and played all but 30 minutes of five games, four of them complete. After the Wisconsin game, Kinnick said of him, "Bergstrom finished a college course in one afternoon."

The 41–0 victory in the opener against South Dakota saw Kinnick score three touchdowns and dropkick five conversions for 23 points, a new school record. But the first real tip on what was to come was given the next week against Indiana in Iowa City.

Iowa had not beaten an Indiana team since 1921, and had not won a Big Ten football game at home since 1933. And Indiana had an ace forward passer named Harold Hursch. George Strickler, covering for the Chicago *Tribune*, wrote of the game,

"The renaissance arrived at Iowa, borne triumphantly on the shoulders of Nile Kinnick and fleet-footed Erwin Prasse. Coming from behind twice, the Hawkeyes marched and passed their way to a 32–29 conquest of Indiana, to rest, virtually hysterical with joy, at the top of the Big Ten championship race."

Iowa, which had led at the half, 20–17, trailed with time running out, 29–26. Then the Hawkeyes put on a final drive. With fourth down and three to go, they were positioned nicely in front of the goalposts, and Kinnick was a superb dropkicker. But in the huddle, Kinnick said, "Forget the tie! We're going all the way!" And all the way they went, with Kinnick eluding three Hoosiers to hit Prasse with a touchdown pass for a 32–29 victory.

The next week at Michigan, the Hawks were temporarily blown off course. A pass from Kinnick to Dean gave them the lead, but Tommy Harmon, enjoying one of his strongest days, scored four touchdowns, the first on a 90-yard run with an interception. This was Iowa's only loss of the year, 27–7.

Dr. Eddie Anderson. *Chicago Tribune Photos*

The Hawks rebounded well the next week at Wisconsin, where Kinnick connected for touchdown passes to Coupee, Evans, and Green and a 19–13 win. In those days, the prospect of small crowds at home impelled Iowa to schedule more than its share of away games, so their date at Purdue was their third straight on the road. This one was won by the odd score of 4–0, when Mike Enich, the big tackle, twice blocked kicks that the Boilermakers downed for safeties in their end zone. Eight of the Hawkeye starters, including Kinnick, played 60 minutes.

Now past the halfway mark in the season, Iowa had a 4–1 record. Dick Lamb and Bert McGrane in their book, *75 Years with the Fighting Hawkeyes,* wrote: "Notre Dame was next. The Irish had not played in Iowa City since Dr. Anderson's playing days, when the Hawkeyes won a memorable victory. This Notre Dame team, like its earlier predecessor, was unbeaten when it arrived in Iowa City and, like its predecessor, it went away a loser.

"Notre Dame's speed and power piled up big yardage. But 16 Kinnick punts, averaging nearly 46 yards, drove them back. Up and down the field the teams surged until Notre Dame fumbled and Ken Pettit recovered for Iowa on the Irish 4-yard line.

"Kinnick strategy helped produce the Iowa touchdown that followed. He switched halfback positions with Buzz Dean, who had been at right half. Improvising, Kinnick took a direct pass from center and bolted into the hole opened by Dean and the Iowa line for the score, then dropkicked the extra point.

"Notre Dame's savage retaliatory onslaught brought a fourth-quarter touchdown but the conversion failed. The Irish got no additional chance for in the waning moments Kinnick boomed one of the mightiest clutch punts on record in Iowa Stadium, putting the ball out of bounds on the Notre Dame 5-yard line. Iowa won, 7–6, with eight Hawkeyes again playing 60 minutes."

Fifty thousand jammed Iowa Stadium the next week to see this storybook kind of team survive probably its most pressurized chapter. At the beginning of the last quarter Iowa trailed Minnesota 9–0, a team it had not beaten in ten years. But the Iron Men hung in their tough.

Starting from their 20-yard line, the Hawks scored on Kinnick's passing. He threw one to Dean for 18 yards, a second for 15, plunged for two yards, and then connected with Prasse on a 45-yarder. On this toss Nile again had to maneuver himself free of several tacklers. Kinnick kicked the extra point, and Iowa was behind 9–7, with 11 minutes to go.

After an exchange of punts, Minnesota's Harold Van Every kicked to Kinnick, who ran it out to the 21. A first pass by Kinnick failed, a second to Dean gained 17, and a third was allowed for interference on the Minnesota 45. Bill Green ran for seven, and Kinnick for 10 to the Gopher 28. Then Kinnick faded, eluded a clutch of Gophers, and hit Green deep in the end zone for a 13–9 victory.

Nile missed the extra point, but that mattered not to the Iowa fans who swarmed over him. Kinnick and six Iowa linemen went the full 60 minutes. One Chicago writer began his lead, "Nile Kinnick 13, Minnesota 9; tersely that tells the story of the most spectacular game in modern history."

Kinnick and the other Iron Men could not quite make it all the way to the Big Ten title. They had to settle for a 7–7 tie at Northwestern, so Ohio State, despite its loss to Michigan, backed into the championship. The Hawkeyes were badly battered, including Kinnick. After 402 minutes, almost seven straight games, he was sidelined by a shoulder injury, with Northwestern ahead, 7–0.

The doctor as a player. *Chicago Tribune Photos*

The Hawks still had enough left to get the tie.

Although the Conference crown was not theirs, Iowa was still the most talked of team of the year; they had won five games in the last quarter. Prasse, Enich and Tollefson attracted All-Team attention. Kinnick was voted the Heisman Trophy and seemingly every other award available. He was even named Male Athlete of the Year, ahead of the Yankees' Joe DiMaggio.

Nobody was inclined to argue the honors, after inquiry into Kinnick's accomplishments. He threw 11 touchdown passes, dropkicked 11 extra points, and was involved in 107 of Iowa's 130 points. His 377 yards returning kicks and eight pass interceptions led the country. He handled the ball 197 plays from scrimmage, 104 rushing and 93 passing, and his run-and-pass yardage of 998 set a new record for an eight-game schedule.

"He was a perfectionist," Dr. Anderson reminisced. "Never satisfied unless he could come as close as he could to absolute perfection in any move he made. He could never feel convinced there was no room for further improvement, and his spirit was transmitted to his teammates.

"More often than not, as a result of his inspiration we had as many as seven or eight players who would go the full 60 minutes with him in a particular game. And they knew Nile

was never wasting himself; when Kinnick wasn't running the ball or passing it, he was blocking for somebody else. There was no such thing as using Nile Kinnick on a fake."

On June 2, 1943, a U.S. Navy fighter plane, its motor conked out, plunged into the Gulf of Paria in the Caribbean Sea, to take the life of its pilot, Nile Kinnick. Kenneth L. (Tug) Wilson, commissioner of the Big Ten, spoke for thousands:

"Throughout the Big Ten, throughout the nation in fact, Ensign Nile Kinnick—athlete, scholar, gentleman, inspiring leader—was considered something quite special and not likely to be duplicated too often."

That 1939 season brought deserved honor and reward to Dr. Anderson. His peers named him Coach of the Year. The Iowa Board in Control of Athletics gave him a new six-year contract at $12,000 a year, and voted him a $1,000 bonus for 1939. Among other things, the Doctor had restored the athletic association books to good health. The department had a net loss of $10,641.19 in 1938; in '39 it showed a net profit of $85,741.56.

That Eddie Anderson, given the tools, would do an outstanding job did not surprise football followers. His six-year chart at Holy Cross from 1933 through '38 had been revealing:

YEAR	W	L	T
1933	7	2	0
1934	8	2	0
1935	9	0	1
1936	7	2	1
1937	8	0	2
1938	8	1	0
TOTALS	47	7	4

The 1935 team's only blemish was a 13–13 tie with Manhattan; the two 1937 ties were scoreless, with Temple and Carnegie Tech; the single loss in '38 was to Carnegie Tech, 7–6. In those years Holy Cross contended regularly for top Eastern honors and some national recognition also.

The teams that gave Anderson the most satisfaction were Holy Cross 1938 and, of course, Iowa in '39.

"We missed the Sugar Bowl bid in '38 by losing to Carnegie," he pointed out, "and the All-America selectors missed the boat on fullback Bill Osmanski. Later, when Osmanski was a sensation in the pro league, we learned that the Sugar Bowl committee regretted not having named us.

"Osmanski was a good defensive player and a good pass receiver. He was not a passer or kicker, but he was, I think, one of the finest ball carriers I've ever seen. In college ranks the other man that I would compare with him would be Tom Harmon, of Michigan.

"Along with Osmanski we had another boy by the name of Ronnie Cahill. A boy of the same type as Nile Kinnick of Iowa, a great triple threat and one that would win a lot of ball games for you."

With the advent of the forties, and without a Kinnick, an Osmanski, or a Cahill, Dr. Anderson still continued to extract the maximum from his personnel but without the same headline success. Following 1939, his next three teams at Iowa accumulated a 13–13 record. Then Anderson served from 1943 through '45 as a major in the Army Medical Corps. He returned to Iowa and from 1946 through '49 his record was 16–19–1. That placed his overall eight-year record with the Hawks at 35–33–2. Notable victories after 1939 included Notre Dame, 7–0, in 1940; Wisconsin, then rated No. 2 nationally, 6–0, in '42; Minnesota, 13–7, in '47; Ohio State, 14–7, in '48; and Northwestern, 28–21, in '49.

Holy Cross, meanwhile, remembering the big years he had given them, wanted him back. He also knew that Ohio State had just given Wesley Fesler something unusual for a football coach —tenure. Anderson asked Iowa for the same and when he was refused, he resigned on January 28, 1950.

His second time around at Holy Cross, 1950 through '64, he made a 15-year record of 82–60–4, and had only three losing seasons. His best records were 8–2 in both 1951 and '52, and 7–3 in 1961. Against traditional rival Boston College, counting both first and second times around, his record was 11 won, 10 lost. In 1971, seven years after his last game, he was inducted into the College Football Hall of Fame.

"Winning," said one of his old players, end Bob Noble, "was important to Dr. Anderson, but it was far from being all-important. Once during my junior year he 'sat down' two of the best players on the team for discipline infractions —and this at a time when victories were less than plentiful and time was running out on his bid to win his 200th game."

That victory came in the eighth game of 1964, his last year, 32–0 at Boston University.

After graduation from Notre Dame in 1922,

Anderson in 1939, his first year at Iowa

Anderson coached Columbia (now Loras) of Dubuque, Iowa, to a three-year record of 16–6–2, and then De Paul to a seven-year mark of 21–22–4. It is an almost incredible testament to his work-load capacity that while he was coaching De Paul and playing pro ball with the Chicago Cardinals, he was qualifying for his degree from Rush Medical College. Throughout his coaching at Holy Cross and Iowa, spanning 31 years, he always practiced medicine.

It was while he was coaching De Paul that he met his bride, Mary Broderick, a model from Manchester, New Hampshire. They were married in 1929 and had three boys and a girl, Nick, Gerry, Jim, and Judy.

The day the Andersons were wed was the same day Eddie started taking his final medical school examinations and had to have his picture taken for the yearbook. He was sitting with his jaw in its usual set, when the photographer said, "For heaven's sake, get that woebegone look off your face, or people will think you were just married."

"We lived the hectic life of a football coach," said Mary Anderson, moving here and there and loving every minute of it. It's an exciting life, a wonderful emotionally exhausting life."

The twin careers of football and medicine left the Andersons little time for entertaining.

"It's a spur-of-the-moment thing with us," Mrs. Anderson said. "If Ed doesn't have a meeting at night, if he hasn't any special reading to do, and if he's not too tired, we may call up a few friends and have them over, or we might just drop in on someone. It works out quite well that way, too."

In his rare moments of relaxation, Anderson enjoyed playing records, especially pianist Frankie Carle's; he had a record player installed in the dressing room at Iowa. One of his close friends was actor Don Ameche, who had tried out for football unsuccessfully at Loras. Ameche followed Anderson's teams assiduously, and once came to a game at Iowa City, where he was introduced at midfield between halves.

Although he was a kindhearted and generous person, there was something about Anderson that discouraged familiarity. He was not the type you'd walk up to, slap on the back, and say, "Hiya, Coach," or, "Hiya, Doc." But as a friend he wore well. He always followed the future of his players and took pride in them.

"A lot of my boys have gone on to become doctors, dentists, lawyers, and the like," he said. "There's a lot of satisfaction in just that.

"Knute Rockne always wanted to be a doctor himself and when he learned I was thinking about going to medical school, he kept after me about it. He made a big impression on me and I suppose that's one reason why I did go on to become a doctor."

The kind of life he led—he was a frequent Catholic communicant—unmistakably influenced his players. One of them, Bob Noble, put it this way,

"I look back on my days in the company of Dr. Anderson as a period when I was exposed to some genuine Americana. I was exposed to a fine man who simply practiced virtue while most of my generation was still trying to define it."

That would seem to say it all about Dr. Eddie Anderson.

Charlie Bachman

A RECORD THAT WEARS WELL

As a kid in short pants on Chicago's South Side around the turn of the century, Charlie Bachman lived only three miles from the University of Chicago, where Amos Alonzo Stagg tutored the football team.

"I spent many hours watching Mr. Stagg coach the Maroons," Bachman said. "Even in those days my mind was made up that I was going to be a football coach."

Few careers ever got an earlier start; in his senior season with Englewood High, Bachman also coached the team.

Over a half century later, in 1972, when he was pushing 80, Charlie Bachman was still thinking, talking, and writing football and still making much good sense about it.

In the years between, Bachman coached 28 seasons, 20 of them in the twenties and thirties, and made notable contributions to football programs at four schools: Kansas State, Florida, Michigan State, and Hillsdale.

His overall record—137 victories, 83 defeats, and 24 ties for a percentage of .611—describes him for what he was: a sound, solid teacher. One who won the respect of opponents for himself and his team, which is, after all, what the game of intercollegiate football is supposed to be all about.

Bachman's .611 stands up well with several coaching names more renowned than his:

	YEARS	W	L	T	PCT.
Charlie Bachman	28	137	83	24	.611
Amos Alonzo Stagg	57	314	197	35	.607
Eddie Anderson	39	201	128	15	.606
Bill Alexander	25	134	95	15	.580
Dutch Meyer	19	109	79	13	.575
Clark Shaughnessy	32	149	116	17	.559

That Stagg, Anderson, Alexander, Meyer, and Shaughnessy are in the Hall of Fame and Bachman is not traces to several factors. James Wallace Butts, who used to be a successful coach at Georgia, once said that most winning coaches, including the immortals, had something going for them beyond their own ability; meaning, of course, superior material and here and there an edge in schedule-making. Too often to qualify for immortality, Charlie Bachman didn't enjoy the edge in context.

His teams, however, had only six losing seasons in 28; there were five years—Kansas State 1922, Florida 1928, and Michigan State 1934, 1936, and 1944—when they lost only one game. But none of them went undefeated, and in his only postseason game, his 1937 Michigan State team lost to Auburn 6–0 in the Orange Bowl game.

For a coach who was around as long as he was, he enjoyed relatively few outstanding stars. Three of his best were Clyde Crabtree, his lefthanded, left-footed quarterback at Florida, Michigan State guard Sid Wagner, and Johnny Pingel, authentic triple-threat ace of the Spartans. Pingel is rated a member of MSU's all-time offensive backfield, with Earl Morrall, Everett (Sonny) Grandelius, and Clinton Jones.

A Big Six championship and a Rose Bowl bid each eluded Bachman by one game. With the Big Six title at stake, his 1922 Kansas State team was overpowered by Nebraska, 21–0. Six years later, in the season's finale for both teams, Florida met Tennessee at Knoxville. (This was not the first confrontation of Bachman and Bob Neyland, famous coach of the Volunteers: Bachman, as a Notre Dame guard, was assigned to blocking Neyland, Army end, in the 1916 Notre Dame–Army game at West Point, won by the Cadets 30–10.)

Florida, whose 336 points were tops for the nation that season, took a perfect eight-game record into Shields-Watkins Field. Tennessee had also won eight but had played a scoreless tie with Kentucky the week before. According to Southern football historian Zipp Newman of Alabama, a victory would have brought Florida the Rose Bowl bid. But with its regular tackles injured, the Gators lost 13–12 on a muddy field. So the Roses

Charlie Bachman

went instead to perfect-record Georgia Tech, which beat California, 8–7, aided by Roy Riegels' wrong-way run.

"I went to Florida when the state was suffering from the boom bust," Bachman recalled. "Our material was the opposite of that at Kansas State. We had several fast, clever backs, but we were short of linemen, particularly tackles."

Despite the loss to Tennessee, that 1928 record of 8–1 still stands, at the time this is written, as the best regular-season record percentagewise in the first 65 years of Florida football. Two more winning years were followed by two losers, but when Jimmy Crowley left Michigan State for Fordham in 1933, the Spartans were glad to hire Bachman as his successor.

He didn't disappoint them. Until he arrived at East Lansing in 1933, Michigan State—or Michigan Aggies, as it was also known—had beaten Michigan only twice in 28 tries: 12–7 in 1913 and 24–0 in '15. Bachman's teams beat the Wolverines four in a row, 1934–37, a feat later tied by Coaches Clarence (Biggie) Munn and Duffy Daugherty, but at the time so totally unprece-

dented as to evoke hysteria. (It should be added that even though Bachman's first Michigan State team [1933] lost to Michigan, 20–6, it scored a touchdown on the Wolverines for the first time since 1918.)

In the 1934 victory, 16–0, which broke an 18-season drought, the only sophomore to start for the Spartans was left tackle Howard Zindel, later chairman of the Department of Poultry Science.

"Charlie and the assistant coaches," said Dr. Zindel, "took turns informing me that I was going to be on the spot. Charlie said that the first play would be directed at me and if I stopped it, they would try again. Then, if I stopped that play, the rest of the game would be easier.

"He was right. The first play and the second play did come to me. I got lucky and stopped both, and had a 'ball' the rest of the game. Charlie was all football and no nonsense. He was alert to new teaching techniques. He not only told us how to do it, but being a big rugged man, he showed us how."

Dr. Zindel also revealed that in his sincere, homespun fashion, Charlie Bachman was an able recruiter.

"While I was still a senior at Union High School in Grand Rapids, Michigan, in 1933, I recall hearing my mother call me. I was out in the garage under my Model A Ford, when I was told that three Michigan State College people were there to see me. I slid out to be confronted by Coach Bachman, Coach Tom King, and Secretary J. A. Hannah. [John A. Hannah, later president of Michigan State University and more recently a State Department administrator of the Agency for International Development, contributed prodigiously to the general growth of MSU, including its athletics, and probably had more to do than any other individual in getting the Spartans accepted into the Western Conference.]

"Mother invited them in for coffee and cookies. Her homemade peanut butter cookies made a hit with Charlie and so he asked for the recipe, which she gave him. In 1971, at the Homecoming Game, he still praised those cookies. He said that both his wife and daughter-in-law made them regularly, and that he thought of me and my family every time he munched one of them."

Bachman's teams were always well prepared in all phases of the game. In his 28 years of coaching, they had kicks blocked only twice. Much of his kicking technique he got from Knowlton A. (Snake) Ames, Princeton back and

a member of the first All-America team picked, in 1889.

"Pingel was the best quick kicker I ever coached," Bachman stated. "His kicks went low naturally ... many of them went 70 yards, and many rolled over the goal line. Usually, there was no return by the safety. ... We always opened up a hole over center for a low kick to go through, or the kicker to convert the play into a run if the ball was mishandled."

Bachman also reminisced about the kicking of Clyde Crabtree, who employed an interesting version of the quick kick:

"Clyde was lefthanded and left-footed and was a fine open-field runner. He frequently lined up at right halfback. On a called left-end run he would start out and watch the safety. If he stayed back, Clyde ran the end. If the safety came up on the run, he would kick the ball left-footed over his head."

It is doubtful any other coach who ever lived was more seriously dedicated to football than Bachman. His strong, rugged face suggested a German U-boat commander's, and it was no facade. Charlie was a tough-fibered man, physically and mentally.

When he was only 27 and a neophyte head coach at Northwestern, he was pitted against the famous veteran Fielding H. Yost of Michigan. Michigan won the game 16–13. Bachman believed that Yost had violated a tenet of sportsmanship, having to do with an eligible man catching the ball out of bounds, and after the game he invaded Yost's dressing room and dressed him down for it.

"I'll have you thrown out of here," Yost threatened.

"Nobody will throw me out of here," Bachman grated. "I came in on my own and I'll go out on my own." Which he did.

Although Bachman's serious mien did not encourage frivolity, his vast experience in the game had given him a chestful of good stories, which he told well. One concerned a game he played in as a sophomore guard for Notre Dame in 1914 at the old Comiskey ball park in Chicago, against the Carlisle Indians, coached by Glenn S. (Pop) Warner:

"As we approached the Carlisle 5-yard line, I noticed that the Carlisle defensive right guard was widely overshifted to the strong side, leaving a big hole to our weak side. I told Dutch Bergman, our quarterback, about this and on the next play he called our 25 play with Ray Eichenlaub, our great

During his Michigan State days

fullback, hitting to the weak side from his fullback position.

"Gus Welch, an oldtime Carlisle star whom Warner had imported for the game from an Indian school in Minnesota where he was coaching, came up to make the tackle and he ran into one of Eichenlaub's knees. Gus hit the ground and Eich scored. They carried Gus off the field and from the Mercy Hospital in Chicago for over a week they issued daily bulletins on his condition. Fortunately he recovered.

"The next time I saw Gus Welch was in Canton, Ohio, in 1917, where our Youngstown Patricians were on hand to play Jim Thorpe's Canton Bulldogs. I played left tackle. Gus, substituting for Jim, started in my direction from a short punt formation and in typical pro style I moved out toward the sideline. They weren't going to run around me.

"Coming to my aid was Bob Peck, our center, who had been All-America under Pop Warner at Pittsburgh. Gus saw Bob following the play, leaving a big hole over center; Gus cut back, ran through that hole and went 60 yards for a touchdown.

"As I saw him running down the field, I thought, 'Pretty good for a dead Indian.'"

In his playing days at Notre Dame, Bachman performed the unusual feat of starting and winning letters three years in three different positions: 1914 right guard, 1915 fullback, and 1916 left guard. In 1916 he made Walter Camp's All-America second team. His head coach was Jesse Harper, a former Stagg quarterback at Chicago, who was instrumental in recruiting him; but it was Harper's assistant, Knute Rockne, who was to exert the most influence on Bachman.

The Rockne charisma convinced each of his former players who went out to coach that he had a special interest in him, which in fact he did. But strong evidence indicates that Rockne did have unusual respect for Bachman's football mind.

"I first met Rockne at a track meet in the old First Regiment Armory in Chicago," said Bachman. "The year was 1911. He was a sophomore at Notre Dame and I was competing for Englewood High. We were both entered in the pole vault.

"The next time that Knute and I met was at Notre Dame in 1913, my freshman year. Fortunately, I was assigned a room in the Corby Hall 'Subway.' Rockne and his roommate, quarterback Gus Dorais, had a room at the end of the hall. Like many boys away from home for the first time, I was homesick, and thought seriously of packing up. I will ever be thankful that after I was on campus about one week, Knute Rockne picked up the mail at the rector's office. I am sure Rock read a postal card from my sister, telling me to grow up and make up my mind to stay in school and get a college education.

"Rockne stopped in my room, handed me the card and told me that he and Dorais were going out through a large screen in our storeroom window that night and they wanted me to go along. The mission was a few beers at Steve Odyssey's saloon, about a mile south of the present stadium. This window procedure in those days was known as 'skiving.' Rockne manipulated the screen and opened it enough for us to step through. He then replaced it in workmanlike fashion.

"We sat in a field behind Odyssey's on empty beer cases with a big harvest moon for company. He told me first of his first week in school when he became homesick and packed his bag and was ready to leave when his friends learned of his intentions and hid his bag. For about an hour we talked about football, the Notre Dame schedule, and the school. After this pleasant hour I decided

Charlie's favorite pastime, talking football

to put off my trip to Chicago until the Christmas vacation."

After his graduation from the Notre Dame Law School in 1917, Bachman was an assistant coach at DePauw and on Sundays played tackle for Youngstown. In 1918, he entered the Officers School at the Great Lakes Naval Training Station. He roomed with George Halas, Paddy Driscoll lived next door, and the three of them played on the Great Lakes team that went through undefeated, was tied twice, and won the 1919 Tournament of Roses game from the Mare Island Marines, 17–0.

By a twist of fortune, Bachman and Rockne coached against each other that season. Charlie not only played center for Great Lakes, but was an advisory coach, and Rockne was in his first year as Notre Dame's head coach. Since the game ended 7–7, honors were even.

Through the twenties, while Rockne was building his Four Horsemen teams of 1923 and '24 and the national champions of 1929 and '30, Bachman was also successful, though on a lower plateau, at Kansas State and Florida.

"I was hired as head coach of Northwestern in 1919," said Bachman. "Paddy Driscoll was my assistant. We never saw our material until the opening day of practice."

His record, 2–5, was not good enough for

Bachman to stay at Northwestern. But he showed enough to get his chance at Kansas State. His eight-year record at K. State, 33–23–9, found him using a strong off-tackle attack and flat passes to hold his own in the Big Six.

Under Bachman, Kansas State finally caught up with Kansas for a while. Previously, K. State had won only once in 17 tries against the university. Under Bachman, the Purple won two, tied two, and won four, in that order. Then Bachman, who had turned down a chance for the Alabama job, accepted the challenge at Florida.

In those years at Kansas State and Florida, Bachman corresponded regularly with Rockne until Knute's death in the airplane crash on a wheatfield near Bazaar, Kansas, March 31, 1931. On March 28, 1928, for example, Rockne wrote Bachman at Gainesville: "I wish you could drop up here sometime after your spring practice is over so we can talk over personally the many things about which you have been writing."

As the twenties advanced, and the traditional seven-box defense gave way to the 6–2–2–1, one of the earliest to move with it was Bachman; it helped him gain a scoreless tie in 1930 with Georgia, also coached by a Notre Dame man, Harry Mehre.

"Rock wanted me to tell him all that I knew about the 6–2–2–1 defense," Bachman reminisced. "He admitted reluctantly that the 7–2–2 defense was in trouble. Teams were quick-kicking over the heads of the deep two, and it was almost impossible to cover a fast wingback going down the middle after the ends had drawn the halfbacks wide. Passes on early downs were very effective and some teams were beginning to flood the flat zone where a second receiver was being covered by the strong-side defensive guard."

Bachman was the last of Rockne's players to visit him, a few days before his death. They got together at Miami Beach to discuss the 6–2–2–1 defense and other football developments.

"I spent three days with him on the beach," Charlie smiled. "Bonnie, his wife, shooed Rock and myself out of their room at the Gulf Stream Hotel. She said she wanted him to get a good rest and to forget about football. We ended up on the beach diagraming plays with seashells."

The most rewarding football years for Bachman had to be from 1934 through '37 at Michigan State, when the Spartans not only beat Michigan four in a row but put together records of 8–1–0, 6–2–0, 6–1–2, and 8–2–0, for a total of 28–6–2. Unbeaten seasons were frustrated in 1934 by Syracuse, 10–0, and in '36 by Marquette, 13–7. These were the years of Wagner and Pingel and the Orange Bowl. But most important, Bachman, like Crowley before him, was building Michigan State up to the level where it could legitimately claim strength worthy of being taken into the Big Ten.

With the coming of Fritz Crisler, the Michigan series turned around on Michigan State and Bachman, as the Wolverines beat them seven in a row. The last two, in 1945 and '46, saw the Spartans badly outgunned, 40–0 and 55–7. Bachman, whose contract would be running out on July 1, 1947, agreed with those who believed he should step down. In accepting his resignation, President Hannah said:

"I checked the record again today. Bach's teams have played 95 major games, at least what I consider major games. I've crossed off all the Waynes and Albions and Illinois Wesleyans. He's won 57, tied 7, and lost 37. He's taught good, hard, clean football here and has never, in any way, either personally or with his teams, done anything to embarrass the institution."

Bachman was 54 when he left Michigan State and coaching. For the next quarter of a century he was successful in the food and real estate businesses. In 1953, at 60, he came out of retirement temporarily to coach Hillsdale College at Hillsdale, Michigan, and showed he hadn't lost his touch.

"We had a 5–3–2 season," he said. "I then turned the job over to Frank Waters, my assistant, who had played for me at Michigan State, and he is still on the job with a fine record."

Charlie Bachman has been the kind who wears well. Dr. Hannah spoke for a big majority when he saluted Bachman recently:

"I have always had great respect for Charlie as a coach and as a man—and for his good wife Grace. For years we lived as close neighbors and close personal friends and while time has not permitted our ways to cross very often in recent years, I have nothing but great admiration for him."

Madison A. (Matty) Bell

THE BIG BOUNCE BACK

It would be hard to find a football coach better qualified to discuss the sudden unpredictable ups and downs of the profession than Madison A. (Matty) Bell. In 1933 Bell was fired by Texas A. & M. Two years later he led Southern Methodist to a 12–0 record, the Southwest Conference championship, a valid claim to the national title, and the only Rose Bowl game played in by a Texas team. SMU lost it, to Stanford, 7–0. Bell proved dramatically that coaching can be "chicken today and feathers tomorrow"—or the other way around.

When at Texas A. & M. the 1933 Southern Methodist team got its last touchdown near the end of a 19–0 victory over the Aggies, Russell McIntosh, SMU line coach, said to head coach Ray Morrison, "I'm afraid that will finish Matty down here."

McIntosh was right. Yet, in three months Bell had McIntosh's job. For some time SMU had lacked a goal-line punch, and alumni blamed it on McIntosh. So he was demoted to freshman coach and replaced by Bell. Morrison left SMU for Vanderbilt, his alma mater, after the 1934 season. He took McIntosh with him as line coach and he did a good job.

Bell—who had been head coach at Texas Christian for six seasons and Texas A. & M. for five—was named to replace Morrison, and he inherited an outstanding team.

"We had a great line and a great backfield," Bell recalled, "but only six or seven first-class subs. Truman Spain and Maurice Orr were the two finest tackles ever to play for SMU." Matty could have added that he also had probably the four best guards in the entire conference: J. C. (Iron Man) Wetzel, Billy Stamps, Paschal Scottino, and Charlie Baker. Wetzel, discussing the team, said in 1953:

"We used a balanced line, single-wing attack primarily. We used the old Minnesota buck-lateral series with great success. At tailback we had two fine breakaway runners in Bobby Wilson and J. R. (Jack Rabbit) Smith. At fullback for power we had Harry Shuford and Bob Finley. At the wingback position were Shelly Burt, Smith and Bob Turner, and at blocking back was John Sprague, who was killed at Salerno Beach in Italy.

"Outside of our two tackles, Spain and Orr, who weighed about 215, the rest of our line averaged about 182–183 pounds. Our backfield averaged about 172–175 with Wilson. This size team gave us great speed, quickness, and alertness. Smith and Finley gave us fine punting."

To win the Southwest Conference championship, Southern Methodist had to get by Texas Christian. The Horned Frogs had a comparable team, led by Slingin' Sammy Baugh, who seemed to throw a football like Walter Johnson pitched a baseball. That day, in fact, Sammy's receivers couldn't hang on to his speed balls as well as they had, which helped SMU.

No game in Texas, before or since, surpassed this one for buildup and fulfillment. The capacity of TCU's stadium, 30,000, couldn't meet the demand.

Matty Bell. *Chicago Tribune Photos*

With both teams undefeated and rated at the top nationally, the game attracted name sportswriters from all over, headed by Grantland Rice. The National Broadcasting System covered the game, the first radio network broadcast to come out of the Southwest.

Dallas and Fort Worth displayed signs, "On to the Rose Bowl." Each team had won ten games. SMU had shut out seven opponents and allowed only one touchdown each to the other three. TCU had averaged three touchdowns a game, and was a six-point favorite.

Matty Bell and Dutch Meyer used different psychologies in readying their teams. Bell played it calmly, while Meyer hopped things up. Bell's predominant pessimism had got him named "Moanin' Matty," and when fullback Shuford was declared out with a wrenched knee, Bell said, "We're going to do the best we can, but without a man like Shuford, I'm afraid we don't have much chance."

Privately, however, Matty told George White, Dallas *News* sports editor, "Now don't you change your selection, but we're going to win this game." As Bell had hoped it would, this got out, and it delighted Dutch Meyer as just the gimmick he needed.

The two teams reflected the opposing psychologies when they came out on the field. TCU ran on, slapping one another's thighs and yelling, "Let's go, gang! Let's go! Let's get 'em, gang!" In contrast, SMU emerged like professional mourners. But Bell knew his Mustangs were ready when he heard Truman Spain say to Maurice Orr, "Those skunks think they're going to the Rose Bowl on our reputation."

Poised as Bell had hoped, the Mustangs moved to a 14–0 lead. With Bob Finley, who replaced the injured Shuford, calling signals, SMU marched 73 yards for a touchdown. SMU relied on the dangerous Bobby Wilson, but he carried only once on the drive, while wingback Burt gained on reverses and Finley, on fake buck laterals, smashed up the middle. Finley finally took it over from the 1.

After a TCU drive that stalled on the SMU 16, the Mustangs struck again, 80 yards in six plays. The big gainer was a 33-yard pass from Finley to Maco Stewart on the 9. Now Wilson, who had handled the ball only twice, took a lateral from Burt and raced across standing up. TCU got one of the touchdowns back, and SMU led at the half 14–7.

Asked afterwards what he said between halves,

Bell replied that he'd made only one comment, which he borrowed from his high school coach, "You have 30 minutes to play, and a lifetime to think about it."

There was no score in the third period but early in the fourth period, Baugh's passing tied it up, 14–14. With 13 minutes to play, Bell sent in Jack Rabbit Smith, who returned TCU's kickoff 27 yards. Smith, five feet nine, 165 pounds, was a competitor and cocky. He shared the play-calling with Finley, and now he took over.

With fourth down, four yards to go, the ball on the SMU 37-yard line, and 10 minutes to play, the book called for a punt. But in the huddle Smith snapped, "Fake punt. Ends down and out. Pass to Wilson." Finley, the regular punter back in kick formation, would throw the ball. As the huddle broke and the players moved into position, Wilson said to Finley, "Listen, Bob, be sure to throw the ball as far as you can. I'll try to be out there. But make sure it gets to the end zone."

While Bell almost fainted on the bench, Finley faked a kick, faded back, and got rid of the ball an instant before being smothered by purple jerseys. Some said that by technical standards it wasn't a great pass. Dutch Meyer said it was thrown on the wrong side of Wilson. But it paid off.

Wilson ran straight down the sideline, looked back, and leaped at the 3. He tipped the ball into control and scrambled into the end zone—for the ball game, 20–14, the SWC crown, and the Rose Bowl bid.

A slightly inebriated rooter, legend has it, gave a toast at the beginning of the game "to the two greatest men in the world, President Roosevelt and Bobby Wilson." At halftime he amended it "to Bobby Wilson and President Roosevelt." At game's end he went all the way, "to the greatest man in the world, Bobby Wilson."

Grantland Rice summed up the press coverage when he wrote, "This was one of the greatest games ever played in the 60-year history of the nation's finest college sport ... a swirl of action that no other section of the country could approach ... the climax game of 1935."

"Coach," said Jack Rabbit Smith to Bell weeks later, "I've been thinking about the fourth-down play. If TCU had got the ball and won the game, they'd have run me out of town."

"Yeah," agreed Bell, "and they'd have run me right out with you."

The billing of Southern Methodist against Stanford caused a new high in demands for Rose

Bowl tickets. The 85,000 pasteboards were over-subscribed 48 hours after they went on sale and three weeks before the game. Al Masters, Stanford graduate manager, was confronted with an unsolvable problem. He had to turn down 200,000 requests.

In past Rose Bowl games the demands from the East and South ran from 1,500 to 3,000. Southern Methodist asked for 8,000, and had to settle for 4,000. Jimmy Stewart, SMU graduate manager, had to lock himself in a hotel room for three days and have his meals sent in.

SMU's big season plus its Rose Bowl share, $78,300, paid off the stadium debt and got Bell a new three-year contract. Artistically, though, the outcome, a 7–0 loss, was to Texans a failure.

This time the psychological edge rested with Stanford. The Indians had lost at Pasadena two straight years, to Columbia and Alabama. They were aching to answer the jeering references to them as "laughing boys."

Stanford scored the only touchdown of the game in the first quarter on a 42-yard drive. SMU's touted aerial circus fizzled except for one march that reached the Stanford 5-yard line only to be aborted by a fumble.

"The Texas Centennial made us its emissary," said Bell, "and we went out there more to put on a show than to win a football game. What I should have done was to have banned banquets, abolished autographs, and taken the team into the desert until the day of the game. After the first few minutes of play, I saw that the team was not mentally right.

"During the intermission, I didn't try the storybook oration. I merely tried to get the team calmed down. I told them that all they needed was to play cool-headed football in the last half and they would win.

"I also told the quarterbacks to call short passes that would be on their way before the Stanford ends, Monk Moscrip and Keith Topping, could get through. A few were called and ground was gained. But, though four quarterbacks were tried, long passes, slower got off, were thereafter used in an effort for a quick touchdown. The boys simply were trying too hard."

Although he never came up with a team that quite matched the 1935 gang, Bell went on coaching successfully. The Mustangs finished second in the Southwest Conference three straight years, 1938–40. During World War II, Bell served as a lieutenant commander in the navy.

In his second go-round with SMU he coached back-to-back SWC champions in 1947 and '48, and the '48 team beat Oregon in the Cotton Bowl, 21–13. His No. 1 player for all time was Doak Walker, truly a back for all purposes.

One of the fabulous games in Texas history was SMU's 1949 gallant but failing effort against national champion Notre Dame, 27–20. The headlines went to two Mustang backs, Kyle Rote and Johnny Champion.

How Bell became a football coach instead of a lawyer as planned makes a study in circuitous fate. As an all-round athlete at Fort Worth's North Side High, he was coached by Robert L. (Chief) Myers, an alumnus of Centre College in Danville, Kentucky.

In 1916, Myers brought Bell, Bo McMillin, Red Weaver, Bill James and others from Fort Worth's "stockyards district" to Kentucky's blue hills. There, under the coaching of Uncle Charlie Moran, Centre lost only three games in four years and gained national attention by beating Harvard in 1921, 6–0. Bell was an end but also played quarterback, linebacker, and guard.

When Bell left Centre in 1920, he had law, not football, in mind. But he needed money for law school. He coached Haskell Institute for two years and Carroll College for one. When he accepted a job as an assistant coach to E. J. (Doc) Stewart at the University of Texas in 1923, it was with the belief that he could finish his law study.

History was working against him, however. In 1923 Texas Christian joined the Southwest Conference, and the name of Matty Bell, a Fort Worth boy who had shown he could coach, appealed to Professor E. W. McDiarmid, chairman of the TCU athletic council. He offered him the head coach's job, Matty took it, and that was the end of law.

In Bell's first year, TCU was bombed by SMU, 40–0, but Bell always credited Ray Morrison, the Mustang coach, with giving him his first real respect for the passing game.

Bell's outstanding player at Texas Christian, and one of the best ever to come out of the Southwest, was Raymond Matthews, better known as "Rags" because his shirt was torn up or off in action so often.

"He was the greatest defensive end I ever saw," Bell said. "He was also a fine all-round football player—one of the best pass receivers, terrific under punts. He was as quick as a cat . . . he would spring out ten or fifteen feet."

In 1925, Matthews' first varsity year, Bell

played him at guard. The other guard was Raymond (Bear) Wolf (later head coach at North Carolina), who was inspired but in a different manner. Said Bell, "I'd look out and there'd be Matthews laughing and Wolf crying, and both playing fine football."

Matthews loved to taunt the opposition into trying his end. "Try comin' around this way, suh!" he'd challenge. In the 1927 East-West Shriners game, All-America Bruce Caldwell of Yale met the challenge five times and was stopped five times. That was the day that Joel Hunt of the Texas Aggies, Jerry Mann of SMU, and Matthews made the All-America selectors, who had passed them over, look foolish.

While Matthews was playing, 1925 through '27, the best that the Texas Aggies and Joel Hunt could get with TCU was a 3–0 loss and two ties, 13–13 and 0–0. Bell's five-year record at TCU against the Texas Aggies (the teams didn't play in 1923) included two victories, two ties, and only one loss. This was a weighty factor when they chose him to replace Dana X. Bible in 1929, after Bible left for Nebraska. Bell's 26-year record —154 victories, 87 defeats and 17 ties—breaks down this way for the three SWC teams he coached:

	W	L	T
Texas Christian (1923–28)	33	17	5
Texas A. & M. (1929–33)	24	21	3
Southern Methodist (1935–41)	47	23	3
(In service 1942–44)			
Southern Methodist (1945–49)	31	16	4
TOTALS	135	77	15

In discussion of the vicissitudes of coaching and the vacillations of alumni, Bell stated:

"Alumni have strange reasoning. They fire a coach instead of giving him sufficient material to produce a team that can win, and when they get hot enough to wield the ax, they usually are aroused enough at the same time to provide material for the new one, who then turns out a good, workmanlike job and is called a wizard.

"The coach without material is usually the coach without a team, despite some occasional masterminding article crediting a Houdini with building a champion out of nothing. A check of histories of members of a championship club will usually show that the individuals were outstanding high or prep school players.

"Marvelous coaching jobs are usually marvelous amounts of work, thought, application and getting the maximum out of the material at hand. Any expert diamond cutter, laboriously, painstakingly, and with delicate craftsmanship, can trim the uneven stone which nature gave him, and polish the facets to gleaming brilliance, but I never heard of anyone doing it with a hunk of coal."

In the fall of 1935, Bell was in a Pullman going down to College Station to scout Texas A. & M. when he was suddenly joined by Roscoe Minton, who was to officiate in the game, and by a Texas Aggie alumnus. Minton winked at Bell and asked the alum: "What's the matter with Bell?"

"Rotten," said the alum. "No coach at all."

"Well," Minton drawled dubiously, "he's doing pretty well this year. He's won eleven straight."

"Ray Morrison left him a team," the old grad snorted.

Minton stuck a fist in his mouth so that his laughing would seem like coughing. When he felt it was safe, he removed his fist and resumed, "Do you think he'll be able to stay at SMU?"

"Naw," said the alum. "Give him one more year and he'll lose every game, like he did at A. & M."

Again, Minton put his fist in his mouth. At this point Bell broke in, "I'm pretty well up on his record. He won the majority of his games at A. & M. every year except one."

"He did not!" yelled the old grad. "I used to make my expenses each year by betting on A. & M., but he never won a Thanksgiving game from the University of Texas."

Minton was coughing. Color was rising in Bell's face.

"As a matter of fact," Bell said, "Texas hasn't beat A. & M. on Kyle Field since 1923."

"Bet you!" the alum shouted.

Minton stopped coughing to ask the old grad, "What do you have against Bell?"

"He didn't care whether he won or lost," said the old grad. "I sat behind the A. & M. bench in 1932 when A. & M. was taking a walloping from TCU and someone asked him for God's sake to do something. Bell laughed and said he didn't care because his pay would go on anyhow."

"Did you hear him say that?" Bell demanded.

"No," the old grad admitted, "but a friend of mine did. I don't even know this fellow Bell. I might be talking to him now, but he didn't care whether he ever won or lost."

Minton could no longer control himself. He ran for the smoker just as Bell got the alum by the collar.

"I'm Matty Bell," he said, "and I worked my gizzard out for A. & M. and every time we lost, I suffered the tortures of the damned."

It was the old grad's turn to color. He apologized, and Bell accepted. Then the old grad brought over two of his boys and introduced them to "that great coach, Matty Bell."

Bell is quick to point out that all alumni are not the same. "That trip home from the Rose Bowl," he wrote, "was a doleful one despite all the jokes and humor my assistants and I could manage. The boys, who had been idols of the Southwest, knew there would be a vacant terminal and thunders of silence when we pulled in.

"I shall never forget the sight I saw a quarter of a mile away as the special finished the long trek. I thought someone was being mobbed. Someone was. It was us! Lining up on the tracks, delaying the train, blocking traffic for half a mile, jammed like a sea of sardines, 25,000 Dallas people were there to give a conqueror's welcome to warriors being brought home on our shields. That, I thought, was the kind of alumni that counted."

After the 1949 season, Bell devoted full time to his duties as director of athletics. By the time he had retired in 1964, SMU had won a national championship in golf and had a total of 20 conference titles in basketball, swimming, tennis, golf, and baseball.

Matty is a member of the National Football Hall of Fame, the Helms Athletic Hall of Fame, was president of the Football Coaches Association longer than any other person, and was on the NCAA Football Rules Committee for many years.

"But to the people of this region," said Les

Matty in November 1970, at a dinner in his honor

Jordan, long-time SMU sports publicist in Matty's time, "he is not known primarily for his record as an athlete, coach, and athletic director, but for his great capacity for leadership and friendship."

Hugo Bezdek

HUGO THE VICTOR

Because Penn State University is located at the foot of Mount Nittany in the central Pennsylvania mountains, its teams have been known since 1906 as the Nittany Lions. The name Nittany comes from Nita-Nee, an Indian maiden who became the beloved of a trader named Malachi Boyer. Nita-Nee's father, Chief O-Ko-Cho, opposed the match and had Malachi im-

prisoned in nearby Penn's Cave. There he died, and the tale of tearful Nita-Nee and her lost love became legend.

Had Hugo Bezdek lived in the time of Nita-Nee and become enamored of her, it is not unlikely that Chief O-Ko-Cho would have regarded him as a suitor less acceptable than Malachi Boyer. For Bezdek, head football coach

at Penn State, from 1918 through '29, and before that at Oregon and Arkansas, would have rubbed the chief the wrong way.

Bezdek did that to a lot of people. He was at his abrasive best on New Year's Day, 1923, in Pasadena, California. That was the first year the Tournament of Roses game was played in the Arroyo Seco and given the name Rose Bowl. Bezdek kept Penn State's opponent, the Southern California Trojans, their coach, Elmer (Gloomy Gus) Henderson, and a capacity crowd of 52,000 waiting a full hour. The scheduled 2:30 kickoff didn't take place until 3:30, and was nearly preceded by an unscheduled fistfight between Bezdek and Henderson. Two explanations have been offered for the lateness of the Lions.

"Bezdek," stated Chester L. Smith, veteran Pittsburgh sports columnist and one of the few writers who ever got along with Hugo, "had held up the game because it was a warm day and he wanted to wait until the sun started to drop behind the Sierra Madre."

The other viewpoint accepts Bezdek's position that the buses carrying the players were without police escort and got tied up in the traffic.

Whatever the reason, it left Henderson understandably irate. His Trojans had warmed up strenuously, and he feared they would lose their edge. Finally, at 3:15, a Penn State manager showed up at Southern Cal's dressing room and informed Henderson that the Penn State starting team had arrived, whereupon Henderson went out and confronted Bezdek in the middle of the field.

"Your manager tells me your first team has arrived," Henderson grated. "Don't you think you've delayed the game long enough? Let's get going."

"All of my players are not here," Bezdek sizzled in turn, "and I don't like it any better than you do. If you say I am responsible for delaying the game, you're a liar."

"I only know what your manager said," Henderson retorted, "and he seems to know what he's talking about. That makes you out a pretty good liar, and you can take it any way you want."

"You're not calling me a liar," Bezdek blazed. "Take off your glasses and we'll settle this thing right here and now."

But the unscheduled preliminary didn't come off.

"I had just climbed out of bed with the flu and could hardly stand up," Henderson explained later. "Also, I knew Bezdek had earned his way

Hugo Bezdek, at Penn State

through the University of Chicago fighting as a pro under an assumed name, so I decided it would be wiser if the two teams decided the issue."

Southern Cal won the game 14–3. The Trojans were better and luckier; one of their touchdowns was set up by a forward pass from Roy (Bullet) Baker, which Harold Galloway caught while sliding on his back at the 2-yard line.

The pregame bad feeling carried over into postgame, and both coaches barred writers from the dressing rooms. Incensed at being denied access to quotes, one scribe fabricated his own. They had a quaint, uncoachly ring.

"The best team won," Gus Henderson was quoted. "Good coaching, like the effect of cigarettes, always tells in the long run. It is my personal belief that USC should have won by four more touchdowns. Thank God for the guy who made it a criminal offense to hit a man wearing glasses. Hugo Bezdek is no gentleman."

"The best team lost," Coach Bezdek was quoted. "A football team with the best coaching in the world could not win against the luck the Trojans had. When playing at its best, my team could beat S.C. by 40 points. My only regret is that Elmer Henderson had left his glasses on."

Penn State, the latest to arrive at the Rose Bowl, had been invited the earliest. It had received and accepted the bid in Seattle almost 13 months before, on December 3, 1921, after beating Washington 21–7. At that time the Lions had an undefeated string of 24, which had begun after losing 19–13 at Dartmouth in 1919.

Joe Bedenk, star right guard for the Lions in 1921–23, later Bezdek's assistant, and head coach for one year, 1949, told what happened to the Lions between accepting the bid and playing the game.

"Our 1921 team was supposed to be Bezdek's best, and prospects were better for the following year, since we were losing only four seniors. That winter, however, Dick Harlow, who'd been an assistant to Bezdek and before that head coach, 1915–17, left to be head coach at Colgate and took with him six talented sophomores. The six went with him because they were mad at Hugo; they had missed out making a letter by about five minutes."

Whatever the effect of the departed six sore sophomores, the Rose Bowl locked-in Lions were savagely shot up through the second half of the 1922 schedule. They were tied by Syracuse and beaten by Navy, Pennsylvania, and Pittsburgh. The loss to Navy, 14–0, terminated a 30-game defeatless string.

Despite his hectic experience with Southern Cal, Bezdek was still one up at Pasadena. He had coached the Oregon team that beat Pennsylvania in the 1917 game 14–0, and the Mare Island Marines that defeated the army's Camp Lewis team in the 1918 wartime game, 19–7. Odds favored Pennsylvania at 5–3, and Bezdek did not discourage them.

"I've got only overgrown high school boys," Hugo cried, "while Penn can field a varsity of big university strength. We haven't a chance."

Meanwhile, he conducted secret practices. In contrast, Bob Folwell, Penn's coach, conducted open practices, and even invited Bezdek. Bez accepted. Bert Bell, later commissioner of the National Football League, was Penn's quarterback.

"Bezdek asked Folwell," Bell said, "if he would show him our reverse-pass play, and Folwell told me to run it. Reluctantly I complied. Imagine what we thought, and said, when Oregon scored its first touchdown on our own play."

Bezdek drove his players so hard during the week that playing a game on Saturday was a relief. Scrimmaging began the second day of fall practice. C. B. (Casey) Jones, former Penn State assistant, noted that a regular in-season practice week under Bezdek was about as follows:

Sunday—Home or away, there was a long, running hike.

Monday—Those who hadn't played on Saturday had a long scrimmage.

Tuesday—It was known as "Bloody Tuesday" because every player scrimmaged until half dead.

Wednesday—Offensive scrimmaging plus passing, and defensive scrimmaging against opponent's plays.

Thursday—Pass scrimmaging and defense.

Friday—Long signal drills up and down the field.

Every day's practice ended in a half hour of wind sprints.

Bezdek was even known to hold full practice the day of the game. Herb McCracken, former coach of Lafayette and later publisher of *Scholastic Coach,* told of shepherding his team to Penn State: "When we arrived at old Beaver Field to dress a couple of hours before the game, we heard a rumpus going on under the stands. It was Hugo conducting a pregame scrimmage."

As a pep-talker, Bezdek was a thespian, known even to put onions on his cheeks to evoke ersatz tears. He seldom praised a player—"Your best is not good enough! I want something better!" All opposing coaches, once scheduled, were classified as despicable villains, practitioners of dirty tricks, continually spying on Penn State practices.

Bezdek didn't get along at all well with Pop Warner. It galled him that in five games with Warner's Pittsburgh teams, Penn State got only one victory, 20–0 in 1919. The undefeated teams of 1920 and '21 both were favored against the Panthers but came away from Forbes Field with no better than scoreless ties. In 1922 and '23, Pitt won 14–0 and 21–3. (From 1924 through '29, his last year as coach, Bezdek's teams lost six straight to Pitt teams coached by Jock Sutherland.)

In the heat of battle, Bezdek had a habit of pulling the bench he sat on practically onto the playing field. To prevent this and the further to bedevil Hugo, Warner had the Forbes Field benches secured to the ground with stakes.

"People admired Bezdek, as his players did," said Casey Jones, a valued assistant, "but, I believe, for his success only. He liked only people who had something that would improve his 'image.' He never gave any of his assistants credit or even mentioned their names."

Hugo in one of his quieter moments. *Chicago Tribune Photos*

Rough cut, belligerent, autonomous—Bezdek was all that. He also had a football mind, sharp and imaginative. As fullback for the University of Chicago early in the century, he had been exposed to that master innovator, Amos Alonzo Stagg.

After graduation, Bezdek coached Oregon in 1906 and immediately won attention with an undefeated team. He moved on to Arkansas, where his five-year record, 1908 through '12, included an undefeated season in 1909 and a one-defeater in '10. In 1913 he returned to Oregon until 1918. His teams gave Gil Dobie's unconquerable Washington its toughest opposition; in three games they held the Huskies to 20 points, while scoring seven. The 1916 team that beat Penn in the Rose Bowl played a scoreless tie with Washington.

In 1908, his first year at Arkansas, the Razorbacks were beaten 24–0 by St. Louis, whose coach, Eddie Cochems, had developed that new weapon, the forward pass, far beyond his contemporaries. To improve his own use of the pass, Bezdek called for help from Stagg, who along with Walter Eckersall, his ace ex-quarterback,

went down to Fayetteville where Eckersall worked with the Arkansas quarterback, Steve Creekmore.

They proved successful clinics; Bezdek was to rate Creekmore, Oregon tackle John Beckett, and Penn State quarterback Glenn Killinger his three top players. Creekmore recalled that Bezdek put in a spread formation for passing, and had a play in which a far flanker or "sleeper" was posted as a receiver. Hugo also was a pioneer in exploiting the screen pass, the quick kick, and the onside kick.

Bezdek was one of the first, if not the first, to use the half spinner and full spinner in his attack. Warner, who developed them to high proficiency at Stanford, gave him credit. Bez came upon the spinner by accident in 1919, according to Dick Harlow, his assistant then:

"A signal was missed and the wingback did not take the ball from Harry Robb. Being a smart back, Robb turned toward the line and a huge hole developed. This was talked over but nothing was done until the same thing happened again. Then it was put in as a play."

Bezdek coached several players at Penn State of All-America ability. Besides Bedenk and Killinger there were end Bob Higgins and backs Charlie Way, Henry L. (Hinky) Haines, Joe Lightner, Lighthorse Harry Wilson, and Mike Palm.

Higgins, who later coached Penn State from 1930 through '48, set a record in 1919. He played eight games with the 89th Division, the American Expeditionary Force champions, and then returned to Penn State, where he played eight more. He captained the team, and in the 20–0 victory over Pitt (last in 20 years for the Lions over the Panthers) he was on the receiving end of a 92-yard touchdown pass play, with the ball thrown by Bill Hess from punt formation in the end zone.

In the 28–7 victory at Pennsylvania in 1920, Hinky Haines returned a kickoff 90 yards for a touchdown. The next week Pie Way paced the 20–0 triumph over Nebraska with scoring runs of 67 and 57 yards; he had 11 touchdowns for the season. In the 1921 win over Georgia Tech, 28–7, in New York's Polo Grounds, Glenn Killinger returned a punt 90 yards for a TD. Killinger made big yardage on Bezdek's spin plays, as did Lighthorse Harry Wilson.

Wilson was called "Lighthorse" after the Revolutionary War cavalry general Henry (Light-Horse Harry) Lee, because he moved with a

dancing elusiveness and unusual balance that made him tough to bring down. In 1923 he accounted for all three touchdowns in the 21–3 victory over Navy by returning a kickoff 95 yards, running 80 from scrimmage, and bringing back an interception 55. He repeated the three-TD trick in the 21–0 win at Penn on runs of 49, 45, and 25 yards.

After Penn State, Lighthorse Harry played four more years at West Point. Although he never as a Cadet matched his Nittany peaks, he was still colorful and dangerous. In seven games involving Wilson, Navy got only one victory; among those who cheered when he received his commission was the Brigade of Midshipmen.

The Penn State–Harvard tie, 21–21, at Cambridge, October 22, 1921, was one of the highlight games of the era. The Lions had going an undefeated string of 18, the Crimson a longer one of 24. By today's standards both teams were light heavyweight; Penn State's starters averaged 186 pounds, Harvard's 179.

Halfback George Owen and quarterback Charlie Buell ran and passed Harvard to a 14–0 lead, but the Lions put on a terrific comeback. Halfback Joe Lightner scored all 21 of State's points, which were set up by Killinger, Wilson, and himself. A big contribution also was made by the blocking of fullback A. H. (Knabby) Knabb. The game ended with Penn State on Harvard's 24, and the Lions won the statistics, 19 first downs to 9 and 294 yards rushing to 105; each team gained 62 yards passing.

Bezdek's six teams from 1919 through '24 compiled a 40–10–7 record. The 1919 team went 7–1, losing only to Dartmouth; the 1920 and '21 teams were unbeaten, but each tied twice. Hugo's 12-year log at Nittany, 1918 through '29, shows 65–30–11.

"Defense was the success of Bezdek's teams," said Casey Jones. "Hugo believed in the principle, 'If they can't score on you, they can't beat you.' One has only to look back at the scores and see that very few teams scored over one touchdown against Penn State." In six years, 1919–24, the Lions gave up more than one touchdown in only eight of 57 games.

Bezdek had comparable success as Penn State's baseball coach. His record, 1920 through '30, was 129–76, including a winning streak in 1919–20 of 29, one short of his defeatless football skein. In 1919, he also filled in as basketball coach with a respectable 11–2.

His baseball record and brand of leadership impelled the Pittsburgh Pirates to hire him as manager. In 1917, he took over a last-place club and in '18 and '19 moved it up to fourth. His stay with the Bucs was also memorable for a Pullman fistfight he had with another intractable character, the bristle-bearded spitball pitcher Burleigh Grimes.

"The fight almost wrecked the Pullman," said Chet Smith, "and when it was over they were both bloody and their clothes were torn. But Bez said to Burleigh, 'Okay, you——— ———, you're still going to pitch tomorrow.'

"I don't know," Smith continued, "any man who could make as bitter an enemy as Bez had the knack of doing. He succeeded in dividing Penn State into two camps, one his friends and the other just as much against him, and the situation, as much as anything else, led to a gradual downcurve of the Nittany Lions on the football field.

"The anti-Bezdeks were led by Ed Yeckley, who captained the 1905 team and turned so completely against his alma mater that he dispatched his talented son, Bill, to Princeton, where the boy captained the Tiger eleven.

"But years later, when Ed and Bez met at an alumni gathering in Youngstown, Ohio, the first thing you know, they were standing shoulder to shoulder at their host's bar, calling each other everything they could think of in the most friendly fashion."

As he grew older, Bezdek did soften somewhat. He remained a harsh taskmaster but became less antagonistic, and when in the mood he could be an entertaining conversationalist.

Gus Henderson pointed out that Bezdek, in his fullback days for Chicago, had done some boxing for money. One bout found him representing the Morgan Athletic Club of the South Side and decisioning a Buck Montgomery. Stagg, hearing about it, visited Frank Ragan, president of the Morgan A.C.

"Is it true," Stagg inquired, "that Bezdek fought for money?"

"No, sir," Ragan replied. "Hugo fought for the love of the game. But I paid him $75."

According to another story, Stagg, who abhorred profanity, is supposed to have broken his rule at the request of Bezdek. Hugo was not having a very good practice, and suggested to the Old Man, "Perhaps I'd do better if you cussed me out."

Bezdek was born in Prague, Czechoslovakia, brought to America at 5, and raised on the rough,

tough Chicago South Side. He had to be tough to climb out of his background, and he was. The record says he succeeded, both as a coach and as an athletic director. His 24-year record reveals 127–58–15 for .672, and he is in the Hall of Fame.

"As an athletic director," said Casey Jones, "Bez was a fighter for his program. He was responsible for our golf course in 1922; Varsity Hall, which housed all athletes, in 1925; the Recreation Building in '25; and the old stadium, between 1921 and '28."

In 1938, he retired to Doylestown, Pennsylvania, to become a chicken farmer. In 1949, he returned to football briefly as a coach and athletic director at National Agricultural College in Doylestown.

"Hugo lived a strenuous life," wrote Chet Smith, "which included a good many triumphs and a number of lickings. If he was inclined to brag a bit over one, you have to admit also that he never cried about the other."

D. X. Bible

THE FOOTBALL CLASSICIST

Dana Xenophon Bible, better known as D. X. Bible, was born in Tennessee, was the son of a teacher of the classics, and now was coaching Texas A. & M. It was halftime of the 1922 Aggies-Texas game, and the score was tied 7–7. Never in the eight-year history of the Southwest Conference had an Aggie team been able to beat Texas at Austin.

Bible called on history. He remembered that in the defense of the Alamo, Colonel William B. Travis drew a line with his sword along the dirt floor, and invited all who wanted to stay to step over the line. They all stepped over except Jim Bowie; since he was seriously ill they carried him across in his cot. So now D. X. Bible drew an imaginary line across the floor with his shoe, and told his players.

"Those who want to go out and be known as members of an A. & M. team that defeated Texas in Austin, step over the line."

Bible was almost knocked down in the rush. Whether calling on the Alamo had anything to do with it, the Aggies won, 14–7.

Joel Hunt, Aggie All-Conference halfback, 1925–27, and one of the very best players in Southwest football history, summed up Bible: "Confident as a banker, astute as a schoolmaster, poised as a preacher, and expressive as a salesman."

This blend of qualities accounted for one of the most distinguished of coaching records. From 1917 through '28 at Texas A. & M. (excluding 1918 when he was an army pursuit pilot in France), Bible's teams won five Southwest Conference championships. In his 1929–36 span at Nebraska, his Cornhuskers won six Big Six titles.

At Texas, 1937–46, his Longhorns won three SWC crowns.

(Those fierce rivals Texas and Texas Aggies both have a fond feeling toward Bible; his Aggies won 5, lost 5, and tied 1 with the Longhorns, and his Horns won 8 and lost 2 with the Aggies.)

That's 14 major conference championships in 29 seasons with three different teams, and that's why Dana Bible, as soon as he was eligible five years after coaching his last game, was named to the Hall of Fame in 1951.

That and a sportsmanship always unquestioned. Once, while he was at Nebraska, an official had to penalize a player more than once for overrough tactics. Finally the official said, "Who taught you that? I know you never were taught it by your coach." The player was repentant and fearful. He asked the official not to report him to Coach Bible. And he mended his ways.

In his 33 seasons—he coached at Mississippi College and Louisiana State before Texas A. & M.—Bible's record shows 192–71–23 for .712. He experienced his share of peaks and valleys, the brightest and the darkest.

His salary negotiations bespoke a sharp knowledge of the market. For coaching the 1917, '19, and '20 Aggies to a 24–1–1 record, he received $2,400 a year. But when he left Nebraska for Texas in 1937, he negotiated one of the best pacts in coaching annals. The Longhorns wanted him so badly that they gave him a 20-year contract, the first ten years as coach and athletic director, the second ten as athletic director, at $15,000 a year.

Before they could agree to the deal, the Texas

D. X. Bible

assigned responsibilities for recruiting good high school football players therefrom.

Bible said it would take five years to build a champion. He missed by one; it took him six years. His 1937 and '38 teams finished last in the SWC, but in the next three years they kept moving up, to 4th, 3rd, and 2nd, and in his last five, they finished 1st, 1st, 2nd, 1st, 3rd; for his last seven years they totaled 53–13–1. The '42 team, first to represent the University of Texas in a Bowl game, defeated Georgia Tech 14–7 in the Cotton Bowl. In two other Cotton Bowl appearances, the '43 team tied Randolph Field 7–7, and the '45 team beat Missouri 40–27.

No victory ever pleased D.X. more than the Texas Aggies' 22–14 upset of Centre, New Year's Day, 1922, in the Dallas Fair Park. It was called the Dixie Classic and was a forerunner of the Cotton Bowl 15 years later. Centre was the glamour team of football. The Praying Colonels were undefeated, had won national attention by upsetting Harvard 6–0, and were 20-point favorites. They also had a special Texas following, because Alvin (Bo) McMillin, their quarterback, lineman Matty Bell, and others came from Fort Worth.

Further to dramatize the setting, the morning of the game Bo McMillin married his childhood sweetheart in Fort Worth and walked onto the field that afternoon with her on his arm. But the niceties were shoved aside with the kickoff. T. F. (Puny) Wilson, who starred at end for the Aggies, said that "Mr. Bible spoke a few well-chosen words, and man, we knew we were ready." Said referee Ernie Quigley, "I've never seen a team as ready to play as A. & M." It was a hard-hitter all the way, and as injuries cut into the Aggies' sparse reserves, a Texas A. & M. tradition was born. Coach Bible recalled a promising sophomore named King Gill, who was sitting in the stands. Dr. Gill, later an M.D. in Corpus Christi, told the story:

"I had played on the football team, but was on the basketball team at that time because those in charge thought I'd be more valuable there. I was in Dallas, however, and even rode to the stadium in the same taxi with Coach Dana X. Bible. I was in civilian clothes and was not to be in uniform. Coach Bible asked me to assist in spotting players for the late Jinx Tucker (sports editor of the Waco *News-Tribune*) in the press box.

"So I was up in the press box ... when near the end of the first half, I was called down to the Texas A. & M. bench. There had been a number

legislature pondered and debated. Fifteen grand meant that Bible would be getting more than the college president. The legislature resolved the impasse by raising the president's salary.

Before he signed, however, Bible came to a clear-cut understanding with the man who had much to do with hiring him, H. L. Lutcher Stark, a multimillionaire. Stark owned more than a half-million acres in Texas and Louisiana, but Bible bearded him.

"Just what part, Mr. Stark," he asked, "would you expect to have in athletics at Texas?"

"Just sitting on the sidelines," said Stark.

"What if I put you off the sidelines," said D.X.

"Well," Stark countered, "I've been put off by worse coaches than you, D.X."

"A lot of people will be involved in our program," Bible pointed out, "and none can be given special privileges."

Stark was pleased with Bible for his forthrightness.

"Then I'll just buy the best seats I can," he said. "And when you need help, holler."

D.X. immediately put in motion "The Bible Plan," by which all 267,399 square miles of Texas were divided into districts, and alumni were

of injuries but it was not until I arrived on the field that I learned Coach Bible wanted me to put on a football uniform and be ready to play, if he needed me.

"There were no dressing rooms at the stadium in those days. The team had dressed downtown at the hotel and traveled to the stadium in taxi cabs. Anyway, I put on the uniform of one of the injured players. We got under the stands and he put on my clothes and I put on his uniform. I was ready to play but never was sent into the game."

That's why, to this day, the Aggie Cadet Corps stands throughout the game, symbolizing the original "Twelfth Man," King Gill, to be "ready if needed."

Comparable to upsetting Centre was the 7–0 shocker the 1940 Texas team pulled on the Aggies and fullback John Kimbrough to wreck their Rose Bowl plans. Pete Layden's running and passing and a doughty defense did in the Farmers. Before that game Bible read his men Edgar Guest's poem "It Can Be Done."

Ironically, what was probably Bible's best team, acknowledged among the best in SWC history, 1941 Texas, gave him his deepest disappointments. Heavily favored both times, it suffered back-to-back upsets in a 7–7 tie by Baylor and a 14–7 loss to Texas Christian. Both games were lost on passes, Baylor with 18 seconds to go, TCU with seven.

Before those two nightmares, the Longhorns, with Layden and Jack Crain in the backfield, Mal Kutner end, and Chal Daniel guard, had whomped Arkansas 48–14, Rice 40–0, and Southern Methodist 34–0. And after the two upsets they beat the Aggies at College Station 23–0, and in a postseason game knocked the whey out of Oregon by the incredible score of 71–7. The Oregon State team that beat Duke in the 1942 Rose Bowl (at Durham, N.C.) had beaten Oregon by only 12–7.

So Texas, showing its real strength, took a lot of the shine off the Rose Bowl game it had blown. The Longhorns finished fourth in the Associated Press national poll, behind Minnesota, Duke, and Notre Dame, while the Aggies, Southwest Conference champions, finished No. 9 nationally. All of this compounded the frustration of Texas.

D. X. Bible first attracted national attention with his Aggie teams of 1917, '19, and '20. The '20 Aggies seemed on their way to a third straight undefeated and unscored-on season and to their 26th defeatless game in a row when they led the Longhorns, 3–0, well into the fourth quarter. But

D. X. at Texas

on a fourth-down play, Tom Dennis, of Texas, made a leaping, falling grab of a tackle-eligible pass to the 4-yard line, and Francisco Dominguez punched it over. What was then a record crowd of 18,300 watched Texas complete its season with a 9–0 record and win its first SWC championship, under Coach Berry Whitaker.

Bible's aces in those years included fullback Jack Mahan, tackle Ox Ford, guard E. S. Wilson, back Rip Collins, a star punter, back Roswell Higginbotham, end Puny Wilson, tackle C. R. Drake, and guard Cap Murrah.

Bible's favorite team and favorite player probably were the 1927 Texas Aggies and halfback Joel Hunt. When Jim Crow, onetime Aggie tackle and 36 years a Southwest Conference scout, picked his all-time SWC backfield, he had Joel Hunt at one of the halfbacks. (The three other backs were Kimbrough at full, Doak Walker, Southern Methodist, quarterback, and Bill Wallace, Rice, halfback.) Few would debate Crow on this.

When Hunt, a high school whiz at Waco, arrived at Texas A. & M. in 1924, he was so small

(five feet ten and 145) they wouldn't give him a uniform. He got one only when Blackie Williams, a tackle, switched to Texas Christian. In 1925, as a sophomore, he got into the first game when Taro Kishi was hurt, and he stayed in for three years. In 1926, his junior year, Bible gave him charge of the team on the field.

By now Hunt weighed 155, and as an example of his versatility he accounted for all 13 points in a tie with Texas Christian, scoring a touchdown, kicking the extra point, place-kicking one field goal and dropkicking another, for 46 yards.

In 1927, his senior year, he weighed 168 pounds and scored 128 points to lead the SWC and finish second in the nation. If the All-America pickers hadn't been myopic, they would have picked Hunt unanimously. Hunt, Jerry Mann of SMU, Rags Matthews, Texas Christian end, and J. V. (Siki) Sikes, Aggies' end, showed up the All-America pickers by taking charge of the 1927 East-West Shriners game.

Hunt was truly an all-purpose player. He punted, passed, place-kicked, dropkicked, kicked off, ran the ball three out of five times, called the plays and was team captain. He was outstanding on defense, and he played all but three minutes of the schedule.

"A flaming competitive spirit drove Hunt to greatness," wrote Weldon Hart, of the Austin *American-Statesman*. "He was a natural player. He liked practice, loved scrimmage. He possessed a congenital elusiveness that led a contemporary to muse, 'He ain't so fast but you couldn't catch him in a telephone booth.'

"The only man who had the Indian sign on Hunt was Rags Matthews. During their three years of battling, Hunt's Aggies never defeated Matthews' Horned Frogs. There was one TCU victory and two ties."

With Hunt in high gear the Aggies won the conference championship in 1925 and '27; in between they finished sixth. The 1927 title hinged on the Aggies–Southern Methodist game at College Station. It pitted Joel Hunt against Jerry Mann. The Ags won it, 39–13, and Hunt had a day unmatched. He scored three touchdowns, passed to two others, and punted eight times for a 44-yard average. Such were the height and accuracy of his kicks and the Aggie coverage that the Mustangs were unable to return them even a foot.

The only flaw in the 1927 Aggie record was a scoreless tie at Texas Christian; as an ironic note, Blackie Williams, whose departure had gained

Hunt his uniform two years before, captained the Frogs. After the game, the bus taking the Aggies back to College Station was slow getting started, and Hunt prodded the driver. "Take it easy, bub," he replied, which was too much for D. X. Bible. He had, when aroused, a bull's bellow to belie his bald friendliness.

"Get this heap going," D.X. roared, "or I'll jerk you out of that seat and take it in myself." In telling the story, Hunt added, "We drove on to the championship."

Bible always imputed that 0–0 tie with the Frogs to Hunt's spirit of team play and modesty:

"Joel got off an especially long run—about 60 yards, as I recall it—to TCU's 1. He called each of the three other backs on the first three downs, but because of Matthews and other Frogs, we found ourselves facing fourth down, not on their 1-yard line but on their 10. Joel finally decided to run himself. He got nine yards, but the ball went over to TCU on its 1, and the game ended 0–0. Bless Joel, I just wish he hadn't been so modest that day."

Hunt and Jack Crain, of Texas, were named by Bible as his two best running backs, and Bobby Layne, who starred for the Longhorns in the midforties, his best passer. "The only way to evaluate Layne," said D.X., "is to say he was electric."

Bible was a fundamentalist, whose teams were thoroughly schooled defensively and in the kicking game. On offense he ran from a single wing, a double wing, and a Y formation. His teams always executed well.

Bible was a realist who knew when the time was ripe to move. It was following a 5–4–1 record, a sixth-place finish, and a shrewd analysis of the future (his successor, Matty Bell, lasted five years with a 24–21–3 record) that D.X. in 1929 accepted the offer of Nebraska. And at least part of his motivation for accepting the Texas job in 1937 was his awareness that the Longhorn alumni, who had gone without a champion for seven years and had just suffered through two sixth-place finishes, would be as patient as is possible for alumni to be.

At Nebraska, from 1929 through '36, his teams failed to win the Big Six conference title only in 1930 and '34, and dropped only three conference games. Bible's Nebraska stars were headed by fullbacks George Sauer and Sam Francis, and tackles Ray Richards and Hugh Rhea.

On the negative side, Bible lost four out of four to Minnesota, coached by Bernie Bierman, and

the best he could get out of eight games with Jock Sutherland's Pittsburgh teams was scoreless ties in 1930 and '32. Yet, this did not detract from his stature very much, if any, because the Gophers and Panthers were top national powers and the Cornhuskers usually pushed them to the limit.

For example, in 1936 the Big Six champion Nebraska team lost to Minnesota 7–0, and to Pitt 19–6, but ranked No. 9 nationally: Minnesota and Pitt vied for the national championship, the AP poll naming the Gophers No. 1 and the Panthers No. 3. The loss to Minnesota rates among the notable "heartbreakers," for there were only 59 seconds left when Andy Uram, taking a lateral from quarterback Bud Wilkinson on a punt return, raced 75 yards for a touchdown.

The aftermath emphasized Bible's ability as a practical psychologist, even though he was, in effect, again calling on "the Alamo." The next game was with Indiana, and the Hoosiers led the Huskers 9–0 at the half in great measure because Bible's team was still "down" from its effort against Minnesota. Paul Amen, star all-round athlete and later head coach of Wake Forest, recalls the halftime scene in the Nebraska dressing room:

"D.X. just threw out technical details and concentrated on psychology. He challenged our desire to win, our courage to fight back. He offered starting positions to the first eleven men who wanted badly enough to beat the rest of us to the exit. We lit out for the door. Bible beat us to it. Then he stood blocking the way, insisting we weren't 'ready.' A real mob scene developed. Friendly players knocked each other down fighting to get out. Some squared off and fought. The pandemonium was indescribable."

And it worked. Nebraska won the game, 13–9, and played the second half with only eleven men.

Dana Xenophon Bible was born October 8, 1891, in Jefferson City, Tennessee, son of Jonathan and Cleopatra Bible. Jonathan Bible taught Latin and Greek in the public schools, but young Dana, although he himself was a Latin scholar, was less impressed by the commentaries of Julius Caesar than by those of the leading coaches of the day, like Fielding Yost, Bob Zuppke, Pop Warner, Amos Alonzo Stagg, and Dr. Henry Williams.

D.X. did his first coaching at Brandon Prep in Shelbyville, Tennessee. Eligibility standards were elastic and sometimes rival coaches, by mutual agreement, suited up and played. Bible played some halfback for Brandon and, since he was already balding at 21, heard rooters call him "Grandpa."

His work at Brandon got him his first coaching job at Mississippi College. In probably his most notable victory there, he beat Tulane, coached by Clark Shaughnessy. In 1916, the Texas Aggies hired him as freshman coach. Near the end of that season Louisiana State lost its head coach and received permission from A. C. Love, chairman of the Aggies' athletic committee, to borrow him. In his three games as coach, LSU beat Ole Miss, and tied Rice and Tulane. As a result, both LSU and the Aggies wanted D.X. for their 1917 coach.

"I felt a moral obligation to A. & M." Bible said. "They had consented to let me go to help out LSU: now they wanted me back. I was delighted and honored to return to A. & M. as its head coach."

D.X. was also delighted that the powerful 1916 Aggie freshman team was available for the varsity.

Every honor football has to offer was bestowed on D. X. Bible. He was president of the Football Coaches Association of America. For 27 years he was a member of the National Football Rules Committee. In 1953 he received the coaches' Amos Alonzo Stagg Award for long service to the game, and in 1954 the Touchdown Club of New York saluted him for his contributions. What Bible meant to his players and to the game of football was eloquently expressed by Joel Hunt:

"He was a gentleman, a forceful leader, and a great moral character. He had courage to match the situation. He could take charge of all situations. He had the ability to organize a squad into a loyal and spirited group. He demanded discipline and respect. He was a man who could have been successful in any profession.

"I can still hear him say, 'Captain, go out there and take charge; take command of the situation.' He was a really great man who has been honored with many words and the recipient of many football honors, but he never shall be honored as he has been by his boys with their respect and admiration."

Bernie Bierman

THE HAMMER OF THE NORTH

Anecdotes growing around Bernard William Bierman were as rare as defeats for his Minnesota teams. And when one did spring up, it had to do with some bit of psychology he'd practiced. Always a driver, Bierman was extra tough with his 1938 squad the week before the final game with Wisconsin. He picked fullback Larry Buhler as his particular target, downgrading Buhler and building up his opponent, Howie Weiss. By the end of the week the Gophers were so mad at Bierman that they took it out on Wisconsin, 21–0.

"I'm lucky," Bierman said after the game. "I'm lucky somebody didn't shoot me this last week."

Just as the Golden Gophers left the cold breath of defeat on their opponents most of the time from 1932 through '41, so did their white-haired, steely-eyed boss leave behind him the chill of aloofness.

It wasn't that Bierman lacked emotion. He showed the tension inside him the way he lit and discarded one cigarette after another on the sideline during a game. But he was not capable of showing sentiment and he admitted it. Even when he visited injured halfback Julie Alphonse in the hospital, his conversation began and ended with "Hello" and "How are you?"

"I had to make most of the conversation," Alphonse said. "The coach was obviously ill at ease. And yet I knew he was concerned about me."

"I don't think I'd be able to make a sentimental dressing room talk," Bierman said. "I'm afraid I would end up laughing at myself."

He believed in long hours of practice at blocking and tackling. He did not believe in a team's running pell-mell onto the field. He called back a Tulane team of his that was rushing out. "Walk out there, and expend your energy after you get out there. Keep your mind calm."

The closest he came to halftime oratory was at Georgia when he was coaching Tulane in 1929. The Greenies would ultimately win, 21–15, but they trailed at the half, 15–14. Lester Lautenschlaeger, Bierman's assistant and a former Tulane backfield ace, was chewing out the players. Lester climaxed his tirade by flinging his hat on the floor, stomping on it, and shouting, "Georgia! I can lick the whole state of Georgia by

myself!" Then—or so the story goes—Bierman drove his own heel into the hat and added, "So can I."

No, Bernie Bierman never had much to say, until after he quit coaching in 1951 and became a radio sportscaster; and then he avoided criticizing anybody.

His teams spoke loudly for him. From 1932 through '41, the Golden Gophers won 64, lost 11, tied 5. They were undefeated five times; won six Big Ten titles—1934, '35, '37, '38, '40, '41; were national champs four times—'34, '36, '40, '41.

A 28-game defeatless string, the last 21 of them victories, was broken, 6–0, on Northwestern's muddy field in 1936. A 15-yard roughness penalty on Ed Widseth, the Gophers' ace left tackle, set up a 1-yard scoring plunge by fullback Steve Toth. That game cost Minnesota the Big Ten title, but it was still ranked No. 1 nationally.

Before returning to his alma mater in 1932,

Bernie Bierman, watching his Northmen

Bierman had coached at Montana, Mississippi State, and Tulane. At Tulane the 1929 team was undefeated and the '31 team went 11–0 in the regular season. They lost 21–12 in the 1932 Rose Bowl game to perhaps Howard Jones' finest Southern Cal team. Turnovers gave the Trojans a 21-point lead, but the Greenies came back to score twice and put Jones and all of Troy on the worry seat. Total yards from scrimmage were Tulane 378, S.C. 233; first downs were 18–11.

That Greenie team, perhaps No. 1 in Tulane history, had several star players, including Don Zimmerman, Wop Glover, and Lowell (Red) Dawson in the backfield, and Jerry Dalrymple at left end.

After he quit coaching, Bierman called the 1934 Minnesota team the best he ever turned out.

"It had great spirit and poise," he said. "It was two deep and in some spots three deep without falloff. It was very well coordinated and this came to some extent from uniform speed. We had no real fast man in the backfield and no real slow one in the line.

"Glen Seidel at quarterback did a great job directing. Pug Lund, captain and left half, gave it great spirit; so did guard Billy Bevan."

Lund starred despite a summer accident that had chopped off part of a thumb. Bevan was the last Minnesota player not to wear a head guard.

Other line personnel included All-America Frank (Butch) Larson, Bob Tenner, and John Romig, ends; Dick Smith, Phil Bengston, and Ed Widseth, tackles; Milt Bruhn, Vern Oech, and Bud Wilkinson, guards; and Dale Rennebohm and Bud Svendsen, centers. Besides Seidel and Lund in the backfield, there were Babe LeVoir and Art Clarkson, halfbacks, and Sheldon Beise and Stanislaus (the Hammer) Kostka at full.

Harry Kipke, Michigan coach, spoke for a majority when he said, "It is the greatest team I ever saw or played against as a coach. Their reserves would beat almost any team in the country."

One of the most important and best-played games of the thirties sent this '34 team against Pitt at Pittsburgh. Although it was played early, October 20, its result, as anticipated, stood up in determining the national championship. By winning, 13–7, Minnesota finished No. 1; by losing, Pitt finished No. 2. Each won all the rest of its games; neither was pressed.

Pitt led at the half, 7–0, on a 64-yard play in which fullback Izzy Weinstock gained nine yards, then lateraled off to halfback Mike Nicksick

(later Nixon) who raced the rest of the way. Pitt earlier had recovered a fumble on the Minnesota 6, but four slams off or inside tackle were thrown back by the Northmen.

Meanwhile, Lund was kicking on second down. The strategy was to wear down Pitt, force mistakes and capitalize on them. This would work out. Milt Bruhn, later a successful head coach at Wisconsin, was first replacement at left guard. He recalled:

"At the beginning of the game, they blocked us like knives. But as physical attrition mounted late in the game, when we blocked them, we could hear them softly groaning."

Bierman's halftime speech would have pleased George Orwell, who advises writers, "Whenever you can leave out a word, leave it out."

"Two touchdowns will win it," said Bernie.

Both Minnesota touchdowns produced a significant clinic for assaying Bierman football, power with precision, yes, but well-conceived, multiple-ball-handling plays and use of the pass judiciously. Minnesota passed three times and completed two, the second for the winning touchdown.

Both touchdowns were set up through hard inside blasting by Kostka alternating with Lund, and then Kostka. A true Hammer of the North who weighed 230, Kostka could start quick and veer at top speed. After his blasting had reached the 22, Seidel called on a reverse by Alphonse who went around Pitt's right side behind sharp blocking all the way.

A fumbled punt soon after, by safety man Bobby La Rue, groggy from punishment, was recovered by Larson on the Panther 45—the winning break. Kostka went blasting again until he reached the 18. Then on fourth down and short yardage, Kostka, faking a smash into the line, handed the ball off to Seidel. Seidel pivoted and pitched out to Lund who, faking an end sweep, stopped and passed to Tenner, the left end. Tenner, cutting diagonally across the Pitt backfield, took the ball in stride and carried into the end zone.

Origin of the buck-lateral sequence, which has been used successfully by many teams, has been attributed to Bierman. He was at least one of the first to use it, as head coach of Montana, as early as 1921.

"Like so many things in football," he added, "it may have been used somewhere, sometime, without my knowledge. But we did install it that week with use in mind for Pitt. Pitt was the best team

we met, the strongest I've played against in college coaching."

Probably the greatest single clinical play in Bierman's dynasty was an extemporaneous lateral of a punt that brought victory when a scoreless tie seemed imminent. Bud Wilkinson, later the superb coach of Oklahoma, played outstanding guard for Bierman in '34 and '35 and was shifted in '36 to quarterback, where again he stood out. He engineered the beginning of the play. Dick Cullum, ace football writer of the Minneapolis *Times*, described it:

"There were 68 seconds to play ... Nebraska had the ball on its 43-yard line ... Sam Francis, Nebraska's best kicker, had been removed in favor of sophomore Ron Douglas. He punted a short, high one to Wilkinson on Minnesota's 28. Wilkinson caught the ball near the sideline, and took the first step to the inside and backwards, drawing all the tacklers toward him.

"It was not until one of them had him by one leg that he let the ball go. Uram caught it on the 25-yard line and ran through a broken field 75 yards to a touchdown. It was unquestionably one of football's finest plays. Bierman called it the most perfectly executed spur-of-the-moment play ever to come to his attention. He also insisted that every man used the maximum of good judgment in clearing the way for Uram, who himself used perfect judgment in setting his pace and choosing his course. At one stage, every Nebraska player was on his back. This phenomenal and brilliant play decided a tough ball game, 7–0, in the final minute."

On defense, Bierman's Minnesota teams were nearly impregnable. In three games, 1938–40, Tommy Harmon, Michigan's famed No. 98, failed to get into the Gophers' end zone. Of the five defeats incurred by Fritz Crisler's Michigan teams, 1938–41, four came from Minnesota.

The headline rivalry of Bierman's pre–World War II years, however, was with Lynn O. (Pappy) Waldorf's Northwestern teams from 1935 through '41. Minnesota won four, Northwestern three. Minnesota's margins were 21–13, 7–0, 13–12, 8–7; Northwestern's 6–0, 6–3, 14–7. Total points were Gophers 59, Wildcats 58.

For those who played under him, Bierman made football a stern challenging task. As a player and coach he gave the game everything. Under his arctic exterior, he harbored an attitude toward his school, Minnesota, that was almost reverence. To him, it was inconceivable that any player wouldn't be willing to sacrifice anything, take anything, to work and win for Minnesota.

"When I have to beg a kid of 16 or 17 to go out for football," he used to say, "then I'll quit."

Beside him, other frigid coaching types seemed almost mellow: Sutherland, a mincing gatherer of nuts and whey; Bob Neyland, a zephyr in Avalon; Red Blaik, caller at a square dance.

But after his players graduated, they discovered that their winning football had made them big men in their state and was helping them get started. Then they began to appreciate what Bierman had done for them. When times turned against him later, his old lettermen stood almost solidly behind him.

If his players found Bierman cold, newspapermen and other communicators found him mostly impossible. He would have liked football to be conducted in a vacuum. A strange blend of shyness and self-possession that bordered at times on arrogance, or seemed to, he consistently refused to extend even average cooperation to a writer or photographer.

As justification, he said they were infringing on his working time. That they, as well as he, had a job to do was something that did not seem to occur to him.

His last national championship team of 1941 completed an 8–0 year with trouncings of Iowa and Wisconsin a few days before Pearl Harbor. He served as a marine colonel for three years, and did some coaching at Iowa Pre-Flight. In 1945 he returned to Minneapolis. He had turned down the job at Southern California because he was sure he could build back at Minnesota.

His failure has been imputed to several causes. One was that he failed to adjust to meet the changes made in the game by rules liberalization, especially in free substitution, and by the T formation.

"Bernie," one of his old players charged, "is too much of an introvert to change."

Except for a few T plays and an abortive triple-wing deploy, Bierman did adhere to his old power blueprints. But he probably could have continued to win with them, just as old-line Neyland football won at Tennessee. The difference was material. Minnesota had not regained prewar standards.

Even so, Bierman, from 1945 through '50, won more games than he lost. But he had set a standard, much higher than that before World War II. And that was to become his undoing.

Bierman's stern aspect toward life and football had its roots in his childhood. Born March 11,

1894, to immigrant German parents, farmers, he suffered from osteomyelitis as a child and had to go around on crutches. Fortunately surgery mended him.

He was an all-round star at Litchfield High and entered Minnesota in 1912. He won seven letters, three each in football and track, and one in basketball. He also won a Big Ten medal for proficiency in both academics and athletics.

"Bernie talks sometimes," a classmate said. "Not at society cotillions, unless some fair coed has cornered him with a question that demands an unequivocal answer. Not at training table. But he does talk. He talks in the classroom. When an instructor asks a question, he answers."

Bierman was captain and halfback of Minnesota's 1915 conference champions, and his approach to the game was deeply influenced by Dr. Henry L. Williams, who coached the Gophers from 1900 through '21. Williams, a former Yale football and track star, built the early tradition of Minnesota power.

He was also an imaginative man who conceived the Minnesota shift that antedated the Notre Dame shift. But the doctor believed that the indispensable basis of winning football was power. He could also be harsh on the field. Let a player hobble around after a pile-up and the doctor would boom, "Get a substitute out here. I've got no use on my team for anybody with a tin knee."

Williams' hard science and ultrarealism found a response in the keen mind, Spartan philosophy, and icy purposefulness of Bierman. In 1916, the fall after his graduation, Bernie began coaching at Butte, Montana High, and showed the winning touch right off with a 7–0 season. Then he enlisted in the Marine Corps for World War I, came out a captain in 1919, and coached the University of Montana from 1919 through '21.

In '21 he met Clara, his wife-to-be, at an M Club dance, and decided to give up coaching in favor of selling bonds.

"Bernie was quiet by nature," says Mrs. Bierman. "He courted me that way. It was I who persuaded him to get back into coaching. He had to travel a lot when he was selling bonds and I was lonely and scared."

Clark Shaughnessy, who had been his teammate under Williams, was now coaching Tulane, and he took on Bernie as an assistant. Unquestionably, he picked up a lot under Shaughnessy. After serving as his assistant, Bierman coached the Mississippi Aggies (now Mississippi State) for two years and upset Tulane in 1926, 14–0. When Shaughnessy resigned to coach Loyola of New Orleans in 1927, Bierman was a natural to succeed him.

Five years after he quit coaching, Bierman's name was brought up to Bud Wilkinson, then on his way at Oklahoma to the modern all-winning record of 47 games. Bud recalled what his father had told him when he chose to accept the job at Oklahoma after Jim Tatum left for Maryland.

"No matter how successful he may be," said Wilkinson, Senior, "every coach eventually reaches a point where a lot of people want somebody else."

"And he was right, of course," said Bud. "Just take the case of Bernie Bierman. Yes, he was frigid and forthright, but he didn't talk out of both sides of his mouth. He had integrity. He was completely fair, honest, and the most thorough, hard-working individual I have ever known. His 10-year record at Minnesota prior to the war is unequaled. Yet, there came a day when he was no longer wanted."

Some 14 years later, from the home he retired to in Laguna Hills, California, Bierman recalled that he was hung in effigy and there were signs that read, "Bye, Bye, Bernie."

"I was saddened," he said. "I had to be after all those years ... and it took me a while to come back. But I know how fickle a fan can be. I see a man like John McKay, a wonderful man, and I'm delighted in his success. But what do you suppose might happen, and what do you suppose people might be saying, if Southern Cal would start losing? Every coach thinks about that, you know."

The answer lies in the late Vince Lombardi's favorite definition of coaching football, "It's a game for madmen." Meaning more than enough to drive a man mad.

The coaches know that when they buy into it. Bernie Bierman could tell you.

Red Blaik

THE EARL OF HANOVER

Earl (Red) Blaik met the new Superintendent of West Point, his old friend Lieutenant General Robert L. Eichelberger, in New York's Ritz-Carlton Hotel, Sunday morning, December 22, 1940, and told him he had decided to tackle the task of raising football at Army, his alma mater, from 20,000 leagues under the Hudson. Blaik, who had sweated out a decision for almost a month, experienced relief but also a profound depression.

"I've never seen a man less happy than Blaik was, the morning after the signing," Colonel Charles Danielson, the West Point adjutant said later. "He was a man in a deep fog. All of us, merely by observation, realized how much of a wrench it was for him to leave Dartmouth."

Almost seven years before, Blaik had been tentatively sold by two old Big Green backs, Eddie Dooley and Red Lowden, and then totally convinced by Ernest Martin Hopkins, Dartmouth's president from 1916 to '45, that a good part of heaven was located in Hanover, New Hampshire.

Blaik found out they were right—and it was no mundane celestial stakeout, either. It was a kind of condominium of clouds, ranging from one to nine and down again, sometimes Spartan, other times intellectual and religious, still others cuckoo. The ex-cavalry officer, deputy chief of staff for Army football seven years, did not, as some charged, try to remake Dartmouth into an Ivy League equivalent of West Point. He had never wanted to. "A small school," said Daniel Webster, "but there are those who love it." Among them stood Red Blaik. He did, however, bring the Indians to attention.

Two feet of snow and a thermometer twelve below greeted Blaik and his assistants on their first visit to Dartmouth in January 1934. He brought Harry (Fats) Ellinger, Army line coach, to coach the Big Green line. For the backs and ends, he had acquired two former Pittsburgh players under Dr. John Bain (Jock) Sutherland: Andy Gustafson and Joe Donchess. The new staff immediately reaffirmed President Hopkins' confidence. His had been the deciding voice in choosing Blaik over Dick Harlow, the finalists of 126 names considered.

"Earl," President Hopkins said, "always remember that football is incidental to the purpose for which the player is in college." Then he added, "Let's have a winner."

President and Mrs. Hopkins invited Blaik and his aides to stay at their home until they got permanently settled and brought on their families. The coaches occupied "the dormitory," a large guest room immediately above the Hopkins' bedroom. That first night they plunged into details of the single-wing offense Blaik had determined on, basically an amalgam of Army's inside tackle thrust, short reverse, and running pass, and Pittsburgh's sweep, off-tackle cutback, and deep reverse.

To demonstrate techniques for one another, they often leaped up from their chairs, thereby causing much scraping, shuffling, and banging, and were too engrossed to note that night was on the wane and one floor below them their hosts were presumably trying to sleep. Finally, about

Red Blaik, during his Dartmouth days

three o'clock, Mrs. Hopkins inquired of the prexy: "Do you plan to have all the season's major games played upstairs?"

A few nights later, in Davis Field House, Blaik met the squad for the first time, introduced his assistants as the best in America at their jobs, and the attack as the game's most advanced.

"We'll be as successful as you men will let us," he said. "If there is anybody in this room who is not ready to do some strong sacrificing, I hope we've seen him for the last time tonight. Because we're going to bring home the bacon."

Looking back almost four decades, Blaik says, "Our major problem at Dartmouth was to replace the spirit of good fellowship, which is antithetical to successful football, with the Spartanism that is indispensable. The successful coach is the one who can sell the Spartan approach, the one who is able to get a willing acceptance from his men that victory or success demands a special price.

"The play-for-fun approach will lead the player to revolt against the coach, and eventually against the game itself, because play-for-fun never can lead to victory. The essence of the game, the only 'fun' of the game, is the soul-satisfying awareness that comes not only with victory but also with the realization that victory more than justifies all the communal work and sacrifice that went into it.

"This savor can also be derived by a losing team to a considerable degree, but only if they know their attempt to win obviously represented their best possible effort.

"Our Dartmouth players accepted discipline, sacrifice, and subordination to team effort as necessary to success. I found them little different from the West Point Cadet. Young men respect authority, and a football team cannot be coached by committee action."

The severity of the new order and the failure of the new coaches to mingle socially engineered resentment among some of the old guard, who precipitated a test at the first opportunity. Blaik's first Dartmouth team, 1934, which had lost only to Yale, 7–2, and had defeated Harvard, was beaten at Cornell. The coach felt it had not played up to its potential and was tempted to fling himself off the high cliffs of Cayuga.

The special train taking them back to Hanover stopped near Syracuse around midnight, and two Dartmouth athletic officials and an alumnus, as had been their custom in recent years, took three of the players into a railroad saloon and more than sufficiently supplied them with beer and Scotch. "Don't worry about that straightbacked soldier," the elders advised the gridders. "These men have had their inning and have proved exactly nothing. They're through even if we have to buy up their contract, and it's back to alumni coaching. At least we won't have to salute them."

In the morning, Blaik sensed something was wrong, extracted the story from the team manager, and by eleven o'clock Monday morning had the affair resolved. He told President Hopkins what had happened and that he was going to relieve the trainer and the other athletic officials. Hopkins backed him to the limit and the incipient rebellion was quelled, all without a word to the squad. But the squad had got the message.

The final game was at Princeton the next week, and at the half, Coach Fritz Crisler's powerhouse led Dartmouth, 38–0. Blaik told the players that what was wrong with them could not be cured by coaching. He and his assistants then walked out of the room. From outside they could hear all hell break loose. The players, thinking they had lost Blaik's respect, accused and threatened one another. Then they charged out and in the second half outscored Princeton, 13–0.

"In that 30 minutes," says Blaik, "the Dartmouth spirit was reborn."

For the new trainer in 1935, Blaik chose a man who had won a wide reputation as a coach and trainer of Ohio high school teams. Blaik knew him but slightly then, but recognized that his ideas on conditioning were identical with his own.

His name was Roland Bevan, but for six years at Dartmouth and later at West Point, he was known as "Beaver," a nickname born in the traditional manner, by accident. One of the Dartmouth players, who didn't have Bevan's name straight, asked another, "What do you think of the new trainer, Mr. Beaver?"

Beaver did not admit to such a word as coddle, could spot a malingerer against a stiff wind, and himself maintained a trim, muscular 148 well into his sixties. He did indulge himself in snappy sport clothes and garish ties, which he thought set off his bald virility; at times his attire seemed patterned after Balch Hill when the leaves are aturn. He also had a yen for ice cream sundaes and other exotic desserts. As a discriminating devotee of physical culture, Beaver considered a burlesque show both artistic and entertaining.

Soon after he arrived, Bevan outfitted a corner of the gymnasium with physical fitness equipment suggestive of the Spanish Inquisition, and the players named it "The Torture Room."

Bevan's philosophy on food was much like that

of Blaik's. Earl, his old friend Stanley Woodward, the sportswriter, charged, considered food sinful, which Beaver obviously did not, though he did agree it could be immoral for a player. Anyone who reported overweight in September was put on a diet that featured lettuce and Ry-Krisp, spiced on occasion by an apple.

When Carl (Mutt) Ray, who became a fine linebacker-center, returned one September at 220, 30 pounds overweight, he was placed on the lettuce list and by the opening game was down to 190 pounds, his right playing weight. The rapidity of his shedding, however, prompted Carl's father to inquire of Beaver if he were training his son to appear not at a stadium but at a séance.

Fullback Johnny Handrahan was also shaved down from 200 to 180 one fall, much to the consternation of his brother Joe, an agile guard with a playing weight of 220, an uninhibited gourmet who worked at Gitsis Restaurant in Hanover. One night Joe left Gitsis with a bag of steak sandwiches for his undernourished brother, but en route to their fraternity house he was intercepted by Beaver. The trainer investigated the bag and was aghast.

"Who are these steak sandwiches for, Joe?" Beaver inquired, putting the bag under his arm.

"For John," Joe replied. "The boy cannot subsist on lettuce and Ry-Krisp."

Beaver was unrelenting. Taking Joe by the arm, he led him across the street to Tanzi's fruit store and bought him an apple.

"Here, Joe," he beamed. "Take this back to John. It will carry him through the night, and tomorrow I'll see that he gets an extra Ry-Krisp."

Beaver met his defeats, however. He did not do much better than break even with Mary (Ma) Smalley, who operated an eating club where many of the players were members. Ma, a large-hearted soul who fed many a boy free, had on call a vocabulary to make Bluebeard blanch. and, to the delight of the players, occasionally used it in discussing Bevan.

Ma thought that football players, like all growing boys, needed cakes, pies, and ice cream, and to catch her violating his caloric commandments, Bevan went in for some sleuthing, which occasioned more than one comic-opera situation.

So there were physical conditioning and dieting and there was also a cold ignoring of injuries, which at first the players thought shocking. When an injured man didn't get up and by habit the others began to gather around him, Blaik would snap, "Move it over and keep going. Take care of

him, Rollie," After such an incident, with a player prone, his nose smashed and bleeding, Blaik called the squad together.

"I want you to understand something," he said. "I was just as concerned about that injured man as you were. But to be consoling an injured man is bad for you and bad for him. It breeds a softness that is inimical to success."

Blaik himself set the example the day in the field house he caught his cleats in the cage netting, tried to cushion the fall with his hand, and broke his elbow, which was placed in a cast that night. But he managed to get up immediately and see the practice through.

The challenge that obsessed Dartmouth was to beat Yale. This was something the Indians never had been able to accomplish, in 17 games over 52 years. They had played nine games in Yale Bowl and though several times favored, their best had been three ties.

Dartmouth felt there was a jinx. This was nonsense, Blaik insisted; Dartmouth had lost because in crises it had played poorly. His first two seasons he never referred to the Yale game, but merely alluded to it as "the game in New Haven." In 1934, nevertheless, the Green lost because it was still too tied up fighting the jinx.

In 1935 he intensified the relaxation theme, and replaced serious practices and repetition of fundamentals with fun games that had linemen playing in the backfield and backs in the line. The attitude was, "Who the heck is Yale? Let's go down there and have a good time."

Blaik was suffering from an ear ailment that caused a mild vertigo and forced him to work from a kneeling position. The week of the game a doctor had to open the ear and it was very painful. He forgot it in New Haven.

On Yale's first sequence, Jack Kenny, Dartmouth captain and center, ran over to the Eli huddle, stuck in his head, and said, "Let's have a lot of fun today, boys."

"Get the hell out of here," one of the Yales threatened, "or I'll punch you in the nose."

"I think he would have, too," Kenny reported to his teammates.

In the second quarter Dartmouth took the lead on a 47-yard drive. Right halfback Frank (Pop) Nairne smashed over from the 9, as tackle Dave Camerer impaled Larry Kelley, Yale's celebrated right end, on a wall-out block. John Handrahan converted. Soon after, Charlie Ewart returned a punt 65 yards for a Yale touchdown, but the extra point was missed. Dartmouth, leading 7–6, was

not home free, however, until Carl Ray intercepted a desperation Eli pass on Yale's 8 and ran it in. Handrahan converted again and the final was 14–6. The jinx was ended.

"Three minutes before the end," Blaik recalls, "the goalposts were down. Laughing and crying, old grads and young grads, students, everybody it seemed, were crowding around our bench and later running over our locker room. It was something none of us who experienced it will ever forget."

If Yale was beaten, President Hopkins had promised Blaik he would make a bonfire of Crosby Hall, today a refurbished building for alumni affairs, but in 1935 an antiquated, wooden-framed dormitory. Blaik has a fine sense of humor, which he usually took pains to conceal, perhaps because he felt it might dilute his Spartan demeanor. Now, returning to Hanover, he asked Mr. Hopkins, "What time are you planning to set the fire?"

"I've decided not to, Earl," said Hoppy. "Beating Yale is all the excitement we can stand."

The Yale jinx-crackers carried an 8–0 record into their game at Princeton. The Tigers, however, were the favorites, perhaps the strongest team ever to come out of Nassau. They would finish the season 9–0, be called Eastern champions, and earn high and well-deserved national rating.

A spillover sellout of 55,000, largest Palmer Stadium crowd in seven years, watched the Tigers overpower Dartmouth, 26–6, in a game that is recalled as "The Rape in the Snow," and "The Twelfth Man Game."

When Dartmouth left its Peddie School headquarters—Blaik never quartered his teams at a hotel—at noon, Saturday, November 23, the sun was shining. By the time they reached the stadium, the sky had turned gray and was spitting snow. By game time, the stuff had covered the field and was turning into a blizzard. As the game progressed, the field became a pudding of slush.

The Indians erred tactically by scoring first; on a Statue of Liberty play, Nairne ran 25 yards to the 2, and Johnny Handrahan plunged over. The aroused Tigers, who were to throw only one pass all day, geared up their grinder. Blaik's line was respectable; Princeton's, schooled by Tad Wieman, Fritz Crisler's valued line teacher, was extra special. Behind its steam-hammer blocking, a galaxy of fine ball carriers made touchdown marches of 43, 48, 40, and 50 yards.

After each substantial ground-gainer, line-backer Jack Kenny would challenge the Tigers, "Come on through here again! Come on! You won't make an inch!" Finally, tackle Dave Camerer, later an All-American but frequently prone this day, reprimanded his leader to the amusement of both sides. "Dammit, Jack," he cried out, "don't forget the sons-o'-bitches are coming through me before they get to you!"

In the final quarter, with Princeton ahead 20–6 and poised on Dartmouth's 2, an alcoholic spectator came tacking down out of the stands in the north end zone to do for dear old Dartmouth—or pass out.

His identity never has been established. A short-order cook in a Rahway, New Jersey, diner claimed to be the man, and was feted by some Princetons until he became conscience-stricken and said he wasn't the man.

Whoever it was, he outdid Walter Mitty, who merely dreamed his heroics. He staggered through the end zone up to the line of scrimmage, and took his own kind of stance between Camerer and guard Joe Handrahan.

"Kill them Princeton bastards!" he bellowed, and before the Tigers could start the play, he lurched into their backfield, made a failing grab at fullback Pepper Constable, and skidded on his stomach along the slush.

The intense Tigers, heeding Jeremy Collier's warning, "Intemperance is a dangerous companion," were not amused. Guard Jac Weller aimed a kick at him and a general laying on of claws was imminent when New Jersey State policemen arrived in powdered blue and rescued the intrepid volunteer. As they led him away, he resembled an underdone mudpie. Then Constable, enforcer without a badge, locked up Princeton's final touchdown.

"The Twelfth Man" epitomized the motto of the mother of Henry of Navarre, "To the valiant heart, nothing is impossible." He had responded to the plight of Dartmouth as if to wild and imperious bugles from a beleaguered castle.

Camerer, later a sportswriter, magazine sports editor, and radio script executive, has a clear picture of "The Twelfth Man."

"He was young, medium-sized, towheaded with crew cut, and wore a jacket. And I don't think he was a college man. At least what he yelled was, 'Kill *them* Princeton bastards.'"

Despite the loss at Princeton, the season was still successful, but it ended sourly in a 13–7 upset at Baker Field, New York, by a Columbia team that had lost four and been tied.

"We thought you were a good team" a chagrined Blaik told them. "You were beaten, badly beaten, by a great Princeton team. So what? So you couldn't forget it and carried it into this one—something a good team doesn't do. That's why I'm horribly disappointed in you!"

While the rest of the team scattered around New York and broke training, Bevan worked on Johnny Handrahan's shoulder separation with ice and heat pads, took him to dinner, and then to a burlesque show. The perfectionist trainer had acquired front seats and when he observed the neat surgical scar of an appendectomy one of the chorus girls had undergone, his sense of artistry quite overpowered him.

"John!" he yelled. "Just look at that beautiful scar!"

That fascinating fall of '35, a young man from Glen Ellyn, Illinois, had enrolled as a freshman at Dartmouth—Robert Frederick MacLeod. Bob MacLeod would play halfback three seasons, captain the 1938 team, and be everybody's All-American. In Mac's three seasons, Dartmouth's records were 7–1–1, 7–0–2, and 7–2–0, for a total of 21–3–3. This included a defeatless string that comprised 19 victories and three ties. The 1936 and '37 Indians were champions of the then informal Ivy League, and in '37 were rated No. 7 nationally. In those three years, Dartmouth never lost to Harvard, Yale, or Princeton, a record unmatched even in Coach Bob Blackman's dynasty.

If these accomplishments and MacLeod were coincidental, so is gin in a martini. "There is no question," says Blaik, "that my top player at Dartmouth was MacLeod."

Mac excelled as runner, receiver, blocker, and on defense. As wingback in right formation of Blaik's single-wing version, he ran the deep reverse behind four blockers, the tailback, and three pulling linemen. The excitement of such mass mobility made the play the most glamorous of its day and prompted Greasy Neale, then Yale's first assistant to Coach Ducky Pond, to describe it as "that play in which the student body comes down out of the stands and gets into the interference."

Whatever the play, when the going was roughest, MacLeod was best. Along with four other starters and seven substitutes, he suffered an attack of dysentery from rancid spinach the Thursday before the 1937 Yale game, and was still in dubious shape before the Friday afternoon practice in Yale Bowl. Blaik called him aside.

"Mac," he said, "the newspapers are all here to watch this practice. Whether we win this game tomorrow or lose it, it is going to look bad if these people think we are using illness as a pregame maneuver to detract from a possible Yale victory, or to lull Yale into some sort of security.

"Now, how do you feel? Are you and the others going to be able to do the full job or more? If the answer is no, I have got to rearrange our pattern. If the answer is yes, I want you to get the other boys who were stricken and tell them individually we are going to put on the darndest practice that has ever been seen in this bowl! I want those writers to go out of here knowing we are a ready ball club!"

Dartmouth had that kind of practice. And the next day, the largest Yale Bowl crowd since before the 1929 depression, 75,000 overflowing into aisles and portals and another 10,000 near rioting outside, saw a game in the dramatic Yale-Dartmouth tradition, a 9–9 tie. And the standouts were two exceptional backs, the Elis' marvelous Clint Frank, and a Dartmouth competitor of the same cast, Bob MacLeod.

Mac's 85-yard run with an intercepted pass for Dartmouth's touchdown was one of the finest ever seen in Yale Bowl. He played through that game well below physical par. For two nights he had had little sleep, and he finished the game at 169, which was under his weight of the previous Wednesday by 18 pounds. The spirit of MacLeod and Blaik, a pair of braw Scots, is summed up in some Scottish lines favored of Blaik, from "Johnnie Armstrong's Last Goodnight":

"Fight on, my merry men all,
    I'm a little wounded, but I am not slain;
I will lay me down for to bleed awhile,
    Then I'll rise and fight with you again."

The competitiveness of MacLeod carried over from football. Mac, a Protestant, could kindle into a bright flame the religious arguments of Harry (Heavenly) Gates, a blocking quarterback who had joined the Holy Ghost and Us, a religious society with a farm near Manchester, New Hampshire. Often halfback Phil Conti, a Catholic, and quarterback Henry (Hank) Whitaker, a self-avowed agnostic, would join the debates.

One such debate could have proved costly to Blaik's Indians. The subject has long been forgotten; it may have been whether the head of a pin can accommodate fewer angels than wingbacks. But it carried from the Dartmouth bus into

the locker room in Harvard's Dillon Field House right up until it was time to go on the field, and Blaik and his assistants had a hard time breaking it up. It did not, however, adversely affect the team that day, as it beat Harvard, 26–7.

Religion and football became incompatible finally to Heavenly Gates, and he did not report for practice the fall of 1938, his senior year. He had decided, apparently, that his fondness for football was a form of sinful exhibitionism. By the week of the Yale game, though, football was luring him. Blaik, who needed him badly, left it up to the squad whether he should be taken back. They welcomed him and the way he blocked the Yale ends in a 24–6 victory was evil indeed.

But remorse must have set in, for when the team returned to Hanover, Heavenly took refuge in the Holy Ghost and Us house, and played no more football. He returned to school, however, to graduate with distinction.

A quarterback who thought football sinful, a "Twelfth Man," the accusation he wanted to make Dartmouth a military institution, the Yale jinx and its smashing—the bizarre, the spectacular, the dramatic seemed to seek out Blaik and his teams, and there was a strangeness in this for he was a conservative by nature.

Strangest of all was that Red Blaik ever became a football coach.

Earl Henry Blaik was born in Detroit, February 15, 1897, second of the three children of William Douglas and Margaret Purcell Blaik. His father, descended from seagoing Glasgow people, came to America at 16, and set up his own blacksmith shop in Detroit. In 1901 he sold it to become a horseshoe company's representative in Dayton, Ohio, and moved his family there when Earl was eight. Later, he went into the real estate and building business. An active Democrat, he became friendly with Governor James M. Cox.

From childhood Earl was fascinated by sports, especially football, and although he weighed only 133 pounds, he was a star pass-catching end for Steele High. Later at Miami University of Oxford, Ohio, where he was influenced to go by his friend Marvin (Monk) Pierce, an outstanding pitcher and back at both Steele and Miami, Blaik developed into an all-round athlete. He played end on the undefeated 1916 team coached by George Little, and made All-Ohio.

At Miami, Blaik also met his future wife, Merle McDowell, an attractive coed from Piqua, Ohio, and was influenced by a teammate, tackle Jack Butterfield, who had been a plebe at West Point,

to apply for an appointment in 1918. His father's friendship helped him get appointed by U.S. Senator Atlee Pomerene.

Under West Point's stepped-up program during World War I, Blaik completed his course in two years and was commissioned with the Class of 1920. As varsity end, outfielder, and guard in basketball, he was awarded the Saber as the outstanding athlete in his class, and though he had but recently recovered from a heavy bout with influenza, his fine end play against Navy earned him a third-team spot on Walter Camp's All-America.

General Douglas MacArthur was then Superintendent of the Academy, and there began between "The Old Soldier" and the young Ohioan a relationship that developed into a lifelong friendship. When Blaik was recovering from the flu in the post infirmary, MacArthur sent by his car and chauffeur to take him on health-restoring rides, and also ordered Blaik to report to the post surgeon three times daily for health-giving ingestions of sherry. Blaik, an abstemious soul, smiles slightly when recalling the liquid nutriment: "The military fashion in which I gulped down this quick builder of strength would have given miseries to a gourmet."

Although Blaik had reputedly the strongest arm in the Academy, and was fast and a ball hawk, he found curve-ball pitching even more of a problem than his mathematics nemesis, *The Theory of Least Squares*.

"General MacArthur," he says, "was sympathetic and tried to give me a personal demonstration of what I was doing wrong; he had played on the Army baseball team in his Cadet days. He unloosened his blouse, high collar, and Sam Browne belt, selected a bat, and instructed me on how to cope with that bedeviling No. 2 delivery. When he had concluded his seminar, I could not even hit a fast ball. This was the one failure in MacArthur's career."

Douglas Blaik and Merle McDowell came on to see Earl graduate, and they also saw him play baseball against the Seventh Regiment team. In part, perhaps, because he had pushed himself in defending successfully the Corps 100- and 220-yard championships in an interclass meet that morning, he struck out all four times up.

"Dad didn't ask me why," says Blaik. "He just looked at me. But I knew he was thinking, 'And you won the Athletic Saber!'"

Blaik chose the cavalry, went to the cavalry school at Fort Riley, and in July 1921 was

Blaik (*right*) chatting with author Cohane

assigned to the Eighth Cavalry Regiment of the First Cavalry Division at Fort Bliss. But with the army being cut back under the illusion there would be no more wars, officers were being encouraged to resign, and in February 1922 Blaik and many of his class put in for resignation.

If, however, a letter written by General MacArthur on March 12 had been sent a day earlier, Blaik would have stayed in the service and very likely would never have become a coach. The General had concluded his tour at West Point, was assigned to the Philippines, and wanted Blaik to come along as his aide.

Earl returned to Dayton and became partner with his father in the latter's real estate and building business, which lasted until his father's death in January 1947. Football, however, was singing to him. In the fall of 1926 he took time out to coach the Wisconsin ends for his old Miami coach, George Little, and from 1927 through '33—three years under Biff Jones, three under Ralph Sasse, and one under Gar Davidson —he took a sabbatical from business to return to West Point as an assistant coach.

His counsel became increasingly important,

and his fame grew. Army had several successful teams in that era, and Blaik's contributions were widely recognized. Since West Point had a rule that only a graduate officer could be head coach, Blaik had no thoughts on the Army job. He received many offers to become head coach at other schools—Ohio State (three times), Yale, Princeton, Michigan, Northwestern, Minnesota, Southern California, California, UCLA, Washington, Texas, Texas A. & M., Nebraska, Mississippi State—and was approached by several pro teams.

"I doubt," says Blaik, "that any man who made a career of coaching ever got to it so late and so circuitously as I did. I was 29, six years out of West Point, before I became even an assistant, and then only temporarily to help out a friend. It was eight years after that, 14 after I left college, that I finally decided to become a head coach and make it my life's work. I was 37 when I went to Dartmouth."

The next-to-the-last game he coached at Dartmouth, Blaik produced his greatest upset. This was the famous "Fifth Down" game, which Cornell seemingly had won, 7–3, on a touchdown

pass in the last six seconds, but conceded to Dartmouth the following Monday, after films affirmed that the touchdown had been scored on an extra down.

The error by referee Red Friesell, one of the best of his time, was traced to an excited scoreboard keeper who never changed the scoreboard down number after turning it to 3.

The excitement surrounding the "fifth down" and the reversed score tended to becloud the magnitude of the upset. Cornell had won 18 straight games, had been rated No. 4 nationally the season before, and was considered now a contender for No. 1.

Dartmouth had been ripped at Ithaca the year before, 35–6, and had no rating. Nobody remembered that Blaik, in a typical prediction before the season, had said, "The mysterious Indians on one occasion will rise to great play."

This was the occasion. Blaik didn't have to get them up emotionally; they got themselves up. His job was to keep them from getting wound too tight. To do this he staged an act that he himself was relaxed; he even indulged in the strictly extraordinary gimmick of clowning on the bus en route to the stadium.

He had also equipped the team with a defensive pattern as complex and elaborate as anything designed until that time. It was based on forgoing an early charge and commitment, angling off in the direction of the ball, and giving up the short gain but no more.

The Indians executed with such abandon they put the left side of the Cornell line out of action with injuries. In the first half, Cornell was stopped cold. In the third quarter, they managed a march, but it was stopped by an end zone interception. Then Dartmouth began to move the ball and set up a field goal by Bob Krieger from the 27. With only four and a half minutes to play and the ball on its 48, Cornell took to the air with a ball slightly damp from a light snow. Halfback Walt Scholl began connecting, and his completion to right halfback Bill Murphy gave Cornell first down on the Dartmouth 5.

With less than a minute to play, fullback Mort Landsberg smashed to the 3. On second down Scholl drove to the 1. Third and one, Landsberg was stacked up for almost no gain. The ball was less than a yard from the goal line with time for, at the most, two plays.

To stop the clock, Coach Carl Snavely called time out, and the Big Red was penalized back to the 6 for delaying the game. On fourth down

Scholl's pass to Murphy in the end zone was batted down, and hit Joe McKenney, the head linesman, in the chest.

McKenney, the only one of the four officials who knew what down it was, knew it was first down. The ball was brought out to the 20-yard line and handed over to the Indians. But Friesell, like the two other officials apparently, was confused by the scoreboard, which still read third down, and signaled fourth down for Cornell coming up.

Captain Lou Young of Dartmouth protested vehemently, but Friesell turned the ball over to Cornell on the 6. There were six seconds left, time for one more play. With two seconds remaining on the clock, Scholl's pass to Murphy in the end zone was good this time. Tackle Nick Drahos converted, the game was over, and the Big Red had apparently won a 7–3 victory.

But the writers knew Cornell had scored on a fifth down and when Cornell had affirmed this after studying the films on Monday, it wired Dartmouth that it was relinquishing claims to the victory.

Dartmouth wired back:

> DARTMOUTH ACCEPTS THE VICTORY AND CONGRATULATES AND SALUTES THE CORNELL TEAM, THE HONORABLE AND HONORED OPPONENT OF HER LONGEST UNBROKEN RIVALRY.

A good part of heaven was in Hanover, Blaik had been told, but they had not specified a football game that was won after it was lost.

From Dartmouth, Blaik was to go on to even greater triumphs at West Point: two national championship teams; four others that were undefeated; six Eastern championships; unbeaten strings of 32 and 28; Coach of the Year and every other honor coaching can bestow; and the prized Gold Medal Award of the National Football Foundation and Hall of Fame. He retired in 1958 with his undefeated "Lonely End" team Eastern kings and No. 3 nationally, and for the next decade was a successful top executive for the Avco Corporation. In his midseventies, Blaik looked much younger, and on the golf courses of the California desert country, the competitor of old.

"Just as football will remain a leading competitive sport in college athletics, so will Earl Blaik be remembered as an outstanding architect on the gridiron," said General MacArthur. "For, apart from his innate grasp of successful strategic and tactical concepts, he possesses those essential

attributes of leadership which mold men into a cohesive fighting team and inspire in them an invincible will to victory."

To which the Sons of Eleazor Wheelock will add a "Wah-Who-Wah!" And toast in rum—but strictly unbuttered.

Frank Cavanaugh

THE IRON MAJOR

Armistice Day was less than three weeks away, and the Allied grand counteroffensive was rolling up the German Army all along the western front. As the battle of Saint-Mihiel raged, there was no smokier pit than LeRavin des Boises des Caures —The Ravine of the Woods of the Hunting Calls—near a town named Samogneux in the area around Verdun.

Early that morning of October 23, 1918, Batteries D, E, and F of the 2nd Battalion, 102nd Regiment Field Artillery, Yankee Division, had begun preparation fire to support their infantry in the north sector of Verdun. Battery E maintained the center, with D on its right and F on its left.

These soldiers were mainly from Worcester, Massachusetts, and surrounding towns. They had been through much together: the Chemin des Dames, the Toul sector, the Second Battle of the Marne. They had seen comrades go down, many never to rise again. They had dragged their caissons over mud-logged roads, under enemy fire, and had slugged it out with the Boches. None of them had not wondered whether he ever would see home again. They had seen and suffered much, and now they were in for it again.

Because there was no alternative, their guns were positioned, contrary to the basics of artillery reconnaissance, on the forward slope of a hill facing the enemy lines, where they were exposed to incessant counterblasts from the German 210s. A German plane, circling like a vulture, signaled the position of the American batteries and battalion headquarters by firing its machine gun in code, as the German shells swept the ravine.

From his post command, a dugout that was a makeshift lean-to, Captain Frank William Cavanaugh, of Worcester, directed the American guns, which were about a half mile to his left. He signaled by stepping out of the dugout and waving his handkerchief, although each enemy round was hitting dangerously near him.

At Battery E, Cavanaugh's signals were followed by First Lieutenant George W. Jones, of Worcester, winner of the Legion of Honor, the Distinguished Service Cross, and the Croix de Guerre. With Lieutenant Jones was Sergeant Earnest E. LaBranche, also a winner of the Croix de Guerre.

Cavanaugh had just given a signal to fire when he disappeared in a cloud of smoke. This meant a shell had landed near him. Between the roars of their French cannon, LaBranche shouted to Jones: "That one must have got the captain." Already, hospital men were rushing from the field dressing station near E's guns down through the precarious shell-ridden field to the post command.

A 210 shell was truly a plaything of Satan, its fragments dispersing upwards and outward, to tear and rend. The medical corpsmen found Cavanaugh lying in blood, hands clutched to his face. Blood seeped from a deep gash in his head, and his left eye was seriously damaged. But the damage to the right side of his face was sickening. Much of the nose and cheekbone had been destroyed. The right eye still had some connection with the socket, but Cavanaugh actually held it in his right hand. Major General C. R. Edwards later wrote, "He was about as grievously wounded a man as I saw who got well and regained his health."

The captain was a big man, six feet one and 230 pounds, and it took six men to carry him on a litter to the dressing station. While they were easing him onto the litter, another shell hit close by. They had thought he was unconscious, but now he counseled them, "Lie still. Lie still, and everything will be all right."

At the dressing station, they put temporary bandages on the remnants of his face, and he held the bandages tight with his hands and set his teeth. They thought he could not possibly last long. A priest came into the dressing room and gave him the last rites.

"Do you know who this is?" the priest asked.

"Sure," said Cavanaugh. "It's the fighting chaplain of Holy Cross."

And it was Father Mike O'Connor, Holy Cross '97, who had known Cav when he coached the Purple football team early in the century.

"Good boy," Father O'Connor said. "It will take more than this to stop you, Cavanaugh."

Finally they got him to a railroad station three miles away. There, on the platform, and for many months after in a French hospital, where the plastic surgeons worked on him, the soldier they were to call the "Iron Major" knew a purgatory. For a long time he thought he would never see again. But he did see again. It would be 15 years before those wounds finally would catch up with him—and in that time he was to do his finest work as a football coach, at Boston College and Fordham.

From the day he led Battery E to its first position on the Chemin des Dames, Cavanaugh proved his qualities as a soldier and a born leader. He was the best artillerist in his regiment, and one of the best in the United States Army. They gave him the toughest, most complex jobs, because they knew he would somehow get them done.

Yet, because he was outspoken and unawed by rank, his promotions were neither rapid nor his decorations appropriate. There can be no other explanation to it, considering his record. Not until after he was hospitalized did his majority come through. He received the Purple Heart and Victory Medal with Battle Clasps—and that was all, and it is ridiculous. It is unlikely, though, that Frank Cavanaugh thought much about it, for to him patriotism was unconditional.

Long before the day he was hit at Samogneux, Cavanaugh had made extraordinary sacrifices to the war. When he was commissioned on May 31, 1917, he was 41, and six of his nine children had been born—they ranged in age from seven, Davie, to one, baby John—and Cav was not wealthy. In their rich life together, Frank and Florence Ayers Cavanaugh always were confronted by budget problems.

During a lull in battle, in a gathering of officers, Colonel John (Long John) Herbert, the Worcester newspaper publisher and Cavanaugh's commanding officer in the 102nd, mentioned his large family and going to war. "Would you do it over again, Lieutenant?" asked Long John.

Cav bit musingly on the stem of his pipe, a characteristic gesture when he was relaxed. "I suppose I would," he said slowly. "I just couldn't

Frank Cavanaugh, at Dartmouth

keep out of it. Impossible after teaching so many hundreds of youngsters how to play and fight on the football fields. I insisted that they keep fit, and to practice what I preached I had to keep fit myself. It wouldn't have looked right for me to tell them to get into the war and then stay home myself, when I was perfectly well enough to go.

"There was a job to be done and we're doing it now, whether we think this war is useless or not. I hope the world won't be foolish enough to get into this kind of mess again, but if it does, I'd want my sons to do exactly as I have, without hesitation and without whimpering. And without heroics, because, after all, we're doing now just what we ought to do—and what they would be doing."

Prophetic words. When World War II came, every one of Cav's nine children, the three girls as well as the six boys, was in it. Lieutenant Frank Cavanaugh, Jr., won the Distinguished Flying Cross and the Air Medal with three Oak Clusters; Dave was wounded at Anzio; Phillip was a staff sergeant in the Marine Corps; Bill, an Air Corps lieutenant; John, a marine corporal; and Paul, a marine flyer. Ann, Rosemary, and Sarah were in defense work. (Phillip and Ann, Paul and Sarah were twins.)

Cavanaugh operated on the principle that the first obligation of an officer was the welfare of his

men. The midafternoon he came upon a technical sergeant fast asleep on duty, an offense for which he could have been shot, Cavanaugh realized that he was not much more than a boy and that he was worn out from a forced march. He reached down and pulled off the sergeant's chevrons, and let it go at that. "These are not professional soldiers," he said later. "You've got to make allowance."

Cav had earned a law degree at Boston University, while coaching Dartmouth, and Judge Webster Thayer, who presided at the celebrated Sacco-Vanzetti trial, stated once, "If Frank Cavanaugh applied himself, he could be the greatest criminal lawyer in Massachusetts." He also might have set a new record for being in contempt of court. As it was, football had its hooks into him so deep that he never approached law as more than an avocation.

Whenever there was an interesting case on the docket in Worcester during the football off-season, however, Cav would sit in. He was on hand for a murder trial the day that the Worcester district attorney, Edward Esty, was pompously interrogating his star witness, a child of seven named Mary Lee.

"What is your name?" inquired Esty, who seemed not to be aware of the child's age or that she was frightened.

"Mary," she finally whispered in a half panic.

"Please state your surname and your given name," Esty commanded. "It is Mary Lee, is it not?"

"Yes," said Mary Lee faintly.

"Now, Mary Lee," Esty went on, "state whether or not on the evening of February the third, nineteen hundred and twenty-one, you were at the corner of Gates Lane and Main Street?"

By now, Mary Lee was in an advanced state of terror, and looked around wildly for help. Cav leaned over the shoulder of a friend in front and said in a loud stage whisper, "A battle of wits."

Cav put his legal ability to work in defense of a 17-year-old soldier who had been accused by a Frenchwoman of rape. Employing his sparse but functional French, Cav trapped the plaintiff into killing her own case by admitting that her real complaint was that she had not been paid.

Although he seldom complimented his men, the Iron Major never ceased praising them to others. A dramatic highlight in their relationship came on the evening of July 26, 1918, in the Marne, where E had fought without relief for 22 days. When orders came that E finally was to be relieved, Cav sighed and ordered preparations for withdrawal. A half hour later, new orders arrived. The 42nd Division Infantry was coming into action and E was to carry on in its support. Cav called his men together.

"Boys," he said, "the 42nd is relieving the 26th, but without artillery support. We are ordered to supply that support. What an honor! We, weary and exhausted, have still the unbounded confidence of those high in command! Shall we fail the 42nd?"

Later, he was to write of this moment.

"A yell of approval was the answer. Shoulders stiffened and a new light came into their eyes. There was a battery, a battery founded on a rock—the foundation rock of all civilization—voluntary obedience."

On the gridiron as on the battlefield, Cavanaugh had no use for anything short of a total effort, but he never asked the impossible or risked a man unnecessarily. He was a hard man with those who soldiered or played football under him, because he felt that this was the only way in which he could truly protect them. The boy who was not willing to learn and practice the ways of a Spartan could not play football for Frank Cavanaugh.

Nobody ever beat a team of Cav's by winning in the last quarter on better physical condition. He whipped his players into shape to go 60 minutes, and seldom substituted unless a player was injured or a game was one-sided. He devised his own set of calisthenics, a torturous series known as the grass drill, which is still used, in part at least, by modern teams. The drill emphasizes flinging the body into a prone position, then scrambling erect, then down again, then up again, up, down, up, down . . .

Cav got the idea from a conversation on a train with Stephen Chase, champion intercollegiate high hurdler, who said he had used such exercises successfully with his five- and three-year-old boys. The grass drill served Cav not only as conditioner but as penalizer. At Fordham, his ends included his son Dave, a good pass receiver, good enough to play more than he did. But some of the other ends were good enough too, so Cav, though bursting to use Dave, wouldn't. Some of the subs won letters, but Dave never did. His old man was funny that way.

Dave saw plenty of scrimmage, however, and on one occasion, to get even after a fashion with Cav, who they felt had been giving them too rough a time, the Fordham first team ran every

play inside or outside Dave's end. Dave took a battering until Cav finally shouted, "Get in and take a shower before you get killed." Then he took the varsity down to another section of the field and put them through a grass drill twice as long as usual and he picked out a spot that heavy rains had turned into a swamp.

Cav's defenses, supported by a sound kicking game, were as obdurate as anything in their day, especially within the 10-yard line. As an offensive thinker, he was well ahead of most of his contemporaries. He was using a hop shift from the T into a tandem right or left at Dartmouth, well before Knute Rockne inherited the Stagg box shift from Jess Harper at Notre Dame. Cav's spot passes to hooking ends have not been improved on. They were the couplings to his dynamic ground game.

Eleven years before Clark Shaughnessy introduced the T with man-in-motion to the college game at Stanford, Cavanaugh was using a T at Fordham, both a normal and a winged T, with quarterback Jack Fisher in motion. His use of Fisher with his back to center was another innovation. His 1928 team may have been the first to be numbered front as well as back. This happened when a tailor put the numbers on the front of the uniforms by mistake. When the error was discovered, Cav told him to leave them there, but also put numbers on the back.

Cav's feat of building the plinth of important major football at three schools—Dartmouth, Boston College, and Fordham—stands unique. His Dartmouth record was 42–9–3; his 1913, '14, and '15 teams each lost only one game. The Indians won three, tied one with Pennsylvania; won two, tied one with Syracuse, and though they won only one of six from Princeton, three of the defeats were by a total of 11 points. They lost to Haughton Harvard teams, 5–3 in 1911 and 3–0 in '12, and then were dropped from the schedule. It was around this time that Cav first got his reputation for teaching exceedingly rough football.

"Cavanaugh," Hugh Fullerton wrote in 1927, "is perhaps the most viciously criticized of all coaches. He teaches hard, fighting football. Harvard gave him a reputation as a dirty coach. I can find only two cases, however, in which one of his players has been put out for roughness."

Harvard, according to what Cav told Fullerton, had started to ruin the reputation of Dartmouth in football two years before dropping them, in order to justify breaking off relations.

"If he produced rough teams," says Hubie McDonough, who quarterbacked Dartmouth for him in 1915 and '16, "it was incidental to his attitude toward life and football, which he regarded as a man's game to be played by men. I don't remember when playing such teams as Penn State, West Virginia, Syracuse, and Princeton of those days, that I ever met many Lord Chesterfields.

"As for profanity, Cav had no need of it, and I don't remember that he ever used it. He had a marvelous vocabulary and a gift for sarcasm that could knock one down. Profanity would have been superfluous.

"Cav was in no sense a lovable character. He had, however, our complete respect and admiration. His constant watchword was 'mental attitude.' He never failed to send us onto the field believing that we could win regardless of odds. His attitude was contagious—completely masculine, courageous, and, above all, defiant under all circumstances. His independent attitude did not endear him to the faculty, but that disturbed him not at all."

Faculty, lay or Jesuit, army brass, Harvard, Yale—they were all one to this disestablishmentarian deluxe. When he was hired by Boston College in 1919, he told them, "You know, I have made many enemies." "Your enemies," B.C. replied, "shall be ours."

If Cavanaugh could get an opposing star out of action by legitimate physical punishment, he would; in this philosophy he is not distinguishable from other coaches. If the punishment produced a broken bone, that was part of the game.

"Football," Cavanaugh told his players, "is a game that should be played to the uttermost limits of respectability."

Cav's attitude was underscored in the 1923 game between Boston College and Marquette at Boston's Braves Field. Marquette won, 7–6, and went undefeated; the B.C. team won every other game. The Marquette ace runner and kicker was Red Dunn, and Cavanaugh instructed B.C. to gang up on him the first time he caught a punt.

They followed orders and Dunn suffered a broken arm—but still played the rest of the game and inspired Marquette. The plan to inactivate him backfired on B.C., because the punter, Joe McKenney, left unprotected when his teammates searched out Dunn, suffered a shoulder separation that terminated his career as a promising college pitcher.

It was in 1919, less than ten months after the

German 210 hit him, that Cavanaugh coached his first team at Boston College. His record was 5–3, but the season was considered a decided success; the Eagles not only finished strong, defeating Holy Cross, 9–7, and Georgetown, 10–7, but also gained B.C. its first football recognition outside New England by upsetting Yale in the Bowl, 5–3. (His eight-year record at B.C. was 48–14–5. The '26 team was undefeated, but tied twice.)

The 1920 team had a perfect 8–0 record and a claim on the mythical Eastern championship. Yale again was defeated, 21–13, and after that B.C. was off the Eli schedule. For this, Cav went out of his way to needle Tad Jones, the Yale coach, until even Cav's friends were embarrassed, and Tad's told him he didn't have to take it. Tad, however, would just look at Cav, and smile, "To the victor belong the spoils," and Cav, who was plenty of man, came out the lesser man this time. Cav sounded better when he settled for needling the Elis with his claim, "All Yale men past the age of 40 have ground out their back teeth from growling 'Yeye-yull!'"

It was mainly because of Cav that the Boston College–Holy Cross rivalry, second only to Yale-Harvard as a New England traditional, knew its brightest years from 1919 through '26. There was a natural enough rivalry between Cav and Cleo O'Donnell, Holy Cross coach—"They got along," said Cav's friend, Dr. Joe O'Connor of Worcester, "like two strange bulldogs." Cav, however, made it worse than it was to build up the gate.

Cav was from Worcester, born in the Belmont Hill section April 28, 1876, son of Patrick and Ann Cavanaugh, and second oldest of four boys and two girls. He and his pal Charlie Boyle were star ends at Worcester High, and were steered to Dartmouth by Ed Hall, a graduate and later chairman of the football rules committee. When Cav and Charlie chose Dartmouth over Holy Cross, the Irish, always a critical lot of one another, sniffed, "Humph! Dartmouth! Is the local Catholic college not good enough for them?"

After leaving Dartmouth in 1898 at 22, Cav did his first coaching that fall at the University of Cincinnati, achieving a 5–1–3 record, climaxed by a victory over his alma mater, which he'd lured onto the schedule. From 1899 through 1902, he turned out winning teams for the Denver Athletic Club, and returned to Worcester in 1903 to coach Holy Cross that season and the next two. He built the Crusaders up, but the Jesuits decided to

return to graduate coaching, and for the next four years Cav tried law. He returned to coaching in 1909 and '10 at Worcester Academy, had a winner as usual, and in 1911 answered Dartmouth's call.

So Cav had 16 years of head coaching—ten college, four club, two prep school—when he began coaching B.C. in 1919. Cleo O'Donnell came from Somerville, Massachusetts, had played under Cav at Holy Cross, and been a head coach at Purdue before World War I. He would build football at Holy Cross as Cav was doing at B.C. In personality, however, they were unalike: O'Donnell, straitlaced, was more serious than Cav, who played on his sensitivities like a demon harpist.

In those days, the home team selected the four game officials, and the start of a game at Braves Field was delayed more than ten minutes, to the intense displeasure of a freezing crowd, while Cav and Cleo argued officials at midfield.

"When you bring your team to Worcester," Cleo protested, "I don't appoint four of my friends to officiate!"

"Of course you don't, Cleo," Cav agreed. "You have no friends!"

On another, less abrasive occasion, Cleo put out his hand and said, "Okay, Cav, may the best team win."

Cav withheld his hand.

"Not here, Cleo," he reminded him. "Not before all these people. We're enemies, remember. Also, not may the best team win, but the better team."

Cav used to make up harmless stories at Cleo's expense and tender them as gospel. Such as the one about Cleo strolling through the gate to watch the crowd come in, and then being stopped by the ticket taker when he tried to come back in.

"But I'm Cleo O'Donnell," he explained.

"I don't care if you're Cleopatra," said the ticket man. "You can't get in without a ticket."

Shortly after fall practice began one September, Cav was walking up Chestnut Hill to the Boston College campus with a friend when he espied a man approaching. "Get a load of this," Cav nudged his friend. "This fellow is from Worcester." The man from Worcester extended his hand with a smile, but Cav refused it with a glower.

"What's the matter, Cav?" the man asked.

"It's a fine thing," Cav grated, voice rising in feigned fury, "when I'm not in Worcester to defend myself, for Cleo O'Donnell to be hanging

around Harrington's Corner, spreading stories about me and my family! A fine thing, I must say!"

"But Cav," the man protested, "surely Cleo wouldn't do anything like that. I just can't imagine it."

"Well, I can!" Cav stormed. "I have it from good sources. I've still got a few friends back there. And you can go back and tell Cleo O'Donnell and all the rest of his backbiting buddies that I know what's going on!" Then he stalked off, as if in a rage, followed by his companion, whom he deliberately had not introduced. After a few paces, he chuckled softly, "That will be all over Worcester tonight. And it won't hurt the ticket sale."

When he went to Fordham in 1927, Cav did his best to keep the feud going, since Fordham and Holy Cross in those days were also strong rivals. In his first formal address to the Fordham players, most of them New England boys he'd recruited and who had heard of the Cav-Cleo feud in their high school days, Cav concluded, "Now, as to how you should address me on the field. You may call me coach. You may call me sir. Or you may call me major. But don't ever call me Cleo!"

In 1930, Cleo was replaced as Holy Cross coach by Captain John McEwan, but continued as athletic director. On Saturday, October 18, 1930, at Worcester, the Rams beat the Crusaders, 6–0, but had to stop little Phil O'Connell four times on the 1-yard line to do it. It was a big day for Cav. Somebody from Worcester handed him the watch and map case he had left behind the day he was hit at Samogneux 12 years before. And in a postgame interview with John Houlihan, of the Worcester *Telegram*, he was speaking strictly for his old feudist, Cleo, when he said pointedly, "John, just as sure as God made little apples, that was simply the *finest organized* Holy Cross team I have ever seen."

Cavanaugh probably would have made an outstanding writer. He had so many tools for it: command of the language, especially the offbeat but apt expression, like Gene Fowler; the deep sense of drama; the imagination; the great sense of humor. It was all this and his resonant voice that made him the king of the football banquet circus long before Bob Zuppke and Knute Rockne, who were good, had been heard from. And Cav was unsurpassed for ad-libbing.

At a banquet before the Boston College–Centenary game in 1924, the principal speakers were the rival coaches, Cav and Bo McMillin. Bo, later coach of Indiana's first Western Conference champions in 1945, had been the famed quarterback of the Praying Colonels of Centre College. It was Bo's long run that had perpetrated the stunning 6–0 upset of Harvard in 1921, so he had a big Boston following.

Bo was given to traditional coachly pessimism. This Centenary team had been culled from all compass points; Cal Hubbard, classic giant of tackle play, came from Missouri; Jim Weaver, later Atlantic Coast Conference commissioner, was from North Carolina; "Mexico" Farrell hailed from Colorado; and so on. When he got up to speak, however, Bo pointed out piously and piteously that his players were just a bunch of "pore" little country boys, all born and brought up within the very shadow of the main building at Centenary, in Shreveport, Louisiana! Soon after Bo finished, Cav got up.

"I have heard of and seen," he said, "some architectural wonders. The Woolworth Building in New York. The Parthenon in Athens. The Leaning Tower of Pisa. The Taj Mahal. The Eiffel Tower in Paris. But none of these could conceivably compare with the tremendous edifice at Centenary that Bo has been describing. Just imagine a building so tall that it can cast its shadow all the way from Louisiana as far westward as Colorado, as far northward as Missouri, and as far eastward as the Atlantic Ocean." Cav paused and purred:

"Some sh-sh-sh-shadow!"

He used humor on the field when he felt the need to let up on the players. He liked to make a joke at the expense of players he liked best. At Dartmouth these included Bill Cunningham, later widely known Boston sports columnist and radio commentator, and at Boston College, Jack Heaphy and Bill Doyle. All three were centers.

"Heaphy," said Cav one day, "what are you going to do after graduation?"

"I intend to be a teacher and football coach, Major," Jack replied.

"A coach?" boomed Cav incredulously. "Heaphy, how in the name of God are you, a center, ever going to teach football after looking at the game upside down all these years?"

Cavanaugh took the Fordham job because he had been advised by his doctors that his life expectancy was not more than six years, an accurate estimate. He still had that large family to take care of, and the $15,000 offer, worth $50,000 in today's dollars, was irresistible.

Fordham had known an occasional good team and some first-flight stars like halfback Frank Frisch, quarterback Earl (Zev) Graham, and end Frank (Bull) McCaffrey, but the Rams never had been a power. Under Cavanaugh, however, they became one. It took him two years to build, but in 1929 he had an undefeated team, and in 1930 a once-defeated. His last four years at Fordham, the last four of his life, the record was 27–4–4. In 1932, with death due the following July, he wore dark glasses, was almost totally blind, and was shriveling up physically. But he insisted on coming out on the field. More than once he inadvertently got in the path of a play and was knocked down. Sad, embarrassed, the players helped him up.

The real coaching was done that final year by his first assistant at B.C. and Fordham, William P. (Hiker) Joy, who later was a successful head coach at Canisius. But it was Cav who rallied the Rams, after midseason upsets by Michigan State and Boston College, to victory in their last three games, over St. Mary's, NYU, and Oregon State. It was the first time an Eastern team had ever defeated Far Western teams twice in the same season.

Cav's greatest victory at Fordham, however, was the one that firmed the cornerstone of the 13-year Fordham dynasty on October 12, 1929. That was the 26–0 victory over NYU by 4–1 underdogs before a sellout crowd of 55,000 at the Polo Grounds and another 10,000 turned away.

Although his old Dartmouth and Boston College players surely would debate this, it is possible that Cav was at his most demanding with his Fordham teams, because the time was short and there was much to be done. Certainly, the players were afraid of him. When they saw him coming down Fordham Road, they would cross to the other side of the street.

The September night in 1927 that Gene Tunney retained his heavyweight crown by decisioning Jack Dempsey in the famous "long count" battle, some of the players were down in Fordham Village listening to the radio broadcast of the fight. Returning to the Fordham campus through the main gate at the Third Avenue elevated station around eleven o'clock, they happened to meet Cav.

"What are you doing down here at this hour?" he growled.

John (Moco) Healey, later Western sales manager of Massachusetts Electric, was one of the group and eating a candy bar. Cav grabbed it,

flung it up on the elevated tracks, and threatened to send Moco home to Worcester in disgrace. Moco not only stayed but won three letters and two degrees, B.S. and M.S., taking honors in both. Furthermore, after Cav went his way that night, Moco proved two-deep in candy bars.

The Fordham classes of '31 and '32 provided the smart, tough, dedicated blond and brunette Poles, Liths, Italians, and Irish, most of them from New England, who formed the backbone and soul of the undefeated 1929 and once-defeated 1930 and '31 teams, and set the foundations of Fordham's golden era, the 13 years from 1929 through '41, the last four of Cav's six years, and the nine of Crowley's.

The rosters included Tony Siano, a 162-pound center-linebacker, captain in both 1929 and '30; Henry (Pistol Pete) Wisniewski, first an end and later a guard; such stalwart tackles as blond, cat-quick, quick-thinking Mike Miskinis, John Cannella, Pat Foley, and Ray Hurley; guards Walter (Rah) Tracey and John (Moco) Healey; and ends Adam Elcewicz, Harry Kloppenburg, John (Giant) Conroy, Frank (Meathead) Davis, and John (Tip) Tobin.

In the backfield there were Charlie (Peck) Pieculewicz and and Henry (Zal) Zaleski, fullbacks; the brilliant running and passing Jim Murphy, hard-hitting, hard-blocking Bill (Bingo) McMahon, spirited Bill (Red) Conway and bullet-plunging Al Cullen, halfbacks; and at quarterback, Frank Bartos, whose field goal beat B.C. at Fenway Park in 1930, 3–0, and Jackie Fisher.

Siano, Wisniewski, and Murphy earned All-America rating. Until injured in his senior year, Fisher was slated to be the first Fordham man to make Grantland Rice's All-America first team. This scrawny, whipcord lad, from Everett, Massachusetts, was a fine passer, astute field general, and born leader. He was good enough to have played on any college team. He was probably closer to Cav than any of the other Fordham players and got to know the whole man. Fisher later became a very successful high school coach at Waltham and Weymouth, and given the opportunity, would have been the same kind of college coach.

"In the 1930 game with Boston College," Fisher recalls, "I cracked my nose late in the game. Trainer Jake Weber stuffed it with cotton, and I finished the game. That night I picked up my girl (now my wife) in Everett, and headed for the B.C.–Fordham dance. My nose ached so much I knew it must be broken. I decided to call

Cav at the Kenmore Hotel and find out what to do, since we were to play at Holy Cross that Saturday.

"As you know, Cav didn't go much for names, but usually called you by position. I told him my story, and without a moment's hesitation he said, 'Quarterback, go to the nearest drugstore and get it fixed up, and have them send the bill to the Fordham A.A.' I finally did find a doctor and he set my nose. Five days later I played against Holy Cross. I never thought too much about it afterward, as you always had the feeling that in view of Cav's playing record and his war record, he wouldn't even have gone to the doctor.

"In contrast was the time I cracked my collarbone against B.C. in 1931, very late in the game. That night, on the sleeper back to New York, Cav sat on my bunk most of the night and talked to me. He knew I'd played my last game."

Fisher ranks as Cav's greatest quarterback at Fordham. His greatest at Boston College was Joe McKenney, who played for him four years, and later from 1928 through '33 was an outstanding head coach himself at Boston College. He had a perfect-record Eastern championship team in 1928, but left coaching for the Boston public school system, ending up as associate superintendent.

The Seven Blocks of Granite lines, now part of football legend, originated with Cavanaugh's 1930 team, which was identical almost with 1929's. The '29 team was unscored on through the line; the '30 team gave up one touchdown there, in its only defeat, 20–12, to St. Mary's. It was after the 1930 feat of shutting out B.C. and Holy Cross, 3–0 and 6–0, within six days, that the Fordham line received the tag, the Seven Blocks of Granite.

Later, in 1936 and '37 when Fordham had another great line under Jim Crowley, I, as sports publicity director, exhumed the Seven Blocks of Granite label, used it again, and this time it stuck. But who originated it is unknown. It's known only that he wrote it as the lead-in to a caption that appeared under an Associate Press picture of the 1930 Ram line, the week after the Holy Cross game. Whoever he was, he did Fordham and football a favor.

Many of Cavanaugh's players, at both Boston College and Fordham, were the sons of immigrants. They appreciated the value of an education and performed as ably in the classroom as on the gridiron. A number of them were on the Dean's List. There were no soft courses. Every-

body worked for a Bachelor of Arts or a Bachelor of Science degree, and majored in philosophy as juniors and seniors.

Cav was at Fordham and had put together his strong 1929 and '30 seasons, when in '31 the Carnegie Investigation Committee, a self-appointed group of busybodies, investigated college football. Suspicious of Fordham's sudden emergence as a power, the committee paid a visit to Rose Hill, site of Fordham's uptown campus.

They were welcomed by the Fordham president, the Very Reverend Aloysius J. Hogan, S. J., who eagerly furnished them with transcripts of the football players' records. Many of the players, like Healey and Miskinis, were at the cum laude level, and the group was well above average. The records affirmed what had been stated before and was later by that razor intellect and great-souled professor of psychology and natural theology, Father Joseph A. Murphy, S. J., later provincial of the New York–Maryland Province.

"It has been my experience," said Father Joe Murphy, "that the football players at Fordham, as a group, are academically superior to the student body as a whole."

In war or football, the Iron Major was a hard man. The tender side of him was something he usually took pains to conceal. Back in 1916, when he was coaching Dartmouth, Cav collaborated with Frank Graham, of the New York *Evening Sun*, in an analytical article on the Yale-Harvard game. Cav was pleased with the way Graham handled the story and sent him a thank-you note in which he said, "I wish I could write like that."

About a year later the Boston *Herald* printed a letter which Cav had written from France to his little boy Dave, then seven. Graham saw the letter in the *Herald* and arranged to reprint it in the *Evening Sun* as part of a story on Cav.

"And this letter, mind you," says Graham, "was written by a man who thought he couldn't write." The *Evening Sun*, like the Boston *Herald*, was flooded with requests for copies of the letter, and had several hundred of them printed. Here is the letter the Iron Major wrote his son:

Somewhere in France

Nov. 12, 1917

Dear Davie Boy:

Your good mother writes me that you have a chum, and she says he is a fine boy and lives next door. Isn't that fine? I wish I had a chum. You and mother used to be my chums, and sometimes Joe

and Billie and even dear little Rosemary, and Phil, too, when he was home.

But, now, that is all changed and I have no chum at all in all the world. I think it's rather sad sometimes, don't you? But I have your pictures, which I take out and talk to when I am lonesome.

I'm happy to know you like your new school and home and I'm sure you'll only play with the clean boys who don't do anything very bad, and who also like to go to school.

Didn't we have the good times together, and wasn't it great fun when you'd come up to the car to meet me; then, when you saw me getting off, do you remember how you'd come and hide behind a tree and run up behind me and scare me after I had passed?

And do you remember how sometimes you and I would race, and you were getting so you could run pretty fast, because you were growing up to be a big boy. And then we'd all go down to see the circus and the parade and hold hands so we wouldn't get separated or lost. And then, Christmas! Oh, wasn't that a wonderful day! Early in the morning how you'd all rush downstairs to see your presents. And then poor tired mother would work and work to give all her boys and girls a big Xmas dinner—turkey, cranberry sauce, and dressing and plum pudding and candy, nuts and "evathin." Oh, Dave, did any little boy ever have such a good mother as you, I wonder.

And now, you are soon to have another Xmas, and old Cav won't be home; but I want you to have the finest time you ever had on that day, so that I may be happy over here thinking of you.

I wish I knew some little boys and girls over here, so that I might talk to them and hold their hands, and then I would call them by my little boys' and girls' names and pretend I was home.

The other night I had a lovely dream, and I was so disappointed when I awoke. I dreamed I was sitting in our kitchen with mother and Dave and all the children, and my chair, which was tilted back against the wall, slipped and I fell gently and without hurting me to the floor. And then mother and you and all the children laughed and laughed like good naughty folks, and you came over and took my hand in yours and lifted me right up easily.

Isn't that funny, Dave? Think of any boy lifting a big, fat father like me from the floor with one hand. Then we laughed some more and suddenly I remembered it was after nine o'clock and I said: "Why kids, what are you doing out of bed at this hour of the night?" And you said: "Well, it isn't very often our father goes away to war, so we thought we ought to stay up to say, 'good-bye.'" And then I was so surprised to learn that I hadn't gone away to war yet, that I suddenly awoke only to find myself in my little lonely barracks, and the rain was coming down hard outside and I was lonesome for my family, my dear family.

And now, Dave "old hoss," everyone is in bed but me, trying to get lots of strength and health for the big fights that we will soon be in, so I must do likewise and end this letter to you.

You must always remember that your father came into this great war for the sake of all little children, and I know that you will, while I am gone, take good care of mother and all the children.

I can see you now growing up, tall and straight, with shoulders back and head up, 'cause that's what old Cav wants and you love Cav, I guess, don't you, Davie boy?

Davie, will you do something for me? I knew you would. Well, then, kiss mother and Ann, and Billie, Rosemary and John for Cav, and send one to Phillip up in Maine.

Excuse me, Dave, for writing in pencil instead of ink, but ink is hard to get. The lights are going out in a few moments, so Good-night, Good-bye, Dave, and God bless you.

Your old man,
CAV

Fritz Crisler

THE FOOTBALL STATESMAN

Nineteen hundred and thirty-one, the year before Herbert Orrin (Fritz) Crisler began his six seasons as coach of Princeton, the Tiger practices for the climactic game with Yale saw 50 or more former players in uniform, trying to help out with the coaching. There was scarcely room left on the field for the players to move about. Result: quiet chaos and a 51–14 licking from Yale.

Crisler, as the first nonalumnus ever to coach Princeton, was regarded warily in some quarters. When he took over, however, one of the first things he did was mail every interested alumnus a

Fritz Crisler

breaks down into two seasons at Minnesota, 10–7–1; six at Princeton, 35–9–5; and ten at Michigan, 71–16–3.

He had three perfect seasons, 9–0 at Princeton in 1933 and '35, and 10–0 at Michigan in 1947. The '47 team, which defeated Southern California, 49–0, in the 1948 Rose Bowl game, surely was one of the top offensive teams ever put together. Certainly, with its spinning and buck-lateral sequences, it was one of the best to watch. Bob Chappuis (pronounced CHAP-pee-us), Bump Elliott, Jack Weisenberger, and Howard Yerges were slick ball-handlers.

Beyond the football field, the athletic building program begun at Michigan under his predecessor, Fielding H. Yost, reached even fuller bloom under Crisler. Michigan Stadium was expanded twice, to 101,001, largest college-owned in the country. And he had added a million-dollar women's swimming pool; the Matt Mann's men's varsity pool; a modern steel baseball pavilion; the golf course clubhouse; the Athletic Administration Building; and had enlarged the rink.

Crisler also exerted much influence on football rules and National Collegiate Athletic Association administrative committees. He was responsible for the two-point conversion, the widening of the goalposts from 20 to 24 feet. But he will be best remembered as the father of the "two-platoon" system at Michigan in 1945.

"It was not from ingenuity on my part," Crisler said, "but out of desperation. When the other fellow has $1,000 and you have a dime is the time to gamble. My spindly, rosy-cheeked lads, including a dozen freshmen, couldn't stand up against the Doc Blanchard–Glenn Davis Army team for 60 minutes, so we had to gamble.

"When Army had ball possession, we lined up in a 4–4–3, with the guards on the heads of their guards and the tackles on the heads of their ends. Our ends played behind our tackles, and our center and fullback behind our guards. The center and the two tackles, independent of one another, would designate a stunt. So far as I know, it is the first time a four-man front ended up in a seven-man line charge. When we had the ball, we substituted for eight people: the four front and the four linebackers.

"By resting those eight defensive players, we went into the fourth quarter 7–7, but the dam broke, as I knew it would, when Blanchard went in for one and Davis for two; someone zigged when he should have zagged.

"It worked so well, however, that for the rest of

pass to practice with two stipulations: that what they saw would remain secret and that they would stay on the sidelines.

The reaction at first was negative, but when Crisler's 1932 team tied Yale, 7–7, and his '33 team capped an unbeaten, untied season by beating the Elis, 27–2, the grumbling faded off.

This was a typically smooth Crisler operation. Of all the coaches whose qualities of leadership indicated they probably would have done well in other careers, Fritz stood out as the diplomat, the statesman. He would have been thoroughly at home in the Court of St. James or as a member of any embassy, including Moscow's.

Although he is generally credited with restoring football muscle at two schools, Princeton and Michigan, it was also Crisler who, before he left Minnesota for Old Nassau, arranged for Bernie Bierman to be his successor. And under Bierman and with the head start of Crisler's recruiting, the Gophers dominated the Big Ten and the national picture for much of the next decade.

In his 18 years as a head coach, Crisler's record of 116–32–9 for .768 was 14th in the all-time totals at the game's centennial, 1969. The record

the season, we platooned eleven men instead of the eight. My mail and phone calls had considerable volume as coaches wanted to know what we were doing. By the following season most of the colleges and secondary schools adopted platooning."

College football rules and athletic statesmanship had no part in the boyhood plans of Herbert Crisler, born January 12, 1899, on a farm near Earlville, Illinois, 72 miles west of Chicago, and educated through high school there (pop. 1,420) and nearby Mendota (pop. 6,154). Brought up in a devout Methodist family, he leaned at first toward the ministry, but his uncle, a country doctor, advised him:

"A minister can do a lot of things, but he can't keep people out of hell. If you really want to help suffering people, you should be a doctor."

Crisler remembered hitching up the horses, driving with his uncle on sick calls, and even watching surgery at a small rural hospital.

In high school Crisler was six feet but weighed only 100 pounds. Earlville High had 15 boys and all but two played football: a cripple and Crisler. Fritz did do some baseball playing, even a little pitching, for the high school and town teams. But he emphasized the books, and a four-year average of 93.4 earned him a full-tuition academic scholarship at Chicago, where he enrolled as a premed student.

He missed Phi Beta Kappa at Chicago by only one honor point, because he lost three points for cutting chapel his senior year. It was traditional for seniors to delegate freshmen to occupy their chapel seats, but Crisler's delegate proved derelict. Fritz actually completed two years of med school; meanwhile, however, by degrees he was becoming one of the Big Ten's outstanding all-round athletes, winning the senior medal for proficiency in scholarship and sports. But he got started in football by accident.

"I was wearing my green freshman cap and watching practice," he said. "My mouth was wide open as a play came my way. Mr. Stagg [Coach Amos Alonzo Stagg], avoiding the players, bumped into me and down we went. He looked at me with great scorn, doubtless spotting my green cap, and asked, 'Why aren't you out here with your classmates?'

" 'I've never played football,' I told him.

"But I did have a curiosity to see the inside of Bartlett Gymnasium. I went there the next day and got equipment, which never came close to fitting a six-footer who weighed no more than 150 pounds at best. I got knocked from here to there in the varsity-freshman scrimmage.

"This was my first introduction to football and, I thought, my last. I turned in my uniform. A week later I saw Mr. Stagg riding across the quadrangle on his bicycle and turned away as he went past, but he circled around.

" 'Weren't you out for football?' he asked.

" 'Yes.'

" 'What happened?'

" 'I quit.'

" 'I never thought you'd be a quitter,' he said, and he rode away. I was back in uniform the next day."

Crisler won nine letters at Chicago, three each in football, basketball, and baseball. As a pitcher he made a tour of Japan with the Chicago varsity in 1920, and even had a brief tryout with the Chicago White Sox.

"After I had completed my eligibility at Chicago," he said, "Ed Walsh, the White Sox pitcher I admired, invited me to pitch batting practice in Comiskey Park. He cautioned me not to try to throw the ball past the batters—just lay it in there. When they started rattling the fences on almost every pitch, I went to my curve ball. But I had no better luck.

"After I'd thrown maybe a dozen pitches, Walsh came out to the mound, lugging shin guards, chest protector, and a mask.

" 'Here, put these on before you get killed,' he said. So ended any hopes I had of playing professional baseball."

In basketball Crisler became a regular the second game of his sophomore season, and as a senior was captain and All-Conference. In football as an end he made Walter Eckersall's first All-America team and Walter Camp's third team. His advancement as a gridder, however, was not rapid. After he had repeatedly flubbed the same play one day, Stagg said to him:

"Crisler, there's a celebrated violinist in this country. The name sounds like yours but it is spelled differently—K-r-e-i-s-l-e-r. He's world-renowned because he has certain attributes and knows how to use them. He has genius, skill, coordination. From now on, Crisler, I'm going to call you Fritz, too, just to remind myself that you are absolutely his opposite."

The nickname stuck, and years later, when the violinist was giving a concert in Hill Auditorium at Ann Arbor, Michigan, students arranged for the two Fritzes to meet. They chatted briefly, found they were not related—the coach's ances-

try was Dutch, the violinist's Austrian—and between his two final encores the artist asked the coach if there was something he could play for him. The request was "Danny Boy."

The depression and the lorelei of coaching combined to phase out the dream of medicine. To supplement his income as assistant to Stagg and the baseball coach, Crisler tutored the son of Morris Rosenwald, prominent Chicago businessman. And the youngster was the one Leopold and Loeb planned to kidnap. That day, however, the headmaster of the school called Crisler to tell him young Rosenwald had a toothache. Fritz called the chauffeur and took the boy to the dentist. When Leopold and Loeb could not locate him after school that day, they took 14-year-old Bobby Franks.

Eight years later, in 1932, when Crisler was conferring with Princeton about becoming its head coach, the kidnapping of the Lindbergh baby took place. Fritz was driving from New York to Princeton in a borrowed car when he was stopped by police who were spreading out and blocking roads.

"There I was," he recalled, "driving alone in a car that wasn't my own, so you can see the police were concerned. It took a telephone call before they would release me."

Crisler followed the Bruno Hauptmann case avidly, and the curious coincidences escalated. En route to a restaurant in Hopewell, New Jersey, scene of the kidnapping, he passed a man driving a mule and a cart filled with hay, and learned that soon after the man stopped and discovered the body of the Lindbergh infant. On another occasion, Crisler was riding in a car with Governor Harold Hoffman, of New Jersey, when an assassin fired two shotgun blasts at them. Fritz realized that there are other dangerous professions than coaching football.

In 1924, only two years after graduation from Chicago, Crisler, 26, was offered the head coach's job at Minnesota, but turned it down when Stagg advised him, "Fritz, you're not ready to fly." When the offer came again six years later, Stagg told him he was ready and advised him to grab it; the Old Man recognized that football was dying at Chicago.

In his first season at Minnesota, 1930, Crisler experimented with various styles of attack ultimately to derive his own blend. For a time, the attack used by an opponent one week would be, in part anyhow, Minnesota's the next. Old grads were critical of this, but Crisler was determined

Fritz as head coach of the Princeton Tigers

not to commit himself until he had first experimented with the best thinking of the best coaches.

Crisler's two best remembered games at Minnesota were a scoreless tie in 1930 with a heavily favored Pop Warner Stanford team at Minneapolis, and a 19–7 triumph over Ohio State in 1931.

Warner called the 1930 team his best at Stanford; they were 26-point favorites. Crisler, adept at bringing a team to an emotional peak, had the Gophers ready, and they repulsed several deep Stanford drives.

At one time Stanford had first down on the 2-yard line, but on fourth down Minnesota's star guard, Clarence (Biggie) Munn, and Stanford's fullback Harlow Rothert were piled atop a mass of tangled humans still inches short of the goal.

For the Ohio State game Crisler was eager to enhance Munn's chances of All-America, and

arranged things thereto. The holes Munn opened enabled Minnesota's backs to pour through. Biggie also punted, carried the ball from fullback for substantial gains, threw two complete passes, and topped it off by pulling out from his guard position to take a lateral off a forward pass all the way to the 4-yard line to set up the clincher touchdown.

"When Crisler and Tad Wieman, who had been Yost's line coach at Michigan came here," wrote Dick Cullum, "the plan was to have them share the coaching assignment equally. Both regarded this as unrealistic. Both had great football minds and they did pretty well because Crisler took the dominant position and Wieman cooperated nobly. I think Wieman had a really profound football mind."

Minnesota football, which had thrashed in turmoil during the twenties, from the last days of Doc Williams through Bill Spaulding and Clarence (Fat) Spears, was pulled together by Crisler. He talked to 103 alumni groups about steering players to Minnesota.

"My last official act at Minnesota," wrote Crisler, "was an effort to entice Bernie Bierman to leave Tulane and cast his lot with his alma mater. We met in the Palmer House in Chicago, where for two hours I reviewed the many advantages and bright future at Minnesota. Bernie was never known to be very loquacious, so I finally suggested, 'Bernie, you probably have some questions you would like to raise about a contract.' His only response was, 'Where do I sign?' Little did I suspect that that act would haunt me in later years."

The Princeton situation Crisler inherited in 1932 resembled Minnesota's, the core of the problem being divergent opinions among alumni groups as to a proper course. In Roper's last two years, 1929 and '30, and Al Wittmer's one year, 1931, the total record was 4–16–2, and the last three Yale games had been lost. One of the prominent ex-Tiger players, Ed McMillan, captain of the 1925 team, wrote:

"On his way East for his first spring practice at Princeton, Fritz stopped off at Pittsburgh, where many of the old Tigers came from. We had a smoker and despite Prohibition, managed to dig up a few kegs. I was sitting beside Fritz when he got up to speak. He adjusted his glasses, which gave him his best professional appearance, and proceeded to give one of his better efforts.

"Near the end he got carried away and gave this goodie, 'I am happy to be coming to Prince-ton and I want you people to know that I would rather lose than win with one player with the taint of proselytism upon him!'

"I held onto the table to keep from falling onto the floor. For the next four years Princeton had the finest material in her history—before or since."

The freshman group that entered Old Nassau that fall of 1932 was mainly responsible for the three-year record of 1933–35: 9–0, 7–1, and 9–0. From the sixth game of the 1932 season through the second game of 1936, Princeton's record was 28–1–1, the only defeat a 7–0 upset by Yale in 1934.

When it was remarked to Fritz that the freshman squad of 1932 (Class of '36) included 30 former high school and prep school captains, he replied without batting an eyelash that it was an interesting coincidence. Thereafter, the Class of '36 was known as "The Princeton Coincidentals."

Soon after Princeton hired him, Crisler asked Grantland Rice, whom Fritz calls "the dean of them all," "What should I do to keep the press happy? Throw banquets, come up to New York frequently to visit them, just what?" "Be cordial, honest, and sincere," said Rice, "but don't go out of your way calling on them. If you win, they will write about you; and if you lose, then nothing is going to help you."

In comparing the perfect-record teams of 1933 and '35, Crisler wrote, "The 1933 team was largely a sophomore group, and the striking thing about it was its defensive greatness. Since it is much easier to teach defensive football, it is understandable why sophomores were able to distinguish themselves. Starting with defense as the basis, I began to build the offensive crew which culminated in the undefeated team of 1935.

"That was a great line in 1933, with Hinman at center, Bliss and Weller at the guards, Captain Lane and Ceppi at the tackles, and Lea and Fairman on the ends. The backfield, Kadlic, Constable, Le Van, and Spofford, had a great scoring punch.

"The 20–0 victory over the Columbia team that went to the Rose Bowl was one of the finest clutch performances during my years at Princeton. It was a game in which every member of the team bore down. The blocking especially was of a high order.

"My impression of this team that went through 1935 largely intact was its tremendous poise and savvy. As the sophomores began to find that they could halt the other team, their confidence and

poise developed and they began to acquire the know-how necessary to assimilate the fine points of attack. That left me more free of defensive worries and permitted me to place more time and emphasis upon attack. And the significant thing about these teams was their great offensive strength."

Crisler always appreciated the necessity of strong assistants, and in addition to Tad Wieman, who was responsible for much of the precision of Fritz's best teams, he had a valuable scout at Princeton in Campbell Dickson, All-America end at Chicago, Phi Beta Kappa, and former FBI investigator. It was Dickson who spotted Columbia end Red Matal's tip-off, adopting a parallel stance when he was going out for a pass."

Jac Weller, star Princeton guard, attests that Crisler believed some players needed a lot of praise and others, including Weller, little or none.

"I was used to playing without a helmet," Weller related, but Crisler had a rule, 'If anyone throws his helmet over to the bench, he comes out of the game immediately. We had a good lead, but not a safe one, against Dartmouth I think it was, and in the fourth quarter they filled the air with passes. The helmets we had in those days interfered with vision, so I waited one play into the fourth quarter and tossed mine. It almost hit Fritz on the feet. He swore at me but left me in. As I recall, I intercepted the last one they threw without my helmet."

Weller was in the middle of the 1935 Princeton-Dartmouth game that saw Palmer Stadium spilling over with 55,000, its biggest crowd in seven years. They stayed to the end despite a snow blizzard that turned the gridiron into a slushy skating rink and caused the Tigers' 26–6 defeat of the Indians to be known as "The Rape in the Snow."

That 1935 team, which was one of Princeton's finest, put on a show that day. Behind steamhammer blocking of a great line against a good line, Old Nassau's assortment of talented backs, despite the wet footing, made four inexorable scoring marches of 43, 48, 40, and 50 yards.

Before the Yale game, Crisler used to receive 3:00 A.M. phone calls from author F. Scott Fitzgerald. One of them suggested a play involving an allegory of red ants and black ants, but it did not fit into Crisler's playbook.

Fitzgerald apparently sought vicarious football adventure. He had been a second-team quarterback at Newman prep school, and when Princeton admitted him, he wired his mother, AC-

As athletic director at Michigan

CEPTED. SEND FOOTBALL PADS AND SHOES IMMEDIATELY. A classmate recalls Fitzgerald, five feet seven and 138, catching punts. He stayed out for three days until an ankle injury ended his career.

Asked to compare his strong Princeton teams with the Tommy Harmon Michigan teams of 1938, '39, and '40, Crisler wrote, "I would not risk picking a winner. A break would probably decide. Both had an abundance of ability and competitive desire."

Crisler arrived at Ann Arbor in 1938 concurrent with Harmon's sophomore year, and for the next three seasons the Wolverines logged a 19–4–1 record, with three of the defeats administered by Bierman's Minnesota teams, two of them 7–6. Fumbles and other misadventures prevented Harmon from ever scoring against Minnesota, but that represented about his only failure.

Before he retired his famous No. 98, Harmon scored three touchdowns against Ohio State to bring his three-year total to 33; Red Grange scored 31 in four fewer games. A fusion of exceptional speed, power, and deception, Harmon lugged the ball 399 times for 2,151 yards, an average just shy of six yards. He completed 101 of 233 passes for 1,346 yards and 16 touchdowns. He averaged 38 yards punting, and place-kicked 33 extra points and two field goals. Like Grange, his favorite running move was the cutback over tackle, going to either side.

At Michigan, Crisler put together the spin series he had developed at Princeton with the

buck-lateral sequence, and the result was a peerless version of single-wing attack blending power and chicanery. Over the 10 years he was head coach, 1938–47, Michigan was the team to beat in the Western Conference. The Wolverines won the title outright in 1947, tied with Purdue in '43, and finished second six times.

Although his later teams included numerous outstanding backs like Bob Chappuis, Bump Elliott, and Jack Weisenberger, none of them ever matched Harmon, who ranks with Red Grange, Chic Harley of Ohio State, Bronko Nagurski of Minnesota, and Nile Kinnick of Iowa, in a special Big Ten pantheon.

Harmon had first reported to Horace Mann High in his native Gary, Indiana, as a 14-year-old freshman who had won a bubble gum contest at a local theater. He ended up as a 14-letter winner in football, basketball, baseball, and track. He was also a good student, and at least three dozen colleges tried to recruit him. But his Gary coach, Doug Kerr, was a Michigan graduate, and this gave the Wolverines the edge.

Against Iowa in his junior year, Harmon scored all of the winning 27 points, and always called that his best individual day. But most critics who covered him would pick the game at California his senior year, when he celebrated his 21st birthday by returning the opening kickoff 94 yards to a touchdown, scored another on a punt return of 72 yards, and a third on an 84-yard run through the entire Cal team and an overheated fan who came charging down out of the stands.

As Harmon went on to score all 21 points in a triumph over Michigan State and all 14 in a shutout of Pennsylvania, his principal blocker was quarterback and captain in 1940, Forest Evashevski, who would later become an outstanding coach at Washington State and Iowa. Evvy exuded a free spirit and sense of humor that neither Crisler nor anybody else could quell.

He often referred to Crisler as Chris Fisler and when Crisler in one of his rousers said he wanted eleven tigers on defense and eleven lions on offense, Captain Evashevski raised his hand and said he wouldn't play unless he could be a leopard. Crisler's Michigan players referred to him as "the Lord" and explained that it never

rained at Michigan practice before six o'clock, because "the Lord" wouldn't let it.

No doubt, Evashevski's unpredictable ways were a salutary leavening for Crisler's highly organized, serious operation. Fritz, of course, never lost command of his teams. The longer he coached, the fewer dressing-room histrionics he invoked.

"Offense is poise, defense is frenzy," was Crisler's No. 1 motto. Since opponents were invariably pointing for Michigan, he was in the habit of assuring his squads, "Our plan is simple, their's, one of desperation."

No matter the halftime score, Crisler would ask the players, "What's the score?" and they would chorus in response: "Nothing to nothing." Inevitably, of course, a sophomore spoke out one day. "You fellows are all wrong," he said. "The score is 21–0 and we're ahead." There was no more halftime seriousness that day.

Crisler was also superstitious. He kept a lucky penny he'd found, and had a lucky pair of socks, tie, and suit. At all home games he and his staff rode in a certain car over a certain route to the stadium.

Away from the gridiron or the council table, Crisler was a sociable soul, who liked to stay up late with old friends, and unlike his old coach and mentor, Stagg, favored a stronger beverage than milk. One Northland legend has Crisler and Bill Hunter, former Southern California athletic director, requisitioning early-morning milk-wagon teams and trying to emulate the Ben Hur–Messala chariot race. Crisler says he has no recollection of that event, which is no doubt the truth.

For anything connected with the playing of football, however, Stagg rubbed off on Crisler, who would not abide dirty or illegal play or any form of unfair advantage. Of the many salutes he has received, none sums him up better than Stagg's:

"Balance, judgment, dependability, and loyalty are his predominant characteristics. In my talks to young people, I have often used him as an illustration of those qualities well supported by eloquent mental gifts."

THE COACH AND HORSEMAN

As Notre Dame was blessed that Knute Rockne happened to coach there, Fordham was fortunate to have had first Frank Cavanaugh and then Jim Crowley. Crowley's record on Rose Hill—56 victories, 13 defeats, 7 ties—was the best in the East in his nine-year span, 1933–41, and one of the four best in the nation among coaches in pressure situations, as this brief statistical survey affirms:

COACH & SCHOOL	W	L	T	PCT.
Bernie Bierman, Minnesota	59	8	5	.854
Frank Thomas, Alabama	68	12	5	.829
Bob Neyland, Tennessee	58	12	3	.815
Jim Crowley, Fordham	56	13	7	.783

(Neyland did not coach in 1941. He was in the army.)

In 1969, when college football celebrated its centennial, a committee of 100 asked to select the top coaches picked Neyland 2nd, Bierman 12th, Thomas 22nd, and Crowley 60th. In 1972, however, the National Collegiate Athletic Association Sports Services records revealed the following on the four coaches:

COACH	ALL-CAREER	W	L	T	PCT.	RANK
Neyland	21 years	173	31	12	.829	5
Thomas	19 years	141	33	9	.795	10
Crowley	13 years	78	21	10	.761	19
Bierman	26 years	147	61	12	.695	53

Obviously, the committee of 100 had given Crowley's record scant notice, and there is a reason. After Fordham defeated Missouri, 2–0, in the 1942 Sugar Bowl game, he became a lieutenant commander in the navy V-5 program, and though he took an abortive whirl at coaching the Chicago Rockets, a short-lived pro team, after the war, 19 years elapsed between his last important coaching and the centennial. (It should be pointed out, however, that the father of modern organized coaching, Percy D. Haughton of Harvard—13-year record of 96–17–6 for .832 and No. 4 rank—was picked by the committee of 100 as No. 29. Obviously, there were members on that committee who had not done their homework.)

Crowley's record at Fordham sparkles even brighter when you consider that he delivered it despite box-office schedules, loaded week after week with the toughest intersectional powers available, and Dr. Jock Sutherland's Pittsburgh teams, so good that even Notre Dame dropped them. These powerhouses marched on the Polo Grounds, Fordham's home field, primed to be at their best before the New York press and public.

"If you want to make All-America," Sutherland told his players before the 1936 scoreless tie with Fordham, the second of an incredible three straight played by Panthers and Rams, 1935, '36, and '37, "here is the place to do it."

Everything a great football coach needs, Crowley had in abundance. He was a natural leader, inspiring talker, assiduous recruiter, shrewd psychologist, sportsmanlike image, and manipulator of football's golden key: defense.

In his first five seasons at Fordham, Crowley's personnel forced him to emphasize conservatism, so he built the best defenses of the day.

Yet, at Michigan State his backfield of Alton Kircher at quarter, Bob Monnett and Abe Eliowitz at the halfbacks, and Bernie McNutt at full had been brilliant and explosive. With them he upset Fordham in 1932 at the Polo Grounds, 19–13, to establish himself as the successor to the ailing Major Cavanaugh, who died the following summer.

In his last four years at Fordham, Crowley began to get some backs like Len Eshmont, Jim Blumenstock, and Joe Andrejco, who could op-

Jim Crowley, at Michigan State

nonentity in football until Cavanaugh got it rolling in 1929, Crowley never was fully appreciated either by the New York press, which was mesmerized by Columbia's Lou Little, an even better promoter than a coach, or by that segment of the Fordham studentry and alumni, real or subway, who can best be categorized as "the nutboys."

Blatant boobery their trademark, they indicted Crowley as "strictly a defensive coach." To support their argument, they cited the three straight scoreless ties with Pitt. Nobody else was scoring much on Pitt in those days, or even getting close to them on the scoreboard—but who are so demanding and omniscient as nouveaux riches well sprinkled with morons and cretins? They should be lined up at midfield on Homecoming Day, and drawn and quartered to band music.

Crowley also worked under some Jesuits who were not exactly conducive to coachly peace of mind. There were exceptions, of course. One was Father John W. Tynan, Fordham's faculty moderator of athletics during Crowley's last six seasons. Father Tynan, for one thing, recognized that Fordham could not expect to win all the time. His predecessor, Father John Pancretius Fitzpatrick, was about as qualified for the job as the Wicked Witch of the West.

Then there was the president of Fordham in Crowley's first four years, the Very Reverend Aloysius J. Hogan. In 1936, when I was completing the first of five years as Fordham's sports information director, Jack Coffey, our graduate manager of athletics, turned out one of his many fine baseball teams. The Rams won 18, lost 2, and had a claim on the mythical Eastern championship. To accomplish this, they naturally had to have some luck; each of the victories over Yale, Harvard, and Princeton was by one run. Andy Palau, fine quarterback and catcher, won the game at Yale Field, 7–6, with a ninth-inning home run.

The next day I had to see Father Hogan about a publicity matter. As a presumably joyous gambit, I offered the dramatic baseball triumph at Yale. "You would have enjoyed it, Father," I began.

Father Hogan reached for his tobacco jar. There was a rumor, not unfounded, that when the rector reached for the jar, he was winding up. In tones as resonantly splendid as his impressive self—he was a handsome, courtly man, with a fine mind, and was a good speaker—he said,

erate behind blocking and on their own. He also modified the Notre Dame shift to exploit them to the fullest. As a result, the 1940 team (7–2, including a 13–12 loss to the Texas Aggies in the '41 Cotton Bowl) and the 1941 team (8–1, including the Sugar Bowl win, 2–0, over Missouri) totaled 344 points in 18 games, an average of better than 19 points a game. That's only a fraction below the *one-year* record of the 1940 Stanford team, whose Modern T with flanker and motion, as developed by Clark Shaughnessy, would soon supplant all forms of single wing as the predominant offense.

Despite what he did for Fordham, a relative

"There is no reason in the world why either of those men [Crowley and Coffey] should have lost a game. A friend of mine who is a sports expert and visits most of America's campuses was here recently and told me, 'Father Hogan, I never have seen such college football and baseball material as you have here at Fordham.'"

The rector packed his pipe and proceeded in dignified melancholia, "I help out as much as I can. But the exigencies of this job are endless, and I cannot be in two places at one time."

Father Hogan's successor, the Very Reverend Robert I. Gannon, who was to fold Fordham football in the embrace of dissolution, was fond of telling graduates of the depression thirties, like myself, that after the war most of us could not have made it at Fordham academically. Intellectually impoverished though we may have been, however, none of us would have been so obtuse as to miss the implications when Father Hogan disclaimed the supernatural power of bilocation.

Clearly, had he only more time to advise Crowley and Coffey, their records would have been better. He still found time to meet Crowley by appointment, shortly after lunch each Monday during football, just outside the Bathgate Avenue entrance to the campus. They would sit there in Crowley's blue Packard while the rector dissertated on strategy and tactics.

It may have been during his education at Cambridge, where he played a spot of Rugby, that Father Hogan derived some of his authority on athletics, football especially. In any event, he spoke ex cathedra, from the chair of infallibility. He was by no means the only Jesuit on Rose Hill or elsewhere so equipped. And such infallibility is not exclusive with Jesuits. Military academy brass rate just as expert, or more so.

It was a tragedy for Fordham football, nevertheless, that Father Hogan didn't stay on. It is better to have a rector who is convinced you should win them all, than one who doesn't want to play. Father Gannon regarded football as Beelzebub's Beanbag. It is ironic that he, one of the church's finest orators, may be even better remembered as the man who gave Fordham football the coup de grace. Maybe he figured that Fordham needed only one outstanding speaker, which would have made Crowley superfluous.

On the dais or any other place, Crowley possessed and still does the quickest, most natural wit I've ever encountered in sports. It is one of the reasons that today he is still in much demand as a speaker. (For several years he has been industrial

Sleepy Jim is anything but somnolent here as he eyes a practice at Fordham

commissioner for Lackawanna County Industrial Department, working out of Scranton, Pennsylvania.) Born mimic, master of the dead pan, naturally articulate, with a genuine sense of the dramatic, Crowley probably could have been a successful actor. If he ever forgot his lines, he could ad-lib without missing a beat. As a Notre Dame undergrad his soft-shoe dancing made him a figure in campus musicals.

Crowley's native sense of humor served him in good stead as an anodyne to the pressures of coaching and the tension that goes with a competitive pride that was white hot. More than one Friday night I sat with him in his apartment on East 96th Street, awaiting the dawn of a game day and the advent, say, of Pittsburgh and its great back Marshall Goldberg. "The Mad Marshall" could give you the willies just by putting on his helmet.

Goldberg finally broke down Fordham's defenses in Pitt's 24–13 victory in 1938. The game was played in Pitt Stadium before 68,918, still the largest crowd ever to see an event in Pittsburgh. Fordham invariably drew well.

Earlier that year Pitt had devastated Wisconsin, coached by Crowley's friend and Four Horseman quarterback, Harry Stuhldreher. Before the

With his 1935 Ram coaching aides, *left to right*: Frank Leahy, assistant line coach; Glen (Judge) Carberry, first assistant and head line coach; Crowley; Earl Walsh, backfield coach; and Hugh Devore, freshmen coach

Wisconsin-Pitt game Stuhldreher and Crowley compared notes on the Panthers. Stuhldreher, who was given to violent dreams during the football season, told Crowley that he had experienced his worse nightmare yet. It was built around Marshall Goldberg.

"He had broken through our defenses and was in the open, streaking for a score," said Harry, reliving the horror of it, "until I couldn't stand it any longer. In my nightmare I leaped off the bench to tackle him. In reality, I sprang off the bed and hit the radiator. And that's how I got this black eye."

"Never mind the shiner," said Crowley, impatiently. "Did you stop Goldberg?"

The 1938 Pittsburgh backfield—Goldberg at full, Dick Cassiano and Hal (Curly) Stebbins at the halves, and Johnny Chickerneo at quarterback—was known as the "Dream Backfield." But it had also played in the third straight scoreless tie with Fordham in 1937.

Fordham practiced in those days on a field to the west of its gymnasium. Farther to the west lay the Fordham Prep field, the New York Central Railroad tracks, and Webster Avenue with its elevated trains, surface trolleys, and automobiles, which sent up a continuous drone during Ram practices.

The week of the 1937 Pitt game, the varsity was about to line up after snapping out of the huddle. Suddenly above the normal noise, a fire engine siren began screaming. The new noise seemed to startle the players.

"Don't mind that," Crowley said. "It's only the Pitt backfield, *walking* through their plays."

A quiet quip, a heaping of praise, a barbed needle—all were used by Crowley to get the most out of a player. When the challenge called for an acknowledged great player to outdo himself, Crowley knew how to build him up to it. Lou DeFilippo was one of an outstanding line of Fordham centers, including Tony Siano, Johnny Dell Isola, Alex Wojciechowicz, and Joe Sebasteanski.

DeFilippo played on the once-beaten 1940 team, which was a pronounced short-ender going into the 1941 Cotton Bowl game with the powerful Texas Aggies.

Crowley's 1936 Fordham team. The Seven Blocks of Granite (*from the left*): Johnny Druze, Al Babartsky, Vince Lombardi, Alex Wojciechowicz, Nat Pierce, Ed Franco, Leo Paquin. The backfield: Andy Palau (54), Frank Mautte (65), John Lock (6), Al Gurske (50). *Fordham Sports Information Office, Roger J. Hackett, Director*

Afterwards, even such a Texan as Dizzy Dean announced publicly that the Aggies, distinctly outplayed, were fortunate to win, 13–12; Crowley called it the toughest game a team of his ever had lost. The Aggies were outplayed mainly because their super fullback, "Jarrin' Jawn" Kimbrough, was well contained by DeFilippo. Kimbrough later shook his head in pained admiration: "Oh, that Dee-fee-*leep*-o!"

DeFilippo had been primed for this performance by Crowley on the train carrying Fordham to Dallas. Somewhat casually Jim mentioned to Lou several times that it was quite possible he might not be able to handle Kimbrough. "It's all right, though, Lou," said Jim. "We'll just have to compensate by adjusting our normal defenses." After hearing this a few times, DeFilippo was impatient to get at Kimbrough.

When Crowley first arrived at Fordham in the spring of 1933, the team's two leading stars were Captain Ed Danowski, left halfback, and Johnny Dell Isola, center.

"You fellows will never play for me," said Crowley. "You're not fast enough."

Later a guard for the New York Giants and so rugged he was known as the policeman of the National Football League, Dell Isola was openly irritated. "Big Ed" Danowski, a tremendous clutch player three years at Fordham, for both Cavanaugh and Crowley, and later a fine passer for the Giants, was quietly simmering. Finally

Dell Isola said sarcastically, "Is it all right if we draw uniforms?"

Crowley smiled. "That," he said, "is what I wanted to hear you say."

Danowski and Dell Isola were the heart and soul of that fine 1933 team—record: 6–2–0—and Grantland Rice put them both on his All-America second team.

To sustain a team that was expected to win all the time, because it won most of the time, against a succession of frightening opponents, Crowley scraped for psychology. He did not try to stir them up every Saturday, because no team can maintain a relentless top pitch. Nor did he always try to arouse them himself. He used Jack Dempsey before a Pitt game. Another time he called on Steve Owen, coach of the Giants. Still another it was Bill (Bojangles) Robinson, who helped relax the boys with a tap dance.

And then there was the time a very fine lady helped out—a lady named Kate Smith—and her manager, Ted Collins. It was still the day of the dramatic dressing-room exhortation, a day which never really has passed away. Only methods and moods change to fit the superficial changes in boys, who remain basically the same. There is no generation gap in college football.

None of those guest rousers, however, could do the job that Crowley did. When he tossed aside the cap and bells and played it straight, he was the closest thing, I suspect, to Rockne himself

that Notre Dame or any other school ever turned out. Jimmy's voice was resonant, dramatic, with a definite shading of Rockne in the inflections and the staccatos.

Before the St. Mary's game in 1936 he mentioned the millions who would be listening to Ted Husing's broadcast of the game on radio. Among them, he said, would be his old mother, sitting there in her rocking chair up in Green Bay and saying her beads for her boy Jim's team. Then he paused, turned slowly to the team manager and, in lowered voice that still reached every corner of the locker room, warned him:

"Son, you better open that door and get out of the way fast! Here comes my Fordham team!"

Crowley never wanted to win a single game more badly than the one with Alabama at the Polo Grounds in 1933. Frank Thomas, an outstanding coach at Alabama for 15 years, had been a Notre Dame quarterback in Crowley's time. Years later, Rex Enright, an old Notre Dame fullback who became head coach and athletic director at South Carolina, and was a close friend of Crowley's, brought Thomas and Crowley together. In 1933, however, they weren't speaking. What the roots of the feud were is unimportant. It was there. Before the game Crowley told his players, "If we lose, I'll not go across the field and shake his hand."

Fordham won, 2–0, when Amerino Sarno, sophomore right tackle, blocked the only kick that Millard (Dixie) Howell, the Crimson Tide's All-America left halfback, ever had blocked in college. It was also Alabama's only defeat that season.

Sarno, heavy in battle, was lighthearted off the field. Dr. Julius M. Winslow, professor of pedagogy, was discoursing on his visit to a museum. "Above the door," said Dr. Winslow, "was the inscription: 'Italy, Mother of the Arts.'" From the back of the room, Sarno responded, "Pray for us!"

Sarno, Dell Isola, Danowski, Joe McArdle, a sawed-off combative guard, later celebrated as Frank Leahy's line coach and known as "Captain Bligh," Joe Maniaci, talented runner but erratic, Les Borden, a nifty pass receiver, quarterbacks Frank McDermott and Freddy Harlow, fullbacks Tony Sarausky and Steve Sorota, halfbacks Jim Cowhig and Bill Curran, tackles Walter Uzdavinis and Joe Ludwinowicz—it was a rugged Fordham team.

And the Alabama side did not comprise nasturtiums or dahlias either. In fact, Paul (Bear) Bryant, a sophomore end, didn't get into the game. Don Hutson, then a junior, didn't start but played some. He had not yet become a great pass receiver, yet he almost won the game for Alabama by getting behind Cowhig. Howell's pass barely slithered off his fingers. "If Hutson had caught that ball," said Cowhig afterward, "he surely would have scored—and I surely would have kept running by him, up the steps to the dressing room, right on out into Eighth Avenue, and kept right on running till I got home to Boston."

It was a hard game, no quarter asked or given. Early in the fray, Fordham knew it was up against a tough line, featuring Bill Lee at tackle, Tom Huppke, a hellcat guard, and Kavanaugh (Kay) Francis at center. The quarterback, Riley Smith, later played for the Washington Redskins.

Lee is reported to have called Uzdavinis a "Yankee son of a bitch," to which Uzdavinis is supposed to have replied, "You are a little mixed up. The Yankees play across the river."

Fordham usually played well against the powerful Southeastern Conference teams. The 1934 team had the poorest record of any of Crowley's nine—5–3–0—yet may have got as much out of what it had as any of the eight others. The big achievement was a 13–12 upset of Bob Neyland's Tennessee team at the Polo Grounds; the Vols' only other loss that year was to Alabama.

The victory was accomplished in an unusual 65-yard run by left halfback Tony Sarausky. Tony tried to sweep Tennessee's left flank, failed, reversed toward the middle of the field, suddenly cut up the field, picked up a couple of blocks, and astonishingly was in the open. Years later I discussed that play with General Neyland, and he blamed Sarausky's run on the failure of the Vol right defensive sideback to pursue early enough. It was unusual for a team to break off such a long gain on a Neyland team. The play also underlined the potential fatality of a mistake against a Crowley team.

In that '34 Fordham-Tennessee game, rival linemen were Vince Lombardi and Murray Warmath, Vince then a tackle but later shifted to guard, Murray a guard. Fifteen years later they would be assistants to Red Blaik at Army, whence Murray went to Mississippi State and Minnesota and Vince to the Giants and then Green Bay.

By 1935, Crowley had his recruiting organized and after an early-season loss to Purdue, the Rams were to go four years before losing again in

the Polo Grounds, to Alabama, 7–6. In the final game of the 1935 season, Crowley's team beat a previously undefeated, untied New York University team, 21–0. The Violets were coached by that humanitarian bone specialist and sportsman, Dr. Marvin A. (Mal) Stevens, earlier a star halfback and coach at Yale. We may have knocked Mal and his team out of a Rose Bowl trip; if so, they returned the compliment the next season.

That year we went into the NYU game unbeaten, but with two ties, the second of the three straight with Pitt and a 7–7 affair with Harry Mehre's Georgia team. Crowley had been Mehre's assistant for one year at Georgia, 1928. Georgia was the underdog but deserved the tie. Fordham still could have had the Rose Bowl bid from Washington by rallying against NYU in Yankee Stadium on Thanksgiving Day, only five days later. As I look back now, I think something went out of the team with that Georgia tie. NYU won 7–6. It was the low point of Crowley's coaching life.

Nevertheless, until the Georgia tie, the season had been a success with victories over Southern Methodist, St. Mary's, and Purdue, and the second successive scoreless tie with Pitt. They gave up only one touchdown through the line that year, to NYU. After the scoreless tie with Pitt on October 24, I exhumed the line that had been used on the lines of the undefeated 1929 and once-defeated 1930 Fordham teams coached by Major Cavanaugh—the Seven Blocks of Granite—and applied it to the 1936 line.

It had not caught on in 1930, because Cavanaugh was still laying the foundation. In 1936 it did catch on. That 1936 line was made up of Leo Paquin left end, Ed (Devil Doll) Franco left tackle, Nat Pierce left guard, Alex Wojciechowicz center, Vince Lombardi right guard, Al (Ali Baba) Babartsky right tackle, and John Druze right end. Equally quick, rugged, and containing on defense were Joe Dulkie and Johnny (Bull) Lock fullbacks, Al Gurske, Warren Mulrey, and captain Frank Mautte halfbacks, and Andy (Handy Andy) Palau quarterback.

After they began to come apart they didn't look like the same team. In blowing the Rose Bowl they lost to an NYU team that had lost its opening game to Ohio State, 60–0. Among the consequences, my wife and I honeymooned not in Pasadena as planned but in Winchester, Massachusetts, where nice New England snow piled up outside the window while we listened to Pitt

Himself one of the Four Horsemen of Notre Dame, Crowley poses before a drawing of that immortal backfield and its equally immortal coach, Knute Rockne

claw Washington, 21–0. (Despite the NYU upset, I would still not learn for many years the hard lesson of just how unpredictable a game football is.)

In 1937, the swollen heads of that black 1936 finish redeemed themselves by going through undefeated, with a climactic 20–7 victory over NYU. Paquin, Pierce, Lombardi, Dulkie, Mautte, and Gurske had graduated, but stalwart replacements were on hand. Harry Jacunski went in at left end and Mike Kochel, Jimmy Hayes, and Joe Bernard played guards. Bill Krywicki and Angelo (Butch) Fortunato were the quarterbacks, Joe Woitkoski, Steve Kazlo, and Joe Granski halfbacks, and Dom Principe fullback. On their record the 1937 version of the Seven Blocks deserved the sobriquet more than their 1929, '30 and '36 predecessors.

They wanted the Rose Bowl bid badly, but California invited Alabama, which had been out there three times before. Cal's Thunder Team beat 'Bama, as it figured to, 13–0. Pitt had been the first choice, but had turned it down. Fordham should have been the second choice.

We were naive, no doubt, sitting by the telephone and waiting for it to ring. We should have dispatched Jack Coffey or some other convincing legates—God knows we had enough able and willing people in high places—to apprise them of what jolly fellows we really were.

To go undefeated, the 1937 team gained Fordham's third straight scoreless tie with Pitt, national champions that year, and defeated Texas

Christian 7–6 (on a last-quarter drive), North Carolina, and Purdue. Pitt had Marshall Goldberg, TCU had Davey O'Brien and Ki Aldrich, Purdue had Cecil Isbell, and North Carolina lost no other game.

The Tar Heels were defeated 14–0 at Chapel Hill, North Carolina. It was a very hot day, and the Rams lost from 10 to 20 pounds a man. Wojciechowicz and Babartsky, I think, lost the most. They still talk about that team in Carolina as one of the finest ever to come into the South. It was quite a team that day—or any day.

Fordham didn't win all its games with Southern teams. On October 14, 1939, at New Orleans the Rams had to fight for their lives to prevent a rout. One of Tulane's finest teams pushed Fordham all over the field, but was thrown back several times near the goal line, and had to settle for 7–0. Sometimes a team will explain its tradition in defeat. Fordham did that day, and a onetime Rockne fullback who was then coaching Loyola of the South and saw the game, pointed it out.

"I never saw Fordham play before," Larry (Moon) Mullins said, "but after watching them play today, after watching them refuse to quit and permit a rout, I know why they have great teams. They have material, coaching, and strong schedules, but they also have that most important ingredient of all: the pride of a winning tradition."

Jimmy Crowley always had been associated with winners. The 1921 Year Book of Green Bay's East High carries these lines with his picture:

Here's to the star of the gridiron,
   To the man who can handle the ball,
Here's to Jimmy, our hero,
   Who sits high in the hearts of us all.

Notre Dame first heard of him as captain and star left halfback of East High's 1920 state championship team. In the 43–6 victory over arch rival West High, Crowley dropkicked a 30-yard field goal, tore off several nifty runs, played defensive linebacker, making tackles all over the field, and called the plays from left halfback. But he was most sensational in passing for four touchdowns.

The little finger on Crowley's right hand was deformed, but he always maintained it helped him steer the ball. Part of his success as a passer is attributed to his East High coach, Curly Lambeau, the same who fathered the Green Bay

Packers. Lambeau had a concept of passing well ahead of his time. He knew how and why it should be integrated into an attack, and he taught Crowley and East's receivers things other high school players never heard of, such as "stop and go" and "buttonhooking."

The football fortunes of Lambeau and Crowley and Lombardi, of Green Bay and Notre Dame and Fordham, have intertwined strangely down through the years. Curly coached Jim at East High, Jim coached Vince at Fordham, and years later Vince came to Green Bay and restored the Packers. Mike Cohen, Green Bay attorney and an old friend of Crowley's, put it this way: "Vince was like a third-generation kid, coming back to pick up the pieces and save the old homestead."

Since Lambeau had attended Notre Dame, it was natural for him to point Crowley there. It was at Notre Dame that Jim's occasional slumbers in class and the sometimes almost somnolent contours of his dead pan while wide awake combined to earn him the nickname "Sleepy Jim." Crowley always has insisted, however, that he was actually a victim of insomnia.

"I sleep all right at night and in the morning," he told Rockne one day, "but in the afternoon I toss and turn something awful."

Rockne did not know quite what to make of him at first. He tried bearing down on him with sarcasm, but soon realized that wasn't working. They did not enjoy any special rapport until near the end of his sophomore season in 1922. It was his performance in the 34–7 victory over Purdue that won him the left halfback job. Elmer Layden, who had been alternating with him, was shifted to fullback.

When they picked an all-time Notre Dame team a few years ago, the halfbacks were Crowley and Creighton Miller.

"Crowley, the sleepy-looking wit," wrote Rockne, "was the nerviest back I've known. He would throw himself anywhere. Also, he was the greatest interferer for his weight I've ever seen, and a particularly effective ball carrier on the critical third down."

All Four Horsemen—Crowley, Layden, Don Miller, and Harry Stuhldreher—were good friends. The most sociable two when they got together were Don Miller and Crowley. Don was United States district attorney for the Northern District of Ohio, and served as national president of the United States Attorneys Association. Before he went into law, however, he served as backfield coach at Georgia Tech under Bill

Alexander and at Ohio State. Even after he quit coaching, he'd occasionally visit Crowley in New York, put on a suit, and work with the Fordham backs.

"This is Don Miller, boys," Crowley would introduce him. "He used to play right halfback and block for me at Notre Dame. He is going to take the backs down to one end of the field and give them some tips. I want them to pay very strict attention—and when he has finished, forget everything he has said."

A few years ago, Don wrote me, in part:

I am enclosing a copy of a letter that Rockne wrote to sportswriter William E. Brandt, which I wish you would show to Crowley and shove it right down his throat. For the past 38 years he has been making statements in public speeches that I was his blocking back. I call your attention to the fact that this letter is dated July 5, 1930, only eight months before Rockne died, and this is a testimonial which even Crowley cannot deny. I am hoping that this letter will close Crowley up for the remainder of his life.

The letter follows:

                                        July 5, 1930
Mr. William E. Brandt,
c/o Sports Department,
New York Times,
New York City

Dear Sir:

Replying to your letter I wish to say that Don Miller, one of the Four Horsemen, was the greatest open-field runner I ever had.

I'm afraid I cannot give you much help on the other questions.

                        Yours very truly,

                        K. K. Rockne
                        Director of Athletics

Crowley claimed the letter to be spurious and protested surprise at Miller. "Usually," said Jim, "Don is the soul of charity. He will never say anything bad about anybody. Of a convicted wife murderer, he might comment, 'The poor fellow probably has his good points.' That's why he turned down the Attorney General when asked to be a prosecutor at the Nuremberg trials. His daughter Gert advised him to, 'because,' she said, 'you would decide the Nazi war criminals were all the finest fellows God ever put in two shoes.'"

And so went the needling between two old friends. (For the full story of how the Four Horsemen came to be, see the profile on Knute Rockne.)

Because he'd played his last college football game in the 1925 Rose Bowl victory over Pop Warner's Stanford team, 27–10, Jim Crowley hoped always to bring one of his Fordham teams back there. In 1936 the Rams blew it, and in 1937 when they deserved it, they weren't invited.

It is known to few, however, that Crowley's last season, 1941, Fordham was invited—and had to turn it down.

The Rams went into the NYU game with a 7–1 record and a commitment that if they beat the Violets, which they did, they would play in the Sugar Bowl. They had made the decision in part because of their 1937 experience in waiting for the Rose Bowl bid, and in part because the Sugar Bowl was getting bigger all the time. The announcement would be made formally on Monday; Missouri would be the opponent.

After the victory over NYU, there was no need to sit around a telephone. The official family, Crowley, Jack Coffey, and the rest, went celebrating at their favorite metropolitan watering spots, like Leone's.

Meanwhile, with three hours difference in time, Oregon State defeated its traditional rival Oregon for the Pacific Coast Conference championship and the role of Rose Bowl host. Coach Lon Stiner had the players vote on whether they wanted to play Duke or Fordham. They voted Fordham.

Then Percy Locey, Oregon State's director of athletics, tried to get Coffey with no luck. Coach Lon Stiner finally reached Crowley at Jim's New Rochelle home about three o'clock Sunday morning.

"Jim," Stiner said, "Oregon State invites Fordham to the Rose Bowl."

So there was Crowley with the Rose Bowl bid, and he had to turn it down. He asked Stiner to wait, while Fordham tried to get out of its verbal commitment to New Orleans. Then he called Coffey. The Sugar Bowl people naturally would not release Fordham, so Oregon State invited Duke.

Then came Pearl Harbor, and the shifting of the site of the 1942 Rose Bowl game, because of West Coast war security regulations, from Pasadena to Durham, North Carolina. The Beavers upset the Blue Devils, while Fordham at New Orleans beat Missouri, 2–0. We got our first look at the split T. Crowley defensed it with a seven-man gap front and a box.

Fordham was situated on Rose Hill. So every fall, no matter what kind of a squad we had, some scribe of no particular imagination would rerun the ghastly cliche, "Fordham's slogan this season is 'From Rose Hill to the Rose Bowl.'"

Well, even if we had been able to accept the bid, we couldn't have gone. And New Orleans beats Durham.

I sat and watched the Rams beat Don Faurot's club on a blocked kick by right tackle Alex Santilli, a boy of such character he was known as "The Saint," and later gave his life in action on Saipan. And I knew this was the end of days that had been too good to last. Fordham played in 1942, gave up the game three years, renewed in 1946 for nine years with a nitwit policy of diluted coaching and material but still tough schedules. Typical of the decisions was the appointment of Lombardi as an *assistant* coach.

After the 1954 season, the game was dropped. From 1964 through 1969, the Rams played club football, and in 1970 renewed the varsity game in the college division.

Fordham was a superior team and Jimmy Crowley a superior football coach. You can't go behind the record.

Gil Dobie

THE MAGNIFICENT SKEPTIC

The 1938 hurricane was one of the worst ever to roar up the Atlantic seaboard. Its backlash whipped across Boston, knocking down trees, snapping branches, and carrying away signs. The air was filled with flying debris as if swept along by some witch's broom. On Alumni Field at Boston College, the wind shook the bleacher seats and separated some of the wood from its iron supports.

Coach Gil Dobie was holding a practice with his Boston College football team. If it kept up, if pieces of trees and wooden seats kept sailing through the air, a decent workout would be impossible. Coach Dobie, however, was not one to permit a practice to be disrupted, even by Mother Nature. Finally, one of the players said, "Coach, this looks like a hurricane building up. Don't you think we should practice indoors?"

"What's the matter with you?" Dobie barked. "Can't you see the opportunity? We might have to play in conditions like this."

Seconds later, a monstrous gust of wind actually lifted Dobie, a tallish, slender man, into the air. A player at hand reached up and pulled him back to the ground.

"I guess," Dobie said, "we'd better go in."

If he had chosen to practice through the storm, however, his players would not have been surprised. The upperclassmen remembered how, in spring practice two years before, he was accidentally sent tumbling by a player and received a fractured collarbone. He stayed with the final 30

Gil Dobie, while at Cornell

minutes of practice, and the next day went right on coaching with his arm in a sling.

There never was a mentally tougher football coach than Gilmour Dobie. Or one who more persistently paraded pessimism. He gave the language of sportswriting an added synonym for sad and gloomy—"Gildobian." There also have

been few coaches who were more successful.

At the game's first century turn in 1969, statistics showed Dobie No. 11 in the all-time lists; in 33 years his teams won 179, lost 45, and tied 15 for a .780 percentage. Dobie turned out a record number of undefeated teams, 14; two at North Dakota Aggies of Fargo (1906–07), nine at Washington (1908–16), and three at Cornell (1921–23).

It has been pointed out that several of his games at Washington were against service teams, athletic clubs, and high schools that could not match his personnel. The best that Washington's principal rivals could get out of 21 games with Dobie's Washington teams, however, was a tie each by Washington State, Oregon, and Oregon State. His stats against them are remarkable:

OPPONENT	W	L	T	PTS. FOR	PTS. AGAINST	SHUT-OUTS
Washington State	5	0	1	136	12	4
Oregon	6	0	1	114	30	3
Oregon State	7	0	1	200	3	7
California	4	0	0	112	10	2
Idaho	4	0	0	120	0	4
Whitman	7	0	0	167	27	3
TOTALS	33	0	3	849	82	23

The coach of such a record, one would assume, might well be a paragon of popularity. Actually, Dobie's approach and method were reminiscent of Dale Carnegie's, because they were so different. Dobie went out of his way to influence people against him. Although campus publications are not necessarily noted for maturity, objectivity, and calmness, the following piece from the student publication, *Argus*, reflected a general reaction after Dobie left Seattle in 1917 to coach the Annapolis team three years:

"The disagreement between Dobie and President Suzzalo is caused by a misapprehension on the part of the president. In some manner Suzzalo has gotten the idea that the educational functions of the university are of more importance than the football team.

"For nine long years, spurred on by Dobie's zeal and profanity, Washington has waged successful football warfare. Any football fan will tell you that the university has grown and prospered solely because of the wonderful record that Dobie has achieved. Now, with a president who puts mathematics over muscle, brain over brawn, the future of the university is indeed shrouded in uncertainty."

Fans, newsmen, and players all found Dobie abrasive. His first day at Washington, he barred everybody from practice but the players. He nearly got into fistfights with Hy Gill, the former mayor, and with George Russell, the postmaster.

He told the team captain, Pete Tegtmeir, town and campus hero, that he was yellow. He advised Wee Coyle, his quarterback, that he played "like a man devoid of a brain," and wouldn't even have a suit if "I didn't have so many cripples." He kicked Penny Westover, another key player, off the field for missing an assignment, and told him never to return.

Westover spent the night muttering and sobbing, "Why didn't I hit him? Oh, why didn't I hit him?" But Penny was the first man out for practice next day, and Dobie promptly stuck him back on the first team. "I knew," Dobie smiled thinly, "that he had too much pride to stay away."

Dobie built up enough ill will in one year to get him fired, should he lose even one game. And the Huskies' semifinal game, at Oregon, was one he figured to lose. He sought some psychological advantage and found it in the six inches of sawdust that Oregon had covered its Multnomah Field with. He knew well enough that the sawdust was for protection against bad weather, but pretended that Oregon had other motivations.

"You've been slickered," he advised his players. "They know we can't move in that sawdust. I will not ask you to play." At the end he had them begging him to let them play. The blaze he built under them, the quarterbacking of Wee Coyle, and the kicking of Max Eakins earned Washington the game, 15–0.

Although Dobie was known justifiably as the arch apostle of the off-tackle play, his players realized he was far more innovative than the public imagined. In 1911, Oregon was again favored to beat Washington at Multnomah Field, and again was beaten, this time 29–3.

The Huskies took the lead—and never were headed—on a play that Dobie had his men practicing for 30 minutes each night that week. It was a delayed, hidden-ball handoff to an end coming around, and it went for 50 yards and a touchdown. The ultimate ball carrier, Wayne Sutton, the right end, had lined up between his left end and left tackle. The center snapped the ball into his own stomach and then faked it to Wee Coyle, who faked carrying it around Oregon's right end.

The ball-handling was so excellent that even the official, George Varnell, who'd had the play explained to him by Dobie that morning, followed Coyle. Oregon never recovered from this humiliating chicanery and was easy prey.

"Oregon had it on us," said Coyle, "but they didn't have it on Dobie."

Most people thought that Dobie would fit nicely into the Annapolis picture, since prime physical condition and discipline are intrinsic to the Academy. And Dobie was successful, losing only three games out of 21, one a year, to West Virginia in 1917, 7–0; Great Lakes in '18, 7–6; and in '19, Georgetown, 6–0. The Great Lakes game produced the first notable tackle by an ineligible man. Midshipman and sub tackle William Hardin Saunders leaped from the bench and tackled Great Lakes' Harry Eileson, who was in the clear. The touchdown was allowed.

Dobie's biggest triumph at Navy was his victory over Army, 6–0, in '19, the Sailors' first against the Cadets since 1912. This impelled Navy to ask Dobie to state his terms for a three-year contract, but he said he was not coming back. He gave no reason but later admitted privately that there were "too many admirals trying to run football at Navy, who should be at sea."

The greatest player ever coached by Dobie was George Pfann at Cornell in 1921, '22, and '23. Pfann was an outstanding field general and runner, with heavy legs that gave him power, speed, and shiftiness. Eddie Kaw, who scored five touchdowns despite rain and mud at Franklin Field in 1921 for a 41–0 victory, was even shiftier than Pfann though not as powerful.

Thanks to Pfann, Kaw, and linemen like Sunny Sundstrom and Swede Hanson, sharp field-goal kicker, the Big Red under Dobie put through three 8–0 seasons in succession.

Cornell's 1923 team was reported by the *Football Guide of 1924* to be "entitled to first rank among the Middle States colleges, and was spo-

ken of by some good critics as the strongest team in the country." Pfann, who was outstanding also as a student and won a Rhodes scholarship, told Allison Danzig, New York *Times* football expert and a scrub at Cornell in those days, that Dobie in conversations with him (Pfann) had called the 1922 team the strongest.

"Aside from insistence on careful execution of fundamentals and careful attention to detail," said Pfann, "I think that the factors which made Dobie an outstanding coach were: 1. His ability to select a team; 2. His ability to keep a team in top condition mentally and physically; 3. Obtaining an extremely high degree of coordinated team play; 4. Getting the best performance of which they were capable out of the team.

"Dobie's whole theory of offensive football was power with timing, mixed with just enough passing and deception to keep the secondary from moving immediately toward the ball carrier, thereby keeping the defense sufficiently off balance to give his power plays a chance to develop ... Backs were instructed and trained to go for three yards on a play, and anything more than that was just so much gravy.

"He believed that in order for a team to really become a team, it must play together constantly, particularly on offense. Consequently, once he had his first team picked in the fall (and the first three weeks were a survival fight to let him pick the best eleven men) no one except Dobie could touch the team. He kept it intact, as far as possible, and he alone worked with its offense, adjusting backfield positions to fit the individual characteristics of the backs so that the entire team would charge *as a unit*. ...

"On defense he placed his men in positions which allowed for the least possible gamble. He never permitted two defensive linemen playing alongside each other to be spaced so that both could be double-teamed. He liked a seven-man line and a box defense and relied on rushing the passer to take care of the extra eligible receiver. His line was taught to play the cup defense and he worked constantly to develop a fast, aggressive charge on the part of the line."

Even when Cornell had them, Dobie's doomsday philosophy was inimical to praising individual stars, and he was one of the first, if not the first, to point out the absurdities of All-America teams.

"The story was once told me," he said, "of the much sought-after campus queen who promised that she'd marry the first football man that made

the All-America. Whereupon the gridiron gladiators fought so valiantly for their alma mater and sweet Adeline that four of them were chosen on various first-string teams picked by critics. Naturally, this unforeseen circumstance caused considerable discomfiture to sweet Adeline, as well as to the players. Finally it was decided to relieve her of her promise to unite in wedlock with them, for she didn't wish to hurt anyone's feelings by marrying just one, and if she married them all, she'd be promptly arrested for polyandry.

"If a player isn't quite good enough to land on the first team chosen by the sports staff of the New York *Telepathy*, he will at least be given mention on the second or third team. But if this gridiron celebrity was received rather coldly by the *Telepathy*'s judges, perhaps he will land on the *Miracle*'s list, or the team selected by his old friend, Joe Pickemgood, of the Chicago *Cyclops*, who has been giving him a break in the news all season as being a product of the Windy City who is an outstanding success in Eastern football.

"Many a tomato has been made to look like a peach through the pressure of publicity. . . . If you sing the praises of a man high enough in this country, it will reach not only to heaven but from Kennebunkport, Maine, to Walla Walla, Washington.

"It may be possible to pick an All-Eastern, an All–Big Ten team, an All–Southern Conference eleven, and others that are sectional with a fair degree of accuracy, but when it comes to All-America choices, some first-string men are sure to be left out.

"The power of ballyhoo may make a few men greater, but it has a tendency to make many of them light-headed. One All-America man was so proud of his marriage that he posed for the tabloids while scrubbing pots and pans in the kitchen with his wife to show how domesticated he had become.

"Tooting one's own horn is frowned upon in sportsmanship, and there is no reason why excessive verbal splurging about a football player should not merit equal disapproval in the eyes of the public."

Although Dobie presented a craggy facade to the world, the few who got to know him—and they had to do most of the getting—found him an articulate, well-read conversationalist, full of pointed wry humor, and sociable with a glass or two or three.

"I knew Gil personally," writes Ben Mintz, Cornell's well-thought-of sports publicity director. "I was a childhood friend of his son, and I had nothing but the greatest respect for him. I cannot fill you in how the loss of his wife affected him [she was killed in an automobile accident], though obviously bringing up two daughters and a son alone must have been quite an undertaking.

"Underneath the exterior he presented, Gil was a most human fellow. I used to sit on the bench at some of the games in the late 20s. My mother would bake a chocolate cake for Gil from time to time, and my father knew him quite well."

Although the Cornell material deteriorated and the record with it, Dobie still had no losing seasons for ten years following the graduation of Pfann's Class of 1924. Three years he broke even, '24, '27, and '28. The other seven seasons were winning; the 1931 team went 7–1, losing only to Dartmouth; the '26 season was 6–1–1, losing only to Columbia; and the '25 and '30 seasons were 6–2. The record for the 1924–33 decade was 50–23–6. But in 1934, the Big Red went 2–5, Dobie's first losing season in 28 and the best he could get out of seven games in '35 was a 7–7 tie with Columbia.

While his teams were winning, Dobie's sour ways and his pronunciamentos of doom for his players were accepted as a brand of humor by those aboard the bandwagon. But like all coaches, he found, as he had known he would, that most football friends are fair weather, and as the late twenties became the early thirties he heard the cry of the pack. He was criticized by Monday-morning quarterbacks for staying with a seven-man line and a box secondary on pass defense. "Everybody," Dobie reminded them, "thought the box was pretty fair, when Kaw, Pfann, [Floyd] Ramsey, and [Charlie] Cassidy were in it."

The 1935 season evoked some acid counterstatements from Dobie. After the loss to Princeton's powerhouse, 54–0, he suggested seriously that the squad publicly absolve him of blame. "After all," he pointed out, "I'm just the coach." The day before the game at Dartmouth he took his squad on a walk around Memorial Field.

"You kick off here," he said, pointing to the 40-yard line. Then he walked over to the bench on the east side and observed, "This is where you sit when you're not playing." And finally he took them down to the 10-yard line. "Here," he advised them, "is where you'll be all afternoon with your backs to the wall."

After Dartmouth proved him an accurate prophet, 41–6, Red Blaik, coach of the Big Green,

sought him out. "I'm sorry we beat you so bad, Gil," said Blaik, himself something of a dour Scot in those days. "But it was a good game."

"Yeah, Blaik," said Dobie. "Yeah, it was a good game as long as you had your fourth team in there."

When Cornell bought up his $11,000 contract for two years, he commented, "You can't win games with Phi Beta Kappas." Earlier that year, a young Midwestern coach had approached him in a hotel lobby with the greeting, "You don't look very happy, Gil. The old master must be slipping." "No," said Dobie, "just forced to play students."

Actually, Dobie had no time for the tramp athlete. He himself had been an assiduous student and had acquired a law degree as a quarterback and an assistant coach under Dr. Henry L. Williams at Minnesota early in the century. When Cornell convinced him he should make known his true feelings on sports and academics, he stated:

"Some people seem to have the idea that I object to a boy's coming to college to study. Let me say that I think this is the only reason a boy should come to college; and if football interferes with his studies, he should drop football."

It didn't take Dobie long to find another job after his separation from Cornell. Jack Curley, graduate manager of athletics at Boston College, signed him to a three-year contract at $10,000 a year. Counting what Cornell paid him, in 1936 and '37, Dobie drew $21,000 for coaching B.C. and not coaching Cornell.

With improved material, Dobie immediately proved he had not lost the winning touch. His three-year record was 16–6–5. His biggest victory was a 13–12 upset of Holy Cross in 1936, and he played a notable 26–26 tie at Philadelphia in '38 with a Temple team coached by Pop Warner.

Gil, a good Presbyterian, never caught on to the religious nomenclature at Boston College, a Catholic school; and to the amusement of all he referred to the Jesuit fathers as "parsons." One story has it that during a conversation with Father Pat Collins, moderator of athletics, Dobie asked, "Parson, how many of these boys are receiving aid?"

"Oh, about 25 or so, Gil," the priest replied.

"And how much aid are they getting?" Dobie inquired.

"In terms of dollars the scholarship for board, room, and tuition comes to about $1,000," the priest explained.

Dobie shook his head.

"You parsons don't care how you spend your money, do you?"

Actually, the material was excellent. The juniors, sophomores, and freshmen of the 1938 season formed the 1939 B.C. team coached by Frank Leahy with only one regular-season defeat. That was a loss in the Cotton Bowl, 6–3, to the Clemson team coached by Jess Neely, with Banks McFadden the star back. And most of the undefeated 1940 Eagles, who beat one of General Bob Neyland's best Tennessee teams in the Sugar Bowl, 19–13, were recruited in Dobie's time.

Leahy, of course, proved what he could do, but so could Gil Dobie, when he had such horses. In addition to missing out on these squads of '39 and '40, Dobie also happened to be at B.C. when arch rival Holy Cross was having its best teams in history, under Doctor Eddie Anderson.

Why did Dobie leave when he could have stayed on for a strong finish? One reason was his health; he never had been too robust, and his condition worsened his last three years of coaching because of an automobile accident that almost killed him. It came soon after his biggest triumph at B.C., the 13–12 upset of Holy Cross in '36. Also, Dobie had no financial worries. He was as keen a student of the stock and bond market as he was of the off-tackle play. Some thought he was a millionaire.

Boston College's games with Temple in Dobie's three years were especially hard fought; the only defeat of 1936 was by the Owls, 14–0, and the 1937 and '38 games ended in 0–0 and 26–26 ties.

"The Temple team was coached by Pop Warner," recalls Til Ferdenzi, a pocket-sized halfback star for the Eagles. "There was only one exit from the playing field to the clubhouse in Fenway Park, through the first base dugout. At halftime, Warner, who then walked with a cane, ducked into the dugout right behind Dobie and made some sneering remark.

"Dobie turned around and cackled something about how nice it must be to have all those great football players to pick from.

"Dobie's feud with Warner stemmed from his belief that what was called the Warner single wing was really the Dobie single wing as rooted in his playing days at Minnesota and developed by him afterwards at Washington, Navy, and Cornell.

"Although he was a single-wing purist, the attack he gave us was as modern as any in its time. In my senior year [1936] our offense was well larded with the buck-lateral series that

Charlie Caldwell got so much publicity from in later years at Princeton. We had a fullback named Al Horsfal [shot down in World War II], who could really make that buck lateral go.

"I think one of Dobie's biggest moments came in my senior year when we tied Michigan State, 1313, in Fenway Park, and came from behind to do it. The Spartans were nationally ranked then, as they are now, and had a great All-America fullback in Jake Pingel."

Because he was a little fellow, Ferdenzi, who had started much of the time as a sophomore and junior, was looked on dubiously by Dobie at first.

"How much do you weigh, lad?" he asked him at their first meeting. "Oh, around 160," Ferdenzi said. Dobie gave his dry cackle, "You mean after a big beef stew dinner with lots of gravy, potatoes, and bread?"

Dobie, a stickler for detail, once dressed Ferdenzi down for the way he scored a winning touchdown.

"We were playing North Carolina State at Fenway Park, and it was a rough game. Late in the fourth quarter, they had us, 3–0, and then I caught a pass deep in the end zone and we won it, 7–3. I was pretty proud and happy, especially when I was awarded the game ball. But just as I made it to the sidelines en route to the dugout, Dobie leaped in front of me, yanked the ball out of my arms, and shouted, 'No little peasant is going to improve on my plays and get away with it!'

"Gil was raging because I made the catch in the middle of the end zone and not in the corner, where I should have been according to the diagram. The reason I wasn't there was because the primary area was all cluttered up.

"Anyway, he gave me the football back a week later and muttered something about my having made a good play. The old bastard made me sweat a full week, though. Later, he and I got along great. A few weeks before I was graduated, he called me into his office and asked if I'd like to be one of his assistant coaches. I couldn't accept, because I'd already been picked as a high school teacher-coach.

"What Dobie did for B.C. has been greatly underpublicized. He gave the school a national big-time image, which Leahy carried on and enlarged. No question about it, B.C. hired a big league coach when they got old Gil."

Ferdenzi's reaction to Dobie typified most of the players who started for him. There were exceptions, of course. Charley Hunt, a sub tackle who later became an admiral, recalled that at Navy classmates often had to hold Ernest Von Heimburg, captain of the 1917 team (later an admiral), from slugging him. "Dobie," Hunt observed, "was no leader—only a slave driver."

But many of his players remained loyal and welcomed the chance to come back and spend an evening with him.

"I remember a gathering at the Warwick Hotel in Philadelphia the evening of the Penn game," said Al Danzig. "It was for Dobie. There were several hundreds of his Cornell players present. Many of them hadn't been East in years, but they came to pay their respects to the Old Man, then in retirement, and they were just as respectful and as much in awe of him as in the days when he was scrimmaging them two hours an afternoon and into the hours of evening with a whitewashed ball. To a few of them he was Gil, but to most of them he was still Mr. Dobie, a man never to get familiar with."

Dave Lucey, Boston College back and later Massachusetts' commissioner of motor vehicles, who used to get his share of tongue-lashings from Dobie, recalled how he and Fella Gintoff, an ace back, visited the coach after graduation, and never spent a brighter evening. Dobie mixed his highballs as he did his off-tackle play, with a concentration of power at the point of impact. His conversation was equally attractive, for he was an inveterate and diversified reader who seemed to soak up everything he read.

Eight years after he coached his last game and three and a half years before he died in Putnam, Connecticut, Dobie received a telegram from Buck Clarey, Cornell's sports information director, requesting statistics on his coaching career. In reply, Dobie wrote:

"Your telegram at hand.

"I graduated from the Hastings, Minnesota, High School, where I played football, in 1899. In the fall of that year, I entered the University of Minnesota where I played football on the first team, one year as left end and two as quarterback and field general. After graduation, I acted as first assistant coach for two years to and including 1905.

"In 1906 I took the job of athletic director and football coach at the North Dakota Agricultural College located at Fargo, North Dakota. I remained there for two years and my teams were undefeated in each year.

"In 1908 I took the position of head football coach at the University of Washington, where I

remained for nine years. My teams were unde-feated in each and every one of those years.

"In the fall of 1917 I became head football coach at the United States Naval Academy and remained there for three years. The team lost three games during this period: one to West Virginia, one to Georgetown, and one to Great Lakes Naval Station.

"In 1920, I went to Cornell. You have that record.

"In the fall of 1936, after leaving Cornell, I went to Boston College. The 1936 team lost one game to Temple, in 1937 the team lost four, in 1938 they lost one and tied two.

"This in brief is the information you called for. Hope it will suffice.

"Truly yours,

"(Signed) Gilmour Dobie."

The reply was again typically Dobie. Without frills of any kind, direct and to the point—Dobie going off tackle.

Although the story has been attributed to many, it belongs to Dobie and should be his, since it so well epitomizes his philosophy of football and life, as well as his humor. He first told it when he was assistant coach to Minne-sota's Dr. Henry L. Williams, whose approach to the game was as severe as Dobie's.

"When I'm traveling," Dobie said, "I ask farm boys how to get to a certain place. If they point with their finger, I move on. If they pick up the plow and point with it, I stop and sell them on the University of Minnesota."

Dick Hanley

A COACHING DYNAMO

The dynamism and aggressiveness of Richard E. (Dick) Hanley characterized the football teams he coached. In the decade from 1922 through '31—his five seasons at Haskell Indian Institute and his first five at Northwestern—his record stands among the very best of his time: 80 victories, 21 defeats, 5 ties.

After he gave up college coaching in 1935, he set a record by selling more than a million dollars' worth of policies in each of his first three years with Equitable Life Assurance Company in Chicago.

And as Lieutenant Colonel Hanley, in charge of physical training and combat conditioning for the entire U.S. Marine Corps in World War II, he once again excelled.

Despite his winning habits, mention of Hanley to those who remember him almost immediately evokes memories of a game his Northwestern team lost to Notre Dame, 14–0, in the Wildcats' Dyche Stadium, November 22, 1930. By winning, Northwestern would have been regarded as the mythical national champion, the honor that went to Notre Dame after it beat Army and Southern California and finished 10–0.

The 1930 Notre Dame team, Rockne's last, is usually rated his strongest. The Irish roster was loaded with stars, including watch-charm guard

Bert Metzger, his running mate Frank (Nordy) Hoffman, tackle Joe Kurth, center Tommy Yarr, quarterback Frank Carideo, and halfbacks Marchie Schwartz and Marty Brill.

But Northwestern was also well stocked with one of the best teams in Big Ten history. The line was peopled by such sparklers as end Frank Baker, tackles Jack Riley and Dallas (Dal) Marvil, and Wade (Red) Woodworth, who played without a helmet. The backfield, perhaps North-western's finest, had Felix (Lefty) Leach at quar-ter, sophomores Ernest (Pug) Rentner and Fayette (Reb) Russell at halfback and fullback, and at the other half "Hard Luck" Hank Bruder.

Few if any stars ever lived more intimately with misfortune than Bruder, who could run, pass, and kick, and who reaffirmed in his career with the Green Bay Packers what he could do when well. In his sophomore year, 1928, he hurt a hip a week before the season opened, missed the first five games and was below par for the last three. In 1929, his junior year, he broke a leg in the third game, with Wisconsin, and was out for the season.

Despite his little playing time, Bruder was elected 1930 captain. In its opener Northwestern beat Tulane, 14–0, a handsome beginning be-cause the Green Wave, coached by Bernie Bier-

Dick Hanley, *right*, with 1927 Northwestern captain Vic Gustafson. *Chicago Tribune Photos*

man, was otherwise undefeated and Southern Conference champions that year. The first and what proved to be the winning touchdown was a 50-yard run by Bruder. A few days later Hank was stricken with smallpox and missed several games. Bruder was back for the Notre Dame game, though not in top shape, and the Wildcats also were hurt by the absence of Rentner, who had hurt himself against Minnesota.

For 53 minutes, however, Northwestern dominated the game: total yards running and passing for the day were N.U. 350, N.D. 40. But Carideo's coffin-corner kicking, critical penalties, and fumbles prevented the Wildcats from capitalizing. Sophomore fullback Reb Russell, behind the blasting of tackles Riley and Marvil, ripped off yardage that brought Northwestern to Notre Dame's 4-yard line. There he fumbled and the Irish recovered.

Again, after center Bob Clark intercepted a pass, Northwestern drove deep, this time to the 1-yard line. Again the 'Cats fumbled, again Notre Dame recovered. And the fumbler was none other than Hard Luck Hank Bruder. Thenceforth momentum went over to Notre Dame, which scored on a touchdown run by Schwartz and on another by Dan Hanley (no relation to the

coach—and no friend either), after Carideo returned an interception to the N.U. 10.

Thus were frustrated a perfect season and a national championship for the Wildcats, but they were still 5–0 in Western Conference play, which gave them a tie for the title with Michigan.

The 1931 team made it two Big Ten crowns in a row for Northwestern and Hanley, a record for the school as the Wildcats won seven and played a scoreless tie at Notre Dame. This time it appeared that the Wildcats had won the "Big Apple" outright, because it was 5–0 in conference play, while Michigan, Purdue, and Ohio State each lost once.

But there was a depression on and the Big Ten agreed to play a set of postseason conference games for charity, yet to count in the standings. Minnesota, which had lost three games, upset Ohio State, Michigan beat Wisconsin, and Purdue surprised Northwestern at Soldier's Field, 7–0. For 50 minutes there was no score. Then Fred Hecker of the Boilermakers returned an interception 40 yards to the Wildcat's 30, and four plays later halfback Jim Purvis broke loose on a 19-yard scoring run. So the Big Ten ended in a three-way tie among Northwestern, Michigan, and Purdue, each with 5–1.

It was an unsettling weekend all around for the Wildcats. The night before the game, the elevator at their hotel, with several players aboard, had gone out of control and fallen several floors. Nobody was hurt, but after what was a sluggish performance by the hitherto unbeaten Purple, the accident was pointed out as an omen.

Those were the dark days, the losses to Notre Dame in 1930 and Purdue in '31, but they were outnumbered by the bright ones. Hanley had inherited some strong players from Glenn Thistlethwaite, who left Northwestern for Wisconsin and lived to regret it. In Hanley's first season at Evanston, Northwestern beat Ohio State for the first time, 19–13. In 1928 the Wildcats edged Minnesota with Bronko Nagurski, 10–9, and won the school's first important intersectional victory, from Dartmouth, 27–6. In 1929, they beat Wisconsin for the first time in 17 games, dating back to 1890, and Illinois, 7–0, for the first time since 1912.

But the most talked of triumph of a Hanley Northwestern team, the most savored in bull sessions, was the 1931 team's victory over Minnesota, in which the Wildcats rallied from a 14–0 scoreboard and Rentner, although he got his shoulder hurt that day, was sensational.

Six special trainloads of rooters accompanied Coach Fritz Crisler's Minnesota team to Dyche Stadium, and when they found they had all been allocated end zone seats they were most displeased. They booed loud and long as the teams left the field at halftime with Minnesota leading 14–7. Hanley, who could dip into psychology with the best of them, incited his team at halftime by reference to the booing and to Minnesota's decision, relayed by an official, to begin the second half by kicking off to the favorite.

"Gentlemen," said Hanley, "—and I call you this because you have been playing such polite football—people play this game for diverse reasons. Some wish to be popular at tea parties. Some hope for a better job some day. Some wish to prove that they are men.

"Why you play I cannot say, but today this team became immortal. At halftime you became the first football team in Northwestern history to be booed off the field by your classmates, your schoolmates, your brothers. I ask you to go back on that field and show these people that you are men, not quitters. Fritz Crisler has insulted you by saying, 'Take the ball on the kickoff. You can't go any place with it.' Run that kickoff right down their backs."

The Northwestern team, feeling the goad of pride, did precisely that: Pug Rentner, a consensus All-America that year, caught the ball and behind some thundering blocks and with his own speed and nimbleness ran it back 95 yards for a touchdown through the entire Minnesota team. The extra point was wide, so the Gophers still led 14–13, and maintained it into the fourth quarter. Then Ollie Olson passed to end Dick Fencl, who lateraled to Jakie Sullivan and Jakie ran 55 yards to a score. Two more long scoring runs, one by Olson and another by Rentner on a punt return, made it 32–14.

Like all superior college teams, Northwestern's of 1930 and '31 were assembled not by chance —not by Coach Hanley driving around the Evanston campus on a sound truck and calling out in decibels of exhortation: "Anybody for football?" A two-week coaching school at Northwestern attracted as many as 480 high school coaches and the contacts he made with them enabled Hanley to enrich his recruiting. The class that entered in 1928 formed the hard core of the back-to-back champions. "There were 125 freshmen," recalled one of them, All-America tackle Jack Riley, "and 36 of them were All-State high

school players. ... Only 16 of the original 125 proved to be important players, but that was enough."

While he was at Northwestern, Hanley and Kenneth L. (Tug) Wilson, athletic director and later Big Ten commissioner, joined with Howard Jones, Southern California coach, in putting on an East vs. West College All-Star game at Soldier's Field as part of the Chicago World's Fair in 1933.

"About two weeks before the game," Wilson recalled, "Hanley and I realized we were $28,000 in the hole. I was learning a lesson in promotion of athletic events, namely, that people will not buy unreserved tickets ahead of time.

"The sportswriters had been very generous with their publicity and there was a great deal of interest, but the day before the game we still were $25,000 in the red. Luckily for us, the weather was good. It was Iowa Day at the fair, and more than a half-million people were in attendance.

"I had traded a handful of tickets to the men who ran the loudspeakers, and in return got announcements that could be heard all over the fairgrounds. I also hired a man to shoot off fireworks, starting a couple of hours before game time.

"People simply jammed the gates. We ran out of printed tickets, so I told the ticket sellers to accept dollar bills and let the people through. Even the ushers and policemen were out at the gates selling tickets. Not all of the money was turned in, but we collected on nearly 60,000 people. It was a good game, too, and the crowd's interest was intense as the East finally won.

"Before the game Hanley and I had tried desperately to get financial backing. We offered it to the Northwestern Alumni Association, but they turned it down. As it turned out, it was a very profitable deal for the two promoters, Hanley and Wilson. It was a thrilling—and lucky —promotion.

"At the meeting of Big Ten faculty representatives and athletic directors the following December, however, legislation was passed forbidding any director or football coach to foster any promotion of this kind."

Arch Ward, sports editor then of the Chicago *Tribune*, which had publicized the game strongly, took it over, and the *Tribune* has staged it annually ever since, earning hundreds of thousands of dollars for charity.

That 1933 world's fair promotion was to have a

Hanley with four N.U. All-Americans (*left to right*): Reb Russell, Jack Riley, Hanley, Dallas Marvil, and Pug Rentner

negative effect on Northwestern football, however, because whatever the reason, it bruised the rapport that had existed between the coach and the athletic director, Hanley and Wilson. And this was a factor in Hanley's leaving Northwestern after the lean seasons of 1932, '33, and '34, in which the Wildcats won a total of only seven games.

The 1933 team logged a peculiar record: it scored 25 points in its only victory, over Indiana, and failed to score in its seven other games. Yet, it gained two upset scoreless ties, with a Bierman Minnesota team and the first of Stanford's "Vow Boy" Rose Bowl teams.

(Hanley again emphasized his ability to teach defense in the first College All-Star game sponsored by the Chicago *Tribune*, in 1934. He was in charge of the defense that blanked the Chicago Bears in a scoreless tie and allowed them only one first down.)

Northwestern under Hanley used the Warner double-wing attack, and each year after the season, Dick would visit Pop in Palo Alto for days of football talk. It was in the early thirties that the defense began to catch up with the double wing—as defenses ultimately catch up with any offense. It was not the offense, though, but the lack of enough horses to run it that eventually undid Hanley at Northwestern.

Dick Hanley was born in Minnesota, but as a small boy was moved to the Pacific Coast. He entered Washington State in 1915 and though he had never played football before, he quarterbacked the Cougar team that made a 6–0 record and defeated Brown 14–0 at Pasadena on New Year's Day, 1916, in the second Tournament of Roses game. (The first had been played by Michigan and Stanford 14 years before.) With the 1916 game, it became an annual, unbroken since. As a junior in 1917, Hanley quarterbacked another undefeated team that won the Pacific Coast Conference championship.

His coach at Washington State from 1915 through '17 was the colorful and astute William (Lone Star) Dietz, who had captained one of the Carlisle Indian teams. Through Dietz, Hanley came to know Pop Warner.

When World War I caused Washington State to drop football in 1918, Hanley joined the Marine Corps and was stationed at Mare Island, California. There he played quarterback and was captain of a team made up of former Pacific Coast college players and coached by Lone Star Dietz. They lost, 17–0, in the 1919 Tournament of Roses game to Great Lakes Naval Training Station. In 1919 Hanley returned to Washington State for one more year and again captained and quarterbacked the team, now coached by another former Carlisle Indian player, Gus Welch.

Hanley was graduated in 1920 with a degree in mining engineering and geology, and his football career appeared ended when he accepted a job with Caribbean Petroleum Co., working out of

Venezuela. But when the United States accused Venezuela of harboring German U-boats during World War I and relations between the two countries grew taut, Hanley's job faded away.

So he gave up engineering and became the athletic director at Pendleton (Oregon) High, where he also coached football, basketball, and track, served as director of physical education, and taught history. His Pendleton teams of 1920 and '21 won Eastern Oregon championships in football, basketball, and track. The football teams' 17–1 record and the recommendation of Warner got him the job of football coach and athletic director at Haskell Institute, the Indian school in Lawrence, Kansas, from 1922 through '26. Hanley made the Haskell Indians almost as well known as the Carlisle Indians had been before them. The five-year record of 51–9–4 shows this breakdown: 1922, 9–2–0; 1923, 11–2–1; 1924, 9–2–1; 1925, 10–3–1; 1926, 12–0–1.

Although the schedules were composed mainly of small colleges, Haskell also did well against major opposition. The 1922 team beat Baylor's Southwest Conference champions 21–20; the 1923 team lost to Minnesota by only 13–12; the '24 team defeated Brown 17–13.

The 1926 team, which had a perfect record except for a 21–21 tie with Major Frank Cavanaugh's Boston College, scored 558 points in 13 games, nearly a 43-point average, to the opponents' total of 63.

Coming and going the Indians also covered a lot of ground. Because of their coast-to-coast schedules, Notre Dame's 1929 and '30 teams were known as "Rockne's Ramblers," but Hanley's Haskells rambled even more. The 1925 team played three times on the East Coast, against Boston College, William and Mary, and Bucknell, and twice on the West Coast, against Gonzaga and the Los Angeles Olympic Club.

In his Haskell days, Hanley's most notable players were John Levi, Mayes McLain, and Theodore (Tiny) Roebuck, backs, and tackle Tom Stidham. Levi led the nation in scoring and touchdowns in 1923 and '24. In '26 McLain set a scoring record of 253 points; he later played fullback for Iowa and tackle for the New York Giants and Pittsburgh. Stidham was later Hanley's line coach at Northwestern and head coach at Oklahoma.

Perhaps the most important, certainly the most unusual game ever played by Haskell came in Oklahoma after the end of the regular 1924

schedule. Following the victory at Brown that season, Hanley had a phone call from Vice President Charles Curtis, asking him to route the team homeward to Kansas by way of Washington, D.C., ostensibly to meet President Calvin Coolidge.

Vice President Curtis, part Indian, wanted the Haskell team to front a drive to raise funds for a stadium on its campus. Money was to be solicited from all the Indian nations, and as part of the buildup the Haskell team would tour Oklahoma. Hanley and Haskell, of course, agreed.

The tour of Oklahoma included a visit to Hominy, which had a game scheduled with Fairfax. The Hominy team was made up of representatives of the Osage nation. When the chief of the Osages discovered that the Fairfax team was freely sprinkled with members of the New York Giants, including tackle Steve Owen, later their coach, he informed Haskell that if it expected a donation for the stadium, it would have to play Fairfax.

Hanley and his brother Pat (an assistant who later coached Boston University) suited up with the graduating seniors. They played and Haskell won, 14–0. John Levi put forth one of his finest games. (Levi probably could throw a football as far as anybody who ever lived.) The Osages were delighted, and being oil-rich, they were able to give $50,000, which assured the Haskell stadium.

It was dedicated in 1926, preceded by a week-long powwow that attracted 9,000 Indians from all the nations. They watched gleefully as Hanley's undefeated team won 36–0 from a Bucknell team coached by Uncle Charlie Moran, who had earlier won fame with his Centre College teams. It was the success of the 1926 team that convinced Northwestern that Hanley was the right man to succeed Glenn Thistlethwaite.

If Dick Hanley had coached at another college after he left Northwestern in 1935, his record suggests he would have matched his success at Haskell and Northwestern.

In 1944, at the age of 50, Lieutenant Colonel Hanley of the Marine Corps had successfully supervised the physical and combat training of all marine divisions and air wings, and was stationed at the Marine Air Station in El Toro, California.

He had rejoined the marines with no idea of coaching. The Marine Corps had decided not to field any athletic teams. But after the commanding general of Marine Aircraft, West Coast,

watched an exhibition game between the Army Fourth Air Force and the Washington Redskins, he determined that El Toro should have a team, and ordered Colonel Hanley to field one.

It was some order. Coach Hanley and his El Toro Marines had a name, and they were able to gather a squad of marines who were former college and pro stars. But they had no equipment, no field, no schedule, and no money. Further to complicate things a local law prevented service teams from charging admission to home games. Hanley got around that by playing in the Los Angeles Coliseum and billing the opponents as the home team. He also borrowed equipment and money from coaching friends. So that football wouldn't interfere with physical training, the team practiced mornings from 7:15 to 9:30.

When Hanley had the players, he knew what to do with them. El Toro's two-year record was 26–3, and they snapped the winning streak of Randolph Field at 25. They also netted $80,000 in two seasons for the Marine Relief Fund.

Not only as a football coach but at anything he put his mind to, Richard Edgar Hanley got the job done.

Dick Harlow

"DO IT MY WAY, DEAR BOY"

Navy, the decided favorite, had been played to a 0–0 tie by Harvard, and now one of the Midshipmen players was sitting in front of his locker and shaking his head.

"We should have beaten that team by four touchdowns," he said. "But we didn't. Every time I went to carry out my assignment by blocking the player in front of me, he moved away from me. I never saw anything like it."

It probably wouldn't have consoled the young sailor even had he known it, but Harvard's football teams of the thirties were pioneers of stunting in their defensive line play. By looping or slanting just before or at the snap of the ball, they were never where they were supposed to be when opponents tried to block them.

These maneuvers were the brainchildren of Richard Cresson Harlow, who coached football for 27 seasons—3 at Penn State, 4 at Colgate, 9 at Western Maryland, and 11 at Harvard—and achieved a record of 150 victories, 68 defeats, and 17 ties for a percentage of .667.

That's an impressive record when you consider that much of the time at Harvard, and frequently enough before that, the other team outgunned Harlow's. Wesley Fesler, one of Harlow's assistants at Harvard, and later head coach at Ohio State and Minnesota, said, "I don't believe anyone could lick him if he had an even break in material."

Harlow's offense at Harvard and before that at Western Maryland was a form of single wing constructed to compensate through timing and deception for lack of power. He and Carl Snavely, at Cornell and North Carolina, led the way in developing a series of single-wing plays with fullback spins, reverses, double reverses, traps, and angle blocking. It was really double-wing football run from single wing. It got results by keeping the defense unsure an extra split second as to who had the ball and was heading where.

Harlow, however, always pointed out that systems and formations are not important: "Sound fundamentals and common sense are what make winning football teams."

Perfectionism to be fulfilled demands a man be stubborn, persevering, and determined. Harlow was all of those things. After Harvard lost to Yale, 20–7, in 1939, he wasted no time in replay or lamentation. He got home as quickly as he could, set up a card table, took a pencil and pad, and began to diagram plays.

"I want you to take a good look at those plays," he told a friend, "because one year from today, they are going to be used to beat Yale."

The score a year later was Harvard 28, Yale 0.

In hiring Harlow, Harvard broke with tradition; previously the head coach was always a graduate. The Harvard *Crimson* viewed it with

alarm, pointing out that Harlow had always coached at schools that proselyted. But Harvard soon welcomed Harlow. At a sports dinner following his appointment, he stood in a reception line and surprised old grads by identifying their sport and year. He had done in a short time a huge hunk of homework; he had studied the Harvard *H Book* loaned him by Vic Jones, an old grad, then sports editor of the Boston *Globe*.

Harlow fitted the Harvard atmosphere as a football coach who exuded scholarship. Although he always claimed he was merely an amateur, he had considerable standing as an oologist. For 25 years he spent his spring and summer roving woods and cliffs in search of rare birds' eggs. His own collection numbered more than 850, valued at $40,000.

Shortly after he came to Harvard, he was appointed an associate in oology, and in 1939, James B. Conant, president of Harvard, named him curator of oology in the Harvard Museum of Comparative Zoology. Harlow was a student of botany too; he grew rare gentians and rhododendrons in the garden of his summer home in the Pocono Mountains. He made six species

flourish that never before had grown in the United States.

Harlow's experiences as a collector of birds' eggs proved to be as dangerous as football. To reach a raven's nest, he lowered himself on a rope down the side of a vertical cliff to a ledge. He was taking notes there when a loose boulder from above hit him on the head and dazed him, and he fell 90 feet to the ground. As he fell he grabbed the rope with one hand, and it burned his skin. When he hit the ground he broke an ankle, went unconscious, and lay there for three hours until rescued. On another occasion he was driving along a country road when a rare bird so preempted his attention that he ran the car into a tree. Harlow also had a third hobby: collecting rare stamps.

Meanwhile he was cultivating some good football at Harvard. Although his first two seasons, 1935 and '36, were building years—3–5 in 1935 and 3–4–1 in '36—he was voted Coach of the Year in '36 by the Football Coaches Association of America. His most successful years spanned 1937 to '41:

YEAR	W	L	T	YALE	PRINCETON	DARTMOUTH
1937	5	2	1	W	W	L
1938	4	4	0	W	W	L
1939	4	4	0	L	L	L
1940	3	2	3	W	T	L
1941	5	2	1	W	W	W

The 1938 team dramatized the improvement of a Harlow team in November over October. After losing their first four games, Brown, Cornell, Army, and Dartmouth, Captain Bob Green's men won their last four, Princeton, Chicago, Virginia, and Yale.

Harlow rated his 1937 and '41 teams his best at Harvard, on a level with his undefeated teams at Colgate in 1925 and Western Maryland in '34. The '37 victory over Yale at Cambridge, 13–7, spoiled an undefeated season for the Elis.

Before a jam-packed 58,000, the Crimson line controlled the play and Clarence (Chief) Boston, the inside blocking back, was doing a job knocking people down. Three times in the second period Harvard penetrated Yale territory before Frank Foley hit Don Daughters with an 18-yard touchdown pass.

Despite a bad knee, Clint Frank, No. 14, possibly the finest of all Yale backs, was making

tackles all over the field to keep Harvard from breaking the game wide open. In the third quarter he led a 67-yard march, and smashed over himself for the score.

Harvard then responded with a winning 80-yard drive. Foley made the touchdown on a 9-yard run around Yale's left end. Harlow had put in the play to take advantage of Frank's bad knee. Foley faked off tackle and then veered to the outside, and Frank could not recover quickly enough to stop him. Since Harvard had defeated Princeton, 34–6, the win over Yale brought the Crimson its first Big Three title since 1915.

The 1941 team gave Harlow great satisfaction by recovering from 19–0 and 7–0 losses to Pennsylvania and Cornell in its first two games to win five and tie Navy in its last six. That team was graced by a rarity in modern Harvard football, a man named to the All-America. He was guard Endicott T. (Chub) Peabody, later governor of

Dick Harlow. *Chicago Tribune Photos*

Massachusetts. It was a dynamic tackle by Peabody that shook the ball loose from Navy ace halfback Bill Busick in the 0–0 upset and forced him out of the game; Chub recovered the fumble.

Next to Peabody, Harvard's best-known player under Harlow was fullback Vernon Struck, who hid the ball so well on spin plays that his coach dubbed him "The Magnificent Faker." In the 34–6 victory over Princeton, Harlow's first Big Three win, Struck scored three touchdowns (one on a 21-yard punt return), gained over 200 yards rushing, and stood out on defense.

Two of the Kennedys, Joe Jr., a halfback, and Bobby, an end, played under Harlow 10 years apart. Neither was a regular, but both were hustlers and battlers. Bobby won his varsity H by getting into the Yale game, but Joe didn't, and the reason reflects Harlow's complete command.

The night before the H-Y game Harlow received a phone call from a man who identified himself only as a friend of Joe Kennedy, Sr. He asked Harlow whether Joe Jr. would get a letter, because, he said, Joe Kennedy, Sr. would like to know. Harlow was so incensed at what he considered pressure that he didn't play young Joe against Yale.

Strangely enough, he had the same kind of pregame phone call about Bobby, and was not going to play him either, until a friend advised him it would be better to be unfair to one boy than to two, and Harlow agreed.

Harlow was the complex kind of character Jack London would have enthused to as the subject for a novel— intellectual and tough. A good man to have on your side in a brawl, be it in a scramble up and down mountainsides between two teams of bird's egg or fern fanciers fighting for firsties of a new species, or between opposite squads dedicated to mayhem in a deadfall.

While he was coaching at Penn State, he also served as a dormitory proctor. In those days campus rioting related to one dorm's taking on another in a free-for-all. Harlow broke up one such set-to by arranging a set of bouts with boxing gloves. From this beginning, Harlow got boxing started as an intercollegiate sport at Penn State, and coached the varsity team from 1919 through '21. A strong, blocky man, Dick himself was adept with the gloves, and probably could have taken any one of the students, if not any two together.

Once when scouting a Penn State rival, a handful of the enemy came into the stands and tried to take away his notebook. Harlow punched the leader in the chin, knocking him back down some ten rows, and eluded the others by jumping off the back of the stands 20 feet from the ground and running.

After his arrival at Harvard, Harlow adjusted his coaching phraseology and intonations along more Chesterfieldian lines. If a particularly backward guard insisted on executing a blind-side block with the wrong technique, Dick would look at him almost sadly and say, "Now will you do it my way, dear boy?"

Tough on the field, Harlow was always approachable off it. He loaned $27,000 to players over the years, and was proud to point out that he got all of it back except $165. That would have been returned, too, he pointed out, if the boy who owed it hadn't been killed in World War II.

Dick Harlow was born October 19, 1889, in Philadelphia, attended Episcopal Academy there, and won Bachelor of Science and Master of Science degrees at Penn State in 1912 and '13. He played four years at tackle under Coach Bill Hollenback, and in 1911 set a record by blocking punts in five games. It was as an undergraduate that he became interested in birds' eggs, and one

The professor explaining some of the finer points to his Harvards

year, when an egg-searching expedition conflicted with spring practice, spring practice lost.

Harlow assisted Hollenback from 1912 to '14, and succeeded him as head coach in 1915. A 20–8 record from '15 through '17 foreshadowed his later success. After the '17 season he served as a lieutenant of infantry, returned to Penn State as as assistant to Hugo Bezdek from 1919 through '21, and became head coach at Colgate in 1922.

In 1923, Harlow's Colgate team, with Eddie Tryon at halfback and Tiny Welsh at guard, upset otherwise undefeated Syracuse in Archbold Stadium, 16–7. Welsh kicked a field goal, and passes from Chet Sanford to end Rae Crowther and Tryon brought the only two touchdowns scored on Syracuse that year. It was one of Harlow's finest triumphs.

Dick's four-year record at Colgate shows 1922, 6–3; '23, 6–2–1; '24, 5–4; and '25, 7–0–2. The 1925 team, tied by Lafayette and Brown, gave the Chenango Valley school its first undefeated season since 1893. Eddie Tryon, who ranked near Swede Oberlander as the best back in the East that year, scored 111 points and 15 touchdowns. One of these came in the 9–0 victory at Princeton, the only defeat suffered by one of Bill Roper's

best teams. To prevent defenses from getting set for Tryon, Harlow used an effective double shift.

"Tryon," Harlow said, "was the answer to a coach's fondest dream. He could do everything, and in addition was a wonderful boy to handle. He was a tremendous competitor in a crisis.

"In that game with Princeton, he was forced to kick from behind his own goal line. The snap from center was bad; also Ed McMillan, the Tiger center, broke through. A blocked punt seemed certain. But Tryon, in a split-second judgment, held the ball out toward McMillan. McMillan was so surprised, he dove for it. Tryon pulled it away from him and then got off the longest punt of his career."

Following the 1925 season, Harlow accepted an offer to coach football and be director of athletics at Western Maryland. There he delivered three undefeated seasons, 1929, '30 and '34. The '34 team, which shut out every opponent but one, was paced by a back named Bill Shepherd, who rated with Tryon and Struck as Harlow's most celebrated.

The sheen of Harlow's Western Maryland teams attracted attention, and in 1935, Bill Bingham, Harvard's athletic director, signed him to succeed Eddie Casey and never regretted it. Arthur Sampson, leading New England football expert, wrote of Harlow:

"Never blessed with outstanding material and frequently forced to resort to all sorts of ingenious tactics to hold the score against some star-studded elevens to respectable margins, Harlow was rated among the top coaches in the country by all those who know football . . . ." This opinion was validated when Harlow was inducted into the College Football Hall of Fame in 1954.

Although he was 53, Harlow in 1942 sought and got overseas duty as a navy commander and was assigned to rehabilitation in the submarine service. He drove himself so hard that he suffered a shock from high blood pressure and physical exhaustion and had to be hospitalized. Weeks of rest, diet, and treatment enabled him to get back the 50 pounds he lost. He was still not well when he returned to Harvard and coached three more years, 1945–47. He was put on a strict diet of rice and fruit juice. After the '47 season, he retired on the advice of his doctor.

There can be little doubt that Harlow's ill health, more than any other single factor, prevented his coaching as well after the war as he had before. This applied especially to his rela-

tionship with the players. He was not himself. On Harlow's death in 1961, Henry E. (Tim) Russell, one of his old centers, wrote this tribute:

"His tenure at Harvard enriched the lives of many Harvard men, particularly those who played football, to whom he referred affectionately as 'my boys.' And his feelings for Harvard are illustrated by an incident on the eve of the Yale game in 1938, at the Choate school where the squad was assembled.

"To conclude the evening squad meeting, he led, in his deep bass voice, the singing of 'Fair Harvard.' About halfway through the second verse he detected several of those present unable to recall the words, which triggered a tirade to the effect that 'the eleven men representing Harvard University tomorrow afternoon are representing the greatest institution of its kind in the world and, in this enviable capacity, they can be expected to know the words of "Fair Harvard," all three verses! Nobody plays tomorrow until they prove to me this lesson is learned!'

"This came from the first nongraduate head coach in Harvard's football history. Harlow loved Harvard. In his passing, hundreds of Harvard men have lost a great and wonderful friend."

Howard Harding Jones

THE THUNDER MAKER

For dominating Bowl play no coach of the twenties or thirties matched Howard Jones, "The Head Man" of the University of Southern California's "Thundering Herd" teams from 1925 through 1940. Five times Jones led Southern Cal to the Rose Bowl, and five times the Trojans not only won but beat teams also directed by coaching masters. The Pasadena scoreboard speaks brilliantly of Howard Jones:

YEAR	USC	OPPONENT		OPPONENT'S COACH
1930	47	Pittsburgh	14	Jock Sutherland
1932	21	Tulane	12	Bernie Bierman
1933	35	Pittsburgh	0	Jock Sutherland
1939	7	Duke	3	Wallace Wade
1940	14	Tennessee	0	Bob Neyland

Nevertheless, the Rose Bowl did not furnish the backdrop for Jones' top victory, which came at Notre Dame in 1931, when the Trojans, trailing 14–0 into the last quarter, scored 16 points, the last three on probably the most celebrated field goal ever kicked, by guard Johnny Baker from the 23-yard line. Baker thus relieved himself of the ready horns, for he had missed the conversion after Troy's first score. N.D. carried a 26-game defeatless record into that game, and the national championship was on the line.

Braven Dyer, veteran Los Angeles football writer and Southern Cal historian, rates that game as the No. 1 of all-time Trojan thrillers. By a fabulous break in timing, Metro-Goldwyn-Mayer had a film crew cover the game, and it was the first time that an entire football game was presented as a full-length feature. Dyer did the voice over.

"They rushed the film," said Dyer, "down to Loew's State Theater, then the top movie house in downtown Los Angeles. When the bill first went on, the football game was one half of a double feature. After the first day, business was so good and everybody admitted it was the football game that lured them to the theater, that the manager jerked the second feature and ran the gridiron picture over and over. It broke all house records at Loew's State."

Notre Dame's 1931 team was coached by Heartley W. (Hunk) Anderson; Knute Rockne had died the previous March 31 in a plane crash on a Kansas wheatfield. Rock had been on the other side of the field, however, ten years before at Iowa City, when the University of Iowa, coached by Howard Jones, had handed Notre Dame its first setback in 21 games, 10–7. (In fact, there was rumor, and not without foundation, that when Jones left Iowa after the 1923 season, to coach one year at Duke before going to Southern Cal, Rockne seriously considered accepting the Iowa job.)

The Hawkeyes, undefeated in 1921 and '22, and with a solid claim on the '22 national title, featured three All-Americans: tackle Duke Slater, quarterback Aubrey Devine, and halfback Gordon Locke. Slater, a black, later named to the

Hall of Fame and to two all-time All-America teams, could fold up one side of a line with his blocking, and behind his charges Devine and Locke seldom failed to gain.

"Slater was the best I ever played against," said Fritz Crisler, noted Princeton and Michigan coach, who was an end at Chicago. "I tried to block him throughout my college career but never once did I impede his progress to the ball carrier."

Aubrey Devine, whom Howard Jones once rated as the best all-purpose back he ever coached, dropkicked the winning field goal against Notre Dame from the 38-yard line. The victory was No. 5 in a 20-game defeatless string that began with the fifth game in 1920 and extended to the fourth game of 1923. The skein-snapper was a 9–6 loss to Illinois. Earl Britton's passes to Red Grange, then a sophomore, and Grange's running brought the Illini touchdown, and Britton place-kicked the winning field goal from the 47-yard line. Grange, who held the ball, called it his greatest thrill.

The big victories over Notre Dame and his royal flush at Pasadena, much as they were savored by Jones, gave him no more satisfaction than his ultimate triumphs over Stanford teams coached by Glenn Scobey (Pop) Warner.

"Howard had great respect for Pop Warner," said Al Wesson, S.C.'s sports publicist in Thundering Herd times, "and he always worked the hardest to get his teams ready for Stanford."

Jones and Warner had first confronted each other in 1908, when Jones, fresh out of Yale, was coaching Syracuse to a 6–3–1 record. One of his three defeats was incurred from Warner's Carlisle Indians, 12–0. Warner's Stanford teams beat Jones' first two S.C. teams, in 1925 and '26, 13–9 and 13–12, and the '27 game ended in a 13–13 tie.

The Warner double-wingback attack, with its single and double reverses and its big fullbacks blasting up the middle after fake handoffs, was as much talked of as Notre Dame's shift from a T into a box. But Jones, as was his custom, caught up with it, and won the next five games with Stanford, 1928 through '32: 10–0, 7–0, 41–12, 19–0, and 13–0.

Over that period, Warner's record at Stanford was a substantial 39–12–5, and Warner's inability to cope with the Thundering Herds caused alumni disenchantment that contributed to Pop's decision to leave Stanford for Temple in 1933. He couldn't have got much farther away and stayed

on dry land. Jones beat the Warner attack by emphasizing position play to his linemen:

"Lick a man and hold your position. You have a spot about a yard or two either side of you to see that nobody gets through. No matter who winds up with the ball, they won't go anywhere if you guard your own small territory and don't get faked out, trying to find where the ball is."

Against the double wing's wide reverse, S.C.'s crashing end play would often dump the would-be reverse runner before the ball ever got to him.

"Opposing teams," Jones explained, "were loath to use a six-man line against Stanford because Warner's team, with its wingbacks in close, was practically a nine-man line offensively, and it looked as if the defense needed every man right up in the forward wall to stop this powerful attack.

"Surprise was manifest, therefore, when we adopted a six-man line against Stanford. The man we pulled into the backfield—generally the center or a guard—was delegated to watch the fullback. If he always went in and cracked the fullback, he was bound to mess up a lot of Stanford plays. The defensive work of guard Aaron Rosenberg in this position ... had much to do with our success, both against Stanford and Notre Dame."

Offensively, Jones used an unbalanced line with the two guards lining up shoulder to shoulder on the strong side. The guard nearest the center pulled out to run interference. The objective of Jones on his end sweeps and off-tackle thrusts was to get three blockers ahead of the runner at the point of play impact, and nobody ever succeeded any better, if as well.

The tailback or the fullback did all the ball carrying except on reverses. There was a single reverse in which the left end, shifting back into a wingback position, took the ball. On the double reverse, he faked to take the ball and it was handed to the blocking back moving in the opposite direction.

It was Earl Sparling on the single reverse once and Ernie Pinckert on the double reverse twice who undid Tulane in the 1932 Rose Bowl. On both of Pinckert's runs, Jerry Dalrymple, Tulane's All-America end, was caught out of position.

That 1931 Trojan team also installed a double shift that enflanked defenses and gave the Thundering Herd a head start. On the whole, however, Jones was a fundamentalist and a conservative; some thought him an archconservative. (He was

surely an imaginative recruiter.)

"More than 60 percent of our total practice time," said Joe Shell, 1939 captain, "was involved with purely fundamental blocking and tackling positions."

Howard Jones scarcely would have struck a casting director as a Hollywood-type coach. But what is more glamorous than victory, and in the twenties and early thirties Southern Cal rated up near Notre Dame in the national headlines and radio broadcasts. If the Notre Dame "Victory March," "Cheer, cheer, for old Notre Dame," was first on the gridiron hit parade, then second belonged to the Trojan "Fight Song," "Fight on for old S.C."

As the Thundering Herds rolled on and over, many moving-picture stars became fans and even attended the practice sessions. Al Wesson collaborated with Jones in a book called *Football for the Fans*, which included a chapter devoted to questions sent in by movie stars and the answers. Several dozens of stars were represented, among them Mary Pickford, Douglas Fairbanks, Sr., Gary Cooper, Richard Dix, Harold Lloyd, Norma Talmadge, Hoot Gibson, Vilma Banky, Ronald Colman, Nancy Carroll, and Reginald Denny. One question sent in by Oliver Hardy had the sound of a Stan Laurel–Oliver Hardy film dialogue:

"Is the quarterback's value today greater than it used to be?" "Yes," Jones replied, "because the introduction of the forward pass broadened the field for the employment of strategy."

Gary Cooper asked, "What is the penalty for coaching from the bench during a game?" Answer, "Fifteen yards."

When Vilma Banky asked him who was the greatest player of all time, Jones picked Tom Shevlin, Yale's 1905 captain and All-America end, because "he not only was powerful physically, but also had great mental characteristics such as dynamic determination."

"Howard lived and breathed football," said Wesson. "If it were not for football he would have starved to death—couldn't possibly have made a living in business. His assistants tried to get him to organize the practices and let them do most of the heavy work.

"He'd promise to do it, but after 15 minutes on the field, he'd be down on the ground showing them personally how to block, following every play on the dead run, and acting as though he were still playing end at Yale. His putting so

Howard Jones in 1920, while at Iowa. *Chicago Tribune Photos*

much into the game was undoubtedly the cause of his premature death from a heart attack in 1941 at the age of 56. He just couldn't relax and let others do the heavy work."

Except when he took time off for bridge, golf, or fishing, Jones thought football all his waking hours, including many in which he should have been asleep. He liked to put the names of players on, ironically, gambling chips and move them about, devising formations, plays, and defenses.

He was so preoccupied that he often lost himself driving home, and usually had to be asked a question a second or third time. Despite his frosty exterior, he was an inwardly sensitive person, and by the end of each season he suffered from tension. Nervous smoking of cigarettes was his only vice. Otherwise he lived the Spartan life he preached to his players. He never took a drink. While coach at Iowa he wrote a book on conditioning that revealed his stern approach.

"I prohibit the boys from hanging around poolrooms," he said, "because the air in such places is usually bad and his associates are not always of the best. There are always a certain number of men hanging around such places who think it their duty to offer suggestions about various phases of the work done on the practice

From Hawkeye to Trojan, Howard eyes a Southern Cal
workout in 1929. *Chicago Tribune Photos*

field, and these men can often do more harm in
one hour than the coach can do good in three or
four practice periods. A boy playing football does
not need the exercise afforded by pool or billiard
playing, which is a waste of time."

He also spoke out, while he was at Iowa, even
against dancing, and his indictment was specific:

"The athlete does not have to participate in
order to keep up his social prestige. The objec-
tions I have against dancing are: first, it breaks in
upon sleeping and eating; second, it is a different
form of exercise than the boy is used to and is
tiring; three, there is the danger of getting heated
up and then cooling off too quickly; fourth, a
midnight lunch is usually partaken of, mostly
because of the obligations to the girl; fifth, the
boy usually does not feel like getting up for
breakfast."

Jones believed that music, however, was a good
thing for the player:

"I like to hear a squad singing popular songs
after a hard practice and while dressing. I know

then that most of the men will leave in good
spirits, that they will have forgotten the unpleas-
ant, unimportant occurrences of the practice by
the time they are dressed."

Jones disliked profanity. Upset over a bad
performance or a poor play, he indulged in
nothing stronger than a "Dad burn it!" In the
midthirties, when his teams were losing, he became exasperated enough to explode in a "God
darn it!" But he was seldom demonstrative. One
notable exception followed the 16–14 comeback
win at Notre Dame in '31, when he kissed
Captain Stan Williamson.

Jones would hardly ever pat a player on the
back coming off the field, but after the game he'd
go around the dressing room and talk one by one
to those who had played, thank them for a good
game, and look into possible injuries. He was not
given, however, to coddling the injured.

"When a player is injured," he said, "he should
say so but not until then. *Nothing* is more harmful
to the morale of the squad while scrimmaging
than the agonizing cry of an injured man. A good
rule to follow is to keep still until one is sure he's
hurt, and then not yell the information from the
housetops, but to report quietly to the physician
in charge."

Although he was severe with his players, he
bred in them a superb team spirit. In 1933 at
Multnomah Field in Portland, Oregon, a Trojan
victory string of 25 was halted when Oregon
State, coached by Lon Stiner, gained a scoreless
tie. Between halves, Jones noticed that star guard
Aaron Rosenberg's face was bloodied and
seemed to have a dent in it. Rosy had suffered a
broken cheekbone and was in much pain.

"Why didn't you call time out when you were
hurt?" the coach asked.

"We'd used three time-outs," Rosenberg replied, "and it would have cost us a five-yard
penalty."

"Rosy," Jones said, "you're about the gamest
guy I've ever seen in football."

Rosenberg became a leading Hollywood film
producer, and long after he'd played his last game
for the Trojans he looked fit enough to suit up.

Jones, no laughing boy, was made to smile at
least once by his ace blocking back, Ernie
Pinckert. In losing to Washington State 7–6 at
Pullman in 1930, the Trojans played a sloppy
game, and when Jones came into the dressing
room, he was full of "Dad burn its!" But he had
to smile when he heard Pinckert singing from a

Coach Jones (*left*) with two of his fellow coaches, Bill Spaulding (*center*) and Edwin (Babe) Horrell, before one of their many rounds of golf

popular song, "I'm nobody's sweetheart, now."

Pinckert was one of 19 Southern Cal All-Americans under Jones; the others: Stan Williamson, center; Brice Taylor, Nate Varrager, Johnny Baker, Aaron Rosenberg, and Harry (Blackjack) Smith, guards; Jesse Hibbs, Tay Brown, and Ernie Smith, tackles; Francis Tappaan and Garrett Arbelbide, ends; and Mort Kaer, Morley Drury ("The noblest Trojan of them all"), Don Williams, Orville Mohler, Gaius Shaver, Irving (Cotton) Warburton, and Granville Lansdell, backs. Pinckert, Hibbs, Rosenberg, and Harry Smith were named for two years.

Warburton, 146-pound cotton top, had glittered as a sophomore in 1932; he tallied the touchdown that beat Washington, 9–6, starred in the 13–0 win over Notre Dame, and scored the two touchdowns that broke open the 1933 Rose Bowl victory over Pitt, 35–0. But his most remarkable run, 60 yards for a touchdown, brought S.C. a 6–3 victory at Berkeley in 1933 over Coach Bill Ingram's California team.

A first-quarter field goal by Arleigh Williams gave the Golden Bears a 3–0 lead that they protected into the fourth period. Warburton was stunned making a tackle in the first half, had to be taken out, and was somehow overlooked in the dressing room after the Trojans ran out for the second half.

Cotton had taken a shower and was sitting naked on a pile of blankets preparatory to dressing when he was discovered by John Lehners, assistant to graduate manager Bill Hunter. Warburton asked Lehners to help him dress. "Let's get out of here," he said. "The game's over." Lehners succeeded in convincing him the game wasn't over and helped him get back into uniform.

"When we finally reached the bench," said Lehners, "the second half was under way. I asked Dr. Packard Thurber, team physician, to take a look at Cotton and check his condition. Quite frankly I had no idea that they'd allow him back into the game. Next time I looked up, there he

The grandest Trojan of them all

was running for the touchdown. I never was so surprised in my life."

Red Christie, who backed up the line for Cal, recalled, "On Warburton's run I guess all of us Cal players had our one miss of the day. I know I did. I had a straight shot at him behind the line but he got away. Then there was a succession of missed tackles—and that was the ball game."

Warburton never remembered scoring the touchdown or much else about that game. His run preserved a defeatless string at 27. The following week, however, in Los Angeles Coliseum, the Trojans lost to Stanford, 13–7. Warburton got the Trojan touchdown on a 44-yard run, but two field goals by Stanford's All-America guard, Bill Corbus, were decisive. (This was the sophomore year of the Stanford Vow Boys teams. They had lost as freshmen to S.C., vowed they'd never lose a varsity game to the Trojans, and didn't.)

That was the Trojans' only loss in a 10–1–1 season, as they finished strong, including a 19–0 victory over Notre Dame. In the next four seasons, though, they struggled to stay near the .500 mark, with a 17–19–6 log. And for the first time Jones heard the cry of the wolfpack. Paul Zimmerman, former sports editor of the Los Angeles *Times*, analyzed why the Trojan material fell off:

"Howard had a lot of fine stars who spent three years on the bench when they could have played at some of the other schools. The high school

players figured that out for themselves and many decided to go elsewhere. Of course, alumni and coaches at other schools were stepping up their recruiting. By the same token, the Jones staff and the alumni naturally got to riding on their oars, assuming every great prep star would want to be part of the Thundering Herd."

While Jones was having his down years, his son, Clark Jones, was the sports editor of the Southern California school paper, the *Daily Trojan*. And though there is no evidence whether Howard read what his son was writing, it is a fact that Clark did not hesitate to criticize the play of the Trojans.

By 1938 and '39, Jones had rebuilt, and the Trojans were back winning Rose Bowl games. For last-minute hijinks and hysteria, no Bowl game ever surpassed the Trojans' 7–3 triumph over Duke at Pasadena, New Year's Day, 1939.

(With its Seven Iron Dukes line, the team from Durham was unbeaten, untied, and unscored upon. It had a superior coffin-corner kicker in Eric [the Red]Tipton. And its victims included Dr. Jock Sutherland's last Pitt team in Jock's last college game, 7–0, on a blocked kick by end Willis [Bolo]Perdue, in a snowstorm at Chapel Hill. That was the Pitt team of the Dream Backfield: John Chickerneo, Dick Cassiano, Hal Stebbins, and Marshall Goldberg.)

With Duke leading 3–0, S.C. on Duke's 34-yard line, and little more than two minutes to play, Jones substituted a fourth-string back named Doyle Nave. Nave had played only 38 minutes all season, but he had practiced forward passing assiduously with end Al Krueger. Now it paid off. Nave completed four straight passes to Krueger, the last a 14-yarder for a touchdown.

The 1939 Tennessee team that Southern Cal beat in the 1940 Rose Bowl was also unbeaten, untied, and unscored upon, and regarded by Coach Bob Neyland as one of his greatest. Bob Suffridge and Ed Molinski were the guards, and a group of superior backs was led by George Cafego, Johnny (Reb) Butler, and Bobby Foxx. But the Trojans were just as talented, bigger by a 10-pound average, and deeper. On both touchdown drives, Trojan second-stringers prevailed, especially backs Ambrose Schindler and Jack Banta.

"We weren't stale or off form," Bob Neyland said afterwards. "We were outclassed. We were badly beaten by a superior team, and my hat is off to Howard Jones."

Howard Harding Jones was born in Excello, Ohio, August 23, 1885, about a year and a half before his brother, Thomas Albert Dwight Jones. Both played in the backfield at nearby Middletown High, then two years at Exeter, before entering Yale.

As a Yale quarterback on championship teams, Tad Jones got more ink that Howard Jones, who played end. But though Tad delivered standout teams as Yale's coach in 1916, '23, '24, and '27, Howard outstripped him as a coach—first at Iowa and later at Southern Cal.

On the two occasions they coached against each other, Howard won; first when Yale beat Syracuse, 15–0, in 1909, second when Iowa beat Yale, 6–0, in 1922. It was with the undefeated, untied, and unscored-through Yale team of 1909, captained by All-America fullback Ted Coy, that Jones first showed his coaching aptitude and his appreciation that the worst mistake a coach can make is to get caught without material. The '09 Yales were so good nobody ever got beyond their 28-yard line.

Howard also coached Syracuse in 1908 (6–3–1), Ohio State in 1910 (6–1–3), and Yale in 1913 (5–2–3). In 1910, '11, '14, and '15, he tried his hand at business. Not until he went to Iowa in 1916 did he commit himself fully to coaching. He stayed with the Hawkeyes eight years and built the teams that went undefeated in 1921 and '22; the '21 team had a valid claim on the national title. Then, after one season at Duke, 1924, he went on to Southern Cal.

Jones's 29-year record as a head coach stands at 194 victories, 64 defeats, and 21 ties for .733. In his 16 seasons at Southern California, the log shows 116–36–13 for .750. The Trojans won seven

Pacific Coast Conference championships, two national titles, 1928 and '31, five out of five Rose Bowl games, and averaged over 480,000 in attendance; the 1933 team played before 645,000.

The only coaching rival to hold a series edge on Howard Jones was probably his best friend among coaches, Knute Rockne. In 1921, Jones' Iowans beat Rock's Notre Dames but of the five games between their Southern Cal and N.D. teams, Jones won only in 1928, 27–14. Three of Rockne's victories, however, were by one point: 13–12 in 1926 and '29, and 7–6 in '27.

It was only in their last meeting, and in Rockne's last game, that Notre Dame prevailed decisively over the tough Trojans, 27–0. Before that game in the Coliseum the two old coaching rivals and friends were trying to make small talk but both were tense. Jones showed it by chain smoking cigarettes, Rockne by chewing on his cigar.

"My gosh, Howard," Rockne quipped, "what are you so serious about? You're chain smoking!"

"Well," Jones retorted, "what about yourself? Your cigar looks like shredded rope."

After his most dramatic triumph, the 16–14 comeback at Notre Dame in 1931, Jones was followed into the Trojan dressing room by Jack Rissman, who sponsored the trophy emblematic of the national championship. S.C., it developed, had clinched it that day.

"You're just the man I wanted to see," said Jones. "Can you direct me to the cemetery where Knute Rockne is buried?"

Jones and his players went from Notre Dame Stadium to the cemetery and the coach led them in a prayer. As Jack Rissman pointed out, it was Howard Harding Jones' most shining hour.

Lawrence McCeney (Biff) Jones

CAPTAIN OF EXCITEMENT

Four schools—Army, Louisiana State, Oklahoma, and Nebraska—benefited from the organization skills, on and off the field, of Lawrence McCeney (Biff) Jones as a football coach. His record, covering 135 games in 14 seasons, during the 1926–41 period, shows 87 victories, 33 defeats, and 15 ties for a percentage of .700. For turbu-

lence, none of his on-field experiences surpassed his first major assignment, Syracuse at Michie Stadium, Army's home field, the third game of the 1926 season.

Army won 27–21 in a game extraordinarily rough. Vic Schwartz, the referee, got his nose punched and broken by a Syracuse player, who

Biff Jones

was put out of the game and suspended for the season. Among themselves players were slugging indiscriminately.

It was evident when the teams left the field at the half, with Syracuse leading 14–6, that all was not going well. Biff Jones and Herman Koehler, Army's director of athletics, walked off gesticulating with Schwartz, the referee, and Pete Reynolds, the Syracuse coach.

In the third quarter, with Syracuse leading 14–13, the ball at midfield, the roughness at its apex, and the crowd yammering ominously, Bill Hollenback, one of the officials, called time and walked over to the Army bench. Brigadier General Merch B. Stewart, Superintendent of West Point, left his box and also came down to the Army bench.

"Say, Biff," Hollenback said, "I think it would be a good thing if you had some police protection for us after the game. That crowd is acting up ugly."

"We'll see it's taken care of," Biff replied.

Then General Stewart stepped in. "Under the circumstances, Captain Jones," he said, "I think it would be wise to stop the game."

"I believe we should go on with it, General," Biff said. "We are behind, and if we stop the game now, the move might be misinterpreted."

General Stewart thought it over and agreed. After the game, Syracuse rooters moved threateningly down out of the stands and onto the field. The officials were escorted away by four military police. One of the MPs drew his pistol and held it in readiness against any overt move. Gradually the crowd scattered.

Captain Jones went down to the gymnasium to congratulate his players and then returned to his quarters, threw himself into a chair, and exhaled.

"I wonder," he asked Mrs. Jones, "if all my games as head coach will be anything like that one."

The telephone rang. It was General Stewart.

"Captain Jones," he said, "did you give that military policeman permission to draw his gun?"

"No, sir," Biff replied, "I certainly did not."

"Well," said the Superintendent, "I'm glad he didn't shoot anybody. It wouldn't help football here to have a civilian shot in Michie Stadium."

Although nobody got shot, Army football boiled with excitement and controversy through the four-year regime of Biff Jones, 1926 through '29. His record of 30–8–2 breaks down into 1926, 7–1–1; '27, 9–1–0; '28, 8–2–0; and '29, 6–4–1.

Jones, a native of Washington, D.C., had played left tackle on the 1915 and '16 teams; the '16 team was undefeated and had a claim on the national championship. Biff was elected captain of the 1917 team, but by the time that season came around he was serving as a lieutenant of field artillery with the American Expeditionary Force in France. After the war he returned to West Point and was a valued assistant coach under both Charlie Daly and John McEwan.

Biff's four years as head coach coincided with the four of his greatest player, halfback Christian Keener (Red) Cagle. Even before the crowd spotted his No. 12, they could tell Red Cagle by the peculiar set of his headgear. He wore it with the chin strap hanging over the back ever since the time a tackler grabbed him by the head and yanked the helmet off, and he thought his head was coming with it.

"Onward Christian" Cagle some sportswriter named him, and that was not only catching but apt, because it was onward Cagle headed when he got the familiar feel of a football in his hands.

Sometimes Cagle moved backward in a circle and from one side of the field to the other in order finally to move onward, retreating 15 yards to take 25 or 35, or all he needed for a touchdown. He ran just as well to his left as to his right.

For four years at Army he delivered the hysteria they had paid for to the thousands that mobbed Yale Bowl and Yankee Stadium and Chicago's Soldier's Field. Crowds pulsated to his escape artistry.

Red Cagle, before entering West Point in the summer of 1926, had been the fifth highest scorer in the nation at Southwestern Louisiana Institute. But it was at Army that he became a national name.

As a plebe Cagle scored one of the touchdowns against Syracuse. There was little time to contemplate that overheated affair, because Yale loomed just ahead. In five previous visits to Yale Bowl, Army had come off with no better than two ties. And there was General Merch Stewart.

Biff Jones had been promoted from lieutenant to captain just before the season began. He had taken the oath in the adjutant general's office; General Stewart was in the next office and the door was ajar. After Biff repeated the concluding words of the oath, General Stewart added:

"And beat Yale."

"Is he really serious about that?" Biff asked Colonel Koehler.

"You bet he is," Koehler laughed.

The general got his wish as the Cadets trounced the Elis 33–0. The plebe Cagle scored one of the touchdowns; others were made by Chuck Born, Johnny Murrell, "Lighthorse" Harry Wilson, and Joe Gilbreth.

If Biff Jones had pointed out that his Cadet teams could have used some luck against Notre Dame, few would have debated him after hearing the facts. One play separated the 1926 Army team from a perfect record, Christy Flanagan's 65-yard run off tackle for a 7–0 Notre Dame victory.

In 1928, Knute Rockne called on the memory of N.D.'s legendary hero, George Gipp, to inspire an Irish eleven at the half. "Win this one for the Gipper," he said, and they did, 12–6. But only after a tremendous effort by Cagle, which brought the ball down to the 1-yard line. There the clock ran out on Army. And in 1929, Notre Dame won 7–0 when Jack Elder intercepted a Cagle pass and ran it back for a touchdown.

In 1927, however, his yearling (sophomore) year, Cagle led the Cadets to an 18–0 victory over the Irish, running 53 yards for one touchdown and catching a pass from Dick Hutchinson for another.

The largest crowd ever to see an Army-Navy game, 111,000, jammed cold, snow-bordered Sol-

Biff and 1936 Sooner captain Connie Ahrens

dier's Field, Chicago, in 1926. Navy had a perfect record; Army had lost only one game, to Notre Dame on Flanagan's run. Coach Bill Ingram's Navy personnel included Tom Hamilton, field general, passer, and kicker; Frank Wickhorst, All-America tackle; Alan Shapley, nifty runner; and two star ends, Whitey Lloyd and Hank Hardwick.

For much of the first half Navy appeared to be headed for a conclusive victory. Biff Jones started the game with an Army lineup heavily mixed with second-stringers. While Colonel Koehler stalked up and down the sidelines in a frightful stew, Hamilton, Jim Schuber, and Howard Caldwell, a 158-pound fullback, passed and ran to two Navy touchdowns and a 14–0 lead.

During the second Navy drive, Biff sent in the rest of the first team. Before the half was over, Lighthorse Harry Wilson and Red Cagle collaborated for one touchdown, and end Skip Harbold scooped up a Midshipman's fumble and ran for another. Wilson, who clinched his All-America rating that day, matched Hamilton's two extra points and the score was tied, 14–14.

Early in the second half, the plebe Cagle streaked off tackle and down the sideline for 44 yards and a touchdown; again Wilson converted. Toward the end of the third quarter, with the first fingers of nightfall reaching out over the field, Navy got a drive under way at its 43. Shapley

finally skirted end from the 8-yard line and Hamilton calmly kicked the extra point. The game ended with the 21–21 scoreboard indistinguishable in the darkness.

That was perhaps the most exciting of all Army-Navy games—or close to it. It had a little bit of everything. The tie score seemed just—but to Army and Navy a tie is unsatisfactory. The Midshipmen took what consolation they could from saying, "Anyhow we're undefeated and have as good a claim as anybody on the national championship." And Army, of course, was saying, "If Biff had only started the first team."

Three straight years, 1927, '28, and '29, Red Cagle ran, passed, blocked, and tackled his way onto the All-America team that counted most, the one picked by Grantland Rice. Swept along by Cagle's brilliance, the 1927 team lost only to Yale, 10–6. The Elis lost only to Georgia that year.

The most exciting runner in Yale Bowl for that Army-Yale game was a well-groomed inebriate, possibly a onetime halfback. He came down out of the Yale stands between halves and entertained the crowd by running up and down the gridiron with his hat under his arm as a football. A score of New Haven police gave chase and tried to trap him. They finally caught him only after he threw himself exhaustedly on a pile of hay that had been used to cover the gridiron during the week.

The 1927 season closed out with a 14–9 victory over Navy at the Polo Grounds. It was Lighthorse Harry Wilson's last game and he scored both touchdowns in the third quarter. When Army got near the goal line, Cagle refused to carry the ball. He told quarterback Spike Nave, "Wilson scores the touchdowns today."

There had been discontent at Annapolis for some time because Army refused to adopt the rule that limited participation in the service game to men who had not played a total of three years of varsity competition, whether at West Point or elsewhere. This rule, in vogue at other colleges, had been adopted by Navy in June 1927.

Army and Navy had entered into a general four-year contract in 1926. On December 3, 1927, Admiral Louis M. Nulton, Annapolis Superintendent, requested that West Point add to the individual contract for the 1928 game a clause stipulating that "no contestant shall take part in this game on either team who has had three years' experience in intercollegiate football." The admiral added that refusal to accede to this request

would be considered "rejection of the contract and the Naval Academy will consider itself free to schedule another game on November 28, 1928."

Major General Edwin B. Winans, who had succeeded Brigadier General Stewart as West Point Superintendent, rejected the request, invoking the precedent that the right of any Cadet not barred by academic deficiencies or tactical discipline to play on an Army team could not be questioned.

So the Army-Navy series, which had gone on since 1899 without interruption, except for World War I years, was broken off. By 1938 the old rivals would be playing again and Army followed the orders of the commander-in-chief, Franklin Delano Roosevelt, to adopt the three-year rule. But at the time of the break, prospects of restoration in the future were not bright.

To compensate for the absence of the Navy game, Army's graduate manager of athletics, the shrewd, imaginative, debonair Major Philip B. Fleming, signed a four-year agreement with Harvard (missing from Army's schedule since 1910), arranged home-and-home games with Stanford and Illinois, and signed Southern Methodist and Nebraska for dates at Michie Stadium.

The immediate results posed Coach Biff Jones a tough 1928 schedule, but the Cadets achieved a solid 8–2 record. The colorful Southern Methodist "Aerial Circus," coached by Ray Morrison, came up from Dallas, Texas, with its famous jazz band, its pony mascot Peruna, and several train carloads of uninhibited rooters. The Mustangs had a dangerous passer in Redman Hume. Cagle had to be at his best, and it was still close: Army 14, SMU 13.

Between halves, Colonel Fred McJunkin—a Texas not a West Point colonel—made a speech over the loudspeaker and invited everybody present, including the plebes, to come down to Texas as his guest. The Corps couldn't accept, but they did follow the team to Boston, where they marched to the Common and were reviewed by Governor Alvan Fuller, who presented them with gold spearheads.

Cagle repaid the hospitality by dazzling Harvard with his runs and his passes to quarterback Spike Nave and a pair of smooth sophomore ends, Ed Messinger and Carl Carlmark. The Corps celebrated a 15–0 victory, Army's first ever over Harvard and on its first visit to Boston.

In Yale Bowl the next week, Cagle ran wild in

With his LSU coaching staff, *left to right*: Frank Wandle, trainer; Coach Moore, freshmen coach; Joel Hunt, backfield coach; Burt Ingwersen, head line coach; Jones; Spike Nelson, assistant line coach; and Ben Enis, end coach

an 18–6 triumph. He broke around Yale's right end and reversed his field on a 51-yard touchdown run. He ran 76 yards for another, breaking off tackle and eluding the clutch of blue shirts.

Although Notre Dame's "win one for the Gipper" spoiled their bid for a perfect season, the Cadets seized the opportunity to do some derailing of their own. Nebraska, Big Six champion, was undefeated and coming off a scoreless tie with powerful Pittsburgh.

For a half the big visitors to Michie Stadium kept Cagle in check whenever he threatened their goal line, and went ahead on Clair Sloan's field goal, 3–0. Early in the third quarter, however, Cagle faked a handoff to Murrell, came back over the left side, twisted loose, and ran 37 yards to a touchdown. Late in the game Johnny Hutchinson threw a 19-yard pass to Charlie Allan and the extra point made the final score 13–3.

The savage battle with Nebraska's big, heavy line contributed to the 26–0 defeat by Stanford in Yankee Stadium a week later. Under any circumstances, however, the Stanford personnel and

the hipper-dipper of Glenn Scobey (Pop) Warner's double-wingback attack, with its spins, fakes, and reverses, would have been too much for the Cadets.

Beyond the result, the game exerted two far-reaching effects. The double-wingback attack so impressed Biff Jones that he installed it with the 1929 plebe team and it was used in the early thirties by Army under Coach Ralph Sasse.

In arranging a site for the game, Major Fleming had played the Yankee Stadium against the Polo Grounds until he got the Stadium for a flat $15,000 rental. Since a sellout throng brought in $340,000 and Army and Stanford each took home over $150,000, the Stadium people were unhappy, and in a mood to listen to Ray McCarthy, advertising man and promoter. McCarthy used the Fleming coup to convince the Stadium and Polo Grounds they should act as a single lessor for college football with a flat 25 percent rental fee and McCarthy as booking agent.

Cagle was elected captain for 1929 and was brilliant in many games, but went unrewarded by

Biff in 1936

Jones visited LSU and Major Troy Middleton, commandant of its ROTC. Finally, Biff said he would come if he could be detailed as an instructor in military science so that he would not have to resign from the army. To bring this about, James M. Smith, LSU's president, and Broussard met in Washington with General Douglas MacArthur, then chief of staff.

"How much are you going to pay Biff Jones?" MacArthur inquired.

"Seventy-five hundred dollars," replied Broussard.

"Okay, you can have him," MacArthur snapped. "You've got yourself a good coach, but don't ever come back and ask for any more favors."

Peter Finney, who wrote *The Fighting Tigers*, excellent history of LSU football, said of Jones:

"An erect 6-foot, 3-inch 200-pounder with clear blue eyes that reflected determination, Jones impressed those around him with his poise and traits befitting an army captain trained at West Point. . . . A congenial mixer at social functions, he was at ease on the banquet circuit, where he spoke with quiet force . . . .On the football field he was a drill master and expected results by operating on the John D. Rockefeller theory—organize, deputize, and supervise.

"Looking somewhat like a director on a Hollywood movie set, Jones was easy to find at any football game, sitting in an elevated chair near the 50-yard line. Rarely did he stand or walk the sideline. Once in a while he would half rise out of his seat to signal a player or member of his staff, but for the most part he sat still in the saddle even during the fiercest set-tos."

Jones' three-year record of 20–5–6 at LSU breaks down into 1932, 6–3–1; 1933, 7–0–3; and 1934, 7–2–2. Against Tulane, the Tigers' traditional rival, he won in 1932, 14–0, tied in 1933, 7–7, and lost in 1934, 13–12. Postseason games in 1933 and '34 were arranged with Tennessee, where Coach Robert R. Neyland, Biff's old West Point teammate and co-assistant coach, had already built a dynasty.

LSU beat Tennessee in 1933, 7–0, and lost in 1934, 19–13. Although the Tigers had the home-field advantage in '33, Tennessee was favored, in good measure because of its ace runner, Beattie Feathers. But it was LSU's ace, Abe Mickal, who scored the only touchdown as the Tigers made 16 first downs to the Volunteers' three, and handed a team coached by Neyland its first shutout defeat in 77 games.

any major victories. First-class (senior) complacency affected some of the veterans, the breaks were far from favorable, and Army was meeting some mighty fine teams.

Cagle resigned from West Point when it was discovered that he had married in August 1928, during furlough at the end of his yearling (sophomore) year. He answered all questions truthfully, and was not in violation of the honor code.

The excitement Biff Jones coached through at Army prepared him for more as Louisiana's head coach in 1932, '33, and '34. In '30 and '31 he was not in coaching, but served as a field artillery officer, and assistant graduate manager of athletics at the Academy.

Meanwhile, Louisiana State sought a new head coach, and James Broussard, chairman of athletics, approached Jones. Biff wanted to get back in coaching, but at first he shied away from LSU. He told Broussard, "Frankly, Huey Long worries me." He had sound cause for worry. "The Kingfish" was in his political prime, and the interest he evidenced in the LSU football team was nothing less than proprietary.

Meanwhile, Senator Huey Long headed up an unprecedented sideshow. He marched and pranced at the head of 2,000 cadets, 200 musicians, and 50 boy and girl cheerleaders down the main streets of Houston, Nashville, or wherever LSU played. He sat on the sideline and led cheers. The newspapers didn't like Huey but they were forced to cover his shows.

It was in the front offices, however, that the Kingfish showed his real muscle. The 1934 schedule listed Southern Methodist as LSU's home opener. To get the Mustangs, T. P. (Red) Heard, who had succeeded Broussard as athletic director after Jones came, had to give them a guarantee of $10,000. Early in the morning of the Tuesday before the game, Long phoned Heard to ask him how the tickets were going.

"Not too good, Senator," said Heard. "They've got a circus scheduled Saturday night and the conflict seems to be hurting the advance."

With the help of a law student, Long dug up an old statute from Louisiana's sanitary code requiring that any animal coming into the state had first to be dipped. Then he got in touch with the advance man for John Ringling North's Barnum and Bailey Circus.

"Did you ever dip a tiger?" the senator asked him. "Or better yet an elephant?"

The advance man phoned North, who took the hint and canceled out his show for Baton Rouge. With this help LSU was able to meet SMU's ten-grand guarantee; a crowd of 20,000 watched a 14–14 tie.

LSU's game at Vanderbilt in 1934, a 29–0 victory for the Bengals, provided the backdrop for Long's most colorful hijinks. "No student," he proclaimed, "should miss this trip for lack of funds." When the Illinois Central Railroad told him that it could not lower its rates for students, Long countered strongly.

"The bridges over which your trains travel in Louisiana," he told them, "are taxed at $100,000. Their value is $4 million. It would be a sad day for you if our legislature was to raise the assessment from $100,000 to $4 million."

The president of the railroad saw the point and agreed to a $6 fare for students, one third of the regular cost; nearly 5,000 made the trip.

It was inevitable, of course, that Long's capers would collide with Biff Jones' sense of organization. Biff was disturbed when the Kingfish ordered the state legislature to name star back Abe Mickal a senator. Mickal was injured against Mississippi State, and his place against George Washington was taken by his understudy, Bert Yates. Bert was greeted by the G.W. players as "Senator." He replied, "My name's not Mickal. It's Yates." LSU was hard pressed to win 6–0.

"Look," Biff Jones told Red Heard, "I can't run a ball club like this. It's bad for morale."

Apprised by Heard of the coach's reaction, Long said, "Hell, Red, I'll make 'em all senators." Heard succeeded in convincing him that this would help the opposition psychologically, so "Senator" Mickal's title was removed.

Back-to-back defeats by Tulane and Tennessee led to a final showdown between Jones and Long. LSU was trailing Oregon at the half, 13–0. Jones was about to outline the problems, depending on reason rather than emotion, when Huey arrived at the dressing-room door and asked Biff, "Can I talk to the team?"

"No," Jones replied curtly.

"Who's going to stop me?" Long asked.

"Well," Jones snapped, "you're not going to talk."

"Well, I'm sick of losing and tying games," said Long. "You'd better win this one."

Biff was outraged; he flushed.

"Well, Senator," he said, "get this: win, lose, or draw, I quit."

"That's a bargain," said Long, and Jones closed the door on him. Huey was shaken. "Ain't I part of the organization?" he asked people near the door. "Why can't I talk to the boys?" Somebody, apparently a pro-Jones man, replied: "Why don't you run the band and lay off the football team?"

After they had cooled off, Long and Jones both regretted the incident, and Heard got them together. But neither wanted to back down publicly, so Biff left. His reasonable halftime approach had helped LSU rally in the second half to win, 14–13.

The foundations laid by Biff Jones at LSU enabled his successor, Bernie Moore (later commissioner of the Southeastern Conference), to build three straight Sugar Bowl teams.

Still an officer in the army, Jones coached Oklahoma in 1935 and '36 to records of 6–3 and 3–3–3. Again he built a firm foundation on which Tom Stidham, his line coach who succeeded him, fashioned an Orange Bowl team in 1938. Harold Keith, director of Oklahoma sports publicity then and during the later dynasty of Bud Wilkinson, said, "Biff Jones gave us our first real organization." Karey Fuqua, one of his O.U. players, said of Biff:

"My one-year experience with him was during the fall of '35, from which time I did not see him until the winter of '41. He was coaching one of the teams for the East-West game, which because of Pearl Harbor had been moved to New Orleans. His team was housed at Louisiana State, where I dropped in to say hello. He immediately said, 'Hello, Karey,' and sat down and visited for a few minutes."

For over a decade, Biff Jones had coached football and remained in the army. In 1937, however, he retired with the rank of major and signed to replace Dana X. Bible as coach of Nebraska. His five-year record with the Cornhuskers was 28-14-4. He delivered Big Six championships in 1937 and '40. He developed Charlie Brock, center; Fred Shirey and Forrest Behm, tackles; and Warren Alfson, guard, into All-America linemen. His 1937 team was the first to beat Minnesota (14-9) since 1913, and his '39 team the first to beat Pittsburgh (14-13) since 1921.

His 1940 Nebraska team, after losing its opener to Minnesota, 13-7, won its eight other regular-season games, and became the first Cornhusker team to play in a Bowl.

The Cornhuskers were beaten, 21-13, in the Rose Bowl by the Stanford team coached by Clark Shaughnessy. Stanford used the T formation with man-in-motion and flankers, the forerunner of all modern offensive sets. More important, Stanford fielded an exceptional backfield of Frankie Albert at quarter, Pete Kmetovic and Hugh Gallarneau at the halves, and Norm Standlee at full.

Nebraska went down only after a magnificent effort. The Huskers took a 7-0 lead on a seven-play, 53-yard march built around its spinning fullback, Vike Francis. Stanford tied it, 7-7, but the Huskers again gained the lead after Allen Zikmund recovered a Kmetovic fumble of Herman Rohrig's 56-yard quick kick. Rohrig passed to Zikmund for the touchdown, but the extra point was blocked.

A 40-yard pass from Albert to Kmetovic and a 39-yard punt return by Kmetovic behind a series of outstanding blocks, gave Stanford two touchdowns and the game.

Nebraska took a special pride in that Rose Bowl team, because 38 of the 39 men on the roster came from within the state. When the bid came, the campus, the city of Lincoln, and the state went crazy. Gregg McBride, veteran newspaperman and Nebraska publicist, said, "It was the greatest thing that happened to Nebraska since William Jennings Bryan ran for the presidency."

Faculty men locked coeds in their dorms, but husky males got stepladders and sprang them. Ten thousand Nebraskans followed the team to Pasadena. The demand for tickets in Lincoln was so intense that businessmen formed what they called the "Last Man Club." The idea was for every native to be sent to Pasadena except one, the last man, who would be left behind to guard the bank.

Through all the hubbub Coach Biff Jones maintained his organizational cool. Excitement was nothing new to the man who had coached Army in the time of Red Cagle and Phil Fleming, and LSU in the time of Abe Mickal and Huey Long.

Tad Jones

TAD'S BIG BLUE

The first letter of his first three names couldn't have missed getting Thomas Albert Dwight Jones the nickname Tad. No way. No way, either, he could have escaped coronation as King of Kings among Establishment Squares by a too prevalent modern school of sportswriters, the CCPs —Creeps, Cheap Shot Artists, and Pinkos.

Devoted to his players; to his school—Yale; to the game it had fathered and raised—football; and to the ideal that this game could help make strong men—what a Square, indeed, was this Tad Jones! How the CCPs would have dripped their rancid prose on his last words to his Big Blues before he sent them out against their blood foe, the redbellies from the Charles.

"Gentlemen, you are now going out to play

football against Harvard. Never again in your life will you do anything so important."

For sure, Tad Jones, Yale's coach in 1916 and from 1920 through '27, was an idealist. He was also a realist, a shipbuilder, and coal shipper, experienced in the harshness and chicanery of men and life. He was a wise enough man to know that life is also idealistic. His was a realism contradicting the half-baked, unconscionable school that preaches negativism exclusively and since it can't eliminate the positive, tries to pretend it's not there. What Tad was saying to his players just before H Hour was really this:

"Harvard is the goal we've worked toward together, long and hard. No matter what happens, the important thing is that you come off the field knowing you have made a total commitment. Knowledge of this could make the difference in your favor the day you are confronted by the ruling crisis of your life."

It was the inner flame of the Holy of Holies, Yale vs. Harvard, that Tad responded to. He didn't care, if in fact he was even aware, that as an epitome of privilege at play, nothing could match it, not even croquet finals between topmost branches of Cabots, with God as guest referee. Modern Yale-Harvard bills itself as The Game. Such a tag in the twenties and thirties would have been up-eyebrowed as superfluity tainted by an ostentation too precious for the digestion. Of course it was The Game. Who the hell needed that spelled out?

Resplendent in raccoons, flasks, and a serenity that cannot be made to fit, nor would it indeed become, any others, the Harvards descended by train or car on New Haven and environs. Every one of Yale Bowl's (then 80,000) seats had been long gone at $3 a ticket. (Scalpers were getting more than that; by 1927 they were getting $60 a pair.) Three hard bucks, good for a crock of some bootlegger's best, or six in the orchestra for six good acts of vaudeville plus a four-star, first-run silent film like Tom Mix in *The Light of Western Skies*.

You might acquire a pair for Yale-Harvard if you could somehow get up $6 and knew somebody. But it had to be somebody like Davey Fitzgerald, New Haven's eloquent hunchback mayor, or that tiger not from Princeton who saw the 1922 game, Premier Georges Clemenceau of France. Radio crystal sets were sparse, and television was dreamed of by few people beyond the two Toms, Edison and Swift.

Tad Jones

You could, however, see the game on the gridograph in front of a newspaper office. If you lived far in the outskirts, two tokens for 15 cents got you a round-trip ride on one of the trolleys that overran Connecticut; today, you'll fine one only in the museum at Branford. In early twenties boyhood as a Yale towner who later moved to Hartford, I saw my first college football—Yale-Harvard, Yale-Princeton, Yale-Army—on the gridograph in front of the Hartford *Times*. I never enjoyed football more.

Never was Y-H in finer flower. From 1910 though 1922 Yale beat Harvard only in 1916. Yale, football's early colossus, was groaning

under the taut leash of the father of modern organized coaching, Percy Duncan Haughton, and his 1911 captain and guard who succeeded him after the war, Robert T. Fisher.

From 1923 through '27, however, Yale fought back to the top, beating Harvard not once but four times and tying (0–0) in 1925. The man mainly responsible was that incredible King of Squares, Thomas Albert Dwight Jones.

Tad Jones was born in Excello, Ohio, near Middletown, February 21, 1887. On August 23, 1885; a brother had arrived—Howard, who at Iowa and Southern California would become a more famous coach than Tad, but not as charismatic. In 1902, the Jones brothers were the halfbacks on the Middletown High team, coached by a Yale man, '02, Bill Oglesby.

Oglesby had been inspired to attend Yale by reading Frank Merriwell, but he couldn't get beyond the freshman team in football. In baseball he made the varsity, and even got a single off the sainted pitcher of John McGraw's New York Giants, Christy Mathewson. Oglesby had shaken off, finally, the euphoria of his hit off Matty, returned home to Middletown, and settled down to banking, his sports behind him, he thought. Twenty years ago, Bill wrote me:

"When fall came around, I heard that the local high school team had a game on and I took it in. They were beaten and as I watched them, I realized how little of football they knew. Over Sunday I thought about how much I could teach them. Monday I talked it over with my fellow bank workers. They were all local boosters. It was decided that they would do my after-closing-time work and that I would go teach the boys football.

"That afternoon I hurried down to the playgrounds and found eleven boys trying to make a team of themselves. No coach, no scrub, not even one substitute. It looked rather bad, and when I offered my help the boys were overjoyed. I was from Yale and that meant plenty.

"Our only agreement was that they were to do just what I said, and they did it faithfully. We went to work and although we had to finish out a couple of games with only ten players, we finished up the season with 143 points to our opponents' 22, and most of these were in that only losing game. They played football the way I had learned it at Yale, and their opponents didn't play it that way.

"My two halfbacks were honeys ... just as good on defense as they were in carrying the ball.

When I took charge of the team, they were inclined toward Princeton. I always liked Princeton, but naturally I talked Yale to them. They did go to Yale, and I look upon them as my gift to my school. They were Tad and Howard Jones."

After preparing at Exeter, where they added to their athletic statures, Tad and Howard arrived at Yale in September 1904, quiet, serious, and straitlaced. All his life Howard remained an ascetic, but after his playing days Tad decided the Gates of Hell did not necessarily wait around the corner from a highball, a cigar, or a flyer in the market.

Admitted with four conditions, including Latin and math, Tad had to study very hard his freshman year, but was straightened away by the time he was a sophomore. That fall, 1905, he played a lot of quarterback, and in the spring he caught for the baseball team. The New York Giants offered him a contract for $5,000, but he didn't want to turn pro, and he preferred football.

Tad bridged the advent of the forward pass in 1906, playing one season before it and two with it. He was in the lineup for the 1906 opener, Wesleyan, October 3, at Yale Field, when probably the first forward pass in an Eastern game, and one of the first anyplace, was thrown by Wesleyan's Sammy Moore to Irvin Van Tassel for 18 yards. Walter Camp equipped Yale with several pass plays, including a tackle-eligible number, called after a meaningless wisecrack of the day, "Twenty-Three Skidoo!" With "Twenty-Three Skidoo," Tad Jones set up the only touchdown in the victory over Harvard at Yale Field, 6–0. (This tackle-eligible pass was still functional over 60 years later until the rules committee outlawed it.)

Tad and Howard Jones never played in a losing game at Yale; in their three seasons, 1905, '06, '07, the record was 28 victories and two scoreless ties, Princeton in '06, Army in '07.

The closest thing to defeat was a memorable comeback victory over Princeton at Yale Field in '07, with Tad first the goat and then one of the heroes. An onside kick Tad had blocked was turned into a touchdown and propelled the scrappy Tigers into a 10–0 lead at halftime. A thunderous upset seemed imminent, and in the Yale dressing room Tad sat against a wall and fought back tears.

Then he went out and turned the game around in the third period with his smart, nifty running and hard-nosed stiff-arm to return a punt 40

yards to the Princeton 32. He was aided by the truckamuck blocking of sophomore Ted Coy, already a Homeric fullback.

With Tad calling the plays and Ted Coy ripping up the Tiger line, Yale rallied to score two touchdowns and win, 12–10, in a context of such drama that William Lyon (Billy) Phelps, beloved professor and football buff, was inspired to tell a mass rally on Tuesday, "If I live to be 85 years old, I will never forget last Saturday's game, for I never have and never will see anything like it."

Tad's last game was a 12–0 victory at Harvard the next week, and he was named All-America quarterback. After graduation in 1908, he stayed on as backfield coach that fall, and in 1909 and '10, at Syracuse, his first head coaching assignment, his teams won half their games in hard schedules. In 1911 he coached a boys school in Pawling, New York, returned to Exeter as an assistant coach in 1912, and the next three years was head coach of superior Exeter teams.

Meanwhile, Yale was sweating through its first real downcurve. Scoreless ties with Harvard were managed in 1910 and '11, but the next four years Haughton's teams trounced the Elis. The 36–0 drubbing that dedicated Yale Bowl in 1914 prompted the gag: "Yale had the Bowl, but Harvard had the punch." At Cambridge the next year, it was worse, 41–0. The story against Princeton was happier, Yale winning three, tying two, losing one. But Army, Brown, Washington & Jefferson, Colgate, Virginia, Vanderbilt, and Maine were able to tie or beat the Elis. In six years, their record was 36–14–7; in six years the ex-scourge lost as many games as it had in the previous 34.

The causes were three: the organized Haughton at Harvard, growing power among more and more teams, and an internal fight for power between Walter Camp and those who would unseat him. In the fight, Camp finally went down, and Yale with him.

Following the 1915 debacle at Harvard, a rugged, spirited guard was elected captain for 1916. His name was Clinton Rutherford Black, who had a torso and head that sort of resembled a rugged Cupid, so he was known as Cupe. An old Exeter boy, Cupe Black knew what Tad Jones could do, and he prevailed on a graduate selection committee to name him Yale's new coach.

Always an intense traditionalist, Tad set about solidifying old mores and mending old fences. He brought Walter Camp back into the picture. That

Tad (*right*) listening to the wisdom of Michigan's Fielding H. Yost. *Chicago Tribune Photos*

mystic temple of Yale football, Room 117, first at the old New Haven House, then the Quinnipiac Club, was now renewed in the old Bradley House on Wall Street. The coaches and players gathered there for blackboard talks, and were pioneers in studying action movies of themselves.

Under the inspiration of Tad Jones and Black, a quick-ranging Cupe who made tackles all over the field, Yale had her best team since Ted Coy's perfect-record 1909 powerhouse. The only defeat, 21–6, by Brown, was perpetrated by the Bruins' All-America Negro back, Fritz Pollard, who ran the ends and tackles for 184 yards and returned a punt through a broken field 60 yards for a touchdown. Colgate's best team until that time outplayed Yale but was upset, 7–3. Princeton was defeated, 10–0, on Jim Braden's field goal and a touchdown set up by a halfback-to-halfback pass from Joe Neville to Harry Legore. Best of all, Harvard was beaten in the Bowl, 6–3.

When Traver (Shorty) Smith, the regular quarterback, came up with a bad throat before the Big Three games, it was typical of the team spirit that Chet LaRoche could step in at quarterback against Princeton and Harvard and do the job. The defense, though, was preeminent, especially in the second half against Harvard, when it made the 6–3 lead stand up. The Yale touchdown, scored by Neville on a fourth-down one-yard smash to climax a 50-yard drive, was Yale's first against the old rival in nine years.

The victory touched off a celebration that didn't back off until after January 19, when a record gathering of Old Blues dined at the Yale Club. Afterwards, 2,000 attended the Century Theater to see Elsie Janis in *The Century Girl*. Yale blue decorated everything even unto stage effects and costuming. Yale songs and cheers filled the intermission, and after the final curtain Miss Janis and the audience beguiled Cupe Black into coming onto the stage and joining her in leading a Yale cheer.

The songs and cheers were soon smothered by the drums of World War I. Yale had hoped that 1916 would be the first year of a new dynasty, but by fall the call to arms had left only a freshman team from the ROTC, which Tad coached until the government's request to build ships in Seattle. In 1918 there was no team. When the game was renewed in 1919, Yale lagged behind Harvard and Princeton again. Haughton was too busy in the bond business to return to Cambridge. (The great P.D. was lured back into football at Columbia and was building the Lions when a heart attack on the field early in the 1924 season caused his death.) He was replaced by Fisher, who delivered undefeated teams in 1919 and '20 and a 25-game defeatless string.

It was snapped in the seventh game of the '21 season, 6–0, by little Centre College of Danville, Kentucky, on a spectacular 32-yard run by the storied quarterback, Alvin (Bo) McMillin, an upset that rocked the nation as no other ever had.

The 1919 Harvard team, first and last to play in a Bowl other than Yale's, defeated Oregon, 7–6, in a bristling dramatic battle at Pasadena, New Year's Day, 1920, an appropriate kickoff of the Golden Twenties.

From 1919 through '22, Harvard won all four games from Yale, but had to accept two defeats and two ties from Princeton. The Tigers, coached by Bill Roper, another titan of inspiration, was undefeated in 1920 and '22, and beat Yale three out of four. The loss by Princeton at New Haven in 1921 was Old Eli's only Big Three victory from 1919 through '22.

In 1919, Tad was still involved in shipbuilding at Seattle, so Yale called on Al Sharpe, halfback on Gordon Browne's 1900 champions, Yale's best of the prepass era. Sharpe's credentials were excellent; his 1915 Cornell team, undefeated and a strong claimant of the national championship, had defeated Michigan, Pennsylvania, and one of Haughton's strongest Harvard teams. A brass-band parade and a welcoming committee escorted Al from the railroad station to the Yale campus. Fumbles and broken signals plagued him, however, as Yale lost to Princeton, 13–6, and Harvard, 10–3. Al left without band, parade, or farewell committee, while Tim Callahan, guard and captain in both 1919 and '20, brought back Tad Jones.

Once again, Tad had to reorganize and build back and it took him longer than in 1916. He was able immediately to establish a strong defense; field goals, a recovered fumble, and a 51-yard end run from a fake kick by Princeton quarterback Don Lourie accounted for the 1920 losses to the Tigers and Harvard, 20–0 and 9–0. But the Crimson's three field goals were set up by mingling passes with runs, while Yale's overdevotion to the off-tackle play resulted in underuse of the pass, except as a dying gasp near the end of the half or the game.

For the first time Tad Jones heard alumni and towner rumblings, but criticism never shook him and he still had much going for him. The big victory over Harvard in 1916 still served him in this and later storms. Malcolm (Mac) Aldrich, brilliant halfback and 1921 captain-elect, wanted him back. He enjoyed the support of Louis E. Goddard, tough-minded chairman of the graduate coaching committee. He also had a prosperous coal-shipping business in New Haven.

His critics didn't have a chance. He was signed to a four-year contract at $10,000 a year, and immediately set about acquiring the unified support of all Old Blues by a series of meetings in the Y Club, above the Yale Co-op then on High Street.

Tad looked forward hopefully to 1921. Such veterans as Aldrich, Ralph (Doc) Jordan, and Cam Beckett in the backfield, and Justin Sturm, Al Into, Phil Cruikshank, and Tubby Guernsey in the line were augmented by sophomores from the

powerful freshman team that beat Harvard and Princeton, 17–3 and 28–3. They included end Tony Hulman, tackle Jack (Tex) Diller, center Houston (Judge) Landis, quarterback Charlie O'Hearn, halfback Newell Neidlinger, and fullback William Neely (Bull) Mallory.

The 1921 season marked the first of 15 annual visits by Army to Yale Bowl, accompanied by the entire Corps of Cadets. An automatic sellout, a classic of color and competition, it has been transcended by few, if any, rivalries. Hitherto, no Army team had been permitted to leave the Academy for a football game, except the one with Navy. Earlier games with Yale and Harvard were always played at West Point. The Yale series had been broken off after the 1912 game was played in an atmosphere of acute asperity between the rival coaches.

Now the Corps was marching out Chapel Street to the Bowl, and the natives were lining the curbs and thrilling to the perfect cadence of the files of gray. One old gentleman, refusing to go overboard, was heard to grump, "No wonder they march pretty. All they do up that place is drill." And a little boy inquired, "Are they Americans, mamma?"

West Point tradition has it that after the first Army game in the Bowl, a plebe was asked the reason for the left-oblique movement in marching. "Sir," he replied, "it is designed to keep the Corps from being run over by one man trolley cars on Chapel Street in New Haven."

The running, passing, and kicking of Mac Aldrich, the running of Charlie O'Hearn, and stout defensive play beat Army, 14–7, and Princeton, 13–7, for Yale's first Big Three victory since 1916.

For a time at Harvard, it appeared the Blue might complete a perfect season. A 28-yard run by Aldrich set up his field goal from the 20, and he made other sizable gains. On one of them he used referee Tiny Maxwell as a blocker, naturally to the irritation of Harvard. Tiny, an excellent official with a stutter and a sense of humor, rode out the situation with a typical comment, "T-t-t-t-time out, w-w-w-while I g-g-get my b-b-b-blue jersey!"

Yale was still in control in the third period, until two of its all-time Harvard tormentors, little quarterback Charlie Buell and halfback George Owen, went to work. Buell, whose passes and two field goals had featured Harvard's 9–0 victory the year before, returned a punt 34 yards to the Yale

11. Owen smashed over on the second play of the fourth quarter, and Buell converted for a 7–3 lead. Late in the game, Owen dropkicked a 31-yard field goal and Harvard won, 10–3

Yale had won seven battles but had lost the war, so there was more grumbling, yet Tad had plenty of supporters, including some radical chauvinists who claimed Yale would rather lose under Tad Jones than win under anybody else.

In 1922, Tad again looked forward hopefully. Captain Doc Jordan led a strong nucleus of returning lettermen, and another vigorous sophomore group was coming up.

The Elis were plagued, however, by injuries, ennui, and the tendency of Yale teams in the immediate postwar years to dissipate scoring opportunities. They were also playing some mighty fine teams. Army, which was undefeated and played a scoreless tie with Notre Dame, was tied, 7–7. Princeton's "Team of Destiny," also undefeated, won, 3–0, by a goal-line stand. Iowa, undefeated Big Ten champions for the second straight year, and on a 20-game winning streak, definitely outplayed the Elis but that season was held to its fewest points in winning, 6–0.

The game was memorable for pitting the Jones brothers, Howard and Tad, against each other. A third brother, Tom Jones, a Yale student, liked to bet and tried to get some inside dope from both his brothers, to no avail. At length, loyalty to college prevailed and Tom bet on Yale. Whether he got odds is unknown.

Against Harvard in the Bowl it was the same story as in 1921; Harvard won, 10–3, with George Owen leading the way by returning a punt 31 yards to the Yale 4, smashing over on third down, and converting. Premier Clemenceau, who looked on, said football was sporting and Harvard agreed, but Old Blues said football was becoming insufferable.

Harvard had won eight of its last nine games with Yale and Tad heard an "Anvil Chorus" that was not emanating from Shubert's Theater. He accepted it philosophically except for the part he felt was coming from those who bet on games, be they alumni or downtown New Haven gamblers.

"I won't be driven out," he said, "by a crowd of tailor-shop gamblers, nor will they dictate Yale's athletic policy."

His sleeves were rolled up when he said it, for he was already at work on the 1923 season.

The 1923 team stood firm as No. 1 in Yale's history. Few, if any, Eastern squads ever had

more diversified talent, depth, and savor for the game, and it played in a day when the old Eastern schools could still compete at the national championship level: Harvard, 1919 through '21; Princeton, 1920 and '22; Cornell, 1921 through '23; Dartmouth, 1925; Yale, 1923 and '27.

In "Memphis Bill" Mallory, Tad had an inspirational 1923 captain. Neely, as he was known to his roomie, Ted Blair, had backed up the line and been a superb blocker for two years. He was an aggressive player who might worry inordinately about a boil on his neck but risk the neck itself in a game.

Through the years, a whisper of a legend grew that Yale, wearied of Harvard's almost invariable success under Haughton and Fisher, built the 1923 team by scouring the country for every tramp athlete on the loose.

That is the legend. These are the facts. The '23 team issued from three founts; first, the development of the strong 1920 freshman team; second, similar escalation of the comparable '21 frosh; third, the availability of four exceptionally talented transfers: tackle Century Milstead, halfbacks Mal Stevens and Widdy Neale, and quarterback Lyle Richeson.

Century Milstead got his unusual first name from being born on January 1, 1900. His father argued the infant had arrived with the new century, but his mother contended correctly that the new century would not begin until January 1, 1901. They named him Century anyhow, and his dad never did agree that the reasoning behind the choice was invalid.

Century had been a powerhouse tackle at Wabash College, Indiana, in 1921, and had created a sensation in a game at West Point by playing with a handlebar moustache. His playing was also sensational and Yale scouts reported it to Tad Jones. Century also heard about Yale, and after a brief stay at Syracuse in the fall of 1922, showed up at Tad's office in the old Y Club.

He would not be eligible until 1923, so Tad ordered him to forget football and concentrate on his studies. Century was crestfallen but obedient. Since he did not have very much money, he got himself a part-time job stoking furnaces in the Hotel Taft. The job didn't tire him much; nothing did. By the Wednesday before the Princeton game, he decided he could stay away from football no longer.

The varsity was polishing up in a scrimmage against the scrubs. They were coached by Dr.

Billy Bull, the old Yale kicking ace, and known as "Bull's Bastards." Although Century had no pads on, he talked Dr. Bull into letting him get in with the "Bastards." On the first two plays, he threw the ball carrier for losses of five and ten yards and Bull quickly got him out before he hurt somebody. He was six feet four, 220, with unusual strength and quickness, and would make the 1923 All-America team without sweat.

The second of the celebrated transfers, Marvin Allen (Mal) Stevens, from Stockton, Kansas, had been an All-State halfback at Washburn College. He came to Yale, however, to study medicine, his childhood ambition. He doubted he was good enough to play for Yale, and didn't go out until the third week of practice. Tad was unimpressed by his lateness and his slight build, but was prevailed on by Johnny Mack, the Yale trainer, to give him a chance. Tad soon found he had a spectacular all-round star on his hands. (For more about Mal Stevens, see his profile herein.)

The third of the transfers, quarterback Lyle Richeson, had earned letters at Tulane in 1918, '19, and '20, but got into some sort of contretemps with the faculty. His father wired Harvard if it would accept him as a transfer. Harvard wouldn't but Yale did. The chairman of the Yale Board of Admissions was Professor Bob Corwin, the old 1886 football captain and later a faculty power in athletics.

Richeson, Stevens, and Milstead entered in '22, sat out the transfer-rule year, and had only the '23 season of eligibility. Widdy Neale had entered in 1921, so he played in '22 and '23. Neale's first name was William, but he was known as Widdy because as a child he was such a "widdy" fellow, unlike his big brother Earle, who was known as Greasy.

Widdy had played a year at West Virginia in 1919, and Greasy tried to get him enrolled at Yale in 1920, but Professor Corwin said no. Greasy then told Corwin he was going to coach at Marietta and asked whether Widdy, if he went there a year and got good marks, would be accepted. Corwin okayed that, and Widdy arrived at New Haven in '21.

All four transfers were stars on a team of stars that included Mallory, Neidlinger, Diller, and Blair. Edwin (Ted) Blair, from Weatherford, Texas, also the home of singer Mary Martin, came up to Yale through Terrill School in Dallas and Hotchkiss Prep. Ted, a Phi Beta Kappa, was an outstanding tackle. It is doubtful Yale

ever had a better pair of tackles than Milstead and Blair.

The 1923 team had a terrific attack, fast, powerful, diversified, and Richeson exploited it beautifully. Stevens, Pond, Neidlinger, and Neale were used in various combinations at left half and fullback, striking from a single wing, a short punt, and a spread. Charlie O'Hearn was a fifth star halfback until he broke an ankle in the Bucknell game.

Mallory, who lined up at wingback, was used primarily as a blocker, and so he could get into the business of scoring a little, worked hard as a place-kicker under Doc Bull. This was to pay off against Harvard.

Teaming with right end Dick Luman, or by himself, Mallory was a master at neutralizing the defensive left tackle, while Dick Eckart, who lined up as inside guard on the strong side of center, was the key pull blocker on the end or the secondary.

Yale, which had been derelict with the pass, now used it to bedevil. Much of the answer, of course, lay in the material; Stevens and Neale could throw the ball, and Luman, Richeson, and others could catch it.

The defense was equally impressive. Bucknell scored 14 points on passes in the second half of a game Yale already had won. Maryland also got 14, mostly in screen passes, but that was the Saturday before Princeton. Tad was in Palmer scouting the Tigers against Harvard, and almost everybody was relaxing. Army's 10 points came on a field goal and a long punt return. That was all the scoring on Mallory's team. With the pressure on and the first string in action, they gave up little ground.

Their all-triumphant march comprised North Carolina, 53–0; Georgia, 40–0; Bucknell, 29–14; Brown, 21–0; Army, 31–10; Maryland, 16–14; Princeton, 27–0; Harvard, 13–0. The margin over Princeton was the biggest since 1890.

It was in the second half against Army, however, that Mallory's team, trailing 10–7, put on perhaps the most spectacular 30-minute offensive show in Yale history. They lined up in a spread, and the Cadets, who had held the once-defeated 1923 Four Horsemen team to 13–0, were run, passed, and kicked dizzy.

Consider it. Neale took the kickoff back to his 20, and he and Stevens bit off 11 yards. Stevens passed 25 to Richeson, but fumbled to Army the next play for a slight delay. Soon Yale was on the

Cadet 48, and Stevens, a Light Brigadier charging Balaklava Heights, went knee churning off tackle for 20 to the 28. Three end runs, by Stevens, Richeson, and Neale, brought it to the 17, whence Neale passed to Luman for a touchdown and Neale converted.

When Army, trailing, 14–10, went into the air, Richeson intercepted and sped back to the Cadet 39. Neidlinger rocketed off tackle, reversed the secondary, and went 39 yards for a score, and Stevens converted. In the fourth period, Neidlinger raced 17 more to preface a 20-yard pass from Stevens to Richeson that set up a Mallory field goal from the 17. Richeson's interception and 32-yard return for a touchdown, and Stevens' conversion made it 31–10.

Yale made 323 yards rushing against Army, averaging four yards a crack, and completed seven of 11 passes for 63 more. Army completed three of nine passes, but had five intercepted, including the two important ones by Richeson.

There was hope of an even finer performance at Harvard. There was even talk of avenging that 41–0 shellacking there in 1915. But ten hours before kickoff it began to rain and blow a nor'easter, and what it was the next day was not football.

The downpour turned the gridiron into a swamp. Yale fumbled 11 times, recovered 10; Harvard fumbled 14 times, also recovered 10. Yale punted 28 times; Harvard 26. Yale, its speed and talent immobilized, needed a break. It came early in the second period. Backed near his own goal line, Neale's punt got only as far as the Yale 32, but when halfback Marion Cheek fielded it, Mallory slammed into him so fiercely, he dropped the ball.

Raymond (Ducky) Pond, coming up the field, scooped it up, evaded one tackler, and headed for the Harvard goal 68 yards away. Luman's block eliminated a mud-daubed Crimson who might have made trouble. Pond, one of the best mudders who ever ran a ball, somehow kept his feet in the quagmire. The last 25 yards he was seen to look back over his shoulder at a small mud-covered figure, Yale or Harvard you couldn't tell which, but giving pursuit. Then the little figure gave Pond a reassuring wave; it was Widdy Neale. Ducky touched the ball down and Mallory gave it a thumping kick for the extra point.

The 7–0 would have been enough, but in the second half, Mallory gave an exhibition of place-kicking that, considering the conditions, must

rank among the finest. He tried three field goals, from the 24, the 31, and the 29, and missed only the second. He was aided considerably by center Winslow Lovejoy, who could snap any kind of football, even one sogged and mud-caked, with the accuracy of a machine. His proficiency would amaze modern centers, who snap the deep pass only for punts and place-kicks. After Mallory's second three-pointer, the Yales felt safe to sing "The Undertaker Song" for the first time since 1916.

The 1924 team, captained by Win Lovejoy, was savagely depleted by graduation, but did an excellent job, winning all its games except ties with Army, 7–7, and Dartmouth, 14–14. The Big Green, returning to the schedule after a 24-year lapse, was in a 22-game defeatless streak under Jess Hawley and well-starred with Swede Oberlander, Eddie Dooley, George Tully, Hank Bjorkman, and others. The exciting flow and counterflow, Yale going ahead, 7–0, Dartmouth recovering to take a 14–7 lead, and the Elis coming back to tie it, had the crowd of 50,000 in several dithers, and set the tempo for a generally mad and marvelous rivalry.

Princeton was beaten in Palmer Stadium, 10–0, on a 43-yard field goal by Harry Scott and a 42-yard punt return by quarterback Tibby Bunnell that set up a tackle-eligible pass from Ducky Pond to Johnny Joss.

Execrable weather again hung over the Yale-Harvard game, as 73,000 sat through a drenching rain. Yale's backs removed all their padding, wore only jerseys, pants, socks, and cleats. They smeared pitch on their arms to hold the damp ball, and committed only three fumbles, as the unerring Captain Lovejoy made not a single bad snap.

With the wind at its back, Harvard led unexpectedly at the half on two field goals by Erwin Gehrke, but in the second half, Pond and another fine mudder, sophomore Bill Kline, pounded through the wet on three hardy, urgent scoring drives, with Pond going over once and Kline twice, for a 19–6 victory.

Somewhere around this time, "Sheriff" Bill McGeehan, conductor of the scintillant "Down the Line" sports column in the New York *Herald Tribune*, advised Harvard, tongue in cheek, that it should offer its president even up for a good quarterback. Although Tad Jones recognized the gag, he was disturbed by the implication that Harvard football was *in extremis*, and wrote a friendly but firm protest to McGeehan, in which he said, "Don't be rediculous."

The misspelling provided the Sheriff with more delightful fodder for columns in which he questioned the caliber of Yale academics, citing as proof the poor spelling by its football coach. This got Tad quite a kidding in New Haven.

Fun was less in evidence through 1925 and '26. The '25 team was beaten 25–12 by Princeton, once defeated (Colgate), and its star running back, Jake Slagle. Harvard, which should have been handled, escaped with a scoreless tie through Yale fumbles and arguments among the backs. The '26 team, first in Yale history to lose four straight—Brown, Army, Maryland, Princeton—scored a redeeming victory over Harvard in the Bowl, 12–7. The Elis led when left tackle Guy Richards blocked a kick and Herb (Cobbles) Sturhahn, outstanding guard, recovered. Yale missed the point and Harvard went ahead 7–6 on a sensational 50-yard scoring pass from Henry Chauncey to Nat Saltonstall, and Chauncey's conversion. But sub halfback Jimmy Wadsworth put Yale ahead with a 23-yard field goal and Captain Bunnell kicked another.

In the long range, Tad had envisioned another outstanding team on the horizon for 1927, and announced it would be his last season. Now 40, he was at his peak as a coach, for he had continually learned and improved.

His '27 team, sometimes overshadowed by '23's, had an even stronger line, perhaps Yale's greatest. Dwight Fishwick and Stewie Scott were exceptionally fine ends, Sid (Red) Quarrier and Max Eddy were well above average tackles, and at the guards, Captain Bill Webster and Waldo (Firp) Greene were comparably able. The center, John (Bud) Charlesworth also was outstanding.

The backfield was not as deep or talented, but until triple-threat Bruce Caldwell was declared ineligible before the Princeton game, for having played two games as a freshman at Brown in '23, the offense could move against the best. It was a tribute to the team that without Caldwell it could still defeat powerful, previously unbeaten Princeton in the Bowl.

The schedule was a tough one, in fact as well as name. The only defeat was by Georgia's finest team up to that time, the "Dream and Wonder Team" with All-America Tom Nash at end. The Bulldogs conquered Alabama and Tulane teams coached by Wallace Wade and Bernie Bierman, and lost only to Bill Alexander's Georgia Tech

club that went through with only a loss to Knute Rockne's Irishmen. Georgia, outplayed but saved by a goal-line stand, was glad to escape. Army, with a dazzling sophomore back, Red Cagle, conquered Notre Dame and lost only to Yale, 10–6. Dartmouth's only loss was also to Yale.

Tad Jones and Bill Roper had entered into a nonscouting agreement that year, so all Yale and Princeton knew about each other was that each was good. How good, they'd have to find out in the Bowl. Tad's old friend Al Jolson was playing at Shubert's, and Tad asked him if he'd say a few words to them in the dressing room.

"They're a little tight, Al," he said, "and I think you could loosen them up with a few words or a couple of jokes."

"I'll do it, Tad," said Jolson. "In fact, if you'll stand for it, I'll even sing them a song."

So Al Jolson sang to the Yale team before it went out for the kickoff. He sang "California, Here I Come." Since Yale wasn't interested in a Rose Bowl bid, he might better have rendered "Blue Skies."

He also talked to the players and he did loosen them up. What he said amounted to a pep talk. Some of them looked at one another and at Tad and back at Jolson. They weren't sure Al wasn't gagging. He wasn't; he was dead serious.

For the first 50 minutes, it looked bad for Yale. Princeton scored on a 75-yard drive in the second period and led, 6–0, with 10 minutes to go. Then with the ball on the Tiger 40, halfback Johnny Hoben threw a deep diagonal pass that Fishwick, in the clear at the 10, gathered in and raced for the score. Not before or since has a single play set off such a crowd detonation in Yale Bowl. Duncan Cox converted for a 7–6 lead and Yale scored another after recovering a fumble on the 20. Cox again converted and the final was 14–6.

In freezing cold at Cambridge the next Saturday, Ted Jones sent his last Yale team against Harvard in his last game. Touchdown runs by Johnny Garvey and Bill Hammersley, for 52 and 42 yards (Garvey's, the first from scrimmage by Yale in Harvard Stadium since 1907), and Cox's conversions accounted for the 14–0 wrap-up and Tad's fourth Big Three championship.

Perhaps something Tad did in his last game best typifies him. John (Mike) Flaherty had been a regular at the beginning of the 1925 and '26 seasons only to be shelved by leg and elbow injuries. He got into the '26 Harvard game, however, long enough to win his letter.

In 1927 Flaherty had looked forward to a change in luck. He saw a lot of action as right tackle substitute to Max Eddy, but again the jinx hit him, this time a broken ankle. He wore a cast on the leg until a week before the Harvard game, but could not possibly play, and didn't expect to make the trip.

To his surprise and joy, Mike heard Tad read off his name among those who'd travel with the varsity to Cambridge. That was swell. He couldn't make his letter, because he couldn't move on his leg, but at least he'd be suited up and on the bench.

Two minutes before the end of the game, Mike got another surprise, when Tad called out, "Flaherty, go in there and report for Quarrier at tackle." Mike went onto the field, but before a play could be run, Tad, who knew he was in no condition for contact, replaced him with another sub. But Flaherty had been in the game officially and had won his Y.

That was Thomas Albert Dwight Jones, King of the Squares all the way.

Andy Kerr

MAKER OF MAGICIANS

Grantland Rice used to lead off his daily syndicated column, "The Sportlight," with a piece of verse, sometimes serious, sometimes light, always catchy. To be the subject of Rice's rhyming meant the team or individual had truly been tapped for fame. Such were the Colgate football teams from 1929 through '34, coached by a tiny, canny, fatherly but demanding kind of man named Andy Kerr. The deceptive Colgate double-wingback attack, with its multiple spinners, reverses, and laterals, evoked these lines from Rice:

Andy Kerr, at Colgate, 1935. *Chicago Tribune Photos*

The call goes up from the battlefield as the Raider backs swing by,

We know how to dive for a flying leg under an Autumn sky,

We can beat the shock of the body crash, whenever the crash is due,

Human to human, we fear no foe when our tackling's sharp and crisp,

But how in the name of the gods of chance, do you tackle a will-o'-the-wisp?

Give us a runner that we can see—slip us a shot at the ball—

Our feet are fast and our hands are quick, our eyes are young and keen,

But how can we follow a flock of ghosts over the churned-up green?

The legerdemain Rice sang of, the magical shell game played by the Red Raiders of the Chenango Valley, was highlighted by their adept use of the lateral pass. The lateral, adopted from Rugby, has always been part of American football. No coach got more out of it than Andy Kerr.

Kerr's Colgate teams used the lateral in three forms:

1. the buck lateral, in which the fullback handed the ball to a pivoting tackle, who flipped it to a back or an end coming around;
2. the forward lateral, or flea flicker, in which the end or halfback who caught the pass pitched it by prearrangement to another player;
3. the extemporaneous downfield lateral, in which a runner about to be tackled tossed the ball to another player.

One of the most spectacular shows ever witnessed by a New York football crowd came in Colgate's victory over Tulane at Yankee Stadium in 1934, 20–6. The Red Raiders' artistry with the lateral bemused the Green Wave. Ironically, the most exciting play ended in a fumble; on a Colgate punt return, the ball was lateraled four times, from Dick Offenhamer to Ike Kern to Don Irwin to Dutch Bausch to Steve Kuk. A fifth lateral was fumbled by Joe Bogdanski, with Offenhamer, the point of origin, standing by hopefully to take No. 6 and go in for a touchdown.

That year Colgate completed 24 extemporaneous laterals and met with only one defeat, by Ohio State, 10–7. Francis Schmidt, Ohio's coach, himself an apostle of the wide-open game, paid tribute to Kerr and his Red Raiders:

"Colgate offers one of the most modern offenses in the country, and they don't think any

more of tossing a lateral than they do of taking a shower after the game ... they fired the pigskin around like a major league baseball team during infield practice. ... We were lucky enough to eke out a 10–7 victory and even now we don't know how."

Colgate reduced the fumble danger of the lateral in long practice sessions driven by Kerr.

"In the developing of lateral passes, I put great stress on ball-handling," Kerr told football authority Allison Danzig in 1951. "For this phase of the game I received much information from Rugby coaches and players of Stanford University, as well as from one outstanding Canadian Rugby coach. Our ball-handling was perfected to the point where the boys could handle multiple passes with accuracy and precision under tremendous pressure in the scoring zone."

Beneath the colorful open-field facade, Kerr also taught the soundest fundamentals, offense and defense. He assisted Glenn Scobey (Pop) Warner at Pittsburgh for seven seasons, 1915 through '21. When Warner after the '21 season agreed to take the coaching job at Stanford, but not until his contract with Pittsburgh expired two years hence, he had such confidence in Kerr that he sent him ahead to Palo Alto. There, as head coach in 1922 and '23, Andy installed the Warner single- and double-wingback attack and stayed on as Pop's backfield coach through 1925.

There were some who thought that Kerr could teach the Warner system better than Warner himself. Lloyd Jordan, who played under Warner and Kerr at Pittsburgh and later was head coach at Williams and Harvard and then commissioner of the Southern Conference, said, "I have never seen a man who could take an idea and develop it to the extent he could."

Whether Kerr, the disciple, surpassed Warner, the formation father, is debatable. But statistics make an interesting point: the two best major independent records in the East, from 1929 through '34, were made by two of Warner's students, Kerr, who had coached under him at Pittsburgh and Stanford, and Dr. John Bain (Jock) Sutherland, who had played guard under him at Pitt:

	W	L	T
Colgate under Kerr	47	5	1
Pittsburgh under Sutherland	47	7	3

In those years the Colgate breakdown shows: 1929, 8–1–0; 1930, 9–1–0; 1931, 8–1–0; 1932, 9–0–0; 1933, 6–1–1; 1934, 7–1–0. The defeats were by Wisconsin, 13–6, in '29; Michigan State, 14–7, in '30; New York University, 13–0, in '31; Tulane, 7–0, in '33; and Ohio State, 10–7, in '34.

As the thirties advanced, defenses caught up with the double wing and the material fell off on Kerr. In contrast to his record for the first six years at Colgate—47–5–1—the log for the last 12 showed 48–45–6.

After he retired from Colgate at 68 in 1946, Kerr coached three more seasons at Lebanon Valley where he still tinkered successfully with imaginative formations. In 1951 he was named to the Football Hall of Fame.

Kerr's outstanding team at Colgate was 1932, which defeated St. Lawrence 41–0, Case 27–0, Niagara 47–0, Lafayette 35–0, New York University 14–0, Penn State 31–0, Mississippi A. & M. 32–0, Syracuse 16–0, and Brown 21–0. The line responsible for the nine shutouts comprised Winnie Anderson, Vernon Lee, Bob Smith, Joe Hill, Ed Prondecki, Bart Ellis, and Glen Peters. Anderson stood out at end; Smith and Hill, superior guards, pulled out of the line to lead interference.

John F. (Count) Orsi, three-year regular at end, captain and All-America in 1931, and for seven years Kerr's assistant, wrote of the '32 team: "This was not a large team, such as the ones in the previous years (not over 200 pounds), but it was strong and fast, averaged about 190 pounds, and had fine precision."

Charlie Soleau was the 1932 quarterback, and he got a lot of yardage out of the double spinner, which Kerr installed that year. "The fullback, Bob Rowe," Andy explained, "took the ball and pivoted as if to give to the quarterback, who spun toward the fullback. The fullback would either keep the ball, give it to the quarterback, or hand it to one of the wingbacks coming round."

The game in which Colgate unveiled the double spinner, the 35–0 victory over Lafayette, was also the day the team first became known as the Red Raiders. Colgate's color is maroon, but Andy dressed them that day and thenceforth in bright red jerseys.

As the season progressed, Kerr reached for fresh motivation. First, it was not to lose, then it was not to be scored on. By the sixth game, with Penn State, he was exhorting the Raiders not to permit a first down. This caused guard Joe Hill to ask, "What in the heck will he ask us to work for in the last two games."

Andy (*left*) with Northwestern's Dick Hanley in 1933.
Chicago Tribune Photos

Whatever it was, it worked.

Kerr told Ellery Huntington, Jr. Colgate All-America and football historian, that the 1932 team was his best, and praised it especially for its coachability:

"I have coached football squads that were more powerful physically than the 1932 squad. No squad ever surpassed them in intelligence. They absorbed everything that they were taught and executed it in an almost perfect manner."

This 1932 team is best remembered, oddly, for a game it never got to play, in the Rose Bowl. That year Southern California was the host team at Pasadena. The Trojans' first choice was Michigan, undefeated and Big Ten champion, but Western Conference policy at that time prohibited postseason games.

Instead of awaiting the formal turndown from Michigan, Bill Hunter, S.C.'s athletic director, invited Pittsburgh, although the Panthers had been badly trounced, 47–14, by the Trojans in the Rose Bowl three years before. Hunter's decision traced in part to Pitt's tougher schedule—the Panthers were undefeated, had beaten Notre Dame, and played scoreless ties with Ohio State and Nebraska. The selection of the Panthers also traced to a high-pressure job by Don Harrison, Pitt's athletic director, who went west and pleaded his case successfully.

In voicing the reaction of Colgate, Kerr coined a line that has become part of the game's lore, "We were undefeated, untied, unscored on, and uninvited." When Southern Cal again drubbed

Pitt, this time 35–0, Kerr's Big Four U's took on added validity.

Although his 1932 team ranks No. 1, Kerr's earlier once-beaten Colgate teams also rate very high. The 1929 team gave up only 19 points and its victims included Michigan State, Indiana, Columbia, Syracuse, and Brown. "I think the '29 team actually was Andy's finest," said John Orsi, a sophomore that year. "It was a group that continuously had reunions with Andy, and will continue to have reunions, even though Andy has passed on. Our 40th anniversary was held in 1969."

Les Hart did the passing in '29, and Tommy Dowler the running; John Cox was a superior center, and quarterback Julius Yablock was smart and a hard blocker.

The 1930 team featured the inside running of Len (Iron Legs) Macaluso, who led the nation in scoring with 145 points. The combination of Macaluso's running and Hart's passing led the Maroon and White to 383 points, and it gave up only 27. Tom Doyle and Les Lockwood ran strong interference from their guard posts, and 245-pound Art Schiebel and Bart Ellis provided superior tackle play.

In a postseason "Charity Bowl" game in New York, the '30 team edged NYU 7–6 as Orsi caught a touchdown pass and blocked the Violets' extra-point attempt. Macaluso carried the ball 32 times, and kicked the winning point.

NYU revenged itself in 1931, 13–0, Colgate's only defeat that year, as Kerr fielded a new but effective backfield: Bob Samuel, blocking quarterback; Howie Controy and Whitey Ask, passers; and Johnnie Litser, almost as effective a plunger as Macaluso. Smith and Hill continued to be outstanding at guard, while Jim O'Hara teamed with Schiebel at tackle.

Although he did not get the credit due him until he later played for the Chicago Bears, guard Danny Fortmann may well have been the equal of any player Kerr coached at Colgate. He was a big reason the 1933 and '34 Raider teams each lost only one game.

When Kerr's career is considered—26 seasons, 137 victories, 71 defeats, and 14 ties for a .649 percentage—it is surprising that he was 36 before he became even a college assistant coach.

Andy was born in Cheyenne, Wyoming, October 7, 1878, of Scot and Irish forebears. His father drove cattle in Wyoming, Texas, and the Indian territory. His mother was born in Chicago,

but she traveled the Midwest by covered wagon with her father, an army officer.

When he was three, Kerr was moved to Carlisle, Pennsylvania, played there with Indian children who later attended Carlisle, and then himself attended Dickinson College, where he was a 130-pound quarterback, outfielder, and high jumper.

After studying some law, he opted for teaching at a business college in Johnstown, and at Johnstown High he did his first football coaching for $25 a week. He commuted between the business college and the high school on bicycle, and his squads were so small that he often scrimmaged one side of the line against the other and got into the action himself.

In 1914 he went to Pittsburgh as a track coach, and became Warner's football assistant the following year. From a 13–10 loss to Washington and Jefferson in the seventh game of the 1914 season until a 24–3 loss to Syracuse in the third game of 1919, Pittsburgh won 33 straight games, and shared in the national championship in 1915, '16, '17, and '18.

The 1915 team included three future coaches of note: guard Jock Sutherland, who built another dynasty at Pitt in the twenties and thirties, tackle Claude (Tiny) Thornhill, who coached three successive Pacific Coast Conference champions and Rose Bowl teams at Stanford in 1933, '34, and '35, and end Harold (Red) Carlson, who coached Pitt basketball for over 30 years.

The 1916 team, rated one of college football's strongest, numbered two All-Americans in center Bob Peck and fullback George McLaren. Later All-Americans were halfback Tom Davies, 1918–20, and center Herb Stein, 1918–21

Pop Warner in those years was at his coaching peak with his brainchildren: the single- and double-wingback attacks, and Kerr as his assistant derived much of the savvy that he later demonstrated at Colgate.

When Kerr went to Stanford in 1922 as Warner's advance man, he inherited a fun-loving squad that he had to discipline by degrees. On his first visit to the training table, baked apple with whipped cream was the dessert. By prearrangement all of the players pushed away the dessert, and when Kerr asked them why, he was told to smell his portion to find out. When he lifted the plate, one player hit it from the bottom and another pushed Kerr's face into it.

Kerr retained coolness; he wiped away the

The master reminiscing

mess on his face, joined in the laugh on him, and commented, "And I thought I was from the big city."

But he soon convinced his players that he could not only take it but dish it out. On a Sunday morning after an overnight train ride from a Saturday game in Oregon, Kerr and most of the squad found their pants missing. Finally, a porter located them in a women's washroom several cars away. The following Monday, Kerr drove his men harder than usual. As they trudged wearily off the field, he ordered three players whom he suspected of the pants theft to stay on for a long series of wind sprints. The starting signal was "pants."

Despite such hijinks, Kerr and Tiny Thornhill, the line coach, built a solid two-year foundation on which Warner, from 1924 through '27, developed a 32–5–3 record and three Rose Bowl teams. Kerr's contributions were well recognized and impelled Washington and Jefferson to extend its first three-year contract.

Truly on his own as head coach for the first

time, Kerr turned out a once-defeated team in 1926, an undefeated team in '27, and both years played scoreless ties with Pittsburgh, which under Sutherland was regaining its former stature under Warner. Andy's three-year record was 16–6–5, and his top player was fullback Bill Amos. In 1929 Kerr answered the call from Colgate.

Consistency was a big thing with Kerr. In his 18 years at Colgate he never missed a practice. He was equally steady in his superstitions; he never entered a room without touching both sides of the doorway.

Although Kerr maintained a fatherly relationship with his players off the field and down the years, he was a stringent taskmaster on the field; he had to be to produce such precisioned teams. When he felt it was called for, he could turn on the sarcasm.

Before one of the 1932 games, he told a substitute center: "I have a son in high school who snaps the ball better than you do." He later berated end Joe Bogdanski, "I have a son who weighs 120 pounds who blocks better than that."

"If the season had three weeks to go," one player commented, "Andy would make his boy the greatest all-round football player in America."

For many years Kerr spent much of his time helping to assemble and coach a team of Eastern senior all-stars against a similar all-West group in the Shriners hospital charity game in Kezar Stadium, San Francisco. This game, which provides money for the care of crippled children, had a special appeal for Kerr. Andy, though in tune with the essential harshness of football, was first of all a humanitarian. He was recognized as such, and reaction was positive to his own description of himself on a national radio program, "This I believe."

"At the center of my philosophy of life," he said, "has been the ideal of service; the desire to help my fellow man. ... I believe in God, the Creator and Ruler of the universe. I hold that a man's religious faith is the greatest single force in his life for good.

"My philosophy of life is based on faith in America ... and in my work. I have faith in my family ... and a necessary faith in myself. I have an abiding faith in God. In my life I have tried to express those faiths in service to my church, my community, and to mankind generally.

"This has given me a happy and satisfying philosophy of life."

If you had asked Andy Kerr to name his most satisfying single football game, his early nominations would surely have included the 13–7 victory over Brown, in 1931. Laterals were chiefly responsible for a hard-fought win. Pop Warner, a visitor, sat alongside Kerr on the Colgate bench that day, as Andy sweated it out.

"Those touchdowns came hard, Andy," said Pop afterwards. "Good thing you had those laterals."

"I suppose you could have done better with straight power, Pop," said Kerr.

"No," Warner replied. "Seriously, Andy, I'm tinkering with this lateral business."

Elmer Layden

THE CLIFF DWELLER COACH

In the years 1934 through '40 when Elmer Layden served as Notre Dame's athletic director and head football coach, Joe Petritz, then N.D.'s sports information director, told him, "Elmer, as an athletic director ... history will prove you great." Petritz was alluding to Layden's success as a schedule-maker, especially his ability to make profitable football dates with Western Conference schools.

Layden, renowned from his playing days as the lean, swift fullback of the Notre Dame Four Horsemen backfield of 1924, restored Iowa and Purdue to the schedule. He arranged games with Ohio State, Minnesota, and Illinois for the first time. As his biggest coup, he got Fielding H. (Hurry Up) Yost, Michigan athletic director and former head coach, to visit the Notre Dame campus. Yost had never got along with Knute Rockne; now, out of his visit, emerged home-and-home football games.

But what of Elmer Layden, the Notre Dame football coach? He too, the record insists, enjoyed success:

YEAR	W	L	T
1934	6	3	0
1935	7	1	1
1936	6	2	1
1937	6	2	1
1938	8	1	0
1939	7	2	0
1940	7	2	0
TOTALS	47	13	3

It's a natural reaction, after scanning that column, to ask: "Why did Layden leave Notre Dame?" Answer: the Very Reverend J. Hugh O'Donnell, president of the university, offered him only a one-year contract; a new policy, the priest said, to affect all lay employees. (Previously, Layden had worked under contracts for two and five years.) Soon after, Layden signed a five-year contract to become commissioner of the National Football League at $20,000 a year, close to double his salary at Notre Dame. In 1946 he became a sales executive with the General American Transportation Company.

Despite his winning record, some elements of the alumni, subway as well as real, were dissatisfied. The Win-'em-All school, the "dynostaurs," looked back fondly on the all-conquering Knute Rockne teams of 1919, '20, '24, '29, and '30, which had laid strong claims to the mythical national championship.

Frank Leahy would bring back such records in the forties. Nevertheless, looked at in historical perspective, Elmer Layden's coaching job at Notre Dame was excellent.

Notre Dame football was nurtured on miracles and lived with cliff-hanger games. As a cliff-hanger coach, nobody—not Rockne, not Leahy, not Ara Parseghian—surpassed Layden, if indeed, matched him. On November 2, 1935, at Columbus, Ohio, Layden's Notre Dame team came from behind for a last-ditch 18–13 victory over Ohio State in what was to become probably the most talked of single game in football history.

Ohio State and Notre Dame were both undefeated. The Buckeyes were deserved favorites, yet N.D.'s 5–0 record, against Kansas, Carnegie Tech, Wisconsin, Pittsburgh, and Navy, in which the Irish allowed a total of only 16 points, signified a respectable short-ender. Ohio State usually sells out its home games, but none had

Elmer Layden, in 1956. *Chicago Tribune Photos*

ever fired up Columbus like this one. Despite the depression, the 81,018 tickets were soon grabbed up.

The buildup for the Buckeyes gave Notre Dame a pregame psychological advantage, and Layden took full advantage of it. In Rockne's day, the South Bend *Tribune* had run an occasional football column under the by-line of Bearskin; nobody knew who Bearskin was, but many suspected Rockne himself. The prime purpose of the column was to deflate any egos that might need it. Layden exhumed Bearskin, and assigned Petritz to writing it. Bearskin's prime target was halfback Andy Pilney, whose talent had been plagued by fumbles. He was accused of having the largest scrapbook on campus.

When writers asked Layden for a prediction, he said, "We'll be lucky to hold Ohio State to 40 points." A Columbus newspaper ran this as a page-one headline.

"While Columbus was having pregame revelry," Layden wrote, "a train pulled out of South

Bend carrying those students who could afford a train ride and a ticket to the game. Each year there was a student trip, and the Ohio State game had been selected for 1935.

"A few of our players were also on this train," Layden pointed out. "We carried only forty players on trips; that was all we were permitted. But when a boy could pay his own way on the student trip and was willing to carry along his own uniform, we welcomed him to join us on the bench. That way he didn't have to buy a ticket.

"Among the handful of players on the student trip, lugging his uniform for his ticket of admission, was Dick McKenna, our fourth-string quarterback. When he arrived at the stadium, he had a devil of a time getting the guards to find one of our student managers to let him into our dressing room. Lucky for us he did get in, because as it turned out, we were to need him badly."

Ohio State dominated the first half to lead 13–0. Layden gave no emotional pep talk, but as calmly as possible pointed out mistakes. He started the second half with the second team that had Frank Gaul at quarterback and Pilney, Bearskin's target, at left half.

Pilney this day played up to his potential. It was his 47-yard return of a punt through an open field that brought the ball to Ohio's 13. On third down Pilney passed to Frank Gaul on the 1-yard line to set up a score by Steve Miller. The extra point was missed, so Ohio State led 13–6. A fumble aborted another N.D. drive on the 1, and the Irish had to start again from their 21 with only three minutes to go.

A third-down pass from Pilney to Wally Fromhart brought N.D. to Ohio's 38. Elmer Layden's brother Mike was in at right halfback. If anything, Elmer had leaned over backward in not using Mike. Mr. Layden, however, had advised him: "If you want a winning team, play your best ten men and your brother." Mike now proved his parent right by catching a touchdown pass from Pilney. A bad pass from center messed up the extra-point try. With less than two minutes to go, Ohio State led 13–12.

Notre Dame tried an onside kick but Ohio got the ball at midfield, and there were only 90 seconds left.

("One widely told story," wrote Layden, "is that my wife was sitting up in the stands near Father John O'Hara, Notre Dame president, who took this moment to console her by saying, 'Don't worry, Edythe, Elmer and his boys have done a fine job.' To which she is supposed to have replied, 'That's easy for you to say. Your job doesn't depend on it.' ")

Then came the decisive break. Ohio's Dick Beltz tried an end run, was swarmed over, and shaken lose from the ball. Since Notre Dame center Hank Pojman was the last to touch it before it went out of bounds, the Irish were in possession of it on their 45. The clock was stopped.

Layden sent in Gaul with a pass play. Pilney, his receivers covered, elected to run. Five Ohio State players had a crack at him and missed. Finally three others drove him out of bounds on the Buckeye 19; he received a severe leg injury on the play and had to be removed.

To replace him, Layden sent in a halfback with the classical name of William Shakespeare. (One of the Bard's plays is titled *All's Well That Ends Well*.) Layden also sent in a quarterback, Andy Puplis, with another pass play. Fifty seconds remained. Shakespeare faded and passed. For a split second Dick Beltz seemed about to intercept the ball, but the luckless fellow couldn't hold it. This made it second down, with 19 yards and 40 seconds to go.

Layden had run out of quarterbacks—or so he thought. At that moment, assistant coach Chet Grant came running up with Dick McKenna, the fourth-string quarterback who'd paid his way on the train. The play he was sent in with was a reverse pass on which the two ends crossed. Again Shakespeare faded. Then he threw. And then Wayne Milner leaped in the end zone and caught the ball. Notre Dame had won, 18–13.

The crowd was so shocked that many did not leave their seats for several minutes. In the press box, author-sportswriter Frank Wallace, who as an undergraduate had been sports publicist for Rockne, was doing a dance with Bill Cunningham, Boston sports columnist, who had played center at Dartmouth. When Wallace asked Cunningham why he was so excited, Bill said he'd just heard that his alma mater had beaten Yale for the first time.

Red Barber, later famous as a baseball announcer, was broadcasting the game. In the pandemonium, his Notre Dame spotter had run out of the box screeching. It was ten minutes before Red could find out who caught the final winning pass.

Dozens of other stories grew out of the game. Somebody finally got around to pointing out that

the Shakespeare to Milner pass play was pulled off by two non-Catholics.

The following week, Northwestern, coached by Lynn O. (Pappy) Waldorf, upset the Irish at South Bend, 14–7. To carry the literary nomenclature one step farther, the winning pass was thrown behind Shakespeare to a fellow named Longfellow.

A 6–6 tie with Army and a 20–13 victory over Southern California closed out the 1935 season at 7–1–1. The closest Notre Dame came to a perfect season under Layden was 1938. The Irish, captained by guard Jim McGoldrick, won their first eight games: Kansas 52–0, Georgia Tech 14–6, Illinois 14–6, Carnegie Tech 7–0, Army 19–7, Navy 15–0, Minnesota 19–0, and Northwestern 9–7.

"Aside from our opening game with Kansas," Layden wrote, "all of them had been tough, close games. Five of them had been sellouts. We arrived in Los Angeles being hailed as the prime candidate for national champion. The Los Angeles Coliseum was filled to, capacity with 104,000, the largest crowd we ever played before, and the sixth sellout of our season. And we lost, 13–0."

(The 7–0 victory over Carnegie Tech, the Tartans' only regular-season loss, involved costly forgetfulness by an official, John Getchell. With Tech in possession near midfield, the Tech quarterback asked Getchell what down it was and was told "third." So he called a running play that failed to make first down. Now Getchell told him that it had been a fourth down, and turned the ball over to Notre Dame, which then moved to the touchdown of a 7–0 victory. Coach Bill Kern and the Tech players naturally put up a howl. Later, however, in a gesture of sportsmanship and in recognition that Getchell, despite his error, was a fine official, Tech selected him to be one of the four to work its Sugar Bowl game with Texas Christian.)

The restlessness of a large segment of Notre Dame rooters was increased by the failure to make a perfect record in 1938, followed by late-season disappointments in 1939 and '40. Both years the Irish won their first six games; both years they ended up 7–2; both years the first defeat was inflicted by Iowa, coached by a onetime Notre Dame end under Rockne, Dr. Eddie Anderson.

"From both games," Layden recalled, "I drew criticism for my choice of starting halfbacks. Our

Layden (*left*) enjoying a pleasantry with Eddie Anderson in 1940. *Chicago Tribune Photos*

left halfbacks generally carried the burden of passing and ball carrying. I also liked a halfback who could punt. I had two great left halfbacks in 1939—Harry Stevenson and Benny Sheridan.

"Harry was the better punter, a good passer, but a bit slow afoot. Benny was the shiftier runner. The 1939 Iowa game was played on a clear, sunny day. I went most of the game playing Harry when my critics felt I should play Benny. The next year, on a cloudy, windy, wet day, I went most of the way with Benny when my critics thought I should have played Harry."

Lack of undefeated seasons reduces a team's chances for All-America notice, and so it was with Layden's seven years. Some were tapped, however; besides Shakespeare and Milner, the last-scene heroes at Ohio State, there were ends Earl Brown, Bud Kerr, and Chuck Sweeney, tackle Joe Beinor, guard John Lauter, and center Jack Robinson. By his election to the 1940 team captaincy, Milt Pupil certified his stature, for it had been a 25-year-old Notre Dame tradition that the captaincy should go to a lineman.

During Layden's regime, Notre Dame decided that a player must maintain a 77 average, seven points above passing, to remain eligible. Layden was opposed at first, but learned to live with it easily enough ... "I can't remember losing a single outstanding boy because he couldn't make the average. I will confess that a few did give me some anxious moments, but it all worked out for the best."

Layden was hampered, however, by a restric-

tion Father O'Hara laid down related to recruiting procedures. The head coach could not leave the campus to sign up any prospects; the boy had to come to the campus.

This may have been a decisive factor in the case of Marshall Goldberg, the All-America back from Elkins, West Virginia, who chose Pittsburgh over Notre Dame. Goldberg spearheaded Pitt's national championship-level teams from 1936 through '38, and had a big part in 1936 and '37 victories over the Irish. Something else was lost by Goldberg's choice of Pitt; one Notre Dame supporter, a moving-picture producer, had promised that if Marshall matriculated at Notre Dame, he would make a movie called *Goldberg of Notre Dame*.

Goldberg at full, Dick Cassiano and Hal (Curly) Stebbins at halfbacks, and John Chickerneo at quarter constituted Pitt's Dream Backfield of 1938, which probably got more press notices than any other backfield in history except Notre Dame's Four Horsemen: Elmer Layden, Jim Crowley, Don Miller, and Harry Stuhldreher.

Layden, a three-sport star at Davenport (Iowa) High, was steered to Notre Dame by Walter Halas, older brother of George Halas, founder, general manager, and coach of the Chicago Bears. Layden believed that there never could have been a more homesick boy than he was. His freshman year he went home several times, made many phone calls, and not until he started the 1922 Army game at West Point (a scoreless tie) was he sure he'd stay at South Bend.

Not until late in the 1922 season, against Carnegie Tech, did Layden, who had been an alternate left halfback, become the starting fullback, when Paul Castner broke a leg. "Layden," Rockne said, "I want you to play fullback." Layden pointed out that there were already two fullbacks who weighed more than he did: Bill Cerney and Bernie Livergood. "Never mind," Rockne said, "I need a small fullback because our line opens small holes."

In his playing prime Layden weighed 162; Crowley and Miller were each 164 and Stuhldreher 158. They beat Carnegie 19–0, but lost at Nebraska the next week. Their record in 1923 was 9–1, losing only to Nebraska, and in 1924, 10–0. Their first touchdown against Carnegie came on a freak. Said Layden:

"Rock started the shock troops against Carnegie, and they worked the ball down to the 5-yard line. Rock called Harry and me over to

him and said, 'I'm sending you in.' Thinking it was fourth down, he gave Harry a pass play to call. I was to be the receiver.

"In we went and Harry immediately discovered it was only third down. Now in those days we did not huddle; the huddle still was several years away. Harry called signals from behind the center in our basic T formation, then we shifted and the play was under way.

"Harry decided since it was third down, he wouldn't pass, but rather send me on a fullback buck into the line. As he called this signal and we shifted, I sensed the change in plans at the split second Bob Reagan centered the ball. The ball bounced off my knee, sailed five yards forward and landed on the goal line, where our end, George Vergara, fell on it for a touchdown. Now you know why I can tell my grandchildren that I had a hand in scoring the first time I played with the Four Horsemen. Or should I say a knee?"

Layden saved his last game for his finest, the 27–10 victory, New Year's Day, 1925, in the Rose Bowl against Coach Pop Warner's Stanford team that had the legendary fullback Ernie Nevers. Layden scored 18 of Notre Dame's points. He scored three touchdowns and set up the fourth with his punting.

Layden went over from the 7 to give Notre Dame a 6–3 lead. With Nevers as steamhammer, Stanford drove deep into Irish territory. Edward P. (Slip) Madigan, coach of St. Mary's and a former Notre Dame guard under Rockne, had scouted Stanford for his alma mater; he had noted that in scoring territory, the Indians liked a screen pass by Nevers into the flat. Layden, recalling this, played wider than usual. Gus Dorais, sitting on the bench next to Rockne, pointed it out. Rock replied, "He knows what he's doing."

Sure enough, Nevers tried the screen pass, and when it was deflected by Chuck Collins, N.D.'s left end, Elmer was in position to grab it off on the Irish 20 and return it 80 yards for a touchdown. Crowley converted to give N.D. a 13–3 lead at halftime.

In the third period, Layden's 55-yard punt was fumbled on the Stanford 20 and grabbed by the right end, Ed Hunsinger, who ran it in for a touchdown. Crowley again converted; 20–3. Then Stanford intercepted a pass on N.D.'s 27, whence Nevers blasted to the 3 and passed to Ted Shipkey for a touchdown. Murray Cuddeback converted; 20–10.

As the fourth quarter opened, Nevers led another drive but this time he was stopped on the goal line. Layden had to punt out, to the Stanford 48, and with Nevers blasting again, the Indians went 22 yards to the Notre Dame 30. Again Nevers tried the screen pass, again Layden intercepted and returned it all the way, 70 yards. Crowley converted to make it 27–10, the final score.

Nevers, a great All-America fullback and competitor, respected on both sides of the scrimmage line, relived those two interceptions by Layden many times. He reminisced:

"The two plays that can never be erased from my memory were the two accurate passes I threw to Layden. One good for 80 yards and a touchdown, and the other for 70 yards and a touchdown. A total of 150 yards in two tries and two touchdowns makes the passing combination of Layden of Notre Dame and Nevers of Stanford the best in Bowl history."

Layden had demonstrated his threat as an interceptor in an earlier victory over Northwestern, 13–6, when he picked off Ralph (Moon) Baker's aerial and returned it 40 yards for the clincher touchdown.

Few fullbacks ever matched Layden in the quick start and swiftness. That is how he managed to get by at 162 pounds spread over 5 feet, 11 1/4 inches. In later life, he took on a few pounds but remained gaunt-looking and came to be known as "The Thin Man." People introduced to him often said, "You must have been heavier when you played." Then Elmer would have to explain that as a player he was 20 pounds lighter.

Layden took a Bachelor of Law Degree at Notre Dame, considered law as a career, and passed the Iowa bar exam while coaching Columbia College in Dubuque, Iowa, in 1925 and '26. His Columbia record was 8–5–2; his 1925 team beat Luther for the Western Interstate Conference championship.

(Columbia had been known as St. Raphael's and St. Joseph's, but a newspaper headline, "Luther Trounces St. Joseph," prompted a change of name. Later it was renamed, for the last time, Loras, after its founder, Matthew Loras, bishop of Dubuque.)

Layden's work at Columbia attracted the attention of Duquesne, which signed him in 1927 to a two-year contract at $6,500 a year. At Duquesne, he learned how to make a little go a long way. The Dukes had only 11 numbered

Elmer viewing the 1940 College All-Star game. *Chicago Tribune Photos*

jerseys, and only enough spare parts for 35 makeshift uniforms. The athletic field, built over an old brick yard, looked less like a gridiron than a dump. At one end a 500-foot cliff made extra-point kicking a costly equipment item. (Duquesne, however, played its home games at Forbes Field.)

The biggest problem was squeezing enough dollars out of the budget to give scholarships. Despite the handicaps, Layden's seven-year record at Duquesne was 48–16–6. His 1928 team, which had an 8–1 record, pulled off a large upset at Washington and Jefferson, 12–6. His 1933 team beat Miami 33–7 in the Festival of Palms game, as the Orange Bowl was then known.

Probably the best player he ever recruited at Duquesne was Mike Basrak, an All-America center, whom he never got to coach. Aldo (Buff) Donelli, a center he switched to fullback, was also a star soccer player, who would have shone as a modern place-kicker, using the soccer sidewinding approach. Donelli later proved himself a fine head coach, with Duquesne, the Pittsburgh Steelers, Boston University, and Columbia.

By 1934 Notre Dame was seeking a head coach to replace Heartley W. (Hunk) Anderson and Father John O'Hara, chairman of the athletic board, approached Layden. (Later, Father O'Hara was the first Holy Cross father to become a cardinal.)

"We signed a contract," Elmer said, "on a table Father O'Hara told me was more than 100 years old and that his mother had brought from Ireland. Next to signing over the Blarney stone itself, this must have been as appropriate a place as you could find to sign up a coach for the Fighting Irish."

Elmer Layden's 16-year coaching record of 103 victories, 34 defeats, and 11 ties for a percentage of .733 placed him No. 29 among the coaches in football's first century who served ten years or more. Broken down, the record reveals:

Loras (1925-26)	8-5-2
Duquesne (1927-33)	48-16-6
Notre Dame (1934-40)	47-13-3

To prove that fame is fleeting, even for the Four Horsemen, Layden likes to tell the story of his grandson, Elmer Layden III, who was playing his first football in grammar school. His coach told him, "You know your grandfather was one of the Four Horsemen of Notre Dame?" When little Elmer got home, he asked his mother, "Mom, what's a Horseman of Notre Dame?"

Lou Little

THE LION KNOWN AS LOU

The 1924 Georgetown team, Coach Lou Little's first, lost to Bucknell 14–6, a game they should have won. At the following Monday's practice, Coach Little was seething, and when he got around to the Hoya center, Jerry Minihan, he crescendoed.

"Minihan," Coach Little roared, "take off that uniform and never put it on again!"

Jerry Minihan, later the Very Reverend Jeremiah F. Minihan, auxiliary bishop of Boston, was by nature respectful of appropriate authority. Instead of reporting for Tuesday's practice, he attended a Keith's vaudeville show in Washington. That night, Coach Little confronted him.

"Where were you today?" he demanded.

"I went to a show," Minihan replied. "You told me to take off the uniform and never put it on again."

Little contemplated the young man querulously.

"Don't you know better," he asked, "than to pay attention to me when I'm mad?"

"Mister Coach," replied Jerry, "when you're mad, I pay strict attention."

Minihan was back in uniform on Wednesday, and as Little gained in coaching experience, his rages decreased. But his authority was never questioned.

Nor his devotion to football. Any thought unrelated to the game didn't distract him for long, not even the contemplation of a full-course dinner at Mamma Leone's; he was a stalwart at table.

"Lou came to my first public Mass in Haverhill, July 27, 1930," Bishop Minihan smiled. "Father Jerry Graham was my archpriest, whose duties may be likened to a prompter's. Actually, I didn't need one, because I'd been saying Mass in Rome for seven months before returning to the States. Well, after that first Mass in Haverhill, Lou walked with me to my house.

"'Jerry,' he asked, 'who was that white-haired man beside you on the altar?'

"'That was my parish priest, my archpriest for the Mass,' I said, and explained the reason for the archpriest. Lou listened and then shook his head.

"'He never should have been there—he was blocking the interference all through the Mass.'"

If Lou Little had the material to work with the last 20 years of his career that he had the first 13, he might well have ranked among the first 25 coaches in all-time winning percentage. His six seasons at Georgetown, 1924–29, show 39–12–2—.755; his first seven at Columbia, 1930–36, 43–15–3—.729; 13-season total: 82–27–5—.741.

Through most of the twenties and thirties, he was recognized for what he was: given "a fair field and no favor," a coach capable of meeting

the best of his contemporaries on even terms. Two of his Georgetown and five of his Columbia teams lost only one game. From 1931 through '34, his record at Columbia—29-4-2, .857—ranked near the top.

After 1936, except for the post–World War II seasons of 1945, '46, and '47, his Columbia teams were almost invariably outmanned by opponents. They had only five winning seasons in 20 for a record of 67-101-7, .403, with the last nine seasons the worst, 26-53-1, .331.

The contrast of Little's record up through 1936 with the two decades that followed provides ultimate proof of an ancient truism: No coach can win with silhouettes. No coach can make chicken salad out of chicken feathers.

In the good days, Little's teams perpetrated several dramatic upsets in settings that captured headline attention. At Georgetown they included the 1926 defeat of Syracuse, 13-7, spoiling an undefeated season; the 7-2 triumph over the 1928 New York University team led by the brilliant back Ken Strong; the 1929 scoreless tie with Navy. At Columbia in his second season, 1931, the Lions hung a 19-6 shocker on Dartmouth, which had run over them the year before, 52-0; it was the Lions' first over the Indians since 1899.

The game that Lou Little and Columbia football will always first be remembered for, however, was the upset of a heavily favored Stanford team in the Rose Bowl, New Year's Day, 1934.

No game better exemplifies how the fate of a team and a coach in much of its context is worked out beyond their control. Columbia began that fourth season under Little, 1933, with a strong starting eleven, a few good substitutes, and a self-belief founting from two 7-1-1 seasons back to back.

In their third game, the Lions played at Princeton, then in its second season under Fritz Crisler. This was a good but predominantly sophomore Tiger team; although it would make a perfect 9-0 record, the schedule was not too taxing. The Princeton 1933 team was by no means equal to the perfect-record team of two falls later, when the sophomores were seniors. The season before, 1932, Columbia had defeated the Tigers 20-7. Perhaps overconfidence played a part, but Princeton won emphatically, 20-0. Little would say afterwards, "The defeat was the making of our team." The Lions won all the rest for a 7-1-0 regular-season log.

At no time during the season, however, did

Lou Little, at Columbia

anybody, including the most chauvinistic around John Jay Hall, even think of the Lions for the Rose Bowl. Princeton, Army, Duke, and Pittsburgh featured the Pasadena talky-talk. But the Big Three ban against postseason games eliminated the Tigers, the undefeated Cadets were beaten in their last game by Notre Dame, 13-12, and the same dose was served Duke by Georgia Tech, 6-0. And Pittsburgh, defeated only by Minnesota, 7-3, and probably the East's best, had lost on all three of its Rose Bowl adventures, the last two to Southern California, 47-14 and 35-0.

Still, Columbia entered the minds of nobody except the people who counted: Stanford and the Rose Bowl committee. When the invitation came it was a major upset in itself. Everybody was happy for the Lions—and sorry for them. While the faculty was deciding whether the bid would be accepted, Lou Little held court to some newspapermen, including John Kieran, the erudite and readable sports columnist of the *Times*, and celebrated pundit on the radio show "Infor-

mation Please," before turning to a career as author-naturalist. Kieran described the scene in some of his neat verse:

> The Eastern coach, with all his staff, was standing in the hall,
> The Rose Bowl bid was in, and they were waiting for the call,
> The faculty was huddling and the Dean still held the ball.
> "If twenty men were used against eleven on their side,
> Do you suppose," the Head Coach said, "that Stanford could be tied?"
> "I doubt it," groaned an aide-de-camp, and broke right down and cried.
> "If all our men wore armor plate with rivets at the seam,
> We still might save the lives of all the players on our team,"
> The Head Coach said. But that seemed just a hopeful Eastern dream.
>
> Then rose a wailing, warning voice the coaching staff amid,
> "From fire and from pestilence please keep the East safe hid,
> From famine and from slaughter and from Bowl of Roses bid."

When the West Coast heard that Columbia had been invited and had accepted, derisive howls arose about Stanford playing "a high school team." For once, Rose Bowl tickets moved slowly, and the usual sellout would have been unlikely, even in good weather. Heavy rains forced the use of fire engine pumps to drain off the gridiron the day before the game. Coach Claude (Tiny) Thornhill, of Stanford, suggested a postponement. Little, however, insisted the game be played; he was aware of the traditional values of "General Mud" as equalizer.

Stanford's "Vow Boys" of 1933, '34, and '35 had vowed they'd never lose to Southern California, and they never did. Along the way, they also won three straight Pacific Coast Conference titles and Rose Bowl bids, losing to Alabama at Pasadena as juniors, and as seniors defeating Southern Methodist. They included many players of All-America caliber: fullback Bobby Grayson, end Monk Moscrip, tackle Bob Reynolds, and halfback Bones Hamilton. They had lost in 1933 to Washington, 6–0, been tied by Northwestern, 0–0, and had scraped through against UCLA and Santa Clara, 3–0 and 7–0.

They were not the team they would be as juniors or seniors, may not have been ready for a top-level Bowl assignment, a factor no doubt in the selection of Columbia. None of this dilutes in the slightest the Columbia accomplishment. Stanford, the bigger, deeper, more talented team, with a two-year All-America guard in Bill Corbus, was a heavy favorite and deserved to be.

If Stanford was overconfident, it was not for long. From the opening kickoff, "the high school team" out of New York laid the wood to them. Part of the Lions' strategy reposed on confidence in their defense, and a decision not to risk interceptions and field position by passing; they threw only two passes.

Throughout the first quarter, Columbia controlled the ball with quarterback Cliff Montgomery, a fine runner and passer, and fullback Al Barabas, a powerful, speedy runner, making goodly dents in the large Cardinal line. In the second quarter, following a punt and a five-yard penalty against Stanford, the Lions were deployed at midfield. On first down, Montgomery threw one of the two passes for the day. Star end Tony (Red) Matal made a leaping catch at the Stanford 20 and skidded three more yards. On first down from the 17, Barabas fumbled and recovered for loss of half a yard.

Now came the coup de grace. Columbia's offense, a single wing behind an unbalanced line, featured a series of tricky spinner-reverse plays, which drillmaster Little had made them run until execution was pristine. Deception by faking and ball hiding was essential. Montgomery called a hidden-ball wide reverse with a fake reverse to another back off tackle, also to the weak side.

On the play, Montgomery, taking the center snap, executed a full spin. On the first half of the spin, away from the line, he fed the ball to Barabas reversing behind him from fullback. On the second half of the spin, toward the line, he faked feeding the ball forward to right halfback Ed Brominski, who faked a slant over the weakside tackle. The key to success was the ability of Barabas to hide the ball by holding it in his left hand against his left leg, and the ability of Brominski to convince the enemy that he actually had the ball. Both rated Oscars.

The play is essentially a flimflam. No matter how well executed or hidden, it cannot work if the defensive right end and right linebacker "play the man," which in later-day semantics has come to be known, because it sounds more scholarly, as "reading the play." Stanford's right end and right

At his Columbia desk, where a coach's work is never done

halfback were bamboozled. Barabas raced into the end zone as unopposed as if it were signal drill. Some San Francisco scribe described it nicely by quoting from John 18:40: "Now Barabbas was a robber."

Stanford was a team easier to fool than to discourage, however. The infuriated Palo Altoans dominated the second half, but Little's light Blue Line from Little Old New York, though bending often to the fury of the storm, refused to snap. Six times the Indians marauded goalward. Six times they were repulsed, thrice within the 20, thrice within the 10. Once they had first down on the 3; after four shots they were still a yard shy, As the clock ran out, Grayson and Hamilton made one mad, furious last attempt, but could not penetrate beyond the 10—and one of the darkest dark horses of all time had locked the favorite in the barn.

What a victory! Even Fordham's sports publicity director, no Columbia enthusiast he, listening by radio in New Haven 3,000 miles away, had to thrill to the plucky Lions. He went so far as to sing a chorus of "Roar, Lion, Roar," which within the hour was suddenly becoming the hit of

the week at every notch on the dial. And bard Kieran once more dipped his nifty quill to speak for everybody:

> Lou—meaning Coach Little—this lightens my fate,
> And this is the lilt that enlivens my song:
> It's bright to be right, but this time I must state,
> I laughed with delight when you proved I was wrong.

As the years went on, the many staunch defensemen of the Columbia line that historic wet day were forgotten; for such is the fate of linemen.

The legerdemain that wove the heady chaplet of laurel—the play known as KF-79—seemed destined for a time to match Abraham Lincoln in belonging to the ages. It became as well known in the thirties and even into the forties as TNT, NTG, FDR, and LS/MFT. For 15 years it reappeared regularly on sports pages, especially New York's, like a vampire violating the sundown rule.

Fourteen years after, at Baker Field, home gridiron of Columbia, a Little team pulled off his

No. 2 all-time shocker. An end named Bill Swiacki made several catches that had to be seen to be disbelieved for a 21–20 comeback upset that ended a 32-game defeatless string by Red Blaik's Army team. Only then was a figurative wooden stake driven into the heart of KF-79 and its great soul given decent requiem. Long live Swiacki!

There was one discordant note to the Columbia Rose Bowl story. Stanley Woodward, ace sports editor, writer, and reporter of the New York *Herald Tribune* and a good friend of Lou Little, got tipped off by an inadvertent remark of Mrs. Little's at dinner, and had himself a scoop. Columbia, however, was in bad odor with the somewhat stuffy sports editor of the *Times*, Captain Bernard Thompson, who threatened to restrict the story to two sticks a day. He relented, of course, but for Columbia to be out of favor with the *Times* or the other media in Lou Little's time was as rare as a stinkweed in the Garden of Allah.

Little, an outstanding football coach, was even more proficient in the field of public relations. He had an instinct for it, firmed on a keen understanding of people, and was guided also by a true expert in the field, Bob Harron, Columbia sports information director and justifiably one of the best-loved men in sports. Little on his own, however, was a Dale Carnegie incarnate.

Who else could have lasted on a coaching job through a 20-year record of 67–101–7 (.404) and only five winning seasons. Little did more than survive. He commanded a press that for consistency and elegance was the envy of many winning coaches. It is a case history unique.

It was made possible basically because Little served under two Columbia presidents, whose approach to football should serve as models: Dr. Nicholas Murray Butler, who headed the school from 1902 to 1945, and his successor, President of the United States and General of the Armies, Dwight David Eisenhower.

Dr. Butler, winner of one half of the 1931 Nobel Peace Prize, president of the American Academy of Arts and Letters, Republican Vice Presidential nominee in 1912, and philosopher in tune with the world, was not concerned with seeing Columbia a football power. He was not concerned with football at all. He abolished the game at Morningside Heights from 1905 to 1915 as "an academic nuisance." He would as soon listen to alumni complaints about football as he'd wed a burlesque queen.

On the other hand, his successor, General Eisenhower, had been an authentic backfield star at West Point in 1911 and '12 until repeated injuries to a knee sidelined him. Ike understood the game and had the horse sense to recognize that winning football meant good horses. He recognized clearly that no coach could extract any more from Columbia's material than Little did.

With presidents like Dr. Butler and General Ike, Little held the key to his own future, a blessing seldom enjoyed by coaches. Usually they are, as Michigan State's Duffy Daugherty so well expressed it, "responsible to the irresponsible."

The doctor and the general, of course, did not account for Little's splendid press through long years of defeat. The writers deserve a salute also, for recognizing that he was doing all that could be done. This was not a consideration, however, that they accorded other coaches who were just as able but had come upon sparse days.

Little himself was mainly responsible.

At first, though, he was a good front man only on the field. He was a rough-cut youngster, the son of a successful Leominster, Massachusetts, contractor, who moved from Lou's birthplace, Boston, when the coach was only four. By his own admission, Little was an indifferent scholar, interested only in sports. Failing to qualify for Yale, he went to Vermont, where his tackle play attracted attention, and resulted in his transferring to Pennsylvania. At Penn, he considered studying dentistry but became convinced it was not a profession for lefthanders.

Between outstanding football seasons at Penn in 1916 and 1919, Little served with distinction as a lieutenant of infantry in the Meuse-Argonne and was promoted to captain. After graduation from Penn in 1920, he played professional football for four years and sold bonds. All the time he was soaking up knowledge of the game that fascinated him, and in 1924 he was hired by Georgetown.

Little's harsh taskmastership on the field traced to the kind of game he'd known as a player, especially in 1919 when college rosters were well peopled with returning veterans who had survived something far rougher and more testing than the gridiron. They were lined up on both sides in a game Pennsylvania lost at Dartmouth, 20–19.

"It was the roughest game I ever played in," Little said. "I was having a rough time with the player opposite me, tackle Gus Sonnenberg, who

later turned wrestler. At the other Penn tackle, John Titzel, a real man but a scrupulously clean player, was working opposite Cuddy Murphy. Murphy was an outstanding player, and a great fellow—off the field." Titzel told Little about Murphy's overrough tactics.

"Listen, you," Little threatened Murphy, "if you don't play the game right, I'm going to take care of you."

Murphy shot a stream of tobacco juice right past Lou's nose, which football collisions had developed to a size near Cyrano de Bergerac's.

"You hook-nosed punk," growled Cuddy. "You'll do nothing."

"Johnny," said Little to Titzel, "it's every man for himself. I've got trouble of my own with that Sonnenberg. You'll have to handle this Murphy yourself."

Except for an occasional lapse into profanity on the field, which came as a sharp contrast to his reproving "Oh, my, my, my, my, my," the later-day Little by contrast became a gruffly urbane diplomat, his pince-nez perched on his great beak giving him the mien of an erudite and amiable eagle.

Little made a tremendous initial impact, and sustained it, the kind of man few would not turn to for a second look. Big and well built, he kept himself in excellent condition by handball, golf, and gardening at his summer home in Barnstable on Cape Cod. He indulged himself in a cigarette or beer occasionally, and in beat food, his principal temptation, by surrounding his gourmand's feats with periods of dieting.

Lou loved clothes. His sartorial depth—40 suits, hats, and coats, dozens of shoes, hundreds of shirts, and perhaps 500 ties, many of them strictly psychedelic—was impressive enough to move Lucius Beebe, the clothes, food, and vocabulary horse of the *Herald Tribune*, to view him with envy.

It was not the facade, however, that won and kept writers friendly. He went out of his way to help them. It was in the early thirties that the long trip uptown to Columbia, Fordham, NYU, and Manhattan to cover football practice led to the formation of the first weekly football writers luncheons, soon to become a national habit. The luncheons, along with the fancy brochures and tons of well-prepared material made available to football writers by college sports publicity departments, are no unmixed blessing. They tend to dilute initiative, enthusiasm, and knowledge of

Lou receiving one of his many awards. *Chicago Tribune Photos*

the game. Sportswriters deserve to be assisted, but not to have their work done for them.

Little recognized the value of keeping the writers coming to the campus. He and Bob Harron instituted a special weekly in-season luncheon at Columbia's John Jay Hall (not too far uptown). It was attended regularly by such top sports columnists as John Kieran, Frank Graham, and Stanley Woodward, with a plurality payoff in pieces they'd write on Lou and his Lions.

To sportswriters who did favorable pieces, and they were the only kind, Lou usually dispensed thank-you notes. If a young writer made the long trip to a Baker Field practice, Little would not only improve his education in the game but usually invite him to have supper at the training table, which featured succulent steaks. Lou even carried his good-will campaign to the extreme of tendering the writer the extra steak.

In all this communication, he drove home to the writers the high academic caliber of Columbia.

"When you have a squad, 60 percent of which are studying to be engineers, doctors, lawyers, architects, you simply must take an interest in it. Their primary purpose in college is academic

development. Football must be subordinated to that purpose."

Columbia's recruiting, handled not by Little but by emissaries, allocated only part-time aid to 20 varsity and 10 freshman players in a given year out of Columbia's then total scholarships available, 300.

Blue-chippers were few. Usually, Little had a superior quarterback-passer—Sid Luckman, Paul Governali, Gene Rossides. And he was one of the best of all coaches at developing the quarterback in every phase.

Despite his appreciation of Columbia's philosophy and a $17,500 salary, tops for the time, Little more than once became fed up with the lack of material and was severely tempted to take one of the many offers tendered him. In 1944 the New York Yankees pro team of the old All-America Conference asked him to be coach and general manager for $25,000 plus five percent of the profits, and the Brooklyn Dodgers, of the National Football League, made an even better offer.

The only time Little seriously considered leaving Columbia, however, came after the 1947 season when Howie Odell resigned at Yale to coach at Washington. At the time Little had put together the only successful segment of his last 20 years, post–World War II seasons of 8–1, 6–3, and 7–2 back to back.

He envisioned that at 54 he would have to move now, if he was ever to move, and he let Yale know he was interested. Yale sparked to the idea. Columbia alumni, hearing about it, prevailed on General Eisenhower, newly appointed president but not yet in office at Columbia, to call Lou to Washington and talk him out of it. Ike did, and

Lou stayed. One cynical coach commented, "It would not have been surprising if, to keep Uncle Lou at Columbia, and all right with the world, university trustees had asked Pope Pius XII to dispense a special papal bull."

The patience, the mental stamina that Little demonstrated in living with losing for so long were matched by his physical fortitude. During the 1942 game that Columbia, outpersonneled, lost to Navy in the last minute, 13–9, Little shouted himself so raw that he injured his larynx. Surgery removed part of the organ, and reduced the booming roar, once a hallmark, to a painful rasp. He also coached for two years with a calcification in his hip joint that required 140 grains of aspirin a day to dull the pain; two operations finally brought relief.

The last football game he ever coached, Little won, when Columbia concluded its 1956 season by beating Rutgers at New Brunswick, New Jersey, 18–12. Among those who congratulated the maestro in the locker room were four players from his first team, 1924 Georgetown: Frank Murray, Andy Gaffey, Eddie Brooks, and Bishop Jerry Minihan. He had not known they were there and was deeply touched. Tears filled the eyes of Lou Little, born Luigi Piccolo, as he gave each of them the Roman man's greeting of true friendship and deep affection—the *baccio Romano*.

Coach Lou Little's old players knew he was interested in each of them not only as an athlete but as a total person. Any coach who can evoke this has succeeded in his mission. The name of the game in college football, contrary to what you have heard in many a boring cliche, is not merely to win.

Dan McGugin

HE STEAMED UP THE COMMODORES

The pep talk, the dressing-room oratory that motivates men to play beyond themselves, will always be a part of college football. The approach may be different, the words changed, but those who play the game still react to the emotional. It was in the twenties and thirties, however, that the pep talk reached classic levels, and there was no

finer practitioner of the art than Daniel Earle McGugin, who coached Vanderbilt 30 years, 1904 to 1934, 1918 excepted.

"It was from McGugin," said one of his former quarterbacks, Henry Russell (Red) Sanders, in his coaching peak at UCLA, "that I learned psychology, particularly the art of handling men."

How well McGugin employed the psychological tack is documented by his record at Vanderbilt: 197 victories, 55 defeats, and 19 ties for a percentage of .762. When totals were tabulated in 1969, college football's centennial year, among those who had coached at major colleges at least ten years, McGugin was No. 17.

In 1922, Vanderbilt dedicated its new 20,000-seat Dudley Field, named after Dr. William L. Dudley, of Vanderbilt, who organized the Southern Intercollegiate Athletic Conference in 1894, and was its president for 20 years.

As an opponent, Michigan was a natural. In 1902 and '03, McGugin had played guard for Coach Fielding H. (Hurry Up) Yost's point-a-minute Wolverines; he had a furious offensive charge. "I had to," he explained, "or Willie Heston would have run through my back." There was also a family bond. When McGugin married a Nashville girl, Virginia Fite, Yost was best man. He met, wooed, and won Virginia's sister, Eunice.

Michigan was favored; it had won six previous games with Vanderbilt. But the game ended in a scoreless tie, and Vandy went on to an undefeated season. The deadlock was distinguished by a punting duel between Michigan's Harry Kipke and Vanderbilt's Scotty Neil, while Captain Jess Neely, who could play end or halfback, had one of his finest days.

A few minutes before the kickoff McGugin pointed out the window to a nearby military cemetery and then to the Michigan team warming up.

"In that cemetery sleep your grandfathers," he said, "and down on that field are the grandsons of the Damn Yankees who put them there."

McGugin was an Iowan, had attended Drake and Michigan, and his father, a Union officer, had marched with Sherman to the sea. Perhaps the Vanderbilt players didn't know this, but if they had, it wouldn't have made any difference. McGugin had adopted the South; everybody knew that.

No coach ever got closer to his men than the big, smiling blue-eyed Irishman.

"A man didn't have to play football under McGugin to get to know him well or to comprehend and admire his coaching philosophy," wrote Fred Russell, sports columnist of the Nashville *Banner*. "He was hearty, convivial, with an infinite deal of wit."

McGugin was not the staccato, fire-eating, rouser type like Knute Rockne. He spoke softly,

Dan McGugin of Vanderbilt

slowly, using a gradual approach to key up his team. His undefeated 1921 team gave Texas its only defeat, 20–0, in Dallas, after a classic McGugin exhortation:

"You are about to be put to an ordeal which will show the stuff that's in you. What a glorious chance you have! Everyone of you is going to fix your status for all time in the minds and hearts of your teammates today. How you fight is what you will be remembered by. If any shirks, the Lord pity him. He will be downgraded in the hearts of the rest of you as long as he lives.

"I heard repeatedly before we left Nashville that this team might win from Texas if it would only fight. Has anybody the right to imply such an insult? And if so, when before now could such a thing be said of men from Tennessee?

"Who the devil started all this bunk about the Texas team? Who thinks they are unbeatable? They say that they have the greatest team in history. They say that Vanderbilt never had a team which could beat theirs this year, but that is not true. Texas has no shield like ours. We have some scars on it, but there are a lot of stars there. Texas has no such athletic tradition and history.

"Now is there any man here who will not fight every inch of the way? Will any man here disgrace himself and live in the contempt of his

teammates the rest of his days? Are you going to establish yourselves in your own self-respect and in the eyes of the thousands watching you? Are you going to make your own record and leave memories for others to live by?"

Modern coaches and even some of McGugin's contemporaries believe that such exhortation did more to harm than help a team. One of them said, "I want my players to go on the field clear-eyed and able to see, not crying."

Yet, there were some wet eyes among the Vanderbilt players who upset a heavily favored Minnesota team 16–0 in 1924; and the eleven Vandy starters went all the way. That was the day McGugin told them quietly:

"With each one of you boys there was a time—you knew nothing about it, of course—a time when you were two months old, or five months, when your mother looked at you in the cradle, and she wondered, she asked herself, what kind of heart beat in that little body; of how this boy, as he grew into a man, would meet his first real test of courage; whether, when that time came, she could feel the pride that only a mother can feel for a son who is courageous—and fearless—or whether there might, perhaps, have to be a different feeling. She knew that such a time, such a day, would come. Today—she may be wondering—"

McGugin's influence extended beyond Vanderbilt players and Tennesseans. In a time when visiting sportswriters were treated as potential spies, he welcomed them and helped them with stories. That explains why he was the most quoted football coach in the South, and why 23 sportswriters gave him a silver tray with the inscription, "Friend of Sportswriters."

And he enjoyed comparable good will among his fellow coaches, who chose him as their president in 1933. It was he who convinced Bernie Bierman he should stay in coaching, in the midtwenties when Bierman was at Mississippi State, the same Bierman who later developed championship teams at Tulane and Minnesota.

"Dan McGugin," said Frank Thomas, who turned out many Bowl teams at Alabama, "was the first coach ever to encourage me when I was probably bluer than at any time. He was brilliant, understanding, and loved by his players."

Will Wedge, of the New York *Sun*, called McGugin "the best-loved coach in his region . . . at Vandy he's as much a part of the place as the statue on campus of Commodore Vanderbilt,

who founded the university in 1873."

In the late twenties and early thirties, when Vandy's fortunes under McGugin decelerated before the new dynasties at Alabama and Tennessee, some alumni complained. But Chancellor James H. Kirkland spoke for the large majority when he said, "If Dan McGugin isn't good enough for Vanderbilt football, then football isn't good enough to be played at Vanderbilt."

McGugin's record stands even taller when one considers that coaching came second to his profession as a successful corporation lawyer, although football was what he liked to be around.

"I believe that McGugin would have gone down in history as the greatest of all coaches," wrote Zipp Newman, veteran Alabama football authority, "had he given all his time to coaching. McGugin pioneered in speed and the forward pass. The South learned the Michigan punting game from McGugin, who believed in a punt, a pass, and a prayer. He was a great playmaker but football was a sport with him and law was his profession."

The venerable Statue of Liberty play, in which a fake pass or punt develops into a handoff and an end run, may have originated at Vanderbilt under McGugin, but with typical forthrightness he refused to take credit for it.

"I had nothing to do with it," he said. "One of my players thought it up. If I'm not mistaken it was Ray Morrison, our quarterback. He was always thinking up plays." But Morrison, queried, didn't remember. As in the origin of most plays, it is probable that different people hit upon the same idea at different times in different places.

The No. 1 player coached by McGugin at Vanderbilt—the only place McGugin ever coached—was Lynn Bomar, 1922–24, who is in the National Football Hall of Fame. Although Bomar, six feet two, and 208, was chosen All-America end, McGugin used him as a blocking back and a linebacker. This way he derived maximum value from the big blond's ability to catch passes, run interference, and tackle opponents at the line. Jess Neely, Bomar's teammate and later a Hall of Fame coach for his work at Clemson and Rice, said, "I've never seen a football team that Bomar couldn't have made."

McGugin began at Vanderbilt in 1904 with an undefeated team, and not until the last game of the 1905 season did a *Southern* team score on the Commodores. That was Sewanee (the University

of the South), which until 1930 played a traditional Thanksgiving Day game with Vandy.

The Vandy record under McGugin shows ten Southern championships: 1904, '05, '06, '07, '10, '11, '12, '21, '22, and '23. The 1904 team was 9–0–0 and led the nation in scoring with 474 points against four for the opponents. The 1910, '21, and '22 teams were undefeated but tied. In 1905, '06, '11, '15, and '26 they lost one game. In 1907, '12, and '16 they lost one and tied one.

Long before Bowl games it was McGugin's Vanderbilt teams that pioneered intersectional football for the South, against Michigan, the Carlisle Indians, Ohio State, Navy, Harvard, Yale, and Minnesota. The Commodores usually lost, but by close scores. They also perpetrated some shocking upsets.

In 1906 they surprised the Carlisle Indians, 4–0, the first time an Eastern team invaded the South. Carlisle had beaten Villanova, Syracuse, Pennsylvania, and Minnesota. Eight thousand cheered Bob Blake's decisive 17-yard place-kick. Vanderbilt's 6–6 tie with Navy in 1907 also provoked excitement, but the No. 1 shocker was the 0–0 tie in 1910 with Yale at New Haven. Eleven Commodores played the entire game against Yale's three-deep team, and Grantland Rice, a proud son of Vandy, wrote that "they were the fastest, best-organized team to meet Yale in a long time." They were also inspired by a Union-Confederate pep talk by McGugin, similar to the one he used 12 years later against Michigan.

That 1910 Vanderbilt team won all of its eight other games and gave up only eight points. The 1911 team lost only to Michigan, 9–8, and was otherwise all-winning and unscored on.

McGugin was in such command of his players that he was able to fraternize with them and still not lose any of their respect. He would always call a player by his correct first name—not Chuck, but Charles—because he felt that the nickname might be offensive. To get the best out of each individual, he diversified his approach. There is at least one case, however, in which he used the same gambit on many.

"In my first varsity year, the night before we played Georgia Tech," recalled Pete Gracey, All-America center at Vanderbilt in 1931, "Coach McGugin casually walked up to me in the lobby of our hotel, put his arm around my shoulder and sort of whispered, 'Peter, I was with some Atlanta newspapermen this afternoon and I told them you were the finest sophomore center I had ever coached. I hope I haven't made it embarrassing for you.'

"We beat Tech, 23–7. Afterward I talked to seven other players and you know, Coach McGugin had told them all the same thing he told me."

In defeat as well as victory, McGugin was adept at shoring up morale. After winning Southern championships in 1921, '22, and '23, Vanderbilt was upset by Tulane early in the '24 season. The hero of the Green Wave was Brother Brown, who frequently outlegged the Vandy defenses. On the train home to Nashville, McGugin called the safety man, who had missed some key tackles, into his drawing room.

"Where were you," the coach asked, "when Brown got away?"

The boy replied nervously, "I just don't know, coach. I just couldn't get him."

McGugin patted the boy on the shoulder.

"That was all right," he smiled. "I yelled at him to stop myself, but he just kept on running."

The story helped the youngster forget his errors.

Not aboard that same train was Vanderbilt's star fullback and punter, Tom Ryan, who also missed Monday's practice, presumably because he could not tear himself away from New Orleans. McGugin said the squad would have to vote on whether Ryan would be allowed to return. While they were voting, McGugin was having a private talk with the miscreant at the other end of the field.

"What would you do," McGugin asked Ryan, "if a fellow said maybe you were yellow?"

"I would stomp him," Ryan said.

"Well, suppose I said you were yellow?"

Ryan was shocked but replied, "Sir, that would have to go for you, too."

After a moment, McGugin spoke, "Tom, you make me think of a certain Indian out West. When he saw his first locomotive, he said he was going to lasso it. I admire your courage, but you've got mighty poor judgment."

Ryan went on to some fine football that year.

To impress upon his players the importance of seizing opportunity, one of McGugin's favorite stories had to do with the bumblebee who was gobbled up by a bull. He decided to teach the bull a lesson by stinging him from the inside but it was so comfortable inside the bull that he decided that first he would have a nap. And when he woke up, the bull was gone.

"The reserves of B team," said Fred Russell, "were McGugin's favorites. At the end of almost every practice he would praise their spirit and hustle and conclude with the remark, 'Who knows but what Team B will start Saturday?' Many times the reserves almost got up the nerve to answer in unison, 'Team B knows,' but they never did."

McGugin savored best those laughs he had at the expense of his old Michigan coach and brother-in-law, Hurry Up Yost. After Michigan finished its season, Yost would hurry to Nashville to see the Vanderbilt-Sewanee game. Then he and McGugin would go on to the football coaches convention. One year Yost was supposed to make the principal address and he rehearsed it on the train in front of McGugin so many times that Dan learned it by heart.

At the meeting McGugin was asked to make some remarks from the rostrum, and he proceeded to deliver Yost's speech, leaving his brother-in-law to extemporize as best he could.

Yost, who fancied himself an authority on many things besides football, is supposed to have been one of the first, if not the first, to argue that the North Pole had not been discovered by Dr. Cook, but that the honor belonged to Admiral Peary.

McGugin arranged at a dinner for the subject to be brought up and a ballot to be taken. They voted 16–3 in favor of Peary. But that did not satisfy Yost; he spent 40 minutes trying to convince the three of their error. Finally, at his request another ballot was taken and this time Cook won 18–1.

When death came to Dan McGugin in 1936, two years after he retired from coaching, not only football at Vanderbilt and in the South but the game everywhere lost a cherished friend.

"They said there would never be another McGugin in Vanderbilt's lifetime," wrote Zipp Newman. "This could have been said for all Southern football—never another McGugin."

DeOrmond (Tuss) McLaughry

TUSS AND THE IRON MEN

The occasion was a homecoming dinner at Brown University in 1956, the 30th anniversary of Brown's 1926 "Iron Men," and the speaker was their coach, DeOrmond (Tuss) McLaughry.

"I'm going to tell you people tonight a story that I've never told before," said McLaughry. "As you know, we had a great team in 1926. My Iron Men went undefeated through 10 games; only a 10–10 tie with Colgate marred an otherwise perfect record. ... One member of that Iron Men eleven made Collier's All-America team that year—Orland Smith. Here's how it happened.

"Grantland Rice, who selected the team, called me on the phone one Sunday following the close of the season. Granny said to me, 'The Iron Men rate a place on my All-America team. I'm calling you to see who it will be.' I told him I couldn't make any choice.

"'It has to be one of the three seniors,' he said, 'either left end Hal Broda, right guard Orland Smith, or halfback Dave Mishel.'

"I said that Captain Broda could play end on

any team in the country. There wasn't a better pass receiver, and he was wonderful on defense. Mishel, in my opinion, could pass with the best of them—including Benny Friedman. His passing to Red Randall and Broda was one of the big factors in our offense. Then we had Smitty, Orland Smith. A tough guy. There was tiger in his heart. When he hit you, he hurt you. He always went for the jugular vein.

"'Well,' Granny replied, 'I've got to put Vic Hanson of Syracuse and Bennie Oosterbaan of Michigan at my end positions. I've just got to do it. And I've got Moon Baker of Northwestern and Mort Kaer of Southern California for my halfbacks. They're all set. But I've got a guard spot open.'

"Now Smith, if you'll remember, played offensive guard and defensive tackle. He was the biggest man on the team at 225 and he could pull out of the guard position on running plays better than any man I ever coached. When he hit a backer-up, he killed him.

"So, Grantland Rice put Smitty on his All-America team that year, and you folks tonight, including Smitty, have heard for the first time how it happened. But that just shows how political all these so called All-America teams are, although with the thousands of men playing the game on gridirons all over the country that's the way it has to be."

In addition to Smith, Broda, Mishel, and Randall, the Iron Men were composed of Ed Kevorkian left tackle, Lou Farber left guard, Charlie Considine center, Paul Hodge right tackle, Thurston Towle right end, Ed Lawrence halfback, and Al Cornsweet fullback.

Before the Colgate tie in their final game they defeated Rhode Island 14–0, Colby 35–0, Lehigh 32–0, Bates 27–14, Yale 7–0, Dartmouth 10–0, Norwich 27–0, Harvard 21–0, and New Hampshire 40–12.

The Iron Men were not a predetermined concept by McLaughry; he substituted in the first four games. Against Yale, first major foe, at New Haven, Tuss planned to substitute at several positions. But when Brown scored and controlled the tempo of the game, he stayed with his starters.

"It wasn't until midway through the final quarter," McLaughry said, "that I realized my starters had gone all the way. In those days you could sit on a 7–0 lead, and I just let the eleven stay in there and do the job.

"When we went to Dartmouth the next week and the same eleven men played all the way again as we won, 10–0, the papers started calling us the 'Iron Men.' This was okay with me because I think it gave my men a morale boost."

Against Harvard, two weeks following the Dartmouth game, Tuss substituted in the last five minutes, and in the tie with Colgate he played 12 men.

That 1926 team ran from single- and double-wing formations behind a balanced line. The sharpshooter passes from Mishel to Broda and Randall were blended with a healthy running game. On defense the Bruins lined up in a 7–2–2 to negate opponents' passes, including those of Dartmouth quarterback Eddie Dooley. The quarterbacking and punting were superior, team spirit and morale high.

McLaughry was not only a fundamentalist but an imaginative innovator. From 1928 through '32 he developed a triple-wing offense.

"I took the tailback from deep double wing," he explained, and put him outside the opposite

Tuss McLaughry, at Brown

end on a double-reverse play which hit that side."

This play was instrumental in the 16–13 victory over Colgate in 1928. The '28 team made an 8–1 record, losing only to Yale, 32–14. Tuss delivered nine winning seasons in his 15 at Brown, 1926 through '40.

(Later at Dartmouth he coached from 1941 through '54, except for 1943 and '44 when he

Tuss (*right*) with son John, in 1939. *Chicago Tribune Photos*

served as a marine officer. His 1948 and '49 teams were the first at Dartmouth to win six major games. Most of the rest of the time Tuss suffered from lack of personnel.)

Ranked high with the 1926 and '28 Brown teams was the 1932 team, which went 7–1, losing only to Colgate 21–0. After four down years, 1933 through '36, McLaughry delivered four winners: 1937, 5–4–0; 1938, 5–3–0; 1939, 5–3–1; and 1940, 6–3–1. The four-year totals were 21–13–2.

In addition to the Iron Men, outstanding Brown linemen under McLaughry would include Tom Nash, Joe Sawyer, Maury Caito, John Prodgers, and John Marsolini ends; Paul Mackesy and John Ciuci tackles; George Lear, Spencer Manrodt, and Jack Hawley guards; Tom Gilbane center. Backs would comprise William

(Linc) Forgarty, Bill Gilbane, Joe Buonanno, Bob Chase, Bill Karaban, Frank Foster, Irving (Shine) Hall, Charlie Blount, Hal Detwhiler, John O'Leary, Ernie Savignanno, and John McLaughry.

John McLaughry, son of the coach, played on the 1938 team and was captain in 1939. Later he followed in the steps of his father by coaching at Amherst and Brown, and by serving in the marines.

Tuss McLaughry played guard, tackle, and end for Michigan State for two years, and was fullback for two years at Westminster, where his father, a judge, was trustee. Tuss captained the 1914 team and was head coach there in 1916 and '17, 1920 and '21 before going to Amherst where he coached successfully from 1922 through '25. He earned a Bachelor of Science Degree at Westminster in 1915 and a Bachelor of Law from Northeastern in 1932.

After the 1954 season, McLaughry was named Dartmouth's professor of physical education and associate director of athletics, and held these positions until his retirement in 1960.

A quiet, reserved, friendly, handsome man who avoided controversy and was soft spoken, McLaughry was not the type that produces anecdotes. Possessor of a fine mind, articulate, and a student of history, he nevertheless made an interesting conversationalist when he opened up.

No coach was more respected and admired. His peers recognized that his losing seasons were ascribable to his disinclination to recruit with high-pressure methods. In 1962 he was elected to the National Football Hall of Fame.

When he had the material at Amherst, Brown, and Dartmouth, he knew what to do with it. He reaffirmed this in 1940 when he coached the Eastern All-Stars to their first victory, 17–7, at the Polo Grounds, over the New York Giants in the New York *Herald Tribune* charity game for underprivileged youngsters.

"McLaughry," said Stanley Woodward, sports editor of the *Herald Tribune*, which sponsored the game, "produced a remarkable team out of unknown players."

John Francis (Chick) Meehan

ORANGE SQUEEZE AND VIOLENT VIOLETS

The tapestries of the twenties in college football were enriched by the coaching ability and show-manship of John Francis (Chick) Meehan, whose Syracuse and New York University teams earned regional and national respect.

In a day when head coaching was far less of a young man's job than it is today, Chick Meehan at Syracuse was acknowledged to be something of a lethal precocity. When he succeeded Frank J. (Buck) O'Neill at Syracuse in 1920, he had just turned 27, and had only one season as O'Neill's assistant behind him. O'Neill, however, recom-mended him without reservation, because as quarterback for O'Neill's pre–World War I Syra-cuse teams, Meehan had demonstrated brains, imagination, and leadership. In his last game, he had kicked the field goal and extra point that brought a 10–9 victory over Nebraska.

"Amid the run of veteran football coaches," Grantland Rice wrote after the 1922 season, "it is interesting to see one of the younger school making the progress that Chick Meehan of Syra-cuse has made. Meehan doesn't look any older than his quarterback, but he made a fine job of a hard schedule this fall, one of the finest jobs of the East."

Meehan's five-year record at Syracuse, 1920–24, shows 35–8–4; his 1922 and '23 teams lost one game each; his '20, '21, and '24 teams, two each. And a closer look attests that Chick was compet-ing well against many of the biggest coaching names, most of them far more experienced than he.

Meehan's rivalry with Pop Warner, then in his early 50s and at the peak of his fame at Pitts-burgh, gave off a special flavor. The games were

Chick Meehan

usually close and toughly waged, but the person-able Meehan enjoyed a pseudo-son-father rela-tionship with the older man, who had earlier won fame coaching Cornell and the Carlisle Indians when Chick was just a small boy.

"Pop Warner was like a father to me," Meehan said. "After each game we played each other, he would analyze both teams."

Grantland Rice spoke of a visit he and Walter Camp made to Syracuse in 1920 for the Pitt-Syracuse game. They wanted to look over two strong All-America candidates, Herb Stein, Pitt center, and Joe Alexander, who played either guard or center for Syracuse. Rice and Camp had breakfast in the Onondaga Hotel with Warner and Meehan.

"I didn't get a chance to scout you this season," said Meehan over his ham and eggs, and with tongue in cheek. "You have anything new? Any-thing I don't know about yet?"

"Not a thing, lad," Warner countered. "We'll use about five plays ... two reverses, an off tackle, a trap play or two, and perhaps a pass. I

AGAINST	W	L	T
Fred Dawson, Nebraska	2	0	0
Hugo Bezdek, Penn State	2	0	1
Dick Harlow, Colgate	2	1	0
Doc Spears, Dartmouth	1	0	0
Wallace Wade, Alabama	1	0	0
Frank Cavanaugh, Boston College	1	0	0
Pop Warner, Pittsburgh	1	2	1
Jock Sutherland, Pittsburgh	0	0	1
Greasy Neale, Washington & Jefferson	0	1	0
Gus Henderson, Southern California	0	1	0
TOTALS	10	5	3

promise not to use anything else, but I won't tell you in what order I'll use 'em."

"That's okay with me," Meehan smiled.

"Pop stuck to his promise," Rice recalled, "as Pitt and Syracuse fought to a 7–7 standoff."

It was to Pitt two years later that the Orange lost in probably the toughest defeat a Meehan-coached team over suffered.

"The score was tied 14–14 with 30 seconds to play," explained Meehan, "when a great idea came to me. I called Roy Simmons and gave him instructions: 'Go in there and throw a pass straight down the field to Giff Zimmerman. If you do it, we can win.'

"The idea was a fairly good one, inasmuch as Zimmerman was the fleetest back on the team. We had a play designed to break him loose, and all our hopes depended on the chance that a forward pass would click. On this play Paul Jappe, our end, was to run out toward the sideline as a decoy and yell excitedly in order to attract attention.

"Simmons called the signal and everything went along nicely until Jappe started out toward the sideline. Then, instead of a subdued yell, he let out a terrific bellow that could be heard throughout the stadium, and Simmons, a sophomore, was too readily convinced.

"He completely forgot Zimmerman. Instead, he threw the ball in the direction of the bellow, where there was no member of our team to receive it except Jaffe, who couldn't have caught a forward pass in a bushel basket.

"Tiny Hewitt of Pittsburgh came galloping into the picture, picked off the pass, and continued down the field for a touchdown."

Meehan indicted himself for not knowing better from an experience the year before in losing 17–10 to Washington and Jefferson. That was the same undefeated W. & J. team that gained a scoreless tie with California's Wonder Team in the Rose Bowl.

"Here again," Meehan pointed out, "the score was tied and less than a minute remained. A break had just gone against us. A minute earlier we had been hammering at the door to victory, but now we had the ball 80 yards from the goal.

"I decided to remove Harry Herbert, the quarterback, because I feared for his judgment. He was a fighting quarterback—the type that would risk a chance. In place of Herbert I sent forth Benny Moses, a smart little quarterback and a great passer. My last instruction was: 'Don't you pass!'

"I did not realize until afterward how deceitful the English language can be. Moses heard, but understood me to mean only that he, personally, was to do no passing.

"On the next play Reeves Baysinger dropped back in kick formation to throw a long spiral down the field. Moses scurried across the turf to make the catch, but the ball never approached him. One W. & J. tackle broke through and blocked the ball as it left Baysinger's hand. The other tackle, Weiderquist, caught it and dashed away to a touchdown."

Two of the most notable victories by Meehan's Syracuse teams came against heavier, favored Nebraska, 9–6 in Archbold Stadium, the Syracuse field, in 1922, and 7–0 at Lincoln in '23. The Cornhuskers, coached by Fred Dawson, were Missouri Valley Conference champions both years, and lost only one other game in that period, to Illinois, 24–7, in '23.

Even more important for headlines, the Huskers in both seasons gave Notre Dame, already established as a national power under Knute Rockne, its only defeats, 14–6 and 14–7. The latter game was the only time the Four Horsemen, used as a unit, were ever beaten. Although the same attention was not accorded the two Syracuse victories, they did gain the Orange wide recognition and respect.

Meehan's stars at Syracuse included Jack McBride, kicker, runner, and passer, whose field goal beat Pitt 3–0 in 1923; tackle Lynn O. Waldorf, later a top coach at Northwestern and California; Vic Hanson, a superb end and all-round athlete; and Evander (Pete) McRae, end. McRae and Waldorf received All-America mention from Camp.

The No. 1 Saltine Warrior for Meehan, however, was Joe Alexander, a two-year All-American at guard or center. In the 14–0 win over Colgate in 1921, Alexander made 11 consecutive tackles. And in the 10–0 victory at Dartmouth in 1920—the Big Green's first loss at home in 16 games—Joe put on a one-man goal-line stand. He made the tackle on each of the first three downs and on fourth down intercepted a pass and returned it past midfield.

That was also the game in which Bert Gulick, tackle and later 1921 captain, place-kicked a 47-yard field goal that carried well over the end zone and out of the park. It is all the more remarkable because Gulick was nearsighted.

The morale developed in his teams by Meehan was expressed fervently by one of his former

players, Walt Nowak, Class of '25: ". . . I pay my respects to John F. Meehan whom I consider one of the finest gentlemen on or off the gridiron. I never heard him use one word of profanity; he taught hard, clean, and serious football. Never tolerated unsportsmanlike conduct. He was fair, gave any candidate equal opportunity, and made football players out of boys who never saw a pigskin. He was a model sportsman and gentleman."

Meehan's teams were fundamentally sound, devoted to the off-tackle play, intransigent on defense, and never beaten by poor condition. When Chick felt the need, he could be a severe driver. When he heard from the Department of Home Economics, which was supervising the football team's diet, that the Saltiners were eating too much butter, he advised the squad, "I'll remove the butter from your systems."

"It would be stating it mildly," grinned Charlie Heck, Class of '26, "to say that he did just that. I was the last one in the dressing room at 7:00 P.M., and found that the boys had gone to bed, just too weary to go over and eat. I write this as no reflection on anyone, and often wished I could be in as good physical condition as I was that day."

Meehan maintained that there was only one sound defense against injuries—a sound body. He also believed that part of a coach's job was to impart as much showmanship as possible to his teams. He made both points in his last game at Syracuse, a 16–0 loss to Southern California. It was, coincidentally, also the last game for S.C.'s coach Gus Henderson, who moved to the Tulsa job.

The Syracusans made the cross-country train ride in three days. "The boys were kept dressed in sweat shirts and sweat pants," Meehan said, "so that they could detrain at every stop to snap through light exercise and signal practice. Naturally, we always attracted small crowds. The train stopped about four times a day.

"From every town news dispatches were sent East, saying that Syracuse had stopped off there for a brief workout. I have been told that newspaper offices doubted the veracity of the reports, because of their great frequency.

"Upon returning home, it took me some time to convince friends that the dozen dispatches in three days were legitimate. Even then they accused me of 'putting on a show'—as if that were something foreign to a football coach's business."

A naturally sociable man, although he never took anything stronger than ginger ale, Meehan

Chick rewarded at a testimonial dinner in his honor

was probably more well and favorably known among his peers than any other coach of his time. He used to arrange the entertainment for the coaches' annual banquet. That was when they used to give a derby every year to the coach adjudged to have told the best story.

"Rockne, Cavanaugh, and Zuppke were always great storytellers," Chick laughed. "They didn't know it, but the coaches used to select the winner even before the speeches were made. Then they would tell each of the three that they were voting for him. Cav won most of the time."

New York University, operating in the world's largest city, had never been a football power, but decided to be one as part of the general sports growth of the Golden Age. In searching for the right man to give it strong, well-known teams, NYU focused unerringly on Meehan. Just as naturally, the flamboyant Chick found the challenge of New York irresistible.

In his seven years on University Heights, 1925–31, Meehan never had a losing season. His 1926 and '27 teams lost one game each; the '25 and '28 teams lost two each; the '29, '30, and '31 clubs, three each.

Two years after Meehan came from Syracuse to NYU, Major Frank Cavanaugh came from

Boston College to Fordham, 1927. And thus came the days of the "Violent Violets" and the original "Seven Blocks of Granite." From 1928 through '31, they staged the Battle of the Bronx in the Polo Grounds or Yankee Stadium before sellout crowds of 55,000 to 70,000. Louis J. Madow, a Fordham Road jeweler, put up the Madow Trophy, which went to the most valuable player in the game, and was the forerunner of the Lambert Trophy, which since 1936 has gone annually to the Eastern team with the best performance.

Meehan dressed up the NYU schedules with name teams like Tulane, Colgate, Nebraska, Carnegie Tech, and Oregon State. He had a cannon shot off after every NYU touchdown. And he equipped his teams with a military cadence that they used in coming out of the huddle to line up on the ball.

"The Meehan military shift," said his ace quarterback, Jack (Dutch) Connor, "was simple but effective. The entire line would line up about three and a half yards away from the ball with their backs to the line of scrimmage. The running guard would always line up the ball as if he were the center.

"With the play and starting signal given in the huddle, the entire line would pivot on their left feet, swinging around in perfect cadence of one-two-three and landing on the line of scrimmage in charging position. The backs, of course, were in step at the same time with the linemen."

John E. (Bing) Miller, another Meehan player, who was later graduate manager of athletics, pointed out that the military movement had purpose as well as eye appeal.

"The unusual part of the huddle, and not a generally known fact, was that any one of the three middle linemen—the center or one of the two guards—could act as center. As a result the team could line up in a balanced line, or in an unbalanced line right or left without changing the position of a single man. Often, the defensive team, trying to meet the shift, would be caught flat-footed.

"Some said that Meehan was a showman," Miller continued, "and I agree; but this certainly does not detract from the man's strong and inspiring personality. His profound ability in completely understanding each lad's personality enabled him to cement unity."

Meehan's personality and industry made him an effective recruiter. He rounded up some of the best prep school material in the Northeast, especially from Dean Academy. By today's standards, however, when 40 recruits a year are not unusual, Meehan's numbers seem few.

"In seven years at NYU," he said, "we gave out 72 scholarships; in five years at Syracuse, about 40." But we have to remember it was single-platoon, iron-man days, not the specialized platoon football of today.

In addition to Connor, Meehan's outstanding NYU players included tackle Al Lassman, and backs Frank Briante, Ed (Cowboy) Hill, and Ken Strong.

Strong was No. 1, one of the most gifted all-round backs ever to wear cleats. He stood six feet one, weighed 201, and could do it all: run, pass, receive, punt, place-kick, block, and tackle. He scored 22 touchdowns and 28 conversions for 160 points to lead the nation in 1928.

That year, although they lost to Georgetown 7–2 on a wet field and to Oregon State in their last game, 25–13, the Violets were the best of Meehan's teams, probably the best in the East, and capable on a given day of beating the best nationally. That's the kind of team they were in Forbes Field, Pittsburgh, the day they beat Carnegie Tech, 27–13.

Carnegie, unbeaten and conquerors in a row of Washington & Jefferson, Pittsburgh, Georgetown, and Notre Dame, featured an outstanding quarterback-passer in Howard Harpster, but the Tartans were undone by Strong, who had his greatest day. He ran 40 yards for one touchdown, hit the line for another, and passed for the other two. After the game, Carnegie's coach Wally Steffen, who was also a former University of Chicago quarterback and a federal judge, told Grantland Rice:

"I've seen Heston. I've seen Eckersall. But Strong is the greatest football player I ever saw. It is the first time I have seen one football player run over my team. We beat Notre Dame 27–7 last Saturday. We were undefeated. But Strong ran, passed, and kicked us into the ground."

Rice himself, in his story of the game, showered Strong unreservedly:

"The NYU attack was led by a runaway buffalo, using the speed of a deer, and his name was Ken Strong. This man Strong weighs 201 pounds and runs the 100 in about ten flat. Today, he ran all over a big, powerful team, smashed its line, ran its ends, kicked 50 and 55 yards, and tackled all over the lot. Today he was George Gipp, Red Grange, and Chris Cagle rolled into one human form and there was nothing that Carnegie had that could stop his march.

"I doubt that any team in the country could have stood off this New York attack as it struck this afternoon. Certainly nothing in the East could have checked it on a dry field. It had manpower, weight, strength, deception, and exceptional speed. It also had the plays."

That year NYU under Meehan beat Fordham under Cavanaugh for the last time. Gradually Fordham caught up with and passed the Violent Violets, yet the chart for their complete rivalry shows that Chick came out one game in front. The Meehan-Cavanaugh chart:

YEAR	MEEHAN		CAVANAUGH	SCORE
1924	Syracuse	10	Boston College	0
1927	NYU	32	Fordham	0
1928	NYU	34	Fordham	7
1929	NYU	0	Fordham	26
1930	NYU	0	Fordham	7
1931	NYU	0	Fordham	0

Away from the field, these two rivals were good friends, and in the years when Cavanaugh's health was fading, Meehan often visited him at his apartment in the Concourse Plaza Hotel.

Once Professor Philip O. Badger, who abhorred big-time football, became chairman of the athletic board, Meehan's regime at NYU was doomed. After the 1931 season, Chick resigned. But he did not resign as a failure. He had accomplished precisely what NYU had asked him to. He had made the Violets violent, a football power that made headlines and drew crowds.

Meehan coached six more years at Manhattan; on a subdued stage there, he compiled a winning record of 31–21–6. This put his all-time record for 18 seasons at 115–44–14 for .705.

On November 9, 1972, Chick, full of years at 79, died. For coaches who combined sell with fundamentalism and leadership, a high place in the twenties belongs to John Francis (Chick) Meehan.

Harry Mehre

THE TRUE ATHENIAN

Only one I know of to hold a grudge, or half a grudge, toward Harry J. Mehre is me. It used to be a whole grudge; even the kind of indignities perpetrated against my youth are assuaged by time. There are some things, though ...

Harry Mehre is a transplanted Hoosier who developed in 1923 a passion for the University of Georgia and the South that has had its ups and downs but has never gone unrequited. When last heard from, both parties to the almost half-century affair were still humming, "I saw you last night and got that old feeling ... ."

As head coach of Georgia for ten seasons and Mississippi for seven, the last three during World War II, Mehre's record, analyzed in its context, can scarcely be rated less than distinguished. Since retiring as a coach after 1945, Mehre has been a success as a soft-drink executive in Atlanta. He has maintained his connection with football and his hold on the heart of Georgia and the South by his pungent football columns, syndicated through the Atlanta *Journal*, and by his frequent banquet appearances.

Georgia thinks so much of Mehre that it has inducted him into its Athletic Hall of Fame, not once but twice, not only as a coach but as a sportswriter.

Football's nutcake fans are not a majority, or even a plurality; they only sound that way because the vacuity of their heads is matched by the fiber of their larynxes and the stamina of their windpipes. Even most fans who could tell a football from a bowl of grits knew that the coaching setbacks Mehre suffered in a 10-year career, 1928–37, at Georgia came in games with Tulane, Alabama, Tennessee, and Southern California, games which found him emphatically outsquadded.

These teams also happened to be coached by people any football genius who ever lived, at even odds, would have found tough to handle: Tulane's Bernie Bierman, Alabama's Wallace Wade and Frank Thomas, Tennessee's Bob Neyland, and Southern Cal's Howard Jones. There was no doubt in the mind of these four titans that they brought superior forces against Mehre's.

Harry Mehre, at Georgia

There was deep respect among all of them for his knowledge of the game, his ability to teach it, his leadership that extracted the maximum from gallant Southern kids of limited talent, and his outstanding qualities as a person.

More than a quarter of a century after Harry coached his last game, these charismatic qualities were touched upon by Dr. Lenox D. Baker, orthopedic surgeon at Duke University Medical Center. While studying he served as trainer under Neyland at Tennessee and Wade at Duke.

"Harry Mehre," Dr. Baker recalled, "never had a greater personal admirer, one who more appreciated his ability to use his wit in putting over a point, than Robert R. Neyland. He would frequently laugh and quote some of the things he had said. And he had a deep appreciation of Harry's knowledge of football. Wallace Wade likewise enjoyed him. At many an Atlanta Athletic Club party, Harry, without trying, scintillated. As he traveled his way, he brought happiness and joy to many people."

How, it is logical to ask, could such a proven paragon be the subject of a half grudge?

Easily, given the facts. In my boyhood as a New Haven towner madly devoted to the Yale football team, Harry Mehre made a habit of beating Yale, and did it in Yale Bowl three times.

The 1929 victory over Yale at Athens was unbecoming but yet not amoral, but who would desecrate a holy place thrice? It was a wonder the Almighty did not interfere. Why didn't West Rock fall on Harry Mehre?

This demon rebel, camouflaged as an apostle of interregional understanding, would have long since been totally forgiven here, however, had he not chosen to visit not only indignity, but catastrophe on the 1936 Fordham football team the author worked for as sports information director.

Fordham's hour was near zenith. The Rams were undefeated, and rumor had a Rose Bowl invitation from Washington awaiting them, if they could get by their last two games, with Georgia at the Polo Grounds, November 14, and New York University in Yankee Stadium on Thanksgiving five days later. Consummation was considered automatic by Fordham fans and by some of the players.

This was the first year of the second version of the Seven Blocks of Granite line. Alex Wojciechowicz at center, Ed Franco and Al Babartsky at tackles, Vince Lombardi at right guard. They hadn't given up a touchdown. Their victims included St. Mary's, then a power, Southern Methodist, and Purdue. They had played the second of the celebrated three straight scoreless ties with Dr. Sutherland's ferocious Pitt Panthers, who would later rip Washington at Pasadena, 21–0.

Fordham followers wore buttons, "From Rose Hill to Rose Bowl." Coach Mehre saw to it the Georgia players got some. The Fordham band, which should have been sent on tour of Outer Mongolia after the Purdue game, paraded into the Polo Grounds playing a premature hit, "California, Here I Come." Coach Mehre saw to it the Georgia dressing room windows were open.

This was not one of Harry Mehre's better teams; nor was it a weak team. Co-captained by guards J. C. Hall and Harry Harman, it had been belted around in October, but had pulled itself together to defeat Florida and Tulane, and would go on to beat Georgia Tech, a habit of Harry Mehre's. At best, however, it shaped up as no better than a 2–1 underdog to Fordham, mainly because of the Ram's tremendous defense.

The Fordham players, even those below the cum laude level of Vince Lombardi and end Leo Paquin, knew that Athens, Georgia, is the South's center of culture. After the game began the Rams thought they had been matched with Leonidas and the 300 Spartans. Such a game as Georgia

played to deserve a 7–7 tie demands many heroes. Leonidas this day, though, was a right guard named Peter Tinsley, an antebellum type, who would have courted Scarlett O'Hara with a bottle of corn and a rebel yell.

Earlier that season, Tinsley, who dropped back to punt, had been warned by Mehre to kick away from the Louisiana State safety man, whose vice was running the ball down the throats of rival safety men, if not farther. Pete kicked for the first time from his 5-yard line. He angled the ball high up to about the 40th row in the stadium seats to his right, but it went out of bounds on Georgia's 9. When Pete came out of the game, he advised Coach Mehre, "That's one they won't run back for a touchdown." Pete could stand up to adversity.

Against Fordham, he dished it out. He helped himself by lining up where he wasn't supposed to, in the gap between the Fordham offensive left tackle and left guard, Franco and Nat Pierce. The unorthodoxy enabled him to play most of the first half in the Ram backfield. There was also a center named Quinton Lumpkin, who bedeviled complacent Fordham. Georgia dominated the first half and took a 7–0 lead on a pass. In the second half, Fordham rallied and managed to come out with a 7–7 tie.

A comeback victory over NYU, a weaker team than Georgia, might possibly have saved the Pasadena invite, but the upset tie by the Georgians put a dent in the hitherto inviolate morale of the Rose Hillers. They looked even more impotent in losing to NYU, 7–6. Looking back, I believe if Fordham had defeated Georgia, it would have defeated NYU also.

In that case, my bride and I, as naively planned, would have honeymooned in Pasadena. Instead, thanks to Harry J. Mehre, we settled for Winchester, Massachusetts, six feet of snow, and the Indian Pudding Bowl.

When Harry Mehre was an athletic star at high school in Huntington, Indiana, 1914–18, football had been suspended because of the death of a student. It was for his prowess in basketball that Mehre was invited to Notre Dame in 1918. But Rockne got him suited up for football, tried him as a back, then shifted him to center-linebacker.

Mehre was called "Horse" then because he was big, especially in the hands he snapped the ball and tackled enemy ball carriers with. He played as first sub in 1919 and regular in '20 on Rockne's first two undefeated teams. Away from the field

there was nothing about this tall, gracious, intelligent, articulate, and witty young man that was suggestive of the equine, so the nickname died.

Notre Dame football as taught by Knute Rockne, which exerted a national influence in the twenties and thirties, was first brought south by Mehre as line coach and Frank Thomas as backfield coach at Georgia in 1923.

In 1925 Thomas left Georgia to begin the four seasons at Chattanooga that tipped off his potential as a head coach. In 1929 he returned to Georgia as backfield coach under Mehre, who had become head coach the year before. In 1931, Thomas succeeded Wallace Wade at Alabama and made a 15-year record that few have matched.

During Thomas's four years at Chattanooga, the Georgia backfield coach was a third Notre Dame man, Jim Crowley. In 1929 Crowley went to Michigan State where in four years he built the foundations of the modern Spartan empire. In nine years at Fordham, he delivered one of the four top coaching records in the country; the three others belonged to Bierman, Thomas, and Neyland.

H. J. Stegeman, who had been an all-round athlete at Chicago under Alonzo Stagg, coached Georgia from 1920 through '22 to records of 8–0–1, 7–2–1, and 5–4–1. His 1920 team, undefeated but tied by Virginia, 0–0, claimed the championship of the South; his '21 team lost only to two powers of the East, then still the dominant area, to Harvard, 10–7, and Dartmouth, 7–0.

In 1921, Stegeman became athletic director and had appointed as his successor Kid Woodruff, who had quarterbacked and captained the 1911 team. Woodruff's record indicates that had he chosen to stay with coaching, he could have done well. He did well enough in his five years, 1923 through '27—30–16–1, and only one losing season. His last team, 1927, the Dream and Wonder team, was Georgia's best through that time. It handed Yale, with its great line, an only defeat, 14–10, and swept over all Southern opposition, including Tulane and Alabama, until the final game at Georgia Tech.

In losing to Tech, 12–0, the Bulldogs also lost a probable Rose Bowl trip. Tech, building up to its 1928 Rose Bowl team, might have won under any conditions, but Georgia was hurt by fumbling on a muddy field and the absence of Captain Chick Shiver, star end and punter, injured against Alabama. Tom Nash, the other end, was All-America, and later starred at Green Bay. Herdis

McCrary, fullback, 210 and a 9.8 sprinter with a quick start, was a Doc Blanchard type.

Woodruff quit after that season according to plan. He was a well-to-do Columbus business-man. Coaching was not his career ultimate. But he was devoted to Georgia's advancement. It was he, with Stegeman's approval and on Rockne's recommendation, who brought Mehre, Thomas, and Crowley to Athens. He felt the football they had learned was ahead of its time and that Mehre and Thomas could succeed him to the advantage of Georgia.

In their six-year varsity span at Notre Dame, 1919 through '24, Mehre as fullback, Thomas as quarterback, and Crowley as left halfback had played in the era of Gipp and the Four Horse-men, which placed Rockne where he will long remain among coaches, at the pinnacle. That six-year record, including three perfect seasons —1919, '20, '24—shows an astonishing log of 54–3–1, .939. Mehre, Thomas, and Crowley, how-ever, were not swept into coaching as products of a dynasty, as were some who went out from South Bend. They were natural strategists, and leaders born to be coaches. Rockne knew it, and told Woodruff and Stegeman when they sought his advice on young promising assistants.

Mehre, however, never recruited as successfully as Thomas and Crowley. Part of this, he admit-ted, traced to himself. "I never cared for the pressures of big-time college coaching," he said. "I really wasn't a very good recruiter. Oh, I went after the boys, all right, but I couldn't demean myself. I couldn't soft-soap a kid and his family to get him to sign when I knew I'd be chewing him out six months later."

The biggest part traced, however, to Georgia's laudable yet unrealistic football philosophy, which the small-in-number but large-mouthed win-'em-all alumni would not let the college live with, if they could make a coach unwilling to live with their savage, unreasoning criticism.

Thomas at Alabama and Crowley at Fordham were issued an identical and unequivocal man-date by their presidents, Dr. Mike Denny and Father Aloysius J. Hogan, who fancied them-selves also football experts. The mandate was: win and keep winning. The mandate Mehre received at Georgia was, on the whole, consid-erably saner. It was expressed by Dr. S. V. Sanford, faculty moderator of athletics, who later became Georgia's president and chancellor. He said in 1929,

"The Georgia ideal is to play the best teams of the land, even those out of our class, to spread the fame and glory of alma mater to the hinterland of New England and the Pacific Coast by presenting Georgia boys who would play with the dash and gallantry typical of our youth, despite the inev-itability of defeat.

"The ideal will be reached when all major colleges in the Southern Conference have such schedules and the squads are of such well-balanced strength that no one else can hope or expect to have a clean slate."

By every conceivable gauge, Harry Mehre carried out Dr. Sanford's mandate. His 10-year record at Georgia—59–34–6, .626—included only two losing seasons, 1928, his first, and 1932. Against No. 1 rival Georgia Tech, the Bulldogs were 6–2–2. No Mehre Georgia team won a conference championship; his 1931 and '33 teams, both 8–2, were derailed by late-season losses, in '31 to Tulane, in '33 to Auburn. Georgia's record against the East was 5 out of 6 against Yale, 3 out of 5 against NYU, the upset tie with Fordham, and in 1937 another near upset, a 7–6 loss at Holy Cross to one of the Crusaders' finest teams coached by Mehre's old Notre Dame end and teammate, Dr. Eddie An-derson.

The fondest memory that Mehre cherishes of his coaching days at Athens was the dedication game of Sanford Stadium against a Yale team making its first visit to the South. It was Old Eli's way of saluting the oldest state-chartered college in America, whose football teams had visited Yale Bowl six consecutive seasons. The game attracted national attention. Nobody could pos-sibly describe Coach Mehre's memories of the historic game better than sportscribe Mehre. Here are excerpts from a column he wrote about it 38 years later.

"Christopher Columbus discovered America on October 12, 1492. On October 12, 1929, 437 years later, Yale University came to Athens, Georgia, and discovered Sanford Stadium.

"Dr. S. V. Sanford, then faculty chairman of athletics and later president and chancellor of Georgia, was the mastermind behind the building of the stadium and the master salesman who persuaded the Yale people to accept our sincere invitation.

"Dr. Sanford not only carried the athletic banner for Georgia, but he was a trailblazer in athletics for the entire South. A brilliant and educated scholar and teacher, he was also one of the first to visualize the impact of football, the

coming of the paved highways, and the magnetism of intercollegiate football in the Southland. It was the natural thing for the stadium to be named for him. No other name was even mentioned or considered.

"The Yale party invaded Athens on Friday, October 11, 1929, and immediately won the hearts of the Athenians as the Yale Band marched down College Avenue hammering out 'Dixie,' and the sidewalk crowd responded with Rebel yells. This was the beginning of Athens celebrated 'football weekends.'

"If you are 50 or older and a Bulldog alumnus or fan, you will know that the Bulldogs of Georgia upset the Bulldogs of Yale, 15–0. To give you a little background on how great an upset it was, my Bulldogs had been upset by Oglethorpe University, 13–6, while Yale, in its opening game, had defeated Vermont by 89–0. We did not enter the Yale game overconfident.

"Let me tell you 1967 Hippies that Yale in the '20s was big league football. Georgia defeated Yale for the first time in 1927, 14–10, Yale's only loss that season. In 1923 Yale was undefeated and untied and under the present ground rules for determining the national champ, the Elis would have been it. They defeated Georgia in the first game between the schools, 40–0.

"The tip on the outcome of the dedication game came Friday night when the University entertained the Yale team, coaches, faculty members, and Eli fans. The late Red Maddox, half of the partnership of Leathers and Maddox, the fiery redheaded guards, was selected by the squad to deliver its welcome. Red thanked the Yale people for honoring Georgia by coming South to dedicate the Stadium. His closing remarks set the tempo for the team's great play the next day.

" 'No one but the Lord knows what the outcome of tomorrow's game will be. But when the sun goes down behind Sanford Stadium tomorrow afternoon, all Georgia and the entire South will be proud of this Bulldog football team.'

"A Yale coach sitting next to me said, 'We're licked.'

"As in all victories a star emerges. That day it was the hitherto unknown sophomore end, Vernon (Catfish) Smith who grabbed the headlines with his brilliant offensive and defensive play. Smitty scored every one of Georgia's 15 points, kicked a point after, and, to top off the afternoon, cornered Yale's brilliant sophomore, later All-America, 'Little Boy Blue,' Albie Booth, in the end zone for a safety. His dramatic play zoomed the Catfish into the national limelight and eventually to All-America status.

"From the safety came an amusing incident. Smith pushed into the Yale end zone and was about to block Booth's punt. Albie, seeing that his kick was about to be blocked, took the football and started running for his life with the Catfish in pursuit. Smitty did not make a shoestring tackle. It was more of a choking exhibition as he wrestled Albie to the end zone turf. Booth got up and told the Catfish, 'That doesn't go around here, Smith.' Smith replied, 'Neither do you, Albie.'

"University of Georgia officials, coaches, players, and alumni and friends have cause to be proud of the New Sanford Stadium with its 60,000 seats but we were pretty proud of the Old Sanford Stadium, filled with 30,000, and the team that dedicated it back on October 12, 1929. I know I will never forget that day or that football team."

It was, indeed, a multikarated form-shaker pulled off by an unusual team that had eight sophomores and two juniors starting; the only senior starter was Captain Joe Boland. It was known as the "Whistlestop Team," because of the hometowns of the players, most of them Georgians.

Marion Dickens was from Ocilla, Herb Maffett from Toccoa, Red Maddox from Douglas, Red Leathers from Athens (if the Culture Center will accept a "whistlestop" designation), Bobby Rose from Valdosta, Spurgeon (Spud) Chandler (later a formidable pitcher for the New York Yankees) from Carnesville, Jack (the Ripper) Roberts from Albany, Weddington Kelly from Newnan, Catfish Smith from Macon, and Theodore Frisbee from RFD Alabama. Gainesville contributed Tommy Paris and Tiger Bennett, and Savannah sent Jimmy Patterson. Captain Boland from Atlanta and quarterback Austie Downs from Chicago were the only real city slickers.

From the great day of dedication, the Whistlestoppers advanced through three years that saw the hopes and dreams of Dr. Sanford, "Steg" Stegeman, and Kid Woodruff achieve fruition in records of 6–4 in 1929, 7–2–1 in '30, and 8–2–0 in '31. Georgia Tech, which had won three of the last four in the post-World War I resumption of the series, was whipped three straight years.

The four losses through the '30 and '31 seasons were 13–0 to Wallace Wade's last and best undefeated Alabama team that smashed Washington State in the Rose Bowl, 24–0; to the 1931

Tulane and Southern California teams, 20–7 and 60–0, each the best turned out at each school by Bernie Bierman and Howard Jones; and 25–0 to a 1930 Tulane team that was second only to Alabama in the South that year, losing one game, at Northwestern, then a Big Ten power.

The tremendous 60–0 thrashing by Southern Cal in Los Angeles traced to two factors. First, the Bulldogs didn't belong on the same field with the Trojans. Second the game was played on a postseason Saturday, following four rugged assignments in a row: the 7–6 victory over a strong Chick Meehan NYU team in Yankee Stadium; the loss to Tulane; a 12–6 victory over Auburn and that great all-purpose halfback Jimmy Hitchcock, one season away from undefeated; and a resounding 35–6 triumph over Georgia Tech.

The Bulldogs were not only outpersonneled against Howard Jones' Trojan Horses, which included eight current or to-be All-America players; they were far from peak form. This was affirmed indirectly by the Rose Bowl game when the Trojans were happy to escape, 21–12, from a Tulane second-half rally, the same Bierman team that Georgia had held to 20–7.

The Trojans heavily outweighed the enervated Southerners and literally knocked them around. The winning teams make the jokes and tell the funny stories. Maddox, who had made that two-edged welcome speech to Yale, was the protagonist of a story told afterwards by Johnny Baker. He was the guard who had earlier in the year kicked the celebrated field goal to cap the Trojans' fourth-quarter comeback victory at Notre Dame, 16–14.

A Georgia guard (Maddox), he said, kept tackling him from behind as he pulled out of the line to lead the Thundering Herd on Howard Jones' fearsome off-tackle play. Finally, Baker said to Maddox, "Look, man, I'll have to belt you good, if you don't cut that out." The weary Maddox grinned, "Don't get mad, Baker, I haven't been able to catch up with you. All I want to know is where can a guy get a gallon of corn liquor after the game?"

Any Whistlestopper who felt need of a gallon of corn, or maybe even five quarts, had it coming after the three seasons he had given alma mater. But the Nutcake Alumni would have voted it down. They had begun to growl in 1930 and in 1931 after the Bulldogs lost the Tulane game and with it the Southern Intercollegiate Conference championship; and following the debacle in Los Angeles, the growl grew in volume and menace.

Mehre, then and for some time afterwards, paid little attention to it, but Stegeman and other friends knew trouble lay ahead.

On the way home from the West Coast, the team changed trains at Atlanta.

"Steg," Mehre said, "lend me a nickel. I want to call up a friend."

"Harry," Stegeman replied, "take a dime and call up all your friends."

Along about then, "Old Timer," the Atlanta *Journal's* influential sports columnist, also gave him friendly warning:

"Look elsewhere for a job. You are riding the crest now, but your boat is only a canoe and you can't paddle it long in an ocean. You can't beat Alabama and Tulane more than one time in five. They have three athletes to your one, and always will have." (He was wrong on Tulane, whose material came back to Georgia's.)

Mehre's love for the university perhaps blinded him to reality. He was hard to convince.

"We don't have to win them all," he said. "We've got a sane situation here. Everybody understands we are playing a big league schedule on a shoestring, and if we can beat Tech two times out of three and win most of the others, we are doing well. . . . It's too much fun, working here with these Georgia boys. They are the right type. They've got character and background and manners, and they are battlers. You won't find boys like them anywhere else. I'm going to stick around as long as I can."

Mehre stuck around for six more seasons. With the Whistlestoppers graduated, the 1932 record, 2–5–2, his only losing season except the first, evoked ever louder complaints from the Nutcakes. Then, in his last five seasons, Mehre's record of 32–16–3, .657, topped that of his first five. But the snipers never let up.

Gradually Mehre became disenchanted. By 1937, he'd had enough. His decision to chuck it was firmed up by ludicrous criticism from the Nutcakes after the Georgia Tech game. The Bulldogs, three-touchdown underdogs, gained a 6–6 tie. Fullback Bill Hartman gave Georgia the lead by returning the second-half kickoff 93 yards.

Even when the background is unhappy, the humor in football is inevitable. Mehre never saw Hartman's 93-yard run. In returning to the field, he had trouble convincing a gate Cerberus that he was the Georgia coach, "Five people have already gone through here," protested the Cerberus, "who said they were Harry Mehre."

Left to right: Harry Mehre, Harry Stuhldreher, Elmer Layden, and Hunk Anderson, in 1963. *Chicago Tribune Photos*

The Nutcakes blamed Mehre for letting Hartman try for the extra point; Hartman, they said, was exhausted from his run, and a fresher man would have made it. Ten years before, they had demanded a coach who could beat Tech. Mehre's record against Tech was 6–2–2. Harry's mistake is clear—he didn't beat Tech ten straight. (Tech's alumni, for obvious reasons, supported the Nutcakes.)

So Mehre wasn't shoved. He was sensitive enough not to want to live any longer with the Nutcakes. Years later he would say, "I often kid about my leaving Georgia. I tell people I had a lifetime contract there and that the school got out of it by declaring me legally dead. But the truth is, I was simply fed up. Georgia wanted big-time football but didn't want to pay for it. I told them that it was best for them and best for me to go elsewhere."

At the time he left, he could have stated the same with justification, but his letter of resignation had the flavor of a farewell note to a lover. Mehre spoke from the heart of his having come to love Georgia as much as he did his alma mater, Notre Dame.

Seldom, if ever, has a resigning coach evoked such support and fervent hope that he would reconsider. The Georgia players wrote President Harmon Caldwell: "We, the football squad of the University of Georgia, do hereby petition that the University of Georgia Athletic Board, under Faculty Chairman of Athletics, W. O. Payne, use its influence in persuading Coach Harry J. Mehre to reconsider his resignation.

"We are behind Coach Mehre 100 percent."

It was signed by Captain Bill Hartman, Alternate Captain Otis Maffett, and every other man on the squad.

O. B. Keeler, the famous sports columnist of the *Journal*, wrote angrily:

"Harry Mehre, who is a sportsman as well as a football coach, apparently got fed up on the howling—he is too much of a sportsman to do any howling about it himself. And Harry Mehre just hauled off and resigned, in a gracefully phrased letter that was a masterpiece of courtesy and consideration for the official family of a school with which he had been connected for 14 years.

"Harry Mehre had nothing to say about the Wolves, thus showing a greater capacity for self-restraint than this correspondent, on the outside looking in, is able to boast. . . . I think, by gum, I'd have asked them (always supposing 'they' can be located and questioned, which ought to be not so difficult now, as 'they' are definitely out on a limb)—I think I'd have asked them what they had expected me to do as a head coach."

"Old Timer" summed it up: "The question is, does the University of Georgia want to make it

Big Time. The other options are to stick with the present compromise plan, or to switch to Small Time.

"*Under which king, Bezonia? Speak or die.*'"

Georgia chose big time under Coach Wally Butts, won four Southeastern Conference championships, and played in eight Bowls.

In February 1938 Harry Mehre went to work on a three-year contract with Mississippi. In the four seasons before Pearl Harbor, he put together records of 9–2, 7–2, 9–2, 6–2–1 for 31–8–1. His 1938 team, beaten only by Vanderbilt and Tennessee, featured an All-America halfback, Parker Hall. Against Mississippi State, traditional rival, he was less successful; after winning the first year, he lost three in a row. In the 1941 loss, 6–0, his cause was not helped when Bobby Yandel, whose 80-yard run for a touchdown had made him a hero in the 18–0 victory over Arkansas the week before, had the misfortune to be so shaken up that he tackled teammate Ray Poole, who was in the clear and headed for a touchdown.

Ole Miss and Mehre got clobbered during the war seasons, and didn't play in 1943; the squads comprised mainly 16- and 17-year-olds, and 4-Fs. Mehre, however, began recruiting the players who would get the regime of his successor, Johnny Vaught, off in high gear. They included halfback Charlie Conerly and end Barney Poole. If Mehre had cared to stay on, he too might have enjoyed a dynasty. But he wasn't interested. He'd had enough coaching. He was leaving Ole Miss in better football shape than he had found her. If the situation had needed more building, he might have stayed.

Perhaps by the time this is read, Georgia and Ole Miss will have been able to place Harry Mehre where he belongs—in the National Football Hall of Fame. And the citation should not overlook the tribute of which he was most proud, written by a columnist:

"The most remarkable thing about Harry Mehre's coaching career was that he compiled such a fine record without cheating."

About the half grudge. It's a quarter grudge now. There are some things, however ...

Dutch Meyer

THE SATURDAY FOX

When Dutch Meyer was about to chew out his Texas Christian football squad, he showed consideration to the ministerial students. "Leave the room," he commanded them. "I'm going to raise hell." TCU raised hell in the Southwest Conference much of Meyer's 19 seasons—1934–52. They won three championships, took four seconds and four thirds, and upset so many favorites that Dutch became known as "The Saturday Fox," a second nickname. The first was "Old Iron Pants."

Seven times Meyer's Horned Frogs got to Bowl games, and the 1938 team was recognized as national champions. That was the team with Little David (Slingshot) O'Brien at quarterback. Little David later joined the FBI, which knew a good brain and a good gun. With Little David calling the shots, TCU went 10–0 and beat Carnegie Tech in the Sugar Bowl.

O'Brien was supported by a typical TCU line, meaning extraordinarily large by SWC standards and equally combative, with probably the best center in Lone Star history, Ki Aldrich, and at least four All-Conference desperadoes in tackle I. B. Hale, end Don Looney, guard Forrest Kline, and fullback Connie Sparks.

A man dumb enough could get into a bad argument in Fort Worth or College Station by naming either the 1938 Texas Christians or the 1939 Texas Aggies the best in Southwest single-platoon days. A man that dumb, of course, should be at least smart enough to pack a gun and be quicker on the draw even than the champion of silent film cowboys, William S. Hart. (Bill's elapsed time from holster to firing was 0:00, with the aid of a film cutter who removed all intervening frames.)

It would have been High Noon in the O.K. Corral for sure, if the Frogs of '38 and the Aggies of '39 had collided. The Frogs were the forward-pass wonders of the age, the Ags the big overland crunch, the College Station Wagon, led by fullback "Jarrin' Jawn" Kimbrough.

Nobody in Texas will give you an argument on

this, though: no college team at any time in any place ever had two such forward passers back to back as Dutch Meyer enjoyed at TCU, from 1934 through '38, in Sammy Baugh and Davey O'Brien. And though they would have been stars on any team, they benefited from playing under such a teacher and strategist, imaginative yet sound, as Leo Robert Meyer.

Credit for fostering the Saturday Shootout that first made the nation aware of football in the Southwest rightfully belongs to Ray Morrison's Southern Methodist "Aerial Circus" of the early twenties, starring the first of many celebrated pint-sized passers in Logan Stollenwerck.

It was Meyer and his TCU teams, however, that made the forward pass less of a gamble and more of a science through the arms and hearts of Slingin' Sammy and Slingshot Davey, some very talented receivers, and incessant drilling by Meyer to execute the patterns and timing of his double-wingback formation. With two split ends and two, later three, wingbacks, it was the most advanced aerial deployment of its time, and earned its innovator fame as "The Meyer Spread." Twenty-five years later, however, Dutch claimed it was an exaggeration.

"They said I had my ends sitting in the stands, spread out so wide they could sell soda water between plays," he stated. "They were hardly spread out at all by today's standards. No two men were ever separated by more than three to five yards, and so spaced that any of them could make the two-way move to block, in or out. We always had a blocking angle in mind."

To support his passing game, Meyer recruited linemen who were quick and powerful and so formidable in their purple shirts they were known betimes as "The Purple People Eaters." Their 7–6 loss in New York's Polo Grounds in 1937, O'Brien's junior season, to Fordham's undefeated Seven Blocks of Granite team was perhaps the No. 1 thriller in Ram annals, still remembered in detail by all who saw it.

The scintillant show put on by Meyer's teams was supported by his own sideline spectacular that featured tantrums, tensions, and tears; screams of rage, woe, exultation, and frustration; and a running commentary at once pertinent and humorous. Dutch would light one cigarette after another, and sometimes put the lighted end in his mouth. He would pluck and nibble blades of grass like a neurotic goat. He would jam his Stetson down over his ears until he resembled a cat with its head halfway in a salmon can. He

Dutch Meyer of TCU, in 1951. *Chicago Tribune Photos*

would tumble off the end of the bench like a drunken troll. And all the time, he'd ad-lib on the ebb and flow:

"Stop that drop-the-handkerchief and let's play some football! ... What luck! Who put the hat on the bed! ... Receiver's as open as a butcher knife! ... They're blowin' us out of the tub! ... Judas H. Priest! We can't hit nobody!"

By the end of a game Dutch was an emotional wreck. Win, lose, or draw, he'd often collapse into tears. After one victory over No. 1 traditional rival Southern Methodist, he wept unashamedly as the team physician wrenched his hat up from around his ears, applied hot and cold towels,

sponged his face, and tried to get him to think soothing thoughts.

A man of profound sentiment, Meyer sometimes broke down at reunions with old players until he had them weeping too.

Dutch's football mind and emotional nature made him a natural on his television show with TCU's business manager, Amos Melton. Viewers sent in questions and Melton deliberately fed Dutch the most exasperating, if not asinine, such as did he think Kyle Rote, the great SMU runner, was really an All-American or just a local build-up. Dutch would wave his arms and scream:

"Is Rote All-America? Why every time that Rote kid has got into a shook-up field against us, it has taken our whole team to bring him down! What do you want Rote to do—pick up the stadium and carry it across the goal line?"

Melton surprised Dutch on the show one night with a bunch of his "old boys" in a sort of this-is-your-life epic. Said Amos, "It turned out to be the greatest crying scene since *Camille*."

The sentiment and native humor of Meyer were cross-grained with ambition, belligerence, and cockiness. He was the only Southwest Conference coach to win his series with Dana Xenophon Bible, in D. X.'s decade at Texas, 6–4.

"I always felt comfortable playing Mr. Bible," Dutch said. "I'd studied him so long I felt I knew what he would do in any situation."

It was his aggressiveness that made the short, blocky Meyer a regular end for Texas Christian in 1919 and '20. "I hunted them up and cut them down," he recalled, "and the bigger they were, the worse it hurt them."

"From Waterboy to Coach" would be the Horatio Alger title for Meyer's life story. He was born in Waco of German parents in a German neighborhood, and spoke his first English after he got to grade school. By third grade, he was fascinated by sports, especially the football team of Texas Christian, which was in Waco until 1911, moving to Fort Worth after fire destroyed its buildings. At nine, Dutch was waterboy and mascot for the Frogs, and related their feats vividly, especially the three intratown games with Baylor.

The Christians and the Baptists conducted their early games in an atmosphere inimical to Lord Chesterfield, Tom Playfair, or prayer. The 1908 series, Dutch said, was especially classic. Loser in the first two games and trailing in the third at halftime, 8–6, Baylor concocted a football equivalent of the Trojan Horse by dressing its ace right end, John Fouts, in TCU colors.

The Frogs chorused a protest, but Babe Gantt, Baylor captain, said there was no rule against it, which there wasn't. With the aid of this unconscionable gamesmanship, Baylor rallied to win, 23–8, and that night windows were smashed in Waco, and trolley cars derailed. It was many years before TCU would acknowledge the game in its record books.

When his stalwarts departed for Fort Worth after the 1910 season, Meyer vowed he'd one day join them. At high school in Waco, he won letters as guard in football, a keen set-shooter in basketball, and a pitcher in baseball, his best sport. In the fall of 1917, he arrived at TCU with something of a reputation, a diploma, and a mind made up not to obey his father's dictum, "Don't you go out for football!"

His TCU ambitions were delayed by World War I, which saw him at Transylvania (Ky.) College as an ROTC instructor and an end on what he termed the worst football team of all time. "Our longest drive of the season reached Marietta's 5-yard line.

"The end zone seats crowded the goal line, so the Marietta quarterback said, 'Lend us five yards so we'll have room to punt. We'll pay you back.' Transylvania agreed, but the Marietta quarterback was no gentleman. He called a fake kick and their fullback ran 90 yards for a touchdown. They beat the devil out of us after that. And they never did pay back those five yards."

Dutch returned to TCU late in 1918, became a three-sports man, and in 1920 played end on the team that won the championship of the Texas Intercollegiate Athletic Association. (TCU didn't join the Southwest Conference until 1923.) The Frogs' coach, Billy Driver, a most appropriate name, agreed to a postseason game with Centre's famous Praying Colonels, coached by his old friend, Uncle Charlie Moran. Dutch found himself pitted against such talented Fort Worth transplants as Bo McMillin, Red Weaver, and Sully Montgomery. Centre won, 63–7, and except for no lend-lease yards, it was almost as bad as Transylvania vs. Marietta.

"We made a mistake by scoring first," Dutch said. "Driver and Moran had agreed there would be no holds barred, and things got pretty rough."

Meyer didn't play football his senior season, 1921, because of some difference with Coach Driver, perhaps the scheduling of Centre. Driver also coached basketball, however, and he needed Dutch's set-shooting, so they patched up their differences.

Dutch also ran into some difficulty with the

department of discipline, and took an enforced sabbatical for participating in the hazing of ministerial students. After his return, a milk cow was found in the dean's office one morning, and suspicion focused on Meyer. Nothing could be proved.

Despite his nip-ups, Dutch graduated on time in 1922, with a degree in geology. Some ten years later, during the Baugh era, Meyer's nephew, Lambert D. Meyer, matriculated at Texas Christian, and his uncle took him aside for a talk.

"L.D.," Dutch said, gravely, "I've been at TCU many years and have a spotless reputation here. So I don't want you to neglect your studies or get into any mischief, because that would reflect on my perfect reputation."

L.D. graduated with honors and was a fine end, pass catcher, and kicker who scored all of the Frogs' points in their 16–6 victory over Marquette in the 1937 Cotton Bowl. It was not until a few days before graduation that he heard of his uncle's tricks as an undergrad, but Dutch said L.D.'s disenchantment was only temporary.

Dutch Meyer might have become a big league pitcher and manager instead of a football coach, had he not hurt a ligament in his right or pitching arm as a sophomore. Even so, his 30–4 varsity record earned him a contract with the Cleveland Indians, but after bouncing around the minors in 1922, his arm still bothering, he gave up baseball and returned to Fort Worth, where he began his coaching career at Polytechnic High.

His duties included girls basketball and the first day 50 reported. Dutch gave them a grim speech and a grimmer workout. "I worked the tar out of those girls," he admitted. When only eight showed up the next day, he bawled them out until a little girl raised her hand.

"Coach," she explained, "we were the only ones able to get out of bed this morning."

In 1923 Dutch became coach of all freshman sports at Texas Christian, beginning a career that would last 40 years, the last 11 as athletic director. His 19-year varsity football record was 109–79–13. He coached 10 All-Americans: Baugh, O'Brien, Aldrich, Hale; tackles Darrell Palmer, Clyde Flowers, and Doug Conoway; center Keith Flowers; and quarterbacks Lindy Berry and Ray McKown.

Meyer also coached varsity baseball 12 seasons for a 92–75 record, and gave the Frogs their first championship in 1933. In 1956, he not only stepped in as emergency baseball coach, but directed the team to the flag.

TCU's 11-year freshman football record under Dutch was 29 victories in 33 games, and a trail of stories. The best one has it that the Polliwogs, as TCU frosh teams are known, were so banged up for a game with Terrell Prep that by the second half Dutch could assemble only ten able-bodied men.

When the referee told him he'd have to produce an eleventh or forfeit the game, Meyer is said to have put one of the injured on a stretcher and placed it just inside the playing boundary, where the wounded man lay quietly while his fellow Wogs played out the game. If this tale is not apocryphal, it was the only time Dutch ever played "a dead one."

It was while he was coaching freshman football in 1932 that Meyer discovered Sammy Baugh. Dutch took the varsity baseball team out to Abilene for some practice games. Baugh, a high school athlete from Sweetwater, was playing for a team known as Mose Sims' Oilers, and he had two great days against the Frogs. He had the quickest, most powerful arm Dutch had ever seen, he moved quick, and he could hit. He was also a blocking back in football, but Dutch thought of him for baseball.

He told Francis Schmidt about him. Schmidt, whose strong TCU teams would get him the Ohio State job in 1934, was also basketball coach and controlled the scholarships. The Sweetwater football player he wanted was a tailback named Red Sheridan, and only when he lost him to Texas did he agree on a scholarship for Baugh. Meyer had put it on this wise, "He's a baseball player, but maybe he can play a little football, too."

When Baugh reported to the Wogs in the fall of '33, Meyer was astonished and delighted to discover that he could throw a football as far, as hard, and as accurately up to 50 yards, as he could a baseball. He threw bullets, but they could be handled. He would also develop into a superior kicker, an able runner, and a smart quarterback.

In 1934, Schmidt departed for Columbus, and Meyer succeeded him, Sammy Baugh in hand. In '33 Dutch had begun thinking about and building the best possible game to use the boy's great arm, and now he did more thinking and building. He drilled Slingin' Sam and a swift, sure-handed end named Walter Roach in every pass pattern then known to man, and a few that weren't. And he began to design the double-wing formation that would have all football talking.

TCU finished second in the conference in 1935 and '36, and both years Baugh made All-American. The 1935 climactic battle with Southern

Methodist, to settle the SWC championship, lived up to its billing as not only the game of the year but the most important played in Texas up to that time, the first to go on a national radio network. SMU won it in a cliff-hanger, 20–14, but Baugh's receivers dropped nine of his bullet passes, the kind they were usually able to hold onto. The Frogs went on to the Sugar Bowl and a 3–2 victory over Louisiana State in the rain, with Baugh's punting and Taldon Manton's field goal decisive.

In 1936, Baugh completed 109 passes for 1,371 yards, but a loss to the Texas Aggies, 18–7, cost the Frogs the crown. They proved their class, however, in a 9–0 triumph over powerful Santa Clara, which was the only undefeated, untied major team at that point, and which later won the first of two straight Sugar Bowls from LSU.

Meanwhile, Slingin' Sammy had an understudy, a five-foot-seven 150-pound bundle of bounce, brains, elusiveness, and arm in O'Brien. Although Little David was a Dallas boy, he had been ticketed from the cradle for TCU. His father died when he was young, but his Uncle Boyd Kieth was a Frog fan and also friendly with Dan Rogers, the banker who chaired TCU's athletic board.

As a youngster Little David was puny and even when he made All-State at Woodrow Wilson High in Dallas, his friends thought him too small for college football and laughed at his plans to play for TCU. One of them, Allie White, a TCU teammate, said later, "We told Davey he was being ridiculous and to forget it. We were wrong. I doubt if there will ever be another his equal."

O'Brien developed slowly as a junior, and TCU for the third year in a row ended up second in the conference. Victories over Texas, 14–0, champion Rice, 7–2, and SMU, 3–0, could not undo an early 7–7 tie at Arkansas and a 6–0 loss at Baylor. In 1938, however, the Frogs did a hop, skip, and a jump beyond frustration, going clean, outscoring the opposition 254–53, being pushed only by Arkansas, 21–14. O'Brien passed for 236 yards against Baylor and Texas, but it was against SMU that he displayed his sparkling field generalship.

As in 1935, the title was up for grabs, and heavy, swirling winds made it a bad day for the forward pass. So O'Brien engineered TCU's first two touchdowns with a neatly diversified ground game, setting up the second with a 39-yard punt return that was a typical squirming, bursting bit of O'Brien business. For the third TD, he caught the Mustangs napping with a 37-yard pass, and a 20–7 victory.

Carnegie Tech posed a tough test in the Sugar Bowl. The Tartans, well coached by Bill Kern, had some fine backs of their own—led by Merlyn Condit—lost only to Notre Dame, 7–0, on an official's error, and brought off the upset of the year in downing Jock Sutherland's last Pitt team with its Dream Backfield.

But Carnegie had not met an all-round threat like Little David, and he did the Tartans in with his passes to Durwood Horner and Earl Clark, tied to a solid running game cored by Connie Sparks. Like all great players, Davey O'Brien was respected and admired on both sides of the scrimmage line. His gameness was recognized; in three varsity years he took only one time out. After the Sugar Bowl game, a Carnegie player was asked why they hadn't tried to give Davey a legitimate beating on the pass rush and perhaps get him out of the game.

"We'd rather lose than to have won that way," the player replied. "After all, we do not feel a bit disgraced losing to a great little guy like that."

O'Brien was the first player to win the Heisman, Maxwell, and Camp Trophies, all three, and TCU did what no opponent had been able to. They retired his No. 8.

Davey's three-year passing totals were 197 of 432 (26 interceptions) for 2,659 yards and a percentage of .456; Baugh's were 280 of 587 (54 interceptions) for 3,384 yards and .459.

"Sammy," said Dutch Meyer, "had the edge as a passer because of that great wrist flick, and he may have been more talented all around. But as a field general, O'Brien was the greatest."

The passing game made famous by Baugh and O'Brien tended to overshadow Meyer's undoubted genius for setting up defenses. His greatest single upset, of Texas in 1941, 14–7, was primarily a defensive masterpiece, based on his knowledge that the Steers would run right from single wing, left from the Y, and pass from the double wing.

The most meaningful tribute to the coaching genius of Leo Robert Meyer was paid by Floyd (Jim) Crow, an outstanding tackle of the Texas Aggies under Uncle Charlie Moran in 1910, and for 40 years with Baylor the best-known football scout in Texas.

"I would say," said Jim, "that Dutch Meyer was one of the finest coaches I ever scouted. Always tough. His defense might change from game to game. And you didn't know whether he

would hit you with single wing, double wing, single wing with man-in-motion, or triple wing with variations, all according to the material he had."

What his "old boys" remember first about Dutch Meyer, however, is that he lived and died with them, in sunshine and shadow, and they never forgot the spirit he imbued in them.

"Fight 'em until hell freezes over," the Dutchman exhorted, "and then fight 'em on the ice!"

And he didn't order the ministerial students out of the room.

Ray Morrison

MASTER OF THE AERIAL CIRCUS

Michie Stadium, home field of the United States Military Academy, has backdropped many a colorful football show, but none to surpass the 14–13 heart-stopper the Army team won from Southern Methodist University's Mustangs, October 6, 1928. And it was the wild and woolly Mustangs who colored the atmosphere cardiac.

The Mustangs arrived complete with their resplendent red and blue uniforms, with their pony mascot Peruna, with their jazz band that never let up promising "She'll be loaded with Peruna when she comes," and with several train carloads of uninhibited rooters. One of them, a Colonel Fred McJunkin, got on the loudspeaker at halftime and invited everybody there, including the plebes, to visit Texas as his guest.

The Mustangs also arrived with a couple of backs, Redman Hume and Sammy Reed, and it was a good thing Army had Christian Keener (Red) Cagle's running to save them that day. For between them, Hume and Reed threw 30 forward passes and completed 16; conservative Army tried four.

SMU was dangerous right down to the final play; Reed caught Hume's last pass in the open but fell on his face from exhaustion. Ironically, the two decisive extra points were kicked by Army tackle Mortimer (Bud) Sprague, who a few seasons before, as a Texas tackle, had been on the losing side against SMU.

Southern Methodist's "Aerial Circus," also known as razzle-dazzle football, thus broke upon the insular East, traditionally myopic about developments in other football sections. But under the coaching mastery of Jesse Ray Morrison, the Mustangs had been darkening the skies with footballs for over five years. They lined up in an orthodox-enough formation, tight with a balanced line and their backs in either a single-wing or a Y formation, but they were just as apt to pass as run, no matter the field position.

Morrison, a scholarly man who taught mathematics, had been an imaginative quarterback at Vanderbilt under an imaginative coach, Dan McGugin. It was second nature for him to study and experiment.

"The thing," said Morrison, "that started me developing the passing game for anytime or anyplace offense was that I so often saw weak and undermanned teams that were behind start passing in the fourth quarter and make touchdowns when everybody in the stands and on the field knew they were going to pass. So I reasoned why not pass when a pass is *not* expected? And I found that our opponents' knowing we *might* pass on *any* down from *anywhere* improved our opportunity to gain on running plays."

In 1921, while still freshman coach at Southern Methodist, Morrison joined Doc Blackwell, business manager of athletics, in recruiting SMU's "Immortal Ten," foundation of the Era of the Aerial Circus. The ten were Logan (Stolly) Stollenwerck, Lawrence (Smack) Reisor, Arnett (Chink) Perason, Hubert (Wally) Walling, William (Blink) Bedford, Collis P. Irby, W. J. R. (Buddy) King, Russell (Dutch) McIntosh, Sidney (Sid) Henry, and Lake (Firpo) Morrison.

Stolly Stollenwerck was the first of a succession of passing-running SMU quarterbacks distinguished for their diminutive size as well as their dynamic arms. Stollenwerck was followed by Gerald Mann, Redman Hume, Bobby Gilbert, Ken Travis, and Bobby Wilson.

In the 13 seasons from 1922 through '34, Morrison's Aerial Circus won three Southwest Conference championships, was runner-up three

Ray Morrison

blocker for powerful fullback Chris Cortemeglia. But against Texas, Morrison used Mann at quarterback and the Mustangs came off with a tie. After that game, Morrison, acutely aware of what he had, wrote Mann a six-page letter in which the main theme was, never let fame change him. And the Little Red Arrow never did.

Mann never used profanity either, and it is part of SMU lore that he once made an unusual request of Cortemeglia. The opponents were being unnecessarily rough, and Gerry asked Chris to "call them what they are. I can't use the proper language." Improper language would have been understandable among the Texas Aggies, Texas, and Texas Christian players who tried to cope with Gerry Mann in 1926. He was a Merriwell-plus, a Mustang not to be roped nohow.

His team trailing the Texas Aggies 7–6, Mann faked a punt and passed to Cortemeglia, to get a drive going that led to a field goal and a 9–7 victory. The field goal, kicked from a difficult angle by Mann, was the only one he ever attempted.

The following Saturday at Texas, however, Mann outdid this. His performance convinced Longhorn rooters that he was in communication with demons. Texas at one time held a 17–0 lead and was ahead 17–7 in the last quarter when Mann passed to Ross Love.

"Figuring the Longhorns wouldn't pass," wrote Weldon Hart of the Austin *American-Statesman*, "with a three-point lead, 17–14, and only a few plays left, Mann came charging up from defensive right halfback just in time to scoop up a Texas fumble and race for a touchdown that won the game, 21–17. Texas fans were left to wonder forever and a day how he happened to be across the line of scrimmage on that play."

In the Texas Christian game, SMU trailed the Horned Frogs 13–7 late in the last quarter. A heavy wind against Mann made it difficult to pass. Nevertheless, Mann did pass over the safety man's head to Co-Captain Stanley Dawson, who went to the 1. On the next play SMU scored and Mann kicked the extra point for a 14–13 victory.

After their senior seasons of 1927, Mann and three other Southwest Conference players—back Joel Hunt and end J. V. (Siki) Sikes of the Texas Aggies, and Raymond (Rags) Matthews, end of Texas Christian—were the stars of the West's 16–6 victory over the East in the San Francisco Shriners game. Matthews recovered a fumble by the East on its 19, and moments later Hunt cut back 12 yards off tackle for the touchdown.

times, and put together a 38–13–13 record in conference play. The three champions were 1923 (9–0–0), 1926 (8–0–1), and 1931 (9–1–1). The 1929 team was undefeated but tied four times.

Morrison's first SWC kings, 1923, placed five men on the All-Conference team: Stollenwerck, end Jimmy Stewart, guard Johnny MacBrooks, center Buddy King, and back Smack Reisor. The Mustangs gave up only nine points, six of them to Arkansas. The passing of Stollenwerck to ends Stewart and Gene Beford, supported by the running of Reisor, Wally Walling, and Mike Dickinon, brought a 13–6 victory over the Razorbacks, whom the Mustangs had never scored against before, and also accounted for the big one against Coach Frank Bridges' Baylor team, 16–0.

The most dramatic of Morrison's backs at SMU was Gerald Mann, 1925 through '27. He was called "The Little Blue Arrow" or "The Little Red Arrow," because SMU's uniforms were red and blue and he threw the football straight as an arrow and moved downfield with the speed of an arrow. Mann, who never weighed over 157, was a picture of direct action, running, passing, or kicking. As a sophomore he was used mostly as a

Matthews and a teammate tackled an Easterner for a safety.

Mann, now entering the game, helped carry the ball to the 18-yard line, whence he caught a sideline pass for a touchdown. All-America pickers, who had overlooked the Texans, were red-faced, and the SWC had made its point: football in Texas was the equal of football anywhere.

Although Morrison was famed primarily for his complete integration of the forward pass, he scarcely neglected other phases of the game. In 1930 Southern Methodist opened N.D.'s season at Notre Dame against Knute Rockne's last team. The Irish, 10–0 national champions that year, were hard pushed by the Mustangs, 20–14, in large measure because of Morrison's defense. He used a five-man line, with the four backs and two ends constituting a rotating secondary toward the direction in which N.D. shifted its backs from the T into the box.

Somehow, Morrison's Mustangs almost invariably were at their best when they played intersectionally against name teams. In 1931 at Navy, it was the passing of Ken Travis to Speedy Mason that sunk the Sailors, 13–7. In 1934 at New York's Polo Grounds, Bobby Wilson, J. R. (Jackrabbit) Smith, and Harry Shuford sparkled as the Mustangs beat the Fordham Rams, 26–14. The night before that game, the Mustang Jazz Band and Peruna visited the Fordham Gymnasium and turned a dull rally into a kind of campus revival meeting.

In 1935, with Wilson, Shuford, and a trio of ace linemen—guard J. C. Wetzel, and tackles Truman Spain and Maurice Orr—SMU had a 12–0 record and lost to Stanford 7–0 in the Rose Bowl. But by 1935, Ray Morrison was coaching Vanderbilt, and his former assistant, Matty Bell, had succeeded him at SMU.

Why would Morrison leave an obviously loaded SMU squad for Vanderbilt? Because Vanderbilt was his alma mater, Mrs. Morrison was a Southern girl, and the salary was probably upped. But mainly because it was his alma mater.

In 1934, McGugin, Vandy's coach since 1904, except for 1918, announced his retirement, to be effective after the season. The morning of his final game, with Alabama in Birmingham, McGugin told Nashville writers that Josh Cody, his line coach, would succeed him.

But Alabama, with Dixie Howell and Don Hutson, was headed for the Rose Bowl. The Crimson Tide, which could have named its score,

With visions of aerials . . .

settled for 34–0. This was high enough to prompt some Vandy alumni to oppose Cody and bring back Morrison, an old hero and master of the Aerial Circus.

Although Vanderbilt lacked the material of Alabama, Tennessee, Louisiana State and other Southern powers, Morrison's five-year record shows 25–20–2. His 1935 team went 7–3; '37, 7–2; and '38, 6–3. In 1935, Vandy finished second in the Southeastern Conference, and missed the Sugar Bowl by losing to LSU, 7–2, for failure to make 12 inches in three downs. And in 1937, the Commodores missed a chance at the Rose Bowl by losing to Alabama (which went), 9–7, on Sandy Sanford's fourth-quarter field goal. Carl Hinkle, an All-America center, and five other linemen played four 60-minute games, one of the last of the iron-man performances.

That 1937 team will always command a page for a hidden-ball play that beat LSU 7–6, the only regular-season loss for that Bengal Sugar Bowl team. Morrison called it the "Henry Frnka" play since Frnka, his assistant and later head coach at Tulane, made it up. It happened on the second play of the game. Vanderbilt had the ball at midfield, second down and four to go.

Dutch Reinschmidt, the Commodore quarterback, took the handback from center and placed the ball on the ground behind the offensive left guard, Bill Hays, who hovered over it to keep it

Ray (*at mike*) and Matty Bell, at a dinner honoring the latter in 1970

from sight. Reinschmidt spun and headed toward the LSU right flank behind a screen of blockers. It looked as if he'd be thrown for a big loss—but he didn't have the ball. Greer Ricketson, a tackle who had lined up as a right guard, had it and was heading for the LSU goal line with no opponent nearer than 25 yards.

"I pulled out from right guard as if to join the interference," Ricketson explained. "Just as I got behind Hays, I tripped—accidentally on purpose —over him. He was squatting over the ball like a hen hatching an egg. I picked up the ball and simply ran down the right side of the field, thinking above all else not to stub my toe."

Just before the game, Morrison had explained the play to the referee, to show its legality. But he said it would take place not on the second play, but the third play. As a result, the referee was fooled as completely as LSU.

Fred Russell, sports editor of the Nashville *Banner*, said that he almost talked Morrison into an even wilder gambit for the Vanderbilt-Tennessee game in late 1939.

"Tennessee had won 20 straight games," said Russell. "Vanderbilt had lost five that season.

The gamblers were laying 8–1 Tennessee would win and 8–5 Vanderbilt wouldn't score. [Tennessee won, 13–0.] It was an extreme situation calling for extreme measures and I wanted Morrison to come on to the field for the pregame workout with a baseball fungo bat and his players dressed in baseball suits. How would it have affected the Tennessee players? And the coaches? I still wonder."

From the time he starred for Vanderbilt, 1908–11, Morrison had been deeply infected by the football bug. But it was his ability to teach mathematics that got him started as a coach. From 1912 through '14 he taught math and coached football at Branham and Hughes Military Academy in Spring Hill, Tennessee.

In 1915, Southern Methodist opened its doors. Frank Reedy, its bursar, heard about Morrison from a mutual friend, Foster Jacoby, who had attended Vanderbilt with Ray. Reedy was not hard to sell because he had seen Morrison stand out for a Southern All-Star team against the Texas All-Stars in 1913.

So in 1915 Morrison was hired at a full professor's salary of $2,000. In return for that he

taught ten hours of math, coached newly formed football, baseball, and track teams, served as manager of all the teams, and was also director of physical education for both men and women.

"If this sounds like an overly busy 44-hour week," wrote Kern Tips, "you have to remember that Morrison, like other football coaches of his day, really wanted to coach football. Not much came of all the activity, however, as his first two SMU teams (1915–16) won just two games. For a two-year-old university that didn't have Alumnus One, there nevertheless arose a gentle cry for Ray's scalp; he gave it to them."

Morrison's 1915 team had a 2–5 record, and in 1916 it played two ties, 0–0 with Austin and 9–9 with Southwestern, and lost eight, including a 146–3 number to Rice. It was a kind of musical-comedy team; the squad comprised 15 men, of which only 12 were able to play.

One was a husky theological student requisitioned by Morrison to send in plays. This was made possible when the Rice coach, Phil Arbuckle, waived the substitution rule, which prevented a player from reentering the game in the same quarter in which he left. At one point the messenger stayed in for a few plays until he remembered to give his instructions. They were, "Get the ball and hold it." Strangely enough, SMU scored first on a field goal, and apparently that made Rice mad.

After he was replaced in 1917 by J. Burton Rix, Morrison did army YMCA work and in 1918 filled in at Vanderbilt for McGugin. He returned to SMU as a freshman coach in 1920, and by 1922 was in charge of the varsity.

Between Ray Morrison, coach and father, and John Ray (Jack) Morrison, quarterback and son, a situation developed that was unusual, if not unique. Jack made the high school team at Highland Park, site of Southern Methodist, and was due to enter college in 1934.

"He broke the news to me," said Coach Morrison "that he didn't want to play for me at SMU. He explained that if he were going to be so good I couldn't leave him off the team, or so poor I couldn't use him in a game, all would be well. But he said he knew he was going to be in between—mediocre was the way he put it—and we would both be criticized whatever we did, as father and son.

"He entered Vanderbilt as a freshman in 1934. Then I decided to leave SMU and go back to Vandy to coach. So Jack and I exchanged places.

He left Vandy and enrolled at SMU in 1935. The Southwest Conference took one year of eligibility away from him as a transfer. That made him eligible as a junior in 1936. Jack broke his leg in the Fordham game—third game of the season —so he really got in only one year of varsity football at SMU, in 1937. My Vanderbilt team beat Jack and his SMU team that year, 6–0."

After a 2–7–1 season in 1939, the alumni grumbled, although Morrison's record for the four previous years, 23–13–1, had been remarkable considering the material. Disenchanted, Ray resigned and went to Temple, where he coached for nine years. While at Temple, he was offered the Yale job, but Mrs. Morrison, a Southern girl, talked him out of it. "If we're going to leave Philadelphia," she said, "why don't we go back to Texas instead of going to New Haven." And that was how Morrison coached his last four years at Austin College, before returning to SMU a second time to fill a public relations role involving academics, athletics, and alumni.

Nobody, including Ray Morrison himself, ever argued that he invented the forward pass or that he was the first to use it as an integral all-times part of his attack, either in Texas or elsewhere. From the time the pass was legalized in 1906, pioneers had recognized its full worth. One such was Eddie Cochems at the University of Missouri.

The University of Texas team, then known as Varsity, scored its first touchdown against the Texas Aggies, then known as Bryant, on a forward pass in 1906. And the same Gus Dorais to Knute Rockne passing team that beat Army on the Plain in 1913, 35–13, closed out that season with a comparably effective air game in defeating Texas—Varsity—at Austin, 30–7.

But no coach in any section ever matched the imaginative Morrison in demonstrating the full worth of the forward-passing game, first to the Southwest and then to the country. No doubt Morrison, Frank Bridges of Baylor, and the other Southwestern pioneers of the all-out air arm were motivated in part because it was somewhat easier to play under torrid Texas suns than the grind-it-out ground game. No matter, the pass, thanks to them and principally to Morrison, became a more popular weapon for all football regions, all football climates.

As the Mustang Jazz Band would put it, "They'll be coming with the passes when they come!"

Bob Neyland

THE GRIDIRON BRIGADIER

America stood deep in breadlines and apple vendors when Tennessee beat New York University, 13–0, in a 1931 postseason charity game at Yankee Stadium for New York's unemployed. The game was arranged by Mayor Jimmy Walker. It was the East's first look at what was then already a well-known Southern football power with a coach whose name was already making headlines, Major Robert Reese Neyland (pronounced *knee*-land).

The Volunteers from Knoxville near the Great Smoky Mountains demonstrated no charity toward the Violent Violets of Coach Chick Meehan. Left halfback Beattie Feathers ran 65 yards for one touchdown, and quarterback Deke Brackett returned a punt 75 yards for another. On defense the Vols were obdurate, especially guard Herman Hickman, who later was Army's line coach and Yale's head coach, and a raconteur, gourmet, and television personality of large parts.

After watching Hickman make piles in the NYU backfield most of the afternoon, Grantland Rice, another Tennessean (Murfreesboro) and dean of American sportswriters, hurried back to his office to rearrange his All-America selections, to make room for Hickman.

One of the spectators that day was the scholarly Carl Gray Snavely, who had just finished coaching a fullback named Clark Hinkle at Bucknell for three years, and would later win fame as head coach at Cornell and North Carolina.

"I had never heard much of Coach Bob Neyland before that day," Snavely said, "but after watching Tennessee play for about five minutes, I became a Neyland fan."

Twenty-six years later, in 1957, when Oklahoma had put together 40 of its modern record winning streak of 47 games (ended by Notre Dame, 7–0, the following fall), Coach Bud Wilkinson co-authored with the late Gomer Jones a book called *Modern Defensive Football*, in which he stated:

"We would like to acknowledge the great debt we owe those whose original ideas are the basis of our theory of defensive football. The foremost of these men, without doubt, is General Bob Neyland, the great coach of the University of Tennessee. In essence, the theory of defense which will be presented in this book is an adaptation of the patterns developed by the great defensive master, General Neyland."

Of all who coached 20 or more seasons, Neyland's record stands No. 1. In 21 seasons spread over 26 years (he took time out for soldiering twice, in 1935, and from 1941 through '45), his record was 173 victories, 31 defeats, and 12 ties for .829. Under Neyland Tennessee won eight Southern championships and finished 1–2–3 fifteen times.

From 1926 through the first two games of the 1933 season, his teams won 63, lost 2, and tied 5. The losses were to Vanderbilt, 20–3, in the eighth game of the 1926 season, and to Alabama, 18–6, in the fourth game of the '30 season. The five ties were three with Kentucky and two with Vanderbilt. And the string of 70 games included two defeatless runs of 33 and 28. In one stretch the Vols lost only once in 62 games.

For some reason, however—in at least two cases he was outpersonneled—success eluded Neyland in postseason Bowl games. His teams won only two of seven, from Oklahoma, 17–0, in the 1939 Orange Bowl and from Texas, 20–14, in the '51 Cotton Bowl.

It was the success of Neyland's teams that made necessary the enlargement of what was then known as Shields-Watkins Stadium, accommodating only 3,200, to the current double-decked horseshoe of 64,000 known as Neyland Stadium.

To Robert Reese Neyland III, a football game was a series of accidents and mistakes and the team that best avoided them and resisted their consequences would almost invariably win.

Neyland did not want his teams to have possession of the ball inside their own 30-yard line. He was the No. 1 High Apostle of vertical field position; the farther from the opponents' goal line you put the ball in play, the greater the number of plays you had to run off, and the greater the chance, by law of averages, for a misplay.

He preached and his teams proved repeatedly that there were more ways of scoring on defense than on offense.

"On offense," he pointed out, "you can score

three ways: on a run, a pass, or a kick. On defense, you can score four ways: by intercepting a pass, by forcing a fumble and catching the ball in midair, by blocking a kick, and by returning a kick. The psychological shock of being scored on any of those ways is so profound that a team so scored on rarely is able to rally for victory."

Neyland, by repeated proof and victory, was able to convince his team, as no coach before or after him, that the keys lay in—and in this order, if order there must be—a sound kicking game, a containing defense, and, say, a couple of dozen plays all thoroughly learned, meaning that none of them is run in a game until it has been practiced at least 500 times.

No coach before or after him had a keener understanding of the kicking game in all its ramifications. The ball shall be snapped and punted in two seconds. The punt shall be high and cover at least 35 yards from the line of scrimmage so that the receiver must call for a fair catch or the coverage will sew him up, perhaps even force a fumble. The punt in enemy territory, from his 45- to 35-yard line, shall be angled out or punted dead to the 10 or inside it.

On early downs in their own territory, his Tennessee teams made valuable use of the quick kick. "The only defense for a good quick kick," Neyland explained, "is to know how to return one." And before Southern teams followed Neyland's example and began study of game films in the thirties, many had thought that the Vols were fortune's favorites, the way they ran back punts for critical touchdowns. Film study revealed there was a definite and deadly pattern to their blocking in a shook-up field.

Other Neyland firsts in Southern football include telephones from press box roof to bench; lightweight jerseys that became known as teara-ways to enable light backs to break away from a tackler; low quarter shoes for more ankle freedom; lighter hip pads constructed of sponge rubber, airplane cloth, and molded fiber; a cover for the football field; and keeping his squad in a tourist motel instead of a hotel. He was impelled toward this when one of his teams couldn't get an elevator to stop at their floor and as a result were almost late for the game.

On defense the Volunteers played a containing or cup defense—they call it perimeter today—to drive all plays to the inside and to restrict the gain on a pass play to the distance of the pass.

Offensively, Neyland used a single-wing balanced line that fused part of the Notre Dame box

Bob Neyland of Tennessee

and some of Gil Dobie's off-tackle mechanics. On old No. 10, Tennessee's off-tackle play, the end and the tackle teamed on the tackle, the fullback and the quarterback teamed on the end, and the two guards pulled to lead the play. Tennessee's toughest-to-defend-against play, as with other formations, was the option run or pass by the tailback, depending on the commitment made by the defensive left halfback.

Although Neyland was known as a single-wing man, his early teams lined the quarterback up over the center and ran dive bucks, split bucks, and fakes that developed into passes from what is much like a winged T. He later incorporated buck-lateral plays into his system, and at one time seriously considered installing a split-T series.

"I was not wedded to the single wing as closely as some thought," he mused. "I used it because we could get quicker power at tackle."

Neyland, who was an excellent scout himself, was unconcerned if the other team knew his plays. "If they're well executed," he said, "they'll go anyhow." Henry (Hank) Crisp, Alabama's star one-armed scout, used to say, "You always know what Bob Neyland is going to do. But try and stop him."

Every coach has the one game he'd like to play over; with Neyland, it was the 19–13 loss in the 1941 Sugar Bowl to Boston College, coached by Frank Leahy. Neyland always felt the Vols had

wasted many opportunities to win. To make it worse, B.C. scored one of its touchdowns after blocking a punt on Bob Foxx, ace wingback, a heresy on the Hill. The runback inside the weak-side tackle for the winning touchdown was a Tennessee play that a B.C. espionage agent had appropriated.

Nevertheless, B.C.'s personnel matched Tennessee's, and Leahy, although in his second year, just before taking the Notre Dame job, was also an outstanding coach even then. Neyland felt that his team peaked too early and that both team and coaching staff may have been overconfident. If so, it was a violation of his first dictum: "The first law of competitive sports is never underestimate the opposition."

In Neyland's single wing, the key man was the tailback, who ran, passed, punted, and was expected to handle his share of the blocking ... "One interferer," Neyland preached, "is worth three ball carriers."

Gene McEver, star of the Flaming Sophomores (Class of 1931), was Neyland's top player, although later he would call Johnny Majors, who played for Bowden Wyatt, the best all-purpose tailback. McEver, a sort of Southern George Gipp, was blessed with superb natural talent, speed, and shiftiness, and later, when an injured knee slowed him down, he proved A-1 also as defender, blocker, and power runner.

Today, 21 years after he coached his last game (1952) and 11 years after his death, in an era of wide-open two-flanker football and passing from every part of the field, Neyland's theories of defense against pass and run still stand up. And most football games are still lost, not won, by mistakes, called turnovers today, and from poor field position.

The theories did not originate with Neyland. He derived them as a star end at Army in 1914 and '15 under head coach Charlie Daly and line coach Ernest (Pot) Graves. Graves' book on line play, *The Linemen's Bible*, was used by Neyland at Tennessee.

Robert Reese Neyland was born February 17, 1892, in Greenville, Texas, the son of Robert Reese Neyland II, a lawyer, and Pauline Lewis Neyland, a teacher. He attended Greenville High and immediately showed promise an an all-round athlete. He also attended Burleson College and Texas A. & M. for a year before a young congressman from Texas named Sam Rayburn got him appointed to West Point in 1912.

Neyland proved to be one of the outstanding all-round athletes of his time. He was an end on the undefeated 1914 Army team, and his record as a pitcher was 35–5, with a 20-game winning streak included, and four victories in four tries against Navy. In the 1915 game at Annapolis, Neyland, who played first base when he wasn't pitching and always batted third, was beaned in the third inning by the Navy pitcher and had to be carried from the field and revived behind the stands. He returned to go on pitching and win. Among the spectators was Newton D. Baker, secretary of war, who later wrote the commandant.

"Would you kindly express to the pitcher on the Academy team my admiration of his courage and determination. I saw the game at Annapolis and am much pleased with his pluck."

"You would think, wouldn't you," said Neyland, showing the letter to Tom Siler, sports editor of the Knoxville *News-Sentinel* years later, "that the————would have known my name."

The New York Giants offered him $5,000 to sign, and the Philadelphia Athletics and Detroit Tigers also wanted him, but he was preoccupied with his Army career. It seems logical to feel that if Neyland had been interested, he could also have entered the professional ring and challenged for the world's title.

How he became heavyweight champion of the Corps underlines his ability to turn disadvantage to his favor—a hallmark of his teams. He had to walk the barracks area for two hours Wednesday and three hours Saturday of his yearling (sophomore) year, after he and eight classmates were found guilty of hazing plebes. Neyland always maintained the punishment was unjust.

His confinement prevented him from seeing the Dorais-Rockne forward passes which enabled Notre Dame to upset Army in their celebrated 1913 game on the Plain. But he was allowed to box for exercise and found he had a natural skill for it that would make him the champion of the Corps. Elmer Oliphant, the super all-round athlete at West Point and before that at Purdue, boasted of his ability to last three rounds with Neyland.

Graduated in 1916 as a young lieutenant of engineers, Neyland served in France, studied at MIT, and returned to West Point for 1921–24, as aide to General Douglas MacArthur, then Superintendent. Neyland was also an assistant coach in football and baseball, and it was then that he decided to try coaching.

"There was an opening at Iowa and at Ten-

nessee," he recalled. "I studied the Tennessee record. It didn't look good. Colonel John J. McEwan, the Army coach, Uncle Charlie Moran, coach of Centre College and my baseball coach at Texas Aggies, recommended me and so did several others. I spent considerable time with Professor N. W. Dougherty, and we came to an understanding."

Neyland arrived at Tennessee in 1925 as a young captain in charge of the ROTC, and an assistant coach of football. His coaching salary was $700. The next year, 1926, he was elevated to head coach by Professor Dougherty and hired two valued, long-time assistants, both former West Point players, Major Bob Britton and Colonel Paul Parker. Later, Neyland succeeded Dougherty as athletic director when Dougherty moved up to chairman of the athletic board and dean of the Engineering College.

"Local sportswriters like to say," said Dean Dougherty, "that Neyland was employed to beat Vanderbilt, whom we hadn't beaten since 1916. This was part of his job, but no such condition was ever mentioned." Neyland's second year, 1927, however, the Vols tied Vanderbilt, beat them in '28 and dominated them thereafter.

"Neyland was not harsh with his players," Dougherty said, "but he was strict. He worked hard with them, expected them to be on time, and to keep training rules. His practice periods were comparatively short [for those days, two hours and a half], but he kept them busy.

"In person he was handsome, had a military bearing, and a military method. He had praise where praise was due, and criticism where it would help."

After three years of play, one of his tackles asked him, "Colonel, I haven't been such a bad player, have I?" "No," Neyland replied, "but you have played in 30 games and you haven't blocked a punt. You should have blocked at least one in each game."

Lenn Coffman, a Neyland fullback of the thirties, has often been quoted, "To play for Tennessee, you've got to get 'wet' all over."

Buddy Hackman, who teamed at halfback with McEver on the Flaming Sophomores of 1928 (Mack and Hack they were known as, and even had a sundae named after them), said later, "We won because we *knew* we were better prepared than the other team. Neyland gave us the edge."

Dr. Dougherty also recalled that Neyland didn't like restrictions on numbers recruited and eligibility, and in making his point would quote

General MacArthur, whom he idolized, "Never make a rule that will deny you freedom of action when the time comes to act." "We make rules," Dougherty would reply, "to get uniformity in action for all teams, rather than to restrict ourselves."

But Neyland's way was to get his way, and he usually did.

In 1938, Neyland and Herman Hickman, then assistant coach at North Carolina State, attended the Pittsburgh-Duke game in Durham. Afterward, they were headed for a restaurant that Herman had scouted and reported on bullishly for its ham hocks and corn liquor. On foot, they were offered a ride by two men in the front seat of a sedan. When they got in, Neyland conducted the introductions in the courtly manner he could summon up on occasion.

"This is Herman Hickman," he said, "and I'm General Neyland."

"That's fine," said the driver, who'd had a few. Pointing to his friend in the front seat, he said, "This is Robert E. Lee and I'm Jesus Christ."

Mention of R. E. Lee would impel Neyland to mention that both of his grandfathers, Texans, were killed at Shiloh, and that if General Albert Sidney Johnston had not been killed early in the battle, the Confederates would have won.

Neyland's own war record suggests that if he had not concentrated on coaching, he would most certainly have been Chief of Staff timber. The job he did as chief supply officer at both Kunming and Calcutta in the China-Burma-India theater, World War II, earned him the Distinguished Service Medal, the Chinese Order of the Cloud and Banner, and the Knight Commander, Order of the British Empire. General Albert C. Wedemeyer, who succeeded General Joseph W. Stilwell in the CBI theater, had high praise for Neyland:

"He was in charge of the reception and disposition of supplies that came into the China theater. The Japanese completely surrounded China so that the only line of communication was over the so-called Hump over the Himalayan Mountains, flying supplies from air bases in India and Burma into Yunnan, the southwestern province of China.

"The capital was Kunming and we had an air base there that was as busy as LaGuardia ever could be, with planes leaving every 90 seconds. There were many demands for supplies being brought across the Hump. Bob Neyland had to exercise tact and firmness in allocating the sup-

The General inspecting his troops

widen the Tennessee River and build Norris Dam, first in the chain that became the Tennessee Valley Authority.

"I served near him," writes Colonel Russell P. (Red) Reeder, World War II hero and author, "when he commanded a battalion of combat engineers in Panama in 1935, and maybe those were his happiest days. The soldiers adored him. They were his boys and could do no wrong. Nobody picked on his boys. I would have loved to see him working on the Burma Road."

Neyland maintained that you ran an army and a football team along the same lines.

"Your men must be in good physical condition. They must have technical ability, and they must have high morale. It was tough at first to use these rules in Calcutta, but in the end they prevailed. India was a land of the underprivileged, with the heat and rains making cholera, dysentery, and bubonic plague commonplace."

Neyland's success as an army leader poses the question: Why did he pick football for his principal career? The answer lies in his makeup. He was born to command, but it was not easy for him to take orders. In football, he felt he would have a clearer shot at running the whole show than he would have as a general officer.

On at least one occasion he bucked rank. In 1942, although he detested it, he was assigned while on duty as a colonel to coach an army team made up of ex-college stars against pro teams. Within four days, Neyland's team defeated the New York Giants and the Brooklyn Dodgers, and lost a third game a few days later to the Chicago Bears by one touchdown. At halftime of the Giant game, with the All-Stars leading 10–0, General Alexander Surles visited the dressing room and requested of Neyland that Joe Louis, the world heavyweight champ, who was a private in the army, be allowed to talk to the team.

"Nobody talks to my team except me," Neyland informed Surles, and when his superior officer tried to persist, Neyland showed him the door. The coach thought this was the reason he was passed up three times before he received his brigadier's star.

The precision with which Neyland planned his approach is emphasized by Bobby Dodd, Tennessee's all-time quarterback, later a successful head coach at Georgia Tech, and still athletic director at Tech.

"We were to put in a hidden-ball play for the Vanderbilt game, my senior year, 1931," Dodd recollected, "and the question was whether or not

plies to the ground forces, to the air forces, and to clandestine forces of OSS and Admiral Miles' Navy Group China. In the short time he was there, Neyland made a wonderful record.

"In his next post in Calcutta, he had to offload ships bringing supplies to the British, to the Chinese, and to the Americans, both ground and air forces. Then he had to shove and push those supplies by rail, water, and truck to the units operating in northeast India, Burma, and to air bases from which supplies would be flown to China. I was told by General Dan Sultan that he (General Neyland) performed in a superior manner and without use of gimmicks but simply through his own fine qualities of leadership and enthusiasm for the job."

Shove and push. That was Neyland. A man who got the job done.

"Neyland," Bob Considine wrote, "had turned the unromantic task of unloading ships into a huge game. He made the listless, wondering Indian laborer conscious of the importance of his record of unloading a Liberty Ship in 44 hours and 5 minutes."

In earlier service Neyland had been effective. He was one of the first engineers to dredge and

I should execute the play, since they thought I would do better hiding the ball, but worried about my lack of speed, figuring that I would be caught from behind.

"The other man is question, Gene McEver, could not handle the ball as well but had terrific speed. Neyland finally said that he wanted me to operate the play, but only inside Vandy's 19-yard line. Well, I called the play on the Vandy 19 and I was tackled on the goal line for a touchdown. So you can see how accurate his thinking was."

Besides Dodd, a partial list of ex-Neyland players who became college head coaches would include Allyn McKeen, Mississippi State; John Barnhill, Tennessee and Arkansas; Herman Hickman, Yale; Murray Warmath, Mississippi State and Minnesota; Phil Dickens, Wofford, Wyoming, and Indiana; Ralph Hatley, Memphis State; DeWitt Weaver, Texas Tech; Bowden Wyatt, Wyoming, Arkansas, and Tennessee; Bob Woodruff, Baylor and Florida; Clay Stapleton, Iowa State.

Neyland was not a believer in dressing-room oratory. "Pregame harangues, as a rule," he said, "do more harm than good. Inspiration at zero hour is a poor thing to rely on. Good mental attitude the day of the game stems almost entirely from attitudes built up over a long period of time." His dressing-room talks constituted a recitation of his maxims, pointing out the failure to apply some of them in previous games and how they had won other games. And always he emphasized that the cornerstone to victory comprised self-faith, resolution, and confidence in ultimate success.

When the situation called for it, he applied psychology with a deft hand. A prime example was the No. 1 victory of a Neyland team, underdog Tennessee's 15–13 upset of Alabama in 1928 at Tuscaloosa. At that time, the Crimson Tide, expertly coached by Wallace Wade, had been to the Rose Bowl twice, and was the paladin of the South.

On the train ride from Knoxville to Tuscaloosa, however, Neyland took each Tennessee player aside and told him he was better than the Alabama man he'd be playing against.

It was in this game that McEver caught the opening kickoff and returned it 98 yards for a touchdown that would prove decisive. "Knock a man down," Gene told his teammates, "and if you can't, step aside and let me through." The Vols deposited the Tidemen like tenpins with their cross-blocking, and at midfield McEver was

clear with an escort of two blockers.

Neyland also tried psyching Coach Wade—with tongue in cheek, no doubt.

"I had never met Neyland before that day," Wade said. "Before the game in Tuscaloosa, he came to me and said it would be a rout for Alabama, and suggested that in order to hold down the score, the last two periods should be cut. I told him Alabama didn't expect to be able to run up a score, but agreed to shorten the last half, if Alabama's lead justified it."

From that day on, the day the Flaming Sophomores were born, Tennessee always brought the fourth dimension into action—the confidence bred from winning.

Had he chosen to, Neyland could have been successful in his public relations, for he was educated and articulate. But though he savored the recognition that came to him through his teams, he did not court the favor of the media, and would not attend luncheons, banquets, or clinics.

When the 1939 Tennessee-Alabama game attracted national attention, Ted Husing, then the ranking radio sportscaster, came down to Knoxville to cover it, and sent an emissary to Neyland with a list of requests regarding the broadcast.

"Tell Ted Husing," Neyland advised the emissary, "to go to hell."

Neyland's stand was predicated on the belief that if his teams won, his press would be good, and if they lost, the press couldn't help him. He also stated that he was hired only to coach football.

He was consistent in his devotion to his job; after the 1937 season, a mediocre one by his standards, he decided that he had spent too much time playing bridge, publicly confessed this to the squad, and said he was giving it up in '38. Whether cause and effect pertained, the '38 team went 10–0 and beat Oklahoma in the Orange Bowl.

Clinics and the banquet circuit missed something when Neyland decided not be a speaker. On one occasion, Professor Dougherty finally prevailed on him to talk to the engineering students.

"He took them by storm," Dougherty reported. "He told a number of stories. One concerned the time he was a young engineer on the Mississippi and his colonel gave him orders to mend the levee. He said he didn't know what a levee was, so he assembled his men and said to his sergeant, 'Sergeant, mend the levee!' And he got the work done."

Neyland's finest hour as a speaker came at the National Collegiate Athletic Association in defense of nine colleges penalized by the so-called Sanity Code for the regulation of recruiting and subsidizing in the early fifties. Thanks in large measure to his speech and the action it stimulated, Southern schools and independents formed a coalition that won legislation for the cost of living code that has proved functional for two decades.

"How can any of us vote to expel these schools," Neyland asked the NCAA convention in New York, "when we are all just as guilty as they are?"

Neyland was adamantly opposed to giving a boy more than he needed to get by, and tossed out a player who sought under-the-table monthly payment at Tennessee after World War II.

While he was chairman of the rules committee, he succeeded in restoring one-platoon or two-way football. He was bitterly opposed to two-platoon.

When it came to getting to the heart of a football matter, Neyland was unerring. Beattie Feathers, a great running back for the Vols in the early thirties, tells about his problems with pass defense when he was a sophomore.

"I asked General Neyland," said Feathers, "what I should do when two receivers entered my territory. Which one should I cover? 'Don't be dumb enough to cover the decoy,' he said. 'Cover the one they pass to.' To save embarrassment I said okay. He got across the point that I should retire into my zone, keeping equal distance between them and playing them with field vision, keeping an eye on the passer and the receiver and playing the ball. And then go for the ball when the passer releases it."

In 1947, Tennessee's 5–5 record proved Knoxville fans were the same as elsewhere. For the first time, Neyland heard the anvil chorus. This bothered the Vols' star tackle Denver Crawford so much that he was about ready not to go into coaching. He stopped by Neyland's office to thank him for giving him the chance for an education.

"I told the General," Crawford recalled, "that I wasn't sure about coaching for myself. I told him if the public would act in such poor taste toward him after the record he'd made, I didn't think I could endure that treatment.

"'Crawford,' Neyland smiled, 'I don't care what endeavor you go into, you can't live on your clippings. You must produce.'

"I decided," said Crawford, "to take up coaching after all."

Neyland was never much for arguing with officials. He felt that over a long period, officiating mistakes evened up. And while he was not by any means a humorist, he did have a fine sense of humor. During the 1953 season, he said to George Gardner, boss of the Southeastern Conference officials, "George, I want you to know that I'm not complaining about the officials. But Mamma [Mrs. Neyland] is sore at the boys who worked the Vanderbilt game."

"I'm burned up," Mrs. Neyland broke in, "because they called back a Tennessee touchdown. It was on a pass and we had an ineligible man downfield."

"What Mamma is sore about, George," said Neyland, "is that the officials took away the only touchdown her boy [Bob, Jr.] ever scored."

The side of Robert Reese Neyland that the public saw was cool, aloof, self-centered, autocratic, proud, sometimes arrogant. But to a chosen few he revealed a side that was warm and charming. He could be a courtly man and a fascinating conversationalist on a wide variety of subjects, including literature, music, history. To hear him talking across coffee at the dinner table of his war experiences was rewarding, and made the listener deplore the General's having decided to write his memoirs when it was too late.

On the football field, on the military field, or socially, Bob Neyland lived the philosophy of *carpe diem* ("seize the day"). His favorite quotation was from the Sanskrit:

"Look to the day—for it is life—the very life of life. In its brief counsel lie all the verities and realities of your existence! The bliss of growth, the glory of action, the splendor of beauty. For yesterday is already a dream and tomorrow is only a vision, but today, well lived, makes every yesterday a dream of happiness and every tomorrow a vision of hope. Look well, therefore, to this day. Such is the salutation of the dawn."

THE SHOWDOWN MAN

Homer, epic poet, would have smote his lyre for Homer, epic football coach and athletic director. When Homer Hill Norton first arrived at Texas A. & M. in 1934, he faced a prospect bleak and dire. The bank held a mortgage of $210,000 on the football stadium, Kyle Field, and in 1933 the athletic association had scraped to pay the interest.

It took gray matter, patience, determination, and grit to do what Norton did. He built three successive Southwest Conference champions, 1939, '40, and '41, and national champions in '39. His teams broke even in four Bowl games, twice in the Cotton, once each in the Sugar and Orange. And when he departed the Texas Aggies in 1947 after 14 seasons, he left the athletic association a surplus of more than $250,000.

To accomplish all this, Norton paid a steep personal price. The succession of crises, the frequent clamor of alumni for his head, bred in him stomach ulcers that required several visits to surgery. He gave to football, the game he loved, more than 80 percent of his stomach.

Before Texas Aggies, Norton had been a successful coach and athletic director at Centenary College in Shreveport, Louisiana. It was his habit of beating Southwest Conference teams that got him the appointment as Matty Bell's successor at College Station in 1934.

After his first spring practice there, he visited all parts of Texas to speak to alumni groups, and he put it on the line. So did the groups. The Houston group, for example.

"The coming season doesn't look good," Norton stated. "We will win a few games, and for the next year I can't raise your hopes by promising any better than we can expect this year. We need scholarships. Perhaps by 1936 we can offer more scholarships and get some of the better high school boys. However, it will be 1937 before they will be eligible to play. So in 1937—"

At that point a rabid ex-Aggie shouted, "Never mind telling us about 1937, Homer. If you haven't started to win by then, you won't be around to worry about it."

The Aggies' financial problem was basic. Since the Texas legislature did not appropriate any money for intercollegiate athletics, Aggie sports had to subsist wholly on the sale of tickets and the contributions of alumni. Norton got around that by getting some influential alumni to influence the legislature to pass an act permitting the college to lend the athletic association $30,000.

That took care of the interest for 1934. But in '35 no interest payment was possible, so for the first time the bonds went into default, and the bank took over the budget. This compounded Norton's problem. There were some things bankers couldn't understand. Why couldn't last year's football shoes be half-soled and used again? Why couldn't last year's uniforms be cleaned and dyed and worn again? And surely Norton could find 11 boys who could play football from a student body of over 5,000.

Even with a tight budget in 1936, there wasn't enough left to pay the interest. So again there was a default—and Norton submitted to stomach surgery. When he had recovered, he advised the bank officials that unless they could loan the athletic association another $25,000 for scholarships, they might find themselves with a stadium and no team to play in it. Grudgingly the bank allowed the loan.

In utilizing the $25,000 for scholarships, Norton and his staff did a recruiting job that would be hard to beat. The best 40 high school players in Texas were scheduled to play in the Texas State High School Coaches Association All-Star game. Of those 40 players, 37 became members of the 1937 Texas Aggies' freshman squad.

The sell line was effective. The boys were told that since the Aggies lacked material, they could make the team as sophomores in 1938, and if they stuck together, by '39 they could win the Southwest Conference championship. As each boy was committed, he helped go to work on the others.

The 37 included two All-Americans, fullback John Kimbrough, and guard Marshall Foch Robnett, and four All–Southwest Conference selectees, Herb Smith and Jim Sterling, ends; Jim Thomason, halfback; and Ernie Pannell, tackle.

Meanwhile, the 1936 and '37 varsities compiled 8–3–1 and 5–2–2 seasons; they were paced by Joe Routt, a two-year All-America guard, and three

Homer Norton, at Texas A. & M.

All-SWC choices, halfback Dick Todd, guard Virgil (Brahma) Jones, and tackle Roy (Spanky) Young.

The 1937 gate receipts and the 1938 advance sale met the interest on the stadium, repaid the $25,000 bank loan, and restored the budget to Norton. After the 1938 season—4-4-1—some alums moaned chillingly for the scalp of Homer, but he was able to beat them off and sign a new five-year contract—with more drain on his stomach.

Before the 1939 season—junior year for the Kimbrough-Robnett class—Norton announced publicly that he had a team of championship caliber. This uncoachly pronouncement, as intended, stimulated advance sales so that the athletic association could repay the $30,000 loan to the college.

As coach and prophet, Norton lived up to his motto, "It's how you show up at the showdown that counts." The Aggies won all 10 of their regular-season games for the first time in 20 years, including a 20–0 triumph over Texas, and then beat a strong Tulane team in the Sugar Bowl, 14–13. With the New Orleans sugar Norton redeemed $120,000 of the $210,000 Kyle Field

bonds, and with the advance sale for 1940, paid off the balance of $90,000.

"Norton had performed two miracles," wrote H. B. McElroy, Aggie sports publicist in those days. "He had taken the Texas Aggies to the very top nationally in football and he had made solvent a business that was one step short of bankruptcy. After his great showing in 1939, that 1938 contract was torn up and a new one was given him at a greatly increased salary."

The 1939 Aggies, which Norton called the "perfect team," was atypical of Southwest Conference champions, which had lived mainly by the forward pass. The Aggies could pass, but they emphasized an overpowering ground attack built around Kimbrough. And they were at least as tough defensively—perhaps tougher. They allowed their opponents an average of 5.4 first downs and 76.3 yards rushing and passing per game. The 1.71-yard average per play they permitted still stands at this writing as a record.

Kimbrough, six feet two and 222 pounds, was the devil to stop, especially behind blockers like Robnett, Thomason, and Pannell. "Jarrin' Jawn," as Texans knew him, is rated tops of all college fullbacks by that eminent football scholar from Nashville, Professor Lacy Lockert. He based his opinion largely on Kimbrough's performance in the Sugar Bowl.

Against a Tulane line that included three All-Americans—guard Tom O'Boyle, tackle Harley McCollum, and end Ralph Wetzel—Kimbrough gained 152 yards on 26 carries, an average close to six yards. He scored the first touchdown on a plunge from the 1, and the second on a 10-yard sweep after taking a lateral off a forward pass.

"I never thought I'd have the honor of tackling a truck," said Tulane's Buddy Banker, "but that's just what it was like to hit Kimbrough."

Kimbrough was also a strong defensive player. After he had tackled Bobby (Jitterbug) Kellogg, Tulane's ace runner (he'd scored earlier on a 75-yard run), Kimbrough helped him up and congratulated him on his good playing. Kellogg appeared to snub Kimbrough, and when asked about it, replied, "Man, when you've been stopped by that Kimbrough, you're lucky to be able to get off the ground, much less have enough breath to say anything."

A 9.8 man in the 100, Kimbrough had speed to match his brawn. In the 1940 victory over UCLA, 7–0, he overtook and tackled Jackie Robinson after letting Robinson get behind him on a pass.

He hit Robinson so hard that Jackie had to leave the game and never reentered.

"I was not running to catch Robinson," Kimbrough explained. "I was running to save my own life, for I would have been killed for letting him get behind me."

Kimbrough ran from both the single-wing box and the double-wing formations that Norton put together by adapting from Knute Rockne, Pop Warner, and Jock Sutherland.

The Aggies carried their winning streak to 19, through the first eight games of 1940. No. 18, against Southern Methodist, was achieved on a rainy day that revealed Kimbrough at his finest and Norton as tactician. He switched Thomason from blocking back to fullback and Kimbrough from full to left half.

With SMU's defense keying on Kimbrough, Thomason gained nine yards, Kimbrough three, and wingback Bill Conatser three for the touchdown on a reverse. Then the Mustangs' ace passer, Ray Mallouf, tied it up with a 33-yarder that Bobby Brown caught in the end zone after it was deflected by an Aggie. In the third period, with the score 7–7, Conatser returned a punt 40 yards to the Mustang 35. Norton sent in the terse message, "Give it to John." So they gave it to John seven times in nine plays, and he at length took it in from the 2. For pile-driving power it was one of the most impressive drives ever seen in the Southwest or any place else.

The extra point failed, leaving it 13–7, and an interception by Kimbrough on the Aggie 10 frustrated SMU's efforts to tie it. A blocked punt gave A. & M. the cushion touchdown in a 19–7 victory.

In acquiring No. 19, over Rice, 25–0, the Aggies went into the air, featured by Bill (Jitterbug) Henderson, who caught eight straight passes for 136 yards.

With an 8–0 record and a Rose Bowl bid awaiting, Norton and his Aggies passed through their deepest valley when they were upset by Texas, 7–0.

The Longhorns, winning the toss and electing to receive, ran the opening kickoff back to their 30. On the first play Pete Layden faked an end run to the right and connected on a cross-over pass to Jack Crain, who was downed on the Aggie 35.

On the second play, Layden failed on a pass down the middle. On the third play, Layden faked a sweep to his left and threw a pass to wingback Noble Doss. Doss made a remarkable diving catch as he went out of bounds on the 1. On the fourth play Layden plunged over and Crain kicked the point.

All of this happened in the first 58 seconds. In the remaining 59 minutes and two seconds Kimbrough led charge after charge, but whenever the Aggies got past the Texas 10, the Horns hooked them. Five times the Aggies tried the bomb pass; five times it was intercepted. In the dressing room, locked to outsiders for the first time in Norton's career, the coach addressed a squad that included many moist eyes, "This is perhaps the bitterest pill you will ever have to swallow, but there is one thing about it: if you will take what happened to you today as a lesson when you get out into life and won't get cocky and overconfident, then this defeat might not be as bad as it seems."

Years later Norton talked about it: "We were all brokenhearted, but you know losing taught many of those boys a valuable lesson; many of them have told me so. And after all, the purpose of football is to teach lessons to young men."

In comparing the 1939 and '40 Aggies, Norton made a distinction, "For my money the 1939 team was one of the greatest I have ever seen. They could do everything well. We had a fine line along with a great backfield. . . . Joe Boyd, All-America tackle, was the outstanding lineman. . . . The 1940 club still had Kimbrough to do the carrying . . . but many times they were overconfident. This was entirely true in November when they lost to Texas and at the same time sacrificed our bid to the Rose Bowl."

With the Rose Bowl bid lost, the Aggies beat a strong Fordham team 13–12 in the Cotton Bowl, and it developed into something just short of a shootout.

"The coaches and the players," said McElroy, "agreed that it was the roughest game they ever played in, and no doubt Fordham agreed. Bill Buchanan, the A. & M. left end, was taking a good fist massage, which drew blood. He turned to Jimmie Higgins, the umpire, and said, 'Jimmie, that bastard is beating the hell outa me with his fist and forearm. Watch him.'

"Higgins said he hadn't seen anything. Buck spit out some blood and inquired, 'What the hell do you think I've been doing? Eating dewberries out here?'"

The Rams slowed down but couldn't stop Kimbrough, who gained 75 yards in 18 carries and scored a touchdown. As a prime blocker, Robnett had an afternoon of confrontations with

Lou DeFilippo, Fordham's ace linebacker.

"After the game," McElroy reminisced, "Robnett was upstairs in his room at the Adolphus Hotel. Rob's knee was torn up and that ruined his pro career. Down in the banquet room, DeFilippo was on crutches with an arm in a sling. He was hunting for Robnett so they could finish the fight and not draw a penalty. The condition of each was caused by the other.

"I don't deny that the Rams got their lumps. Many of Kimbrough's 'short gainers' were aimed at DeFilippo to punish him."

After the game, Kimbrough saluted DeFilippo merely by voice inflection. "Oh," he ohed, "that De-fee-LEEP-o!"

According to Norton, Kimbrough didn't really like to play football, "but when he found out that he could, it never occurred to John not to play football, because he felt that he'd be letting other people down. You know if John Kimbrough had really *loved* football—the way Joe Routt did, for example—he'd have been triple All-American —the greatest fullback who ever put on a shoe. For sheer ability and speed, I've never known his like. Don't misunderstand me, whether or not he liked football, he was still great."

It was natural for Norton to single out Joe Routt, because Routt's development gave him special satisfaction. Joe came from Chappell Hill, Texas, a town of less than 1,000, and went to high school in the nearby town of Brenham, where he was an all-district back. But he failed to make his freshman numerals at A. & M. in 1933.

In 1934, Norton's first year, Routt was ineligible because of academic shortcomings. But he made use of the time by practicing to play guard the way Norton wanted it played, Homer being an old tackle. In 1935 Routt not only started but made All-Conference.

Routt's case underscored again that Norton, to stimulate ticket sales, was not averse to climbing out on a high and wind-tossed limb. Before the 1936 season he promised the Aggie alums their first All-American. "That man," he said, "will be Joe Routt." Joe lived up to the prophecy; he was All-America not only in '36 but also in '37.

Even after the Kimbrough-Robnett class was graduated in 1941, the Aggies won a third straight conference title, but lost to Texas 23–0. In the Cotton Bowl they were outscored by Alabama 29–21.

In the 1943 wartime season, with the two freshman Marions—Flanagan, the back, and Settegast, the end—back Jim Hallmark and tackle Goble Bryant, the Aggies lost only one game, but again it was to Texas, 27–13, and it cost them the conference crown. In the Orange Bowl they lost, 19–14, to the Louisiana State team that had top-drawer runner Steve Van Buren.

The 1944 and '45 teams had winning records, but lost to Texas 6–0 and 20–10, and after the '45 season, Norton again was in surgery. To stay off his feet while coaching, he invented what he called a "Coaching Sky Buggy." It consisted of the body of an old coupe atop a 15-foot-high steel scaffold; from it Homer coached through a loudspeaker.

"It was the world's greatest coaching invention," he said, "and I'd use one today, even in the best of health. Frank Leahy at Notre Dame got the idea for a Sky Buggy and had his own raised platform built. Frank got national publicity for it, but my alumni thought I was nuts and told me to stop using it. Unfortunately, I guess, I agreed."

Homer Hill Norton, son of a Methodist minister, was a four-sport star—football, basketball, track, and baseball—at Birmingham-Southern, and named the best all-round athlete in the Southeast. From 1916 through '18 he played minor league baseball as an outfielder, but in 1919 he accepted an offer from Centenary to become athletic director and coach of its struggling football team.

In 1922, Centenary named a new president, Dr. George S. Sexton, an ambitious and aggressive administrator. He wanted Centenary to have big-time football and a place in the Southwest Conference. So he hired Bo McMillin, whose feats as quarterback of Centre College had got him a national name. Norton agreed to step down and be an assistant to Bo.

McMillin, a disciple of direct action, recruited from all compass points, and his finds included Cal Hubbard, who was to become one of the all-time tackles, in both college and pro. Bo's Centenary teams won, but Bo's methods were not conducive to gaining membership in the SWC. By 1926 Bo had left—Hubbard with him—for Geneva, and Norton had picked up the pieces.

Norton recruited in a more temperate manner and showed he knew what to do with the material. He delivered two undefeated teams, 1932 and '33, and in 1930 lost only to the Texas Aggies. In '32 and '33, Centenary's victims included Arkansas, Southern Methodist, and the Aggies. His eight-year record, 1926–33, against SWC teams was an even .500—13–13–2.

Despite that record and strong annual appeals

by Dr. Sexton and himself at the annual SWC spring meetings—including a special train of prominent Shreveport citizens one year for moral support—the SWC rejected Centenary. They were invariably polite, and just as invariably negative. So in 1934 Norton himself joined the SWC by accepting the Texas Aggies job.

Whether Homer Hill Norton would have grown ulcers faster or slower at Centenary is problematical. That he developed them at College Station is undeniable.

After the 1946 season, in which the Aggies lost to Texas, 24–7, for the seventh straight time, the alumni called for his resignation. But Homer still had three years to go on a five-year contract at $10,000 a year, and he advised them to pay up or shut up.

A year later, after the eighth straight loss to Texas, 32–13, the alums decided to pay up. So Norton pocketed the $20,000 and bid all a fond adieu. He was 50, and until his death in 1965, he was in the motel and restaurant business.

Norton is where he belongs, in the Football Hall of Fame, with such old familiars as Cal Hubbard, Joe Routt, and John Kimbrough. He lived up to the code he preached to his men, "It's how you show up at the showdown that counts." Homer Norton's showdown record stands tall.

He finally built Coach Norton's Pancake House and Restaurant across from the Texas A. & M. campus. From there he could still see Kyle Field—the old homestead where he and his teams lifted the mortgage.

Knute Rockne

THE ROCK OF NOTRE DAME

The blind man was groping his way around the Pennsylvania Station in Manhattan this October day in 1930, when Bill Ainsworth, of the New York Advertising Club, took him by the arm.

"Where would you like to go, sir?"

"Thank you. I'd like to get up on the street and walk over to 34th Street and Park Avenue," the blind man replied. His tone was clear, eager. Ainsworth led him to the stairway. When he felt the stairway under foot the blind man almost raced up the steps to the street, as if he could see. Ainsworth, intrigued, remarked about this.

"Four years ago," the blind man explained, "I lost my eyesight from scarlet fever. For months I deplored my loss. My life seemed useless, and I didn't care about living on.

"I'd always been a football fan, and I asked a friend to take me to see Notre Dame play the Army. I meant to listen and have him tell me the plays. I enjoyed it so much, and after the game we waited until the crowd was out of the stands before we left. As we were making our way out, someone bumped into me and then I heard a voice. 'Well,' the voice said, 'here is one for the book. Here's a guy who likes his football well enough to come out and listen to it.'

"It was a voice I could never forget.

" 'Who are you?' I asked this voice.

" 'Just a fellow interested in football,' the voice said. 'But I can see it all and I wonder what I would get out of it if I couldn't see it.'

"I told him I had seen Rockne teams play so often I could always anticipate what was happening by just a word or two from my associate. Then this voice said: 'I'm Knute Rockne.'

"You can imagine how thrilled I was. He took me down to the dressing room and introduced me to a lot of the players. They were packing and hustling to get away, but he sat down and talked to me. That talk was the beginning of a new lease on life for me. I left that dressing room, determined to have eyes—and I have had them ever since. I owe that fact to Knute Rockne."

When he died in the plane crash on a lonely Kansas wheatfield the last day of March 1931, our generation was in college. We who had never seen him in the flesh still felt that we knew him. All across the country in movie houses, when talkies were new, we saw the bald head, the homely but intelligent face, the lively eyes, and we heard the unforgettable voice. Even had there been no picture but just a soundtrack, we would have sat silently enthralled by the spell of the voice with its crisp, almost stuttering staccatos, its Gatling gun of conviction.

Over the years, we knew and heard him again

Knute Rockne of Notre Dame

in the stories told by his old players who became coaches. Jimmy Crowley, left halfback of the 1924 Notre Dame backfield, the Four Horsemen, and later a successful coach at Michigan State and Fordham, could give an imitation of Rockne that was, old Notre Damers agreed, so true that all you had to do was close your eyes and you'd think it Rockne ...

"The Army ... the Army say they're going to kick us off that schedule and they're going to kick us off that field. Well, they may be able to kick us off that schedule, but they're not going to kick us off that field. ... Now you ends today ... Hunsinger and Collins ... I want you ends to be nice, loose, and liquid when you go up to catch that ball. ... No crowbars up there today ... "

The voice belonged to an unusual man of many and varied facets, for Knute (pronounced Ca-nute) Kenneth Rockne, son of a Voss, Norway, carriage maker, was an orator, an actor, a scientist, a teacher, a humorist, a psychologist, but most of all he was a salesman.

The voice, indeed, belonged to somebody special, but first it was his team that commanded attention as it played from coast to coast, seldom

was defeated, and brought a new dimension of glamour nationally to the game. Rockne and his teams sold football to the butcher and the baker and the man in the street, until his name and his face were as well known as the President's. Notre Dame became the team of the masses, and Rockne their coach.

"Rockne," said Harry Mehre—who played center for him and later coached successfully at Georgia and Mississippi—"sold football to his players with a positive approach, not 'to die gamely,' but to 'fight to live.' He made football an American mania. He brought it up from the thousand-dollar class to the million-dollar class. Rockne captured the imagination of America."

The record—13 seasons, 105 victories, 12 defeats, 5 ties, an .881 percentage—still stands No. 1, and Rockne himself was voted the No. 1 coach of football's first century in 1969, 38 years after his death. Four of his teams were national champions: 1919, 1924, and his last two, 1929 and 1930.

Of the 12 defeats, half of them came in two seasons, four in 1928 and two in 1925. His five victories in '28 still made it a winning season. Of the 11 other seasons, five were unbeaten, six had only one defeat. Four of the defeats were major upsets: Iowa, 7–10, in 1921; Nebraska, 7–14 and 0–17, in 1923 and 1925; and Carnegie Tech, 0–19, in 1926. He coached 14 All-America players.

It figured that when a coach of Rockne's stature did pull a boner, it would be a record one. In 1926, Notre Dame was 8–0 with games remaining at Carnegie Tech and Southern California at home. November 27, date of the N.D.–Carnegie game, also saw Army playing Navy in Soldier's Field, Chicago, before a crowd estimated at close to 110,000, though no official count is available. Rockne decided to attend the Army-Navy game and leave the team in Hunk Anderson's care at Carnegie. One reason he decided on Chicago was to visit with Navy. The Midshipmen were coming onto the Notre Dame schedule for the first time in 1927.

Rockne saw one of the most exciting of all service school battles, 21–21. But it's doubtful he enjoyed it, because in the press box, where he was sitting, he got word that the Irish had been upset by Carnegie, 19–0. The next week, thanks to a lefthanded passer named Art Parisien, N.D. edged Southern Cal, 13–12, for a 9–1 record.

Only Rockne could shake off that kind of a rock, and he did it with automatic aplomb. Whenever the Carnegie game was mentioned to

him on the banquet circuit that winter, he replied, "The Pope has annulled that one."

"Rock could be wrong," says Frank Wallace, Rockne and Notre Dame historian, "and Rock could be cute. But when the chips were down, Rock was a stand-up guy."

Rockne made a habit of visiting the Army dressing room after the game and offering congratulations, win or lose. One year, however, he used his visit to complain about the play of a tackle. He called it dirty play. But Army coach Biff Jones disagreed and the situation was taut. Rockne knew he was wrong, later admitted it, and the old rapport between the rivals was restored.

In 1929, Rockne instituted the all-major-game schedule. Six years earlier, he had introduced the Shock Troops, a form of platooning in which a second team started and the regular team—Four Horsemen and Seven Mules up front—took over after half a period. Both platoons, of course, played both ways.

As an athletic director alone, Rockne would have been extraordinary. Old Cartier Field, Notre Dame's home gridiron until 1930, at one time held only 2,900. Notre Dame Stadium, opened in 1930, seats 59,000. It is noteworthy that Notre Dame football schedules from 1972 through '76, 41 to 45 years after his death, include eight games he arranged or solidified: Navy, Northwestern, Army, Purdue, Michigan State, Southern California, Georgia Tech, and Pittsburgh.

From 1918, when he first became head coach, through 1927, Notre Dame doubled its enrollment and its funds. Rockne's salary, however, was never more than $11,000. In the few years before his untimely death at 43, he was beginning to pick up more than that in speaking, writing, and sponsorship. The Studebaker Company alone paid him $10,000 for giving a series of lectures to its sales force and planned to name a car after him.

"There were many other great football teachers in that era," Paul Gallico wrote, "There were Pop Warner, Hurry Up Yost, Amos Alonzo Stagg, and Percy Haughton, but none of them had that extra star quality that Knute possessed and the ability to fuse eleven men into a unit representative of his own peculiar and often impish spirit. ... Every so often a genuine colossus appears whose influence and teaching cannot be underestimated, and Rockne towered head and shoulders over the best of his profession."

When he was five, Rockne, along with his three sisters and mother, was brought to America by his father, Lars Rockne, a Voss, Norway, carriage maker, who had gone ahead to Chicago to enter his carriage in world's fair competition. The family settled in Logan Square, and Knute got his first taste of football and baseball on the sandlots near 35th Street. He worked in a post office as a mail dispatcher, able to memorize the times of hundreds of trains. Meanwhile, since he weighed only 145 and stood five feet eight, he tended toward track and became an outstanding amateur pole-vaulter and half-miler.

He wanted a college education and managed to save $5,000. He picked Notre Dame because it was cheaper than other schools and he'd be able to work and help pay his way. He took the science course and had for four years a magna cum laude average of over 92. His favorite subject was chemistry, and Father Julius Nieuwland, discoverer of a base for synthetic rubber, took him on as an assistant after his graduation. He sparked so brilliantly in the classroom that all science students wanted to be in his section.

Rockne often looked back on his arrival at Notre Dame. He was 22, much older than the average freshman and already balding. He was, he said in his autobiography, "a lone Norse Protestant in a stronghold of Irish Catholics." But he was soon at home, and in 1925 he embraced the Catholic faith. He had waited until the death of his mother, who was a devout Lutheran.

Like many traditional Rockne stories that blend humor with heroism, there is one that says he became a Catholic the morning of the 1925 home game with Northwestern; that afternoon the Wildcats led 10–0 at the half. In the dressing room Rockne excoriated his players.

"This is a hell of a religion you got me into," he said. "On my first day in it you let yourself be pushed around by a Methodist school."

In the second half Notre Dame scored two touchdowns to win 13–10. The outcome is unimportant. But Rockne delighted in the story because Rex Enright, the fullback whose short gains were at the core of the comeback, scored, lived, and died a Lutheran.

Probably the most brutalized story in the Notre Dame and Rockne legend says that they introduced the forward pass to the East in the 35–13 upset of Army on the Plain in 1913. It is true that Gus Dorais, the quarterback, and Rockne practiced the pass as lifeguards that summer, and that they used it to cut up the Army. But the pass had been legalized seven years before and all teams

were cognizant of it. What Rockne and Dorais did do was show Army and the East how to integrate it as a regular part of the attack. Army, benefiting by the lesson, used it to defeat Navy later that year.

When Rockne succeeded Jess Harper after four years as an assistant, his publicity man was Arch Ward, a student, and later sports editor of the Chicago *Tribune* and founder of both the baseball and the football All-Star games.

"I'm running this team," Rockne told Ward. "Nobody else has anything to say about its makeup or play. If it's a flop, pan me. I have worked around here for four years, and have seldom seen my name in print."

The principle of the shuttling end to get a blocking angle on the tackle was Rockne's invention. The rest of the Notre Dame shift, from T to box formation right or left, had been taken by Harper who had been a quarterback for Alonzo Stagg at the University of Chicago. And Stagg was a Yale end who made the first All-America team ever picked, in 1889. That is what Rockne was talking about when he was asked where the Notre Dame shift came from and he replied: "Where everything else in football came from. Yale."

Beneath the realism and pragmatism that were part of Rockne, below that dynamo that threatened to explode, lay a wide plinth of romanticism. This is underscored in a story by Allen Messick, Notre Dame backfield coach in Rock's playing days.

"Rockne," said Messick, "was basically a romantic with powerful emotions which he usually kept under firm control. But where Notre Dame was involved, he sometimes found himself overcome.

"One night in the twenties—the team was leaving the next morning for Los Angeles and the Southern California game—Knute asked me to take a walk with him. We first strolled aimlessly but eventually found ourselves near the football field. Rock led the way to the turf in front of the goalposts.

"I followed, somewhat puzzled as to why he should on this moonlit night and at this hour wish to visit those empty stands, but I noticed that he seemed moved by strong emotion. He walked in silence to a point directly in front of the goalposts, stood for a moment with eyes closed in reverence, then knelt down and kissed the sacred sod."

Messick told the story a couple of nights later

to an alumni dinner where he preceded Rockne as a speaker. After he had finished, Rockne leaned over and said in his ear *sotto voce*, "You————!"

Rockne admitted the story later to a revered Ivy League football fan, Robert Jackson, former president of Dominion Stores, Ltd., Canada's largest food chain.

"Yes, it's true!" the coach laughed. "But I got even with him by the help of God and considerable prevarication. I'm glad I followed and did not precede him."

It is a strange thing that Rockne, who seemed always in such utter command before an audience, at one time had little confidence in his speaking ability. George Strickler, who was Notre Dame's publicity man in the twenties, tells how he conquered it.

"He went into the woods north of school and practiced. He would stand on a stump near where Brother Leo had Notre Dame's slaughterhouse. I know, because I heard him. In fact, he scared the hell out of me the first time. My dad was in charge of the slaughterhouse and I was hustling his lunch this day when I suddenly heard this voice giving a helluva talk. Looking around a tree, I saw Rock on a stump, going at a lively clip. Eventually, of course, he became one of the greatest speakers in the country. He could make an audience understand and react."

One of Rockne's speeches, which he gave hundreds of times, was an answer to those who said he represented overemphasis in football. To a scholar, which Rockne was, the charge was ridiculous. And he wanted football for as many participants as possible. Under his inspiration and direction, Notre Dame's hall teams numbered 600 players. He felt that sports, football especially, were needed to keep men from going soft. In this speech he foresaw what would happen, if football's critics prevailed, and cited an imaginary football game of the future between Notre Dame and Northwestern:

"Receiving at fullback for Northwestern was the scion of the famous North Shore family, M. Bickerdash Pix III. The entire Northwestern team was gaily clad in purple-mauvette tunics, and about the waist was a white girdle with a Louis XIV buckle.

"Kicking off for Notre Dame was T. Fitzpatrick Murphy, who is better known to his cronies as 'Two Lump,' because he always asks for two lumps of sugar in his orange pekoe.

"The Notre Dame team also presented a strik-

ing appearance with their green shirtwaists and their headgear resembling a woodman's toque. Giving a very neat appearance, without being at all gaudy, were their hip pads trimmed with Georgette. Hanging from the necks were pendants, lavalliere type, on which was engraved the motto of the university: 'Fight fairly but furiously.'

"Precisely at 2:30 P.M., the referee, dressed in regulation costume of plus-fours and crepe de chine blouse, blew his whistle. Two Lump met the ball squarely and sent it soaring down the field right into the arms of Bickerdash, who catching it brought it back fifteen yards before he was tagged by a deft tag on the shoulder by Nouveauriche Gilhooley, the Notre Dame left end.

"Northwestern lined up and tried three running plays to no avail. Notre Dame's tagging defense was impregnable. So, on fourth down, old Bickerdash dropped back in kick formation and sent a long spiral soaring sixty yards down the field to old Two Lump, who was tagged in his tracks. He couldn't move.

"Then, as Notre Dame took the offensive, they found to their dismay that Northwestern was just as clever at defensive tagging as they were. As a result, neither team could gain at all, so throughout the first half a punting duel resulted between old Two Lump and Bickerdash with little advantage to either. Between halves both teams had tea.

"Up until about five minutes to the end of the fourth quarter, it looked as though it were destined to be a tie game, which, you know, is so unsatisfactory.

"Suddenly, out of the rhythmical gavotte, a sort of hidden-ball evolution, old Bickerdash broke loose and went streaking up the field with a clear road to the goal line. The Northwestern stands were in pandemonium; but in the Irish stands was deathly stillness because it looked like a sure defeat for Notre Dame.

"But they failed to reckon on the resourcefulness of old Two Lump. Now when Two Lump, who was back playing safety, the last man on defense, saw Bickerdash streaking toward the goal line and no one there to stop him, did he give up and become panicky?

"Not old Two Lump. With a savoir faire for which he was justly famous, he called in a loud, clear voice that could be heard all over the amphitheater: 'I say, Bickerdash old thing, there's a terrible run in your stocking.'

"Imagine the intense embarrassment and mortification of poor old Bickerdash. What could he

The Rock in battle garb

do to hide his discomfiture but drop the ball and sneak away to the clubhouse, and the game was saved."

Rockne's 13 seasons break down into four parts. Part I—the Gipp era, 1918 through 1920. Part II—the Four Horsemen era, 1921 through 1924. Part III—the between years, 1925–1928.

Rockne's Four Horsemen (*from the left*): Don Miller, Elmer Layden, Jim Crowley, and Harry Stuhldreher

Part IV—the last years, 1929 and 1930. (See scores in Appendix I.)

The Gipp story has stood the test of time and the attempts by the smart-pants school of mod sportswriters to debunk it.

Gipp for sure went out for football only after Rockne saw him kick a stray ball 50 or 60 yards. Gipp for sure was a law unto himself, a pool player and card player who broke training as it suited him. Gipp for sure remained nonchalant under the dynamism of Rockne, and since he was Gipp, a one-only kind, Rockne let him get away with it. Gipp, when the crisis arose, could for sure kick or run or pass a football or defend like a natural, which is what he was. A seven-star natural.

And Gipp, dying of a strep throat infection that developed into pneumonia, for sure said to Rockne before he passed out, "Some day when the going is tough, ask the boys to win one for the Gipper."

Eight years later Rockne judged the time had come to fulfill Gipp's request. Notre Dame was going through its four-defeat season, and at the half in Yankee Stadium it was 0–0 against Army. Rockne asked them to "win this one for the Gipper," and they did, 12–6. In the New York *Daily News* of the following Monday, Frank Wallace broke the story. Years later, when debunkers tried to attack it, Wallace traced down the roots.

"Rockne," he wrote then, "was capable of having invented the Gipp request. But Gipp was also capable of having made the request. A Notre Dame priest told me that an old chaplain who had been in the hospital room at the time had confirmed Gipp's request."

Since it is clearly emblazoned in the records, the Four Horsemen story never has been challenged. As a unit they played in only one loss, to Nebraska in 1923, 14–7, an upset. They were 9–1 in 1923, 9–0 in 1924 and 1925 Rose Bowl victors over Pop Warner's Stanford team with Ernie Nevers at fullback, 27–10.

The name *Four Horsemen*, however, did not come into being until the third game of the 1924

season, against Army at the Polo Grounds on October 18. The name was not given to the 164-pound backfield by Grantland Rice. Rice did make the name famous by using it in the lead of his story, but George Strickler, then Notre Dame publicity man, had the idea.

On Wednesday night, October 15, the night before the team left for New York, Strickler saw the movie *The Four Horsemen of the Apocalypse* for the sixth time. It was being shown in Washington Hall by Brother Cypian as the movie of the week.

"Those heroes got me," says Strickler. "I didn't care for the tangoing Rudolph Valentino did, but when Bull Montana and his associates sped across the screen as the Four Horsemen, goose bumps popped out.

"Between halves of the Army game [Notre Dame was leading 13–0], I stood in the jerry-built press box in the upper left field stands in the Polo Grounds with Granny, Dave Walsh, Damon Runyon, and Jack Kofoed. When we got to talking about the precision of the backfield —Harry Stuhldreher, Jim Crowley, Don Miller and Elmer Layden—I said they were just like the Four Horsemen.

"The last time I saw Granny, shortly before he passed on, we had a good laugh about what might have happened if all four writers had picked it up."

But Grantland Rice alone picked it up. After Notre Dame had won, 13–7, he sat there in the Polo Grounds and typed out what has stood up for almost a half century as sports journalism's most famous lead:

"POLO GROUNDS, NEW YORK, OCT. 18, 1924—Outlined against a blue-gray October sky, the Four Horsemen rode again. In dramatic lore they are known as Famine, Pestilence, Destruction, and Sudden Death. These are only aliases. Their real names are Stuhldreher, Miller, Crowley and Layden."

Strickler, as publicity man, stayed over in New York and read Rice's piece in the Sunday *Tribune*. He immediately sensed the picture value and phoned his father to arrange for four horses.

"Dad handled the assignment with ease," George recalls. "He just stepped next door from Al Breese's, his favorite saloon, to an ice, coal, and wood establishment that dabbled in rent-outs to would-be cowboys. I returned to South Bend on Monday, went from the station to the bar, crawled into a saddle for the first time in my life, and led the other three horses along behind me.

"It was quite an experience. The horses didn't care much about leaving the bar. Three times on the way out from the East side to the campus they pulled me off my mount.

"There was secret practice that day; we were leaving again on Thursday for Princeton. The guards at the gate took a great deal of convincing before they would let me in. My photographer was waiting. We put the four up on horses and he made the picture. Rock grumbled audibly. He didn't like interruptions, but he also appreciated the value of publicity, especially this kind."

Notre Dame had played at Princeton the first time the year before. The Tigers were coming off their 1922 Team of Destiny season and Rockne talked Bill Roper into a two-game series, both at Palmer Stadium. Roper may have realized he was overmatched, but he never had been one to blanch at odds. Notre Dame won the two games, 25–2 and 12–0.

On the first visit, the *Princetonian* ran an interview with Rockne, who said that it was a great honor for Notre Dame to play in this historical revolutionary place and that he was sure his players would benefit from their contacts with Princeton men. He was right.

One of the Princeton halfbacks, Charlie Caldwell, who was to become an outstanding coach himself two decades later, said that his education in football began that day. "I realized," he said later, "that there was much more to this game than I had thought. We were being beaten but we weren't being overpowered. We were being finessed. Every time I was about to do something, I was being nudged or pushed away."

Rockne's teams of the early twenties did not come to a stop after they shifted from the T to the box, which drove the opposition to the rules tables for relief. When the rules were rewritten to demand a full-second stop after the shift, Rockne countered. He put in a series of halfback spins on which the halfback or the fullback cut back to the weak side on sweeps, slants, and thrusts.

The stop after the shift also impelled him to use heavier material. That's why the 1930 backfield of Frank Carideo quarterback, Marchie Schwartz and Marty Brill halfbacks, and Joe Savoldi fullback, averaged 186, outweighing the Horsemen by 22 pounds.

The Notre Dame system, as taught by Rockne, and the single- and double-wingback deploy, as devised by Pop Warner, were the dominant formations of the twenties and thirties. A partial list of Rockne pupils who became successful head

coaches would include Frank Leahy, Boston College and Notre Dame; Frank Thomas, Chattanooga and Alabama; Jim Crowley, Michigan State and Fordham; Harry Mehre, Georgia and Mississippi; Elmer Layden, Loras, Duquesne, and Notre Dame; Slip Madigan, Gonzaga and St. Mary's; Harry Stuhldreher, Villanova and Wisconsin; Charlie Bachman, Kansas State, Florida, and Michigan State; Adam Walsh, Santa Clara and Bowdoin; Jimmy Phelan, Purdue and Washington; Buck Shaw, Santa Clara and California; and Eddie Anderson, Loras, Holy Cross, and Iowa.

In 1969, when the top winning percentages were listed of those coaches of football's first century who had coached at least ten years, not only did Rockne lead but three of his old players, Leahy, Thomas, and Crowley, finished 2nd, 9th, and 18th.

As a psychologist playing on the emotions of his players to bring them to peak form for certain games, Rockne had almost as deft a hand as Bob Zuppke. When he suspected the Four Horsemen needed to be reined in, he would scrimmage them behind a second-string line. After they had been piled up regularly, the first line, the Seven Mules, would be sent in, and Adam Walsh, center and captain, would inquire of the Horsemen, "What's the matter boys, having trouble?"

The charge that Rockne stooped to gimmickry founders on three facts. His players were too intelligent for that. He did not crescendo his pregame and halftime talks too often. If he did seize a situation to step up the adrenaline, it always had a foundation in credibility.

Before the 13–0 victory over Georgia Tech in 1925, Rockne read the players a telegram from his young son Jackie which carried the message, "I want my daddy's team to win." Frank Wallace reports that he dated the girl who was babysitting for the Rockne's and that she sent the wire. At Rock's instigation? Possibly.

But the players believed in Rockne because they themselves knew he would sacrifice himself to win, even risk the chance of death. He did just that during the undefeated 1929 season, twice coaching from the sidelines in a wheelchair, at the

Carnegie Tech and Southern Cal games, and against doctor's orders.

He was suffering from phlebitis and had a blood clot in his left leg that could at any time have gone to his head and heart. In fact, during one of his operations, the clot did travel, but carried through to his other leg. The players knew about this, and it contributed to their compulsion.

Possibly no single game underlined Rockne's ability to get a team "up" better than his final game, an upset of Southern California in Los Angeles Coliseum. The Irish had managed to come through nine major games unbeaten, but in the last two, 14–0 over Northwestern and 7–6 over Army, they had shown the attrition.

Several players were injured, including the two ranking fullbacks, Joe Savoldi and Larry (Moon) Mullins. Southern Cal, meanwhile, despite a 7–6 loss to Washington State, was considered to be perhaps the strongest team Howard Jones (longtime friend of Rockne's) had yet turned out. The Trojan backfield of Orville Mohler at quarter, Gus Shaver and Ernie Pinckert at the halves, and Jim Musick at full was believed unstoppable behind a comparably talented line.

Meanwhile, Rockne projected gloom. He also kept well under cover his fullback plans. Paul (Bucky) O'Connor, who was to start at fullback, wore somebody else's number, and got no publicity. Early in the game O'Connor ran 80 yards for a touchdown and scored again before the Trojans knew who he was. The final score was Notre Dame 27, Southern Cal 0.

When Rockne's life was suddenly snuffed out in an airplane crash, the story received the same attention as a Presidential election or death. Nobody since in sports has received such public tributes, except Vince Lombardi, after his passing in 1970. But Lombardi had received television exposure, Rockne had not. Not even Lombardi had Rockne's impact.

Many tributes have been paid Knute Rockne over the years. Lines not written of him but most applicable to him, perhaps, are Joanna Baillie's:

E'en to the dullest peasant passing by
Who fashioned still on him a wondering eye
He seemed the master spirit of the land.

Bill Roper

A TEAM THAT WON'T BE BEAT

John Prentiss Poe, nephew of the poet and Class of 1854 at Princeton, sent his six sons there, and they all played football. The second son, Johnny Poe, coined the expression, "A team that won't be beat, can't be beat."

In the 1899 Yale-Princeton game at Yale Field, New Haven, Yale led with the clock running out. Early leavers picked up early extras that flashed headlines, YALE WINS, 10–6. Then a roar was heard from inside. Yale had fumbled on its 35-yard line, and the ball had been recovered by a Princeton end.

The Tigers huddled. Arthur Poe, who had beaten Yale by running 95 yards with a fumble at Princeton the year before, was telling Captain Bill Edwards, "All we've got time for is a field goal." "Who's to kick it?" Edwards asked. "I will," said Arthur Poe. "You?" said Edwards. "Why, you've never even tried a field goal before in a game." "I know it," said Poe, "but I can kick this one." Edwards stared at him. "I believe you can," he said. So Arthur Poe kicked the 35-yard field goal and Princeton won, 11–10. It was not the first time a gambling headline failed, nor the last.

The Princeton end who had recovered the fumble to set up that storybook finish was Bill Roper, who later would coach Princeton 17 years to a record of 89 victories, 28 defeats, and 16 ties. And Roper coached far more by inspiration than technique—inspiration based on Johnny Poe's motto, "A team that won't be beat, can't be beat."

The team for which Roper is best remembered lived every week by that motto, Princeton's 1922 Team of Destiny, which won all eight of its games: Johns Hopkins 30–0, Virginia 5–0, Colgate 10–0, Maryland 26–0, Chicago 21–18, Swarthmore 22–13, Harvard 10–3, and Yale 3–0.

The personnel included Herb Treat, All-America, and Harlan F. (Pink) Baker, tackles; Howard (Howdy) Gray and Saxby Tillson, ends; Captain Melville Dickenson and Barr Snively, guards; Oliver Alford, center; Johnny Gorman, quarterback; Charlie Caldwell and Harry Crum, halfbacks; and Jack Cleaves, fullback. Caldwell, who later won fame as a head coach at Williams and Princeton, told Allison Danzig, ranking football historian:

"We were a strong defensive team and we won on Ken Smith's kicking and the breaks. We were truly a team of destiny. Every Saturday they picked us to lose and we won, even though we weren't much on offense. Herb Treat at left tackle and Howdy Gray at left end were very fine players, and Captain Mel Dickenson, a guard, was, too. We had no outstanding back except Jack Cleaves. He was by far the best. The rest of us were just so-so. Cleaves was a fine football player, fast, a good runner, and a good competitor.

"We had no blocking. We couldn't make a first down at times if we had to. When Cleaves passed to Johnny Gorman from behind our goal line against Chicago, the play was made up in the huddle. Gorman went from our 2 to the 40 before he was caught from behind.

"We played a 7–1–2–1 defense all the time and I was the linebacker. I played wingback on offense, but we never ran reverses. I carried the ball once all season and had more actual playing time than anyone else on the team.

"Roper felt that football was 90 percent fight, and all the rest was 10 percent. He was a great psychologist. He would use anything to advantage. He was wonderful in talking to the team. Football was just a fall proposition with him. It was not his profession. He was a lawyer, insurance man, and councilman—and a great man.

"His offense consisted of the best plays other teams used. West Virginia and Ira Rodgers beat us in 1919. He kept Rodgers here for the week. We tied Harvard and beat Yale with the West Virginia spread, which was new that year. The players were crazy about Roper as a person. He was a Princetonian and he would say that if you had a Princeton jersey on and the other man didn't, you had him licked. My senior year we had three different attacks. Roper would like something and put it in. We could have used a little more technique."

Princeton's 21–18 victory at Chicago in 1922 stands tall among the dramatic comeback upsets of the two decades, stands with Yale's 21–13 victory over Army in the Bowl in 1929, Southern California's 16–14 conquest at Notre Dame in 1931, and Notre Dame's 18–13 triumph at Ohio

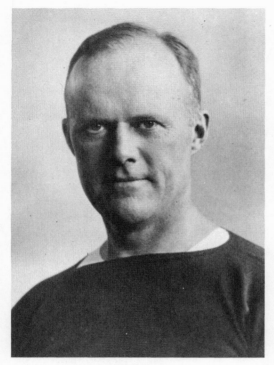

Bill Roper

State in 1935. In his book *Touchdown,* Amos Alonzo Stagg tells of the '22 game with Princeton.

"Chicago held a two-touchdown lead in the final quarter of the Princeton game and lost, 18–21, in a mad, wild last twelve minutes into which enough heart palpitation for forty games was packed.

"It ended with Chicago only a yard away from the winning touchdown and the crowd shrieking, "Hurry! Hurry!" and our quarter, confused in so desperate a crisis, hammering futilely at the Tiger's center. Never before or since has Chicago lost a game which it had tucked away so safely.

"John Thomas, with his brother Harry and Jim Pyott, had ripped the Tiger line to shreds and marched 60 yards in the first quarter for our first score, the bulk of the attack going inside the defensive tackles. We added a second touchdown early in the second quarter and a third near the end of the third quarter without once using a forward pass. ...

"Pyott opened the last quarter auspiciously with a smart 15-yard run. Princeton stiffened and Chicago kicked. Gorman caught the ball and attempted a daring backward pass to Cleaves, who was posted wide. But the pass was thrown

forward, making it illegal, and Princeton was set back to her 2-yard line on the penalty—and we were leading, 18–7, with the end not far off.

"A second time the Tiger outsmarted us. Instead of punting, they passed (from the end zone) to their quarter, Gorman, who was out in end position, and he ran to the 40-yard mark. The tide turned swiftly here. Chicago next got the ball on her 42-yard line. King, our center, was hurt. A substitute took his place. On the first play he passed inaccurately to Zorn. The ball bounded off Zorn's shoulder and bounced into the hands of Gray, the Tiger left end, who continued in full flight for 43 yards and a touchdown.

"The score was 18–14. A 23-yard pass by Princeton carried the ball to our 33-yard line. Strohmeier, playing left defensive half, used his left hand on a Princeton end who was leaping for an out-of-range pass, giving the ball on a penalty to Princeton on our 15. They made four yards on the next play, gained five more on Chicago's offside play. From the 6-yard line Princeton carried it over by an eyelash in four downs. Chicago was behind, 18–21, and time almost up.

"Running the ball back to our 34 from the kickoff, we cut loose with the neglected forward pass and, intermingled with five line bucks, swept down to the Princeton 1-yard line. The attack was irresistible, but suddenly our tactics changed. With the frenzied crowd screaming a prayer for haste in the belief that only seconds remained ... Princeton defended magnificently and John Thomas butted his head into a stone wall. [Herb Treat made the tackle.]

"They had a smart and able team and played brilliantly the tricky, daring strategy of their coach, Bill Roper. No other athletic event in my memory so depressed the university for so many hours."

Although he was not celebrated as a strategist or tactician, Roper's 1922 team at Princeton was the first, in the East anyhow, to use the huddle before each play for the purpose of calling the next play. He did not, however, have any playbook or system.

"Our plays," wrote Ted Drews, of the early-twenties teams, "were a collection of plays that had been used successfully against Princeton and which Roper 'adopted' for our use. There was no rhyme or reason about them and none was 'keyed' to any other play. I don't remember that we even had a 'reverse' play.

"Bill was quite a swearer and most of his speeches were filled with unprintable words.

After our second game in 1924, a 0–0 tie with Lehigh, Bill really lit into the squad at our meeting on Monday, but for some strange reason he used no cuss words until his very last sentence. All the players were looking at one another, amazed at his performance. His closing words were, 'And from now on, don't you guys get so inde-God Damn-pendent.' That really broke up the meeting."

Roper, ire up, was capable of "fighting" words to officials. In the 1907 Yale game at New Haven, the short-end Tigers led at the half, 10–0, but were beaten, 12–10, mainly by the second-half running of Ted Coy. The Elis took more than the allotted 10-minute rest period, and while waiting for them, the Princeton players did calisthenics to keep warm.

"Get them out here!" Roper stormed at the referee, Mike Thompson. "Get them out here! My team will be cold! Get them out here!"

"I've already sent a messenger after them," said Thompson. There was a story that the messenger, another official, got lost underneath the stands. Anyhow, by the time the Yales showed up, Roper was about ready to commit murder. As a result of the incident, a 25-yard penalty for arriving late for the beginning of a half was written into the book. And Thompson was prevented by Roper from officiating at any subsequent Yale-Princeton games.

To prevent Roper from running onto the field in protest, Princeton's track coach and trainer, Keene Fitzpatrick, sat next to Bill on the bench. During the first half of the 1928 Yale game, played at Princeton on a cold, wet day, Roper decided that the referee, Tiny Maxwell, was giving the Orange and Black a bad deal. "I'm going to tell that————what I think of him!" said Roper. Bill Barfield, a Princeton player, recorded the scene.

"Before Keene could stop him, Bill rushed out to Tiny and proceeded to trace his ancestry back to the original cell in most uncomplimentary terms, and lamented with him upon his regrettable future. Listeners claimed that skyrockets soared, pinwheels spun, and the pyrotechnic display was unbelievable. They said that Tiny visibly lost 40 pounds, which he could easily stand.

"Finally, Bill returned to the bench and informed Keene that he had really fixed Tiny. Keene, in his quiet voice, said, 'Bill, do you realize you've got another half of this game to play?' 'By God, Keene,' said Roper, 'you're right.

I'll fix this up.' So he went back onto the field to Tiny, who was still immobile from their previous conversation. 'Tiny,' he said, 'in spite of what I've said, you're not doing such a God damn bad job for such a God damn wet day.' "

Roper saved his best psychological shots for the Yale game. In 1925, the Bulldogs had lost only to Pennsylvania, 16–13, and the Tigers only to Colgate, 9–0, but Yale was the favorite for the game, in New Haven that year. All that week, Roper asked his squad,

"Why should Yale be such a top-heavy favorite? There are only eleven men on each side. And you are not spotting the Yale team anything when it comes to physical qualifications. So why should they be such a top-heavy favorite?"

The night before the game, Princeton stayed at a hotel not far from New Haven. Saturday dawned a bad day, drizzling and the wind strong from the northeast. Jake Slagle, Princeton's best back, and quarterback Dan Caulkins were roommates.

"About dawn," wrote Slagle, "who should come busting into our room but Bill Roper, arms waving. In a rather loud, excited voice he said, 'Hi Dan, hi Jake, great day, just right, how do you feel, fine? Little rain won't hurt, not much wind, time to get up, we all have to be ready for this one. The weather won't hurt your passing or kicking, Jake, the ground doesn't look slippery, a day like this ought to help us.'

"There was nothing really wrong with this enthusiasm but in looking out the window and our hotel being near the coast, it was pretty plain it was an awful day—northeaster blowing, drizzle, and strong wind. When you think about the situation it seems silly but that was Roper's way of getting Caulkins and me ready for the two o'clock kickoff."

Roper was in good form for his dressing-room oratory that day. So much so that when he'd finished, Sayre McLeod, the team manager, had to be restrained from running onto the field with the troops. "I know he wasn't talking to me," McLeod said, "but by the time he stopped, I just naturally started out there to do what he said."

Whatever the impact of Roper or the weather, Princeton won, 25–12, with Slagle returning a punt 75 yards for a touchdown, and Joe Prendergast scoring twice behind the blocking of guard Caleb (Turk) Gates.

The week before, at Princeton, the Tigers had hammered Harvard, 36–0, with Prendergast carrying the ball on nine consecutive plays to score the last touchdown.

Princeton and Harvard broke relations in football for seven years, 1927 through '33, because of the atmosphere surrounding the 1926 game. At the mass rally before the Tigers left for Cambridge, Roper turned to the team on the railroad platform and said, "If you don't beat Harvard tomorrow, I'll cut your throats, throw you in the Charles River, and make you walk home." Prendergast had vivid memories of that game.

"My jersey was literally torn off my back during the game and my signet ring was the one that was supposed to have imposed itself on Al Miller's nose, thereby making the initial stand for 'Prendergast' not 'Princeton.' It was a tough game against a good Harvard team under psychological conditions I have never experienced before or since.

"There was the famous cartoon in the *Lampoon* of pigs in a pigsty, with the caption, 'Come, brother, let us root for dear old Princeton,' and an editorial which stated that this should be the last game between the two universities because Princeton was so inferior in every way to Harvard and the 'Big Three' had always been only the Big Two-and-a-Half.

"The Princeton band leader handed a copy to Roper as he was giving his usual pregame fight talk. He looked at the cartoon, glanced through the editorial, and then read the editorial to us. Then he said, 'Now, go out there and give them your answer.'

"I remember as we came out on the field, you could feel the electricity in the air because by that time everyone had read the *Lampoon* and the Princeton stands gave the team a greater reception than ever before.

"The game was tough but clean in every respect and the resulting break ... was not the wish of the players or the students, but only of Bill Bingham, director of athletics at Harvard. I knew because I was chairman of the Princeton Senior Council and had worked out with Leo Daley, chairman of the Harvard Student Council, whom I had known at Exeter, a solution to the problem satisfactory to both sides.

"Bill Roper was a rough-and-ready guy and a good talker. ... He believed in the game of football and believed that every team and every player should play to the very limit of their capacities, or beyond. He didn't like lazy players or quitters no matter how tough the going was. But he would not tolerate any dirty playing or infraction of the rules. To him football was a great game worthy of great players."

In saluting Roper after his retirement following the 1930 season, Dean Christian Gauss, of Princeton, related the story of the mysterious moving-picture photographer who arrived at the field house to see Bill privately. Roper was busy and called him in, in the presence of a few friends.

The photographer explained that he had been engaged by the coaches of a rival team to take slow motion pictures of their practices and early games. They showed precisely the position of every man on every play.

At first Roper assumed that the photographer had come down to obtain a contract to do the same thing for Princeton. It became plain, however, that this was not his intention. He had made a duplicate set of films, had brought them with him, and was offering to sell Princeton the secrets of a rival.

Before the photographer had time to finish his proposal, Bill grabbed him, pushed, shoved, and literally drove him from the field house with a tongue-lashing such as no football traitor ever had received.

"There are other coaches," said Dean Gauss, "who would have done much the same thing. But it is doubtful if anyone would have kept the secret to himself. To him it was a personal insult, and it was mercenary sneaks like that who were ruining the game. I doubt whether the rival institution has ever learned of the incident to this day.

"It was perhaps episodes somewhat of this sort and Bill's feeling that football should remain a game that led him with Tad Jones to start the movement to abolish scouting. [The movement failed.] It was for the same reason that he opposed football by night, or playing during the spring or summer.

"It was a cool-weather game for the enjoyment and recreation of vigorous young men to be played in the autumn and out of doors. That is why he also objected to mechanizing the game by year-round drill and 'hippodroming' it under lights."

"Bill Roper," wrote author Hugh MacNair Kahler, "was the most *forceful* character in football history ... whatever Bill does, he contrives to throw himself at it with the same irresistible drive that began his football career in the Yale game of 1899.

"Listen to him as he talks insurance to a client or a group of agents. Lend your ear in the Philadelphia City Council when he stands up, the only member of the opposition, to shoot at the pursy, complacent grafters who can outvote him

Bill (*left*) firing up three of his 1930 Princeton Tigers. *Chicago Tribune Photos*

twenty to one, but who hate him, for all that, with the hate that is four parts fear. Sit in the back row of Alexander's at a football rally, and watch the sleek, sophisticated little undergraduate revert, while Bill pours fire into him, into the roaring, artless enthusiasm of your own college days.

"Follow him about the field in the fall and watch him at the work he loves best, with all the power of him driving everybody as it drives Bill himself. Play golf with him and see his face as his lefthanded niblick sweeps down at a buried ball. Look over his shoulder when he writes far and away the best football ever packed up in packages of words.

"Whatever he's doing and wherever and whenever he's doing it, there's never any room for doubt about how much of him is going into it. He's never crossed his fingers in his life."

As the 1930 Tigers team went out to play Yale in Palmer Stadium, their last game under Bill Roper, they had a 1–4–1 record. Their only victory had come in their opener with Amherst, and they had come away from Chicago with a

scoreless tie. Their four defeats had been incurred from Brown 7–0, Cornell 12–7, Navy 31–0, and Lehigh 13–9. Yale, with a 4–1–2 record, Harvard yet to be played, was the distinct favorite.

But Princeton, wanting badly to win this one for Bill Roper, came asnarling. Albie Booth's 18-yard field goal put Yale ahead 3–0 in the first quarter. In the second quarter, the Tigers began whipsawing the Yale line. Quarterback Trix Bennett was playing with a bum knee but he was going to town. So was halfback Jack James. They marched 58 yards to a touchdown, converted, and led at the half, 7–3.

In the third quarter, a lefthanded pass from wingback Tommy Taylor to quarterback Pat Sullivan, good for 36 yards, and Sullivan's conversion restored Yale to the lead, 10–7. With the ball on its 15-yard line and not much time left, Princeton made a final effort. With Bennett and James using flat passes, they moved all the way to the Yale 1-yard line. It was fourth down and a yard to go when Bennett was stopped six inches short of a touchdown. Stuart Hockenbury, who

played the entire game for Princeton, left tackle on defense and weak-side running guard on offense, recalled,

"A fog had settled over the upper half of Palmer Stadium, and literally the people in the high seats could not see the play and understand what the cheering was about. Yale kicked out of danger and in less than a minute had won, 10–7."

No coach, walking from the field, ever received a more heartfelt ovation than Bill Roper after that last game. In the Yale dressing room, Coach Mal Stevens spoke for thousands of Princeton and Yale men when he said, "I hated to see Bill lose it." Then Stevens added, "But I sure wanted to win it. It was the toughest game I ever had to sit through."

For sure that day, just as on the day eight seasons before when Princeton had upset Chicago, 21–18, the words applied that were favorites of Bill Roper, "There is a certain flame of the spirit which can overcome every handicap." Another way of saying, "A team that won't be beat, can't be beat." At least in its inmost heart.

Francis Schmidt

THE SPOT THAT WOULD NOT OUT

It happened 38 years ago, but in bad weather the wound still aches in Columbus, home of the Ohio State Buckeyes, and justifiably regarded as the pinnacle of football madness. Those who remember the date—November 2, 1935—and follow football, in or out of Columbus, will not forget how Notre Dame came from behind in the last quarter to score three touchdowns and defeat, 18–13, an Ohio State team deemed invincible.

That was a memorable date on many fronts, November 2, 1935. Dartmouth broke an old jinx to defeat Yale for the first time. Pittsburgh and Fordham played the first of their three consecutive scoreless ties, an accomplishment not soon to be matched. And Mississippi State invaded West Point and beat the Cadets, 13–12. The Mississippi State coach, a former West Pointer and Army head coach, Major Ralph Sasse, inspired his Bulldogs by reminding them they had come "to avenge Sherman's march to the sea." Major Sasse was a native of Delaware.

But all that had to give way in the headlines to what has been, probably, the most talked-of game ever played. Notre Dame and Ohio State, both unbeaten and untied, were meeting for the first time, and the Buckeyes were the favorites. Top sportswriters from all over the country came to Columbus. Although the depression still gripped the economy, three-dollar tickets were going for $50 a pair. Ohio State was the emphatic favorite.

For the first half, a one-sided triumph for the Bucks seemed a strong possibility. On its second defensive sequence, back Frank Antonucci intercepted an Irish pass, and following Coach Francis Schmidt's injunction, "Look for a guy to lateral to," looked for and found Frank Boucher. Behind a beautiful block by Trevor Rees, Boucher ran 70 yards for a touchdown, and Dick Beltz kicked the point.

In the second quarter, Ohio State's line opened up Notre Dame's and the Scarlet and Gray marched for a second touchdown, with Jumping Joe Williams, a nifty sophomore halfback, knifing over tackle from the 3. This time the conversion was missed. At halftime, press box conversation was concerned with how much Ohio would win by. Notable scribes climbed out on high limbs.

Damon Runyon said, "I'm glad I was here to see 'em. I wouldn't have believed it otherwise."

Grantland Rice: "The Ohio State team in the first half has shown me the greatest display of football I've ever witnessed."

Paul Gallico, "It'll take congressional action to stop those guys."

But in the third quarter, there came a change, gradually. Notre Dame's defenses began throttling Ohio State's attack. And on the last play of the period, halfback Andy Pilney returned a punt from Ohio's 35 to its 12. On third down, Pilney passed to Frank Gaul on the 1, and Jim Miller smashed over. The Irish missed the point, leaving it 13–6.

Another Notre Dame drive foundered on a fumble by Miller on the 1-yard line. But the next time N.D. got the ball, Pilney began clicking on his passes again and hit Mike Layden, brother of

Elmer, the N.D. coach, for a touchdown. Again the Irish missed the point after. Again the Buckeye supporters among the 81,018 sellout roared their relief. Ohio State still led 13–12, and there was only a minute and a half to play.

Notre Dame tried an onside kick but failed. Then Dick Beltz, playing under an ill star this day, committed the first of two errors. He fumbled and Notre Dame recovered. Pilney, back to pass, failed to find a receiver, but stormed to Ohio's 19, where he was knocked out of bounds, again stopping the clock. Pilney was injured and replaced by Bill Shakespeare.

The Irish still had enough seconds left to try two pass plays. On the first, Shakespeare's pass headed straight for the arms of Beltz, who had 90 yards of clear field ahead of him. But he dropped the ball. Then Shakespeare, whose namesake wrote *All's Well That Ends Well*, threw a pass to a spot five yards deep in the end zone and twelve yards from the sideline. An end named Wayne Milner leaped up and caught it. Final score: Notre Dame 18, Ohio State 13.

Probably nobody realized it at the time but from the moment Milner caught the ball, Coach Francis Schmidt's days at Ohio State were numbered. He would never be allowed to forget that by giving a badly needed rest to backs Dick Heekin, Boucher, and Jim McDonald, he had weakened the mobility of his backfield against passes. None of the replacements, it would be pointed out, was over five feet nine. Milner was six feet three. Schmidt would be reminded he should have rested his starting backs near the end of the third period, so he could bring them back in. Nobody, however, explained why Beltz should not have fumbled or dropped the pass.

Schmidt actually lasted five more seasons, even delivered a second conference title in 1939. But that same year the favored Buckeyes—who always seem to be long-enders in Columbus—blew another lead, this one 14 points, to Cornell, pride of the then informal Eastern Ivy League.

Affairs came to a sad climax for Schmidt in 1940, when Michigan, traditionally Ohio's first rival, ran over the Bucks, 40–0, with Tom Harmon enjoying a strong day. Toward the end, the Wolverines were letting themselves be tackled, a compounding of humiliation. This triggered the firing of Schmidt, who coached Idaho in 1941 and '42, and died. Died, some said, from heartbreak over his misadventures in Columbus.

Schmidt had got along well enough with the Grandstand Quarterbacks on High Street, but his

Francis Schmidt, at Ohio State

outspoken ways abraded not only L. W. St. John, athletic director, but members of the faculty as well. "Shut the Gates of Mercy"—the nickname given Schmidt for such victories as 76–0 over Western Reserve and 60–0 over New York University—could be brusque, crude, and profane.

At a social dinner of the Faculty Club he loudly advised a waitress to "take this damned pigeon away and bring me some food."

Whether or not Schmidt downgraded defense, as charged, it's safe enough to say that no coach ever lived who was more offense-minded, and to emphasize this, anecdotes abounded.

Francis was devising offensive tactics one time when an assistant tendered him a scouting report almost as thick as a telephone book. He took the book and tore it to shreds.

"Don't you know better," he roared, "than to bother me when I'm making up plays."

His concentration on offense made it difficult for him to relate to personnel during a game. There was the tale of two Ohio State tackles, who shall be known here as Nitro and Oxman,

"Nitro," said Schmidt, "go in for Oxman."

"Nitro's already in there, coach," said Oxman. "I'm Oxman."

After a very brief pause, Schmidt said, "Okay, whoever you are, go in for whoever he is."

Schmidt had already attracted attention for his excitable ways as coach of Texas Christian from 1929 through '33. He had two undefeated teams with the Horned Frogs, 1929 and '32. On the '32 team, a favorite target of his was Red Oliver, an excellent back whose running defeated traditional rival Texas, 14–0. In an earlier game, Schmidt had yanked Oliver and made him sit by him on the bench. When Oliver's substitute busted a signal, Schmidt yelled, "Look at that Oliver —can't do anything right—that dumb so-and-so."

"Coach," said Oliver mildly, "it's me—Red—I ain't even in the ball game."

Schmidt stared at Oliver.

"What difference does that make," he said. "If you were in there, you'd have made the same mistake."

The Notre Dame game of '35 and the stories told about his excitability under pressure tended unfairly to dilute his image as a coach. The record says he was an excellent coach.

Schmidt, a graduate of Nebraska, served in the infantry in World War I, came out a captain, and began his coaching career at Tulsa University —then known as Kendall—in 1919. His three-year record, 24–3–2, included a trouncing of Arkansas, 63–7, and helped him get the job there.

His seven years at Arkansas, 1922 through '28, showed a good record, 43–19–3, although he won no Southwest Conference championship. He was already well known for his wide-open offense,

well larded with laterals. It is said that he woke up assistant George Cole at three one morning to diagram a trap play that had been keeping him awake.

When Matty Bell, who was coaching Texas Christian, left to succeed D. X. Bible at Texas A. & M. in 1929, he was replaced by Schmidt. In five years, Francis' teams won 46, lost 6, tied 5, and his SWC record was 22–3–2. His 1929 team was TCU's first champions, with quarterback Howard Grubb, later SWC commissioner, and a speedster at halfback named Cy Leland.

The 1932 team, also undefeated, with a 10–0–1 record, ranks higher than 1929's. The Frogs became the first SWC team to defeat all six conference rivals, and placed six of its seven linemen on the All-Conference team. Johnny Vaught, guard and later well-known coach of Mississippi, made All-America.

The TCU years added to the legend of Schmidt. He is supposed to have been working out some plays in his car, while it was raised over a grease pit, and forgetting where it was, he stepped out and into a sudden drop of five feet. Another tale has him reproving a player for dropping a pass in the end zone during signal drill.

"This Saturday you'll be playing before 10,000 people," Francis advised the offender, "and if you dropped a ball like that, do you know what they'd all say?" The player answered, "No." "Well," said Schmidt, "what they'd all say is: 'Aw, hell!' "

When Schmidt moved on to Ohio State in 1934, Buckeye adherents reminded him that the big game was Michigan and that Ohio'd won only nine of the last 12. To which Francis replied, "Michigan puts their pants on the same way we do, one leg at a time." And for four years, he made it stand up as the Scarlet and Gray triumphed over the Maize and Blue by 34–0, 38–0, 21–0, and 21–0. Then the Wolverines caught up with him and beat him three in a row.

But his seven-year record stood out: 39 victories, 16 defeats, 1 tie; and in the conference, 30–9–1. His teams won two Big Ten crowns, one outright, finished second three times, fourth once, and fifth once.

When you look the record over, it stands tall.

But there was always the ghost of the Notre Dame game.

Twenty-five years after Milner caught Shakespeare's pass, a young sportswriter visited an empty Ohio stadium and walked down the grid-

iron to a certain spot in the end zone. There he stopped and stared down. A veteran groundkeeper looked at him, smiled, and said, "That's the spot."

The spot that for Francis Schmidt, a fine offensive football coach, was never rubbed out.

Andy Smith

THE WONDER MAKER

Smith and Jones, common names, had uncommon coaching success, Andrew Latham Smith at the University of California, 1916 to '25, and Howard Harding Jones at the University of Southern California, 1925 to '40. By an odd coincidence they never coached against each other, because their one season in common, 1925, there was no California–Southern Cal game.

Many a team in the twenties and thirties evoked the adjective *wonder*. But the term "Wonder Teams" belongs formally to California's for the five-year period of 1920 through '24. The Golden Bears were given that tag by a San Francisco *Call* sportswriter, Clinton R. (Brick) Morse, and the record insists that he wasn't dreaming.

Veteran West Coast observers argued which of the Wonder Teams was best. Some held out for the 1922 club, captained by 143-pound quarterback Charley Erb. It had only one close game —Southern Cal, 12–0—and it drubbed, 45–7, Coach Enoch Bagshaw's Washington team that lost no other game.

But the 1920 team evoked even stronger support. Lee Cranmer, who played right guard three seasons, 1919–21, told L. H. Gregory, sports columnist of the Portland *Oregonian*, "Good as the 1921 team was, and its successors, to my mind none of them quite came up to the 1920 eleven. What made the 1920 team so great was the fire and inspiration of youth, plus fine material and the most wonderful collective team spirit I believe ever existed on a football eleven.

"The difference between that team and the one of 1921 was that in 1920 we knew we were good, that we had the stuff, but we were out to demonstrate it. In 1921, we knew we were good —so good that we sometimes felt we didn't have to prove it. The 1921 team felt its oats at times and was hard to handle."

Cranmer also pointed out that Andy Smith was well ahead of the field.

"One thing that made Andy Smith so great a coach," Cranmer said, "was his ability to inspire a team in a few words, but that was not all. Andy knew football so thoroughly and his rival coaches so completely that, in his blackboard talks and lectures before any specific game, he would tell us just what to expect. He never missed.

"Andy sized up everything that was ever sprung on us by another team and warned us about it in advance. He seemed to have analyzed the character of the other coach and to know exactly what kind of football he would use. In 1920 we listened to everything Andy told us. In 1921 we were so good and knew we were so good that Andy had his troubles.

"For years you have heard that Andy in the tough spots would signal his team from the bench. The story always went that Andy, who in the nervous excitement of a game drank so copiously of water that he kept a tin dipper in almost continuous motion ladling up sips from the waterbuckets, had an elaborate system of signs, depending on what bucket he dipped water from.

"Nothing to it at all," Cranmer emphasized. "In the three years I played under Andy I never once knew him to signal from the bench. . . . Andy was too smart a coach to signal. . . . When the Bears went on the field, running the team was in the hands of Charley Erb, and it was Charley who called every play. One reason why Erb was such a great quarterback was that Andy Smith, after the game started, left him absolutely alone."

The 1920 Wonder Team outscored its regular-season opponents 482–14, an approximate point-a-minute production, in winning from all eight and being held fairly close only by the Oregon Aggies, 17–7. Despite that record, the Bears were 8–5 underdogs to Ohio State in the 1921 Tournament of Roses game. But they whipped the Buckeyes decisively, 28–0, to enter a valid claim on the national championship.

Andy Smith, 1925. *Chicago Tribune Photos*

Until that game, the East and the other parts of the country had looked down on Pacific Coast football. Condescension was underscored when Walter Camp placed one of the outstanding ends of all time, California's Harold (Brick) Muller, on his third All-America team. By sunset New Year's Day, Camp's face was redder than the sun. Walter tried to make up for the boo-boo by picking Muller on his first team in 1921 and '22.

The one-sided victory over Ohio State certified the Golden Bears' "Wondership." From 1920 through the first two games of 1925, Cal won 46 and tied four. A noncollege team, the Olympic Club of San Francisco, snapped the defeatless string of 50 games by blanking the Berkeley boys, 15–0, in the third game of 1925. The Golden Bears won four consecutive Pacific Coast Conference championships before losing a bitter 7–0 game to Washington in '25.

But it's always the Ohio State game of New Year's 1921 that the oldsters get around to first.

The game was notable also for the first appearance of ticket skulduggery at a Bowl game. Phony pasteboards were printed at $2.50 a copy (prices on the real tickets ran from $1.00 to $6.00), and the tournament committee bought newspaper ads to warn the public. The crowd was 42,000, capacity for old Exhibition Park (the Rose Bowl in the Arroyo Seco was not ready until the 1922 season), and another 58,000 were disappointed. The gate receipts were $90,000, a record, but California and Ohio State received only traveling expenses and a small percentage.

The Golden Bears' roster comprised several standout players, including Cort Majors, captain, and Cranmer, guards; Don MacMillan and Stan Barnes, tackles (Barnes later became a federal circuit judge); George (Fat) Latham, center; Erb, quarterback; and Archie Nisbet, Duke Morrison, Albert (Pesky) Sprott, and Crip Toomey, backs.

Muller was unquestionably preeminent. Called Brick because of his flaming thatch, he was an all-round athlete, football, track, and baseball. In the 1920 Olympics at Antwerp, he finished third in the high jump. He was six feet, 193 pounds, and the possessor of large, strong hands and long powerful arms. He could throw and catch a football, which was bigger then, as if it were a baseball. He could throw a ball as far as 60 to 70 yards at a 12-foot trajectory, and any pass he could get one hand on he could catch. He was also fast and tough under punts, and an exceptional blocker and defensive end.

Elmer (Gus) Henderson, coach of the 1921 Southern Cal team, which had been a strong candidate for the Roses, called Muller "the best player I ever saw in a football suit." Dr. John Wilce, Ohio State's coach, said Brick was "about" the greatest he'd ever seen. Bill Roper, Princeton's coach, said he "was the peer of any end the game has produced."

The long forward pass that gave California a 14–0 lead in the second quarter was the blow the Buckeyes could not recover from. It was a trick number that the Bears had rehearsed thoroughly, and was set up by the previous play, a line plunge by fullback Archie Nisbet to Ohio's 37-yard line.

Nisbet got up slowly and stood near the ball, talking to one of the six other Cal players strung along the line. The three other Cal backs stood with their hands on their hips. Muller stood off to the left of them.

Suddenly, Nisbet stooped and flipped the ball back to Pesky Sprott. Sprott faked a run and then lateraled the ball to Muller coming around from

his left. With Sprott and a guard providing interference, Muller moved laterally to his right and backwards until he'd reached his own 47-yard line.

Meanwhile, Erb and Toomey had decoyed as pass receivers. Brodie Stephens, the right end and intended receiver, went deep downfield. As he passed Pete Stinchcomb, Ohio's ace halfback, who was playing safety, Stinchcomb asked him, "Just where do you think you're going?" (In later years when friends met Stephens they often asked him, "Hello, Brodie, where do you think you're going?") After the game Stinchcomb admitted, "I simply didn't believe anybody could throw the ball that far."

As he neared the goal line, Stephens turned and took Muller's pass in stride. The ball, which hit him in the chest, had covered 53 yards. Ed Hughes, of the San Francisco *Chronicle*, said the pass resembled a catcher's peg to second base, and at no time was more than ten feet off the ground.

For over 20 years Muller was credited with a 70-yard pass, but exhaustive research by Maxwell Stiles, well-known Los Angeles sportswriter, established the distance at 53 yards; since the pass was diagonal it actually covered more than 53. Later in the game Muller completed an even longer one of 55 yards, but it was disallowed by the head linesman, who said Cal had only six men on the line of scrimmage.

Muller completed two other passes, but if he hadn't thrown the ball once, he still would have starred. He caught two passes for 33 yards, several times dumped Stinchcomb after he caught punts, and though he often played eight yards off the line of scrimmage, he still came up to tackle Stinchcomb on attempted sweeps for no gain.

When Jimmy Phelan, who would coach Missouri to the Big Six championship the next fall, read the January 2 newspaper stories of the game, he recalled a conversation he'd had with Andy Smith a year before. Cal had lost to Washington State and Washington, and there was talk of firing Smith. Phelan, visiting him at Berkeley to talk football, warned him.

"I'm not worried," said Andy. "Next year I'll have 'em where I want 'em."

Then he drew Phelan a play in which the left end dropped back and threw a long pass.

"What do you think of it?" Smith asked.

"It's fine," Phelan agreed, "if you've got a man with a shotgun arm."

"I've got one," Smith nodded. "A freshman who'll be eligible next fall."

"I've never asked Andy the player's name." Phelan reminisced, "but a year later I read it in the papers—Brick Muller."

When Andy Smith first came to California from Purdue in 1916, he set forth his formula for a winner, "There are four qualifications necessary for success—aggressiveness, obedience, concentration, and determination. Add to this harmonious cooperation and you have the making of a real team."

Whether squad attitude was a factor—and Cranmer implies it might have been—the Golden Bears, Pasadena's Golden Boys the year before, were well tarnished in the 1922 Tournament of Roses game. They were tied by Washington & Jefferson, 0–0, and thoroughly outplayed.

More than once in Rose Bowl history, the Pacific Coast team was placed at a psychological disadvantage by the West Coast writers downgrading and disparaging the invited team. Such were Stanford's headaches against Columbia in the 1934 game and Alabama a year later; it was the same migraine that beset Washington against Pittsburgh in 1937. But none of those teams was as ridiculed as Washington & Jefferson, which was selected after Cornell, Lafayette, Penn State, and Centre had been mentioned and dropped out.

"Who and what is, or are, Washington and Jefferson?" one scribe inquired. "All I know about Washington and Jefferson," stated another, "is that they're both dead." Still another suggested that Washington and Jefferson were two different colleges that had banded together to make things equal against California. The Presidents were further belittled as "Willie and Jake," and "Whitewash U." The credentials of their coach, Earl (Greasy) Neale, were questioned. He was then known mainly as an outfielder for the Cincinnati Reds, although he had already coached five years—at Muskingum, West Virginia Wesleyan, and Marietta—before taking over W. & J.

Odds were as high as 3–1 in favor of California, and points were freely given. The few rooters accompanying W. & J. grabbed up the bets. They knew their team was sadly underrated; the Presidents' 10–0 record included victories over Syracuse, Pittsburgh, and West Virginia.

A heavy rain left a muddy but playable field. Led by its All-America tackle Russ Stein, who might also line up as an end or a back, W. & J. allowed California only two first downs, both by

Andy watching a Golden Bear scrimmage

persisted, talking about a man who was a dead ringer for me. In the meantime Charley Erb was calling signals and there I was, paying no attention because a fictitious Pittsburgh uncle was on my mind. Luckily, I hollered 'signals over' on time, but even then I didn't get back into the game, the way I should have been in it, for several minutes."

Brick Muller, who was recovering from injuries, was held out until late in the second period. When he was sent in, the Washington and Jefferson players, led by end Herb Kopf, surrounded him and rubbed their muddied hands on his jersey. Brick was mad enough to swing on somebody, and said later that he would have, except it would have evoked a penalty and put him out of the game. Later, Kopf asked Muller if he thought it was going to rain any more.

"How should I know?" Muller growled.

"I thought you would," said Kopf. "You've been on your back all afternoon."

Actually Muller played a good game, but he could not complete a pass and the Golden Bears could not make any meaningful tracks in the heavy going against the derided and bristling Easterners. Andy Smith had called the turn the night before, while chatting with two old friends, officials Tom Thorp of Columbia and Walter Eckersall of Chicago. Andy had looked out the window and commented, "It's still raining. We'll kick. The score will be nothing to nothing."

California's 1924 team played another celebrated tie, 20–20, this with Glenn S. (Pop) Warner's Stanford team. A crowd of 77,000 saw that one in Memorial Stadium at Berkeley, with another estimated 24,000 watching from nearby "Tightwad Hill." Ernie Nevers, Stanford's colossal fullback, had to sit it out with a bad ankle, but the Cardinal still rallied with two touchdowns near the end. A scoreless tie with Nevada in 1923 and a 7–7 deadlock with Washington in 1924 were California's only other nonvictories in the five years from 1920 through '24.

Andy Smith prepped at DuBois High in Philadelphia, played fullback for Penn State in 1901 and '02, and then transferred to Pennsylvania for 1903 and '04. In '04 he was All-America fullback on a Red and Blue team that won all of its 12 games and is regarded as one of the strongest in the school's history.

Smith had majored in chemistry with the intention of entering the steel business, but instead went into real estate. He loved football, however, and snatched up the chance to coach

rushing, and a total of 49 yards to the Presidents' 114 running and 23 passing. Only a bad break prevented a W. & J. victory: a 36-yard touchdown run by Wayne Brenkert was called back because of holding. Ironically, the holding, which was on the side of the line away from Brenkert, was committed by the best man on the field that day, Stein.

W. & J., which had brought along only 19 players, started and finished with the same 11. And Coach Neale, wearing a white cap and cream-colored polo coat despite the downpour, so he could be quickly identified, called every W. & J. play from the bench. The visitors also psyched the Bears by conversation and gimmicks.

"I'll never forget that W. & J. outfit," halfback Don Nichols said. "It not only had a bunch of tough monkeys, but they looked the part. And they were mighty cute at getting us off our guard. Stein fixed me up beautifully. We were lining up on offense when he looked my way and said, 'Say, Nichols, don't you have an uncle in Pittsburgh?'

"I told him I had no relation there, but he

the Penn freshmen in 1905 and '06. He became varsity backfield coach in 1907 and '08, and head coach from 1909 through '12. His four-year record at Penn was 29–11–3, and his best season 1910: 9–1–1. Two of his outstanding players were center Ernest Cozens and back Roy Mercer, who is in the Hall of Fame.

From 1913 through '15, Smith coached Purdue to a 12–6–3 record. His star with the Boilermakers was halfback Elmer (Ollie) Oliphant, who later went on to even brighter fame at West Point.

California, which had played Rugby nine years, 1906–'14, returned to football in 1915, and in '16 John Stroud, graduate manager of athletics, after a thorough search, hired Smith. As one of his assistants, Andy took on Clarence (Nibs) Price, who succeeded him later but was even better known as a basketball coach.

Price had coached at San Diego High, one of the few in California that did not switch over to Rugby. When Cal returned to football, Price encouraged his San Diego players to accompany him there, and one of them was Brick Muller.

After the 1925 season, Andy Smith went back to his hometown, Philadelphia. A thin, spare-looking man who drove himself as a coach, he got pneumonia and died January 8, 1926. He willed his personal estate to the University of California and to his fraternity, Sigma Alpha Epsilon, and requested that his body be returned to Berkeley.

At noon on January 15, 1926, as the campanile sounded the funeral peal, the student body, led by members of the Wonder Team, walked to Memorial Stadium, there to watch an army plane fly over and drop Andy Smith's ashes on the turf.

On the Andy Smith Bench, on the California side of the field, is inscribed, "We do not want men who will lie down bravely to die, but men who will fight valiantly to live … winning is not everything. And it is far better to play the game squarely and lose than to win at the sacrifice of an ideal."

Carl Snavely

THE FOOTBALL SCHOLAR

Among the occupational ailments that plague football coaches, *oandxema* and *sprocketholitis* stand tall. *Oandxema* breaks out in rashes of plays, diagramed with X's and O's on anything handy, from the margin of a life insurance policy to a wife's new tablecloth. *Sprocketholitis* is the study of football films around clock and calendar, play by play, frame by frame, forward and backward and forward again, until eyeballs pop, nerves twang, and minds blow.

Sprocketholitis first showed up in the thirties, when coaches began to use films as a serious tool. And nobody was more responsible than a scholarly, balding fellow named Carl Gray Snavely.

"Just as the doctor uses X rays to tell us what's wrong with the body," said Snavely, "we use movies to tell us what's wrong with our teams. I didn't know a thing about movies when I thought of the idea. At first we used 55-millimeter film. It ran too fast, we couldn't slow it down, and we couldn't reverse it because it would burn up. Then I bought my own projector, compared notes with Coach Jock Sutherland of Pittsburgh, and the plan began to pay off. My first photographer was my wife—and she did a pretty good job of it."

Study of films characterized the scholarliness of Carl Snavely, who entered the Hall of Fame in 1965. His 32-year record—at Bucknell, North Carolina, Cornell, and Washington U. (Mo.) —shows 180 victories, 96 defeats, and 16 ties for .644. His 1939 Cornell team, which won all eight of its games, including a titanic upset at Ohio State, ranked near the top nationally.

Within the four-year span of 1946 through '49 at North Carolina, his teams won two Southern Conference championships and played in three major Bowl games. (They lost all three: to Georgia, 20–10, in the '47 Sugar Bowl; to Oklahoma, 14–6, in the '49 Sugar Bowl; and to Rice, 27–13, in the '50 Cotton Bowl.)

In his first college coaching, at Bucknell, 1927–33, Snavely did not use films at first. Instead, to check the movements of his players, he employed six student bookkeepers known as "watchdogs." Said a story out of Lewisburg, Pennsylvania, site of Bucknell, "Their identity hidden from everybody but Carl Snavely, the six

Carl Snavely. *Chicago Tribune Photos*

sleuths, minus fake whiskers and iron hats, stalk the gridiron. Their notebooks are concealed in their sleeves, their pencils are disguised as cigarettes, and they jot down every mistake of the gridmen.

"As the plan works in practice, one lad watches the guards, another takes the tackles, a third eyes the ends. The remaining three follow the moves of the three backfield men not carrying the ball. Snavely keeps his eye on the ball carrier."

Snavely rated with Dick Harlow, of Western Maryland and Harvard, in development of the fullback-spin series from the single-wingback attack, with its traps, buck laterals, reverses and end-arounds, and in jumping defensive people around, before and at the snap of the ball.

Nobody ever believed in the single wing more deeply than Snavely. For 17 seasons, 1939 through '55, he conducted "The Snavely Survey of Scoring," to prove that single-wing teams outscored T teams. "Yet 80 percent or more of the teams," he pointed out, "are using the T, which the statistics don't warrant."

For his soundness, imagination, and ability to adapt and improve, Snavely always enjoyed the respect of his peers. In 1939, for example, when Snavely and Bob Neyland of Tennessee were coaching an all-star team in the Chicago *Tribune* game, Neyland paid him, though in a negative way, a fine compliment. Snavely had been discussing the advantages of a running shift from the single wing to the short punt.

"Carl," Neyland said, "that's the first unsound idea I've ever heard you express on football."

Two of Snavely's assistants later won laurels as head coaches, George (Lefty) James at Cornell, and Jim Tatum at Maryland. James had played for Snavely both at Bellefonte Academy, where Carl first attracted national attention, and at Bucknell. He had also coached under him at North Carolina and Cornell. They were together 21 years, 1924 through '44.

"When I played under him at Bellefonte," James smiled, "he said 'gosh.' When I played under him at Bucknell, he said 'gosh.' When I coached under him at North Carolina, he said 'gee whiz.' Here at Cornell, and when he began frequenting the golf course, he would cut loose with an occasional 'hell's fire.'" For Snavely, son of a Methodist minister, that was about as far as he could go.

Snavely stated that the two best players he ever coached were Clark Hinkle, Bucknell fullback, 1929–31, and Charlie (Choo Choo) Justice, All-America tailback at North Carolina in 1948 and '49. Of Hinkle, he said.

"He was great in every phase of the game —kicking, running, passing, defense against the pass and the running game. He was a spirited and determined competitor."

Curly Lambeau, who coached Hinkle on the Green Bay Packers, told Snavely that he thought him the best player he'd ever known. At Bucknell, Hinkle was involved in three furious games with Fordham in the Polo Grounds. The Rams won the first and second, but in the third Hinkle's last-period running gave Bucknell a 14–13 victory, Fordham's only defeat that year. Fordham players, in tones of respect, called Hinkle "the country boy"; they respected him as a give-no-quarter gladiator who spat tobacco juice as he drove the ball up the gut or off tackle.

Snavely refused to give an edge to either Hinkle or Justice over the other, because they were different types, one the fullback, the other the tailback.

"Justice," he said, "was a great open-field runner, an excellent passer, and an exceptional

kicker, particularly effective as a quick kicker. He was a spirited leader and possessed amazing stamina. He was not big or rugged in appearance, but during his four years at North Carolina he played in every game but one. Although he was banged up occasionally, his recuperative powers were so great that he was always ready to go full speed on Saturday."

The first time Justice ever met Snavely was in January 1946. "I had just visited another school," Charlie said, "and had gone back to High Point, North Carolina, to meet Coach Snavely and Chuck Erickson, the athletic director. After waiting for over an hour, I happened to look out and see these two men going from house to house. Finally, I went out and asked if they were looking for Charlie Justice.

"The first one I talked to turned out to be Mr. Erickson and then we ran down Coach Snavely. My wife was with me, and as we started to get into the car, Coach asked her if she would sit in the back with Mr. Erickson, as he wanted to talk to me. She agreed and we started out for a place 40 miles away, where we were supposed to meet some people for lunch.

"Coach asked me how much I weighed. I said 155. [Charlie, five feet ten, later played at 165.] Coach's mouth fell open and he did not say another word during that 40-mile drive and then the 60-mile ride to Chapel Hill. In fact, I did not see him any more until about a month later, as he left early the next morning to see some boys in Pennsylvania."

Although Snavely's seriousness precluded a colorful personality to write about, one of Justice's stories revealed that "Coach" was not without humor. When Charlie announced he was enrolling at North Carolina, a writer asked Snavely how he felt about it.

"Good," he replied. "I sure hope he decides to come out for football."

High among Snavely's stars stands Jerome Heartwell (Brud) Holland, Negro end who won All-America honors in 1937 and '38, and later became president of Delaware State College and Hampton Institute, and United States ambassador to Sweden. Holland was superb at running Snavely's end-around, and his strong defensive play bottled up Yale's All-America halfback Clint Frank.

Beneath a dour facade that sometimes seemed hard, Snavely maintained a close relationship with his men. When a 20-year reunion was held for him at Ithaca in 1959, of the 137 Cornellians who had played for him from 1936 through '44,

61 showed up—46 percent. And of those living within 2,000 miles of Ithaca, 68 percent were on hand.

"Carl Snavely has the most unusual method of rehashing a game with his players that I have heard of," wrote Grantland Rice. "Instead of calling them together on Monday and criticizing them for their mistakes, he spends Sunday writing letters to them. Each player . . . finds a letter from his coach at the breakfast table on Monday morning.

" 'I wish I could give you some of those letters to print,' a friend of Snavely's told me. 'They would make great reading. They are letters such as a father would write to his sons. The criticisms are thoughtfully expressed and when a kid is entitled to praise for the way he played, he gets it.' "

The two most notable games in Snavely's career involved Cornell, in 1939 and '40. First was the upending of Ohio State at Columbus in 1939, 23–14, probably the No. 1 upset in Cornell's history. The heavier and heavily favored Buckeyes put on two scoring drives of 86 and 72 yards, led 14–0 well into the second quarter, and looked unstoppable. It seemed as if the Western Conference people were indeed right; the East didn't belong on the same field.

Then the game turned abruptly around. Walter (Pop) Scholl, behind picture-book blocking, ran off tackle 79 yards to a touchdown. Soon after, he tossed a pass 26 yards to Swifty Bohrman and Swifty ran another 37 for the TD. Bohrman's exhilarated swan dive into the end zone for the last couple of yards was recorded by newsreel cameras for the nation.

"Ohio State had scouted us," said Snavely, "and they were truly sorry for us. However, they were nonetheless eager for the kill. Cornell had no delusions of grandeur, but inasmuch as the game was on our schedule, we would play it and suffer the consequences. From Bohrman's run on out, Hal McCollough's passing, Mort Landsberg's running, tackle Nick Drahos's field goal, and an astonishing display of stamina on the part of all, the Cornell boys put the game on ice."

Snavely always maintained that his 1940 team, up through its first six games, was superior to 1939's; victims again included Ohio State, at Ithaca this time, 21–7. But the Cayugans were upset in their last two games, by Dartmouth, 3–0, and Pennsylvania, 22–20.

The Dartmouth game is unique in history as the "Fifth Down" game. Cornell left the field apparently the winner, 7–3, on a last-ditch pass,

Snavely instructing three Tar Heel linemen; *from the left*: Del Leatherman (guard), Ed Twohey (guard), Snavely, and Arthur Collins (tackle)

but when films revealed that the touchdown had come on a fifth down, because of an error by Red Friesell, a highly regarded official, Cornell on Monday conceded the game to Dartmouth, 3–0. The reaction would seem to have contributed to the upset the next week by Penn, led by Frank Reagan.

(Friesell received a wire from Asa Bushnell which ended, "Don't let this get you down ... down ... down ... down ... down." Red said that 16 days after the Fifth Down game, he was working a game at Sing Sing between the inmates and the Port Jervis Cops, when one of the inmate players commiserated with him, "We all make mistakes. That's why we are up here.")

Snavely said that the most "nearly perfect" game ever played by a team of his was the 26–0 victory over Penn in 1939.

"Quarterback Walt Matuszczak was sharp with his calls, taking advantage of Penn's line maneuvers. That was the last time Penn used a looping line on us."

Born in Omaha, Nebraska, July 31, 1894, Snavely was moved as a boy first to Indiana, where he went to Danville High, and then to Pennsylvania, where he attended Lebanon Valley College in Annville. At Lebanon he captained football and basketball, played first base in baseball, and won academic honors.

The football virus first went to work on him when he was 12 and sneaked in to watch Penn State's practices. He always hoped that he might one day coach Penn State. Instead, he enjoyed exceptional success coaching against them. His Bucknell teams beat the Nittany Lions four out of four, and the best they could get against his Cornell teams in six tries was a scoreless tie in 1942.

Snavely thought for a time that he might become a major league ball player, and played two years in the Tri-State League until a bad arm washed him out. He always maintained that a man good enough to play major league baseball could play football or any other sport.

"They're competitors big league players are," he said. "They've poise, nervous control, temperament. A big leaguer's got to be tough to survive, to get to the majors. For everyone who does, thousands don't. The fragile ones fade out of the picture."

Where would Stan (the Man) Musial, the superb St. Louis Cardinal, play in football, Snavely was asked. "I'd play him at end. He says he's never been exceptionally fast, but with his body control, his anticipation, he'd be the greatest pass receiver. He sure could play end, he'd be so doggone slick."

While Snavely was playing baseball at Chambersburg, Wilmington, Trenton, and Lancaster in 1915 and '16, between seasons he was also beginning his career as a football coach at Kiski Prep. After he gave up baseball, he coached at Vandergrift (Pa.) High, Franklin School, Cincinnati, University of Cincinnati, Marietta, and again at Kiski before going to Bellefonte Academy. There, from 1924 through '26, he turned out three teams that laid claims to the national prep school championship.

His total Bellefonte record was 34–4–1 and all four defeats came from college freshman elevens. His Bellefonte stars who went on to more glory at college included Stan Keck, Princeton; Dutch Schwab, Lafayette; Jap Douds and Bill Amos, Washington & Jefferson; Tom Davies, Gibby Welch, Andy Cutler, Ralph Dougherty, and Josh Williams, Pittsburgh; John Dresher and Ted Rosenzweig, Carnegie Tech; and Jerry Nemecek and Ed (Cowboy) Hill, New York University.

His Bellefonte success got him his chance as a college head coach at Bucknell, and after seven successful years, including an undefeated if thrice-tied 1931 season, he went to North Carolina in 1934 for the first of his two go-rounds there. His '34 Tar Heels lost only to Tennessee, 19–7, and in '35 they again were beaten only once, but this was by bitter rival Duke, 25–0.

That Carolina-Duke game bred a coolness between Coach Wallace Wade of the Blue Devils and Snavely, who was quoted as charging Wade with unfair tactics. Of all things, he charged Wade had taken movies of Carolina games. This was a switch for sure, because Wade had never placed much faith in films until he heard Snavely enthuse about them at a service club luncheon.

When he left Carolina for Cornell in '36, Snavely gave this reason: "It is not enough just to coach winning football. Sometimes they want you to jump like a puppet on a string for a governor."

Snavely in 1950. *Chicago Tribune Photos*

After his nine seasons at Cornell, Snavely returned to North Carolina in 1945. There would seem to be two reasons, Cornell's material had been turned off and there was no indication as to when it would turn on again, and the political climate at Chapel Hill looked improved. Aided by a brilliant freshman class that matriculated in 1946, Snavely had four excellent seasons totaling 32–9–2.

"I believe," Snavely wrote, "that the 1947 team was the strongest I had at North Carolina. This team did not start out so well, being defeated decisively in two early games [Texas, 34–0, and Wake Forest, 19–7]. From there on, however, it developed rapidly and gained momentum with every game."

In his last three seasons at North Carolina, the material fell away. Snavely had losing records, and in 1953 he decided he'd had enough of "pressure" football: "I found out I was doing more fund raising, backslapping, and after-dinner speaking than coaching."

At Washington University, St. Louis, Snavely found the deemphasized atmosphere he wanted

to coach in. Once again he was successful, a six-year record of 33–19, before he retired at the mandatory age of 65 and opened a car-wash business. Snavely's college record, broken down by schools and years:

		W	L	T
Bucknell	1927-33	42	16	8
North Carolina	1934-35	15	2	1
Cornell	1936-44	46	26	3
North Carolina	1945-52	44	33	4
Washington (Mo.)	1953-58	33	19	0
TOTALS	32 seasons*	180	96	16

*He had only five losing seasons in 32, two at Cornell, three at Carolina.

In 1965, Snavely said, "From my present viewpoint, I find the game very wholesome. The colleges have eliminated many evils which were present in my time. At one time the sky was the limit. Yet, on every team we had boys who came out without any advance notice or reputation and made the squad. This was especially true at Cornell."

Charlie Justice summed up a general feeling shared by his players toward Carl Gray Snavely:

"Coach Snavely was a man of few words. He treated everyone alike, no matter who they were. There was no time that a boy, regardless of his value to the team, could not go and talk to Snavely man to man."

It is doubtful, however, if Snavely would draw a popular vote from the wives of football coaches, who spend so many of their waking hours studying films, incurable victims of *sprocketholitis*.

Bill Spaulding

THE BELOVED BRUIN

In the ankle-deep mud of Eugene, Oregon, a University of California at Los Angeles football team of the twenties may have set the all-time record for goal-line stands. The exact number cannot be documented, but Norm Duncan and Bobby Decker, who shared the punting for the Bruins, kicked out from behind their own goal line 23 times. And they were kicking a ball so logged with water that it felt like a sack of cement.

Such experiences were common with UCLA football in the days when William Henry Spaulding was building it from small-college to major status. There is an oft-told story that the typical Bruin practice session in those days comprised ten minutes of calisthenics and two hours of practicing goal-line stands against the junior varsity. Who played for the jayvees is not known. Out-of-work Hollywood extras, possibly; stuntmen would have looked down on the assignment.

The Augean-styled problems that beset those early Bruins were matched by an incomprehensibly mad spirit, exemplified by that muddy goal-line day against the well-named Oregon Ducks. Late in the gooey game, Coach Spaulding substituted a lineman named Maurice MacGoodstein. Mack MacGoodstein, later a law-yer who probably never turned down a tough case, ran in and lined up alongside a weary-unto-death tackle named Fat Norfleet.

"Oh, you apple knockers! Oh, you bums!" screamed Mack MacGoodstein at the Oregons. "Just aim one of those plays this way and see what happens to you!"

Fat Norfleet rose from his stance, and stared sadly at the belligerent Bruin.

"Good gawd, Goodie," he pleaded, "don't antagonize them! They're tough enough as it is!"

When Bill Spaulding became football coach and athletic director in 1925, UCLA was a small group of buildings downtown on Vermont Avenue, with an endowment something short of Harvard's, and a history of six years. The football team, a member of the Southern California Conference, had a six-year record of 4–30–4, and had yet to win its first game from Pomona, Occidental, or Whittier.

When Spaulding retired to concentrate on being athletic director in 1939, after 14 seasons as coach, UCLA had been in the Pacific Coast Conference 11 years, and in 1935 had got its first taste of a championship in a three-way tie with Stanford and big brother California at Berkeley. The Bruins had also been occupying their pic-

turesque campus out in Westwood for ten years.

When Spaulding, at 66, retired as athletic director in 1946 and became a public relations executive for a food company, his choice of Edwin C. (Babe) Horrell, a former California star center, as his successor had been vindicated. In 1939, Horrell, who learned about coaching from Spaulding, gave UCLA its first undefeated (though tied four times) team and a share in the PCC championship with Southern Cal. In one of the great games of Pacific Coast history, the Bruins and Trojans had settled nose to nose for a 0–0 tie. S.C. saved itself by a goal-line stand near the end and went on to the Rose Bowl and beat Tennessee 14–0.

Under Horrell in 1942, UCLA won its first PCC title outright, and got its first invitation to the Rose Bowl, where it lost 9–0 to a superior Georgia team. In 1946, under Coach Bert LaBrucherie, the Bruins had their first perfect season, 10–0, but again lost at Pasadena, to Illinois, 45–14.

In the quarter of a century since the retirement of Spaulding, the foundations he so painstakingly set in place have been further augmented by six conference championships, seven second places, four more Rose Bowl bids (the last, in 1965, finally resulting in a victory, the cataclysmic upset of Michigan State, 14–12), one national championship, 1954, and frequent finishes among the top ten ranked teams nationally. Against the cross-town magnificos who once dominated them, the Bruins have won 10, lost 13, tied 1.

Of all the large cities where there is both college and professional football, the superior college game has been able to maintain its posture against the pro football propaganda machine (the loudest since the word-of-mouth from the Circus Maximus) only in Atlanta with Georgia Tech, in Minneapolis with Minnesota, and in Los Angeles with both Southern Cal and UCLA.

This story of UCLA's growth into a power, in football and other sports, all traces back to Bill Spaulding, who lived until he was 86 in 1966 to see the fruits of his labor and love.

The best part of Bill Spaulding's record, however, is engraved in the hearts of those who knew him. No coach or athletic director ever was more beloved by a college or more respected and admired by his opponents and the rest of the intercollegiate world.

When Spaulding first arrived in the City of the Angels, he was already well acquainted with the devils of football. He had three seasons behind

Bill Spaulding

him as head coach at Minnesota and, before that, 15 at Western State Teachers of Kalamazoo, Michigan.

Bill lost no time in putting some growl in the Bruins. They put together three straight winning seasons, including a 6–2–1 record against Pomona, Occidental, and Whittier. In 1928, his fourth year, they were taken into the Pacific Coast Conference. In 1929 they concluded the season with their first PCC victory by defeating Montana, 14–0.

This was heady stuff—like drawing Clara Bow, a Cadillac, and weekend expenses in Shangri-la. The more imaginative students decided to tear down the goalposts. Was that not *de trop*? Perhaps because of physical exhaustion from the delirium of victory, they spent most of an hour in a futile attempt to bring down the wood. Finally they gave up and went home, enthusiasm undimmed.

Spaulding for a time moved a little too fast. His friend Pop Warner was in 1925 in his second season at Stanford, and he gave Bill a game. The Bruins, however, weren't up to giving the Indians

Spaulding with Bruins' 1932 captain and All-Coast center, Homer Oliver

Bill with another UCLA coach, Bert LaBrucherie

one. Pop went up to Berkeley to scout California, which would meet Stanford in the Big Game the next week, and left his team in the hands of Andy Kerr. Stanford was so deep that even at this point in the season there were 23 men fighting for the starting 11 positions, and Kerr couldn't hold them back. They macerated UCLA, 82–0.

"Phew!" said Coach Spaulding. "What a track meet! But we'll be back."

UCLA dropped off the Stanford lists until 1928, lost four more to the Palo Altoans, and in 1932, Pop Warner's last year, supplemented a stout defense with two blocked kicks to upset, 13–6, a team of emphatically superior personnel. When Spaulding was asked by a young writer how the Bruins did it, he replied, tongue in cheek, "We just kicked and waited for the breaks."

The young fellow was running off with what he regarded as an earthquake of an exclusive. Then Spaulding showed the kindliness that was always part of his humor. "Hey," he called after the youngster, "you might add that we've been kicking and waiting for the breaks against Stanford for six years!"

The win over Oregon two weeks before that, Bill always claimed, was his biggest thrill. "It was

our first over a major PCC opponent. Mike Frankovich passed to Pantsey Livesay on a rain-drenched field to give us a 12–7 victory with seconds to play. I was still looking for substitutes when the game was over. It was five minutes before we could restore order to attempt a conversion."

Spaulding's old players, however, would argue that Bill's No. 1 upset at UCLA came in 1935 when the Bruins spoiled, 7–6, a perfect season for the PCC championship Stanford team that went on to defeat Southern Methodist in the Rose Bowl, 7–0. That was the senior season for the Stanford "Vow Boys." They had vowed as freshman they'd never lose to Southern Cal, and they never did. Meanwhile they won three straight PCC championships.

It was a defeat by Stanford, 12–6, four years earlier, in 1931, by another deep underdog UCLA team that tells even more clearly the story of Spaulding as coach and man. One of Pop Warner's early quarterbacks, Dick Hyland, who later wrote sports for the Los Angeles *Times*, told the story.

"No one gave the Bruins a chance, but the score was 6–6 with but five seconds left to play; if it finished that way it would mean the first tie for the Bruins with a major team.

Spaulding flanked by Bruin coach Henry R. (Red) Sanders (*left*) and Chancellor Raymond B. Allen.
Occasion was the naming of the Bruins' football field after Bill

"The stupid Bruin safety man," said Hyland, as controversial a writer as he had been a quarterback, "had been warned specifically that he should *never* do what he did. On a wild third-down pass by Stanford, instead of catching it, he knocked it down. On the next play Stanford heaved a 50-yard pass over his concrete head for the game-winning points.

"I had coached that Bruin backfield for the Stanford game for free, to help the understaffed Bill Spaulding, and after the game I wanted to tie into that safety man. Bill said to me, 'Wait a minute. If you've never made a mistake, go ahead and jump him.' And he winked at me."

The very next week, UCLA sprang a shocker by beating, 12–0, a St. Mary's team that lost to no other intercollegiate opponent, and was high in the national rankings. That could have been Bill's No. 1 upset. It certainly emphasized the value of his patience.

For the joys of every upset there had been many glooms. Some of the players Bill coached in his early years resembled evacuees from Singer's

Midgets, or as I think another Bruin coach, the great Red Sanders, might put it, what they lacked in size, they made up in slowness. When the Bruins first moved out to Westwood, those lush green playing fields of today constituted a large-size honest-to-God dust bowl, in which a short player might get lost after dark and have to be searched for with dogs and flares.

Coaching such material tends to make a man preoccupied, which may have accounted for Spaulding's difficulty in remembering names. "Got a great tackle prospect up from the freshmen," he'd beam to a writer. "What's his name?" the writer would ask, and Bill would admit, "Damned if I know." Then he'd go off looking for the tackle to find his name, but by the time he got back to the writer with it, he sometimes would have forgotten it a second time.

The same year Spaulding came to UCLA, Howard Jones arrived at Southern California. They had coached against each other in 1922 and '23, Bill at Minnesota and Howard at Iowa, and each won one. Howard, however, inherited much

more of an operation at S.C.; the Trojans had already established themselves as a power. Their 1922 team had defeated Penn State in the Rose Bowl. UCLA had had only four graduated classes, and it would take years for its alumni to catch up with the Trojans in organized, effective recruiting.

Both schools were eager to get a rivalry going because of its obvious box-office value. They tested it in opening games in 1929 and 1930, but the Trojans' 76–0 and 52–0 triumphs showed the Bruins were far from ready, and by mutual agreement they did not renew until 1936.

Since then the game has been an annual spectacular, the biggest and best of all college backyard battles. It has set a beautiful example of how an intracity rivalry can be maintained at fervent Fahrenheit, but with the football hard and clean and the partisanship unmarred by rowdyism. This is especially impressive because so often the game decides the PCC champion and the Rose Bowl representative.

The foundation for the spirit of this rivalry was built in by Bill Spaulding and Howard Jones through a close, firm friendship that found them together for card games and golf matches.

"Howard was the finest friend I ever had," Bill said, after the death of the great Trojan coach. "We sure had fun together. Howard used to outdistance me off the tee, but I had the edge on the greens. I remember one big hole when Howard was on the green in two, while I needed three. I sank a 20-foot putt for a birdie, and it took him three putts to get down. He really suffered.

"We had a running gag going before every round. One of us would say, loud enough for all to hear, 'Let's make it 50–50–50 today.' Naturally, everybody thought we were talking dollars, but we were really talking cents."

When the Spaulding and Jones teams renewed their rivalry in 1936, they were pretty well matched. S.C.'s 1938 team, which won the PCC crown and defeated Duke in the Rose Bowl, 7–3, was too much for the Bruins in Bill's last year, 42–7. But in '36 they played a 7–7 tie, and in '37 the Bruins almost shook the Trojans loose from helmets, spears, and shields before losing 19–13.

The star of the Bruins from 1937 through '39 and their first All-America was halfback Kenny Washington. Spaulding coached some excellent people at UCLA, including Mike Frankovich, Lee Coats, Homer Oliver, Norm Duncan, Len Wellendorf, Hal Hirshon, and George Dickerson.

But Bill's and UCLA's all-time No. 1 was Kenny Washington, a crowd-pleasing, all-purpose natural, whose career running total of 1,915 yards still stands as the school's tops.

It was the running and the passing, especially the passing, of Washington that scored two touchdowns in the last quarter of that 19–13 game, almost scored another, had Los Angeles Coliseum in an uproar, and had the Trojans and head man Howard Jones in several dithers. After the game, Spaulding went to pay his usual visit to the S.C. locker room, and knocked on the door.

"Who's there?" asked a voice.

"Bill Spaulding," said the coach.

"Whaddaya want?" asked the voice.

"Tell Howard he can come out now," said Bill. "We've stopped passing."

Scaring the favorite, if not beating him, had been a habit of Spaulding's before he got to UCLA. No matter the size of the challenge, no matter the number of setbacks, his faith, hope, and confidence, never diminishing, were grafted onto his teams. That is how he got the job done at UCLA.

The son of Phineas Spaulding, a Black Rock, Wisconsin, farmer, Bill got his first licks in at football as a Black Rock High fullback in 1899. When he arrived at Wabash (Indiana) College as a freshman in 1903, he started at left half, because he had announced confidently that he was "too fast to play fullback." Bill captained the team in 1905 and '06, and in 1905 sparked the upset at Notre Dame, 5–0, the last time the Irish were to lose on their home grounds (Cartier Field before 1930) until 1928, when they were beaten by Carnegie Tech.

After graduating from Wabash with a B.A. degree in 1907, Bill coached football, basketball, and baseball at Western State (Kalamazoo) for 15 years, and had only two losing seasons on the gridiron. Among his Wabash players was a stubby quarterback from Gary, Indiana, named Frank Thomas, who later quarterbacked at Notre Dame for Knute Rockne and went on to become one of the great coaches of all time at Alabama.

Spaulding's record at Kalamazoo and the recommendation of Fielding Yost, Michigan's coach, got Bill the coaching job at Minnesota in 1922. He succeeded Dr. Henry L. Williams. Dr. Williams had given the Gophers many powerful teams before World War I, but when his 1921 team took a series of pastings, his days were finished.

The selection of Spaulding evoked a predom-

Bill being told that his former players and associates have established a UCLA football Grant-in-Aid Fund in his name, to honor top student athletes. *Left to right*: Al Gibson, former guard; Spaulding; Wilbur Johns, Bruin athletic director; and Jack Remsberg, another Spaulding lineman

inant reaction, "Who's he?" His Wabash credentials were looked down at. Administration, alumni, students, public, and press all wanted to run Minnesota football; no matter who got the job, some factions would have been displeased. "Spaulding was a high-class man," wrote Charlie Johnson, veteran sports editor of the Minneapolis *Star*, "but his choice never received unanimous support."

Bill's three seasons with the Gophers produced records of 3–3–1, 5–1–1, and 3–3–2. He used All-America halfback Earl Martineau smartly in 1923, as the Gophers beat Howard Jones' last Iowa team in the final game on Minnesota's old Northrup Field, but a 10–0 loss to outstatisticked Michigan ruined the season. In 1924, Minnesota dedicated its new Memorial Stadium by upsetting Illinois, 20–7, as Bill's astute defenses held Red Grange to one touchdown on a 17-yard run. The next week, however, the Grophers lost to Vanderbilt, 16–0, and reaction was summed up in a page-one, four-column editorial with the head,

WANTED, A NEW COACH. The regents renewed Bill's contract but advised him to find a new job, which he did.

Whether it was Minnesota's loss, who can tell? None can deny it was UCLA's gain.

On Restaurant Row in Los Angeles, La Cienega Boulevard, the nights of great sports parties have been many. There never was a more deserving and warmer one, however, than the one newspapermen, radio men, and other friends tossed for Spaulding when he retired. All his old Bruin Bears were there "to let loose their thunder," and they gave him a scroll, to "Bill Spaulding, Our Friend" over these lines by Dick Hyland:

We who praise at morning what we blame at night,
But always think the last opinion right,
Have searched the fields of sport far and wide to find,
One man, one kind, ever man, ever kind.

THE FEROCIOUS CHERUB

His name was Clarence Wiley Spears, but he was known as Fat, Cupid, and Doc. He had the face of a cherub, and the body of a gorilla. He stood five feet seven and in fighting trim weighed about 236; the fastest Dartmouth backs could edge him only by a yard in the 50. For a player his size, he had amazing quickness. "He walked with a springing stride," his schoolmate Judge Amos Blandin recalls, "the way I've seen bulls walk—and he was as powerful as one."

Spears made All-America guard at Dartmouth in 1914 and '15. As a player and coach, he thought of football primarily as a game of condition and contact. In Cuddy Murphy and Gus Sonnenberg, Doc coached two outstanding tackles at Dartmouth, but he could handle both of them at one time in a scrimmage. "If the scrimmage wasn't measuring up," recalls quarterback Hubie McDonough, "Doc would take a hand himself, and then all hell broke loose."

"He was the driving, crackdown type of coach," says Dick Cullum, veteran Minneapolis *Tribune* scribe and a good friend of Doc's in his five seasons at Minnesota, 1925–29. "He would have been too tough on the field for today's football. But he was a warm man with his players, excepting at practice. The good players loved him, the rest did not."

An excellent example of Doc's practice procedure was offered by Neil Hyde, six feet tall but a little light for a tackle. Doc took Hyde, a wingback, and an end to one corner of the field and had them work Hyde over with two-on-one blocking. The tackle stood up well to that drill, but it went on and on until it seemed Spears had forgotten about them. Finally, he strolled over and asked, "How are you getting along?" One of the blockers replied, "Okay." Doc then walked away, saying over his shoulder, "Keep it up. I'll be back to check on you." Hyde took a beating, but became a fine tackle.

"Doc was a cruel man at practice," Cullum recalls. "This came from his own fierce play at Dartmouth. He was so good, such a furious competitor that he could never fully understand why the average player couldn't put out more than he had in him to put out. In this respect, Doc was a lot like Norm Van Brocklin."

Spears' competitive nature carried beyond the football field and into his dealings with administrators. He had no tolerance for going through channels. He couldn't wait. This no doubt holds part of the explanation for his moving from job to job, although he did well at all of them: Dartmouth, West Virginia, Minnesota, Oregon, Wisconsin, Toledo, and Maryland.

"Socially," says Cullum, "he was the most cordial person you could find, capable of the most genuine friendship. His circle of closest friends included some of the jolliest stay-out-late people in town."

His relationship with sportswriters, however, was not always smooth. "Twin Cities guys got together," says veteran Minneapolis scribe, Charlie Johnson, "and agreed to give him the absent treatment. They wouldn't call him until he came around and asked why. From the end of one season until the following May, writers never saw him, called him, or mentioned his name. Finally, he barged into one newspaper office with his jaw sticking out and demanded to know why he was being treated shabbily. He got the answer in no uncertain terms. From then on he was a nice boy."

Because of the bruising type of game he insisted on (his teams also had the reputation for clean play), Big Ten teams shied away from scheduling Minnesota, and in 1925 the Gophers had only three conference games, with Michigan, Iowa, and Wisconsin, when a minimum of four was required to qualify for the championship. "You may beat Minnesota," said Dr. John Wilce, coach of Ohio State, "but the next week you can't beat anybody."

At the 1926 winter meeting, Wisconsin, Iowa, and Michigan again were the only teams that would engage the Gophers. Fielding H. (Hurry Up) Yost, Michigan coach and athletic director, solved the problem by agreeing to meet Minnesota twice, early at Ann Arbor and late in the season at Minneapolis.

In the first game, Spears was forced to play many sophomores, and Michigan won decisively, 20–0. In the second game, however, the Gophers pushed the Wolverines all over the field, making 18 first downs to 3 and rushing 314 yards to 50. Yet, they lost the game when halfback Mally Nydahl fumbled and Bennie Oosterbaan, the

superb Michigan end, scooped up the ball and ran 55 yards for Michigan's only touchdown in a 7–6 victory.

This game was one that Doc Spears never got out of his craw. Red Blaik felt the same way about Army's 1957 loss to Notre Dame, 23–21, and Bob Neyland about Tennessee's 1941 Sugar Bowl defeat by Boston College, 19–13.

The next year at Michigan, Minnesota again pushed the Wolverines around in winning, 13–7. Dick Cullum pointed out to Spears that the score didn't represent the margin enjoyed by the Gophers. To which Doc replied, "Yes—but didn't we give 'em a physical beating."

That 1927 team was Doc's best at Minnesota. The Gophers were undefeated but tied by Indiana, 14–14, and Notre Dame, 7–7. A sophomore from International Falls, who is regarded as one of the greatest all-time players, Bronko Nagurski, appeared in the Minnesota lineup. "When I asked him what position he played," said Spears, "he answered, 'All of them.'" He proved himself so right that after his senior season, when Grantland Rice asked Spears where he should place Bronk on his All-America, Doc replied seriously, "Just pick your first ten men and then put Nagurski in any slot that's left." Nagurski was used mainly at tackle and fullback by Spears, although Doc always maintained that end would have been the ideal position for him.

Minnesota went down to Notre Dame for a game in '27. It was played in a blizzard. Rockne respected them so much that he did not start his second line, which was his custom. Meanwhile, Spears started his second team, so N.D. could count on no psychological or chemical edge. Bronk Nagurski forced and recovered a fumble deep in Irish territory. After two shots at the line, fullback Herb Joesting passed to Len Walsh for the touchdown. Walsh was later a judge in Washington. Notre Dame tied it on a 20-yard run by halfback Christy Flanagan. It ended 7–7. The next week Notre Dame was beaten by Army, 18–0.

Spears' biggest upset and probably Nagurski's single greatest game came in a 6–0 upset at Wisconsin in 1928. Joesting and other key people were sidelined with injuries; in Joesting's fullback spot at practice, Spears used Nagurski—who had a special brace on his back at fullback, but kept it a secret. Wisconsin, which had heard the Nag wouldn't play, was rattled when he showed up in a new spot and began tearing holes in its line. He recovered a fumble on the Badger 17 and in six

Doc Spears. *Chicago Tribune Photos*

successive shots scored the game's only TD. Late in the fourth quarter, Bo Cuisinier, fleet Wisconsin back, caught a pass and seemed in the clear, but Nagurski tackled him on the 8.

"I wasn't sure where Bronk was on the play," said Cuisinier, "but I expected if he tackled me, he'd at least knock me forward a few yards. But instead he grabbed me by the shoulder, thrust one big leg between mine, and yanked me backward. I couldn't budge."

Doc feuded with Fred Leuhring, the athletic director, accusing him of pinching pennies, but it was Minnesota's president, Lotus D. Coffman, who really got under Doc's skin. In 1927, Illinois had a conference record of 5–0–0, while Minnesota's was 3–0–1. On a percentage basis they were all even at 1,000, but Illinois had the better-looking record. Doc Spears, however, thought this was no reason for President Coffman to send a wire to Illinois, conceding. Irritations from this burn impelled Doc to quit Minnesota for Oregon after the 1929 season.

When Doc departed, he left word with friends in high places that he could be reached en route

to Eugene at a town in Montana. But nobody contacted him so he went on to Oregon. His two-year record there was 13–4–2, and he had a star back in Johnny Kitzmiller.

The 1931 team of Doc's traveled 12,000 miles, including a transcontinental trek to play one of Chick Meehan's New York University teams in Yankee Stadium. Fat's old coach, Frank Cavanaugh, was coaching Fordham, and his first assistant, William P. (Hiker) Joy, scouted NYU and knew it as well as he knew Fordham. On Thursday, Spears brought his Oregon team up to Fordham Field to scrimmage the Ram Freshmen, who put on the entire NYU play repertory. Such helping hands across the scrimmage line aided Oregon in upsetting NYU, 14–6.

It is no overstatement that Nagurski, the greatest player Spears ever coached, would have regarded the Spears who played guard at Dartmouth in 1914 and '15 as a worthy teammate. Dr. Raymond H. (Slats) Baxter, a tough end and teammate of Spears' under Major Frank Cavanaugh, was Fat's roommate.

"It was on my first day at Dartmouth in 1913," recalls Dr. Baxter, "that I met a disreputable character named Clarence Wiley Spears, who like me had a football scholarship of $140, and one pair of pants. Fortune smiled on us as we took in a roommate who had money, Archie B. Gile. Archie furnished one room on the top floor of Sanborn Hall. It was palatial, but the beauty did not last long. Spears had a curious habit of throwing all the furniture out the window to hear the crash four floors below, and to startle Jake Bend on his midnight rounds of the campus. We wound up sitting on wooden boxes for two years.

"Spears was a transfer from Knox College, where he had played football; this restricted his Dartmouth eligibility to two years. Knox was the place Corey Ford had in mind when he wrote so many wonderful football stories in the *Saturday Evening Post*. Like the one about the village blacksmith who was hired as a fullback. While he was running for a touchdown, he heard the town whistle for the mill to close, dropped the ball on the 1-yard line and left the field."

According to Baxter, Fat Spears' job at Dartmouth was to sweep out the chapel daily, but he later confessed that he had swept all the dirt under the church organ, which annoyed the maiden lady organist no end.

"During one summer vacation," says Dr. Baxter, "Spears worked in a steel mill and made a long vicious knife with which he would welcome

our janitor by placing it in the region of his navel and backing him into a corner. We got poor janitorial service thereafter."

In 1915, Dartmouth played a scoreless tie at Syracuse on a rainy day with the field chopped up into small craters and mud puddles. On one play, Baxter, whose bad knee was protected by a hockey shin guard and multiple pads, got clobbered and lay in one of the deeper puddles.

"Fat," he recalls, "came over to look at me and convulsed Eddie O'Brien, the referee, by saying, 'Poor Raymond in there drowned and cold, and a long way from home.' Between halves, the players were so wet and cold, trainer Harry Hillman produced a large bottle of brandy, which he said was for medicinal use only, and everybody got a good slug."

As any game figured to be that Spears played in, this was a rough one. A Boston *Globe* cartoon showed Fat "blocking" a 280-pound tackle named Christopher (Red) Schlachter, who had long hair. Spears blocked him by grabbing the long hair and pulling him out of the way. Referee O'Brien slapped a 15-yard penalty on Fat for ungentlemanly conduct.

In his senior fall of 1916, since he was not eligible for Dartmouth, he kept his hands in by playing with the Massillon (Ohio) Tigers every Sunday for $35 and traveling expenses. According to Baxter, Spears now had two pairs of pants and two shirts.

When Frank Cavanaugh, Spears' coach, went into service, Fat succeeded him.

It was a big job. He had been an undergraduate only the previous season. He worked alone in handling a full squad of 100 or more. His four-year record was 21–9–1. While coaching, he completed work for his medical degree, and was tireless in the Hanover hospital during the 1918 flu epidemic.

One of the roughest games in history was the 1919, post–World War I fracas at Dartmouth, with the Big Green shading Pennsylvania, 20–19. Bert Bell, later commissioner of the National Football League, and Lou Little, later Georgetown and Columbia head coach, were on the Penn team; ex-servicemen decorated both lineups.

In his first year as coach, 1917, Fat's team upset the West Virginia team that had Ira Rodgers at fullback, 6–2. This game and Fat's ingrained flair for being tactless and fractious with alumni and committees—he would tell alumni gathering bluntly that they knew nothing

about football and should leave the coaching up to him—resulted in his leaving Dartmouth for West Virginia in 1921.

At WVU he made an even stronger record for four years: 30–6–3. The 1922 team (one tie —Washington and Lee) put together a record of 10–0–1, the only undefeated season in Mountaineer annals. The rest of his record showed: 1921, 5–4–1; '23, 7–1–1; '24, 8–1–0. Old-timers in Morgantown call it the Golden Era.

Probably Doc's biggest victory was the 9–6 game with Pittsburgh in '22, first time WVU ever beat the Panthers. The game was won in the last minute on a 39-yard dropkick by a freshman back from Dayton, Ohio, named Armin Mahrt; few people knew that Mahrt, a fine runner, could even kick the ball. After the seventh game of the season, Mahrt was declared ineligible for having violated the one-year residence rule by playing for Dayton in 1921.

In beating Pitt, Dr. Spears dipped into his psychology bag. He convinced the Mountaineers that they had been beating themselves because of a jinx. As one way of dismantling the Pitt spell, he had his team dress in drab gray jerseys, a custom they adhered to in Pitt games for several years.

Midway in the season of '23, West Virginia fought Penn State to a 13–13 tie in the Polo Grounds, New York City, before a record West Virginia crowd of 35,000. Spears blamed himself for the tie:

"I had scouted them in their 21–0 victory over Navy, one of the games in which Lighthorse Harry Wilson, their star halfback, ran wild. I didn't think much of their line, though. I came away confident we would win, maybe too confident, and I think our players sensed that feeling. I should have let Rodge [former star fullback Ira Rodgers] do the scouting."

In the 14–7 loss to Pitt, the only defeat of the 1924 season, Mike Narducci, 155-pound Mountaineer back, made what Spears called the greatest defensive play he'd ever seen. Narducci's forward pass at the Panther 10 was deflected into the hands of a Pitt guard named Hangartner, who seemed to have a clear field, with three blockers in front of him.

Narducci, pursuing diagonally, feinted three times as if to try a tackle. Each time a Pitt man tried to block him and failed. When he finally got Hangartner stripped of his blockers, he closed in on him at the WVU 14-yard line. Nevertheless, Pitt won. But WVU avenged a 1923 7–2 loss to Washington and Jefferson by beating them 40–7

Spears, *left*, with Jim Robertson, captain of Doc's 1920 Dartmouth team

at Morgantown, and W. & J. had defeated Pitt, 10–0.

While he was at WVU, Spears was accused at a coaches' meeting by his former coach, Major Frank Cavanaugh, of stealing away a 220-pound tackle from him. Spears said it couldn't possibly be true, because he didn't have a single tackle who weighed less than 230.

During the undefeated 1922 season, a Boston *Post* reporter went down to Morgantown to interview Spears, who fed him colorful material, which he printed. This included a reference to hillbilly fans coming in the night before the game and camping on the football field in their covered wagons. When the West Virginia folks heard about this, some of them, including possibly people named Hatfield and McCoy, left a note under the door of the writer's hotel room, advising him to get out of town before sunset. He got.

Soon after, Bill Cunningham, feature sports writer on the Boston *Post*, who had formerly played for both Cavanaugh and Spears at Dartmouth, was sent down to interview Fat. "Well, Fat," he began, "you and I didn't get along too well at Hanover, but I would like to write a story about your unbeaten season. Now go ahead and throw me out."

Cunningham's frontal assault appealed to Spears, however, so he bought him a drink, gave him a good story, and invited him to a meeting of the West Virginia athletic council, which he said would have to be off the record for reasons that would become clear.

The committee comprised the professors of Greek, archaeology, and the social sciences, but all the power appeared to be vested in the chairman, a businessman who said: "The meeting

Doc, *right*, watching his Wisconsin Badgers tackle Notre Dame in 1934. *Chicago Tribune Photos*

bench, he'd be penalized. Spears looked at the ball and asked, "Where to?"

A fight started in the stands and boiled over onto the field, and some of the crowd got to pushing Spears around. So Fat tore a 2 by 4 from the scoring platform and began laying it on anyone within target range, including the Lehigh police. Tom Keady, who had a little high-pitched voice, came running across the field, yelling: "My God, Spears! I told them what a wonderful gentleman you were, and you're beating the whole damned police force of Lehigh!"

Gene Stauber, Indiana State assistant, who played end for Toledo, recalls Doc Spears' working methods:

"Modern coaches talk about their winter program with the emphasis on weights. In Doc's day there wasn't any ban on working out, and we worked on football techniques the winter semester every night for at least one and a half hours in the field house before it was blacktopped.

"By the time outdoor spring practice came, we were well advanced and scrimmaged the first day. There weren't any 20-day limitations and practice usually lasted until final exams came up and Doc was satisfied. Two hours was a short practice. We usually went two and a half to three hours.

"One afternoon the tackle on my side and I were doing well stacking up things. I was new and eager to impress the good doctor. The practice dragged on and on, as Doc was determined the fullback and the blocking back should obliterate me and open things up. Between plays, in a huddle, veteran linebacker Chuck Lyskawa, who had played a couple of years under Doc, said, 'Men, if we don't miss some tackles, old Doc will have us out here until dark.' I was kind of indignant and shocked, but the veterans knew Doc and hated to miss their supper."

Since Spears was an M.D., it was not easy to feign injuries with him. And he was a great believer in mind over matter. One day Stauber tore a fingernail, so Doc reached into his hip pocket of his baseball pants, pulled out his pocket knife, and cut the excess nail off. When Stauber sprained his ankle in an early game, Doc taped it up and told him to test it. Stauber put some weight on it, but could still feel pain.

"Doc," he said, "I can't seem to put all my weight on it, but would like to try to go on it."

"Stauber," Doc said, "the good Lord will take you by the hand and see you through."

One of Spears' players at Toledo was Emlen Tunnell, who transferred to Iowa after World

will come to order. I have the seating plans and the cost for the Lafayette game, but I don't suppose any of you academic bastards know anything about business, so I will take care of that."

Then the chairman gave a hard rap with his gavel. This went on for three items, the chairman monopolizing the floor and giving a hard rap of the gavel each time. He concluded, "If there is no further business, the meeting is adjourned." Each person present, except Spears and Cunningham, spat into his cuspidor and walked out. Nobody but the chairman had said a word.

For a long time West Virginia had sought a game with Lehigh. To help arrange a 1921 game at Lehigh, Tom Keady, Lehigh scout who had also scouted for Cavanaugh at Dartmouth, praised Spears highly. The Engineers won the game, 21–12, and a mild riot ensued.

During the second period, WVU was pushed back by penalties to its 6-inch line, and Spears rushed onto the field to debate with the referee. The ref told Fat that if he didn't return to his

War II and later played for the New York Giants. Emlen was lost to Toledo for three games because of a fractured vertebra in the cervical region.

"Before X rays," Doc grumbled, "they would have propped Emlen up and he would have played the next week."

Doc's favorite technique in getting his players up for a game was to go down the line and address each one individually in front of the others. For example, "At guard we'll start Slutzger. Now, dammit, Slutzger, you've got a ball game left in you. Get out there and do something for someone who's done something for you."

Joe W. Berry, one of Doc's players at Toledo, could give a good imitation of him. To simulate Doc's girth, he'd stuff a pillow under his shirt, and don a slouch hat such as Doc wore at games. Then he'd pace up and down and give Doc's routine of "doing something for someone who's done something for you." One day, Spears caught him in the act and commented, "Berry, I wish you could play football as well as you can act."

Dr. Norman Crisp, a teammate at Dartmouth, says of Doc Spears: "Football's gain was medicine's loss, because he could have been a hell of a doctor." When his 28 years of coaching were done, Doc devoted full time to his practice at Ypsilanti, Michigan. His son Bob, a fullback, captained Yale's 1951 team.

Amos Alonzo Stagg

FOOTBALL HIS MINISTRY

To Amos Alonzo Stagg football was much more than a game. It was a manifestation of faith that called for clean living, honest thinking, level dealing. That's what he exemplified and demanded in a life that honored all of its nearly 103 years.

"The coaching profession," Stagg said, "is one of the noblest and farthest reaching in building manhood. No man is too good to be the athletic coach for youth."

Stagg was a head football coach 57 seasons: two at Springfield College, 41 at the University of Chicago, and 14 at College of the Pacific. He began in 1890 at 28, finished in 1946 at 84. His victories total 314, one more than Glenn Scobey (Pop) Warner. He also surpassed Warner as the game's most prolific innovator.

It was not his career span, his victories, or his long line of brainchildren, however, that make Stagg, in the finest meaning of the word, No. 1 in the pantheon. What made him No. 1 was his personal approach to coaching, the framework in which he presented football to his players and to the world.

Stagg intended to become a minister, and entered Yale Divinity School in 1889. That fall he also played right end for Yale, and made the first All-America team ever picked. The following June he left the Divinity School and enrolled at Springfield, then known as the International YMCA College. He had decided to forgo the ministry, and to become a teacher of physical education and a coach.

It was not Stagg's football prowess that influenced him, but rather his fear that he would never be able to deliver a telling sermon. A future Nobel Prize winner had said of him, "It's too bad Stagg can't speak on his feet." A Nobel Prize winner is not necessarily infallible. But Stagg agreed with him and for many years did not shake off what ultimately proved to be an erroneous notion.

If he had become a minister, it is doubtful that Stagg, in pulpit or parish, by precept or example, could have influenced more people for good than he did in college athletics—if as many.

To Stagg, football *was* a ministry.

"The Grand Old Man of the Midway," they called him, not only in the Big Ten—the first conference, which he did so much to help found in 1895—but all across America.

What he stood for rang out clear as carillons that memorable day on Stagg Field in 1922, when his Chicago team, pride of the Midway, was upset by Princeton, pride of Old Nassau, in high drama unsurpassed on any gridiron of the Golden Twenties.

This was Coach Bill Roper's Princeton Team of Destiny, which won all eight of its games, several of them by making breaks, coming from behind,

Amos Alonzo Stagg, 1926. *Chicago Tribune Photos*

finding a way when there seemed no way. They were not expected to beat Chicago, and for over three quarters the favorite prevailed. Paced by the last of Stagg's All-Americans, guard Joe Pondelik, the Maroons' superior line fronted the charge of a powerful running set: the school's all-time fullback, John Thomas, his brother Harry, and Jim Pyott.

Chicago led, 18–7, and the Tigers, following a penalty for an illegal pass, were penned up at the 2-yard line with 12 minutes left. Then, 11 invisible wands began tapping out a message on 11 helmets, "Out from a prospect bleak and dire," the Tigers struck for two quick touchdowns.

A 40-yard pass on a fake kick got them out of chancery, and soon after a Chicago fumble was recovered and run 43 yards for the first touchdown. (Running with a fumble was allowed until 1929.) The second touchdown was helped by two critical penalties, and came after four charges, the first from the 6-yard line, the fourth reaching the goal line—just. Both conversions were made, the Easterners led 21–18, and now the clock was beginning to mock Chicago.

The Maroons returned the kickoff to their

34-yard line. With shell-shocked supporters imploring them to hurry, hurry, they behaved like a Stagg team under pressure. Mixing runs with passes, they moved surely, steadily down to the Tigers' 1-yard line. There was time then for only one more play. John Thomas hurled himself at the line. Tackle Herb Treat met and stopped him a smidgen shy of the goal line.

"No other athletic event in my memory," Stagg said, "so depressed the university for so many hours."

Football being a game of emotions sometimes unleashed, a few of the depressed criticized him—even though it was Stagg—for not sending in a play instead of letting the quarterback call a plunge by Thomas, which they seemed metaphysically certain Princeton was expecting. The Old Man met them as head-on as Herb Treat met John Thomas.

"The rules committee," he said, "deprecates the use of a substitute to convey information."

Although he would not break a rule, Stagg would indulge guile. Against Iowa, a Chicago fullback suddenly pointed behind the line and asked, "What's that?" When the Hawkeyes turned to find out, he ran through them for 20 yards. Anyone who would fall for such a thing should be encouraged to, Stagg reasoned, for the same type would also snore through Gethsemane.

The Old Man was like other coaches in believing football had elements of predetermined damnation. For 30 years Chicago beat Purdue, yet for 30 years the pregame newspaper headlines carried the message, "Stagg Fears Purdue."

It is doubtful that Stagg invented coachly gloom: it came with the first coach, like the forbidden fruit with Eden. The Old Man didn't invent the game, either; it just seemed that way. His coach at Yale, Walter Camp, was the inventor; at the rules conventions of 1881 and '82, Camp put through his two brainchildren, the scrimmage and yards-in downs, the individuating notes that first distinguished the game from Rugby.

There was not much else, though, that was not thought up by Stagg.

Through the twenties and thirties the predominant offensive formations were the wingback attack, single and double, and with an unbalanced line, and the Notre Dame shift from the T formation into a box right or left with a balanced line. The wingback deploy was invented and popularized by Pop Warner and his desciples, while the shift was glamorized at Notre Dame by

Knute Rockne and by his dozens of ex-players who became successful head coaches in every part of the country. When Rockne was asked, however, where the Notre Dame shift came from, he said, "Where everything else in football came from. Yale."

To be explicit, Notre Dame had been taught the shift by Rockne's coach at Notre Dame, Jesse Harper, who had learned it as a Chicago quarterback under Stagg. All that was added at Notre Dame, Rockne said, was the flexing end to get a blocking angle on the tackle.

His first year coaching at Springfield in 1890, Stagg employed a double-wingback principle by pulling his ends off the line for blocking momentum and to run reverses. He also installed a hidden-ball play that he sprang for a touchdown against Harvard. He played himself on what was billed as "Stagg's Team." The Springfield student body numbered only 41, so he couldn't afford to be picky about eligibility rules, which were then almost nonexistent anyhow. In 1891, Stagg's Team played the first indoor game, in Madison Square Garden against a team of former Yale players.

A partial list of other Stagg firsts would include the onside kick, the quick kick, the short punt formation, the handoff from a fake kick, the huddle, numbering of players, practice under lights (and a white football for such), padded goalposts, and the charging sled.

The forward pass was legalized in 1906 by the rules committee he was an important part of. All Stagg did with it at Chicago was install 64 patterns that included a pass by a reversing wingback after a handoff, single- and double-flanker receivers, a guard eligible after a shift, a "shoestring" or "sleeper" to the sidelines, and a fake pass and run. He didn't overlook much.

The modern T formation features four distinct Stagg contributions: the stand-up quarterback behind center, the split buck, the man-in-motion, and the quarterback keeper, although that play and its companion, the pitchout, are inherited from, and as old as, Rugby.

In sum, any time anybody thinks he has come up with something new, he soon discovers it is merely a reclamation with modification of something first used 65 to 75 years ago, and probably by Stagg.

If Stagg had given football nothing but his time, that alone would have made him astonishing. In 1889 he was an All-America end at Yale. In 1932, 43 years later, at 70, he brought his last

The Grand Old Man towards the end of his Chicago tenure

Chicago team back to New Haven to tie his alma mater in the Bowl, 7–7, a mild upset. The occasion inspired George Emanuel Phair, peerless weaver of light verse, to sing,

> Alonzo Stagg, a bright young lad,
>   Came back to Dear Old Yale,
> And all the afternoon he had
>   The Bulldog turning pale.
> Ah, what a coach that kid will be
> When he has reached maturity.

In 1943, 11 years later, his College of the Pacific team logged a 7–2 record and scared Southern California's Rose Bowl team before losing 6–0. This earned him honors as Coach of the Year, chosen by the Football Coaches Association of America, and Man of the Year, chosen by the Football Writers Association of America. He was then 81.

For 20 years now they have been saying that coaching is a young man's game. Whose is that coachly chuckle we hear, coming all the way from the head table at Valhalla? Could it belong to young Lonnie Stagg?

The long haul was something Stagg conditioned himself for, body, mind, and spirit, a rock the storms and high tides of football, as of life, would break upon and be scattered.

"Live in a way that makes you feel good," he preached, "and get your fun out of feeling good."

Stagg's pudgy look was deceptive; he was very strong, always well conditioned. At no time did his five feet seven carry more than 166 pounds, 16 over his top playing weight at Yale. He was still scrimmaging with his Chicago players at 40; he was jogging a mile a day at 70; he was taking walk-and-run hikes at 80. He never wore glasses until he was 50, and he kept all his tough, waved, iron-gray hair. He even conducted a survey among former players to prove that athletes were less prone to baldness than nonathletes.

Alcohol and tobacco had no place in his life, and the oldest returning letterman would not dream of drinking or smoking in front of the Old man. He ate carefully; his 89th birthday party comprised pea soup, two ears of corn, peaches, and milk.

Stagg preached relentlessly against the hot dog; he consigned it to the shelf just above red whiskey in Satan's Supermart. The hot dog and those who devoured it were equally ersatz and should stay in the stands. Ice cream, cookies, and soft drinks were by contrast godly, and fitting for "get-acquainted" gatherings in the Stagg home, or as reward for good playing.

Abuse of food by one of his earliest All-America men, halfback Clarence Herschberger, cost Chicago's first championship team in 1897 a perfect record and he never forgot it. The '97 team was given to a general wildness that kept the former divinity student on sharp edge, but Herschberger overdid. The night before the Wisconsin game, he and Walter Kennedy, captain and quarterback, had to see who could gain the most weight.

After feats of ingestion to have impressed the Giant Jack killed, Henry VIII, and a Harvard heavyweight crew, Kennedy gained seven and a half pounds, to win by eight ounces. Perhaps to prove the victory a fluke, the next morning Herschberger ate 13 eggs and got so sick he couldn't play. His absence, his kicking especially, was sorely missed as Chicago lost to Wisconsin 23–8.

Thereafter, Stagg allowed each player a certain sum for each meal on road trips; if he ate more, he had to pay the coach the difference.

To entrench discipline even deeper, in 1898

Stagg seized every last one of his bearded players, and using his own straight razor, slashed off their whiskers to produce Chicago's first clean-shaven team. Another Stagg first.

Thus did many atone for Herschberger's sin of mad gluttony. And while Clarence may not have been the cause of its foundation, he did become a charter member and, indeed, perennial honorary board chairman of a select organization with stature equal to the varsity letter club. This was Stagg's "Jackass Club," which had two degrees, "The Jackass" and "The Double Jackass."

"Jackass" was the nearest Stagg would permit himself to profanity. "Like all forms of over-statement," he said, "cursing is an opiate, and progressively increasing doses are necessary for effect. Too, cursing is likely to leave a personal wound on the object, no matter how impersonally it is delivered."

No profane coach, however, could have cut or stung a player more deeply than a nonprofane Stagg who'd had enough of selfishness or individualism.

"Heaven help you in later life if you don't take a tumble to yourself," he excoriated one derelict. "You are a self-satisfied, opinionated young Jackass who is bigger than the team, the coach, and the school together! Take a good look at yourself!"

Humor, however, usually attended the initiation of a Jackass, and it was possible to become a double without first being a single. Part of a crowd watching Chicago play at Cornell free-loaded from a bluff overlooking the field. During a critical huddle, a Chicago player looked up at them and startled his teammates by asking, "Say, what do you suppose would happen if that bluff should cave in with all those people?" When this was relayed to Stagg he immediately dubbed the youth a Double Jackass.

His Chicago players were calling Stagg the Old Man as early as 1899, when he was only 37. They looked upon him as a second father, firm but just, and his wife Stella as a second mother. Stella Robinson was an 18-year-old Chicago coed when the 32-year-old coach married her in 1894, and they were together the remaining 70 years of his life. Stella served as assistant coach-at-large, presiding at the ice cream, cookie, and soda parties, typing up scouting notes, and listening to the latest initiation into the Jackass Club.

She gave football priority even over her honeymoon. On their wedding day, September 10, fall practice was already under way for a 21-game

schedule—the 21-game schedule, made possible by playing Wednesday as well as Saturday, was another concept Stagg had absorbed at the New Haven fountainhead. So there was no time for a wedding trip. After the season, however, Alonzo scheduled three postseason games in California, and invited Stella along. It was put this way by his 1893 captain, Andy Wyant: "Stagg must have loved the boys on that team, because he had 22 of them on his honeymoon."

The first college football game in America, a soccer match between Princeton and Rutgers on November 6, 1869, at New Brunswick, New Jersey, was still over seven years away when in West Orange, a little place not far to the east in Jersey, Amos Alonzo Stagg was born, April 16, 1862.

The Union and Confederate armies were gearing for the Seven Days' Campaign in front of Richmond. The South was outsquadded but their quarterback was Bobby Lee, and the signal-callers for the North—McClellan, Pope, and Porter—were no match for him, especially with the bad scouting reports received from Pinkerton, who always had the boys in butternut deeper than they were.

The North, which hadn't yet moved U. S. Grant up to first string, could have used Stagg, a born field general whose forebears on both sides had fought two wars before in the Revolution. "My father, though poor," Stagg said, "was superbly honest and just, and as fearless as was his ancestor, Micah Tompkins of Milford, Connecticut. At the risk of his neck Micah for many weary months harbored in his cellar the regicide judges, Whalley and Goffe, who had been forced to flee England after passing the death sentence on Charles I."

Stagg's early life was not easy, but he had the stern stuff to thrive on it. He was the sixth of eight children, and his father, apprenticed to a shoemaker at seven, took any and all jobs he could find to maintain a home for his family in a neighborhood of Irish laborers as poor as himself.

Food was about enough to go around. When his mother peeled apples, Alonzo would catch and eat the skins, and to supplement their meager larder he often roamed nearby woods for berries, chestnuts, and hickory nuts.

By working summers and part time during the school year, Alonzo was able to attend Orange High School, and by diligence graduate in three years. Reared to respect God even before education, he was steered toward church affairs and the ministry by a friend, Grace Livingston Hill,

who would become a well-known writer of novels for girls.

Alonzo's goal was the Yale Divinity School, which required he first earn a bachelor's degree. To prepare himself for Yale, he managed to put by enough to matriculate at Phillips Exeter Academy, where he budgeted 18 cents a day for food that featured oatmeal, stale bread, and milk at 3 cents a quart.

When he entered Yale as a freshman in 1884 at 22, he had $32 and no overcoat against the New England winter. As a future divinity student, he got $20 off the semester tuition of $50, but even $30 plus board and room posed enough of a problem to make an Algerian hero tremble. Alonzo found an unheated attic room for a dollar a week, and allowed himself 5 cents for breakfast, 10 cents for dinner, and 5 cents for supper.

Even as tough and determined a young man as Stagg could not bear up under this regimen, and on his way to class one day, chills and fever seized him and forced him to bed. The doctor recognized undernourishment and warned him to eat sensibly. Those early privations explain Stagg's devotion to plain, nourishing food, and his impatience with any abuse of food by those who never had known the want of it. Herschberger's sin was not so much the loss of the game as the waste of food.

When young Stagg had recovered his strength, Harry Beecher, a football player, helped him earn good meals by waiting tables, and soon his older brothers and sisters were able to give him some help. By fall 1885, his sophomore year, he had back all his blocky power.

That fall's freshman class tried to brush aside tradition by sitting on the sacred Yale fence at the corner of College and Chapel Streets, but the sophomores, including Stagg, would not abide it. Alonzo personally picked out a freshman named George Woodruff. George would later be a star guard and teammate of Stagg's on Captain William (Pa) Corbin's undefeated 1888 Yale powerhouse. Later he would become the outstanding coach of Pennsylvania, a leading strategist of the pre-forward-pass era, and originator of the guards-back play that preceded the tackle-back formation, favored ground weapon of the early century.

In the fall of '85, however, George was only a big freshman who had gone out for football wearing a straw hat, a pair of running pants, and a set of black whiskers. He was also as strong as a yoke of oxen, and when Stagg ordered him off the Yale fence, he twined his legs around the top and

middle bars and defied Alonzo to take him off. It was a long and fierce struggle, but Stagg finally succeeded in prying the freshman loose with a headlock.

Stagg did not go in seriously for football until the fall of 1888. By that time he had established himself as college baseball's leading pitcher. He had been inspired to take up pitching when he was 15 and heard about the discovery of the curve ball. The day he himself made the ball curve for the first time, he rushed to his mother and cried out, "Mamma! I've got it! I've got it!"

At Yale he mixed the curve with a live fast ball, and Jesse Dann, who might have turned into a pitcher even better than Stagg, became his catcher because he was the only one at Yale who could hold him. The battery of Stagg and Dann may have been Yale's finest. In one game, Alonzo fanned 20 Princetons. From 1886 through '90 his record against Harvard was 17–3; the old rivals then played four or five games a year, and there were no eligibility rules excluding freshmen or postgraduate students. Stagg pitched Yale to five consecutive championships.

Six National League teams made him offers, the largest from New York, $4,200. Such an unheard of amount prompted one editorial writer to sound off, "So long as a pitcher gets $4,200 for six months and a preacher $600 for a year, so long will there be good pitching and bad preaching." Stagg turned the offer down; he was invincibly an amateur, who 50 years later at College of the Pacific was dissuading his best football players from becoming professionals, and helping them get established in businesses.

Yale's fall baseball practice, and the possibility of injuring his arm, delayed Stagg's football advent until 1888. More significantly, that year he had a long talk about his future with Dr. William Rainey Harper, his Bible teacher. Four years later, when Stagg was completing his two years of study at Springfield, Dr. Harper was named president of the new and yet unbuilt University of Chicago, endowed by America's richest millionaire, John D. Rockefeller.

Dr. Harper wanted Stagg to head up the new university's physical education and intercollegiate athletic programs. "I'll give you $1,500," he said. When Alonzo was too stunned to reply, the doctor raised it to $2,000 and an assistant professorship. Stagg was still muted with amazement. "I'll give you $2,500," Dr. Harper almost shouted, "an associate professorship, and tenure for life!"

Stagg pulled himself together and said he wanted time to think. After he had thought it out, he wrote Harper, "After much thought and prayer I have decided that my life can best be used for my Master's service in the position you have offered."

When Stagg arrived at Chicago in 1892, only one building was far enough advanced for him to enter it even on a plank. His first football squad numbered only 13; he himself played the first two years, as he had in Springfield. "The game was too young and weak," he explained, "for such a situation to be thought particularly unusual."

Chicago's first game against a college team, Northwestern, resulted in a scoreless tie and gate receipts of $22.65. Early cash flow of Rockefeller dollars also was slow, and Stagg had to go into his own pocket to rent a dressing room for practice.

With wedge, mass, and mass momentum plays predominating, the game was so rough anything went, short of outright murder. The last game Stagg played in, Purdue in 1893, got so bad that the district attorney for Tippecanoe County strode onto the field and threatened indictments for assault and battery.

Amidst the brawling, Stagg's integrity still managed to shine forth, and he was even invited to officiate games in which Chicago played. On one of these assignments he rushed to the Chicago dressing room as soon as the half was over and gave the only mercenary fight talk of his career. "Boys," he said, "you've got to win! John D. Rockefeller is in the stands!"

From these hardy beginnings, Stagg brought Chicago football to championship stature, regionally and nationally. He coached seven Big Ten champs: 1896, 1899, 1905, 1907, 1908, 1913, 1924, and all but '96, '07, and '24 were undefeated. His teams from '02 through '09 lost a total of seven games.

The 1905 team, which won all nine of its games, scoring 212 points to five, was adjudged national champion. "The greatest that ever wore the C in the days of five-yard football," Stagg saluted them. (The first-down rule was five yards in three downs until 1912, when it was changed to 10 yards in four downs.) The ace of the team, Stagg's greatest player and named by Walter Camp to his All-America team in '04, '05, and '06, was Walter Eckersall, a little fellow, five feet seven and 142, out of Chicago's Woodlawn area and Hyde Park High. Eckersall ranks with Charley Daly, of Harvard and Army, as supreme among quarterbacks of the prepass era; he did play one season of the pass, '06.

Eckie was a shrewd field general, a clever, lively runner with a tough stiff-arm, an expert kicker, and a sure, hard tackler. His generalship, kicking, and tackling contributed much to what was probably the most satisfying victory a Stagg team ever won.

In 1905 Michigan invaded Chicago's Marshall Field with a 56-game defeatless streak (one tie) that had begun in 1901 with the advent of Fielding H. (Hurry Up) Yost as coach. The "point-a-minute" team Michigan was known as, and for four years its victims had included Chicago, 22–0, 21–0, 28–0, and 22–12.

Yost, a brilliant coach, was also a nonstop talker and sometimes abrasive. At a track meet in the spring of 1905, he got into an argument with Stagg and promised Chicago another beating in football that fall. "We'll give you plenty!" Yost warned, and five minutes before the 1:45 kickoff, the Old Man told his players about it. "Don't," he asked them, "let him cram this game down my throat!"

The stands, with extra seats added, were jammed with 25,700, most of them there since the gates had opened at 11:30. Everybody in Chicago who had $2 and could get a ticket had come, and the gate receipts, $35,000, were unheard of. Among the distinguished guests were the two All-America seers, Walter Camp and Caspar Whitney, come down out of their ivory towers and west for a look at Eckersall.

They watched a first half of hard, quick, brainy defensive play, and a standoff punting duel between Eckersall and Ike Garrels. When Stagg followed his players to their dressing room at the half, he was stopped at the door by a lady member of the Chicago faculty who gave him a message from President Harper. He was dying of cancer but listening to the game on a special telephone hookup. His message was, "You must win for me."

Through a furious, sullen second half, the defensive and kicking battle raged on. With time running out and a scoreless tie imminent, Eckersall punted at midfield, driving the ball low and hard behind a head wind into the end zone. Danny Clark tried to clear it for Michigan, but Mark Catlin and Art Badenoch of Chicago tackled him for a safety, the only points scored on the Wolverines all season.

The 2–0 lead was jeopardized twice before the end on runs by Garrels and Tom Hammond, but twice Eckersall made saving tackles. Fans didn't tear down goalposts then because they hadn't

One of the few times Stagg was caught off guard.
Chicago Tribune Photos

thought of it. But Chicago rooters tore down the fences.

There were to be four more Big Ten championships, with a lag of eleven years, 1913 to '24, between the last two, but some of the nontitle teams Stagg turned out probably matched some of his champions—or were better. The 1921 and '22 teams missed the crown because of a seven-point loss the first year and a tie game the second.

In 1923, Illinois finished first with a 5–0 record, Chicago second with 5–1. The difference was their confrontation. In the opening game of their new Memorial Stadium in Champaign-Urbana, the Illini won, 7–0, on a 60-yard run by a sophomore halfback who was to become the most publicized single football player, not only of the twenties and thirties but of all football annals.

His name was Harold Edward (Red) Grange.

Grange's 60-yard run that did Stagg out of the championship for the third straight year was setting the stage, though neither, of course, realized it, for a far more individual and dramatic duel between them the next season, 1924. That year, because of a mad scramble characteristic of well-balanced conferences, a record of three victories, one defeat, and three ties was good enough to win the championship for Stagg, and his key game was the tie with Illinois, 21–21.

The Illini invaded Stagg Field, November 8. Three weeks before, October 18, at the dedication game of Memorial Stadium, they had run over Michigan, 39–14. Or rather Grange had. He had run back the opening kickoff 95 yards for a touchdown, and broken three touchdown runs from scrimmage of 67, 56, and 44 yards, and all in 10 minutes. In the second half, he had run 15 yards for a fifth touchdown, and passed 23 yards to Marion Leonard for a sixth. In 41 minutes he carried 21 times for 402 yards, passed for 64, ran for five touchdowns and threw for the other. No running back has had a day quite like that before or since, and none is likely to.

Scouting the game for Chicago was Stagg's former star end and young assistant, Herbert Orrin (Fritz) Crisler, who would later win coaching laurels of his own at Princeton and Michigan. Fritz raved about Grange. Stagg listened and when Crisler had finished, the Old Man asked, "Fritz, did you ever see Grange score without the ball?" Fritz, wonderingly, said, no, he hadn't. Then Stagg asked him a lot of questions about the Illinois line and the defense Coach Bob Zuppke was using.

Stagg's strategy to slow down Grange was old, but sound. You couldn't stop Grange if he had the ball. Therefore, don't let him have the ball. How do you do that? By controlling, by keeping possession, by moving it. Fine, if you have the man to move it, and a good enough line to block open the Illinois six-man line.

Stagg thought he had the line, and he was certain he had the back. His name was Austin McCarthy, and he's in the Stagg all-time Chicago backfield with Herschberger, Eckersall, and John Thomas. But after that windy, snowy day against Red Grange and Illinois at Stagg Field, he would always be known as "Five Yards" McCarthy.

Five yards was his shortest gain as he hammered out 56 in six plays from the opening kickoff, behind a big, strong Chicago line. The drive was aborted when Illinois recovered a fumble on its 4, but after Earl Britton punted on first down, back came McCarthy, pounding out gains of five yards or more on a march of 49 and this time to a touchdown.

Illinois, apparently unimpressed, kicked off again. Chicago and McCarthy shook the Illini for a second touchdown, and led 14–0. So far Stagg's plan had worked to perfection. It was well into the second quarter, and Illinois had been in possession only one play, Britton's punt. Grange had yet to handle the ball.

It couldn't go on, of course. Illinois had religion now, and chose to receive. And Grange got the ball. In eight plays he gained 69 yards, scoring from the 4. Chicago scored again. Then Red gained 40 yards in nine runs, mixed with two passes he caught for a total of 44 yards, going over from the 5. But at halftime, Chicago led 21–14.

In the second half, Zuppke changed to a seven-man line and box defense that shut off Five Yards McCarthy, while Grange broke loose on one 80-yard touchdown run, had another for 55 yards called back for holding, and spent most of the half scaring Chicago near to death. But Red was not able to get to pay dirt a fourth time, and the game ended 21–21, an emphatic upset triumph for Stagg and his players, who went on to win the conference title.

Ironically, although Stagg accomplished his objective by keeping the ball away from Grange long enough to cut back his production, Red ran for 300 yards, passed for 177, and scored three times. Considering the context, some rate it even higher than his spectacular against Michigan. He also made believers out of those who, seeking desperately to flaw him, had pontificated that he could not run to his left. Against Chicago he ran mostly to his left. "Grange," Stagg said, "single-handedly carried his outplayed team to a draw."

The thwarting of Grange, and the "Big Apple" of 1924 marked the last of the hero lore for Stagg on the Midway. The next four years the best his teams could get in the Big Ten was a fourth in 1927. In 1929 football at Chicago fell prey to a terminal disease that ate away at it until the end in 1939.

The doom was sealed when Robert Maynard Hutchins was named president of the university in 1929. Hutchins wanted Chicago to become a university for the intellectually elite, only as he saw them. Chicago, he thought, had the academic

prestige, large endowment, and freedom from responsibility to government and public that placed it above football.

He did not know, but Chicago would discover that a university must be more than a hive of students without a unifying spirit, or it becomes only part of a sterile way of life. There is no college spirit, however, unless there is something to be spirited about. Football is the incomparable contributor to that spirit, that character a more recent University of Chicago chancellor, Lawrence A. Kimpton, called the *geist*. In 1970, Chicago fielded a football team again, on a small-college basis, which is at least more than Hutchins felt it needed.

Hutchins had come too far too fast to be entrusted with determining on his own the kind of university Chicago should be. Like Stagg, he was a Yale man, Class of 1921, 33 years after Alonzo's. He had been secretary of Yale at 24, a teacher in its Law School at 26, dean of the Law School at 28. At 30, he hadn't lived as long as Stagg by 37 years. He certainly didn't know as much about life and youth and it may be seriously doubted that he knew as much about education.

He never considered this, of course, and if it had been mentioned to him, he probably would have dismissed the notion as ludicrous. For obduracy, as blissful as it is unaware, nothing matches the pseudo-god world of the intellect that becomes insularized.

When Hutchins came on, Stagg had three years to go until 1932, and mandatory retirement at 70. In 1930, Crisler took the head coach's job at Minnesota on the advice of the Old Man. "The game is finished here," he told Fritz. "This man is going to kill it." For the last three years under Stagg and seven under Clark Shaughnessy, the once powerful Maroons became the breather game of the Big Ten, and after 1939, dropped the sport.

Hutchins, who could not have been without respect for Stagg, gave him the choice of two advisory jobs, each worth $8,000, but the Old Man saw them as pensions. "I cannot and will not accept a job without work," he said. "I am fit, able, and willing. I refuse to be idle and a nuisance."

Several colleges thought him fit and able and made him offers. The president of one, Tully Knoles, of College of the Pacific, had always idolized Stagg, had bicycled 30 miles as a youth to see Chicago play at Stanford. Knoles' enthusiasm touched a responsive spark in the Old Man, who, when he accepted, showed his new boss the letter he had written President Harper 40 years before, "After much thought and prayer I have decided that my life can best be used for my Master's service in the position you have offered."

Amos Alonzo Stagg, 71, then added, "I come to College of the Pacific in the same spirit."

At Pacific, he emphasized that given reasonable personnel, he could still produce. His 14-year record of 60 victories, 75 defeats, and 7 ties is deceptive. He usually was outpersonneled by such opponents as Southern California, UCLA, and St. Mary's, but he sometimes upset them, usually made it close, and his teams were invariably interesting to watch. The best were 1938 and '43 with 7-3 and 7-2 records. And his regime made the school a profit of $230,000 that paid off some debts.

"Stagg's hold on his squads," recalled one of his players, "was so remarkable that we played not for the school, not for the girl friend, not for publicity—not for anything or anybody but Stagg."

College of the Pacific tried to make him a "consultant" after the 1946 season, when he was 84, but he said he still wanted to be on the field with boys and help coach them. So the next six years he did just that, as an assistant to his son, Amos Alonzo Stagg, Jr., at little Susquehanna College in Selinsgrove, Pennsylvania. In 1951, at 89, he was assistant coach of an undefeated team. After the next season, now 90, he went back to Stockton, California, to retire finally, although Stockton College gave him the honorary title "kicking coach."

Stagg died in Stockton on March 17, 1965. He had outlived by 40 years his old coach at Yale, Walter Camp, who was born in 1859, three years before him. After Camp died in his sleep during the night of March 13–14, 1925, in a New York hotel, where he was attending the annual rules meeting, Grantland Rice, whose prose and poetry best caught the spirit of the Golden Gridiron, wrote a tribute. Granny Rice, we think, would have agreed that his tribute to Camp would be fitting also for the Grand Old Man, who by serving his Master had left the game he loved an imperishable heritage:

"How often must have come to Amos Alonzo Stagg the memory of old football battles in rain

and snow, in sun and shadow—the flying tackle and the savage line thrust—the forward wall braced for the shock—the graceful spiral careening against a sky of blue and gray—the long run down the field—the goal-line stand—the forward pass—the singing and cheering of great crowds —young and old America gathered together on a golden afternoon, with bands playing and banners flying—

"It may have been in the midst of such a dream that the call to quarters came and taps was sounded as the Great Knight came down the field."

Mal Stevens

MEN IN BLUE

A bland, harmless, professional pessimism is a malady few coaches fail to acquire after a couple of years' exposure to the insidious influences of their strange profession. It is necessary to them in their fight for self-protection and bread and butter against the day of defeat, the inevitable day, when every man's voice, it seems, is turned against them, and the most uninformed is the loudest.

Dr. Marvin Allen (Mal) Stevens, who coached Yale from 1928 through '32 and New York University from 1934 through '41, was almost unique among coaches. He was well enough acquainted with defeat, yet he always spoke, with a slight touch of his native Kansas twang, what was on his mind and he cared nothing about who heard him. He may not have been quite as blunt as, say, Rogers Hornsby, that bluntest of baseball players and managers, but he was blunt enough. His justification was simple: that was the way he felt.

The nature of football coaching is such, its practitioners are afforded little chance to develop whatever latent potentials they might have in the field of humanitarianism and philanthropy. Again, there have been exceptions. In Mal Stevens, the compulsion to help people had been driving him almost from the time he was a small boy.

Bob Zuppke, celebrated Illinois coach, painter, and philosopher, once told Mal Stevens, "You'll never be a great football coach. You have too kind a face."

Stevens wanted to be a doctor. He became a leading bone specialist of his time, and was also a front-rank worker in the war against polio. Few people knew about it, because he did not talk of it, but he did many surgeries for charity.

That in this same Dr. Stevens there was a discernible cynicism need not seem strange. A man who coaches or has coached football without becoming somewhat cynical might be considered to have a strong foot forward on the path to sainthood.

Mal Stevens found it difficult to tell a Yale team, as Tad Jones had told them, "You are going out there now to play football against Harvard. Never again in your life will you do anything so important."

Not that Stevens didn't work hard to beat Harvard. But Stevens found richer rewards in straightening the twisted bones of some small boy. Perhaps the boy would never play football in Yale Bowl or Harvard Stadium or any other college amphitheater, but if he could just play, that was the thing.

Stevens always was the doctor first, the football coach afterward. Graduated from the college in 1925, he entered Yale Medical School that fall, was graduated in '29. He became an instructor in surgery, gynecology, and obstetrics in Yale Medical School and later an assistant professor of orthopedics. In 1936, he began his private practice, both in New Haven and in New York.

He became backfield assistant to Tad Jones in 1924, and continued in that capacity for the next three years. His teaching ability and personality made him a natural to succeed Tad after the '27 season, and on March 1, 1928, he was appointed head coach for a term of three years. Mal received $8,000 salary, then the Yale-Harvard-Princeton limit, but back in Osborne, Kansas, where he had played high school football, the local newspaper ran a story that said Yale was

reportedly paying Stevens $55,000 a year. This worried Mal's mother. She cut out the story and sent it to him.

"Son," she wrote, "I hope you are saving most of that money."

That coaching Yale was worth $55,000 a year was something Stevens didn't doubt on occasion during his five years on the job. Like Tad Jones before him, he found the downcurves in Yale's football chart overemotionalized the Old Blues. Phone calls, letters, and telegrams piled in on Mal at times, some of the less temperate offering gratuitous advice on the more dignified as well as certain methods of self-extinction.

One self-appointed group signed its wires, "The Committee of Ten." Another, "The Committee of Fifty." After a Georgia victory over Yale one year, they wired Mal, "You are the worst coach Yale has ever had." After a victory over Princeton the same year, they wired, "You are the finest coach Yale has ever had."

Before the 19–0 victory over Dartmouth in 1928, on a rainy day, the Walter Camp Memorial Gateway was dedicated. It is the entrance to Walter Camp Field, of which Yale Bowl is regarded as a unit. The gateway is a series of lofty stone pillars, flanked on each side by low walls of stone and brick extending 400 feet. On tablets, set into walls on each side, are inscribed the names of 224 colleges and 279 high and prep schools all over the nation that joined Yale in honoring the man whose scrimmage and yards-in-downs gave American football its basic individuating notes.

Stevens welcomed the sophomore candidates to the 1929 varsity, because it was better than average. He was especially interested in one halfback, just a little fellow, about 144 pounds and five feet seven inches, but built heavily from the hips down.

He wasn't exceptionally fast—Charlie Heim and Harlan (Hoot) Ellis and a few more backfield contemporaries at Yale could outsprint him at any distance up to a hundred yards. But he had a demoniac shiftiness, a perfected talent for stopping on a penny and veering the other way. He could sidestep, shift speeds, pivot, spin. He was as slippery as a striped adder, as unpredictable in his course as quicksilver. He made tacklers look foolish, and at times drove them into an insensate rage.

His ball carrying was only one, though the most exciting, of his skills. He could dropkick from midfield. He could kick off over the goal line. He could angle punts out of bounds. He was

Mal Stevens

not a great passer, but he was a good one. Defensively, he was sure-handed, reliable. He played football with a steady verve and calm courage. When opponents, purposefully if legitimately, set about removing him from the scene, he was never heard to complain, then or thereafter.

A natural athlete, he played basketball and baseball well. He was a forward and a shortstop. He was always at his best in the clutch; he hit a home run with the bases full to beat Harvard.

But it was football, the great spectacle, that provided him the perfect arena. Saturday after Saturday, great throngs packed Yale Bowl, titillated by the prospect of what Albie Booth was going to do.

Little Albie. The Mighty Mite. Number 48. The Mighty Atom. Little Boy Blue.

The most popular football heroes are the escape artists—the Red Granges, the Tommy Harmons, the Glenn Davises. Beyond the visual thrills they provide—not once but several times —on the long touchdown run, their ability to avoid the violent traps and pitfalls prepared for them stimulates and fulfills the spectator, gives him a vicarious victory over the cave-ins, the

thorns, and the enemies that surround and en-snarl his own everyday existence.

When a little fellow like Albie Booth repeatedly escaped, frustrated, and defeated the giants and dragons of the gridiron; when, like some diminutive Ivanhoe, he entered the lists and rattled his lance against the shields of the mighty in tournament, then the thrill for the spectator was increased manifold. The underprivileged watched Booth and became rich. The meek saw him, and in their minds turned on and slew their own private bullies.

The exciting kinship the public and the press felt for Booth was surpassed in specific understanding of his worth by his teammates. The Yale teams he played on in 1929 through '31, though not of championship caliber, included several fine players.

There were Firp Greene and later the combative Fred Linehan at guard, and Kemp Dunn, dependable blocker at either wingback or fullback. Dud Parker was another excellent blocker and clutch punter, while Joe Crowley and Walter Levering backed up the line and barreled through for important yardage.

The smart and fiery Pat Sullivan was at quarterback and Freddy Loser played center as if he loved football, which he did. Then there were his dynamic little successor, the competitive Benny Betner, and Herty Barres, an end who would do the job for you, the tough job when you most needed it.

Fay Vincent, Tom Hawley, Bob Lassiter, Johnny Wilbur, Ed Rotan were other standouts. Linehan was an All-America selection, and Barres and Vincent won a lot of mention. But they all agreed that the top football player in their midst was Booth.

Booth was honored with five captaincies at Yale: leadership of freshman football, basketball, and baseball; and varsity football and basketball. He might have been elected varsity baseball captain also, but he himself led the movement to have it go to deserving Eddie Warren.

Albert James Booth, Jr. was born in New Haven, February 1, 1908, the son of a foreman in the Winchester's firearms factory. An older brother Bill was stockier and a younger brother Fred was taller, but it was Albie who from neighborhood sandlot days up, shone in sports. As a youngster from the time he was 11 until he reached 15, he played for the Dixwell A. C. At New Haven Hillhouse High, Albie at 125 was too small for football, but he captained the baseball

team and played basketball. Later, at Milford Prep, where he got ready for Yale, he also captained three sports.

Zippy performances as a sophomore in early games with Vermont and Brown won Booth some attention, but it was against Army that his fame skyrocketed nationally. Army was coming to the Bowl, where Red Cagle had run wild in 1928. Cagle, in a 20–20 tie at Harvard the week before, had displayed all his old, flashy open-field skills as runner and passer. Booth, it was agreed, was a terrific sophomore; it was asking too much, though, to expect him to outdo the veteran West Point ace, twice All-America. But 80,000 packed the Bowl to see what would happen.

Army got off to a 13–0 lead. Cagle intercepted a pass and ran it back 55 yards for a touchdown. Army converted. Fullback Johnny Murrell ran 27 yards off tackle for another touchdown. Then Stevens pulled the blankets off Albie and sent him in.

He took Army's kickoff back to the 21. He gained one yard, four yards, and then punted. Army fumbled the punt and Firp Greene recovered on the Cadets' 33. Booth twisted up the middle for six. He circled end nimbly for 10 yards to the Army 17. The Elis, inspired by his presence, and playing with a fire and confidence heretofore lacking, took it to the 10.

Then Booth sent Kemp Dunn, the fullback, into the line, and Kemp picked up five. Albie then drove four yards to the 1. On the next play he took it over. He dropkicked the extra point. Army now led, 13–7, and before long the half was over.

Early in the third period, Booth missed a field-goal attempt from the Army 17. It was about the only thing he did miss all day. Presently, he was sparking another drive to the Cadets' 12. He picked up a yard to the 11, lost it on the next play. Tommy Taylor, wingback, made four to the 8. Booth and Taylor alternated in jamming to the 1. On fourth down Albie flung himself over the seething scrimmage for the touchdown. He dropkicked the extra point and Yale was ahead 14–13.

Meanwhile, the Yale line was extracting the zip from the Army attack. The Cadets seemed to be growing demoralized by the antics of the 144-pound demon, who was everywhere. Following Booth's second touchdown, Yale kicked off. Army couldn't gain and Murrell punted.

Booth gathered in the punt on his 30-yard line and started up the field. He got nice blocking along the way from Ned Austen, Herb Miller,

Fay Vincent, Hoot Ellis and Tuffy Phillips, the sub center. It was Tuffy who put Cagle, the last man, on his back with a kind of belly block or "poot" block.

But much of Booth's run was an incredible piece of open-field chicanery that had the Bowl in an uproar. Several times he seemed to be hemmed in, surrounded, but he somehow got away. Army men hurled themselves desperately at him, ended up on the ground as he shadowed away from them, in and out of them, around them.

Two tacklers bore down on him from opposite directions. He stopped dead, allowed them to smash head-on, then danced around them. It seemed as if he eluded each Army player at least once and some of them more than once. Finally he danced, weary but triumphant, over the goal line. He had enough zing left to dropkick the extra point. Yale was ahead and would stay ahead, 21–13.

Booth had scored all 21 of Yale's points. He had carried the ball 33 times from scrimmage for a net gain of 223 yards. He had punted. He had called the plays. Dunn and Taylor and the others had done fine work. But it was Booth who had pulled them together and inspired them. It was Booth who had murdered the Cadets, literally murdered them, with the greatest single-game performance any Yale player ever delivered.

When he came off the field, the stands rose and greeted him in one resounding ovation that echoed from the walls of West Rock and the like of which was not heard in New Haven before or since. His name sang out over the wires to every outpost of the country, and beyond, and became a byword. The newsreels of the game, reaching out to theaters everywhere, showed millions of people who never had been near New Haven the magic of this new hero of the gridiron.

The torrents of fan mail annoyed the Yale Post Office Station in Berkeley Oval, and also bothered Albie. A lot of letters were from girls. They had no interest for Booth, who was already engaged to Marion Noble, the girl he later married. So he turned those letters over to his Yale friends, who impersonated him on dates the length and breadth of Connecticut, with what credit to his reputation is extremely debatable.

Booth's saga against the Army in a sense did him a grave disservice. It was a standard he or no other back could have lived up to, yet it was almost expected of him. And, of course, he was a marked man by all opponents. He continued to be outstanding. At times, he touched off fire-works of the Army game brilliance, but the Army game, October 26, 1929, was to remain his masterpiece.

For Mal Stevens the 1931 season was to be mad, tragic, exciting, and, in the end, glorious. Booth came back to the headlines. Stevens put in the Notre Dame offense. He didn't have his backs shift from the T into the box, but lined them up in the box, left or right, behind a balanced line. Paul (Bucky) O'Connor, who had played spectacularly in Notre Dame's 1930 victory over Southern California, was requisitioned to help install the new pattern. Benny Friedman, the old Michigan quarterback and passer, also was taken on to work with the passers and to help put in some aerial formations along Michigan lines.

Friedman inadvertently helped repeal one manifestation of a strange influence that was touching Yale football at the time. The Harkness millions had made possible many good things for Yale, for one thing the house system of athletics, providing competitive sports for kids not up to the standards of the college team. But some dispensers of the Harkness largesse thought Yale should adopt the Oxford and Cambridge approach to varsity competition and play only Harvard and Princeton. Word of this got to the Old Blues, the men who had made Yale football, and they fought the trend and beat it.

The Oxford-Cambridge movement at Yale dictated the nonscouting agreement with Princeton in 1927. And in 1931 it was suggested the game be given back to the boys a little more by having the coaches sit in the stands during the game. This was tried out in an early game. The coaches occupied a box adjoining that of President James Rowland Angell. President Angell was in perfect earshot when Benny Friedman delivered criticisms of the play of his passers in loud, striking language. The next game the coaches were back where they belonged.

In the 6–6 tie with Army, black tragedy enshrouded the Bowl. On an Army kickoff to halfback Bob Lassiter, Dick Sheridan, 169-pound Army end, was first downfield. Sheridan hit Lassiter head-on and Lassiter's churning knees hit Sheridan in the back of the head. Dick hit the ground and lay there. Everybody realized he was seriously hurt. They got him to a hospital where X rays revealed a fracture of the fourth cerebral vertebra and a partial fracture of the fifth. Two days later Sheridan died.

His death and numerous other casualties and serious injuries that year brought about rule

changes to make a safer game. The flying block and tackle were banned. Restraining lines prevented flying wedges on kickoff returns. Defensive players were penalized for striking opponents on the head, neck, or face. The ball carrier was down when any portion of his body, except his hands ŏr feet, touched the ground.

The fatal accident to Sheridan preceded by only one week quite the wildest, most exciting game ever seen in the Bowl. Yale vs. Dartmouth usually guarantees schizophrenic behavior. But not before or since has the rivalry produced anything on the delirious level of the 33–33 tie game of 1931. In this maelstrom of scoring and long runs, Booth came back again to the Army game level of his sophomore year. But he was matched by the Big Green's Wild Bill McCall. No adjectives can describe that game adequately, or so well as a simple chronology of what happened.

There was no score in the first quarter.

In the second quarter all hell broke loose and stayed loose. Bill (Air Mail) Morton put Dartmouth ahead with a 34-yard field goal. Booth took the ensuing kickoff on his 6-yard line. Using his blockers with excellent judgment, weaving and sidestepping all over the place, he ran it back 94 yards for a touchdown. Albie missed the point. Yale 6, Dartmouth 3.

Kay Todd, right halfback and lefthanded passer, connected with Booth on a 22-yard aerial for a touchdown. Ed Rotan, Yale guard, missed the point. Yale 12, Dartmouth 3.

Booth broke off tackle and ran 53 yards for a touchdown. He dropkicked the extra point. Yale 19, Dartmouth 3.

Morton threw a 22-yard pass to McCall. The ball bounced off a Yale player's hands, Wild Bill grabbed it and raced 54 yards for a touchdown. Morton added the point. Yale 19, Dartmouth 10.

Lassiter ran 50 yards to the Dartmouth 7. On the third play following, Clem Williamson went over from the 2. Carl Sandberg converted. Yale 26, Dartmouth 10.

Early in the third quarter, Lassiter connected with Barres on a 20-yard pass play for a touchdown. Rotan converted. Yale 33, Dartmouth 10.

McCall ran the next kickoff back 92 yards for a touchdown. Morton place-kicked the conversion. Yale 33, Dartmouth 17.

Roger Donner, Dartmouth end, blocked a kick on Yale's 30, picked up the bounding ball on the 17, and ran for a touchdown. Morton converted. Yale 33, Dartmouth 24.

In the fourth quarter McCall intercepted a pass and ran 60 yards for a touchdown. Morton missed the extra point. Yale 33, Dartmouth 30.

Morton kicked a 23-yard field goal. Yale 33, Dartmouth 33.

Darkness was settling in as Yale tried desperately to score again. Booth and fullback Joe Crowley brought the ball to the Green's 20. Booth was readying for a try at field goal when time ran out.

The crowd was left limp, exhausted. Yale was left exhausted and bitter over blowing a 23-point lead. Coach Mal Stevens was heard to mutter, "We threw too many flat passes." Old Blues were heard muttering for the scalp of Stevens.

The final dramatics for Stevens and Booth fittingly came against Harvard. The Crimson, undefeated in seven games, was beaten 3–0 on Little Boy Blue's 14-yard field goal near the end.

The high, shrill notes of the victory at Harvard pleased Stevens. But he was weary of the clamorous criticisms and second guesses following defeats that had punctuated his regime as they had some of the Tad Jones era, and he was not at all uneager to appease segments of the Old Blues by stepping down and letting another, Reggie Root, take over. Which he did after the '32 season.

Stevens, who was to be an assistant professor in the Yale Medical School, agreed to coach the freshman team in 1933 for $6,000. The following year, Mal began an eight-year term as head coach at New York University.

Stevens did well at NYU as long as he had half-decent material. He brought his 1935 team, undefeated and perhaps headed for a postseason game, into the final game with Fordham, but a superior Ram team, which had lost only to Purdue in a more rugged schedule, beat the Violets, 21–0.

The next year, however, Stevens repaid in kind, upsetting an undefeated Fordham team, 7–6, and denying his friends on Rose Hill, of whom he had won many for his sportsmanship, a trip to the Rose Bowl. The running of halfback George Savarese and the coffin-corner punting of end Howard Dunney, scintillated in this multicarated upheaval.

After a time, Stevens' material fell off to out-and-out anemia, and NYU was badly overscheduled. After 1941 Stevens stepped out to concentrate on orthopedics and polio, but he often found time to drive up to New Haven to watch the Yale games.

As doctor, coach, and man, Mal Stevens always walked tall, handsome, and socially handy. More important, beneath this facade there were generosity, tolerance, and forthrightness that won him many friends.

Jock Sutherland

THE OVERLAND MAN

No football teams ever demonstrated the running attack with more precision, power, and sheen than the Golden Panthers of Pittsburgh in the coaching era, 1924–38, of Dr. John Bain (Jock) Sutherland.

Those Pitt teams exuded the fundamentalism and the sportsmanship of their coach, a man who by nature, undramatic in many ways, dramatized through his teams and himself the American Dream.

One of seven of a widowed mother, Johnny Sutherland emigrated from Scotland and joined his older brother Archie in Pittsburgh at 18, a boy of little means or property. He rose to become a Fellow of the American Dental Society, a man of means and influence, and in the minds of many football students, as fine an all-round coach as ever lived.

In the exclusive pantheon of those who coached 20 years or more, Sutherland's record over five years at Lafayette and 15 at Pittsburgh, 1919 through '38, was surpassed in football's first century only by Knute Rockne, General Robert Reese Neyland, and Fielding (Hurry Up) Yost.

Pittsburgh under Sutherland was the only team Notre Dame ever dropped because it was too tough. From 1932 through '37, Pitt beat the Irish five of six, and shut them out four times. The one loss was in 1935, 9–6.

Sutherland's peers acknowledged his genius, and none more than Rockne and Neyland. The only Rockne team to play Sutherland's, Knute's greatest and last, 1930, was clearly superior and won in Pitt Stadium, 35–19. Leading 35–0 at halftime, Rockne thereafter used reserves, for which Sutherland tendered appreciation with congratulations. Later that season in Chicago, two games away from the national championship, Notre Dame was to meet a strong Army team on a rainy, muddy Soldier's Field, and Rockne was concerned.

"If this was your team, Jock," he asked Sutherland, "how would you attack the problem?"

"I'd keep shooting Schwartz off tackle," replied the Scot. "Sooner or later, he must break loose."

A Pitt yearbook editor once wrote, "Whatever the Old Man says is right." He was right in his advice to the coach rated all-time No. 1. Notre Dame beat Army 7–6 when Marchie Schwartz,

Jock Sutherland

after trying most of the day, finally broke off tackle and ran 56 yards through the mud to a touchdown.

Neyland, voted all-time No. 2, was like Sutherland in his reserve, his disinclination to make public statements. Yet, of Sutherland, he said, "I consider him perhaps the best all-round football coach that ever lived. His teams were invariably fundamentally sound, resolute, and formidable in the clutch. As a man, he was loyal, sincere, devoted, and honest to a fault, and I count it as one of my greatest privileges to have had his friendship."

Sutherland had a strength of mind, body, and purpose as unshakable and craggy as the hills enveloping his native Coupar Angus. Tall, strong, conservatively handsome, with formidable jaw, high cheek bones, blue eyes, and grayish hair parted in the middle and brushed back as sharp

as his off-tackle cutback, he was not a type that encouraged a pat on the back, small talk, or quick friendship. Only his few intimates would think of addressing him otherwise than as "Doctor."

"The Great Stone Face," they called him behind his back. The enemies such a man cannot escape making accused him of vanity, stubbornness, autocracy, all no doubt with some reason. That was only one side of Jock Sutherland. There was another that comprised sentiment, kindness, sensitivity, humor, and conviviality by late candle. Yet, he never married, and asked why, he said: "You know, I don't think a football coach —like me anyway—should be married. Living the game as I live it would be too tough on my partner."

He did have two great loves. The first was his mother, Mary Burns Sutherland, a milliner's assistant descended from the poet Robert Burns. When Mary was 32, her spouse, Archibald Bain Sutherland, a molder who had served abroad with the Highland Light Infantry, suffered a fatal internal rupture trying to save the life of a workman pinned under a fallen girder. His mother's early struggles to support her brood left a deep impression on Sutherland. Until her death, he visited her every summer with gifts and bought her a house. And he would return with gifts for a Scotland Room in Pittsburgh's Tower of Learning skyscraper.

His second love was America, especially the city of Pittsburgh. He felt no other country would have offered him the same warmth and opportunities. It enraged him to hear a speaker attack the United States. He served in both world wars, and passed a rigid physical examination to get into the second at 53, as a naval lieutenant commander in charge of Eastern rehabilitation centers.

For the university, where he earned excellent grades in dentistry and won wide fame as a football guard, weight man in track, and wrestler, his affection was deep-grained. To Dr. H. Clifford (Red) Carlson, his teammate on Pop Warner's 1916 national champions, he wrote years later, "My undergraduate days were the happiest of my life."

Coaching Pitt was no mere job to Jock Sutherland, but a crusade of gratitude. After he resigned in 1938, Navy, Yale, Washington, Ohio State, and others wanted to sign him. Instead, he coached pro teams, the Brooklyn Dodgers and Pittsburgh Steelers, driving ordinary personnel to a competitive plateau by the same methods he had used at Pitt. But he did not choose pro ball by preference; he just could not see himself coaching any college team but Pitt.

"He loved that university," said his Scot friend Jimmy Brown. "By golly it was an obsession with him."

Even when he was coaching the pros, he kept his Pittsburgh residence, Room 514 in the Pitt Athletic Club, because it commanded a view of his beloved campus.

Although he was a driver, an exacting teacher, a stern disciplinarian, Sutherland's players knew he was interested in their futures; he steered many of them into the professions. They knew also that he was inwardly warm, sympathetic to their problems, always their defender. When they lost, they had a feeling they had betrayed him.

Sutherland never criticized a player publicly, and was privately considerate with them, especially in bad times. One of the classic games of the college gridiron was Minnesota's 13–7 victory over the Panthers at Pitt Stadium in 1934. It decided the national championship, the Gophers finishing No. 1, Pitt No. 2. Bernie Bierman stamped his team the best he ever coached, and Pitt the best he ever coached against.

Minnesota came from behind to win in the second half on two superbly executed plays, a reverse to Julie Alphonse and a pass out of a buck lateral from Pug Lund to Bob Tenner, but the decisive factor was the superior line reserves of the Northlanders.

"At the beginning," says guard Milt Bruhn, later a winning coach at Wisconsin, "they blocked us like knives; their technique was beautiful. But . . . late in the game, when we blocked them, we could hear them softly groaning."

Even so, the Gophers probably wouldn't have won without a break, the recovery of a fumbled punt. The receiver was Bobby Larue, then a sophomore, who took a severe battering all afternoon from Bierman's ends, Tenner and Frank (Butch) Larson, and could not be rested because his replacement, Leon Shedlosky, was injured. Two hours after the game, Jock was walking down the hill from the stadium in the gloaming, when a hand tapped him on the shoulder. It was Larue, and he was choked up.

"Doctor," he said, "I'm sorry about fumbling that punt."

"Why that's all right, Bob," the coach said. "Not just one thing, but many went into our losing."

Later in Room 514, Sutherland's eyes were wet

as he told his good friend Chet Smith, sports editor of the Pittsburgh *Press*, "Dammit, Chet, I don't want the lad thinking he's to blame. He's not, you know. If Shedlosky wasn't hurt and I could have used him to give Bobby a little rest, he'd not have fumbled that punt."

Sutherland's coaching characteristics carried over into his dentistry. A dental plate had to be as precisely wrought as an off-tackle thrust, and he would recast until it was.

At the annual picnic of Clan Macpherson No. 5 (Order of the Scottish Clans) which Jock, as a member, usually attended, he was of course a celebrity. On one occasion, with a crowd edging around him, he was approached by a burly Scotsman with a little boy.

"Jock," the man said, "my bairn's got a bad tooth. Have a look at it for 'im, eh? Open your mouth, Gavin, so the doctor can look in."

Although it was hardly the place for such a request, the supposedly cold coach bent down and peered into the mouth of the lad, who scarcely reached his hips. Then Jock straightened and patted him.

"Aye, the lad's mouth needs attention," he said. "Bring him over to the university clinic tomorrow and we'll see what we can do for him."

Helping other men, afflicted as well as gifted, appealed to Sutherland. As a young immigrant, one of his early jobs was attendant in a mental hospital, for which he'd had some training in Scotland. His great strength enabled him to control berserk patients, yet he always did so gently and with compassion.

This almost cost him his life. A violent case he was carrying removed from his sleeve surreptitiously a metal stay he had filed to razor sharpness, and before Sutherland could stop him, he slashed Jock from under his left ear to halfway down his throat, barely missing the jugular. Bleeding profusely, Jock held his struggling charge until help came, and then slumped to the floor. After a critical period he recovered, but he bore the scar all his life.

"The tinsel of life has little appeal to the doctor," a rival coach once said. He didn't know the Scots. Jock was no hail fellow well met, but with his own, in his few hours of relaxation, he savored a glass and a song. His physical stamina enabled him to imbibe richly of the dew from his native hills with no outward signs beyond a slight flush of the cheekbones and accentuation of the burr.

With Clan Macpherson No. 5, he preferred his Scottish favorites, "I'm Sittin' on the Stile, Mary," "The Land of the Leal," and "Oh, But I'm Longin' for My Ain Folk." With alumni friends, he would render "Hail to Pitt." Jock's club was the mystical "College of the North"; members included Bill McClintock—Jock's closest friend —referee Red Friesell, and sportswriters Chet Smith and Les Biederman. McClintock was the college's president and janitor, Jock was coach and dean of women. The curriculum, majors and electives, was exclusively social.

Sutherland had authentic natural wit. He and Chet Smith were driving to a dinner for Jock's greatest back, Marshall Goldberg, in Marshall's native West Virginia. Near an old covered bridge leading into Philippi, West Virginia, where an early Civil War skirmish was fought, they approached a bearded old mountaineer driving a buckboard with an ancient squirrel rifle across his lap. As they passed him, Jock leaned out and yelled: "You're too late, Mister! It's all over and *we* won!"

At a Coach of the Year dinner in Leone's restaurant, New York, in 1946, Sutherland had some fun with one of his earliest Pitt players, Andy Gustafson, later coach and athletic director at Miami of Florida. Gus soon after went on the wagon for keeps, but that night he was in orbit. Several times he tacked up to Sutherland at the bar, leading Dave Camerer, New York *World-Telegram* sportswriter, who had been a star tackle at Dartmouth when Gus was an assistant to Red Blaik there.

"Jock," Gus would say with alcoholic gravity, "what kind of a fullback was I at Pitt? This boy played for me at Dartmouth, and I think a lot of him. I want him to hear it. What kind of fullback was I, Jock?"

Sutherland, who had probably taken on three times as much Scotch as Gustafson, was refusing to answer and enjoying it. Finally, however, after a plea that was piteous, he relented.

"Ondy," he said, "you wur a fair runner—but you never could block worth a dom!"

Early in the fall of 1937, Sutherland was invited to Hanover by Blaik, who had incorporated some of his single wing into the Dartmouth attack. At the time, Jock's Pitt teams, with Goldberg, were at high tide, but his relationships with W. Don Harrison, the athletic director, and John Gabbert Bowman, Pitt's president, were worsening.

Jock watched Dartmouth practice accompanied by President Ernest Martin Hopkins, who had picked Blaik for the job. Blaik's teams were

good, but somewhat below Pitt's in personnel. When President Hopkins asked Sutherland, in earshot of Blaik, what he thought, however, the Scot stuck his tongue back over a wisdom tooth and burred: "I wish I could coach a squad like this at Pittsburgh just once, Mister Hopkins. Just once."

Blaik, who recognized the rib, blanched, nevertheless, but he too had a sense of humor. He recovered quickly and offered Jock a trade, President Hopkins even up for Marshall Goldberg. Jock shook his head.

"Much as I would like to have Mister Hopkins," he said, "I still must have someone to carry the ball."

Today it seems a fiction that in 1935, '36, and '37, before sellout crowds in New York's Polo Grounds, nationally ranked Pitt and Fordham played three successive scoreless ties, a record not likely to be matched. Much Ado about Nothing to Nothing, but fierce, tense games that had the crowd continuously on edge. In 1935 Fordham had the edge, in '36 it was even, but in '37 Pitt probably would have won except for eight fumbles, five by the superb Panther right halfback, Hal (Curly) Stebbins. After the game, a writer made so bold as to ask Sutherland why he hadn't removed Stebbins after the fourth fumble.

"I'd no way of knowing," replied Jock, "that he was going to fumble a fifth time."

That eight fumbles by a Pitt team was atypical is an understatement. Paucity of turnovers, traceable to meticulous execution, was one of the things that made the Panthers a scourge. Cremo, a popular cigar of the time, advertised, "Spit is a horrid word, but it's worse on the end of your cigar." A punster parodied, "Pitt is a horrid word, but it's worse on your five-yard line." Or any place else. Said Dick Harlow, himself an outstanding single-wing innovator:

"The coach with the greatest ground attack against the strongest teams in my time was Jock Sutherland. Remember, everyone was shooting at him. ... He ran Notre Dame right off the schedule. ... The Pitt team could pick off, check, and destroy a shifting defense better than any team I ever saw."

Pitt would begin by attacking the flanks and off tackle by sweeps, cutbacks, and reverses, and after the defensive line widened to compensate, would attack inside tackle and up the middle. Jock designed his plays to get four blockers against two defenders at the critical point. "If we can do that," he said, "we'll gain ground." First-down objective was a minimal four yards;

then the next two plays should make first down.

Sutherland, like Neyland, rehearsed every play as if it were an investment representing millions. He would trace the blocking routes with a stick until the pulling linemen ran them to the inch and split second. No other coach came closer to reducing the running game to a pure science.

His naked reverse, or "Sally Rand," in which the wingback reversed without even one blocker, worked time and again because the execution tricked smart defenses. The deceptive key was the wingback's fake block on the defensive tackle; he threw his shoulder into him then reversed away from him, and the ball, well hidden, was handed to him by the tailback right at the off-tackle hole.

Sally Rand wasn't Pitt's only long gainer. Jock liked to control the ball, clock, field position, and scoreboard by long, grinding marches that punished the defense, but the Panthers also could win explosively. In the 1927 victory over a powerful Nebraska team, 21–13, one of Sutherland's Pitt Stadium classics, the Panthers scored on a 90-yard return of the opening kickoff by left halfback Gibby Welch, a 63-yard off-tackle run by Jim (Whitey) Hagan, and a 76-yard reverse pass play from Hagan to Welch.

Pitt's devotion to the running attack caused Jock's friends to kid him that he considered the forward pass not only cowardly but immoral. It's true his greatest team, 1937, used it sparingly, because it had no outstanding passer. But from 1930 through '32, when he had Warren Heller, a superior passer, Pitt used the pass often; three-year record: 22–4–3. And when he lacked a passer in '38, and Southern Methodist packed its defense against the run, Pitt went into the air almost exclusively to win 34–7, a strategy not only sound but ironic, since no team was more famous for the pass than SMU.

In an era when the punt on third down or earlier deep in one's own territory was dominant, Pitt kicked only on fourth down, regardless of field position, because Jock wanted to keep the ball as long as possible. Naturally, with that running game. He was unorthodox also in having his center not snap the ball in spiral but flip it end over end. "I don't have the time to teach the spiral," he claimed. Actually, he felt the spiral snap was more likely to be fumbled, and that it put needless pressure on his center.

He selected his centers carefully for their ability to keep clearheaded in the severest situation. "If the ball is not fed to the back on the exact count and to exactly the right spot, the timing of the play must suffer," he explained. An

effective play cannot be faster than your slowest man, he reasoned, and he insisted his offensive linemen have superior mobility.

Accurate centering and sure protection gave Pitt's punters a confidence that paid off. Pitt's first victory over Notre Dame, 1932 in Pitt Stadium, 12–0, came after the Irish had dominated the game for three periods. A kick by quarterback Bob Hogan turned things around. Standing well back in the end zone, he hoisted one 80 yards over the safety man's head to gain Pitt field position, from which right halfback Mike Sebastian went off right tackle for a 46-yard scoring run behind beauty blocking. Then, when Notre Dame went into the air, left end Ted Dailey intercepted a pass on Pitt's 40 and took it in.

Perhaps because of his success against Notre Dame, the following week Hogan was too confident. Pitt beat Pennsylvania at Franklin Field, 19–12, but had to fight for its life after Don Kellet returned Hogan's kick all the way for the Red and Blue's second touchdown. Kellet got free because Pitt's coverage wasn't there. They had acceded to Hogan's request that they concentrate in protecting him because he said he was going to boot the ball clear out of the stadium, which he didn't.

Pitt players were recruited as they were coached, to meet calibrated specifications. Most of them came from the nearby lush Western Pennsylvania soft-coal region. Jimmy Hagan, who joined the coaching staff after graduation and later succeeded Harrison as athletic director, recruited the great players of the thirties, about 19 to 23 a year. He seldom picked them by position, but went after the toughest, most mobile athletes. Jock would fit them into the right spots. Many of Pitt's guards, quarterbacks, and centers had been high school fullbacks.

Many of the players were recruited on their potential to fill two jobs. The quarterback not only had to call the plays and block, but also had to play left linebacker on defense. The right linebacker on defense was the offensive center. Both halfbacks had to be good blockers, because the left halfback was the wingback from formation left, the right halfback from formation right. On defense the right halfback played safety, the left half fullback, and the fullback right half. When Sutherland went from a 6–2–2–1 defense into the 6–3–2 that imprisoned Notre Dame, the fullback became middle linebacker.

Sutherland's mastery as leader, teacher, disciplinarian, strategist, and tactician bred in his

The Scotsman, *left,* with assistant Bill Kern, observing his 1934 Panthers in action. *Chicago Tribune Photos*

players a confidence, individually and collectively, that was almost arrogance.

Jock was much more of a psychologist than credited. The Pitt team never came onto the field until just before the kickoff. The players sat in their dressing room while the opponents warmed up for 20 minutes, running through plays, passing, punting—and finally wondering when those fierce Panthers would show up. About two minutes before the kickoff, Pitt, helmets on, would come racing out of the dressing room. Three units would run one series of plays the length of the field, and then gather around the doctor while the coin was flipped. This didn't bother the Minnesotas or Fordhams, but it had its effect on others.

Since Pitt in Sutherland's time had no dormitories or food service, and there was a depression on, the players roomed and ate where they could on money channeled from alumni, $48.50 a month. Under the bastard philosophy, a hangover from the British, that he only is an amateur who can afford to play sports without help, the National Collegiate Athletic Association, thanks mainly to the Western Conference, had declared this illegal.

Technically then, Pitt was breaking a rule. Practically, without the money the players could not have stayed in college. What Pitt did was not

only proper but more honest than the jobs, aids, and grants employed by the Big Ten and others who also ignored the not infrequent under-the-table gratuities.

The Carnegie Investigation Committee of the early thirties knew all about this. And Pitt's position has long since been vindicated by the NCAA's cost-of-living code.

Perhaps because he did not want his players, who lived humbly at Pitt, to be upset by elegance abroad, Sutherland demanded that the pregame atmosphere on the road be comfortable but ungaudy. For the 1934 game at Navy, the Panthers were booked at Washington's Wardman Park Hotel. But when Jock walked in and surveyed the sumptuous lobby, he ordered Hagan to find a modest country club nearby. Then Jock, followed by the team, stalked out.

Sutherland himself never had been exposed to luxury. As a boy of eight in Coupar Angus, he was up at four and to his job as a "loon," a light farmhand. He caddied, once for the famous Harry Vardon. He worked for the railroad as a youthful porter and baggage clerk. He meanwhile managed to complete grammar grades.

One of his first jobs in America was policeman in Sewickley, Pennsylvania, and it was the director of the YMCA there, Leslie Mold, and another friend, Lou McMaster, who encouraged Sutherland to study on the side and aspire to college. At Oberlin (Ohio) Academy, where he prepped for Pitt, Jock waited tables, shoveled snow, and ran a laundry agency.

Although he had played a bit of soccer in Scotland, Sutherland played in the first football game he ever saw, as a freshman guard for Pitt in 1914 under Coach Joe Duff. The Panthers lost only one game that year, and none the next three under Pop Warner, who had already won fame as coach of the Carlisle Indians. Jock's strength, competitiveness, and sure instinct for the game made him an All-America guard. He also won honors in track and wrestling, and probably would have made a rated professional boxer. He won the Middle Atlantic States AAU boxing championship by a second-round knockout of a touted local fighter, one Charleston, reputed about to turn pro and take on the redoubtable Gunboat Smith, who once had Jack Dempsey in trouble.

Between his second and last year of dentistry, Jock took other courses, to diversify his education and also be eligible for sports a fourth year. He got his dental degree in 1918, enlisted in the army, and was stationed in Chickamauga, Georgia. It was there he did his first coaching, of the championship Camp Greenleaf team. After the armistice, while practicing in Duquesne, he accepted an offer to become head coach at Lafayette, and for the next five years he handled the Leopards in the fall and the rest of the year was a dentist in the University of Pittsburgh clinic.

His five-year record at Lafayette was 33–8–2; his 1921 team went 9–0. That year and in '22 he beat Warner's Pitt team 6–0 and 7–0, and when Pop left to coach Stanford in 1924, there was little debate about who'd succeed him. Jock's 15-year record at Pitt was 111–20–12, seven Eastern, two national championships, four Rose Bowl games (a fifth bid turned down), and 24 All-America selections.

The Rose Bowl was the backdrop of his worst hours and his finest. The first year, 1928, the Panthers visited the Arroyo Seco (dry gulch) where sits the storied saucer, and were edged by Warner's Stanford team, 7–6, in a grueling battle of lines.

That was unsatisfactory but respectable. On the second and third visits, however, 1930 and '33, the Panthers were all but skinned by two of Howard Jones' Southern California powerhouses, 47–14 and 35–0. To Sutherland, a proud man, especially proud of coaching his alma mater, the humiliation was hard to bear.

To explain what happened to Pitt, some arrant nonsense was circulated: Sutherland's pass defense was unsound, the players had been seduced by Hollywood glitter.

The real answers made some sense. In both games, Southern California's personnel was superior. Pitt stayed in the 1930 game until the third quarter and might have done better, except for the one dissension ever seriously to impede a Sutherland team. It was caused by that not unmitigated blessing, All-America. Halfback Toby Uansa, end Joe Donchess, and guard Ray Montgomery made it. The other guard, Captain Luby DiMeolo didn't, but thought he should have, as did several of his teammates. The thing developed rival factions, and by kickoff time feeling was bitter.

The 1932 team, tied by Ohio State and Nebraska, was ordinary by Sutherland standards. The Rose Bowl bid should have gone to Andy Kerr's Colgate team, "unbeaten, untied, unscored on, and uninvited," but Don Harrison, the Pitt athletic director and a very good one, had friends

Jock's Dream Backfield, *left to right*: Harold Stebbins, Marshall Goldberg, Richard Cassiano, John Chickerneo

on the selection committee. What Harrison spent on good-will booze and caviar was more than covered by the check he brought home.

"That Pitt team," said Chet Smith, "had to be one of the poorest to play at Pasadena. The paper was on a poverty kick at the time, so I listened to the horrible details at the University Club midst friends and liquor."

Four years later, again partly through the offices of Harrison, Pitt got the bid, despite a campaign mounted by Louisiana State and supported by the Los Angeles press, which wanted to see Huey Long, the LSU band, and the Tiger mascot; the team was also attractive. The writers belabored the selection, recalling Pitt's last two appearances, which gave Sutherland a psychological weapon he didn't need.

Despite an upset by Duquesne, then a strong team, and the second goose-egg affair with Fordham, Pitt had thrashed Notre Dame 26–0 with sophomore Goldberg running 156 yards, a fan-

tastic total then, and had shut out Ohio State while not throwing a single pass. The 1936 Panthers at their best were a match for any team.

As the Pitt bus with police escort approached the descent into the Arroyo Seco, Sutherland ordered the driver to stop. Then he got up and pointed to the Bowl.

"There it is," Jock told his players. "There's the place two Pittsburgh teams were beaten by a total of 68 points."

As the bus moved on Bobby Larue said quietly, "That is not going to happen today."

With Larue, Goldberg, and fullbacks Frank Patrick and Bill Stapulis driving behind blackout blocks and supported by an intractable defense, Pitt beat Washington 21–0. Larue scored the first two touchdowns. How Pitt scored the third can now be told under protection of the statute of limitations.

Pitt had wanted to exchange films with Washington, but Jimmy Phelan, the Huskies coach,

demurred. Joe E. Brown, the famous comedian, a Sutherland friend and fan who even traveled across country to see the team, now took a hand. His son attended UCLA, which had played Washington, and young Brown somehow acquired films of the Bruin-Husky game, for study by Pitt at its San Bernardino headquarters.

Washington had a favorite play in which a trailing back took a lateral, and after Bill Daddio, Pitt's All-America left end, had watched it a few times, he said to Sutherland, "Doctor, I believe I can pick off one of those." And Daddio did, for a 60-yard touchdown run.

The aftermath was less pleasurable for Pitt. Both teams had been invited to a dinner-dance. Washington's players had the necessary walking-around money. Most of Pitt's didn't until Sutherland divided among them $300 he had received for a radio appearance.

This aggravated the asperity between Sutherland and Harrison, and things got worse after the undefeated 1937 season when another Rose Bowl bid was extended and voted against by the players, all without Jock's knowledge. Harrison resigned soon after, but the 1938 season was played under future uncertainty and foreboding.

This was the season of Pitt's Dream Backfield: Marshall Goldberg at fullback, Dick Cassiano and Curly Stebbins at left and right halfbacks, and Johnny Chickerneo at quarterback. To make it possible, Goldberg, a selfless player, shifted to fullback and was All-America there as he had been at left half. It was truly one of the all-time great backfields, but time and fortune caught up with it.

Sutherland's last high hour came when the

Panthers rallied from a 7–3 deficit for three fourth-period touchdowns and a 24–13 triumph over Fordham, as first Cassiano and then Goldberg, twice, finally crossed the Rams' goal line. It was a sensational, collisive struggle witnessed by 75,857, to this day a record crowd for an event in Pittsburgh of any kind.

Jock rated that game, the 1934 loss to Minnesota, the 1927 victory over Nebraska, and the 1932 win over Notre Dame as the four classics played by his teams in the hillside stadium that opened in 1925, his second year as coach.

After the Fordham game, it was downhill. A splendid Carnegie Tech team, beautifully coached by Sutherland's former tackle and first assistant, Bill Kern, beat the Panthers, 20–10. Goldberg, who had injured a knee against Ford-

Jock in 1934. *Chicago Tribune Photos*

ham, had to leave early in the Tech game. With the shadows lengthening and Pitt facing defeat, Marshall wanted to get back in so badly that Sutherland almost had to use force to restrain him.

Two weeks later, at Durham, Duke's Seven Iron Dukes line, Eric (the Red) Tipton's controlled kicking, and a snowstorm combined to beat Pitt 7–0 in its last game under Jock Sutherland. He resigned because Pitt's football future, as planned by Hagan, now athletic director with the support of Chancellor Bowman, called for less material but continuing strong schedules.

The Big Ten and Notre Dame were influencing the move. The Irish had dropped Pitt, Wisconsin had begged out of a two-game series. A general blackball was on, citing the $48.50 a month the Pitt players received as the reason, when the true reason was their inability to cope with Sutherland's teams.

Hagan and his faction also labored under the illusion that if Pitt deemphasized its material and adopted a less-direct aid program, it might get the Western Conference slot left by Chicago. This was a misconception. Pitt's scheduling traditionally had its roots eastward, and it could have made good schedules by continuing as it was.

In resigning and afterwards, Sutherland made no comment that would embarrass the school. In the statement he released, he did include that he had written Chancellor Bowman, "The future athletic course is so indefinite and vague that ... it will be for the best interests of all concerned if I ask you to accept my resignation."

At a testimonial dinner a month later, he said, "I have tried hard to give back part of what I have owed to Pittsburgh since I came to this city as a youth ... and found here teachers and good friends to guide me on my way. I shall not say good-bye, but rather good-night and God bless you."

With Sutherland and the good material gone, Pitt got Notre Dame and the Big Nine back on its schedules. The Panthers lost 10 of 11 to the Irish and 24 straight to the holy conference teams. And Michigan State, not Pitt, got Chicago's old spot, in what surely was poetic justice. Meanwhile, Sutherland was reaffirming his coaching genius, first at Brooklyn, later with the Pittsburgh Steelers. His Steeler teams sold out Pitt Stadium.

The Steelers were astonished when suddenly he put down the chalk and walked out of the room. An excruciating headache had seized him, as it had continually for weeks. He was too busy, he thought, to undergo examination during the season. He planned to afterwards, but kept putting it off. On March 25, despite the pleas of his favorite sister, Marion, he drove south on a scouting trip. He visited Wally Wade at Duke and Peahead Walker at Wake Forest, and then, which was unusual, the office didn't hear from him for several days.

Soon after sunup on April 7, near the little town of Bandana, Kentucky, a milkman stopped his truck. The tall man walking along in a daze, his car in a nearby ditch, seemed to need help. All he would say, though, was, "I'm Jock Sutherland. I'm Jock Sutherland." He accepted a ride from the milkman into town and to the sheriff's office. The sheriff questioned him, and he repeated, "I'm Jock Sutherland."

"Do you think you ought to carry this wallet around? Don't you think somebody might take it from you?" the sheriff asked.

Jock's dazed blue eyes blazed briefly. "Do you think anybody could?" he asked.

John Michelosen, his quarterback of 1937 championship days, and other friends came down and flew him home. He underwent two brain operations of two hours each, but there was no hope. The tumor was rampant, and at 4:15 the morning of April 11, John Bain Sutherland passed on.

The Cathedral Episcopal Church overflowed with old players, football men from all over, state and city officials, Pittsburghers who knew him only by name but who admired him. Somebody said, "The Old Man always did pack them in." In his brief eulogy, Right Reverend Austin Pardue, Episcopal bishop of Pittsburgh, spoke of "the stalwart training, the goodly influence he exerted on men ... the joy he gave to lovers of football." Afterwards, hundreds stood around the grave in Homewood Cemetery, while in the background rose the melancholy strain of a bagpipe. His old friend, Grantland Rice wrote:

There's a fog now over Scotland, and a mist on Pittsburgh's field;
No valiant hand to flash the sword or hold the guiding shield.
There's a big, braw fellow missing from the golden land of fame,
For Jock Sutherland has left us—and the game is not the same.

Frank Thomas

TOMMY

When the college football Hall of Fame first opened its doors in 1951, the original 22 coaches to enter included two Notre Dame men. One was Knute Kenneth Rockne. The other was Rockne's 1922 quarterback, Frank William Thomas.

Even after a few social glasses, Frank Thomas was not one to gush with sentiment or let money slip through his fingers faster than mucilage. Nevertheless, Tommy would have bought a round, had he known that he alone would accompany his old coach into formal immortality.

Tommy, indeed, would have ordered a second round in memory of George Gipp, who was among the original 22 players inducted. For Gipp

had been roommate, friend, and teacher to the five foot eight rotund but tough little Welshman from the iron-foundry district of East Chicago, Indiana. If Tommy had an idol beyond his wife Frances and his three children, Rita, Frank Jr., and Hugh Rowe, it had to be that real legend from Calumet, Michigan, the Gipper.

Endorsement of Frank Thomas as Rockne's most successful postgraduate in football was no surprise. His 15-year record at Alabama, beginning in 1931, plus his earlier four years at Chattanooga, stands No. 10 in all-time winning percentages. No question about his belonging in the top ten; the question is: No. 10—or higher? If you consider the challenge and pressure he faced and conquered, probably higher.

The man Tommy succeeded at Alabama, Wallace Wade, had made the Crimson Tide —also known then as the Red Elephants—a national name. In three visits to the Rose Bowl, the Tide had swept over Washington and Washington State, and played a tie with Stanford. The 20–19 victory over the Huskies, through an incredible seven-minute, 20-point comeback in the third quarter, gave Southern football the final push to equality with the best of the nation.

The 1930 team, however, Wade's last at the Capstone, was his best. At Pasadena it whipped, 24–0, a Washington State team built around two classic linemen, center Mel Hein and tackle Turk Edwards. Before he began that 1930 season, Wade had accepted an offer from Duke, and had recommended to Dr. Mike Denny, president of Alabama, that Thomas be named his successor.

After graduating with a law degree in 1923, Thomas had been hired, on Rockne's recommendation, by George (Kid) Woodruff to be his assistant at Georgia. He thus became the first man to introduce the Notre Dame system to the South. The following year, Harry Mehre, a Notre Dame teammate at center, joined him at Georgia, and under Kid Woodruff they built the Bulldogs into a power.

In 1925, Thomas began four impressive years at Chattanooga. In 1928, Mehre succeeded Woodruff as head coach and convinced Tommy that if he'd return to Georgia as an assistant, it would be a higher springboard to a major head coaching post than top man at Chatty. Probably he also got Tommy more money.

Mehre's prediction proved sound. Although Dr. Denny and Wallace Wade, neither a square-dance leader type, sometimes got along like hostile lions, Denny respected Wade and told him

Frank Thomas, at Alabama

to sound out Thomas. Tommy also had the support of Borden Burr, old Alabama quarterback and a power in its athletic policies, and Ed Camp, influential conductor of the Atlanta *Journal*'s sports column, "Old Timer."

On Sunday, July 15, 1930, Tommy, Dr. Denny, Burr, and Camp sat in Burr's Birmingham office. The day was more stifling than an illegal huddle in hell, and the smoke from Dr. Denny's well-known pipe enhanced the humidity. So—after Tommy had signed the contract—did Dr. Denny's advice.

"Mr. Thomas," he said, "now that you have accepted our proposition, I will give you the benefit of my views, based on my years of observation. It is my conviction that material is 90 percent and coaching is 10 percent. I desire further to say that you will be provided with the 90 percent, and that you will be held to strict accounting for the 10 percent."

Tommy and Camp left Burr's office together. On the stairs Tommy said, "Those were the hardest and coldest words I ever heard in all my life. Do you reckon those 90 and 10 percentages are right?"

"I think that they are considerably off," replied Camp. "But there is no doubt that the good doctor means what he says."

Dr. Denny's mandate would have been difficult to digest *after* Wade's 1930 season; the

coach who follows a dynasty is red meat to "dynostaurs." Tommy had to digest it all *through* that '30 season. As Wade's guest at the Rose Bowl, he also had to watch a starting lineup from which only one man would return.

On the whole, it is difficult to conceive of a coach facing a more severe challenge. It is impossible to conceive of a coach giving it a stronger answer.

Wade's eight-year record at Alabama was 61–13–3, .811; Tommy's 15-year record was 115–24–7, .812. (His 19-year mark, including Chatty, is 141–33–9, .795.) Wade and Tommy each notched three perfect regular-season records plus one marred only by a tie. Like Wade, Tommy brought three teams to the Rose Bowl: they defeated Stanford 29–13, lost to California 13–0, and beat Southern California 34–14. Give Wade a half-game edge there, if you will.

Wade's and Thomas' Bowl game monies began and fattened the 'Bama savings account that by 1955 had reached $2 million. It built the natatorium and coliseum, supported the entire athletic program without recourse to state funds, and assisted the College of Engineering and other academic areas.

Tommy and his astute business manager, who is now director of alumni affairs, Jefferson Jackson Coleman, operated on a principle of Bowls and black ink. Tommy, as athletic director, watched the money as if it were his own. No halfhearted block or derelict officiating angered him as much as fiduciary wastefulness.

Outward anger was something he learned to control as he grew up. Instances of his flaring up are few. Once, a St. Louis linebacker tackled him with such enthusiasm that he arose with an incipient shiner. He wanted to fight, but teammates interposed. The offender was Bob Hannegan, later United States Postmaster General.

Another time, Bill Lee, who later became an All-America tackle, reacted with open negativism to a dressing down by Tommy. Lee had maybe seven inches and 50 pounds on the little coach, but Tommy grabbed him by the shoulders, stood on tiptoe in a vain attempt to look Bill straight in the eye, and screamed at him, "You *will* be impudent! You *will* be impudent! I'll kick you over the gymnasium! Right over the gymnasium!"

It was a humorous but meaningful vignette. Lee—and the rest of the squad—got the message. The little man was the boss man.

Neither Hannegan nor Lee, however, roused the ire of Thomas like a dubious athletic business proposition that was proposed to him early in his career at Alabama.

The whole thing was a gag, perpetrated by Tommy's fellow Southeastern Conference athletic directors, and a couple of newspapermen, Fred Russell, veteran sports editor and columnist of the Nashville *Banner*, and Bill Tucker of United Press. Tucker had just been assigned to the UP's Atlanta office, so was relatively unknown in the South.

The background was the annual SEC outdoor track meet in Birmingham, an occasion for athletic directors and coaches of all sports to get together for business and fun. They even got around sometimes to watching the track meet, although outdoor track, even to athletic directors and perhaps especially in the South, has spectator appeal and box-office impact somewhere east of croquet and west of an international chess championship conducted by mail.

The scene was a chamber of commerce luncheon staged for the visiting sport folks. Tucker, known to few other than the plotters, was listed as a speaker under an assumed name, and introduced as the promoter of a five-man traveling professional track troupe: discus thrower, javelin man, shot-putter, broad jumper, and two-miler. Tucker informed his audience that he wanted to schedule his troupe into five carefully chosen Southern campuses to put on exhibitions.

The audience heard him in curiosity and wonder. Was he a mad visionary, or just a naive amateur track buff with more cash than cool?

A professional five-man track troupe giving exhibitions on Southern campuses? It would do less business than the *Cyclorama* in Atlanta advertising a new mural devoted exclusively to William Tecumseh Sherman.

"I am in a position," Tucker continued, beaming by now, "to deliver these scintillant specialists preferably to the campuses of those fine institutions at Athens, Georgia; Auburn and Tuscaloosa, Alabama; and Oxford and Starkville, Mississippi. And"—pause for effect—"at a guarantee from each school for only $750."

Request for such a patently absurd sum turned audience wonder to astonishment. This must be an escaped madman! A few began to sense a gag. But Frank Thomas was seething. He was ready to fight when, by prearrangement, first Wally Butts and then Dudy Noble, athletic directors of Georgia and Mississippi State, got up and declared that such an attraction would sell out for sure at

Athens and Starkville, and that they would be happy, here and now, to pledge the $750 guarantee.

Then Tommy got up to state Alabama's reaction. He not only turned down the offer, but gave Tucker, Butts, and Noble sulfurous hell.

"Tommy was so impressive in his denunciation," Fred Russell recalled, "that all stags present had their supply of salty phrases enriched immeasurably."

Tommy's business acumen augmented his income through real estate and an automobile agency. He socked the money away to provide well for the family he was so proud of. (It also came in handy when illness all but immobilized him the last ten years of his life.)

"Frances was always my inspiration," he said. "From the day we were married she spurred me on to greater efforts, and when things looked gloomy, she cheered me up. Except for that first season of 1931. Even Frances couldn't cheer me up that fall."

Johnny Cain, the lone returning regular from 1930, was a superior punter and runner, and had also called signals for Wade. Cain, Tommy decided, however, was too modest for his own good; he was calling other people to carry the ball too often. So Tommy switched the generalship duties to halfback Hillson Holley.

Tommy got criticized for this, and also for the 25–0 defeat by Robert Reese Neyland's Tennessee team. Neyland came into that game with a five-season record (plus three games) of 43–2–3, America's best. But Wade had beaten him the year before, 18–6, after losing two tight ones, 6–0 and 15–13.

(No Southern coach ever ended up ahead of Neyland. He scored 6–3–1 against Tommy, but it was closer than that, really. Tommy narrowed the margin to 7–3 his second year, and got three victories and a tie his next four jousts with R. R., before losing to the best three Vol teams that Neyland ever put back to back, 1938–40. And Tommy was a sick man in their last confrontation, a 12–0 Vol triumph in '46.)

When the final returns for 1931 showed 9–1, however, even the most rabid Tuscaloosan rebels allowed the new man hadn't done too poorly his first year. He had also recruited a very talented freshman squad. In 1932 and '33, the records were 8–2 and 7–1–1, the three losses to Tennessee, Georgia Tech, and Fordham by a total of 12 points. In 1934, Tommy had the Tide ready to roll for real.

Remember Rube Goldberg's simpleton hero, Bob McNutt, and his little brother, who because he was always asking for things from the moon, up or down, was known as Wanna McNutt? Wanna McNutt would have made the perfect patron saint for nutboy football fans, who wanna win 'em all and who wanna always be No. 1, so they can chant, like the nutboys they are, "We're No. 1."

The Wanna McNutts of the twenties and thirties were not totally unreasonable; they never said, "We wanna be an instant dynasty." They inspired, however, the Associated Press and United Press to institute in 1936 the weekly and final national ratings of the teams, a guessing game not altogether harmless to teams and coaches. Not that they influence the Wanna McNutts, who are their own authorities.

Now, 1934 was truly a vintage year for the Wannas. Each season since 1920 had developed more and more quality teams, but none produced such quality packed near the top. Undefeated Minnesota under Bernie Bierman had its best team. Except for 1937, Pitt had its best. The Navy, which lost only to Pitt, had one of its best. Pitt's lone defeat, 13–7 to Minnesota, was regarded in the East and West as the game that decided the national championship. It was not so regarded in the South and with some foundation.

The '34 Alabama team stands today as the best ever to come out of the South, at least in single-platoon times. It has a high place among the very best of the twenties and thirties: Minnesota '34, Notre Dame '30, Pittsburgh '37 and '34, Southern California '31, Tennessee '38, Yale '23, Michigan '25, Georgia Tech '28, Texas Christian '38, Texas Aggies '39, and California '20.

The '34 Tidemen had everything a team needs, including quality depth. The top star was one of the authentic triple-threat backs of history, a kid from the little town of Hartford, Alabama, Millard (Dixie) Howell. Howell was an outstanding kicker—in one game, against St. Mary's, he booted the ball from his end zone in the air past midfield four times. He could run a broken field, and get short crisis yardage inside like a fullback. He was also a superior passer. His No. 1 receiver had developed that year into one of the best any college team ever knew, Don Hutson. For all-time college passing combinations, Howell-to-Hutson must rate at or near the top.

The team the '34 'Bamans met at Pasadena was also distinctly superior, the Stanford "Vow Boys." They had vowed as freshmen they never would

lose to Southern California, and they made it good. Meanwhile, under Coach Claude (Tiny) Thornhill, they won three straight Pacific Coast championships and were in three Rose Bowls —1934, '35, and '36.

Stanford's supporters believed with some reason that the '34 team was on a par with Minnesota or Pittsburgh. They also believed without reason that it was superior to Alabama. Their squad was studded with stars, especially fullback Bobby Grayson, end Monk Moscrip, tackle Robert Reynolds, and halfback Bones Hamilton. True, they had been beaten as sophomores by Columbia's KF-79 team in what still rates as the daddy of all Bowl upsets, but that, they felt sure, was an accident, and the best way to prove it would be by beating the best.

Their first choice was Minnesota, but the Gophers couldn't come; the Big Ten then had a ban on postseason games. So Alabama was a second choice, by necessity as well as by right. But the Wanna McNutts, Palo Alto Chapter, still clamored publicly, "We want Minnesota!" And Alabama, already requiring no psychological impetus, heard. Tommy said afterwards, "No fight talk was needed that day."

When Stanford scored first, segments of their rooters chanted, "We want Minnesota!" The chant was soon muted; Howell went to work. Howard Jones, the great Southern Cal coach, said, "Never did I see one player so dominate a game." He scored the first touchdown from close up, and put the Tide ahead to stay with a 67-yard run from short punt formation through a broken field, with the Tuscaloosans upending the Altoans like candlepins.

Then Dixie put the game beyond reach of Stanford by hitting Hutson with passes in front of and behind Hamilton, a good defensive man. Don proved that day, as he reaffirmed in professional ball, that he simply could not be covered by one man. Even Jock Sutherland, in his days coaching the Pittsburgh Steelers, finally admitted it.

Long before the first fingers of evening, as the poet would say, reached out across the Arroyo Seco, a new Wanna McNutt detachment was in action: Alabama rooters were chanting, "We want Minnesota!"

If Frank Thomas had a coaching weakness, nobody ever discovered it. To begin with, he surrounded himself with strong assistants. His teams always enjoyed ultimate physical condition, fourth-quarter "bottom." To help keep them

Thomas watching his Tidemen work out. *Chicago Tribune Photos*

fresh as long as possible, he originated the idea of halftime sponge baths from the waist up. In getting a team ready for a Bowl game, he was among the best.

"Getting mentally and physically ready for a postseason game," he said, "is a coach's toughest job. You are invited to play about a month before the game, and many things can happen that will interfere with preparation. Teams have lost Bowl games because they weren't psychologically keen. They have lost because they mislaid the physical edge by too much work or by not enough. I always kept in mind the definition of condition, 'that fleeting moment between getting ready and going stale.'"

Like all successful coaches, Tommy was conservative, but not hidebound. He modified the Notre Dame balanced line, shift from T to box right or left attack by also shifting into a short

punt. From this he ran traps and power sweeps, slants and thrusts to the weak side that forced the defense to overcommit and set up passes. One of football's most scholarly coaches, Carl Snavely incorporated some of Tommy's plays into his own brilliant offense.

Although he did not buy Dr. Denny's 90 and 10 percentages, Tommy genuflected to the truism, the worst mistake a coach can make is to get caught without material. Even when he didn't enjoy the edge, however, he won his share. In fact, he always thought he would win, or looking back, thought he should have, sometimes even against the evidence. He felt that he did his best coaching job with his 1937 team; it went through the regular season undefeated, but four of the wins were by a total of 19 points.

California had its very fine "Thunder Team" that year and invited Pitt to the Rose Bowl. The Panthers, who had carved up Washington there the year before, 21–0, declined. Alabama again was second choice, and had the impulsion of having been sidetracked for Pitt the year before, even though undefeated while the Panthers were beaten by Duquesne. Cal figured to win and did, 13–0, but Tommy blamed himself. "I was told we couldn't run on Cal," he said. "I found out too late that we could run but couldn't pass on them."

Tommy gave off the appropriate amount of coachly pessimism, yet he did not parade ludicrous gloom. Before the 1941 team beat the Texas Aggies in the Cotton Bowl, 29–21, he told writers, "I do not see how they can stop our backs." The press found him good copy, and also a good social companion. He arrived in street clothes and less than pristine health for a morning practice before the '38 Rose Bowl game. As he tried to follow the first team racing up and down the field in a signal drill, he huffed and puffed. In an aside to his reveling press companions, he asked, "Why do they have to run these plays so fast?"

In his early coaching years, he was not inclined to restrain the horses, but with the years he learned to ease up. He enjoyed relating how his 1942 team had a 29–0 lead at the half on South Carolina, coached by his good friend and 1926 Notre Dame fullback, Rex Enright. Getting Enright aside, he said, "Don't do any more passing, and don't kick until fourth down. Keep the ball as long as you can."

The kindly conniving worked; the second half was scoreless. But when Tommy walked into the Gamecocks' dressing room to shake with Enright, a South Carolina player, spotting him from the showers, shouted, "If we got going in the first half like we did in the second, you lucky bums never would have scored!"

If one of his coaching assets transcended all others, it was one that many a top coach has been short on, the ability to make quick and effective decisions during game crises. No matter how nervous he got—and the morning of his first victory over Tennessee he put the lighted end of a cigar in his mouth—once the whistle blew opening kickoff, his mind worked as coldly as a computer.

This faculty was underscored, for example, in the 1943 Orange Bowl victory, 37–21, against an offensively explosive Boston College team. The Eagles were running from the T with flanker in motion. It had been introduced to the college game by Clark Shaughnessy's Stanford Rose Bowl team two seasons before, and in a few years would be universal. But at this time Alabama had not encountered it.

When Mike Holovak, Boston's All-America fullback, broke loose on two long scoring runs for a 14–0 lead, a possible rout loomed, for the Tidemen were obviously shaken. On the spot, Tommy ordered a change in defensive end play that slowed down and gradually shut off the Eagles. Alabama regained its poise, and outscored B.C. the rest of the way, 37–7.

Even though it fell short of fulfillment, perhaps his sharpest job of direction came in the 1945 Sugar Bowl game, lost to Duke, 29–26. With Navy V-12 personnel, the Blue Devils approached their normal peacetime power, while Alabama, which had canceled out football the season before, fielded eight freshmen on the starting team.

Tommy pegged his entire game on one of these 18-year-olds, a blond, whipcord kid named Harry Gilmer. Harry enjoyed unusual peripheral vision and poise, a strong and unerring arm, and the spectacular ability to fire the ball while leaping. He completed all eight of his passes against Duke, five of them to secondary targets, two of them beaded jewels of 57 and 42 yards that set up scores. With time running out, he saw his last completion fail of winning the day only because receiver Ralph Jones was brought down by the last man.

In 1945, Gilmer and the other beardless boys were supported by some returning veterans of talent and had a perfect season, culminating in a

34–14 victory over Southern Cal, the Trojans' first loss at Pasadena. But the 1944 team was Tommy's favorite. "Oh, how I loved those War Babies," he would reminisce. "They were just kids, but they gave everything."

In 1943 'Bama didn't play football. That year Tommy's players saw him in a new light, as he conducted a wholesale correspondence with them overseas.

"We never appreciated him more than when we got those letters," enthused halfback Don Salls. "He'd give us all the dope at home, and where the other players were. I know I got my letter while I was in a hospital. And I suspect a lot of other guys did too."

Tommy had been less communicative with them on trips, even Bowl trips, when it came to handing out money. Where other coaches figured a boy could "live it up" for a night on $5, Tommy figured 50 cents would do it. "Frank Thomas had low pockets and short arms," said one of his ex-players, but he didn't say it vindictively.

After all, there was plenty of partying for free, and sights to be seen, like visiting the palatial estate of Dallas tycoon Clint Murchison, even deeper in millions than the Alabama team in backs. After touring Murchison's fabulous home, one of the players said, "Have you seen the upstairs? Man, even the bathrooms have bathrooms!"

One bathroom had been the limit at home for Frank Thomas. James and Elizabeth Williams Thomas emigrated from Cardiff, Wales, in 1892, settled first in Scranton, Pennsylvania, then followed James' work in the iron foundries to Lima, Ohio, and Muncie, Indiana, where Frank arrived, the youngest of six, November 15, 1898. When the Thomases made their last move to East Chicago, Frank was 10.

The goading scarcity of income, the struggle of a poor man, subject to industrial layoffs, to raise his six children bred in Tommy a deep respect for money. When he arrived at Western State Normal, Kalamazoo, Michigan, in 1917, he owned $7.50 and two changes of clothes. Although he had a full scholarship to Notre Dame law, he always needed money for extra academic fees, for sending home, for buying clothes and other necessities, and for walking around. He used much of his first year's salary at Georgia in 1923 to pay off debts.

From the time he was big enough—which wasn't very big—to handle a basketball, Tommy found sports his fascination, and ultimately his

ticket. His academic consciousness was slower to emerge; the neighborhood was not tuned in to Oxford. That Tommy beat up the truant officer until that official stopped visiting him may or may not be true. It is true that when he decided to make the two-mile walk to grammar school at Hammond, he had to win six fights of increasing size divisions before he won acceptance.

Tommy also got a few good breaks. Andrew Jackson's mother advised him, a man cannot get ahead without friends, and Tommy was fortunate in his. Rockne and Gipp, of course, and before them, Floyd R. Murray, Ralph Young, Bill Spaulding, and Maurice (Big Clipper) Smith.

Floyd Murray, from Earlham College, happened to become the first full-time coach at Washington High School in 1914, the year Tommy entered. He helped him develop in football, basketball, baseball, and track. When he wanted to quit school to help out at home, during one of his father's layoffs, Murray persuaded him not to. It was Murray who first convinced him that despite all obstacles, he could acquire the education his dad had been denied.

Ralph Young, Kalamazoo's athletic director who later set the foundations for Michigan State's modern sports program, encouraged him to come to Kalamazoo. His coach there was Bill Spaulding, who did the same job later for UCLA that Young did for Michigan State. Both Young and Spaulding were strong, smart, and kind men. Any boy exposed to them had something extra going for him.

At Kalamazoo, Tommy starred at halfback, and had his best day in a victory over the Notre Dame freshmen. So Big Clipper Smith, former Notre Dame guard who would later become a superior coach at Santa Clara and Villanova, did not have to sell him to Rockne. What Smith did sell was the idea to Tommy that he could make it at Notre Dame.

The Irish have had more physically talented quarterbacks than the little, blocky, hustling guy they called "Rat." It's doubtful they've ever had a smarter one. Before he got to Notre Dame, he thought he would like to become a football coach. After he met Rockne, he was sure. The Norseman sensed and was pleased with the obvious ambition and instinct for the game in the little guy, although some of the players were unhappy with Tommy's habit of dogging after Rock to ask questions. But insatiable was his hunger to learn all that could be learned.

"Frank Thomas," said Johnny Mohardt, Notre

Dame All-America left halfback, Chicago White Sox second baseman, and later a doctor, "was the most serious fellow about his football I've ever seen."

Although he did not play enough to win his letter in his sophomore season, 1920, he got into five games, and had the thrill of lining up with Gipp. Against, coincidentally, Kalamazoo, Notre Dame was stymied at midfield, so Tommy called on Gipp to punt. Instead, the Gipper dropped back to his 38-yard line and dropkicked a 62-yard field goal.

As a junior, Tommy ran second string to Chet Grant, and as a senior he won the starting job. Notre Dame never lost a game in which Tommy started. He was also a good enough baseball player to make shortstop on the varsity. Summer baseball teams paid good money, and at the end of his sophomore year Tommy wrote letters to several managers offering his services. When he had no takers, he went up to Detroit to see Gipp, who was playing with an industrial team.

"George," he said in desperation, "I'm broke. I've got to get a job. You've got to get me on your team."

The Gipper, always resourceful, talked the manager into taking Tommy on, and then took the little quarterback out and bought him a steak. They roomed together that summer and remained roomies when they returned to school in September.

"I have never seen Gipp's equal as a football player," Tommy would glow, "and I don't expect to. He could do everything. He was also one of the smartest players I've ever run into. We would lie awake nights talking football, and he taught me a lot. He could show you your faults and then show you how to correct them. If he had wanted to, he could have been a great coach, one of the greatest."

Soon after his senior season, Tommy's sophomore season, Gipp suffered a throat infection that developed into pneumonia and caused his death. The hard-bitten little Welshman grieved as for a brother. For the first time in his life, he received a blow, a hurt, that he was slow to recover from.

With his short, blocky build, the weight that came on, the pressures he handled, it was inevitable, probably, that a heart condition and high blood pressure would end Tommy's coaching career and his life when he was still young. He was only 48 when he coached his last game in 1946, only 56 when he died in 1954.

Even when he was coaching the undefeated 1945 team, he was obviously not well. "We could see him fight things," said Don Salls. The 34–14 Rose Bowl victory should have been his bow-out. He deserved that. But it was on his own insistence that he coached in 1946; on doctor's orders he coached sitting down, from the back of a trailer.

He continued as athletic director until 1951. Even after that he kept in touch with football through his TV program; ever competitive and aggressive, he spoke out fervently against single-platoon football.

When they presented him with his Hall of Fame plaque at Birmingham's Legion Field, he received it in a wheelchair.

What Frank Thomas, had he not been forced to quit in his prime, would have accomplished as a coach must be conjectural. The thought occurs that there was a fate in such as Rockne, Gipp, Tommy, and Vince Lombardi facing the final whistle of their last game while still in their full glory.

Wallace Wade

RED TIDE AND BLUE DEVIL

Alabama defeated Washington in the 1926 Rose Bowl game, 20–19, by scoring all of its points within a span of seven minutes in the third quarter. No other game, no other bridge of time exerted so much influence on the ascendancy of the South in the national football picture and the development of Alabama as a major Bowl power.

The Alabama coach, William Wallace Wade, had come to the job the same way Alabama had come to Pasadena—by indirection that seems fateful.

After the 1922 season, Kentucky was seeking a new head coach. High among the candidates was Wallace Wade; he had been a valued assistant coach at Vanderbilt under Dan McGugin through undefeated seasons in 1921 and '22.

Wallace Wade

Wade met with the Kentucky selection committee at Lexington, presented his credentials, and then waited in the lobby for their decision. The committee took a long time, longer than need be, it seemed to Wade. Finally, he burst in on them, and told them off collectively and individually.

He also promised them that no matter where he coached, no team of his would ever lose to Kentucky. As an irony, the committee had voted to hire Wade. As a postscript, his teams—eight at Alabama and three at Duke—never lost a game to Kentucky.

By his second year at Alabama, 1924, Wade fielded a Southern Intercollegiate Conference champion, which lost only one game, to Centre, 17–0. His 1925 team, undefeated in nine regular-season games, shared the SIC crown with Tulane.

At that time the Rose Bowl was a buyer's market, and Jack Benefield, University of Oregon graduate manager, was sent east by the Pacific

Coast Conference to find a suitable opponent for Washington. Benefield's first choice was Tulane, and he tendered the invitation to its coach and athletic director, Clark Shaughnessy, in Chicago's Auditorium Hotel. Shaughnessy, however, couldn't get the approval of Tulane's president, Dr. A. B. Dinwiddie, to accept the bid. So he recommended Alabama to Benefield.

"I've never heard of Alabama as a football team," Benefield said dismally, "and I can't take a chance on mixing a lemon with a rose."

Nevertheless, Benefield agreed to check into it, and Shaughnessy phoned Wade.

"Are you interested in the Rose Bowl?" he asked.

"Definitely," Wade responded.

"Just sit tight, then," Shaughnessy advised. "I'm with a man named Benefield who can extend the invitation. I'll send him to Tuscaloosa to talk to you."

Alabama had a rule against postseason games. Dr. George (Mike) Denny, its president, and Wade disagreed on many things, principally what Wade's salary should be. But on one vital point Dr. Denny and Coach Wade agreed: football was important to Alabama. Dr. Denny rescinded the rule.

Champ Pickens, promoter and Alabama football enthusiast, also helped the Crimson Tide by having Governor Bill Brandon, a Tuscaloosa resident, sign a wire to the Rose Bowl committee, asking them to invite Alabama.

Wade himself had a special interest in the Rose Bowl. Born in Trenton, Tennessee, he had prepped in Chicago, attended Brown, and played right guard on its team that lost 14–0 to Washington State in the 1916 Tournament of Roses game.

Alabama was so little known outside the South that Washington was quickly installed a 2–1 favorite. Most of the Tidemen, however, had played together for three years. They listened with interest to the heroic tales concerning Coach Enoch Bagshaw's Washington team, especially its storybook left halfback, George (Wildcat) Wilson. But they were not awed. Wade, of course, used 'Bama's short-endedness to fan a fire that already blazed.

"This is what a trip to the Rose Bowl means: three weeks of hard work," he said. "I want you to realize that to the full. But remember this, too. Southern football is not recognized as being anywhere near what it is in the East, West, and Midwest. So here's your chance."

General regard for Alabama's chances was epitomized by Will Rogers, the rope-twirling cowboy-philosopher from Oklahoma, who called 'Bama "a team from Tuska-*loser*."

For the first half, Rogers and other Alabama detractors seemed correct. With Wildcat Wilson showing his claws, Washington stormed to a 12–0 lead. After Wilson's second touchdown, however, he was knocked unconscious, had to be removed, and didn't return until the fourth quarter.

Meanwhile, Wade was proving himself as a halftime coach. He rearranged his defense by shifting his two guards, Captain Bruce Jones and Ben Enis, to ends for the purpose of slowing down Washington's attack, especially Wilson. He also altered his attack to make more use of quarterback A. T. S. (Pooley) Hubert's inside running, the passing of right halfback Grant Gillis, and left half Johnny Mack Brown's speed as a pass receiver. Moreover, Alabama enjoyed top physical condition.

In the third quarter, Hubert carried the ball every time on a 41-yard scoring drive, gaining 26, 10, 1, 3, and 1 for the touchdown. Bill Buckler converted to make it 12–7. Next time the Tide got the ball, it went ahead. Gillis, easing back to his 41-yard line, tossed a 34-yard pass that Johnny Mack Brown grabbed at top speed on the Washington 25 and raced for a score: Buckler again converted, and it was 14–12.

A recovered fumble near midfield by Enis set up 'Bama's third touchdown. This time Hubert passed 30 yards to Brown, who caught it in top stride at the 20 and took it in. That made it 20–12.

Wildcat Wilson, showing championship class, returned to the game and sparked an 88-yard scoring drive, which he began with a 17-yard end sweep and capped with a 15-yard scoring pass. He had lived up to his clippings.

On its play-by-play, Alabama's 20–19 victory had fulfilled dramatic demands. The Hollywood touch was enhanced when Johnny Mack Brown, whose matinee-idol features matched the speed of his legs, went on to a movie career. But he never played in a script more action-packed than those seven minutes in which Alabama scored three touchdowns, himself two of them.

Alabama's 1926 team, with Hugh (Wu) Winslett returned at end and new backfield names in a pair of redheads, Captain Emile Barnes and Tolbert Brown, won its third SIC crown in a row, and was promptly invited back to Pasadena, to meet the second of Coach Pop Warner's three Stanford Rose Bowl teams.

This time the Tide was outplayed most of the way, but seized a break to gain a 7–7 tie. Near the end of the game, 'Bama center Clarke Pearce blocked a punt that rolled from Stanford's 47-yard line to its 14. Here Wade called on halfback Jimmy Johnson, who had been out with a bad shoulder, and he plunged over from the 1 on the fifth play. Herschel (Rosy) Caldwell kicked the tying point. (Stanford used only four substitutes, Alabama seven; it was the day of the two-way ironmen.)

Wade said after the game that he had learned a valuable lesson, "I learned that the man-to-man defense against passes is no good. Pop's zone defense, in which his defenders played the ball, not the man, stopped our air attack cold."

The 7–7 deadlock was notable also as the first football game to be carried on a national radio hookup, with Graham McNamee, best-known announcer of the day, at the microphone. This was the day Graham enthused so often about the Sierra Madre that they became known as "the Graham McNamee Mountains."

A sellout crowd of 57,000 brought gate receipts of $226,514. Al Masters, Stanford's graduate manager of athletics, had to return more than $105,000 worth of ticket applications. This impelled enlargement of the Rose Bowl to 72,000. For many years now it has seated more than 100,000.

"Those early Bowl games," said Jeff Coleman, Alabama's business manager in that era, "gave us a start in our savings account, which enabled us to spend half a million on the natatorium and coliseum. We had about two million dollars saved by 1955. Athletic funds were used to assist the College of Engineering and other academic affairs, and enabled the university to develop its entire athletic plant without using any state funds."

Like all football coaching success, Wade's had its built-in future trap. From 1923 through '26 his teams totaled 34-3-2, took three SIC titles, and made two Rose Bowl visits. The Crimson Tide had swept to national recognition. Its football fight song, "Yea, Alabama!" became known by radio to thousands of fans all over the country.

Then, from 1927 through '29, the reaction set in. Wade continued to field winning teams—5-4-1, 6-3, and 6-3—but he had spoiled the fans. The wolves, especially the Tuscaloosans, began howling. His relationship with President Denny continued taut.

Zipp Newman, Alabama's football historian,

recalls the return of one of the early Rose Bowl teams. Thousands were at the Tuscaloosa station. They had requisitioned a large flatbed truck on which the football team and party were to ride in a parade. Dr. Denny and Coach Wade both rode on the truck, each looking away from the other.

Wade recognized the value of publicity. He took newspapermen from all over the South to the Rose Bowl, and was responsible for setting up an Alabama-sponsored radio network. On leaving Alabama for Duke after the 1930 season, he told Jeff Coleman that when he got to Durham, North Carolina, he was going to get to know every "soda jerk" in the state.

"I took that to mean," said Coleman, "that he realized he had not done a good job in public relations among the alumni, or more particularly the people of Tuscaloosa."

To his players, Wade was the supreme, severe drillmaster, who'd get down on the ground with them to teach technique. He had little time for life's tinsel. To most outsiders, he was blunt, unapproachable. Coach Paul Bryant, Alabama's coach since 1958, is known as "The Bear" because he is supposed to have wrestled one at a fair in Fordyce, Alabama. Few people remember that Alabama had an earlier "bear." For that's what his players and others called Wally Wade, behind his back—"The Bear."

Beneath the harsh exterior, however, there was the sensitiveness that had erupted when the Kentuckians made him wait. It erupted again when his nonchampionship, non-Bowl teams and himself were criticized in the late twenties. He knew there were other places he could coach.

Before the 1930 season, Wade determined it would be his last at Alabama. He accepted an offer from Duke, and signed a contract to begin in 1931; after he signed with Duke, California made him an even better offer.

Wade knew he'd have a strong team at Alabama in '30, but it's doubtful he realized how strong. Zipp Newman called it the strongest seen in the South until that time. The Tide rolled over its nine regular-season opponents and Washington State in the Rose Bowl, 24–0. What had once been known as the "Thin Red Line" was now referred to as the "Red Elephants."

The popular song of a few years later, "Stars Fell on Alabama," could have applied to the 1930 team. They included tackle Fred Sington and halfback John (Sugar) Cain, both All-America. Other stars were John (Monk) Campbell, fullback, adept at spin plays and open-field running,

guards Frank Howard (later Clemson coach) and John Miller, center Jess Eberdt, end Jimmy Moore, a top receiver, and John (Flash) Suther, a strong reverse runner and tough to tackle in the open.

"This team was exceptionally well balanced," Wade said. "It was a good defensive team, and it had a good running attack, both through the line and in the open field. The team made many long runs for touchdowns and it used deception effectively in its running attack.

"It had a good forward passing attack which was effectively mixed with the running. It had very good punting. The line play was outstanding on both offense and defense. Good replacements were available and the so-called second team or shock troops were used to start all games, including the Rose Bowl game. The first team usually started the second quarter, when much of the scoring occurred."

Mel Hein, Washington State center and later the star of the New York Giants, said of the 1930 Alabama team, "They taught us that passing was becoming a great weapon in football. They scored three touchdowns by passing. They had a fellow by the name of Sugar Cain who could really throw the ball." Cain was also an exceptionally fine punter and defensive man.

Judged by all available testimony, Wallace Wade's 1930 team was his best.

Although Dr. Denny and Coach Wade often got along like strange bulldogs, Denny respected Wade's football astuteness and followed his recommendation in signing his successor, Frank Thomas, who had demonstrated his head coaching ability at the University of Chattanooga.

Late in the 1930 season, Thomas followed the team as an observer. He got closer to the players than Wade wanted; after the tough 13–0 victory over Georgia, he visited the dressing room and congratulated the victors. As a result, when he accompanied the team to Pasadena, Wade had him assigned to a berth in the last Pullman, or as far from the players as possible.

At the Alabama football awards dinner, Wade delivered a speech as laconic as it was bitter: "There are many things you might like to hear me say, but I cannot say them. There are many things I might like to say but cannot, so I'll just sit down."

To make sure his message would not be mistaken, he left behind him on the dais the silver tray that had been presented him.

Wade's eight-year record at Alabama was 61–

13–3; his first eight years at Duke it was 61–15–3. They would be hard to top for consistency.

At Alabama, his great coaching rivals were Bill Alexander of Georgia Tech and Bob Neyland of Tennessee. At Duke his bitterest rival came to be Carl Snavely at North Carolina; this figured because of the natural neighborhood feud of the Blue Devils and the Tar Heels. Probably few games pleased Wade more than the 25–0 trouncing the Devils gave Carolina in 1935, to wreck its Rose Bowl dreams.

Wade's 1936 Duke team, beaten only by Tennessee on Red Harp's late-in-the-game punt return, featured halfback Clarence (Ace) Parker. Wade rated Parker tops in all categories: open-field runner, passer, receiver, punter, and safety man. The Ace ran from tailback and also switched occasionally with wingback Elmore Hackney, another talented player. Through the years, Wade's formations were the single wing and the short punt.

The best runner Wade coached at Duke, and perhaps including Alabama, was George McAfee, later a star with the Chicago Bears. Wade was looking in '38 to a superior attack built around McAfee, but George was injured and played very little. So Wade built one of football's finest defensive units. The line, led by Captain Dan Hill at center, was known as the "Seven Iron Dukes." They shut out everybody in the regular season.

"It was an outstanding defensive team," Wade wrote, "and had exceptional punting from halfback Eric Tipton, who was also a hard runner, a good passer, and excelled on defense. Fullback Bob O'Mara was good both ways, as was Frank Ribar at guard. Bob Haas, tackle, was very good on defense; end Willis (Bolo) Perdue and guard Fred York were too. Bill Bailey, an end, was a good blocker and good on defense."

One of the most notable contests of the thirties was this Duke team's victory in a snowstorm at Durham in the last game ever played by a Pittsburgh team coached by Dr. Jock Sutherland. Pitt had its Dream Backfield of John Chickerneo, Dick Cassiano, Hal Stebbins, and Marshall Goldberg, but it was stopped by the Seven Iron Dukes and a remarkable coffin-corner punting job by Tipton. The game's only touchdown in a 7–0 victory for Duke came on a blocked punt by Bolo Perdue.

Undefeated, untied, unscored on, Duke accepted the bid to meet Southern California in the Rose Bowl. A field goal by Tony Ruffa gave the Blue Devils a 3–0 lead that stood up until there was little more than two minutes to play. Then Southern Cal put in a sub halfback named Doyle Nave who had practiced passing. Now it paid off. On a 66-yard advance, Nave completed four straight passes to end Al Krueger against a wearied Duke secondary, the last for 14 yards and a touchdown with 41 seconds left.

The first defeat of a Wade-coached team in the Rose Bowl was laden with acerbity. The choice of Duke had been criticized by some of the newspapers, which wanted Texas Christian and Davey O'Brien. Afterwards, Wade was criticized for not congratulating Doyle Nave. Under intense pressure, since his wife was seriously ill, Wade was quoted as saying, "This is a helluva place to bring a football team!" Doyle Nave himself later defended Wade:

"After all, he was preoccupied with the suddenness of Duke's defeat, and the one thing on his mind was to congratulate Coach Howard Jones. I wrote a letter to Mr. Wade ... expressing my feelings. His reply is one of the most treasured possessions I have. During World War II, I had a wonderful visit with him in his home. He is a fine man. I feel he was the victim of extremely poor taste."

Wade was to send one more team into a Rose Bowl game, not in Pasadena this time, however, but in Durham, because of a government ban on large West Coast crowds after the Japanese bombed Pearl Harbor. Oregon State upset the Blue Devils, 20–16, yet this was still Wade's outstanding offensive team at Duke. With Steve Lach leading the way, they gained 3,350 yards in nine games and outscored their opponents 311 to 41.

The awe in which Wade's players held him is spelled out in a story by Tommy Prothro, Duke quarterback and later head coach of Oregon State and UCLA. On short football trips away from home in Carolina, Wade often took the starting backfield in his own car and drove ahead of the bus carrying the other players. On one occasion he pulled up at the side of a road to let the bus catch up; he did not know that his wheels were perched on the brink of a ditch.

"Tell him," Prothro nudged George McAfee. "No," whispered McAfee, "you tell him." A third back, Jap Davis, maintained silence. So Wade started up again and the car plunged into the ditch. Wade and his backfield left it there and hitchhiked a ride to the game.

In his 16 seasons at Duke, Wade's teams won six Southern Conference championships. Their

complete record was 110–36–7; more than half of his defeats came in his last five years, 1946–50, after he returned from war service. His total figures, Alabama and Duke, 171–49–10 for .765, placed him, in 1969, No. 16 on the all-time list of coaches who lasted at least ten years.

After he resigned in 1950 from Duke, where he was also athletic director, Wade served ten years as commissioner of the Southern Conference. He was also a distinguished member of the rules committee. In 1955, or as soon as he was eligible, he was named to the National College Football Hall of Fame.

Wade had grown up as one of five sons of a prosperous farmer in Trenton, Tennessee. So it was the natural thing for him, when he had broken all ties with football, to become a prosperous cattle farmer himself near Durham.

Along with his football trophies, there is his record as a soldier. He served in both World War I and II; in 1942, at the age of 50, he was commissioned as a major of field artillery, and later promoted to lieutenant colonel. He served through the European campaign without a day's leave, and was in the Normandy landing, the Battle of the Bulge, and the crossing of the Rhine.

He was awarded the Bronze Star and the Croix de Guerre with Palm.

War did something to Wade that football couldn't. It mellowed him. In fact, he suspected it had mellowed him too much for effective coaching.

"I'm just not tough enough," he told his friend Jack Horner, sports editor of the Durham *Herald*. "The truth," Horner wrote, "was that Wade mellowed after seeing 135-pounders die for their country as gloriously as 200-pounders."

Wade even came around to mellowing toward Alabama. Between 1930 and 1960, he had visited Tuscaloosa only once, on business connected with a savings and loan company. But in 1960, he returned for a get-together with his old players and associates. There were a series of parties and luncheons and a banquet, where he was presented a $3,000 silver service. After returning to Durham, he wrote Jeff Coleman:

"I am humbly grateful for the wonderful party given for the old boys, Peg, and me. It was certainly a wonderful occasion beyond my fondest expectations and something that we both will cherish always."

Pop Warner

THE COACH WHO WENT AWINGING

Glenn Scobey (Pop) Warner, a head coach in 451 college football games over 44 seasons, often said that the toughest game any team of his ever played in was Stanford's 7–6 victory over Pittsburgh in the 1928 Rose Bowl.

"I have seen many games," Warner said, "where one team or the other played itself to exhaustion, but in yesterday's contest both sides fought with equal fury, and when the last whistle blew, every player on the field was well used up."

The edge Stanford enjoyed, not only on the scoreboard but in yards rushing, 203–125, and in first downs, 13–8, traced largely to the line smashes of fullback Clifford (Biff) Hoffman, especially on a play Warner had put in for this game.

Hoffman got the snap from center, and stood up with arm raised as if to pass. Sometimes he did pass, over the line to left end Ted Shipkey. He

also had the option to hand off the ball to left wingback Dick Hyland on the old Statue of Liberty play. On the third option, he kept the ball and drove straight over his right guard. The first two options were mainly camouflage leading up to the inside smash by Hoffman.

After the game, Hyland ran into Alec Fox, Pitt's left guard, who moaned, "Dammit, Hyland, if I didn't know enough to back out when I see a pass coming, Hoffman would not have made a yard."

Hyland told Pop Warner what Fox said, and he chuckled, "You know I scouted their Penn State game. That Fox fellow seemed to handle himself very well. Sometimes you put in a play to fool a smart player that a dumb one would not react to. I thought Fox pretty smart."

Special plays were needed in that Stanford-Pitt grueler, because it was teacher against pupil.

Coach Jock Sutherland of Pittsburgh had played guard for Warner on the 1916 Pitt team that many regarded as the national champion and the best Pop ever turned out. Both Stanford and Pitt ran from the double-wing and single-wing formations. Both formations originated with Warner; precisely when is obscure, but sometime between 1906 and 1912.

The double wingback was just what it said: one halfback lined up a little behind and outside the left end, and the other half posted himself in the same manner near the right end. The quarterback and fullback deployed behind the center, either one taking the snap to start the play. The line was unbalanced left or right in a 4–2 split, with two tackles or two guards lined up shoulder to shoulder on the strong side.

From it Warner used a bewildering set of spins, reverses, double reverses, fake reverses, runs from fake passes, and passes from fake runs. Eventually, like all formations, the double wing was caught up with by the defenses, which crashed their ends and drilled their other linemen not to go for the fakes. But it had its day in the thirties, when it was copied widely by other coaches.

No game did more to popularize it than Stanford's 1928 victory, 26–0, over a strongly favored Army team in Yankee Stadium. Half the time Army appeared not to know who had the ball. Just as bad off if not worse, from the favorable vantage point in the press box, were the scribes.

On one play, for example, quarterback Herb Fleishhacker took the snap, executed a half spin, faked to the two wingbacks crossing behind him, and then smashed up the middle. Here's how one of the writers described that play:

"Fleishhacker took the ball from Hoffman and gave it to Sims, who gave it to one of the guards pulling out of the line. The next thing I knew, Fleishhacker had the ball again and was 20 yards down the field. How the hell he got the ball I'll never know."

Nobody ever blended deception and power with more precision and effectiveness over a longer haul than Pop Warner. His coaching record, from 1895 through 1938, shows 313 victories, 106 defeats, and 32 ties for .729. Only Amos Alonzo Stagg topped him in victories—and by only one, 314. Warner developed football successfully at Georgia, Cornell, Carlisle Indian School, Pittsburgh, Stanford, and Temple. In any all-time ranking, his name stands very near the top.

Pop Warner. *Chicago Tribune Photos*

Besides the single- and double-wingback formations, his firsts include the rolling body block, the spiral punt, the blocking dummy, fiber padding, and the numbering of players. Of all innovators, it seems safe enough to say that Pop again was topped by only one and the same Alonzo Stagg. Stagg himself stated that Warner was more responsible than any other man in the enactment of rules that improved football.

"Glenn was never very active *on* the rules committee," Stagg said. "But we'd make a rule and Glenn would think up a way to get around it within the rules and we'd have to meet his challenge. He kept us on our toes, I can tell you."

Pop perpetrated his most spectacular flimflam with the Carlisle Indians against Harvard in 1903. Harvard won 12–11, but the story of the game was the ruse of the Redmen, a blend of deception, notoriety, finesse, and hilarity that tickled the football world, Harvard included except for the coaches and players. It was termed, appropriately, "The Hunchback Play."

Warner had planned to use it at Pennsylvania

the week before, but bad weather made him change his mind. So Harvard became the setup, and the occasion happened to be the last game ever played on the old Soldier's Field gridiron; Harvard Stadium, America's first for football, was opened two weeks later against Dartmouth. As was his custom with any new play, Warner outlined its detail and legality to Mike Thompson, a leading referee of the era.

Carlisle brought it off after Harvard made the first score. On the ensuing kickoff, Jimmy Johnson, diminutive Carlisle quarterback, took the ball inside his 5-yard line, while his mates fronted him in a V wedge, common formation of the time. To insure that a forward pass, then illegal, would not be involved, halfback Charlie Dillon turned to face his own goal line. Johnson then thrust the football up under the back of Dillon's jersey, where a two-inch rubber band had been sown to hold it in place. Long rehearsal made for rapid execution.

The Indians' wedge, with Dillon tucked behind it, charged up the field like a plowshare. As the Harvards tore into it near the 25-yard line, Dillon detached himself from the mass and casually trotted toward the sideline.

Harvard, meanwhile, was struggling to get at one of the Indians, who had under his arm what they thought was the football. It was only his headgear. The alerted referee, Thompson, however, was shadowing Dillon, who suddenly broke into a dead run for the Harvard goal line.

"I went flying behind him," Thompson said. "The Harvard team ignored us. And many of the 25,000 spectators thought I was chasing Dillon off the field for some infraction of the rules. When a few detected the hump on his back and guessed what it was, a hum arose and grew into a roar."

By now, Captain Carl Marshall of Harvard had detected the trick and was giving chase, much too late. When Dillon crossed the goal line, however, he was confronted by a problem, as was Mike Thompson. The rules stated that the ball must be touched down; ground and ball were separated by Dillon's jersey.

Dillon lay on his hunchback and kept asking Thompson, "Down yet, Mike? Down yet?" The impasse was solved by Johnson, who had initiated the play. He had also later extricated himself from the wedge and followed Dillon down the field. Now he functioned as a field general, indeed. He reached up under Dillon's jersey, pulled out the ball, and touched it down.

Harvard entered a strong complaint after the game, arguing the play was illegal because Johnson had passed the ball forward to Dillon. Thompson explained what had happened and showed them Dillon's jersey with the rubber band inside the back of it. Harvard insisted that such a play was "not honest" and that there should be a rule against it. And such a rule was written in.

It should not be inferred from the Hunchback Play that Warner was a dubious character who toyed with ethics. To find loopholes in the rules was generally accepted behavior then. In serious matters Warner maintained the finest standards. He was averse to dirty play. "I don't believe anyone," he said, "can play two kinds of football, good and dirty, at the same time. I want my boys to play good football."

Before the 1927 Rose Bowl game, he told his Stanford players, "Last year Alabama played Washington here. It was a rough game. We don't want Wallace Wade and his boys to think *all* Coast football is played like that. The first man I see doing anything he shouldn't will come off the field and he's through."

Warner came to Stanford from Pittsburgh in 1924 by an unusual arrangement. At Pitt he had become probably the most talked of coach in the country. He put together four straight undefeated seasons, 1915–18; his Panthers went 31 straight before losing to Syracuse in 1919. When Stanford first contacted him in the winter of 1921–22, he still had two years to go on his Pitt contract. So he sent two assistants, Andy Kerr and Tiny Thornhill, ahead of him to coach Stanford in 1922 and '23, and then took over himself in '24.

In his 44 seasons Warner handled many fine players. Any list of Pitt's would have to include centers Bob Peck and Herb Stein; guards Thornhill, Sutherland, Dale Seis, and Jack Sack; tackles Len Hilty and Pud Seidel; fullbacks George McLaren and Andy Hastings; and halfback Tom Davies.

A list of Pop's top Stanford players would comprise centers Walt Heinecke and Hal McCreery; guards Fred Swan, Seraphim (Dynamite) Post, Don Robesky, and Bill Corbus; tackle Ray Tandy; ends Jim Lawson, Ted Shipkey and Don (Mush) Muller; and backs Ernie Nevers, Dick Hyland, Biff Hoffman, Phil Moffitt, Harry Hillman, and Ernie Caddel. His top player at Temple was an exceptionally fine fullback named Dave Smukler.

There was no doubt in Warner's mind that his two greatest players were Nevers, Stanford full-

back, and Jim Thorpe, Carlisle halfback. Both were great natural all-round athletes. For sheer skill, the edge probably lay with Thorpe. But the Sac and Fox Indian (he was also part French and Irish) was not always amenable to coaching. Warner finally gave up trying to teach him technique, because Thorpe got results doing it his way.

"I tell you what the damn-hell to do," Warner would explode, "and you start a debate."

That was one reason Warner went on record as rating Nevers over Thorpe. In 1942, Pop stated, "many veteran coaches . . . argued my selection of Ernie Nevers as the greatest player I ever coached, when I had also coached the great Jim Thorpe. I still pick Ernie, because I never saw him do anything but his best, in any situation. He was always putting on the pressure, whether it was a big game or a little one, or a drill against the subs. He knew only one way to compete and that was all-out.

"Jim, on the other hand, would ease up when he felt safe in doing so. Sometimes he found it wasn't as safe as he thought it was, and this made him a bit of an in-and-outer. I'll pick the all-outer over the in-and-outer any day, if their skill is about the same."

Nevers was a junior in 1924 when Warner took over at Stanford. He was sidelined for six weeks with a broken ankle, however, and when he returned to action against Utah, he broke the other ankle. So he was not able to play against California in "The Big Game," as Coast writers had dubbed it. Even with Nevers injured, Stanford rallied with two last-quarter touchdowns to tie Cal, 20–20, in what both Warner and Walter Camp, father of American football, thought the most dramatic game they'd ever seen.

His weak ankles so tightly taped that he had little feeling from the knees down, Nevers played 60 minutes in the 1925 Rose Bowl game against Notre Dame's Four Horsemen team. And even though two of his passes were intercepted by Elmer Layden and run back for touchdowns in a 27–10 defeat, he was still the outstanding player on the field.

"Big Dog" his teammates called him because he was so easygoing—but strictly off the field. Against Notre Dame that frustrating day, Big Dog carried the ball 34 times for 114 yards, passed for a touchdown, punted for a 42-yard average, blocked, faked, and was in on three quarters of the tackles.

There is always one defeat that lives with a coach deeper than any other, and such was that 27–10 defeat by Notre Dame with Pop Warner. He pointed out many times that the Indians had outgained the Irish from scrimmage, 298 to 179, in first downs, 11 to 7, and in completed passes, 11 to 3.

"We spotted Notre Dame 21 points" [two touchdowns by interceptions, a third by a recovered fumble], said Warner, "while they actually earned but six. Except for those errors we completely outplayed them. Notre Dame was great, but I think I had the better team."

The 7–7 tie with Alabama in the 1927 Rose Bowl was almost as hard to take. To increase speed, Warner equipped Stanford with silk pants, an innovation that evoked from the Alabamans such comments as "Take 'em off, we wanna peek" and "Shall we dance?" They soon quieted when Biff Hoffman completed a 38-yard pass play to "Tricky Dick" Hyland, who almost got away.

The Crimson Tide stiffened and forced George Bogue to try a field goal that went wide from the 16. Next time the Indians got the ball, however, the running and passing of Hoffman, Hyland, Bogue, and ends Shipkey and Ed Walker put together a 63-yard scoring drive, capped by a 20-yard pass from Bogue to Walker. Bogue converted and the 7–0 looked good. But near the end of the game a blocked punt rolled back to Stanford's 14, a break the Crimson Tide turned into a 7–7 tie. After the conversion, only three plays remained.

"When it was all over," reported Rube Samuelson, Rose Bowl historian, "neither the Stanfordites nor the fans could believe what they read on the scoreboard. Outplayed all afternoon, the Tide had struggled up off the floor to avert what looked like a certain defeat.

"Any way you figure it, Stanford should have won. The Indians were by far the better team. They gained 305 yards by runs and passes to only 98 for Alabama. They chalked up 12 first downs to six. They gathered in 12 out of 16 forward passes for 175 yards against the Tide's one . . . Stanford showed its superiority everywhere except on the scoreboard."

The Stanfords finally shook off their Pasadena hoodoo in that 1928 victory over Pitt, 7–6. The victory had a special savor for Frankie Wilton, Indians' left halfback, because it helped him shed what looked like a permanent pair of goat horns. It was Wilton's blocked punt that had set up Alabama's touchdown in the 1927 Rose Bowl.

And it was a Wilton fumble, turned into a 17-yard scoring run by halfback Jimmy Hagan, that gave Pitt a 6–0 lead. (Fortunately for Stanford, Heinecke broke his nose blocking Allen Booth's extra-point attempt.)

Warner, however, never gave up on a player who wouldn't give up on himself. From the kickoff following Pitt's score, Wilton alternated with fullback Hoffman on a drive that reached the Pitt 2. There Hoffman completed a flat pass to Bob Sims, who was hit by several Pitt players and fumbled. Four men went after the ball, three of them Panthers, the fourth an Indian named Wilton. In one swoop he grabbed the ball, scooted over for a touchdown and—with Hoffman converting—gave his horns the heroic heave ho.

In his excellent history of Stanford athletics, *The Color of Life Is Red*, Don Liebendorfer, sports publicist for the Indians in Pop's day and very close to him, wrote:

"Warner was a strangely contradictory character, whose gruff, sometimes almost surly and sullen exterior concealed a big and very warm heart. The great coach was penurious and 'tighter than the paper on the wall' about little things. But let a former player or associate come to Pop with a hard-luck story, and the purse strings loosened immediately. A fierce competitor, both as a player and as a coach, he came up with surprising exhibitions of compassion, and never poured it on.

"Pop loved to tinker, and was quite inventive and skillful in an amateurish sort of way. In his tiny workshop adjacent to his garage he created or repaired all kinds of things, partly as a pursuit of the hobby but in most cases to save a few nickels. One of his most famous 'inventions' was a wooden-handled, wooden-headed golf club, which had a head shaped like that of a catfish. Warner used this monstrosity for every shot on the course, and the old codger played a pretty fair game at that."

The $500,000 estate Warner left testifies that he was not loose with his money. His saving ways, though, did not always pan out well. When his dentist charged him $75 for a partial upper plate, he was incensed, especially since it irritated his gums and made it uncomfortable to chew. He attempted to fix the plate with a file in his workshop, but succeeded only in cracking it in two. So he had to have a dentist make him a new plate—which cost him another $75.

Pop in 1934, while at Temple. *Chicago Tribune Photos*

Pop's hobbies also included songwriting and painting. He liked apple pie, Turkish Trophy cigarettes, and on occasion, a dram of liquor—on a cold game day, he instructed Wallace Denny, his trainer, to have available on the bench a bottle containing a liquid that looked like cough medicine. Pop also invented a tasteful cherry cordial, grinding the cherry pits to a powder and mixing with the wine.

Warner was born near Springville, New York, April 5, 1871. Baseball was his teenage game, and he played it around the country. He never played football before entering Cornell in 1892, but he soon became a stalwart 200-pound guard, and was also the college's heavyweight boxing champion for two years. Since he was a few years older than the average student, they got to calling him "Pop."

He was graduated in 1895 with a law degree, passed the New York State bar exam, and opened a law office—but not for long. Football had its hooks in him, and in 1895 and '96, in an unusual arrangement, he coached two teams, Iowa State and Georgia. He coached Iowa State from Au-

gust 15 until its first game, and then took over Georgia. Warner's record broken down shows:

YEARS	COLLEGE	W	L	T
1895-1896	Georgia	7	4	0
1897-1898	Cornell	15	5	1
1899-1903	Carlisle	33	18	3
1904-1906	Cornell	23	10	2
1907-1914	Carlisle	74	23	5
1915-1923	Pittsburgh	59	11	4
1924-1932	Stanford	71	17	8
1933-1938	Temple	31	18	9
TOTALS		313	106	32

The football world was surprised, if not shocked, when Warner announced after the 1932 season that he was leaving Stanford for Temple. He was 61 and still had four years to go on his contract. True, there had been some rumbles of alumni discontent over a 6–4–1 season in '32, and five straight defeats by Southern Cal. But Pop and Palo Alto seemed to go together. The 82 football players he left behind him thought so; they petitioned him to stay, some of them in tears.

Why did he go? Two reasons apparently.

First, he had become convinced that the future at Stanford would not provide him the personnel to beat the other Coast teams, especially Southern Cal. Trojan defenses had shut out the double wing four of the previous five seasons, giving up only 12 points in a 1930 41–12 rout.

Second, Temple, desirous of escalating its football program, had been after him for several years and posed him a challenge he liked. He had built winners every place he had coached. He would do it once more.

He was not a failure at Temple. He had only one losing season there in six, and his 1934 team, posting a 7–1–2 record, lost only to Tulane, 20–14, in the first Sugar Bowl game. But he lacked the showcase of schedules as well as the personnel to fashion the headlines of Carlisle, Pitt, and Stanford.

Meanwhile, his successor at Stanford, Tiny Thornhill, inherited a band of sophomores of unusual talent. They had vowed as freshman that they'd never lose to Southern California, and they made it good. And thus they became known as the "Vow Boys."

They won three straight Pacific Coast Conference championships. They became the first team to play in the Rose Bowl three straight years; they lost to Columbia, 7–0, in 1934; to Alabama, 29–13, in '35; and beat Southern Methodist, 7–0, in '36. Four of them made All-America for two years, 1934 and '35: fullback Bobby Grayson, halfback Bob (Bones) Hamilton, end Monk Moscrip, and tackle Bob (Horse) Reynolds. Reynolds played a total of 180 minutes, the maximum, in three Rose Bowl games, a record not likely to be equaled.

What Warner would have done with the Vow Boys he left behind him makes a good question, even if unanswerable. Two things seem certain enough. He couldn't have done much better than Thornhill, and he wished he'd had the chance. "Leaving Stanford," he said, "was the worst mistake I ever made."

In 1926, the University of California had a sophomore guard who later became All-America, Bert Schwartz. Bert was strong, quick, aggressive, and, as often true with a sophomore, overzealous. To exploit the Schwartzian zeal, Warner put in a fullback smash on a play in which Dick Hyland, left wingback, trapped Schwartz from the blind side and then rolled away from him.

As Warner had predicted, Schwartz didn't know who was blocking him and whence. Neither, apparently, did the other Cal players. The play was used five or six times for goodly chunks of yardage. After the fourth time, Schwartz rose to his knees, raised his hands high, looked up, and before a jam-packed crowd of 80,000 in Cal's Memorial Stadium, screamed: "God Almighty, please tell me where they're coming from!"

That had to be one of Glenn Scobey Warner's most precious moments; he had designed a play that forced a good opponent publicly to ask God to help him stop it.

Fielding Yost

HURRY UP!

"Hurry up" was his battle cry, and Hurry Up his nickname. He was always in a hurry, but he always knew where he was going. And so did the team that he called—in the native West Virginia accent he never shed—"Meeshegan." He pronounced it wrong, but coached it right. Few football teams could put a stop to Fielding Harris Yost's Meeshegan.

Nobody ever put a stop to his monologues. He relinquished the floor only to an earthquake. "Did you ever have a conversation with Yost?" one sportswriter named Grantland Rice asked another named Ring Lardner. "No," Lardner replied. "My parents taught me never to interrupt."

Granny Rice bet Herbert Bayard Swope, editor-reporter of Joseph Pulitzer's old New York *World*, himself a nationally rated gabber, that he could not outtalk Yost. Swope accepted the wager confidently, and Rice brought them together for lunch.

It was a mismatch, a stentor against a Trappist. By three o'clock Swope had been able to get in only five "uhs." At five o'clock, flushed and frustrated, he finally got in his first words, "Bring me the check."

Even when he permitted anybody else to talk, Yost was invincible. He and Lardner were discussing the 1908 Michigan-Pennsylvania game.

"Penn won that one," Lardner stated. "The score was 29–0."

"No, Meeshegan won it," Yost contradicted. "That was the year we had Garrels, a great fullback."

"Penn won it," Lardner repeated. "That was the year they had Scarlett and Greene."

They finally made a $5 bet, and checked the record book. Penn had won, 29–0.

"I told you Pennsylvania won," Yost said.

"You're right," Lardner agreed.

Yost refused to accept the bet, but he reveled in his conviction he was right.

For all his talking, Yost outdid it with his doing. Of those who survived 25 years or more, none matches his record of 198–38–13. In his 25 seasons at Michigan he had eight undefeated teams, and eight Western Conference champions. His first five Michigan teams, 1901

through '05, played 56 games without a loss until beaten at Chicago in '05, 2–0. They outscored opponents, 2,821 to 56 They were known as the "point-a-minute" teams.

The 1901 team, which scored 550 points to its opponents' 0, thrashed Stanford 49–0 on New Year's Day, 1902, in the first Tournament of Roses game at Pasadena. The classic was not renewed for 14 years.

The star of the point-a-minutes was halfback Willie Heston, All-America in 1903 and '04, and an automatic member of any all-time team in the era before the forward pass, if not after. Heston, five feet eight, 184 pounds, was born in Galesburg, Illinois, but his family moved to Grants Pass, Oregon; he attended San Jose State with plans to become a teacher.

"Heston," said Yost, "never had an equal. He was the quickest runner who ever lived, he could hit the line with the best, and he had unusual balance. In moving through an open field, he proved his motto, 'Use your searchlight and jump the dead ones!' "

When he came to Michigan at 30, Yost already had a national reputation. He had developed a state championship team in his first coaching job, Ohio Wesleyan in 1897; it tied Michigan and beat Ohio State, 6–0, for the only time. To see the country, Yost coached Nebraska in 1898, and Kansas in '99, winning Missouri Valley titles. Missouri wanted him to do the same for her in 1900, but he decided in favor of Stanford, where he produced another winner, state champion with a 7–2 record.

If Yost was not sleeping, or talking football, he was coaching it. That season, 1900, he coached four other teams successfully; Stanford Freshman, Lowell High of San Francisco, the California Ukiah team, and San Jose Teachers. Heston, captain of San Jose, was articulate as well as athletic; later he'd become a lawyer and a judge. He not only talked Yost into coaching his team but got him to do it for expenses—and Yost was not eleemosynary.

In those days, football was still an infant. Eligibility and recruiting standards were vague or nonexistent. Yost himself had played at three schools, Ohio Northern, West Virginia (three

Hurry Up Yost, at Michigan

the increasing popularity of football forced the colleges to police their own recruiting and subsidizing, and Yost became a staunch disciple of amateurism purer than Galahad's. Hughie Fullerton, a leading sportswriter of the day, who broke the Chicago "Black Sox" World Series scandal story, wrote of Yost after his retirement from coaching:

"He had run the gamut of coaching methods from the 'tramp on the injured and hurdle the dead' days to today, when he ranks high as a preacher and practicer of the highest morality in sport. He has developed from a rough, fighting coach to an idealist, and is living proof of what football can do as a moral force.

"He is as much bigger today than the Yost of 29 years ago as that huge stadium he is building at Ann Arbor is bigger than the little stand on the gravelly field at Delaware, Ohio."

Another veteran Big Ten observer gave a harsher estimate of Hurry Up.

"Yost was a schemer," he wrote. "He did much to establish Michigan as the political as well as the football power of the Big Ten. He was a sanctimonious man who preached a good line, then did what was necessary to win.

"As a coach he was all alone for a long time, with the only really well manned squad in the Big Ten, but when Stagg and Williams [Dr. Henry L. Williams, Minnesota coach, 1900–21] began to give him trouble, he ran out of the Big Ten and turned eastward for his opponents. During the period he was out of the Big Ten, Williams had his best teams and would have played him even."

The athletic plant Yost built at Michigan stands at least as impressive as his coaching record. It comprises Michigan Stadium (capacity today, 101,001, nation's largest on campus), Yost Field House, Women's Athletic Building, the Indoor Sports Building, the Ice Rink, and the 18-hole golf course. As an intercollegiate athletic plant, it is unsurpassed. His chief objective was to make sports as available to as many students as possible. He succeeded.

A tough, shrewd businessman, Yost made a typically thorough study of the construction business before giving out contracts. George Burke, Ann Arbor attorney, who represented the contractor chosen by Yost, said:

"I always thought I knew my business, but I sure got a lesson in building from the coach. Why, he knows wood from the chopping of the tree to the nailing of the board. He knows the number of nails being used in the building and

years), and Lafayette. (He was an assiduous A student, however, and earned a law degree.) After Heston finished San Jose, Yost talked him out of teaching and into getting his law degree at Michigan.

When Yost needed a player to keep the point-a-minute people on time, he just reached out and took one. In 1904 he was short a good tackle, so he importuned Tom Smull, Ohio Northern captain, to transfer to Ann Arbor, where he starred for two years. Smull returned to Ohio Northern much later—as dean of its engineering school. Yost didn't care where or how he got them, but to play for him they had to be students.

Hurry Up had only two major recruiting failures. One was the decision of quarterback Walter Eckersall to attend Chicago. The other was a challenge Wisconsin had posed by using as its mascot a live badger. Yost decided Michigan must have a live wolverine, and after a hunt that would have done credit to Frank Buck, he rounded up ten. They were all so vicious, however, he had to give them away to zoos. One of them, Biff, was given to the campus zoo, and became the mascot. But though he was live, Biff could not be brought to Ferry Field, and Yost regarded the affair as a defeat.

As he grew into an elder statesman and Michigan became known as "Champions of the West,"

how far apart. He knows how many grains of sand and how many pebbles should be used in the concrete. But if you think I got a lesson, you should have heard the hell he gave those so called pine-tree experts, before I came in."

When the stadium was finished in 1927, Yost and his old friend Fred Lawton stood at the top and looked down. "Gee," said Lawton, "what a lot of seats." "Yeah," Yost replied, "and the best part is folks pay $3 for 'em, then go away and leave 'em, y' know."

Yost, it has been written, had no sense of humor. He didn't, unless he made the jokes. When one of his better players was suspended for trying to pass off as his own composition a short story by Edgar Allan Poe, the Old Man drawled, "It's a wonder he didn't turn in a Shakespearean play, like *Hamlet* or *Romeo and Juliet*, y' know."

Hollywood hired him as technical adviser to a football movie called *The Quarterback*, and after he returned to Ann Arbor, he shook his head. "You should have seen the actors they gave me for football players—a bunch of Ping-Pong players and dancing boys. They couldn't even catch a football in a butterfly net."

The line he enjoyed the most came at the expense of perhaps his most intense rival, Bob Zuppke of Illinois, and Zuppke's storied back, Harold (Red) Grange.

The background was provided in 1924. That year Yost, who had become athletic director in 1921, announced his retirement and appointed George Little coach. Little had proved himself capable at Miami (Ohio) and Wisconsin, and his 1924 record with Michigan was a respectable 6–2. He had the misfortune, however, to play Illinois at the dedication of its new stadium in Champaign-Urbana. That was the day Grange scored five touchdowns, four on long runs in the first 10 minutes, to demolish Michigan, 39–14.

Yost watched from the stands, accompanied by his wife, Eunice, a good and charming creature who wrote verse and left football to her spouse, wisely, and knew rather less about the game than a Mongol princess. She is credited with asking Yost such questions as, "How many halves are there in a football game?" and, "Why don't you play that boy, he's so nice looking?" After Grange's fourth touchdown run, Eunice tugged Yost by the sleeve and said, "Fielding, why don't you *do* something about it?"

What Fielding did was a Sarah Bernhardt; he returned to coaching for two more years. Little was not unrelieved. "When we won," he com-

mented, "it was Yost's team. When we lost, it was mine."

The next season, 1925, Illinois came to Ann Arbor, and the Maize and Blue had its revenge. Aided somewhat by a muddy field, the big Michigan line hung four horsecollars on the Galloping Ghost, and Benny Friedman's place-kick won the game, 3–0. Grange gained 25 yards, but lost 26, and Yost got off his self-savored nifty: "Grange didn't gain enough ground to bury him in, y' know. Even if they'd a buried him head daown!"

Somebody else's joke, though, failed to penetrate Hurry Up. Adolph (Germany) Schulz, fabulous center of the point-a-minutes, took the coach for a ride in his new car. As the interurban trolley cars sped by them, Yost remarked, "Dutchman, those interurban cars go fast." Germany replied with a straight face, "Yes, but they're hard to steer." Yost maintained silence for 30 seconds, then asked Schulz seriously, "What d' ye mean—hard to steer?"

Granny Rice purposely asked Pop Warner in Yost's presence who invented the spiral pass. Warner looked straight at Yost, and said, "Yost did. He also invented everything else in the game—including the football." Yost, who thought Warner serious, thanked him.

No coach who ever lived took defeat harder than Yost, which is quite a claim. "How he hated to lose!" said his friend Lawton. "If he lost a card game, he wouldn't be friends until noon next day. He always said he liked to play *against* a good loser."

In victory, Yost enjoyed being a cynosure; in defeat he searched out solitude. After Michigan lost at Harvard, 7–0, in 1914, Bill Frackelton, general manager of the New York Central, walked through the Michigan sleeper to make sure all was in readiness for the team, which was supposed to board at eleven. It was only eight, but Yost sat alone in the car, on the edge of a lower berth, overcoat and hat still on, munching cookies but disconsolate.

Yost and Michigan, as stated, were as unyielding at the council table as his teams were on a goal-line stand. From 1907 through '14 Michigan dropped out of the conference and operated as an independent; the reason was an argument on institutional control of athletics. Their intersectional games included an intermittent series with Vanderbilt. This was arranged because of the close relationship between Yost and Dan McGugin, who as Vanderbilt coach from 1904 to

Grayer but still in love with his "Meeshegan"

'34 (except for 1918) was a widely respected pioneer of football in the South.

McGugin had played guard for the point-a-minutes. He had a strong charge; he had to, or suffer Heston to run through his back. Dan met a charming Nashville belle named Virginia Fite and introduced her sister, Eunice, to Yost. Both couples married, and until 1921 Yost made his off-season home in Nashville.

Naturally he did not permit his coaching to be diluted by nepotism, and Michigan won the first seven games with Vandy. In 1922, however, the Commodores made the Wolverines settle for a scoreless tie in an otherwise spotless season, and in 1923 Michigan won 3–0, on Jack Blott's field goal.

Michigan was favored, but after three plays Yost recognized he was in for a nervous afternoon. McGugin had built a furnace fire under the Commodores. A few minutes before the kickoff he pointed out the window to a military cemetery near the stadium and then to the Michigan team warming up.

"In that cemetery sleep your grandfathers," he said, "and down on that field are the grandsons of the Damn Yankees who put them there."

After the game Yost remarked to him on the frenzy of Vanderbilt's play, and McGugin told him of the pep talk. Yost didn't think it funny. He refused to shake hands, and was still fuming on the train ride home.

"Him and his phony Southern accent," Yost growled. "Why until he got that coaching job at Vanderbilt, he was never south of Toledo."

Except for self-centeredness and incessant maceration of cigars, Yost had no bad habits. His personal life was exemplary, a reflection of his bringing up. He never told an off-color story, and used *damn* or *hell* only for "medicinal purposes." In demonstrating a forward pass in a hotel room, he inadvertently threw a Gideon Bible, and apologized afterwards.

Alcohol was taboo with him, and trainer Keene Fitzpatrick had to talk him into giving the players ale before Friday night dinner as an unwinder. One Friday they got to the ale early and by Yost's arrival, were obviously high. He gave strict orders that henceforth the ale should not be touched until he got there.

"Some people can drink," he told them, "and it doesn't harm them. But it doesn't do them any good. And ye want to be good, don't ye?"

Yost was good, and worked hard at it. Born April 30, 1871, and reared in a Fairview, West Virginia, cabin, in rough and rowdy mining company, he had to grow up and toughen fast. While still in his teens he acquired a certificate to teach backwoods school, which meant pounding it into some of his pupils physically, and he learned to handle more abrasive types as a deputy town marshal.

Later, he had become comfortable financially, by augmenting his salary as coach; he was part owner of a hydroelectric plant and a credit company, and also served as a bank official. And he was careful of his money. He made friend Lawton pay the photographer for the picture he'd promised to autograph, with the comment, "I don't throw my money to the birds."

But he provided well for his family, was reasonably indulgent of his wife, two children, and three grandchildren, supported the Boy Scouts (who gave him their cherished Golden Buffalo award), donated $1,000 to a soldier's memorial in the Illinois Stadium, and supported an indigent farm couple.

"As an example of clean living," said Captain Bob Brown of the 1925 team, "Yost was tops. He had a talk that always impressed me about the sacrifices made by athletes. 'Why, ye know,' he

would say, 'the athlete doesn't sacrifice anything by being out in the fresh air with a planned objective and work to do. That's the way to build a good, clean, sound body, mentally alert, with a will to fight for a place in the world.'"

Frank Murphy, former associate justice of the United States Supreme Court, said of him, "Fielding H. Yost has done more to inculcate high ideals of clean Christian living in the minds of Michigan students than any other one man."

Yost, the coach, was fundamentalist, psychologist, and leader with an enthusiasm, self-exacting and contagious. Asked why his Michigan teams invariably exuded morale, he explained, "Morale is something ye don't put on like an overcoat. Ye build it on, day by day, the way ye think, the way ye live, and the way ye act, y' know."

Although field position is intrinsic to successful football, Yost was its arch apostle. Teams defeated by Michigan often outstatisticked the Wolverines—on the wrong side of midfield.

"We play percentage," Yost explained. "We let the other fellow run the ball and waste his energy in his own territory. Football games aren't won —they're lost. Meeshegan's record is due to a policy of letting the enemy take the risks of fumbling inside his 40. Then we cash in on his mistakes."

Yost was a favorite target of Zuppke's sharp, barbed wit, but he had a deep respect for Hurry Up's football. "Fielding H. Yost?" he asked. "Yes, I'll buy that. But don't give me any of that Fielding Harris Yost stuff. His name is Fielding *Hitting* Yost. His teams knock you down and run away from you, but when you try the same thing on them, they knock you down again."

Dick Hanley, who coached some excellent teams at Haskell and Northwestern, said that for balance between defense and offense, Yost's Michigan teams were unexcelled.

Yost, who regarded himself as without doubt the No. 1 coach, was irritated by all the publicity accorded the Rockne system and the Warner system. He especially resented the ascendancy of Rockne, who began to dominate the scene before Hurry Up retired. "Even mention of Rockne's name in Ann Arbor," said an old Michigan player, "would cause the Old Man to hit the ceiling." In disparagement of systems, Yost referred to Michigan's as "a punt, a pass, and a prayer." This got wide attention, as he knew it would.

Michigan's opening practice in 1905 was at-

tended by Bill Reid, himself an outstanding coach at Harvard, who wanted to talk with Yost and study his methods. Yost began the practice by taking the squad down to one of the goal lines.

"This game is simple, y' know," said Yost. "It consists of two things, this ball yere, and this goal line yere, and the purpose of the game is to get the ball over the line, and like an express package, without delay or derailment, y' know."

Later, during a scrimmage, Yost blew his whistle and addressed a player we'll call Jones. "Jones, didn't you know that only players are allowed on the field. Spectators are supposed to sit up in the stands. If you will sit up there, you can see much better."

Jones went up into the stands, and the scrimmage went on. After about 20 minutes, Yost yelled up to him, "Jones, would you like to play?" Jones came racing down onto the field. The next play, an end run, was away from him, and he had no chance to make the tackle. So he tackled another player.

Practice didn't necessarily end after Michigan left the field. If Yost happened to meet a player on campus, he'd talk to him, hitting and being hit, usually before a fast-gathering audience of students. Same thing downtown in Ann Arbor. Unknowledgeable bystanders were afraid a fight would erupt momentarily between the middle-aged man and youth who kept pushing and shoving each other on the sidewalk. "It's all right," a student said. "That's Coach Yost showing Stan Wells how to play end."

One day, in front of Huston's Billiard Hall on State Street, Yost staged an informal clinic to prove Pennsylvania had beaten Michigan the year before on an illegal pass. For players, he pressed passersby into service. The town policeman was ordered to play center, and use his helmet for a ball. By the time Yost stopped, so had all traffic.

A stranger recognizing Hurry Up in a Minneapolis hotel made the mistake of asking him to explain a play. Yost requisitioned everybody in the lobby to run through the play, but was still two shy of eleven, when a serene lady marched by, a bellboy carrying her bag. Yost grabbed the bellboy and the lady's bag to fill out the team.

"This is disgraceful," the lady protested. "Where is the manager?"

"Hold yer horses just a minute," said Yost. "The manager is playing quarterback."

In Grand Central, Yost demonstrated the art of dropkicking so well that he inadvertently kicked a

hole in the valise of a perfect stranger.

Because its strategy and tactics bear a certain similarity to football, Yost—like many coaches —found a fascination in military history, and eventually became an authentic expert. He visited Little Big Horn to study the layout and decide whether Custer should be blamed for what happened to the Seventh Cavalry; he never did decide.

On the Civil War he was an unbiased scholar. Nashville people were used to seeing him put his bags of groceries on the sidewalk to demonstrate how the Confederates had deployed at the Battle of Franklin, and he spent many hours retracing the Battle of Gettysburg with Mrs. Yost's uncle, Colonel John Fite, of Lebanon, Pennsylvania, who had been in Pickett's charge.

He had visited the Waterloo battlefield and would discuss it at every opportunity. Andy Baker, his secretary for years, said that whenever they drove by a piece of landscape that resembled the site of the Wellington-Napoleon confrontation, Yost would stop the car, back up, and shout, "There it is! There's Hougoumont Farm! There's the sunken road! Over there's where Napoleon sat on his white horse, y'know."

During World War I, he placed a huge map on the wall of the dressing room, and designated the French in red, the British white, the Americans blue, and the Germans red, and for 20 minutes before football skull practice, the squad got a lecture in military maneuvering.

"The French will withdraw from yere, y' know, because of the bad terrain; the British will advance yere; the Americans will move from yere to yere. Here's what Marshall Foch did. Naow, here's what he should have done. Here's what I would've done."

Although Yost's point-a-minutes will always hold their ancient place, his last five seasons, 33-3-2, with Big Ten championships the last four, stand even more impressive, when you consider the testier opposition, and Yost in his fifties with 24 years of coaching already behind him.

In 1931, Hurry Up surprised a writer very close to him, Harry Salsinger, sports editor and author of the fine column "The Umpire" in the Detroit *News*, by naming the 1925 team the greatest he ever coached; this team lost one game, 3-2, to Northwestern on a mucky Soldier's Field.

"Do you mean to say," Salsinger asked, astonished, "that your 1901 team could not have beaten your 1925 team?"

"No," said Yost, "I don't think they could. The 1925 team had Bennie Oosterbaan and Bill Flora ends, Tom Edwards and Harry Hawkins tackles, Ray Baer and John Lovette guards, Bob Brown center, Benny Friedman quarterback, Bruce Gregory, Lou Gilbert, and, later, Wally Weber halfbacks, and at fullback Bo Molenda. A team hard to fault."

Friedman, brilliant passer, place-kicker, and big playmaker in the crisis, understood Yost's game plans as if they were his own, and gave his plays an indigestible mixture. In Oosterbaan he had one of the great all-time pass receivers and all-round atheletes. Benny made good use of "Old 83"—the chicanery that had scored 50 touchdowns over the years for Michigan—a double fake, first to the right end coming around and then to a bucking back, with the tailback ultimately getting the ball on a sweep around the defensive left end.

It was Friedman's 44-yard place-kick that was the turning point in the dramatic 17-16 victory at Ohio in the next to the last game of the Old Man's last season, 1926. The championship was at stake and the players never forgot old Hurry Up's pregame words:

"We have come to the test. Ohio is strong —very strong. We're glad they are strong. Ye wouldn't be happy tonight if ye won from a weak team. A strong opponent is the test of yereselves. Ye are going out there to fight—for Meeshegan. I know ye won't fail."

Fielding Yost truly loved Michigan, everything about her, the players, the students for whom he planned the vast athletic complex. He doted on Michigan's songs, the inspiring "Victors," the nostalgic "Yellow and Blue."

Sentiment ran deep in him. When he was 74 and the shadows were moving in, he fished through his pockets and showed Fred Lawton a letter he'd received from his mother on his birthday 18 years before. His eyes were wet as he read:

"There have been many ups and downs since we lived in the old log cabin. I can say my children never gave me any trouble. I'm proud of them."

The Old Man rubbed his eyes with the back of his hand. Then he pointed to a word in the letter, "enrichment," and he broke down and sobbed. When he had pulled himself together, he said, "Ye'd wonder how she even knew the meaning of such a word, with the education she had."

About a year later, Lawton was with him again. Yost sat in his blue-striped pajamas and blue

robe. They talked for an hour and then Lawton prepared to leave. Mrs. Yost said, "Finish the orangeade before you go." The coach, with Lawton's help, got to his feet, and they touched glasses. "We've traveled a long road," said Fielding (Hurry Up) Yost. And then he gave his farewell toast:

"To the end of destiny—Meeshegan!"

Bob Zuppke

THE PAINTER OF UPSETS

For unbroken job longevity at one college, Robert Carl Zuppke's 29 seasons at Illinois are topped only by Amos Alonzo Stagg's 41 at Chicago. For coaching genius and personal color, not even his good friend Knute Kenneth Rockne surpassed the Dutch Master. Zuppke the coach was the compendium of Zuppke the man: philosopher—strictly pragmatic, he claimed—psychologist, dreamer, doer, driver, artist, strategist, tactician, leader.

As a painter of oils—colorful, sometimes raw landscapes of desert, forest, and ocean—Zuppke was no mere dabbler. In galleries as well as stadia, he had his exhibitions. "Football," he said, "is not the only physical expression of a mental exercise; the great singer, the great pianist, violinist, the painter all express their thoughts physically."

As a speaker, Zup had few equals; only Frank Cavanaugh and Rockne of his time were in his class. His wit was enhanced by the smidgen of stutter and a German accent; he was born in Berlin and brought to Milwaukee when he was only two.

Whether Zuppke's Fighting Illini made a better show on the gridiron than Zup did on the dais is debatable. Both, at best, were four-star. Zup on the dais was preferred by opposing coaches. For one thing, until the material began to fade off after 1929, his Illini were tough, either contending for the Big Ten championship or upsetting pretenders in a manner to give odds-setters the vapors. For another, when Zuppke had something to say, it was invariably worth hearing or reading.

"It is foolish," he said, "to claim that football is all good. There are both good and bad in the game, as there are in all human beings. A thing that is all good is no good. We wouldn't learn anything, if everything was good."

That was the serious philosopher. The droll Zup trained some of his most pleasurable wit on his coaching rivals.

"It's true," he said, "that Amos Alonzo Stagg never swears at his men—because he doesn't have any men. He calls this man a jackass, then that man a jackass, then another. By the end of the workout there are no men playing—just jackasses grazing."

Zuppke and Rockne shared a wide range of interests beyond football. Both were interested in science, literature and art. Coming upon them suddenly, one might discover to his surprise that the subject under discussion was not a new method of applying power off tackle, but eurythmics, the art of harmonious and expressive bodily movement. Eurythmics, they agreed, was something the ballet virtuoso and the classic open-field runner had in common.

For consumption by press and public, Zup and Rock carried on a mock vendetta of wisecracks and stories at the expense of each other. Zup was often invited to grace the dais at Notre Dame dinners as the principal speaker; Rock also would be scheduled. The same at Illinois dinners. Whoever was up last usually won. If Rockne, with tongue-in-cheek modesty, said, "My assistants do all the work. All I do is blow up the balls," Zup would counter, "I haven't that much wind."

Zuppke liked to kid Rockne about his escalating fame, and told of visiting him at his home in South Bend. A footman—the wild note to begin with—was supposed to have answered Zup's ring.

"I'm Zuppke," said the short, blue-eyed, crinkly cheeked bouncing biscuit of a man. "Zuppke of Illinois."

"Zoopy? Soupy?" the footman began to close the door in his face. "Never heard of you."

"Look," Zuppke snapped. "I want to see Rockne. I'm a coach."

"No! No!" the footman protested. "Mister

Bob Zuppke of Illinois

of only one instance where he seemed tasteless. At a dinner with his good friend, the dean of sportswriters, Grantland Rice, Zuppke referred to New York sportswriting as "the cesspool of journalism." Rice, who worked out of New York, was a gentleman but when irritated, a rough fellow. When he got up to speak, he said, "My friend Zup's remarks on New York journalism remind me of the advice my old grandmother gave me before I left Tennessee. 'Grantland,' she said, 'never get into an argument about cesspools with an expert.'"

The harsh note did not predominate in Zuppke, but as with all coaches who compete successfully, it was there on call. If life called for a counterpunch, Zuppke could throw it, and would. He told Harold (Red) Grange, his greatest player and the No. 1 player of the twenties and thirties, "Red, I know there have been occasions during the stress of getting ready for an important game that some of my boys must have been almost mad enough at me to swing at my chin." Zup paused, then added, "If anyone did that, he'd be busy for a while."

The toughness shows up in some of his painting, which critics, while applauding its violence and dynamism, criticized occasionally as too brutal. Zup, who did not speak of himself as a professional in art, replied with his ready smile, "Why shouldn't art be brutal when and if nature is brutal? Why shouldn't I paint the forests as they are? When I go into the forest, the trees scratch and scrape me. Am I expected to come back and paint a lovely scene?

"Football is brutal, too. But brutes can't play it. The value of all paintings, whether in pigment or pigskin, lies to some degree in their resemblance to life."

Grange has several of his old coach's paintings, one of them a crayon of Red carrying the ball. Usually, Zup did his first landscape sketches in crayon for speed's sake in catching light and shadow, and later copied in oil. He didn't copy "Grainche"—as he called him—in oil, because he considered his movement as difficult for the artist to capture as for the tackler.

Unlike Rockne's or Warner's, Zuppke's name was never used to describe an offensive system. Zuppke adjusted his formations from year to year, according to the available personnel. Had he cared to concentrate on it, he probably could have matched Stagg or Warner as an originator. As it is, he has a long line of firsts credited to him: 1) The Flea Flicker—a predetermined lat-

Rockne's the coach!"

"No, yourself!" Zuppke roared. "Rockne's the genius. I'm the coach!"

Rockne's teams in the first half of the twenties propelled much controversy about whether they came to the full-second stop required by the rules after shifting from the T to the box. Zuppke used this as background for the story of another visit to Notre Dame.

"When I got on the campus," he said, "three freshmen came out of a building hollering, 'One-two-three-shift!' From another building farther along, two young priests came out, listed their cassocks, and shouted, 'One-two-three-hike!' Then I visited the office of the president of Notre Dame. He rose to greet me and advanced yelling, 'One-two-three-hike!' But he's getting old and can't move as fast as the others. In fact, he was the only one I saw on the campus whose shift was legal."

Zuppke's humor, ranging from far-out lunacy to the brisk jab or the stinging barb, was his own. He didn't back up and he didn't pull his punches, but he never was consciously brutal, and I know

eral off a forward pass, getting its name from the finger flick used by the receiver in executing the lateral. Still a functional play today. 2) The onside kick. 3) The screen pass. 4) The guards pulling back to protect the passer. 5) The guards (first one, later two) coming back on pass defense. 6) The spiral snap by center. 7) The huddle.

The huddle, perhaps his most notable gift to the game, was introduced in 1919, but was criticized at first and not accepted universally until the midtwenties. Its advantages, as enumerated by Zuppke, comprise simplifying of signals, helping the quarterback who lacks a strong voice, helping the player who has trouble remembering signals, and enabling the quarterback, by stepping out of the huddle, picking his play, stepping back in, and calling it, to quell would-be quarterbacks among the ten others —the "Mexican Generals."

"That is the big point," he said. "The huddle is much simpler when the quarterback is not in it, as at Illinois, until he has decided on his play."

From 1913, when George Huff, "G" Huff, Illinois' famous athletic director, hired him from Oak Park, Illinois, through 1920, the pigskin pigments in Illini Blue and Gold ran rich for Robert Zuppke, and he used them well. The Illini won five Big Ten titles outright, tied for two others, and finished second once. The 1914, '15, '23, and '27 teams were undefeated; in '14, '23, and '27 the Illini had a good claim on the national championship.

Zuppke called his 1914 team the best. He said that its diversification in talent enabled him to give it a more complex offense than any of his later teams. He considered quarterback George (Potsy) Clark and halfback Harold Pogue of that team his greatest players next to Grange.

Harold (Red) Grange, it says here and a lot of other places, was the greatest back who ever carried a football, including O. J. Simpson and Jim Brown. Grange was born, June 13, 1903, in Forksville, Pennsylvania, near lumber camps where his father bossed 300 men because he could lick any one of them. It took him four hours to prove one case. "With a father like mine," Red says, "I was not apt to be overimpressed with my athletic skills."

Grange's mother died when he was five, and his father moved the family to Wheaton, Illinois, where they had relatives. Red's two sisters returned to Pennsylvania to live with grandparents. The father, Red, and a younger brother, Garland, who played end for Illinois, lived in a five-room

The sun in Bob's eyes—or a new play in his head?

apartment over a store and took turns cooking and keeping house.

As a high school athlete in Wheaton, Grange won 16 letters in football, basketball, baseball, and track, but colleges at the time did not offer formal athletic scholarships. Red chose Illinois, because it cost the least. Wheaton High friends were going there, and when he was on campus for an interscholastic track meet in May 1922, he met Zuppke.

The Dutch Master taking personal charge

"Is your name Grainche?" Zup asked. It was. "Where are you going to college?" He didn't know. "I hope you come here," Zup said, putting an arm around his shoulders. "You may have a chance to make the team here."

Grange arrived at Champaign-Urbana that September with a second-hand trunk, one suit, two pairs of pants, and a sweater. He'd bought them with the savings of four summers' work on a Wheaton ice wagon. He didn't think that he was good enough to make the football team, and went out only because his Zeta Psi fraternity urged him.

After one look at the freshman squad of 300, he returned to the frat house and said, "I'll never make that team. I'm not going out." The frat brethren paddled him and pressured him, especially a fellow named Johnny Hawks, and he went back out. In the first scrimmage with the varsity, he scored two touchdowns, one on a 60-yard punt return.

The famous number he wore, 77, was handed to him as a sophomore. In his first varsity game, against Nebraska, he scored three touchdowns on runs of 35, 60, and 12 yards, as Illinois won 24–7.

Somebody in Georgia wrote him, "I know why they didn't throw you on those runs Saturday. Your number is 77, and I know from experience that you can't throw two consecutive sevens. I've been trying a long time." After that, Red regarded 77 as lucky; later Illinois would retire the number.

Red could not explain his running gifts beyond saying he seemed able to size up a field and plot his moves while in movement. He was quick-starting and fast, seemed to glide, and could sweep or cut back, run to his right or his left, and operate in mud and rain as well as on a dry field. He used a cross-over step, but didn't spin. "If I tried to spin," he said, "I'd have broken a leg."

With Illinois and later the Chicago Bears, Grange was respected and admired for his innate modesty, his fine blocking, his tendency to play down himself and praise others, his deep sense of team play. As such he provides a shining contrast to the overpublicized, pampered stars of today, who labor under the illusion they are bigger than the game.

Between Zuppke and Grange, a deep reciprocal fondness developed.

Zuppke imparting some wisdom to his Illini (it's a lesson in oratory as well)

"I will never have another Grange," Zuppke told Grantland Rice, "but neither will anybody else. They can argue all they like about the greatest football player that ever lived. I'm satisfied I had him when I had Grange."

Zuppke, of course, didn't let him know it. After he had taken him out for a breather that first game against Nebraska, Zup said, "You're learning, and you're also giving the plays away."

"I may be learning, I thought," Grange laughed later, "but I'm not giving the plays away, because I don't know where I'm going myself."

Zuppke didn't drive Grange, he gentled him. "You were sensitive," he told him later. "You were the lone-wolf type. It was only necessary to explain to you the how and why of things, and to convince you that you really could do what I told you you could. Of course, that first year it seemed that it would take an eternity to teach you to cut back, to make you understand that it was better to gain one yard down the field than 20 yards *across* the field—toward the sideline."

Grange's shiniest hour, the finest any running

back ever has known, all things considered, was also one of Zuppke's. The opponent was Michigan, the date was October 18, 1924, the occasion was the formal dedication of the $1,700,000 Illinois Memorial Stadium, and the crowd of 67,000 was the largest to see a football game in the Midwest at that time.

An unusual coaching situation obtained at Michigan. Fielding H. (Hurry Up) Yost, Michigan's head coach and athletic director, had announced his retirement as coach after the 1923 season. He was succeeded by George Little, who had proved his competence at Miami (Ohio) and Wisconsin, and who now, in 1924, coached Michigan with Yost looking over his shoulder. Yost returned to coaching in 1925 and '26, and he was impelled by what happened to Michigan at Illinois.

The teams had not played in 1923, but the Wolverines knew all about Grange. Yost scouted the Illini in the 1924 opener, two weeks before, against Nebraska. Zuppke, knowing he was in the stands, set a trap for him. To lure Yost into

Zup with his greatest, Red Grange

setting a defense to the outside, Zuppke had Grange run mainly to the outside against the Cornhuskers. Yost was seldom trapped, but he was this time.

Michigan, unbeaten in 20 straight, was favored and took the field confidently. It tried to kick off to Harry McIllwain but Grange moved over under the ball, and said, "I've got it." He took the ball on the 5. McIllwain, called by Zuppke the king of open-field blockers, upended the first Wolverine downfield, and Earl Britton, the full-back and star punter, dumped the second.

Grange started to his left, reversed to avoid one man, and then broke back diagonally to his left and through the rest of the Wolverines. At Michigan's 40 he was in the clear except for safety man Tod Rockwell, who made a futile dive at him.

Michigan was shocked, and didn't come out of it. In 10 minutes Grange made four touchdowns. Following the kickoff he carried the ball five times. Three times he scored on touchdown runs of 67, 56, and 44 yards. He began the runs by cutting back inside end or tackle, either to the right or to the left. He was assisted by fine blocking from McIllwain, Britton, quarterback Jimmy Holt, and some strong linemen like Jim McMillen. But it was his running that was mainly responsible.

After the fourth touchdown, the Illini called time out, and Grange told trainer Matt Bullock, "I'm dog tired. You'd better tell Zup to get me out of here." When Red got to the bench, Zuppke said, "You should have scored five touchdowns. You didn't cut right on that one play."

Grange returned in the third quarter and scored his fifth touchdown on a 15-yard end sweep, and in the fourth quarter he threw a forward pass for another TD. Illinois won 39–14. Grange carried the ball 21 times, gained 402 yards, ran for five touchdowns, and passed for a sixth.

"It was," said Alonzo Stagg, "the most spectacular single-handed performance ever delivered in a major game."

"I remember only one thing about those runs against Michigan," Grange recalled. "In the opening kickoff, when I got downfield and saw that only one man was still in front of me, Rockwell, the safety, I thought to myself, 'I'd better get this guy, because after coming all the way, I'll sure look like a bum if one guy tackles me.' I can't tell you, though, how I got by him."

Yost, who was at least one of the top five worst losers of all time, said, "All Grange can do is run." To which Zuppke replied, "All Galli-Curci can do is sing."

For the rest of the season, it was a question of who was coaching Michigan, Yost or Little. Whichever, the Wolverines had a good record, 6–2. But the aftermath of the Illinois game continued through the off-season and into the 1925 campaign.

Yost was planning to run for president of the Football Coaches Association for 1925, and had prepared a self-nominating speech. He made the mistake, however, of showing it to Dan McGugin, Vanderbilt coach; he and Dan were good friends, had married sisters, and were in business together. McGugin, who liked a lark, had a copy of the speech made and gave it to the Army coach, Captain John McEwan, who was always ready for a bit of fun.

The coaches held their convention in New York, in December. The 1924 president, John Heisman, was out of the country, so Zuppke, as first vice president, occupied the chair. Zup had controlled the nominating committee for two years, but had previously turned down the presidency. Now, however, he had been persuaded to run, probably because he wanted to heckle Yost. Anyhow, Zuppke, McGugin, and McEwan had set another kind of trap for Hurry Up.

When Yost got up to read his speech, Zuppke interrupted, "I object. This organization is for coaches only. Yost is not a coach. He's an athletic director. He hasn't been a coach since Michigan played Illinois. He quit coaching that afternoon, and scouting too."

Then McEwan asked for and got the floor. He

read Yost's speech, slightly modified:

"Gentlemen and coaches, I nominate for president a man from the North. A man as tall and straight and strong as the great timbers of the Northwest. A man whose heart is as pure and white as the snow-white flurries over the Dakotas. A man whose name scintillates from coast to coast. Gentlemen and coaches, I nominate Fielding H. Yost, of Michigan!"

Bill Roper, coach of Princeton, said, "I second the nomination." Zuppke, who knew Roper as well as he knew Grange, asked him sternly, "Who are you?"

"I'm Roper of Princeton," Bill said.

"Okay," Zuppke said. "I guess I'll recognize Princeton."

George Little then moved that nominations be closed.

"I'll entertain no such motion," Zuppke thundered. He asked one of the officers to take over the chair, and moved out onto the floor.

"I'm also a candidate for the presidency," he said. "Will anybody nominate me?" Before anybody could speak, he added, "All right, I'll nominate myself."

Coaches who attended that meeting said that Zup's nominating speech for himself was a classic. It is a tragedy it was not recorded in its entirety.

"Captain McEwan," he began, "has said that we want a man from the North. What do you think of that, you Southerners? Do you want a damn Yankee ruling you? Where's that hot Southern blood I've heard so much about?

"If the situation calls for a man from the North, why pick a man as tall and straight and strong as the great timbers which grow in the Northwest? Why not pick a little guy like me, whom you can push around?"

On he went, and he had them in the aisles. He was elected, and is reported to have got every vote but his own.

Harassed by Grange and heckled by Zuppke, Yost had his revenge at Ann Arbor the following fall, when a big Michigan line, aided somewhat by a muddy field, hung four horsecollars on Red Grange, whom they were now calling by the nickname Rice had given him, "The Galloping Ghost." Michigan won 3–0 on a field goal by Benny Friedman.

Grange, however, showed his value on defense. Michigan's famous "83" play, a weak-side run by Friedman after two fakes to and feints by backs in other directions, had scored some 50 touchdowns for the Wolverines over the years. So

The Galloping Ghost in action

Grange was instructed by Zuppke to play a yard outside the end in the secondary and every time Michigan got inside the Illinois 40 to hold his ground and wait.

"Sooner or later," Zuppke told him, "somebody will be coming around our left end carrying a football, and I want you to tackle him. Some one did, Friedman, and Grange tackled him. Thus the Wolverines had to settle for a field goal.

Grange's only appearance in the East as a college player came in the semifinal game of his senior season, against Pennsylvania in Franklin Field. The East acknowledged him, but knew him only by newsreels or radio. Twenty-four hours of rain and snow on a gridiron covered only by straw left the players lining up in mud for the opening kickoff.

Grange ignored the mud. On the third play, his first carry, he broke 55 yards for a touchdown, cutting back to the weak side. He returned the ensuing kickoff 55 yards to Penn's 25, whence the Illini took it over. He scored again in the third and fourth quarters on runs of 12 and 20 yards. Illinois won 24–2, with Grange gaining 363 yards in 36 rushes, scoring three touchdowns and setting up the other. Nobody was inclined to argue with Grantland Rice's lines:

A streak of fire, a breath of flame,
Eluding all who reach and clutch,

Calling it quits, Zuppke congratulates successor Ray Eliot

A gray ghost sent into the game
That rival hands may rarely touch,
A rubber, bounding, blasting soul,
Whose destination is the goal—
Red Grange of Illinois!

Grange gave Zuppke's football brush its liveliest dramatic hues, but the Dutch Master rendered some other masterpieces, especially in pulling off major upsets.

There was the defeat of Ohio State at Columbus, 9–7, in 1919, with the Big Ten championship at stake, and Chic Harley, the legendary Buckeye back, in his last game. Extra newspapers printed ahead of time ran an "if win" streamer, "Ohio State Smears Illinois." One of them reached Zuppke's hands. Trailing 7–6 with five minutes left, the Illini marched from their 20 to Ohio's 20 on passes from quarterback Laurie Walquist to ace end Chuck Carney. With only time enough for a field-goal try and Ralph Fletcher, the regular kicker, sidelined by injury, Ralph's brother Bob, who never had attempted a placekick in a game, came off the bench to boot a perfect one.

The 7–0 upsetter at Columbus in 1921 was even more of a shocker, because Ohio State had a perfect record and Illinois hadn't won a conference game. But the Illini, using only eleven men, stopped halfback Pete Stinchcomb, and got a break when one of the two Illinois passes thrown by halfback Don Peden bounced off the arms of a Buckeye and into the hands of Walquist, who ran for the game's only touchdown.

"We will play only eleven men," Zuppke told the squad that day. "Nobody but a dead man can come out of the game." Nobody died, so nobody came out. The line, "Nobody but a dead man," became something of a legend. Against Iowa the next year, Zuppke was again short of reserves and the starting eleven went all the way. Near the end of the game, however, an Illinois lineman was stretched out, and Zuppke sent in a sophomore replacement. The sophomore reported to the referee, but after looking at the prone player he returned to the bench.

"What's the matter?" Zuppke asked.

"Why, coach," the boy replied, "you said nobody but a dead man can come out, and he's still breathing."

"The referee penalized us," said Zuppke, "which put the ball on our 5-yard line, and we lost the game."

Zuppke's No. 1 upset, probably No. 1 of all time in college football, was the 14–9 defeat of Minnesota at Minneapolis in 1916. Zuppke began the season with a good team, but injuries hurt. Even at full strength, however, the Illini would have been given sparse chance against the Gophers, coached by Dr. Henry Williams, and believed by many to be the strongest team ever assembled in the West.

Minnesota had beaten four opponents by a total of 241 to 14, and would beat its last two, Wisconsin and Chicago, 54–0 and 49–0. It was expected to do the same kind of job on Illinois. It was being called "the perfect team." Captain Bert Baston had twice been All-America end, and the backfield was considered all-star: Joe (Galloping) Sprafka and Hal Hansen at the halves, A. D. (Pudge) Wyman at full, and Clair (Shorty) Long at quarter.

Walter Camp and other Eastern All-America pundits were coming West for the game, and Doc Williams, an old Yale man, hoped to have the Gophers put on their best show. In his Chicago column, Ring Lardner wrote a funny letter to Zuppke, advising him to take his team off the train at Chicago, go to a theater Saturday afternoon, and just not show up at Minneapolis.

Such a situation was not to be overlooked by Zuppke. "Camp is going to put seven Minnesota players on his All-America," he told his players. Every night he scrimmaged them furiously. "We're supposed to be killed Saturday," he explained, "so we might as well have the satisfaction of killing ourselves rather than letting Minnesota do it."

When the team arrived in Minneapolis Friday afternoon, Zuppke suspended training rules, told

them to go out on the town and relax, but to get to bed by midnight. Relaxing wasn't easy; even the bellhops were laying 20 to 1 on Minnesota to win in a walkover, and 10 to 1 that Illinois wouldn't score.

On Saturday Zuppke deliberately set his watch behind so they were on the field practicing when Minnesota came out. Ed (Dutch) Sternaman, the 139-pound Illini halfback, remarked to Zuppke, "Why, coach, they don't look so big." "Not only that," said Zuppke, "but not one of them can add two and two."

Then he took the team into the dressing room for final instructions.

"Today," he said, "I want you to have some fun. Get beaten 100 to 0 if you want to, but have fun. Now I want to tell you something. I've had this great team scouted. On the first play, Galloping Sprafka will take the ball. I want all eleven men to tackle Sprafka. On the second play Wyman will take the ball. I want all eleven men to tackle him. On the third play, Hansen will take the ball. All eleven will tackle him."

"But, coach," one of the players asked, "suppose somebody else takes the ball?"

"Then," said Zuppke, "I'll tackle him. I am Louis the Fourteenth, and you are my court! After us the deluge!"

The Illini didn't know what he meant, but it sounded good. They gave a yell and went running out.

Psychology alone, however, was not Zuppke's only weapon. He supplemented it with sound, special preparation. In this, rival coaches found him a bedeviler. "If Zuppke takes dead aim on a game," they said, "you're in trouble." As planned, Illinois kicked off a flat ball that Minnesota fumbled around and finally recovered on its 5. Already the Gophers were feeling the pressure. Then, as Zuppke had predicted, Sprafka, Wyman, and Hansen carried. They were inundated by Illini.

The Gophers had to punt, and Illinois lined up in a complicated spread. Captain Bart Macomber, quarterback, passed to Sternaman for 25 yards, and running plays brought the ball to the Minnesota 5. The rattled Gophers went offside. Macomber sneaked over from the 1 and kicked the point.

Galloping Sprafka took the kickoff back to his 30 and the Gophers pounded out 15 yards. Then came the killer diller. Wyman's pass intended for Baston was intercepted by left end Ren Kraft, who ran it back 50 yards for a touchdown, and

Macomber again converted. The Illini led 14–0, and Minnesota was having a nightmare.

The Gophers stormed back in the second half, scored nine points. They kept throwing in fresh men in the final quarter, and the Illini were hard put.

"I never acted more than I did in that last quarter," said Macomber. "I kept tying my shoes, breaking string on my shoulder pads, losing my helmet, deliberately fouling up signals. But we managed to hang on."

The headline atop the story in the Chicago *Tribune* the next day read:

> Hold on Tight
> When You Read This

Behind the facade of wit, the planning, the psychology, an intense competitive fire burned in Bob Zuppke. Before the 1933 game with Army at Cleveland, Red Blaik, then Army assistant, asked Zup if coaching bothered him.

"You bet," said Zup. "Why right now I'm as nervous as an old cat! My stomach is burning up on me. But if it wasn't I wouldn't be coaching. When you stop burning up inside, then you better quit—because you've had it."

An Illinois official said of Zuppke, "On the street, during the season, he walks with his head down, thinking football. He is grim. He is in a mental state which he wishes to encourage in his men."

Yet, he did not take football home with him.

"Fannie is not forced to listen to shoptalk," he said. "We seldom discuss football, we have so many other interests and diversions. She kept a scrapbook of all Illinois games, but pasted only the newspaper accounts of the contests which we won. When we lost, she couldn't understand why we played such people."

Unlike Stagg, Yost, and Howard Jones, Zuppke took a social drink to help relax. Once, visiting Jones, he said, "Howard, you are a great coach, but you'd be a greater one, if you'd take a drink once in a while. You'd have more imagination."

"I never heard of a drink yet figuring out a play," Jones replied.

"You haven't?" said Zuppke. "Well, I've just had two drinks and figured out three new plays."

Most of the plays Zuppke used at Illinois he had early put on successfully in his three seasons as coach of Oak Park High, where he turned out two national championship teams, and before that at Muskegon High.

Zup himself had left high school in Milwau-

ROBERT CARL ZUPPKE
1879 - 1957

BOB ZUPPKE WILL ALWAYS BE AN INSTITUTION AT THE UNIVERSITY OF ILLINOIS AND A NEVER-TO-BE-FORGOTTEN FIGURE IN THE HISTORY OF AMERICAN FOOTBALL.
BORN IN GERMANY, ZUPPKE CAME AT AN EARLY AGE TO AMERICA, WAS GRADUATED FROM THE UNIVERSITY OF WISCONSIN IN 1905 AND EMBARKED UPON A CAREER OF COACHING WHICH LED HIM FROM MUSKEGON, MICHIGAN TO OAK PARK, ILLINOIS AND THENCE TO THE UNIVERSITY OF ILLINOIS IN 1913.
FROM THAT MOMENTOUS DAY WHEN HE STEPPED FROM HIGH SCHOOL TO THE BIG TEN "ZUP" SHOWED THE INTELLECTUAL CURIOSITY, INTENSE CONCENTRATION, AND THE SUSTAINED DRIVE WHICH MADE HIM A GREAT FOOTBALL COACH. HIS PHILOSOPHIC ATTRIBUTES AND ARTISTIC INTERESTS ALSO SERVED TO MAKE HIM ONE OF THE MOST INTERESTING PERSONALITIES OF HIS GENERATION.
UNDER ZUPPKE ILLINOIS WON OR SHARED SEVEN BIG TEN CHAMPIONSHIPS AND TWICE WAS RUNNER-UP. FOUR OF HIS TEAMS RECEIVED RECOGNITION NATIONALLY AND WHEN HE RETIRED IN 1942 ZUPPKE'S ALL-TIME RECORD STOOD AT 131 VICTORIES, 81 DEFEATS, AND 12 TIES. HE WAS LOVED BY THE PUBLIC, RESPECTED BY HIS PLAYERS AND FEARED BY OPPONENTS.
HIS INNOVATIONS SUCH AS THE SCREEN PASS, USE OF THE HUDDLE, THE SPIRAL PASS FROM CENTER, AND THE FLYING TRAPEZE LEFT THEIR MARK UPON THE INTERCOLLEGIATE GAME. FEW COACHES HAVE EXERTED SO PROFOUND AN INFLUENCE ON AMERICAN FOOTBALL AND INTERCOLLEGIATE ATHLETICS. NONE PROVIDED MORE KNOWLEDGE OF THE GAME, MIXED IN CORRECT PROPORTIONS WITH THE TRUE "COLOR" OF A GREAT CHARACTER, THAN BOB ZUPPKE OF ILLINOIS.
By Action of The Board of Trustees of The University of Illinois, this Field is Dedicated in Memory of Robert Carl Zuppke - November 12, 1966.

The rewards of greatness

kee at 13 to work as a sign painter's apprentice, returned to school, attended teachers' college to gain a certificate, taught country school, and then entered Wisconsin, where he was graduated at 25. He was a quarterback in football, but too small to play much.

According to Rockne, a big varsity fullback piled up the tough little Dutchman and said, "I guess this will pound some sense into your head!" And Rockne had Zuppke replying: "The whole team couldn't knock any sense into my head!"

From 1905 until 1909, when he began his

coaching at Muskegon, Zuppke bounced around, saw something of the country, studied life and people. He did some scaffold painting in New York, but got fired, "because my lions looked like rats." He drew pictures to go with poetry written by a newspaper cartoonist's wife. He got $18 a week for that, but it lasted only three weeks. He even tried designing feminine apparel, but all his dresses seemed to have polka dots.

From New York he returned to the Midwest, to Grand Rapids, Michigan, where he worked in the art department of an advertising agency, but got himself fired by trying to make it into a part-time athletic club. The boss blew up the day he walked in and found everybody squared off for boxing.

Obviously, sports was to be his career, art his avocation.

After the 1929 season, when Zup's material fell off, Illinois was in the Big Ten second division much of the time. He talked then of the bad in football, as he saw it.

"They tell me," he said, "that I should go around kissing babies and talking to mothers of poor boys to persuade them to send their sons to Illinois. And they say this is one of the duties of a modern coach. I told them that if that was the duty of a modern coach, then I wasn't capable of being a modern coach."

In his last 12 seasons, 1930–41, Zuppke had a fair team in 1933—record 5–3—and a very good one in 1934—record 7–1. A 7–3 loss to Wisconsin that year cost him a chance to tie Minnesota for the Western Conference crown. He had one big upset left, against Michigan in 1939, 16–7.

Tommy Harmon, then a junior, was at the peak of his wonderful career for the Wolverines. Michigan was undefeated, had lost only one game in Harmon's varsity career, to Minnesota, 7–6, in 1938. Illinois had lost four out of four, and was considered to have as much of a chance as its 1916 predecessor against Minnesota.

The Wolverines were coached by the sagacious Herbert O. (Fritz) Crisler, but Crisler let himself be quoted that Harmon was a better back than Red Grange.

Zuppke seized on it. The week of the game, he never stopped repeating it. "So, Crisler says Harmon is better than Grange. Did you read it? Harmon is better than Grange." He worked on a defense built around seven- and six-man fronts and a secondary rotating into the side where Michigan was strong after its deploy. And all week long to everybody he met, Zuppke kept saying, "Crisler says Harmon is better than Grange."

Harmon was well contained. As Yale's Tad Jones once said, "You can hold the greatest back with a cotton thread, if you can get to him behind the line of scrimmage."

After his retirement in 1941, Zuppke divided his time between his painting and raising prize hogs. He left some memorable aphorisms, all original with him, but quoted by many:

My definition of an All-American is a player who has weak opposition and a poet in the press box.

In most colleges the leading contact games are football, wrestling and dancing.

The sheik may be God's gift to women, but the second guess is God's gift to the football coach.

All quitters are good losers.

We don't care how big or strong our opponents are, as long as they are human.

Football is still a great kicking game. The kicking, however, is in the stands.

No athletic director holds office longer than two unsuccessful football coaches.

The tough mug may have a trembling knee.

Football made the nation college-conscious and bathtub-conscious.

Some backs run very fast on one spot.

The hero of a thousand plays becomes a bum after one error.

On the first two downs, play for a touchdown. On the third down, play for a first down.

The undefeated team is not always the strongest team. It might be the luckiest.

The game of football is to college life what color is to painting. It makes college life throb and vibrate.

Never let hope elude you. That is life's biggest fumble.

COACHES' RECORDS—GAME BY GAME, YEAR BY YEAR

(Exclusive of Bowl Games)

BILL ALEXANDER

Record: 131–93–15
Hall of Fame 1951

GEORGIA TECH 1920–44

1920

44	Wake Forest	0
55	Oglethorpe	0
66	Davidson	0
44	Vanderbilt	0
3	Pittsburgh	10
24	Centre	0
7	Clemson	0
35	Georgetown	6
34	Auburn	0

1921

42	Wake Forest	0
41	Oglethorpe	0
70	Davidson	0
69	Furman	0
48	Rutgers	14
7	Penn State	28
48	Clemson	7
21	Georgetown	7
14	Auburn	0

1922

31	Oglethorpe	6
19	Davidson	0
33	Alabama	7
0	Navy	13
3	Notre Dame	13
19	Georgetown	7
21	Clemson	7
14	Auburn	6
17	N. C. State	0

1923

28	Oglethorpe	13
10	VMI	7
7	Florida	7
20	Georgetown	10
7	Notre Dame	35
0	Alabama	0
0	Penn State	7
3	Kentucky	3
0	Auburn	0

1924

19	Oglethorpe	0
3	VMI	0
7	Florida	7
15	Penn State	13
0	Alabama	14
3	Notre Dame	34
28	LSU	7
0	Vanderbilt	3
7	Auburn	0

1925

13	Oglethorpe	7
33	VMI	0
16	Penn State	7
23	Florida	7
0	Alabama	7
0	Notre Dame	13
7	Vanderbilt	0
3	Georgia	0
7	Auburn	7

1926

6	Oglethorpe	7
13	VMI	0
9	Tulane	6
0	Alabama	21
19	Wash. & Lee	7
0	Notre Dame	12
7	Vanderbilt	13
13	Georgia	14
20	Auburn	7

1927

7	VMI	0
13	Tulane	6
13	Alabama	0
13	North Carolina	0
7	Notre Dame	26
0	Vanderbilt	0
23	LSU	0
19	Oglethorpe	7
18	Auburn	0
12	Georgia	0

1928

13	VMI	0
12	Tulane	0
13	Notre Dame	0
20	North Carolina	7

32	Oglethorpe	7
19	Vanderbilt	7
33	Alabama	13
51	Auburn	0
20	Georgia	6

1929

27	Miss. A. & M.	13
7	North Carolina	18
19	Florida	6
14	Tulane	20
6	Notre Dame	26
7	Vanderbilt	23
0	Alabama	14
19	Auburn	6
6	Georgia	12

1930

45	South Carolina	0
0	Carnegie Tech	31
14	Auburn	12
0	Tulane	28
6	North Carolina	6
0	Vanderbilt	6
7	Pennsylvania	34
7	Florida	55
0	Georgia	13

1931

25	South Carolina	13
0	Carnegie Tech	13
0	Auburn	13
0	Tulane	33
7	Vanderbilt	49
19	North Carolina	19
12	Pennsylvania	13
23	Florida	0
6	Georgia	35
6	California	19

1932

32	Clemson	14
6	Kentucky	12
0	Auburn	6
43	North Carolina	14
0	Vanderbilt	12
14	Tulane	20
6	Alabama	0
6	Florida	0
0	Georgia	0
7	California	27

1933

39	Clemson	2
6	Kentucky	7
16	Auburn	6
0	Tulane	7
10	North Carolina	6
6	Vanderbilt	9
19	Florida	7
9	Alabama	12
6	Georgia	7
6	Duke	0

1934

12	Clemson	7
12	Vanderbilt	27
0	Duke	20
2	Michigan	9
12	Tulane	20
0	North Carolina	26
6	Auburn	18
0	Alabama	40
12	Florida	13
0	Georgia	7

1935

33	Presbyterian	0
32	Sewanee	0
6	Kentucky	25
6	Duke	0
13	Vanderbilt	14
0	North Carolina	19
7	Auburn	33
7	Alabama	38
39	Florida	6
19	Georgia	7

1936

55	Presbyterian	0
58	Sewanee	0
34	Kentucky	0
6	Duke	19
0	Vanderbilt	0
13	Clemson	14
12	Auburn	13
16	Alabama	20
38	Florida	14
6	Georgia	16
13	California	7

1937

59	Presbyterian	0
28	Mercer	0
32	Kentucky	0
19	Duke	20
0	Auburn	21
14	Vanderbilt	0
7	Clemson	0
0	Alabama	7
12	Florida	0
6	Georgia	6

1938

19	Mercer	0
6	Notre Dame	14
0	Duke	6
7	Auburn	6
7	Vanderbilt	13
19	Kentucky	18
14	Alabama	14
0	Florida	0
0	Georgia	0
0	California	13

1939

14	Notre Dame	17
35	Howard	0
14	Vanderbilt	6
6	Alabama	0
6	Duke	7
13	Kentucky	6
7	Auburn	6
21	Florida	7
13	Georgia	0

1940

27	Howard	0
20	Notre Dame	26
19	Vanderbilt	0
7	Auburn	16
7	Duke	41
7	Kentucky	26
13	Alabama	14
7	Florida	16
19	Georgia	21
13	California	0

1941

20	Chattanooga	0
6	Notre Dame	20
7	Vanderbilt	14
28	Auburn	14
0	Duke	14
20	Kentucky	13
0	Alabama	20
7	Florida	14
0	Georgia	21

1942

15	Auburn	0
13	Notre Dame	6
30	Chattanooga	12
33	Davidson	0
21	Navy	0
26	Duke	7
47	Kentucky	7
7	Alabama	0
20	Florida	7
0	Georgia	34

1943

20	North Carolina	7
13	Notre Dame	55
35	Georgia Navy P-F	7
27	Ft. Benning	0
14	Navy	28
7	Duke	14
42	LSU	7
33	Tulane	0
41	Clemson	6
48	Georgia	0

1944

51	Clemson	0
28	North Carolina	0
27	Auburn	0
17	Navy	15
13	Georgia Navy	7
13	Duke	19
34	Tulane	7
14	LSU	6
0	Notre Dame	21
44	Georgia	0

EDDIE ANDERSON

Record: 201–128–15
Hall of Fame 1971

Loras 1922–24

1922

14	Wisconsin School of Mines	0
21	Wisconsin State Normal	0
29	Campion	0
31	Mt. Morris	0
50	De Paul	6
12	Luther	0
13	St. Viator	0

1923

6	Platteville Miners	0
13	Mt. Morris	3
0	LaCrosse	19
6	Notre Dame Reserves	6
12	Des Moines	0
0	St. Viator	3
0	St. Thomas	3
7	Luther	13
44	Campion	0

1924

13	Wisconsin School of Mines	2
7	Coe	3
3	Detroit	19
14	De Paul	0
13	Valparaiso	10
0	St. Viator	0
6	LaCrosse	7
6	Luther	0

De Paul 1925–31

1925

7	Ft. Sheridan	6
44	Elmhurst	10
12	Columbia (Iowa)	0
7	St. Norbert	10
7	Valparaiso	6
13	LaCrosse	13
0	St. Viator	13

1926

7	St. Mary's (Minn.)	13
7	Columbia (Iowa)	8
6	Niagara	28
37	Valparaiso	14
19	LaCrosse	0
7	St. Viator	0

1927

0	St. Viator	21
14	Columbia (Iowa)	14
7	Tulsa	0
14	Loyola (Chicago)	7
7	Niagara	14
L	St. Mary's (Minn.)	W
L	North Dakota	W

(Scores of last two games not available.)

1928

27	Crane Junior College	0
0	Detroit	39
20	Illinois Reserves	0
27	Minnesota Reserves	14
0	Des Moines	0
0	Tulsa	27

13 Niagara 0
13 St. Mary's (Minn.) 16
0 Loyola (Chicago) 7

1929

7 Detroit 27
0 Michigan St. Teachers Coll. 27
51 St. Viator 0
0 Loyola (Chicago) 13
12 St. Mary's (Texas) 19
25 Niagara 32
19 St. John's 7

1930

28 Buena Vista 13
13 St. Mary's (Minn.) 7
6 Loyola (Chicago) 0
14 Louisville 0
6 Illinois Reserves 6
0 San Francisco 13
0 St. John's 4

1931

(Scores not avilable.)

HOLY CROSS 1933–38

1933

50 St. Michael's 0
17 Catholic U. 7
21 Providence 0
10 Harvard 7
19 Brown 7
0 Detroit 24
27 Manhattan 6
19 Springfield 6
9 Boston College 13

1934

22 St. Anselm's 0
51 St. Joseph's 0
25 Providence 0
17 Catholic U. 6
26 Harvard 6
7 Colgate 20
0 Temple 14
12 Manhattan 6
20 Brown 7
7 Boston College 2

1935

32 Rhode Island 0
12 Providence 0
47 Maine 0
13 Harvard 0
13 Manhattan 13
3 Colgate 0
34 St. Anselm's 0
7 Carnegie Tech 0
79 Bates 0
20 Boston College 6

1936

45 Bates 0
21 Providence 6
7 Dartmouth 0
13 Manhattan 7
7 Carnegie Tech 0
0 Temple 3
20 Colgate 13
32 Brown 0
0 St. Anselm's 0
12 Boston College 13

1937

21 St. Anselm's 0
7 Providence 0
27 Georgetown 6
7 Georgia 6
6 Western Maryland 0
0 Temple 7
12 Colgate 0
7 Brown 0
0 Carnegie Tech 0
20 Boston College 0

1938

28 Providence 0
46 Rhode Island 13
19 Manhattan 6
6 Carnegie Tech 7
29 Georgia 6
21 Colgate 0
33 Temple 0
14 Brown 12
29 Boston College 7

IOWA 1939–42, 1946–49

1939

41 South Dakota 0
32 Indiana 29
7 Michigan 27
19 Wisconsin 13
4 Purdue 0
7 Notre Dame 6
13 Minnesota 9
7 Northwestern 7

1940

46 South Dakota 0
30 Wisconsin 12
6 Indiana 10
6 Minnesota 34
6 Purdue 21
6 Nebraska 14
7 Notre Dame 0
18 Illinois 7

1941

25 Drake 8
0 Michigan 6
0 Wisconsin 23
6 Purdue 7
13 Indiana 7
21 Illinois 0
13 Minnesota 34
13 Nebraska 14

1942

26 Washington 7
27 Nebraska 0
0 Great Lakes 25
33 Camp Grant 16
7 Illinois 12
14 Indiana 13
13 Purdue 7
6 Wisconsin 0
7 Minnesota 27
14 Michigan 28

1946

39 North Dakota St. 0
16 Purdue 0
7 Michigan 14
21 Nebraska 7
13 Indiana 0
6 Notre Dame 41

0 Illinois 7
21 Wisconsin 7
6 Minnesota 16

1947

59 North Dakota St. 0
7 UCLA 22
12 Illinois 35
27 Indiana 14
13 Ohio State 13
0 Notre Dame 21
0 Purdue 21
14 Wisconsin 46
13 Minnesota 7

1948

14 Marquette 12
0 Indiana 7
14 Ohio State 7
13 Purdue 20
12 Notre Dame 27
19 Wisconsin 13
0 Illinois 14
21 Minnesota 28
34 Boston U. 14

1949

25 UCLA 41
21 Purdue 7
14 Illinois 20
35 Indiana 9
28 Northwestern 21
34 Oregon 31
7 Minnesota 55
13 Wisconsin 35
7 Notre Dame 28

HOLY CROSS 1950–64

1950

21 Dartmouth 21
41 Brown 21
28 Colgate 35
27 Syracuse 34
13 Yale 14
26 Harvard 7
19 Marquette 21
14 Georgetown 21
26 Temple 21
32 Boston College 14

1951

33 Harvard 6
54 Fordham 20
14 Tulane 20
53 NYU 6
41 Brown 6
34 Colgate 6
39 Marquette 13
39 Quantico 14
41 Temple 7
14 Boston College 19

1952

27 Dartmouth 9
12 Fordham 7
35 NYU 0
46 Brown 0
19 Syracuse 20
7 Marquette 0
13 Colgate 7
18 Quantico 27
28 Temple 0
21 Boston College 7

1953

28	Dartmouth	6
19	Colgate	6
40	Bucknell	0
0	Quantico	17
0	Brown	6
0	Syracuse	21
20	Boston U.	7
7	Marquette	13
20	Fordham	7
0	Boston College	6

1954

26	Dartmouth	27
0	Colgate	18
20	Miami	26
14	Marquette	19
14	Boston U.	13
20	Syracuse	25
7	Penn State	39
20	Fordham	19
46	Connecticut	26
13	Boston College	31

1955

42	Temple	7
29	Dartmouth	21
15	Colgate	14
7	Quantico	0
20	Boston U.	12
9	Syracuse	49
13	Dayton	7
6	Marquette	18
0	Connecticut	6
7	Boston College	26

1956

13	Dayton	14
20	Colgate	6
0	Penn State	43
7	Dartmouth	7
13	Quantico	0
21	Boston U.	12
20	Syracuse	41
41	Marquette	0
7	Boston College	0

1957

21	VMI	21
32	Dayton	6
26	Marquette	7
7	Dartmouth	14
28	Boston U.	35
33	Quantico	14
20	Syracuse	19
10	Penn State	14
14	Boston College	0

1958

0	Pittsburgh	17
14	Syracuse	13
14	Dartmouth	8
16	Boston U.	8
26	Dayton	0
20	Colgate	0
0	Penn State	32
14	Marquette	0
8	Boston College	26

1959

31	Dartmouth	8
20	Villanova	0
8	Dayton	0
6	Syracuse	42
34	Columbia	0
14	Colgate	12
17	Boston U.	8
0	Penn State	46
12	Marquette	30
0	Boston College	14

1960

6	Harvard	13
14	Boston U.	20
6	Syracuse	15
9	Dartmouth	8
27	Columbia	6
20	Marquette	0
36	Dayton	6
8	Penn State	33
30	Connecticut	6
16	Boston College	12

1961

6	Villanova	20
20	Buffalo	8
20	Boston U.	7
17	Dartmouth	13
6	Syracuse	34
28	Dayton	0
44	Massachusetts	7
14	Penn State	34
14	Connecticut	3
38	Boston College	26

1962

16	Buffalo	6
22	Colgate	0
34	Harvard	20
0	Dartmouth	10
20	Syracuse	30
36	Dayton	14
20	VMI	14
20	Penn State	48
34	Connecticut	16
12	Boston College	48

1963

6	Buffalo	6
0	Syracuse	48
6	Boston U.	18
8	Dartmouth	13
6	Quantico	7
14	Villanova	22
14	VMI	12
14	Penn State	28
9	Boston College	0

1964

0	Villanova	32
8	Syracuse	34
0	Colgate	10
16	Quantico	0
20	Buffalo	14
36	Richmond	22
6	Massachusetts	25
32	Boston U.	0
20	Connecticut	6
8	Boston College	10

CHARLIE BACHMAN

Record: 137–83–24

NORTHWESTERN 1919

20	DePauw	0
6	Wisconsin	10
13	Michigan	16
0	Chicago	41
7	Iowa	14
3	Indiana	2
0	Rutgers	28

KANSAS STATE 1920–27

1920

14	Fort Hays State	0
55	Camp Funston	0
7	Emporia	7
3	Creighton	0
0	Kansas	14
7	Missouri	10
0	Iowa State	17
7	Oklahoma	7
0	Washburn	0

1921

7	Emporia	3
21	Washington (St. Louis)	0
7	Creighton	14
7	Missouri	5
7	Kansas	21
21	Grinnell	7
0	Iowa State	7
14	Oklahoma	7

1922

47	Washburn	0
22	Washington (St. Louis)	14
7	Oklahoma	7
7	Kansas	7
14	Missouri	10
12	Iowa State	2
0	Nebraska	21
45	Texas Christian	0

1923

25	Washburn	0
6	Creighton	0
7	Iowa State	7
2	Missouri	4
34	Grinnell	7
21	Oklahoma	20
12	Nebraska	34
0	Kansas	0

1924

23	Washburn	0
19	Emporia	6
6	Kansas	0
7	Missouri	14
0	Iowa State	21
6	Drake	7
0	Nebraska	24
7	Oklahoma	7

1925

26	Emporia	7
16	Oklahoma	0
0	Drake	19
14	Kansas	7
0	Missouri	3
2	Marquette	0
0	Nebraska	0
12	Iowa State	7

1926

13	Texas	3
12	Creighton	0
27	Kansas	0
15	Oklahoma	12
16	Arkansas	7

0	Marquette	14
0	Nebraska	3
2	Iowa State	3

1927

30	Fort Hays State	6
6	Missouri	13
13	Kansas	2
20	Oklahoma	14
7	Iowa State	12
7	Texas	41
0	Nebraska	33
18	Oklahoma State	25

FLORIDA 1928–32

1928

26	Southern	0
27	Auburn	0
73	Mercer	0
14	N. C. State	7
71	Sewanee	6
26	Georgia	6
27	Clemson	6
60	Washington & Lee	6
12	Tennessee	13

1929

54	Southern	0
18	VMI	7
19	Auburn	0
6	Georgia Tech	19
18	Georgia	6
0	Harvard	14
13	Clemson	7
20	South Carolina	7
25	Washington & Lee	7
20	Oregon	6

1930

45	Southern	7
27	N. C. State	0
7	Auburn	0
19	Chicago	0
13	Furman	14
0	Georgia	0
0	Alabama	20
27	Clemson	0
55	Georgia Tech	7
6	Tennessee	13

1931

35	N. C. State	0
0	North Carolina	0
12	Syracuse	33
13	Auburn	12
6	Georgia	33
0	Alabama	41
6	South Carolina	6
0	Georgia Tech	23
0	UCLA	13
2	Kentucky	7

1932

19	Sewanee	0
27	Citadel	7
6	N. C. State	17
12	Georgia	33
13	North Carolina	18
6	Auburn	21
0	Georgia Tech	6
13	Tennessee	32
12	UCLA	2

MICHIGAN STATE 1933–42, 1944–46

1933

14	Grinnell	0
6	Michigan	20
20	Illinois Wesleyan	12
6	Marquette	0
27	Syracuse	3
0	Kansas State	0
0	Carnegie Tech	0
0	Detroit	14

1934

33	Grinnell	20
16	Michigan	0
13	Carnegie Tech	0
39	Manhattan	0
13	Marquette	7
0	Syracuse	10
7	Detroit	6
6	Kansas	0
26	Texas A. & M.	13

1935

41	Grinnell	0
25	Michigan	6
42	Kansas	0
6	Boston College	18
47	Washington (St. L.)	13
12	Temple	7
7	Marquette	13
27	Loyola (Calif.)	0

1936

27	Wayne State	0
21	Michigan	7
7	Carnegie Tech	0
13	Missouri	0
7	Marquette	13
13	Boston College	13
7	Temple	7
41	Kansas	0
7	Arizona	0

1937

19	Wayne State	0
19	Michigan	14
0	Manhattan	3
2	Missouri	0
21	Marquette	7
16	Kansas	0
13	Temple	6
13	Carnegie Tech	6
14	San Francisco	0

1938

34	Wayne State	6
0	Michigan	14
18	Illinois Wesleyan	0
26	West Virginia	0
19	Syracuse	12
6	Santa Clara	7
0	Missouri	6
20	Marquette	14
10	Temple	0

1939

16	Wayne State	0
13	Michigan	26
14	Marquette	17
7	Purdue	20
13	Illinois Wesleyan	6
14	Syracuse	3
0	Santa Clara	6

7	Indiana	7
18	Temple	7

1940

14	Michigan	21
20	Purdue	7
19	Temple	21
0	Santa Clara	0
32	Kansas State	0
0	Indiana	20
6	Marquette	7
17	West Virginia	0

1941

7	Michigan	19
13	Marquette	7
0	Santa Clara	7
39	Wayne State	6
0	Missouri	19
0	Purdue	0
46	Temple	0
31	Ohio Wesleyan	7
14	West Viriginia	12

1942

0	Michigan	20
46	Wayne State	6
7	Marquette	28
14	Great Lakes	0
7	Temple	7
13	Washington State	25
19	Purdue	6
7	West Virginia	0
7	Oregon State	7

1944

40	Scranton	12
2	Kentucky	0
45	Kansas State	6
8	Maryland	0
32	Wayne State	0
7	Missouri	13
33	Maryland	0

1945

0	Michigan	40
7	Kentucky	6
12	Pittsburgh	7
27	Wayne State	7
13	Marquette	13
14	Missouri	7
7	Great Lakes	27
33	Penn State	0
7	Miami (Fla.)	21

1946

42	Wayne State	0
20	Boston College	34
0	Mississippi State	6
19	Penn State	16
7	Cincinnati	18
14	Kentucky	39
7	Michigan	55
20	Marquette	0
26	Maryland	14
26	Washington State	20

HILLSDALE 1953

14	Manchester	0
13	Eastern Michigan	28
32	Grand Rapids JC	7
20	Alma	7

Continued on next page

7	Hope	28
7	Olivet	6
14	Adrian	14
0	Adrian	14
0	Albion	0
13	Kalamazoo	6

MATTY BELL

Record: 154–87–17
Hall of Fame 1955

HASKELL 1920–21

1920

44	Kirksville Osteopaths	7
33	Fort Hays	6
6	Marquette	3
47	Kansas Wesleyan	0
14	Baker	0
21	St. Louis	6
33	Oklahoma Aggies	7
7	Phillips	7
6	Xavier	21
14	Pittsburg	14

1921

0	Nebraska	41
14	Friends	7
2	Marquette	41
89	Kansas Wesleyan	0
7	Notre Dame	42
21	Tulsa	0
14	Pittsburg	0
14	Texas Christian	0
7	Des Moines	24

CARROLL (WIS.) 1922
(Record not available.)

TEXAS CHRISTIAN 1923–28

1923

7	Oklahoma A.&M.	6
16	Hardin-Simmons	0
47	Daniel Baker	6
0	Centenary	23
0	SMU	40
0	Austin	26
7	Howard Payne	20
10	Trinity U.	16
6	Rice	0

1924

43	East Texas State	0
13	Daniel Baker	12
17	Oklahoma A.&M.	10
7	Hardin-Simmons	0
3	Rice	7
0	SMU	6
0	Texas A.&M.	28
0	Texas	13
0	Arkansas	20

1925

31	East Texas State	0
12	Daniel Baker	0
7	Baylor	7
28	Hardin-Simmons	16
7	Oklahoma A.&M.	22
21	Abilene Christian	9
3	Texas A.&M.	0
3	Arkansas	0
21	Austin	0

1926

5	Daniel Baker	3
24	Centenary	14
7	Baylor	7
7	Austin	0
3	Oklahoma A.&M.	0
28	Texas Tech	16
13	Texas A.&M.	13
10	Arkansas	7
13	SMU	14

1927

27	Daniel Baker	0
0	Texas	0
16	Texas Tech	6
20	Austin	13
0	Texas A.&M.	0
14	Baylor	0
3	Arkansas	10
3	Centenary	7
6	SMU	28

1928

21	East Texas State	0
19	Daniel Baker	0
19	Hardin-Simmons	3
21	Austin	0
6	Texas A.&M.	0
28	Texas Tech	6
6	Baylor	7
7	Rice	0
0	Texas	6
15	SMU	6

TEXAS A. & M. 1929–33

1929

54	Southwestern	7
10	Tulane	13
19	Kansas State	0
7	TCU	13
13	Arkansas	14
54	Austin	0
7	SMU	12
26	Rice	6
13	Texas	0

1930

43	Southwestern	0
0	Nebraska	13
9	Tulane	19
0	Arkansas	13
0	TCU	3
7	Centenary	6
7	SMU	13
0	Rice	7
0	Texas	26

1931

33	Southwestern	0
21	John Tarleton	0
0	Tulane	7
29	Iowa	0
0	TCU	6
33	Baylor	7
7	Centenary	0
0	SMU	8
7	Rice	0
7	Texas	6

1932

7	Texas Tech	0
14	Tulane	26
26	Sam Houston	0

14	Texas A.&I.	0
0	TCU	17
0	Baylor	0
0	Centenary	7
0	SMU	0
14	Rice	7
0	Texas	21

1933

38	Trinity	0
13	Tulane	6
34	Sam Houston	14
17	Texas A.&I.	0
7	TCU	13
14	Baylor	7
0	Centenary	20
0	SMU	19
27	Rice	0
10	Texas	10

SOUTHERN METHODIST 1935–41,
1945–49

1935

39	North Texas State	0
60	Austin	0
14	Tulsa	0
35	Washington	6
10	Rice	0
18	Hardin-Simmons	6
20	Texas	0
21	UCLA	0
17	Arkansas	6
10	Baylor	0
20	Texas Christian	14
24	Texas A.&M.	0

1936

6	North Texas State	0
61	Texas A.&I.	0
0	Fordham	7
16	Vanderbilt	0
14	Texas	7
6	Texas A.&M.	22
0	Arkansas	17
7	Baylor	13
0	Texas Christian	0
9	Rice	0

1937

14	North Texas State	3
6	Centenary	7
14	Washington	0
0	Vanderbilt	6
0	Arkansas	13
13	Texas	2
0	Texas A.&M.	14
13	Baylor	7
26	UCLA	13
0	Texas Christian	3
7	Rice	15

1938

34	North Texas State	7
29	Arizona	7
0	Marquette	7
7	Pittsburgh	34
7	Texas	6
10	Texas A.&M.	7
19	Arkansas	6
21	Baylor	6
7	Texas Christian	20
14	Rice	25

1939

7	Oklahoma	7
16	North Texas State	0
19	Notre Dame	20
16	Marquette	0
10	Texas	0
2	Texas A.&M.	6
0	Arkansas	14
21	Baylor	0
14	Texas Christian	7
13	Rice	6

1940

9	UCLA	6
20	North Texas State	7
7	Pittsburgh	7
20	Auburn	13
21	Texas	13
7	Texas A.&M.	19
28	Arkansas	0
7	Baylor	4
16	Texas Christian	0
7	Rice	6

1941

54	North Texas State	0
10	Fordham	16
34	College of Pacific	0
20	Auburn	7
0	Texas	34
10	Texas A.&M.	21
14	Arkansas	7
14	Baylor	0
13	Texas Christian	15
0	Rice	6

1945

51	Blackland AAF	0
7	Corpus Christi NAS	22
7	Missouri	10
12	Oklahoma A.&M.	26
21	Rice	18
7	Tulane	19
7	Texas	12
0	Texas A.&M.	3
21	Arkansas	0
34	Baylor	0
34	Texas Christian	0

1946

7	Temple	7
0	Texas Tech	7
15	Oklahoma A.&M.	6
7	Rice	21
17	Missouri	0
3	Texas	19
0	Texas A.&M.	14
0	Arkansas	13
35	Baylor	0
30	Texas Christian	13

1947

22	Santa Clara	6
35	Missouri	19
21	Oklahoma A.&M.	14
14	Rice	0
7	UCLA	0
14	Texas	13
13	Texas A.&M.	0
14	Arkansas	6
10	Baylor	0
19	Texas Christian	19

1948

33	Pittsburgh	14
41	Texas Tech	6
14	Missouri	20
33	Rice	7
33	Santa Clara	0
21	Texas	6
20	Texas A.&M.	14
14	Arkansas	12
13	Baylor	6
7	Texas Christian	7

1949

13	Wake Forest	7
28	Missouri	27
27	Rice	41
20	Kentucky	7
7	Texas	6
27	Texas A.&M.	27
34	Arkansas	6
26	Baylor	35
13	TCU	21
20	Notre Dame	27

HUGO BEZDEK

Record: 127-57-15
Hall of Fame 1954

OREGON 1906

12	Idaho	0
16	Washington	6
4	Willamette	0
10	OAC	4
8	MAAC	4
10	Whitworth	0

ARKANSAS 1908–12

1908

8	Haskell	0
33	Mississippi	0
0	St. Louis	24
51	Henderson Brown	0
5	Oklahoma	27
42	Kansas State Normal	12
72	Ouachita	0
4	LSU	35
0	Texas	21

1909

24	Henderson Brown	0
12	Drury	6
23	Fairmount College	6
21	Oklahoma	6
16	LSU	0
56	Ouachita	0
34	Washington	0

1910

33	Drury	0
63	Henderson Brown	0
0	Kansas Aggies	5
13	Southwestern	12
50	Washington	0
6	Rolla Mines	0
51	LSU	0
5	Texas A. & M.	0

1911

0	Kansas Aggies	3
100	Missouri State Normal	?
65	Drury	5
44	Hendrix	0

0	Southwestern	0
43	Rolla Mines	3
11	LSU	0
3	Washington	0
0	Texas	12

1912

38	Henderson Brown	6
53	Hendrix	0
6	Oklahoma A. & M.	13
27	Southwestern	0
7	Wisconsin	64
6	LSU	7
13	Washington	7
6	Texas A. & M.	20
0	Baylor	7
0	Texas	48

OREGON 1913–17

1913

42	Oregon Alumni	3
43	Bremerton	6
27	Idaho	0
3	Willamette	6
10	OAC	10
7	Washington	10
0	MAAC	19

1914

29	Whitman	3
7	WSC	0
13	Idaho	0
61	Willamette	0
0	Washington	10
3	OAC	3
0	MAAC	14

1915

7	MAAC	16
3	WSC	28
19	Idaho	7
21	Whitman	0
48	Willamette	0
34	USC	0
47	Pacific	0
9	OAC	0
15	MAAC	2

1916

97	Willamette	0
28	MAAC	0
39	California	14
0	Washington	0
12	Washington St.	3
27	OAC	0
27	MAAC	0

1917

14	MAAC	7
3	Washington St.	26
14	Idaho	0
14	Willamette	0
0	Mare Island	27
21	California	0
7	OAC	14

PENN STATE 1918–29

1918

6	Wissahickon Barracks	6
3	Rutgers	26
7	Lehigh	6
6	Pittsburgh	28

1919

33	Gettysburg	0
9	Bucknell	0
13	Dartmouth	19
48	Ursinus	7
10	Pennsylvania	0
20	Lehigh	7
20	Cornell	0
20	Pittsburgh	0

1920

27	Muhlenberg	7
13	Gettysburg	0
14	Dartmouth	7
41	N. C. State	0
109	Lebanon Valley	7
28	Pennsylvania	7
20	Nebraska	0
7	Lehigh	7
0	Pittsburgh	0

1921

53	Lebanon Valley	0
24	Gettysburg	0
35	N. C. State	0
28	Lehigh	7
21	Harvard	21
28	Georgia Tech	7
28	Carnegie Tech	7
13	Navy	7
0	Pittsburgh	0
21	Washington	7

1922

54	St. Bonaventure	0
27	William & Mary	7
20	Gettysburg	0
32	Lebanon Valley	6
33	Middlebury	0
0	Syracuse	0
0	Navy	14
10	Carnegie Tech	0
6	Pennsylvania	7
0	Pittsburgh	14

1923

58	Lebanon Valley	0
16	N. C. State	0
20	Gettysburg	0
21	Navy	3
13	West Virginia	13
0	Syracuse	10
7	Georgia Tech	0
21	Pennsylvania	0
3	Pittsburgh	21

1924

47	Lebanon Valley	3
51	N. C. State	6
26	Gettysburg	0
13	Georgia Tech	15
6	Syracuse	10
6	Navy	0
22	Carnegie Tech	7
0	Pennsylvania	0
28	Marietta	0
3	Pittsburgh	24

1925

14	Lebanon Valley	0
13	Franklin & Marshall	0
7	Georgia Tech	16
13	Marietta	0
13	Michigan State	6

0	Syracuse	7
0	Notre Dame	0
0	West Virginia	14
7	Pittsburgh	23

1926

82	Susquehanna	0
35	Lebanon Valley	0
48	Marietta	6
0	Notre Dame	28
0	Syracuse	10
20	George Washington	12
0	Pennsylvania	3
9	Bucknell	0
6	Pittsburgh	24

1927

27	Lebanon Valley	0
34	Gettysburg	13
7	Bucknell	13
20	Pennsylvania	0
9	Syracuse	6
40	Lafayette	6
13	George Washington	0
13	NYU	13
0	Pittsburgh	30

1928

25	Lebanon Valley	0
12	Gettysburg	0
0	Bucknell	6
0	Pennsylvania	14
6	Syracuse	6
0	Notre Dame	9
50	George Washington	0
0	Lafayette	7
0	Pittsburgh	26

1929

16	Niagara	0
15	Lebanon Valley	0
26	Marshall	7
0	NYU	7
6	Lafayette	3
6	Syracuse	4
19	Pennsylvania	7
6	Bucknell	27
7	Pittsburgh	20

DELAWARE VALLEY

1949

12	Montclair Teachers	7
32	Long Island Aggies	7
0	New Haven Teachers	12
13	Kings College (Pa.)	19
13	Potomac State	19
6	Glassboro State	20
7	Wilkes	53
13	Lycoming	7

DANA X. BIBLE

Record: 190–71–22
Hall of Fame 1951

MISSISSIPPI COLLEGE 1913–15
(Scores not available.)

LOUISIANA ST. 1916*

24	Southern Louisiana Inst.	0
59	Jefferson	0
13	Texas A. & M.	0
50	Mississippi College	7

0	Sewanee	7
17	Arkansas	0
13	Mississippi St.	3
41	Mississippi	0
7	Rice	7
14	Tulane	14

*Coached only last three games.

TEXAS A. & M. 1917, 1919–28

1917

66	Austin College	0
98	Dallas	0
20	Southwestern	0
27	LSU	0
35	Tulane	0
7	Baylor	0
7	Texas	0
10	Rice	0

1919

77	Sam Houston	0
28	San Marcos	0
16	SMU	0
12	Howard Payne	0
42	Trinity	0
28	Oklahoma A. & M.	0
10	Baylor	0
48	TCU	0
7	Southwestern	0
7	Texas	0

1920

110	Daniel Baker	0
3	SMU	0
0	LSU	0
47	Phillips	0
35	Oklahoma A. & M.	0
24	Baylor	0
7	Rice	0
3	Texas	7

1921

14	Howard Payne	7
13	SMU	0
0	LSU	6
17	Arizona	13
23	Oklahoma A. & M.	7
14	Baylor	3
7	Rice	7
0	Texas	0
22	Centre College	14

1922

7	Howard Payne	13
10	Tulsa	13
33	Southwestern	0
46	LSU	0
19	Ouachita College	6
7	Baylor	13
6	SMU	17
24	Rice	0
14	Texas	7

1923

53	Sam Houston	0
21	Howard Payne	0
13	Southwestern	0
14	Sewanee	0
28	LSU	0
0	SMU	10
0	Baylor	0
6	Rice	7
0	Texas	6

1924

40	John Tarleton	0
33	Trinity	0
54	Southwestern	0
7	Sewanee	0
40	Arkansas A. & M.	0
7	SMU	7
7	Baylor	15
28	TCU	0
13	Rice	6
0	Texas	7

1925

20	Trinity	10
23	Southwestern	6
6	Sewanee	6
7	SMU	0
77	Sam Houston	0
13	Baylor	0
0	TCU	3
17	Rice	0
28	Texas	0

1926

26	Trinity	0
35	Southwestern	0
6	Sewanee	3
63	New Mexico	0
7	SMU	9
9	Baylor	20
13	TCU	13
20	Rice	0
5	Texas	14

1927

45	Trinity	0
31	Southwestern	0
18	Sewanee	0
40	Arkansas	6
0	TCU	0
47	Texas Tech	6
39	SMU	13
14	Rice	0
28	Texas	7

1928

21	Trinity	0
21	Southwestern	0
69	Sewanee	0
0	Centenary	6
0	TCU	6
12	Arkansas	27
44	North Texas	0
19	SMU	19
19	Rice	0
0	Texas	19

NEBRASKA 1929–36

1929

0	SMU	0
13	Syracuse	6
7	Pittsburgh	12
7	Missouri	7
12	Kansas	6
13	Oklahoma	13
10	Kansas State	6
31	Iowa State	12

1930

13	Texas A. & M.	0
7	Oklahoma	20
14	Iowa State	12
53	Montana State	7

0	Pittsburgh	0
12	Kansas	6
0	Missouri	0
7	Iowa	12
9	Kansas State	10

1931

44	South Dakota	6
7	Northwestern	19
13	Oklahoma	0
6	Kansas	0
10	Missouri	7
7	Iowa	0
6	Kansas State	3
23	Iowa State	0
0	Pittsburgh	40
20	Colorado State	7

1932

12	Iowa State	6
6	Minnesota	7
20	Kansas	6
6	Kansas State	0
14	Iowa	13
0	Pittsburgh	0
5	Oklahoma	0
21	Missouri	6
21	SMU	14

1933

26	Texas	0
20	Iowa State	0
9	Kansas State	0
16	Oklahoma	7
26	Missouri	0
12	Kansas	0
7	Iowa	6
0	Pittsburgh	6
22	Oregon State	0

1934

50	Wyoming	0
0	Minnesota	20
14	Iowa	13
6	Oklahoma	0
7	Iowa State	6
6	Pittsburgh	25
3	Kansas	0
13	Missouri	6
7	Kansas State	19

1935

28	Chicago	7
20	Iowa State	7
7	Minnesota	12
0	Kansas State	0
19	Oklahoma	0
19	Missouri	6
19	Kansas	13
0	Pittsburgh	6
26	Oregon State	20

1936

34	Iowa State	0
0	Minnesota	7
13	Indiana	9
14	Oklahoma	0
20	Missouri	0
26	Kansas	0
6	Pittsburgh	19
40	Kansas State	0
32	Oregon State	14

TEXAS 1937–46

1937

25	Texas Tech	12
0	LSU	9
7	Oklahoma	7
10	Arkansas	21
7	Rice	14
2	SMU	13
9	Baylor	6
0	TCU	14
0	Texas A. & M.	7

1938

18	Kansas	19
0	LSU	20
0	Oklahoma	13
6	Arkansas	42
6	Rice	13
6	SMU	7
3	Baylor	14
6	TCU	28
7	Texas A. & M.	6

1939

12	Florida	0
17	Wisconsin	7
12	Oklahoma	24
14	Arkansas	13
26	Rice	12
0	SMU	10
0	Baylor	20
25	TCU	19
0	Texas A. & M.	20

1940

39	Colorado	7
13	Indiana	6
19	Oklahoma	16
21	Arkansas	0
0	Rice	13
13	SMU	21
13	Baylor	0
21	TCU	14
7	Texas A. & M.	0
26	Florida	0

1941

34	Colorado	6
34	LSU	0
40	Oklahoma	7
48	Arkansas	14
40	Rice	0
34	SMU	0
7	Baylor	7
7	TCU	14
23	Texas A. & M.	0
71	Oregon	7

1942

40	Corpus Christi	0
64	Kansas State	0
0	Northwestern	3
7	Oklahoma	0
47	Arkansas	6
12	Rice	7
21	SMU	7
20	Baylor	0
7	TCU	13
12	Texas A. & M.	6

1943

65	Blackland AAF	6
7	Southwestern	14
13	Oklahoma	7
34	Arkansas	0
58	Rice	0
20	SMU	0
46	TCU	7
27	Texas A. & M.	13

1944

20	Southwestern	0
6	Randolph Field	42
20	Oklahoma	0
19	Arkansas	0
0	Rice	7
34	SMU	7
8	Oklahoma A. & M.	13
6	TCU	7
6	Texas A. & M.	0

1945

13	Bergstrom Field	7
46	Southwestern	0
33	Texas Tech	0
12	Oklahoma	7
34	Arkansas	7
6	Rice	7
12	SMU	7
21	Baylor	14
20	TCU	0
20	Texas A. & M.	10

1946

42	Missouri	0
76	Colorado	0
54	Oklahoma A. & M.	6
20	Oklahoma	13
20	Arkansas	0
13	Rice	18
19	SMU	3
22	Baylor	7
0	TCU	14
24	Texas A. & M.	7

BERNIE BIERMAN

Record: 147-60-12
Hall of Fame 1955

MONTANA 1919–21

1919

26	Montana Wesleyan	7
0	Utah Agricultural	47
28	Montana Mines	6
6	Whitman	6
0	Idaho	7
6	Montana State	6
14	Washington State	42

1920

133	Mt. St. Charles	0
18	Washington	14
34	Montana Wesleyan	0
0	Washington State	31
7	Whitman	13
28	Montana State	0
7	Idaho	20

1921

25	Idaho Tech	0
7	Washington	28
6	Whitman	14
7	Idaho	35

14	Montana State	7
7	North Dakota State	6
0	Gonzaga	0

MISSISSIPPI STATE 1925–26

1925

34	Millsaps	0
0	Ouachita	3
3	Tulane	25
6	Mississippi	0
0	Alabama	6
46	Mississippi College	0
9	Tennessee	14
0	Florida	12

1926

19	Birmingham	7
41	Mississippi College	0
7	Alabama	26
34	Millsaps	0
7	LSU	6
0	Tennessee	33
14	Tulane	0
6	Indiana	19
6	Mississippi	7

TULANE 1927–31

1927

19	Mississippi	7
6	Georgia Tech	13
6	Miss. State	13
0	Vanderbilt	32
0	Georgia	31
6	Auburn	6
6	Sewanee	12
13	LSU	6

1928

65	Louisiana Normal	0
51	Miss. State	6
0	Georgia Tech	12
6	Vanderbilt	13
14	Georgia	20
27	Millsaps	0
13	Auburn	12
41	Sewanee	6
47	Louisiana College	7
0	LSU	0

1929

40	Louisiana Normal	6
13	Texas A. & M.	10
60	Southwestern	0
20	Georgia Tech	14
34	Miss. State	0
21	Georgia	15
52	Auburn	0
18	Sewanee	0
21	LSU	0

1930

84	Southwestern	0
0	Northwestern	14
19	Texas A. & M.	9
21	Birmingham Southern	0
28	Georgia Tech	0
53	Miss. State	0
21	Auburn	0
25	Georgia	0
12	LSU	7

1931

31	Mississippi	0
7	Texas A. & M.	0
40	Spring Hill	0
19	Vanderbilt	0
33	Georgia Tech	0
59	Miss. State	7
27	Auburn	0
20	Georgia	7
40	Sewanee	0
34	LSU	7
28	Washington State	14

MINNESOTA 1932–41, 1945–50

1932

12	South Dakota State	0
0	Purdue	7
7	Nebraska	6
21	Iowa	6
7	Northwestern	0
26	Mississippi	0
13	Wisconsin	20
0	Michigan	3

1933

19	South Dakota State	6
6	Indiana	6
7	Purdue	7
7	Pittsburgh	3
19	Iowa	7
0	Northwestern	0
0	Michigan	0
6	Wisconsin	3

1934

56	South Dakota State	12
20	Nebraska	0
13	Pittsburgh	7
48	Iowa	12
34	Michigan	0
30	Indiana	0
35	Chicago	7
34	Wisconsin	0

1935

26	North Dakota State	6
12	Nebraska	7
20	Tulane	0
21	Northwestern	13
29	Purdue	7
13	Iowa	6
40	Michigan	0
33	Wisconsin	7

1936

14	Washington	7
7	Nebraska	0
26	Michigan	0
33	Purdue	0
0	Northwestern	6
52	Iowa	0
47	Texas	19
24	Wisconsin	0

1937

69	North Dakota State	7
9	Nebraska	14
6	Indiana	0
39	Michigan	6
6	Notre Dame	7
35	Iowa	10
7	Northwestern	0
13	Wisconsin	6

1938

15	Washington	0
16	Nebraska	7
7	Purdue	0
7	Michigan	6
3	Northwestern	6
28	Iowa	0
0	Notre Dame	19
21	Wisconsin	0

1939

62	Arizona	0
7	Nebraska	6
13	Purdue	13
20	Ohio State	23
7	Northwestern	14
20	Michigan	7
9	Iowa	13
23	Wisconsin	7

1940

19	Washington	14
13	Nebraska	7
13	Ohio State	7
34	Iowa	6
13	Northwestern	12
7	Michigan	6
33	Purdue	6
22	Wisconsin	13

1941

14	Washington	6
34	Illinois	6
39	Pittsburgh	0
7	Michigan	0
8	Northwestern	7
9	Nebraska	0
34	Iowa	13
41	Wisconsin	6

1945

34	Missouri	0
61	Nebraska	7
14	Fort Warren	0
30	Northwestern	7
7	Ohio State	20
0	Michigan	26
0	Indiana	49
19	Iowa	20
12	Wisconsin	26

1946

33	Nebraska	6
0	Indiana	21
7	Northwestern	14
46	Wyoming	0
9	Ohio State	39
0	Michigan	21
13	Purdue	7
16	Iowa	6
6	Wisconsin	0

1947

7	Washington	6
28	Nebraska	13
37	Northwestern	21
13	Illinois	40
6	Michigan	13
29	Pittsburgh	0
26	Purdue	21
7	Iowa	13
21	Wisconsin	0

1948

20	Washington	0
39	Nebraska	13
16	Northwestern	19
6	Illinois	0
14	Michigan	27
30	Indiana	7
34	Purdue	7
28	Iowa	21
16	Wisconsin	0

1949

48	Washington	20
28	Nebraska	6
21	Northwestern	7
27	Ohio State	0
7	Michigan	14
7	Purdue	13
55	Iowa	7
24	Pittsburgh	7
14	Wisconsin	6

1950

13	Washington	28
26	Nebraska	32
6	Northwestern	13
0	Ohio State	48
7	Michigan	7
0	Iowa	13
0	Michigan State	27
27	Purdue	14
0	Wisconsin	14

EARL (RED) BLAIK

Record: 166–48–14
Hall of Fame 1964

DARTMOUTH 1934–40

1934

39	Norwich	0
32	Vermont	0
27	Maine	0
27	Virginia	0
10	Harvard	0
2	Yale	7
21	New Hampshire	7
6	Cornell	21
13	Princeton	38

1935

39	Norwich	0
47	Vermont	0
59	Bates	7
41	Brown	0
14	Harvard	6
14	Yale	6
34	William & Mary	0
41	Cornell	6
6	Princeton	26
7	Columbia	13

1936

58	Norwich	0
56	Vermont	0
0	Holy Cross	7
34	Brown	0
26	Harvard	7
11	Yale	7
20	Columbia	13
20	Cornell	6
13	Princeton	13

1937

39	Bates	0
31	Amherst	7
42	Springfield	0
41	Brown	0
20	Harvard	2
9	Yale	9
33	Princeton	9
6	Cornell	6
27	Columbia	0

1938

46	Bates	0
51	St. Lawrence	0
22	Princeton	0
34	Brown	13
13	Harvard	7
24	Yale	6
44	Dickinson	6
7	Cornell	14
13	Stanford	23

1939

41	St. Lawrence	9
34	Hampden-Sydney	6
0	Navy	0
14	Lafayette	0
16	Harvard	0
33	Yale	0
7	Princeton	9
6	Cornell	35
3	Stanford	14

1940

35	St. Lawrence	0
21	Franklin & Marshall	23
6	Columbia	20
7	Yale	13
7	Harvard	6
26	Sewanee	0
9	Princeton	14
3	Cornell	0
20	Brown	6

ARMY 1941–58

1941

19	Citadel	6
27	VMI	20
20	Yale	7
13	Columbia	0
0	Notre Dame	0
6	Harvard	20
7	Pennsylvania	14
7	West Virginia	6
6	Navy	14

1942

14	Lafayette	0
28	Cornell	8
34	Columbia	6
14	Harvard	0
0	Pennsylvania	19
0	Notre Dame	13
19	VPI	7
40	Princeton	7
0	Navy	14

1943

27	Villanova	0
42	Colgate	0
51	Temple	0

Continued on next page

52	Columbia	0
39	Yale	7
13	Pennsylvania	13
0	Notre Dame	26
16	Sampson	7
59	Brown	0
0	Navy	13

1944

46	North Carolina	0
59	Brown	7
69	Pittsburgh	7
76	Coast Guard Academy	0
27	Duke	7
83	Villanova	0
59	Notre Dame	0
62	Pennsylvania	7
23	Navy	7

1945

32	Louisville (AAF)	0
54	Wake Forest	0
28	Michigan	7
55	Melville, R.I. (USN)	13
48	Duke	13
54	Villanova	0
48	Notre Dame	0
61	Pennsylvania	0
32	Navy	13

1946

35	Villanova	0
21	Oklahoma	7
46	Cornell	21
20	Michigan	13
48	Columbia	14
19	Duke	0
19	West Virginia	0
0	Notre Dame	0
34	Pennsylvania	7
21	Navy	18

1947

13	Villanova	0
47	Colorado	0
0	Illinois	0
40	VPI	0
20	Columbia	21
65	Washington & Lee	13
7	Notre Dame	27
7	Pennsylvania	7
21	Navy	0

1948

28	Villanova	0
54	Lafayette	7
26	Illinois	21
20	Harvard	7
27	Cornell	6
49	VPI	7
43	Stanford	0
26	Pennsylvania	20
21	Navy	21

1949

47	Davidson	7
42	Penn State	7
21	Michigan	7
54	Harvard	14
63	Columbia	6
40	VMI	14
35	Fordham	0
14	Pennsylvania	13
38	Navy	0

1950

28	Colgate	0
41	Penn State	7
27	Michigan	6
49	Harvard	0
34	Columbia	0
28	Pennsylvania	13
51	New Mexico	0
7	Stanford	0
2	Navy	14

1951

7	Villanova	21
14	Northwestern	20
14	Dartmouth	28
21	Harvard	22
14	Columbia	9
6	Southern Cal	28
27	Citadel	6
6	Pennsylvania	7
7	Navy	42

1952

28	South Carolina	7
0	Southern Cal	22
37	Dartmouth	7
14	Pittsburgh	22
14	Columbia	14
42	VMI	14
6	Georgia Tech	45
14	Pennsylvania	13
0	Navy	7

1953

41	Furman	0
20	Northwestern	33
27	Dartmouth	0
14	Duke	13
40	Columbia	7
0	Tulane	0
27	North Carolina State	7
21	Pennsylvania	14
20	Navy	7

1954

20	South Carolina	34
26	Michigan	7
60	Dartmouth	6
28	Duke	14
67	Columbia	12
21	Virginia	20
48	Yale	7
35	Pennsylvania	0
20	Navy	27

1955

81	Furman	0
35	Penn State	6
2	Michigan	26
0	Syracuse	13
45	Columbia	0
27	Colgate	7
12	Yale	14
40	Pennsylvania	0
14	Navy	6

1956

32	VMI	12
14	Penn State	7
14	Michigan	48
0	Syracuse	7
60	Columbia	0
55	Colgate	46

34	William & Mary	6
7	Pittsburgh	20
7	Navy	7

1957

42	Nebraska	0
27	Penn State	13
21	Notre Dame	23
29	Pittsburgh	13
20	Virginia	12
53	Colgate	7
39	Utah	33
20	Tulane	14
0	Navy	14

1958

45	South Carolina	8
26	Penn State	0
14	Notre Dame	2
35	Virginia	6
14	Pittsburgh	14
68	Colgate	6
14	Rice	7
26	Villanova	0
22	Navy	6

FRANK CAVANAUGH

Record: 145–48–17
Hall of Fame 1954

CINCINNATI 1898

12	Ohio	12
22	Miami (Ohio)	0
12	Vanderbilt	0
0	Oberlin	5
0	Indiana	0
12	Alumni	0
57	Ohio Wesleyan	0
11	Indiana	11
17	Dartmouth	12

HOLY CROSS 1903–05

1903

6	Massachusetts	0
0	Dartmouth	18
11	Wesleyan	5
10	Yale	36
6	Tufts	5
36	Amherst	0
27	Springfield	5
5	Maine	0
41	Worcester Tech	0
32	Tufts	0

1904

0	Massachusetts	0
0	Bates	0
0	Yale	23
34	Tufts	0
4	Dartmouth	18
4	Georgetown	17
6	Amherst	40
4	Harvard	28
12	Springfield	9

1905

17	Massachusetts	0
6	Dartmouth	16
0	Yale	29
12	Worcester Tech	6
32	Springfield	0
9	Amherst	0

4 Syracuse 15
12 Tufts 2
27 Fordham 5

DARTMOUTH 1911–16

1911

18 Norwich 3
22 MAC 0
23 Bowdoin 0
12 Colby 0
6 Holy Cross 0
23 Williams 5
12 Vermont 0
18 Amherst 6
0 Princeton 3
3 Harvard 5

1912

26 Bates 0
41 Norwich 9
47 MAC 0
55 Vermont 0
21 Williams 0
7 Princeton 22
60 Amherst 0
24 Cornell 0
0 Harvard 3

1913

13 MAC 3
53 Colby 0
33 Vermont 7
48 Williams 6
6 Princeton 0
21 Amherst 7
34 Pennsylvania 21
10 Carlisle 35

1914

29 MAC 6
74 Norwich 0
21 Williams 3
42 Vermont 0
12 Princeton 16
32 Amherst 0
68 Tufts 0
41 Pennsylvania 0
40 Syracuse 0

1915

13 MAC 0
34 Maine 0
20 Tufts 7
60 Vermont 0
7 Princeton 30
26 Amherst 0
7 Pennsylvania 3
29 Bates 0
0 Syracuse 0

1916

33 New Haupshire State 0
32 Boston College 6
47 Lebanon Valley 0
62 MAC 0
0 Georgetown 10
3 Princeton 7
15 Syracuse 10
7 Pennsylvania 7
7 West Virginia 7

BOSTON COLLEGE 1919–26

1919

20 USS Utah 0
0 Harvard 17
25 Middlebury 0
5 Yale 3
0 Army 13
7 Rutgers 13
9 Holy Cross 7
10 Georgetown 7

1920

20 Fordham 0
21 Yale 13
12 Springfield 0
34 Boston U. 0
37 Tufts 0
13 Marietta 3
30 Georgetown 0
14 Holy Cross 0

1921

13 Boston U. 0
25 Providence 0
23 Baylor 7
0 Detroit 28
0 Fordham 0
14 Marietta 0
10 Georgetown 14
0 Holy Cross 41

1922

20 Boston U. 6
27 Fordham 0
8 Detroit 10
0 Lafayette 19
15 Villanova 3
33 Baylor 7
13 Canisius 7
0 Georgetown 0
17 Holy Cross 13

1923

28 Providence 0
20 Fordham 0
21 Canisius 0
6 Marquette 7
21 Georgetown 0
14 Centenary 0
41 Villanova 0
0 Vermont 0
16 Holy Cross 7

1924

47 Providence 0
28 Fordham 0
0 Syracuse 10
13 Allegheny 0
34 Haskell 7
34 Marquette 7
9 Centenary 10
33 Vermont 7
0 Holy Cross 33

1925

6 Catholic U. 0
7 Haskell 6
51 Boston U. 7
14 Allegheny 7
51 Providence 0
0 West Virginia 20
6 W. Va. Wesleyan 7
17 Holy Cross 6

1926

28 Catholic U. 0
27 Fordham 0
61 St. Louis U. 0
27 W. Va. Wesleyan 6
19 Villanova 7
21 Haskell 21
39 Gettysburg 0
0 Holy Cross 0

FORDHAM 1927–1932

1927

34 Bethany 0
13 Lebanon Valley 3
0 NYU 32
0 George Washington 13
7 Boston College 27
2 Holy Cross 7
26 Providence 19
0 Georgetown 38

1928

27 Saint Bonaventure 0
20 George Washington 0
7 NYU 34
19 Holy Cross 13
34 Washington & Jefferson 0
0 West Virginia 18
7 Boston College 19
0 Detroit 19
7 Georgetown 27

1929

43 Westminster 0
33 Saint Bonaventure 0
26 NYU 0
7 Holy Cross 0
6 Davis and Elkins 6
0 West Virginia 0
7 Boston College 6
40 Thiel 7
14 Bucknell 0

1930

73 Baltimore 0
71 Buffalo 0
3 Boston College 0
6 Holy Cross 0
7 NYU 0
18 West Virginia 2
13 Detroit 7
12 Saint Mary's (Calif.) 20
12 Bucknell 0

1931

28 Thiel 0
20 West Virginia 7
20 Boston College 0
6 Holy Cross 6
46 Drake 0
33 West Liberty State 0
39 Detroit 9
0 NYU 0
13 Bucknell 14

1932

69 Baltimore 0
30 Bucknell 0
52 Lebanon Valley 0
13 Michigan State 19
0 Boston College 3
14 Saint Mary's (Calif.) 0
7 NYU 6
8 Oregon State 6

FRITZ CRISLER

Record: 115–32–9
Hall of Fame 1954

MINNESOTA 1930–31

1930

0	Wisconsin	14
0	Michigan	7
6	Northwestern	27
6	Indiana	0
59	South Dakota	0
48	South Dakota St.	0
0	Stanford	0
7	Vanderbilt	33

1931

14	Wisconsin	0
34	Iowa	0
0	Michigan	6
14	Northwestern	32
19	Ohio State	7
47	Cornell (Iowa)	7
13	North Dakota St.	7
20	Oklahoma A. & M.	0
30	Ripon	0
0	Stanford	13

PRINCETON 1932–37

1932

22	Amherst	0
7	Columbia	20
0	Cornell	0
0	Navy	0
7	Michigan	14
53	Lehigh	0
7	Yale	7

1933

40	Amherst	0
45	Williams	0
20	Columbia	0
6	Washington & Lee	0
33	Brown	0
7	Dartmouth	0
13	Navy	0
26	Rutgers	6
27	Yale	2

1934

75	Amherst	0
35	Williams	6
14	Washington & Lee	12
45	Cornell	0
19	Harvard	0
54	Lehigh	0
0	Yale	7
38	Dartmouth	13

1935

7	Pennsylvania	6
14	Williams	7
29	Rutgers	6
54	Cornell	0
26	Navy	0
35	Harvard	0
27	Lehigh	0
26	Dartmouth	6
38	Yale	7

1936

27	Williams	7
20	Rutgers	0

0	Pennsylvania	7
7	Navy	0
14	Harvard	14
41	Cornell	13
23	Yale	26
13	Dartmouth	13

1937

26	Virginia	0
7	Cornell	20
16	Chicago	7
6	Rutgers	0
6	Harvard	34
9	Dartmouth	33
0	Yale	26
26	Navy	6

MICHIGAN 1938–47

1938

14	Michigan State	0
45	Chicago	7
6	Minnesota	7
15	Yale	13
14	Illinois	0
19	Pennsylvania	13
0	Northwestern	0
18	Ohio State	0

1939

26	Michigan State	13
27	Iowa	7
85	Chicago	0
27	Yale	7
7	Illinois	16
7	Minnesota	20
19	Pennsylvania	17
21	Ohio State	14

1940

41	California	0
21	Michigan State	14
26	Harvard	0
28	Illinois	0
14	Pennsylvania	0
6	Minnesota	7
20	Northwestern	13
40	Ohio State	0

1941

19	Michigan State	7
6	Iowa	0
40	Pittsburgh	0
14	Northwestern	7
0	Minnesota	7
20	Illinois	0
28	Columbia	0
20	Ohio State	20

1942

9	Great Lakes	0
20	Michigan State	0
14	Iowa Pre-Flight	26
34	Northwestern	16
14	Minnesota	16
28	Illinois	14
35	Harvard	7
32	Notre Dame	20
7	Ohio State	21
28	Iowa	14

1943

26	Camp Grant	0
57	Western Michigan	6
21	Northwestern	7

12	Notre Dame	35
49	Minnesota	6
42	Illinois	6
23	Indiana	6
27	Wisconsin	0
45	Ohio State	7

1944

12	Iowa Pre-Flight	7
14	Marquette	0
0	Indiana	20
28	Minnesota	13
27	Northwestern	0
40	Purdue	14
41	Pennsylvania	19
14	Illinois	0
14	Wisconsin	0
14	Ohio State	18

1945

27	Great Lakes	2
7	Indiana	13
40	Michigan State	0
20	Northwestern	7
7	Army	28
19	Illinois	0
26	Minnesota	0
7	Navy	33
27	Purdue	13
7	Ohio State	3

1946

21	Indiana	0
14	Iowa	7
13	Army	20
14	Northwestern	14
9	Illinois	13
21	Minnesota	0
55	Michigan State	7
28	Wisconsin	6
58	Ohio State	6

1947

55	Michigan State	0
49	Stanford	13
69	Pittsburgh	0
49	Northwestern	21
13	Minnesota	6
14	Illinois	7
35	Indiana	0
40	Wisconsin	6
21	Ohio State	0

JIM CROWLEY

Record: 77–20–10

MICHIGAN STATE 1929–32

1929

59	Alma	6
0	Michigan	17
0	Colgate	31
74	Adrian	0
40	N. C. State	6
38	Case	0
33	Mississippi State	19
0	Detroit	25

1930

28	Alma	0
0	Michigan	0
32	Cincinnati	0
14	Colgate	7

45	Case	0
13	Georgetown	14
19	North Dakota State	11
0	Detroit	0

1931

74	Alma	0
47	Cornell (Iowa)	0
7	Army	20
34	Illinois Wesleyan	6
6	Georgetown	0
10	Syracuse	15
100	Ripon	0
0	Michigan	0
13	Detroit	20

1932

93	Alma	0
0	Michigan	26
27	Grinnell	6
27	Illinois Wesleyan	0
19	Fordham	13
27	Syracuse	13
20	South Dakota	6
7	Detroit	0

Fordham 1933–41

1933

52	Albright	0
57	Muhlenberg	0
20	West Virginia	0
32	Boston College	6
2	Alabama	0
6	Saint Mary's (Calif.)	13
20	NYU	12
6	Oregon State	9

1934

57	Westminster	0
6	Boston College	0
9	Saint Mary's (Calif.)	14
14	Southern Methodist	26
13	Tennessee	12
27	West Virginia	20
0	Purdue	7
39	NYU	13

1935

14	Franklin & Marshall	7
19	Boston College	0
0	Purdue	20
13	Vanderbilt	7
15	Lebanon Valley	0
0	Pittsburgh	0
7	Saint Mary's (Calif.)	7
45	Muhlenberg	0
21	NYU	0

1936

66	Franklin & Marshall	7
7	Southern Methodist	0
20	Waynesburg	6
7	Saint Mary's (Calif.)	6
0	Pittsburgh	0
15	Purdue	0
7	Georgia	7
6	NYU	7

1937

66	Franklin & Marshall	7
48	Waynesburg	0
0	Pittsburgh	0
7	Texas Christian	6

14	North Carolina	0
21	Purdue	3
6	Saint Mary's (Calif.)	0
20	NYU	7

1938

47	Upsala	0
53	Waynesburg	0
6	Purdue	6
26	Oregon	0
13	Pittsburgh	24
3	Saint Mary's (Calif.)	0
0	North Carolina	0
13	South Carolina	0
25	NYU	0

1939

34	Waynesburg	7
6	Alabama	7
0	Tulane	7
27	Pittsburgh	13
13	Rice	7
13	Indiana	0
13	Saint Mary's (Calif.)	0
18	NYU	7

1940

20	West Virginia	7
20	Tulane	7
24	Pittsburgh	12
6	Saint Mary's (Calif.)	9
14	North Carolina	0
13	Purdue	7
27	Arkansas	7
26	NYU	0

1941

16	Southern Methodist	10
27	North Carolina	14
27	West Virginia	0
28	Texas Christian	14
17	Purdue	0
0	Pittsburgh	13
35	Saint Mary's (Calif.)	7
30	NYU	9

GIL DOBIE

Record: 179–45–15
Hall of Fame 1951

North Dakota State 1906–07
(Scores not available.)

Washington 1908–16

1908

22	Lincoln HS	0
23	Washington HS	5
24	Whitworth	4
6	Whitman	0
6	Washington State	6
15	Oregon	0
32	Oregon State	0

1909

52	USS Milwaukee	0
34	Queen Anne HS	0
20	Lincoln HS	0
50	Idaho	0
17	Whitman	0
21	Oregon State	0
20	Oregon	6

1910

20	Lincoln HS	0
51	College Puget Sound	0
29	Idaho	0
16	Washington State	0
12	Whitman	8
22	Oregon State	0

1911

42	Lincoln HS	0
90	Fort Worden	0
35	College Puget Sound	0
17	Idaho	0
34	Oregon State	0
29	Oregon	3
30	Washington State	6

1912

53	College Puget Sound	0
55	Bremerton Sailors	0
24	Idaho	0
9	Oregon State	3
30	Oregon	14
19	Washington State	0

1913

26	Everett HS	0
23	All-Navy	7
100	Whitworth	0
47	Oregon State	0
40	Whitman	6
10	Oregon	7
20	Washington State	0

1914

33	Aberdeen HS	6
81	Rainier Valley AC	0
45	Washington Park AC	0
28	Whitman	7
0	Oregon State	0
10	Oregon	0
45	Washington State	0

1915

31	Ballard Meteors	0
64	Washington Park AC	0
21	Gonzaga	7
27	Whitman	0
72	California	0
13	California	7
46	Colorado	0

1916

28	Ballard Meteors	0
62	Bremerton Sub.	0
37	Whitman	6
0	Oregon	0
35	Oregon State	0
13	California	3
14	California	0

Navy 1917–19

1917

27	Davidson	6
0	West Virginia	7
62	Maryland State	0
62	Carlisle Indians	0
89	Haverford	0
95	Western Reserve	0
28	Georgetown	7
80	Villanova	3

1918

47	Newport Tr. St.	7
66	St. Helena Tr. St.	0
37	Norfolk Naval Base	6
127	Ursinus College	0
6	Great Lakes	7

1919

49	N. C. State	0
66	Johns Hopkins	0
21	Bucknell	6
20	W. Va. Wesleyan	6
0	Georgetown	6
121	Colby	0
6	Army	0
15	USS Utah	0

CORNELL 1920–35

1920

13	Rochester	6
55	St. Bonaventure	7
60	Union	0
42	Colgate	6
24	Rutgers	0
3	Dartmouth	14
34	Columbia	7
0	Pennsylvania	28

1921

41	St. Bonaventure	0
55	Rochester	0
110	Western Reserve	0
31	Colgate	7
59	Dartmouth	7
41	Columbia	7
14	Springfield	0
41	Pennsylvania	0

1922

55	St. Bonaventure	6
66	Niagara	0
68	New Hampshire	7
14	Colgate	0
56	Columbia	0
23	Dartmouth	0
48	Albright	14
9	Pennsylvania	0

1923

41	St. Bonaventure	6
84	Susquehanna	0
28	Williams	6
34	Colgate	7
32	Dartmouth	7
35	Columbia	0
52	Johns Hopkins	0
14	Pennsylvania	7

1924

56	St. Bonaventure	0
27	Niagara	0
7	Williams	14
0	Rutgers	10
14	Columbia	0
91	Susquehanna	0
14	Dartmouth	27
0	Pennsylvania	20

1925

80	Susquehanna	0
26	Niagara	0
48	Williams	0
41	Rutgers	0

17	Columbia	14
13	Dartmouth	62
33	Canisius	0
0	Pennsylvania	7

1926

6	Geneva	0
28	Niagara	0
49	Williams	0
24	Michigan State	14
9	Columbia	17
41	St. Bonaventure	0
24	Dartmouth	23
10	Pennsylvania	10

1927

41	Clarkson	0
19	Niagara	6
53	Richmond	0
10	Princeton	21
0	Columbia	0
6	St. Bonaventure	6
7	Dartmouth	53
0	Pennsylvania	35

1928

20	Clarkson	0
34	Niagara	0
18	Hampden-Sydney	6
0	Princeton	3
0	Columbia	0
0	St. Bonaventure	0
0	Dartmouth	28
0	Pennsylvania	49

1929

60	Clarkson	0
22	Niagara	6
40	Hampden-Sydney	6
13	Princeton	7
12	Columbia	6
36	Western Reserve	0
14	Dartmouth	18
7	Pennsylvania	17

1930

66	Clarkson	0
61	Niagara	14
47	Hampden-Sydney	6
12	Princeton	7
7	Columbia	10
54	Hobart	0
13	Dartmouth	19
13	Pennsylvania	7

1931

68	Clarkson	0
37	Niagara	6
27	Richmond	0
33	Princeton	0
13	Columbia	0
54	Alfred	0
0	Dartmouth	14
7	Pennsylvania	0

1932

72	Buffalo	0
7	Niagara	0
27	Richmond	0
0	Princeton	0
0	Columbia	6
40	Albright	14
21	Dartmouth	6
7	Pennsylvania	13

1933

48	St. Lawrence	7
28	Richmond	7
0	Michigan	40
7	Syracuse	14
6	Columbia	9
7	Dartmouth	0
20	Pennsylvania	12

1934

14	St. Lawrence	0
0	Richmond	6
7	Syracuse	20
0	Princeton	45
0	Columbia	14
21	Dartmouth	6
13	Pennsylvania	23

1935

6	St. Lawrence	12
19	Western Reserve	33
14	Syracuse	21
0	Princeton	54
7	Columbia	7
6	Dartmouth	41
7	Pennsylvania	33

BOSTON COLLEGE 1936–38

1936

26	Northeastern	6
0	Temple	14
12	New Hampshire	0
12	Providence	0
13	Michigan State	13
7	N. C. State	3
12	Western Maryland	7
0	Boston U.	0
13	Holy Cross	12

1937

35	Northeastern	2
21	Kansas State	7
0	Temple	0
0	Detroit	14
7	N. C. State	12
27	Western Maryland	0
13	Kentucky	0
6	Boston U.	13
0	Holy Cross	20

1938

63	Canisius	12
13	Northeastern	0
9	Detroit	6
26	Temple	26
33	Florida	0
14	Indiana	0
21	Boston U.	14
0	St. Anselm's	0
7	Holy Cross	29

DICK HANLEY

Record: 87–35–8

HASKELL 1922–26

1922

(Scores not available.)

1923

89	Central Missouri	0
12	Minnesota	13
26	Creighton	0

63	Friends	0
23	Carlisle	3
98	Kansas City U.	0
35	Tulsa	0
38	Xavier	0
34	Pittsburg	0
34	Still	7
14	Quantico Marines	14
13	Butler	19
13	Oklahoma Baptist	0

(Record incomplete.)

1924

0	Nebraska	20
7	Creighton	7
28	Midland	0
26	Tulsa	3
47	Xavier	6
12	Still	0
20	Butler	7
55	Oklahoma Baptist	0
7	Boston College	34
17	Brown	13
14	Fairfax	0

(Record incomplete.)

1925

16	Creighton	7
39	Carlisle	0
40	Kansas Wesleyan	0
29	Midland	0
33	Kansas City U.	0
34	Xavier	8
6	Boston College	7
36	Bucknell	0
10	Gonzaga	9
2	Dayton	6
14	William & Mary	13
0	Loyola (Chicago)	6
12	Los Angeles AC	10

(Record incomplete.)

1926

57	Wichita	0
65	Drury	0
38	Morningside	0
27	Tulsa	7
27	Xavier	0
55	Still	0
21	Boston College	21
36	Bucknell	0
30	Dayton	14
27	Loyola (Chicago)	7
40	Michigan State	7
40	Hawaii All-Stars	7
95	Jackson	0

NORTHWESTERN 1927–34

1927

47	South Dakota	2
13	Utah	6
19	Ohio State	13
6	Illinois	7
19	Missouri	34
6	Purdue	18
7	Indiana	18
12	Iowa	0

1928

14	Butler	0
0	Ohio State	10
7	Kentucky	0
0	Illinois	6
10	Minnesota	9
7	Purdue	6

0	Indiana	6
27	Dartmouth	6

1929

27	Cornell (Iowa)	18
13	Butler	0
7	Wisconsin	0
14	Minnesota	26
66	Wabash	0
7	Illinois	0
18	Ohio State	6
14	Indiana	19
6	Notre Dame	26

1930

14	Tulane	0
19	Ohio State	2
32	Illinois	0
45	Centre	7
27	Minnesota	6
25	Indiana	0
20	Wisconsin	7
0	Notre Dame	14

1931

19	Nebraska	7
0	Notre Dame	0
19	UCLA	0
10	Ohio State	0
32	Illinois	6
32	Minnesota	14
7	Indiana	6
19	Iowa	0
0	Purdue	7

1932

27	Missouri	0
6	Michigan	15
26	Illinois	0
7	Purdue	7
0	Minnesota	7
6	Ohio State	20
0	Notre Dame	21
44	Iowa	6

1933

0	Iowa	7
0	Stanford	0
25	Indiana	0
0	Ohio State	12
0	Minnesota	0
0	Illinois	3
0	Notre Dame	7
0	Michigan	13

1934

21	Marquette	12
7	Iowa	20
0	Stanford	20
6	Ohio State	28
7	Wisconsin	0
3	Illinois	14
7	Notre Dame	20
13	Michigan	6

DICK HARLOW

Record: 150–68–17
Hall of Fame 1954

PENN STATE 1915–17

1915

26	Westminster	0
13	Lebanon Valley	0
13	Pennsylvania	3

27	Gettysburg	12
28	W. Va. Wesleyan	0
0	Harvard	13
7	Lehigh	0
33	Lafayette	3
0	Pittsburgh	20

1916

27	Susquehanna	0
55	Westminster	0
50	Bucknell	7
39	W. Va. Wesleyan	0
0	Pennsylvania	15
48	Gettysburg	2
79	Geneva	0
10	Lehigh	7
40	Lafayette	0
0	Pittsburgh	31

1917

10	U.S. Army Amb. Cp.	0
80	Gettysburg	0
99	St. Bonaventure	0
0	Wash. & Jeff.	7
8	W. Va. Wesleyan	7
7	Dartmouth	10
0	Lehigh	9
57	Maryland	0
6	Pittsburgh	28

COLGATE 1922–25

1922

50	Clarkson	6
19	Allegheny	0
0	Princeton	10
0	Cornell	14
87	Susquehanna	6
35	Lehigh	6
40	Rochester	0
7	Syracuse	14
59	Columbia	6

1923

14	Alfred	0
42	Clarkson	0
55	Niagara	0
23	Ohio State	23
7	Cornell	34
27	Ohio Wesleyan	0
0	Navy	9
49	Rochester	0
16	Syracuse	7

1924

35	Alfred	0
41	Clarkson	0
7	Nebraska	33
49	Hobart	0
42	Providence	0
2	West Virginia	34
33	Springfield	0
3	Syracuse	7
6	Brown	20

1925

28	Canisius	0
60	Clarkson	0
49	St. Bonaventure	0
7	Lafayette	7
9	Princeton	0
14	Michigan State	0
19	Providence	7
19	Syracuse	6
14	Brown	14

WESTERN MARYLAND 1926–34

1926

12	Gettysburg	3
13	Dickinson	0
34	Swarthmore	7
14	Holy Cross	20
60	Washington (Mo.)	0
33	Loyola (Balt.)	0
40	Bucknell	0

1927

6	Washington & Jefferson	15
13	Schuylkill	0
43	Dickinson	0
32	Albright	0
41	Gettysburg	0
26	Loyola (Balt.)	0
48	All Army	0
2	Muhlenberg	6

1928

14	Dickinson	0
0	Temple	7
6	Maryland	13
19	Schuylkill	0
69	Loyola (Balt.)	0
21	Mt. St. Mary's	0
19	Gettysburg	19
18	St. Francis	0
59	Muhlenberg	0

1929

34	Baltimore U.	0
7	Georgetown	0
12	St. Thomas	6
21	Albright	6
23	Temple	0
20	St. John's (Anna.)	0
33	Loyola (Balt.)	7
6	Mt. St. Mary's	0
7	St. Francis	0
7	Muhlenberg	0
12	Maryland	0

1930

58	Baltimore U.	0
18	St. John's	0
10	Georgetown	0
40	Loyola (Balt.)	7
20	All Marines	0
27	John Carroll	0
33	Mt. St. Mary's	0
7	Albright	7
25	Muhlenberg	0
7	Maryland	0

1931

7	Georgetown	25
59	St. John's	0
12	Washington & Jefferson	13
0	Duquesne	0
7	Loyola (Balt.)	7
13	Boston College	19
40	Johns Hopkins	0
20	Mt. St. Mary's	0
34	Muhlenberg	0
6	Maryland	4

1932

12	St. Thomas	6
13	Marshall	13
33	Mt. St. Mary's	6
12	Georgetown	6
28	Loyola (Balt.)	6
13	Bucknell	14
20	Boston College	20
39	Maryland	7

1933

2	St. Thomas	12
7	Mt. St. Mary's	0
0	Duquesne	13
20	Georgetown	0
13	Maryland	7
14	Bucknell	13
54	Loyola (Balt.)	0
9	Boston College	12

1934

0	Villanova	0
49	Albright	0
40	Boston College	0
20	St. Thomas	0
2	Catholic U.	0
35	West Chester Teachers	12
6	Bucknell	0
26	Mt. St. Mary's	0
13	Georgetown	0

HARVARD 1935–42, 1945–47

1935

20	Springfield	0
0	Holy Cross	13
0	Army	13
6	Dartmouth	14
33	Brown	0
0	Princeton	35
41	New Hampshire	0
7	Yale	14

1936

38	Amherst	6
28	Brown	0
0	Army	32
7	Dartmouth	26
14	Princeton	14
65	Virginia	0
13	Navy	20
13	Yale	14

1937

54	Springfield	0
34	Brown	7
0	Navy	0
2	Dartmouth	20
34	Princeton	6
6	Army	7
15	Davidson	0
13	Yale	6

1938

13	Brown	20
0	Cornell	20
17	Army	20
7	Dartmouth	13
26	Princeton	7
47	Chicago	13
40	Virginia	13
7	Yale	0

1939

20	Bates	0
61	Chicago	0
7	Pennsylvania	22
0	Dartmouth	16
6	Princeton	9
15	Army	0
46	New Hampshire	0
7	Yale	20

1940

13	Amherst	0
0	Michigan	26
6	Army	6
6	Dartmouth	7
0	Princeton	0
10	Pennsylvania	10
14	Brown	0
28	Yale	0

1941

0	Pennsylvania	19
0	Cornell	7
7	Dartmouth	0
0	Navy	0
6	Princeton	4
20	Army	6
23	Brown	7
14	Yale	0

1942

0	N. C. Pre-Flight	13
7	Pennsylvania	19
7	William & Mary	7
2	Dartmouth	14
0	Army	14
19	Princeton	14
7	Michigan	35
7	Brown	0
3	Yale	7

1945

6	Tufts	7
21	Rochester	13
7	N. L. Sub-Base	18
25	Coast Guard	0
28	Kings Point	7
14	Brown	7
60	Boston U.	0
0	Yale	28

1946

7	Connecticut	0
49	Tufts	0
13	Princeton	12
69	Coast Guard	0
13	Holy Cross	6
0	Rutgers	13
21	Dartmouth	7
28	Brown	0
14	Yale	27

1947

52	Western Maryland	0
19	Boston U.	14
0	Virginia	47
7	Holy Cross	0
13	Dartmouth	14
7	Rutgers	31
7	Princeton	33
13	Brown	7
21	Yale	31

HOWARD JONES

Record: 189–64–21
Hall of Fame 1951

SYRACUSE 1908

0	Carlisle	12
0	Colgate	5
18	Hamilton	0
51	Hobart	0
23	Rochester	12
28	Michigan	4

0	Princeton	0
28	Tufts	0
23	Williams	0
0	Yale	5

YALE 1909

11	Wesleyan	0
15	Syracuse	0
12	Holy Cross	0
36	Springfield	0
17	Army	0
36	Colgate	0
34	Amherst	0
23	Brown	0
17	Princeton	0
8	Harvard	0

OHIO STATE 1910

14	Otterbein	5
62	Wittenberg	0
23	Cincinnati	0
6	Western Reserve	0
3	Michigan	3
5	Denison	5
10	Case	14
6	Ohio Wesleyan	0
0	Oberlin	0
53	Kenyon	0

YALE 1913

21	Wesleyan	0
10	Holy Cross	0
0	Maine	0
27	Lafayette	0
37	Lehigh	0
0	Wash. & Jeff.	0
6	Colgate	16
17	Brown	0
3	Princeton	3
5	Harvard	15

IOWA 1916–23

1916

31	Cornell	6
17	Grinnell	7
24	Purdue	6
0	Minnesota	67
13	Northwestern	20
19	Iowa State	16
17	Nebraska	34

1917

22	Cornell	13
0	Nebraska	47
0	Grinnell	10
0	Wisconsin	20
14	Great Lakes	23
35	South Dakota	0
14	Northwestern	25
6	Iowa State	3

1918

0	Great Lakes	10
12	Nebraska	0
27	Coe	0
34	Cornell	0
0	Illinois	19
6	Minnesota	0
21	Iowa State	0
23	Northwestern	7
0	Camp Dodge	0

1919

18	Nebraska	0
7	Illinois	9
9	Minnesota	6
26	South Dakota	13
14	Northwestern	7
6	Chicago	9
10	Iowa State	0

1920

14	Indiana	7
63	Cornell	0
3	Illinois	20
0	Chicago	10
20	Northwestern	0
28	Minnesota	7
14	Iowa State	10

1921

52	Knox	14
10	Notre Dame	7
14	Illinois	2
13	Purdue	6
41	Minnesota	7
41	Indiana	0
14	Northwestern	0

1922

61	Knox	0
6	Yale	0
8	Illinois	7
56	Purdue	0
28	Minnesota	14
12	Ohio State	9
37	Northwestern	3

1923

44	Knox	3
20	Oklahoma A. & M.	0
7	Purdue	0
6	Illinois	9
20	Ohio State	0
3	Michigan	9
7	Minnesota	20
17	Northwestern	14

DUKE 1924

0	N.C. State	14
33	Guilford	6
0	North Carolina	6
14	Richmond	0
3	William & Mary	21
54	Elon	0
0	Wake Forest	32
12	Wofford	0
13	Davidson	20

SOUTHERN CALIFORNIA 1925–40

1925

74	Whittier	0
32	Cal Tech	0
80	Pomona	0
28	Utah	2
9	Stanford	13
56	Arizona	0
51	Idaho	7
29	Santa Clara	9
27	Montana	7
18	Iowa	0
12	Washington St.	17
28	Oregon State	0
12	St. Mary's	0

1926

74	Whittier	0
42	Santa Clara	0
16	Washington St.	7
28	Occidental	6
27	California	0
12	Stanford	13
17	Oregon State	7
28	Idaho	6
61	Montana	0
12	Notre Dame	13

1927

33	Occidental	0
52	Santa Clara	12
13	Oregon State	12
13	Stanford	13
51	Cal Tech	0
13	California	0
46	Colorado	7
27	Washington St.	0
6	Notre Dame	7
33	Washington	13

1928

40	Utah State	12
19	Oregon State	0
19	St. Mary's	6
0	California	0
19	Occidental	0
10	Stanford	0
78	Arizona	7
27	Washington St.	13
28	Idaho	7
27	Notre Dame	14

1929

76	UCLA	0
21	Oregon State	7
48	Washington	0
64	Occidental	0
7	Stanford	0
7	California	15
66	Nevada	0
12	Notre Dame	13
72	Idaho	0
27	Washington St.	7
45	Carnegie Tech	13

1930

52	UCLA	0
27	Oregon State	7
6	Washington St.	7
65	Utah State	0
41	Stanford	12
33	Denver	13
74	California	0
52	Hawaii	0
32	Washington	0
0	Notre Dame	27

1931

7	St. Mary's	13
30	Oregon State	0
38	Washington St.	6
53	Oregon	0
6	California	0
19	Stanford	0
69	Montana	0
16	Notre Dame	14
44	Washington	7
60	Georgia	0

1932

35	Utah	0
20	Washington St.	0
10	Oregon State	0
6	Loyola	0
13	Stanford	0
27	California	7
33	Oregon	0
9	Washington	6
13	Notre Dame	0

1933

39	Occidental	0
51	Whittier	0
18	Loyola	0
33	Washington St.	0
14	St. Mary's	7
0	Oregon State	0
6	California	3
7	Stanford	13
26	Oregon	0
19	Notre Dame	0
31	Georgia	0
13	Washington	7

1934

20	Occidental	0
40	Whittier	14
6	COP	0
0	Washington St.	19
6	Pittsburgh	20
6	Oregon State	6
0	Stanford	16
2	California	7
33	Oregon	0
7	Washington	14
0	Notre Dame	14

1935

9	Montana	0
19	COP	7
0	Illinois	19
7	Oregon State	13
7	California	21
0	Stanford	3
20	Washington St.	10
13	Notre Dame	20
2	Washington	6
7	Pittsburgh	12
33	Kamehameha	7
38	Hawaii	6

1936

38	Oregon State	7
26	Oregon	0
24	Illinois	6
0	Washington St.	0
14	Stanford	7
7	California	13
0	Washington	12
7	UCLA	7
13	Notre Dame	13

1937

40	COP	0
0	Washington	7
13	Ohio State	12
34	Oregon	14
6	California	20
0	Washington St.	0
6	Stanford	7
12	Oregon State	12
6	Notre Dame	13
19	UCLA	13

1938

7	Alabama	19
7	Oregon State	0
14	Ohio State	7
19	Washington St.	6
13	Stanford	2
31	Oregon	7
13	California	7
6	Washington	7
42	UCLA	7
13	Notre Dame	0

1939

7	Oregon	7
27	Washington St.	0
26	Illinois	0
26	California	0
19	Oregon State	7
33	Stanford	0
20	Notre Dame	12
9	Washington	7
0	UCLA	0

1940

14	Washington St.	14
0	Oregon State	0
13	Illinois	7
13	Oregon	0
7	Stanford	21
7	California	20
0	Washington	14
28	UCLA	12
6	Notre Dame	10

LAWRENCE (BIFF) JONES

Record: 87–32–15
Hall of Fame 1954

ARMY 1926–29

1926

21	Detroit	0
21	Davis & Elkins	7
27	Syracuse	21
41	Boston U.	0
33	Yale	0
55	Franklin & Marshall	0
0	Notre Dame	7
21	Ursinus	15
21	Navy	21

1927

13	Boston U.	0
6	Detroit	0
21	Marquette	12
27	Davis & Elkins	6
6	Yale	10
34	Bucknell	0
45	Franklin & Marshall	0
18	Notre Dame	0
13	Ursinus	0
14	Navy	9

1928

35	Boston U.	0
14	Southern Methodist	13
44	Providence	0
15	Harvard	0
18	Yale	6
38	DePauw	12
6	Notre Dame	12
32	Carleton	7
13	Nebraska	3
0	Stanford	26

1929

26	Boston U.	0
33	Gettysburg	7
23	Davidson	7
20	Harvard	20
13	Yale	21
33	South Dakota	6
7	Illinois	17
89	Dickinson	7
19	Ohio Wesleyan	6
0	Notre Dame	7
13	Stanford	34

LOUISIANA STATE UNIVERSITY 1932–34

1932

3	TCU	3
8	Rice	10
80	Spring Hill	0
24	Miss. State	0
14	Arkansas	0
38	Sewanee	0
6	South Carolina	0
0	Centenary	6
14	Tulane	0
0	Oregon	12

1933

13	Rice	0
40	Millsaps	0
0	Centenary	0
20	Arkansas	0
7	Vanderbilt	7
30	South Carolina	7
31	Mississippi	0
21	Miss. State	6
7	Tulane	7
7	Tennessee	0

1934

9	Rice	9
14	Southern Methodist	14
20	Auburn	6
16	Arkansas	0
25	Miss. State	3
29	Vanderbilt	0
6	George Washington	0
14	Mississippi	0
12	Tulane	13
13	Tennessee	19
14	Oregon	13

OKLAHOMA 1935–36

1935

3	Colorado	0
25	New Mexico	0
7	Texas	12
16	Iowa State	0
0	Nebraska	19
0	Kansas	7
20	Missouri	6
3	Kansas State	0
25	Oklahoma Aggies	0

1936

0	Tulsa	0
8	Colorado	0
0	Texas	6
14	Kansas	0
0	Nebraska	14
7	Iowa State	7
6	Kansas State	6

14 Missouri 21
35 Oklahoma Aggies 13

NEBRASKA 1937-41

1937

14 Minnesota 9
20 Iowa State 7
0 Oklahoma 0
7 Missouri 0
7 Indiana 0
13 Kansas 13
7 Pittsburgh 13
28 Iowa 0
3 Kansas State 0

1938

7 Minnesota 16
7 Iowa State 8
0 Indiana 0
0 Oklahoma 14
10 Missouri 13
16 Kansas 7
0 Pittsburgh 19
14 Iowa 0
14 Kansas State 7

1939

7 Indiana 7
6 Minnesota 0
10 Iowa State 7
25 Baylor 0
25 Kansas State 9
13 Missouri 27
7 Kansas 0
14 Pittsburgh 13
13 Oklahoma 7

1940

7 Minnesota 13
13 Indiana 7
53 Kansas 2
20 Missouri 7
13 Oklahoma 0
14 Iowa 6
9 Pittsburgh 7
21 Iowa State 12
20 Kansas State 0

1941

14 Iowa State 0
32 Kansas 0
13 Indiana 21
0 Missouri 6
6 Kansas State 12
0 Minnesota 9
7 Pittsburgh 14
14 Iowa 13
7 Oklahoma 6

TAD JONES

Record: 66–24–6
Hall of Fame 1958

SYRACUSE 1909–10

1909

11 Carlisle 14
5 Colgate 6
5 Fordham 5
20 Hamilton 0
8 Illinois 17
0 Michigan 43
5 Tufts 0

39 Niagara 0
17 Rochester 0
0 Yale 15

1910

6 St. Louis 0
14 Carlisle 0
6 Colgate 11
12 Hobart 5
3 Vermont 0
0 Illinois 3
0 Michigan 11
6 Rochester 0
0 St. Bonaventure 0
6 Yale 12

YALE 1916, 1920-27

1916

25 Carnegie Tech 0
61 Virginia 3
12 Lehigh 0
19 Virginia Tech 0
36 Wash. & Jeff. 14
7 Colgate 3
6 Brown 21
10 Princeton 0
6 Harvard 3

1920

44 Carnegie Tech 0
21 North Carolina 0
13 Boston College 21
24 West Virginia 0
21 Colgate 7
14 Brown 10
0 Princeton 20
0 Harvard 9

1921

28 Bates 0
14 Vermont 0
34 North Carolina 0
23 Williams 0
14 Army 7
45 Brown 7
28 Maryland 0
13 Princeton 7
3 Harvard 10

1922

48 Bates 0
13 Carnegie Tech 0
18 North Carolina 0
0 Iowa 6
38 Williams 0
7 Army 7
20 Brown 0
45 Maryland 3
0 Princeton 3
3 Harvard 10

1923

53 North Carolina 0
40 Georgia 0
29 Bucknell 14
21 Brown 0
31 Army 10
16 Maryland 14
27 Princeton 0
13 Harvard 0

1924

27 North Carolina 0
7 Georgia 6

14 Dartmouth 14
13 Brown 3
7 Army 7
47 Maryland 0
10 Princeton 0
19 Harvard 6

1925

53 Middlebury 0
35 Georgia 7
13 Pennsylvania 16
20 Brown 7
28 Army 7
43 Maryland 14
12 Princeton 25
0 Harvard 0

1926

51 Boston U. 0
19 Georgia 0
14 Dartmouth 7
0 Brown 7
0 Army 33
0 Maryland 15
7 Princeton 10
12 Harvard 7

1927

41 Bowdoin 0
10 Georgia 14
19 Brown 0
10 Army 6
19 Dartmouth 0
30 Maryland 6
14 Princeton 6
14 Harvard 0

ANDY KERR

Record: 137–71–14
Hall of Fame 1951

STANFORD 1922–23

1922

9 Olympic Club 27
7 Santa Clara 0
9 St. Mary's 0
6 Oregon State 0
17 Nevada 7
0 Southern Cal 6
8 Washington 12
0 California 28
7 Pittsburgh 16

1923

82 Mare Island 0
27 Nevada 0
55 Santa Clara 6
42 Occidental 0
7 Southern Cal 14
40 Olympic Club 7
14 Oregon 3
17 Idaho 7
0 California 9

WASHINGTON & JEFFERSON 1926–28

1926

13 Waynesburg 0
17 Bucknell 2
19 Rutgers 6
17 Carnegie Tech 6

Continued on next page

28 Fordham	13
10 Lafayette	16
26 Bethany	0
0 Pittsburgh	0
13 West Virginia	3

1927

14 Waynesburg	0
15 Western Maryland	6
31 Bethany	0
20 Carnegie Tech	6
14 Lafayette	0
33 Thiel	0
0 Pittsburgh	0
19 Bucknell	3
6 West Virginia	6

1928

24 Bethany	0
24 Waynesburg	0
6 Duquesne	12
0 Carnegie Tech	19
0 Fordham	34
13 Lafayette	13
0 Pittsburgh	25
0 Bucknell	0
0 West Virginia	14

COLGATE 1929–46

1929

59 St. Lawrence	0
6 Wisconsin	13
31 Michigan State	0
21 Indiana	6
52 Providence	0
60 Hampden-Sydney	0
33 Columbia	0
21 Syracuse	0
32 Brown	0

1930

38 St. Lawrence	0
99 Bethany	0
41 Lafayette	0
7 Michigan State	14
40 Penn State	0
34 Mississippi A. & M.	0
54 Columbia	0
36 Syracuse	7
27 Brown	0
7 NYU	6

1931

40 Niagara	0
45 St. Lawrence	0
16 Lafayette	0
33 Manhattan	0
0 NYU	13
27 Mississippi A. & M.	0
32 Penn State	7
21 Syracuse	7
13 Brown	7

1932

41 St. Lawrence	0
27 Case School	0
47 Niagara	0
35 Lafayette	0
14 NYU	0
31 Penn State	0
32 Mississippi A. & M.	0
16 Syracuse	0
21 Brown	0

1933

47 St. Lawrence	0
25 Rutgers	2
7 NYU	0
0 Lafayette	0
0 Tulane	7
72 Ohio Northern	0
13 Syracuse	3
25 Brown	0

1934

32 St. Lawrence	0
62 St. Bonaventure	0
7 Ohio State	10
20 Holy Cross	7
20 Tulane	6
13 Syracuse	2
14 Rutgers	0
20 Brown	13

1935

30 Niagara	0
31 St. Lawrence	0
12 Amherst	0
6 Iowa	12
52 Lafayette	0
0 Holy Cross	3
6 Tulane	14
27 Syracuse	0
27 Rutgers	0
33 Brown	0

1936

0 Duke	6
54 Ursinus	0
26 St. Lawrence	6
6 Tulane	28
41 Lafayette	0
14 Army	7
13 Holy Cross	20
13 Syracuse	0
32 Brown	0

1937

21 St. Lawrence	0
7 Cornell	40
34 St. Bonaventure	0
6 Tulane	7
0 Duke	13
7 NYU	14
7 Holy Cross	12
7 Syracuse	0

1938

6 Cornell	15
0 Duke	7
12 Columbia	0
14 Iowa	0
0 Holy Cross	21
0 Syracuse	7
7 NYU	13

1939

6 NYU	7
0 Duke	37
10 Brown	0
31 St. Lawrence	0
7 Holy Cross	27
12 Cornell	14
0 Syracuse	7
0 Columbia	0

1940

44 Akron	0
0 Cornell	34
20 Brown	3
0 Duke	13
31 Mississippi College	0
6 Holy Cross	0
7 Syracuse	6
17 Columbia	20

1941

66 St. Lawrence	0
7 Penn State	0
6 Holy Cross	6
6 Dartmouth	18
14 Duke	27
2 Cornell	21
19 Syracuse	19
30 Columbia	21

1942

49 St. Lawrence	0
18 Cornell	6
27 Dartmouth	19
0 Duke	34
10 Penn State	13
6 Holy Cross	6
35 Columbia	26
14 Syracuse	0
13 Brown	0

1943

7 Rochester	0
0 Army	42
0 Penn State	0
6 Rochester	14
20 Cornell	7
7 Holy Cross	14
26 RPI	0
21 Brown	14
41 Columbia	0

1944

13 Rochester	20
14 Cornell	7
0 Penn State	6
6 Columbia	0
13 Holy Cross	19
13 Syracuse	43
20 Brown	32

1945

48 Rochester	0
7 Penn State	27
47 Lafayette	0
7 Columbia	31
0 Holy Cross	21
6 Cornell	20
7 Syracuse	6
6 Brown	6

1946

6 Yale	27
9 Cornell	13
47 Kings Point	7
2 Penn State	6
39 Lafayette	0
6 Holy Cross	21
25 Syracuse	7
20 Brown	14

LEBANON VALLEY 1947–49

(Scores not available.)

ELMER LAYDEN

Record: 103–34–11

Loras 1925–26

1925

14	Wisconsin Mines	6
0	Detroit	6
0	De Paul	12
7	Valparaiso	6
27	LaCrosse	0
0	St. Viator	0
0	Simpson	10
21	Luther	14

1926

20	Wisconsin Mines	6
8	De Paul	7
19	DeKalb	0
0	St. Thomas	0
12	LaCrosse	0
7	St. Viator	24
6	Luther	14

Duquesne 1927–33

1927

0	St. Bonaventure	13
33	Broaddus	0
0	Geneva	20
7	Bethany	7
8	Thiel	7
10	Westminster	0
12	St. Francis	0
0	Waynesburg	18
12	Ashland	13

1928

9	Slippery Rock	0
10	St. Thomas	0
12	Wash. & Jeff.	6
6	Loyola (Balt.)	0
20	Westminster	6
13	Thiel	7
13	Bethany	6
0	Geneva	7
35	Waynesburg	0

1929

14	Edinboro	0
12	Slippery Rock	0
7	West Virginia	7
18	Albion	0
7	Loyola (Chicago)	6
27	Geneva	7
19	Catholic U.	13
31	Westminster	7
7	Haskell	6
14	Waynesburg	7

1930

0	West Virginia	7
27	Slippery Rock	0
38	Detroit Tech	0
7	Loyola (Chicago)	6
14	Howard	9
12	Catholic U.	0
6	North Dakota	14
0	Geneva	7
12	W. Va. Wesleyan	7
15	Providence	6

1931

13	Geneva	7
6	West Virginia	14

6	Oglethorpe	0
0	W. Va. Wesleyan	12
0	Georgetown	0
0	Western Maryland	0
12	Catholic U.	20
0	Holy Cross	12
13	North Dakota	7
6	Howard	13
0	Carnegie Tech	0

1932

20	Westminster	0
3	West Virginia	0
26	Grove City	0
0	Pittsburgh	33
21	Oglethorpe	6
6	W. Va. Wesleyan	7
19	Wash. & Jeff.	0
34	South Dakota St.	12
0	Catholic U.	0
3	Geneva	0

1933

18	Waynesburg	6
25	W. Va. Wesleyan	0
19	West Virginia	7
6	Bucknell	0
13	Western Maryland	0
14	Detroit	0
31	Westminster	0
21	Wash. & Jeff.	6
0	Pittsburgh	7
26	Geneva	0
33	Miami	7

Notre Dame 1934–40

1934

6	Texas	7
18	Purdue	7
13	Carnegie Tech	0
19	Wisconsin	0
0	Pittsburgh	19
6	Navy	10
20	Northwestern	7
12	Army	6
14	Southern Cal	0

1935

28	Kansas	7
14	Carnegie Tech	3
27	Wisconsin	0
9	Pittsburgh	6
14	Navy	0
18	Ohio State	13
7	Northwestern	14
6	Army	6
20	Southern Cal	13

1936

21	Carnegie Tech	7
14	Washington	6
27	Wisconsin	0
0	Pittsburgh	26
7	Ohio State	2
0	Navy	3
20	Army	6
26	Northwestern	6
13	Southern Cal	13

1937

21	Drake	0
0	Illinois	0
7	Carnegie Tech	9

9	Navy	7
7	Minnesota	6
6	Pittsburgh	21
7	Army	0
7	Northwestern	0
13	Southern Cal	6

1938

52	Kansas	0
14	Georgia Tech	6
14	Illinois	6
7	Carnegie Tech	0
19	Army	7
15	Navy	0
19	Minnesota	0
9	Northwestern	7
0	Southern Cal	13

1939

3	Purdue	0
17	Georgia Tech	14
20	SMU	19
14	Navy	7
7	Carnegie Tech	6
14	Army	0
6	Iowa	7
7	Northwestern	0
12	Southern Cal	20

1940

25	College of Pacific	7
26	Georgia Tech	20
61	Carnegie Tech	0
26	Illinois	0
7	Army	0
13	Navy	7
0	Iowa	7
0	Northwestern	20
10	Southern Cal	6

LOU LITTLE

Record: 148–128–12
Hall of Fame 1960

Georgetown 1924–29

1924

21	King	7
0	Quantico Marines	6
6	Bucknell	14
20	Furman	0
0	Pennsylvania	3
6	3rd Corps Area	0
25	Loyola (New Orleans)	0
6	Fordham	9

1925

25	Drexel	0
19	Mt. St. Mary's	13
50	Lebanon Valley	0
24	Detroit	0
2	Bucknell	3
37	King	0
40	Lehigh	0
41	Centre	3
27	Fordham	0

1926

42	Drexel	0
6	Pittsburgh	6
78	Washington College	0
10	West Virginia	13

Continued on next page

60 Elon	13
34 Lebanon Valley	7
13 Syracuse	7
7 Navy	10
39 Fordham	0
19 Detroit	0

1927

80 Lenoir Rhyne	0
57 Susquehanna	0
39 Davis & Elkins	0
6 Syracuse	19
25 West Virginia	0
58 Waynesburg	0
27 Lafayette	2
47 Boston College	0
38 Fordham	0

1928

31 Mt. St. Mary's	0
88 Susquehanna	0
52 Lebanon Valley	0
34 W. Va. Wesleyan	7
35 Duke	0
7 NYU	2
0 Carnegie Tech	13
12 West Virginia	0
13 Detroit	33

1929

27 Mt. St. Mary's	0
0 Western Maryland	7
13 St. Louis	0
19 W. Va. Wesleyan	0
27 Lebanon Valley	0
14 NYU	0
0 Navy	0
13 Detroit	14

COLUMBIA 1930-56

1930

48 Middlebury	0
25 Union	0
48 Wesleyan	0
0 Dartmouth	52
3 Williams	0
10 Cornell	7
0 Colgate	54
0 Brown	6
7 Syracuse	19

1931

61 Middlebury	0
51 Union	0
37 Wesleyan	0
19 Dartmouth	6
19 Williams	0
0 Cornell	13
27 Virginia	0
9 Brown	7
0 Syracuse	0

1932

51 Middlebury	0
41 Lehigh	6
20 Princeton	7
22 Virginia	6
46 Williams	0
6 Cornell	0
7 Navy	6
6 Brown	7
0 Syracuse	0

1933

39 Lehigh	0
15 Virginia	6
0 Princeton	20
33 Penn State	0
9 Cornell	6
14 Navy	7
46 Lafayette	6
16 Syracuse	0

1934

12 Yale	6
29 VMI	6
7 Navy	18
14 Penn State	7
14 Cornell	0
39 Brown	0
13 Penn	12
12 Syracuse	0

1935

12 VMI	0
20 Rutgers	6
0 Penn	34
7 Michigan	19
7 Cornell	7
2 Syracuse	14
7 Navy	28
18 Brown	0
13 Dartmouth	7

1936

34 Maine	0
16 Army	27
38 VMI	0
0 Michigan	13
20 Cornell	13
13 Dartmouth	20
17 Syracuse	0
7 Stanford	0

1937

40 Williams	6
18 Army	21
26 Penn	6
6 Brown	7
0 Cornell	14
6 Navy	13
6 Syracuse	6
0 Dartmouth	27
0 Stanford	0

1938

27 Yale	14
20 Army	18
0 Colgate	12
13 Penn	14
7 Cornell	23
39 Virginia	0
9 Navy	14
12 Syracuse	13
27 Brown	36

1939

7 Yale	10
6 Army	6
7 Princeton	14
26 VMI	7
7 Cornell	13
19 Navy	13
0 Tulane	25
0 Colgate	0

1940

15 Maine	0
20 Dartmouth	6
19 Georgia	13
0 Syracuse	3
0 Cornell	27
7 Wisconsin	6
0 Navy	0
20 Colgate	17
0 Brown	0

1941

13 Brown	6
21 Princeton	0
3 Georgia	7
0 Army	13
7 Cornell	0
16 Penn	19
0 Michigan	28
21 Colgate	30

1942

39 Ft. Monmouth	0
34 Maine	2
21 Brown	28
6 Army	34
12 Penn	42
14 Cornell	13
26 Colgate	35
9 Navy	13
13 Dartmouth	26

1943

7 Princeton	26
7 Yale	20
0 Army	52
0 Penn	33
6 Cornell	33
13 Dartmouth	47
0 Navy	61
0 Colgate	41

1944

21 Union	0
26 Syracuse	2
10 Yale	27
0 Colgate	6
7 Cornell	25
7 Penn	35
0 Brown	12
0 Dartmouth	18

1945

40 Lafayette	14
32 Syracuse	0
27 Yale	13
31 Colgate	7
27 Brown	6
34 Cornell	26
7 Penn	32
32 Princeton	7
21 Dartmouth	0

1946

13 Rutgers	7
23 Navy	14
28 Yale	20
14 Army	48
33 Dartmouth	13
0 Cornell	12
6 Penn	41
46 Lafayette	0
59 Syracuse	21

1947

40	Rutgers	28
13	Navy	6
7	Yale	17
14	Penn	34
21	Army	20
22	Cornell	0
15	Dartmouth	0
10	Holy Cross	0
28	Syracuse	8

1948

27	Rutgers	6
24	Harvard	33
34	Yale	28
14	Penn	20
14	Princeton	16
13	Cornell	20
21	Dartmouth	26
13	Navy	0
34	Syracuse	28

1949

27	Amherst	7
14	Harvard	7
7	Yale	33
7	Penn	27
6	Army	63
0	Cornell	54
14	Dartmouth	35
0	Navy	34
7	Brown	16

1950

42	Hobart	12
28	Harvard	7
14	Yale	20
0	Penn	34
0	Army	34
20	Cornell	19
7	Dartmouth	14
7	Navy	29
33	Brown	0

1951

35	Harvard	0
14	Yale	0
13	Penn	28
9	Army	14
21	Cornell	20
21	Dartmouth	6
7	Navy	21
29	Brown	14

1952

0	Princeton	14
16	Harvard	7
28	Yale	35
17	Penn	27
14	Army	14
14	Cornell	21
14	Dartmouth	38
0	Navy	28
14	Brown	0

1953

14	Lehigh	7
19	Princeton	20
7	Yale	13
6	Harvard	0
7	Army	40
13	Cornell	27
25	Dartmouth	19
6	Navy	14

27	Rutgers	13

1954

7	Brown	18
20	Princeton	54
7	Yale	13
7	Harvard	6
12	Army	67
0	Cornell	26
0	Dartmouth	26
6	Navy	51
12	Rutgers	45

1955

14	Brown	12
7	Princeton	20
14	Yale	46
7	Harvard	21
0	Army	45
19	Cornell	34
7	Dartmouth	14
0	Navy	47
6	Rutgers	12

1956

0	Brown	20
0	Princeton	39
19	Yale	33
26	Harvard	20
0	Army	60
25	Cornell	19
0	Dartmouth	14
6	Penn	20
18	Rutgers	12

DAN MCGUGIN

Record: 197–55–19
Hall of Fame 1951

VANDERBILT 1904–17, 1919–34

1904

61	Mississippi State	0
66	Georgetown (Ky.)	0
69	Mississippi	0
29	Missouri Mines	4
97	Central (Ky.)	0
22	Centre	0
22	Tennessee	0
81	Nashville	0
27	Sewanee	0

1905

97	Maryville	0
34	Alabama	0
0	Michigan	18
45	Tennessee	0
33	Texas	0
54	Auburn	0
41	Clemson	0
68	Sewanee	4

1906

28	Kentucky	0
29	Mississippi	0
78	Alabama	0
45	Texas	0
4	Michigan	10
33	Rose Polytechnic	0
37	Georgia Tech	6
4	Carlisle	0
20	Sewanee	0

1907

40	Kentucky	0
6	Navy	6
65	Rose Polytechnic	10
0	Michigan	8
60	Mississippi	0
54	Georgia Tech	0
17	Sewanee	12

1908

11	Southwestern	5
32	Maryville	0
32	Rose Polytechnic	0
41	Clemson	0
29	Mississippi	0
6	Michigan	24
16	Tennessee	9
6	Ohio State	17
28	Washington (Mo.)	0
6	Sewanee	6

1909

52	Southwestern	0
28	Mercer	5
28	Rose Polytechnic	3
0	Alumni	3
17	Auburn	0
17	Mississippi	0
51	Tennessee	0
0	Ohio State	5
12	Washington (Mo.)	0
5	Sewanee	16

1910

34	Mooney	0
23	Rose Polytechnic	0
14	Castle Heights	0
18	Tennessee	0
0	Yale	0
9	Mississippi	2
22	LSU	0
23	Georgia Tech	0
23	Sewanee	6

1911

40	Birmingham-Southern	0
46	Maryville	0
33	Rose Polytechnic	0
45	Central (Ky.)	0
8	Michigan	9
17	Georgia	0
18	Kentucky	0
21	Mississippi	0
31	Sewanee	0

1912

105	Bethel	0
100	Maryville	3
54	Rose Polytechnic	0
46	Georgia	0
24	Mississippi	0
13	Virginia	0
3	Harvard	9
23	Central (Ky.)	0
7	Auburn	7
16	Sewanee	0

1913

59	Maryville	0
48	Central (Ky.)	0
33	Henderson-Brown	0
0	Virginia	34

Continued on next page

2 Michigan 33
7 Tennessee 6
6 Auburn 14
63 Sewanee 13

1914
42 Henderson-Brown 6
3 Michigan 23
59 Central (Ky.) 0
9 North Carolina 10
7 Virginia 20
14 Tennessee 16
0 Auburn 6
13 Sewanee 14

1915
51 Middle Tennessee 0
47 Southwestern 0
75 Georgetown (Ky.) 0
60 Cumberland 0
100 Henderson-Brown 0
91 Mississippi 0
35 Tennessee 0
10 Virginia 35
17 Auburn 0
28 Sewanee 3

1916
86 Southwestern 0
42 Transylvania 0
45 Kentucky 0
35 Mississippi 0
27 Virginia 6
67 Rose Polytechnic 0
20 Auburn 9
6 Tennessee 10
0 Sewanee 0

1917
41 Transylvania 0
0 Chicago 48
5 Kentucky 0
69 Howard 0
0 Georgia Tech 83
7 Alabama 2
7 Auburn 31
13 Sewanee 6

1919
41 Union (Tenn.) 0
3 Tennessee 3
0 Georgia Tech 20
7 Auburn 6
0 Kentucky 0
16 Alabama 12
10 Virginia 6
33 Sewanee 21

1920
54 Birmingham-Southern 0
20 Tennessee 0
0 Georgia Tech 44
6 Auburn 56
20 Kentucky 0
7 Alabama 14
34 Middle Tennessee 0
7 Virginia 7
21 Sewanee 3

1921
34 Middle Tennessee 0
42 Mercer 0
21 Kentucky 14
20 Texas 0

14 Tennessee 0
14 Alabama 0
7 Georgia 7
9 Sewanee 0

1922
38 Middle Tennessee 0
33 Henderson-Brown 0
0 Michigan 0
20 Texas 10
25 Mercer 0
14 Tennessee 6
9 Kentucky 0
12 Georgia 0
26 Sewanee 0

1923
27 Howard 0
0 Michigan 3
0 Texas 16
17 Tulane 0
0 Miss. State 0
51 Tennessee 7
35 Georgia 7
7 Sewanee 0

1924
13 Henderson-Brown 0
61 Birmingham-Southern 0
13 Quantico Marines 13
13 Tulane 21
0 Georgia 3
13 Auburn 0
18 Miss. State 0
3 Georgia Tech 0
16 Minnesota 0
0 Sewanee 16

1925
27 Middle Tennessee 0
41 Henderson-Brown 0
14 Texas 6
34 Tennessee 7
7 Georgia 26
7 Mississippi 0
0 Georgia Tech 7
9 Auburn 10
19 Sewanee 7

1926
69 Middle Tennessee 0
7 Alabama 19
48 Bryson 0
7 Texas 0
14 Georgia 13
50 Southwestern 0
13 Georgia Tech 7
20 Tennessee 3
13 Sewanee 0

1927
45 Chattanooga 18
39 Ouachita 10
53 Centre 6
6 Texas 13
32 Tulane 0
34 Kentucky 6
0 Georgia Tech 0
7 Tennessee 7
39 Maryland 20
26 Sewanee 6
14 Alabama 7

1928
20 Chattanooga 0
12 Colgate 7
13 Texas 12
13 Tulane 6
34 Virginia 0
14 Kentucky 7
7 Georgia Tech 19
0 Tennessee 6
26 Centre 0
13 Sewanee 0

1929
19 Mississippi 7
26 Ouachita 6
6 Minnesota 15
41 Auburn 2
33 Maryville 0
13 Alabama 0
23 Georgia Tech 7
0 Tennessee 13
26 Sewanee 6

1930
39 Chattanooga 0
33 Minnesota 7
40 Virginia Tech 0
27 Spring Hill 6
7 Alabama 12
24 Mississippi 0
6 Georgia Tech 0
0 Tennessee 13
27 Auburn 0
22 Maryland 7

1931
52 Western Kentucky 6
13 North Carolina 0
26 Ohio State 21
0 Tulane 19
0 Georgia 9
49 Georgia Tech 7
39 Maryland 12
7 Tennessee 21
6 Alabama 14

1932
20 Mercer 7
39 North Carolina 7
26 Western Kentucky 0
6 Tulane 6
12 Georgia 6
12 Georgia Tech 0
13 Maryland 0
0 Tennessee 0
0 Alabama 20

1933
50 Cumberland 0
0 Oklahoma 0
20 North Carolina 13
0 Ohio State 20
7 Miss. State 7
7 LSU 7
9 Georgia Tech 6
27 Sewanee 14
6 Tennessee 33
0 Alabama 7

1934
7 Miss. State 0
27 Georgia Tech 12
32 Cincinnati 0

Continued on next page

7 Auburn 6
0 LSU 29
7 George Washington 6
19 Sewanee 0
6 Tennessee 13
0 Alabama 34

TUSS MCLAUGHRY

Record: Not available
Hall of Fame 1962

WESTMINSTER 1916–17, 1920–21
(Scores not available.)

AMHERST 1922–25

1922

7 Bowdoin 28
6 Columbia 43
6 Massachusetts St. 10
0 Oberlin 7
41 Trinity 0
13 Union 0
6 Wesleyan 21
0 Williams 27

1923

0 Bowdoin 13
0 Columbia 0
7 Massachusetts St. 3
7 Oberlin 14
41 Trinity 12
0 Union 0
12 Wesleyan 10
7 Williams 23

1924

18 St. Lawrence 3
6 Princeton 40
14 Bowdoin 16
33 Wesleyan 13
48 Hamilton 0
7 Massachusetts St. 17
13 Union 20
6 Williams 27

1925

23 Rochester 6
0 Princeton 20
27 Bowdoin 0
19 Hamilton 0
73 Wesleyan 6
27 Massachusetts St. 0
16 Springfield 0
13 Williams 7

BROWN 1926–40

1926

14 Rhode Island 0
35 Colby 0
32 Lehigh 0
27 Bates 14
7 Yale 0
10 Dartmouth 0
27 Norwich 0
21 Harvard 0
40 New Hampshire 12
10 Colgate 10

1927

27 Rhode Island 0
20 Albright 0
6 Penn 14
0 Yale 19
12 Lebanon Valley 13
0 Temple 7
7 Dartmouth 19
6 Harvard 18
31 New Hampshire 13
0 Colgate 0

1928

32 WPI 0
13 Dayton 7
14 Yale 32
19 Tufts 13
6 Holy Cross 0
14 Dartmouth 0
20 New Hampshire 0
33 Rhode Island 7
16 Colgate 13

1929

6 Springfield 7
14 Rhode Island 6
13 Princeton 12
6 Yale 14
0 Syracuse 6
15 Holy Cross 14
6 Dartmouth 13
66 Norwich 6
14 New Hampshire 7
0 Colgate 32

1930

7 Rhode Island 0
54 WPI 0
7 Princeton 0
0 Yale 21
13 Holy Cross 0
16 Syracuse 16
32 Tufts 7
6 Columbia 0
0 New Hampshire 7
0 Colgate 27

1931

22 Colby 0
18 Rhode Island 0
19 Princeton 7
38 Tufts 12
33 Lehigh 0
0 Holy Cross 33
26 Ohio Wesleyan 13
7 Columbia 9
19 New Hampshire 13
7 Colgate 13

1932

19 Rhode Island 0
13 Springfield 6
7 Yale 2
11 Tufts 0
14 Harvard 0
10 Holy Cross 7
7 Columbia 6
0 Colgate 21

1933

26 Rhode Island 0
13 Springfield 6
6 Yale 14
7 Holy Cross 19

0 Princeton 33
10 Syracuse 7
6 Harvard 12
0 Colgate 25

1934

18 Boston U. 0
13 Rhode Island 0
0 Harvard 13
0 Yale 37
0 Syracuse 33
13 Springfield 7
0 Columbia 39
7 Holy Cross 20
13 Colgate 20

1935

7 Rhode Island 13
0 Springfield 20
0 Dartmouth 41
0 Syracuse 19
0 Harvard 33
0 Yale 20
14 Boston U. 0
0 Columbia 18
0 Colgate 33

1936

0 Connecticut 27
7 Rhode Island 6
0 Harvard 28
0 Dartmouth 34
6 Penn 48
38 Tufts 7
6 Yale 14
19 Colby 6
0 Holy Cross 32
0 Colgate 32

1937

20 Connecticut 0
13 Rhode Island 6
7 Harvard 34
0 Dartmouth 41
7 Columbia 6
19 Tufts 0
0 Yale 19
0 Holy Cross 7
7 Rutgers 6

1938

20 Harvard 13
20 Lafayette 0
13 Dartmouth 34
40 Rhode Island 21
48 Tufts 0
14 Yale 20
12 Holy Cross 14
36 Columbia 27

1939

34 Rhode Island 0
20 Amherst 14
0 Colgate 10
0 Holy Cross 20
12 Princeton 26
54 Tufts 7
14 Yale 14
41 Connecticut 0
13 Rutgers 0

1940

41	Wesleyan	0
20	Rhode Island	17
3	Colgate	20
26	Tufts	6
9	Holy Cross	6
6	Yale	2
13	Army	9
0	Harvard	14
6	Dartmouth	20
0	Columbia	0

DARTMOUTH 1941–42, 1945–54

1941

35	Norwich	0
47	Amherst	7
18	Colgate	6
0	Harvard	7
7	Yale	0
0	William & Mary	3
20	Princeton	13
19	Cornell	33
0	Georgia	35

1942

17	Holy Cross	6
58	Miami (Ohio)	7
19	Colgate	27
14	Harvard	2
7	Yale	17
14	William & Mary	35
19	Princeton	7
19	Cornell	21
26	Columbia	13

1945

6	Holy Cross	13
0	Pennsylvania	12
0	Notre Dame	34
8	Syracuse	0
0	Yale	6
13	Princeton	13
13	Cornell	20
0	Columbia	21

1946

3	Holy Cross	0
20	Syracuse	14
6	Pennsylvania	39
13	Brown	20
13	Columbia	33
2	Yale	33
7	Harvard	21
7	Cornell	21
20	Princeton	13

1947

0	Holy Cross	0
28	Syracuse	7
0	Pennsylvania	32
13	Brown	10
14	Harvard	13
14	Yale	23
0	Columbia	15
21	Cornell	13
12	Princeton	14

1948

13	Pennsylvania	26
19	Holy Cross	6
41	Colgate	16
14	Harvard	7
41	Yale	14

26	Columbia	21
26	Cornell	27
33	Princeton	13

1949

0	Pennsylvania	21
31	Holy Cross	7
27	Colgate	13
27	Harvard	13
34	Yale	13
35	Columbia	14
16	Cornell	7
13	Princeton	19

1950

21	Holy Cross	21
7	Michigan	27
26	Pennsylvania	42
14	Lehigh	16
27	Harvard	7
7	Yale	0
14	Columbia	7
0	Cornell	24
7	Princeton	13

1951

6	Fordham	14
14	Pennsylvania	39
28	Army	14
14	Syracuse	0
26	Harvard	20
14	Yale	10
6	Columbia	21
13	Cornell	21
0	Princeton	13

1952

9	Holy Cross	27
0	Pennsylvania	7
7	Army	37
29	Rutgers	20
19	Harvard	26
7	Yale	21
38	Columbia	14
7	Cornell	13
0	Princeton	33

1953

6	Holy Cross	28
9	Navy	55
0	Army	27
14	Colgate	24
14	Harvard	20
32	Yale	0
19	Columbia	25
26	Cornell	28
34	Princeton	12

1954

27	Holy Cross	26
7	Navy	42
6	Army	60
7	Colgate	13
13	Harvard	7
7	Yale	13
26	Columbia	0
21	Cornell	40
7	Princeton	49

CHICK MEEHAN

Record: 115–44–14

SYRACUSE 1920–24

1920

55	Hobart	7
49	Vermont	0
45	Johns Hopkins	0
7	Pittsburgh	7
10	Dartmouth	0
0	Holy Cross	3
14	Wash. & Jeff.	0
7	Maryland	10
14	Colgate	0

1921

35	Hobart	0
38	Ohio	0
14	Colgate	0
14	Dartmouth	7
13	McGill	0
42	Maryland	0
10	Wash. & Jeff.	17
0	Pittsburgh	30
28	Brown	0

1922

28	Hobart	7
47	Muhlenberg	0
34	NYU	0
0	Brown	0
14	Pittsburgh	21
0	Penn State	0
9	Nebraska	6
32	McGill	0
14	Colgate	7

1923

33	Hobart	0
61	William & Mary	3
23	Alabama	0
3	Pittsburgh	0
44	Springfield	0
10	Penn State	0
49	Boston U.	0
7	Colgate	16
7	Nebraska	0

1924

35	Hobart	0
26	Mercer	0
24	William & Mary	7
10	Boston College	0
10	Penn State	6
7	Pittsburgh	7
3	W.Va. Wesleyan	7
23	Niagara	6
7	Colgate	3
9	Columbia	6
0	Southern Cal	16

NEW YORK UNIVERSITY 1925–31

1925

14	Niagara	0
12	Union	3
23	Connecticut Aggies	0
41	CCNY	0
33	Middlebury	0
6	Fordham	26
6	Columbia	6
27	Trinity	3
6	Rutgers	7

1926

34	Niagara	0
13	Allegheny	0
24	W. Va. Wesleyan	7
21	Tulane	0
30	Rutgers	0
27	Fordham	3
6	Carnegie Tech	0
10	Davis & Elkins	0
7	Nebraska	15

1927

27	Niagara	0
29	W. Va. Wesleyan	13
65	Alfred	0
32	Fordham	0
60	Rutgers	0
0	Colgate	0
20	Carnegie Tech	0
13	Penn State	13
31	Allegheny	0
18	Nebraska	27

1928

21	Niagara	0
26	W. Va. Wesleyan	7
34	Fordham	7
48	Rutgers	0
47	Colgate	6
2	Georgetown	7
71	Alfred	0
27	Missouri	6
27	Carnegie Tech	13
13	Oregon State	25

1929

77	Vermont	0
26	W. Va. Wesleyan	0
0	Fordham	26
7	Penn State	0
13	Butler	6
0	Georgetown	14
27	Georgia	19
14	Missouri	0
20	Rutgers	7
0	Carnegie Tech	20

1930

35	Hobart	0
41	W. Va. Wesleyan	6
20	Villanova	6
38	Missouri	0
0	Fordham	7
20	Carnegie Tech	7
6	Georgia	7
2	Georgetown	0
33	Rutgers	0
6	Colgate	7

1931

65	Hobart	0
54	W. Va. Wesleyan	0
34	Georgetown	0
27	Rutgers	7
13	Colgate	0
6	Oregon	14
6	Georgia	7
0	Fordham	0
7	Carnegie Tech	6
0	Tennessee	13

Manhattan 1932–37

1932

6	St. Bonaventure	6
32	St. Joseph's	2
31	Seton Hall	0
0	St. Thomas	7
7	Catholic U.	12
20	Oglethorpe	7
13	CCNY	6
28	Clarkson	0
0	Holy Cross	0
7	Rutgers	6
0	Miami (Fla.)	7

1933

0	Villanova	47
0	Oglethorpe	6
24	CCNY	0
6	Holy Cross	27
7	Catholic U.	0
6	St. Bonaventure	0
13	Clarkson	6
20	Georgetown	20
28	Brooklyn College	21

1934

6	St. Bonaventure	0
19	Clarkson Tech	7
13	Kansas State	13
0	Georgetown	9
0	Michigan State	39
0	Catholic U.	31
21	CCNY	0
6	Holy Cross	12
0	Villanova	39

1935

25	Niagara	6
32	St. Bonaventure	13
59	Brooklyn College	7
0	LSU	37
13	Holy Cross	13
0	N. C. State	20
65	CCNY	0
54	La Salle	13
0	Georgetown	13

1936

32	St. Bonaventure	7
33	Niagara	7
13	N. C. State	6
7	Holy Cross	13
0	Detroit	20
28	CCNY	7
13	Kentucky	7
13	Georgetown	0
0	Villanova	12
6	Texas A. & M.	13

1937

21	St. Bonaventure	12
7	Texas A. & M.	14
3	Michigan State	0
0	Villanova	20
0	Kentucky	19
20	Georgetown	12
7	Detroit	0
15	N. C. State	0
13	Niagara	7
0	Tulsa	0

HARRY MEHRE

Record: 98–60–7

Georgia 1928–37

1928

52	Mercer	0
6	Yale	21
7	Furman	0
20	Tulane	14
13	Auburn	0
6	Florida	26
12	LSU	13
0	Alabama	19
6	Georgia Tech	20

1929

6	Oglethorpe	13
27	Furman	0
15	Yale	0
19	North Carolina	12
6	Florida	18
15	Tulane	21
19	NYU	27
24	Auburn	0
12	Alabama	0
12	Georgia Tech	6

1930

31	Oglethorpe	6
51	Mercer	0
18	Yale	14
26	North Carolina	0
39	Auburn	7
0	Florida	0
7	NYU	6
0	Tulane	25
0	Alabama	13
13	Georgia Tech	0

1931

40	VPI	0
26	Yale	7
32	North Carolina	6
9	Vanderbilt	0
33	Florida	6
7	NYU	6
7	Tulane	20
12	Auburn	6
35	Georgia Tech	6
0	Southern Cal	60

1932

6	VPI	7
25	Tulane	34
6	North Carolina	6
33	Florida	12
7	NYU	13
32	Clemson	18
7	Auburn	14
0	Georgia Tech	0
6	Vanderbilt	12

1933

20	N. C. State	10
26	Tulane	13
30	North Carolina	0
13	Mercer	12
25	NYU	0
14	Florida	0
7	Yale	0
6	Auburn	14
7	Georgia Tech	6
0	Southern Cal	31

1934

42 Stetson	0
7 Furman	2
0 North Carolina	14
6 Tulane	7
6 Alabama	26
14 Florida	0
14 Yale	7
27 N. C. State	0
18 Auburn	0
7 Georgia Tech	0

1935

31 Mercer	0
31 Furman	7
40 Chattanooga	0
13 N. C. State	0
7 Alabama	17
7 Florida	0
26 Tulane	13
0 LSU	13
7 Auburn	19
7 Georgia Tech	19

1936

15 Mercer	6
13 Furman	0
7 LSU	47
6 Rice	13
13 Auburn	20
0 Tennessee	46
26 Florida	8
12 Tulane	6
7 Fordham	7
16 Georgia Tech	6

1937

60 Oglethorpe	0
13 South Carolina	7
14 Clemson	0
6 Holy Cross	7
19 Mercer	0
0 Tennessee	32
0 Florida	6
7 Tulane	6
0 Auburn	0
6 Georgia Tech	6
26 Miami	8

MISSISSIPPI 1938–45

1938

20 LSU	7
27 Louisiana Tech	7
14 Miss. Teachers	0
7 Vanderbilt	13
47 Centenary	14
25 George Washington	0
6 St. Louis	12
39 Sewanee	0
20 Arkansas	14
19 Miss. State	6
0 Tennessee	47

1939

14 LSU	7
41 Southwestern	0
34 Centenary	0
42 St. Louis	0
6 Tulane	18
14 Vanderbilt	7
24 Miss. Teachers	7
46 W. Tenn. Teachers	7
6 Miss. State	18

1940

37 Union	0
19 LSU	6
27 Southwestern	6
28 Georgia	14
14 Duquesne	6
20 Arkansas	21
13 Vanderbilt	7
34 Holy Cross	7
38 W. Tenn. Teachers	7
0 Miss. State	19
21 Miami	7

1941

6 Georgetown	16
27 Southwestern	0
14 Georgia	14
21 Holy Cross	0
20 Tulane	13
12 Marquette	6
13 LSU	12
18 Arkansas	0
0 Miss. State	6

1942

39 W. Ky. Teachers	6
6 Georgetown	14
13 Georgia	48
7 LSU	21
6 Arkansas	7
48 Memphis State	0
0 Vanderbilt	19
0 Tennessee	14
13 Miss. State	34

1943

(No football.)

1944

7 Kentucky	27
26 Florida	6
7 Tennessee	20
0 Tulsa	47
18 Arkansas	26
0 Jackson Air	10
6 Alabama	34
13 Miss. State	8

1945

21 Kentucky	7
13 Florida	26
14 Vanderbilt	7
26 Louisiana Tech	21
0 Arkansas	19
13 LSU	32
0 Tennessee	34
7 Miss. State	6
6 Chattanooga	31

DUTCH MEYER

Record: 106-75-13
Hall of Fame 1956

TEXAS CHRISTIAN 1934–52

1934

33 Daniel Baker	7
27 North Texas State	6
10 Arkansas	24
14 Tulsa	12
13 Texas A. & M.	0
34 Baylor	12
0 Centenary	13

7 Loyola	0
19 Texas	20
7 Rice	2
0 SMU	19
9 Santa Clara	7

1935

41 Howard Payne	0
28 North Texas State	11
13 Arkansas	7
13 Tulsa	0
19 Texas A. & M.	14
27 Centenary	7
28 Baylor	0
14 Loyola	0
28 Texas	0
27 Rice	6
14 SMU	20
10 Santa Clara	6

1936

0 Texas Tech	7
6 Howard Payne	0
18 Arkansas	14
10 Tulsa	7
7 Texas A. & M.	18
0 Mississippi State	0
28 Baylor	0
27 Texas	6
26 Centenary	0
13 Rice	0
0 SMU	0
9 Santa Clara	0

1937

0 Ohio State	14
7 Arkansas	7
20 Tulsa	13
7 Texas A. & M.	7
6 Fordham	7
0 Baylor	6
9 Centenary	10
14 Texas	0
7 Rice	2
3 SMU	0

1938

13 Centenary	0
21 Arkansas	14
28 Temple	6
34 Texas A. & M.	6
21 Marquette	0
39 Baylor	7
21 Tulsa	0
28 Texas	6
29 Rice	7
20 SMU	7

1939

2 UCLA	6
13 Arkansas	14
11 Temple	13
6 Texas A. & M.	20
21 Centenary	0
0 Baylor	27
16 Tulsa	0
19 Texas	25
21 Rice	0
7 SMU	14

1940

41	Centenary	6
20	Arkansas	0
14	North Carolina	21
7	Texas A. & M.	21
0	Tulsa	7
14	Baylor	12
0	Detroit	3
14	Texas	21
6	Rice	14
0	SMU	16

1941

6	Tulsa	0
9	Arkansas	0
20	Indiana	14
0	Texas A. & M.	14
14	Fordham	28
23	Baylor	12
35	Centenary	7
14	Texas	7
0	Rice	0
15	SMU	13

1942

7	UCLA	6
13	Arkansas	6
41	Kansas	6
7	Texas A. & M.	0
21	Pensacola NAS	0
7	Baylor	10
6	Texas Tech	13
13	Texas	7
0	Rice	26
14	SMU	6

1943

13	Arkansas	0
0	Texas A. & M.	13
25	Oklahoma A. & M.	0
0	LSU	14
20	Texas Tech	40
7	Texas	46
6	Rice	13
0	SMU	20

1944

7	Kansas	0
34	South Plains AAF	0
6	Arkansas	6
13	Texas A. & M.	7
19	Oklahoma	34
19	Chatham AAF	7
14	Texas Tech	0
7	Texas	6
9	Rice	6
6	SMU	9

1945

18	Kansas	0
7	Baylor	6
14	Arkansas	27
13	Texas A. & M.	12
12	Oklahoma A. & M.	25
13	Oklahoma	7
0	Texas Tech	12
0	Texas	20
14	Rice	13
0	SMU	34

1946

0	Kansas	0
19	Baylor	16
14	Arkansas	34

12	Miami	20
0	Texas A. & M.	14
6	Oklahoma A. & M.	7
12	Oklahoma	14
14	Texas	0
0	Rice	13
13	SMU	30

1947

0	Kansas	0
7	Oklahoma A. & M.	14
0	Arkansas	6
19	Miami	6
26	Texas A. & M.	0
20	Oklahoma	7
14	Baylor	7
0	Texas	20
0	Rice	7
19	SMU	19

1948

14	Kansas	13
21	Oklahoma A. & M.	14
14	Arkansas	27
7	Indiana	6
27	Texas A. & M.	14
18	Oklahoma	21
3	Baylor	6
7	Texas	14
7	Rice	21
7	SMU	7

1949

28	Kansas	0
33	Oklahoma A. & M.	33
7	Arkansas	27
13	Indiana	6
28	Texas A. & M.	6
33	Mississippi	27
14	Baylor	40
14	Texas	13
14	Rice	20
21	SMU	13

1950

14	Kansas	7
7	Oklahoma A. & M.	13
13	Arkansas	6
19	Texas Tech	6
23	Texas A. & M.	42
7	Mississippi	19
14	Baylor	20
7	Texas	21
26	Rice	14
27	SMU	13

1951

13	Kansas	27
28	Nebraska	7
17	Arkansas	7
19	Texas Tech	33
20	Texas A. & M.	14
26	Southern Cal	28
20	Baylor	7
21	Texas	32
22	Rice	6
13	SMU	2

1952

0	Kansas	13
0	UCLA	14
13	Arkansas	7
47	Trinity	0
7	Texas A. & M.	7

20	Baylor	20
27	Wake Forest	9
7	Texas	14
6	Rice	12
14	SMU	7

RAY MORRISON

Record: 152-123-33
Hall of Fame 1954

SOUTHERN METHODIST 1915–16

1915

0	Texas Christian	43
13	Hendrix	2
0	Austin College	21
7	Dallas	0
0	Daniel Baker	30
0	Southwestern	21
0	Trinity	14

1916

6	Dallas	14
0	Texas	74
0	Austin College	0
0	Texas A.&M.	62
0	Daniel Baker	27
3	Rice	146
6	Trinity	14
9	Southwestern	9
0	Baylor	61
3	Texas Christian	48

VANDERBILT 1918

0	Camp Greenleaf	6
6	Camp Hancock	25
33	Kentucky	0
76	Tennessee	0
21	Auburn	0
40	Sewanee	0

SOUTHERN METHODIST 1922–34

1922

16	SMU Frosh	0
66	North Texas State	0
51	LSU	0
7	Austin College	10
32	Oklahoma A.&M.	6
46	Southwestern	14
17	Texas A.&M.	6
0	Arkansas	9
0	Baylor	24
0	Texas Christian	0

1923

41	North Texas State	0
33	Henderson-Brown	0
10	Austin College	3
35	Missouri Mines	0
10	Texas A.&M.	0
40	Texas Christian	0
13	Arkansas	6
9	Oklahoma A.&M.	0
16	Baylor	0

1924

7	North Texas State	0
14	Trinity	3
7	Austin College	0
10	Texas	6
7	Texas A.&M.	7

Continued on next page

6 Texas Christian 0
14 Arkansas 14
7 Baylor 7
13 Oklahoma A.&M. 13
7 W. Va. Wesleyan 9

1925

48 North Texas State 0
52 Abilene Christian 0
20 Washington 6
0 Texas A.&M. 7
0 Oklahoma 9
0 Texas 0
0 Arkansas 0
7 Baylor 6
21 Drake 6

1926

42 North Texas State 0
48 Trinity 0
37 Centenary 0
7 Missouri 7
9 Texas A.&M. 7
21 Texas 17
20 Rice 0
31 Baylor 3
14 Texas Christian 13

1927

68 North Texas State 0
32 Howard Payne 0
12 Centenary 21
34 Rice 6
32 Missouri 9
14 Texas 0
13 Texas A.&M. 39
34 Baylor 0
28 Texas Christian 6

1928

60 North Texas State 6
31 Howard Payne 0
13 Army 14
6 Simmons 0
53 Rice 13
60 Trinity 7
6 Texas 2
19 Texas A.&M. 19
0 Baylor 2
6 Texas Christian 15

1929

13 North Texas State 3
13 Howard Payne 13
0 Nebraska 0
16 Austin College 0
52 Mississippi 0
0 Texas 0
12 Texas A.&M. 7
25 Baylor 6
34 Rice 0
7 Texas Christian 7

1930

26 Howard Payne 0
14 Notre Dame 20
34 Austin College 0
14 Baylor 14
27 Indiana 0
7 Texas 25
13 Texas A.&M. 7
20 Navy 7
32 Rice 0
0 Texas Christian 13

1931

13 North Texas State 0
27 Simmons U. 10
19 Centenary College 0
42 Arkansas 6
21 Rice 12
9 Texas 7
8 Texas A.&M. 0
6 Baylor 0
0 Texas Christian 0
13 Navy 7
2 St. Mary's 7

1932

0 North Texas State 0
0 Texas Tech 6
0 Rice 13
16 Syracuse 6
7 Centenary 18
6 Texas 14
0 Texas A. & M. 0
13 Arkansas 7
0 Baylor 19
0 Texas Christian 8
14 Nebraska 21
26 Texas Mines 0

1933

0 North Texas State 7
14 Texas Tech 0
27 Texas Mines 6
13 Rice 7
7 Oklahoma A.&M. 7
0 Arkansas 3
0 Texas 10
19 Texas A.&M. 0
0 Centenary 7
7 Baylor 13
6 Texas Christian 26
6 St. Mary's 18

1934

33 North Texas State 0
33 Austin College 0
14 LSU 14
0 Rice 9
41 Oklahoma A.&M. 0
26 Fordham 14
7 Texas 7
28 Texas A.&M. 0
10 Arkansas 6
6 Baylor 13
19 Texas Christian 0
7 Washington 0

VANDERBILT 1935–39

1935

34 Union (Tenn.) 0
14 Mississippi State 9
32 Cumberland 7
3 Temple 6
7 Fordham 13
2 LSU 7
14 Georgia Tech 13
46 Sewanee 0
13 Tennessee 7
14 Alabama 6

1936

45 Middle Tennessee 0
37 Chicago 0
0 Southwestern 12
0 SMU 16

0 Georgia Tech 0
0 LSU 19
14 Sewanee 0
13 Tennessee 26
6 Alabama 14

1937

12 Kentucky 0
18 Chicago 0
17 Southwestern 6
6 SMU 0
7 LSU 6
0 Georgia Tech 14
41 Sewanee 0
13 Tennessee 7
7 Alabama 9

1938

20 Washington (Mo.) 0
12 Western Kentucky 0
14 Kentucky 7
13 Mississippi 7
0 LSU 7
13 Georgia Tech 7
14 Sewanee 0
0 Tennessee 14
0 Alabama 7

1939

13 Tennessee Tech 13
13 Rice 12
13 Kentucky 21
13 VMI 20
6 Georgia Tech 14
6 LSU 12
7 Mississippi 14
25 Sewanee 7
0 Tennessee 13
0 Alabama 39

TEMPLE 1940–48

1940

64 Muhlenberg 7
0 Georgetown 14
20 Boston College 33
21 Michigan State 19
0 Penn State 18
10 Bucknell 7
28 Villanova 0
6 Holy Cross 6
6 Oklahoma 9

1941

31 Kansas 9
28 VMI 13
17 Georgetown 7
14 Penn State 0
41 Bucknell 14
0 Boston College 31
14 Villanova 13
0 Michigan State 46
31 Holy Cross 13

1942

0 Georgetown 7
7 VMI 6
7 Bucknell 7
6 SMU 6
0 N.C. Pre-Flight 34
7 Michigan State 7
0 Boston College 28
0 Holy Cross 13
14 Oklahoma 7
7 Villanova 20

1943

27	VMI	0
13	Swarthmore	6
0	Army	51
6	Ursinus	10
6	Bucknell	7
6	Holy Cross	42
0	Penn State	13
7	Villanova	34

1944

34	Swarthmore	12
0	Holy Cross	30
25	NYU	0
7	Syracuse	7
7	Bucknell	7
0	West Virginia	6
6	Penn State	7
14	Tennessee	27

1945

7	Syracuse	6
59	NYU	0
64	Bucknell	0
28	West Virginia	12
6	Pittsburgh	0
20	Lafayette	0
0	Penn State	27
14	Holy Cross	6

1946

7	SMU	7
7	Georgia	35
0	Pittsburgh	0
6	West Virginia	0
7	Syracuse	28
0	Penn State	26
27	Bucknell	6
7	Holy Cross	12

1947

32	NYU	7
13	Holy Cross	19
12	Syracuse	28
7	Muhlenberg	6
21	Bucknell	0
0	Oklahoma A.&M.	26
0	Penn State	7
6	Michigan State	14
0	West Virginia	21

1948

7	Lebanon Valley	7
7	West Virginia	27
20	Rutgers	34
7	Boston U.	13
7	Oklahoma A.&M.	41
20	Bucknell	0
20	Syracuse	0
0	Penn State	47
7	Holy Cross	13

Austin College 1949-52

1949

0	Midwestern	28
12	Howard Payne	19
19	McMurry	34
28	Southwestern (Tenn.)	0
27	Abilene Christian	14
20	Texas A.&I.	19

27	East Central Oklahoma	7
0	Southwest Louisiana	30
0	Corpus Christi	14
33	Southwest Missouri	0

1950

26	Southeastern Oklahoma	0
27	Midwestern	13
6	Howard Payne	14
0	Trinity (Texas)	27
6	McMurry	27
15	East Texas State	40
14	Abilene Christian	33
13	Texas A.&I.	18
7	Southwestern (Tenn.)	27

1951

34	East Central Oklahoma	13
12	Midwestern	34
20	Howard Payne	35
12	Trinity	20
7	McMurry	19
33	Abilene Christian	50
7	Texas A.&I.	41
7	East Texas State	12

1952

(Scores not available.)

BOB NEYLAND

Record: 171–26–12
Hall of Fame 1956

TENNESSEE 1926–34, 1936–40, 1946–52

1926

13	C-N College	0
34	North Carolina	0
14	LSU	7
6	Maryville	0
30	Centre	7
33	Miss. A.&M.	0
12	Sewanee	0
3	Vanderbilt	20
6	Kentucky	0

1927

33	C-N College	0
26	North Carolina	0
7	Maryville	0
21	Mississippi	7
57	Transylvania	0
42	Virginia	0
32	Sewanee	12
7	Vanderbilt	7
20	Kentucky	0

1928

41	Maryville	0
41	Centre	7
13	Mississippi	12
15	Alabama	13
26	Washington & Lee	7
57	C-N College	0
37	Sewanee	0
6	Vanderbilt	0
0	Kentucky	0
13	Florida	12

1929

40	Centre	0
20	Chattanooga	0
52	Mississippi	7
27	Auburn	0
39	Washington & Lee	0
6	Alabama	0
73	C-N College	0
13	Vanderbilt	0
6	Kentucky	6
54	South Carolina	0

1930

54	Maryville	0
18	Centre	0
27	Mississippi	0
6	Alabama	18
9	North Carolina	7
27	Clemson	0
34	C-N College	0
13	Vanderbilt	0
8	Kentucky	0
13	Florida	6

1931

33	Maryville	0
44	Clemson	0
38	Mississippi	0
25	Alabama	0
7	North Carolina	0
25	Duke	2
31	C-N College	0
21	Vanderbilt	7
6	Kentucky	6
13	NYU	0

1932

13	Chattanooga	0
33	Mississippi	0
20	North Carolina	7
7	Alabama	3
60	Maryville	0
16	Duke	13
31	Miss. A.&M.	0
0	Vanderbilt	0
26	Kentucky	0
32	Florida	13

1933

27	VPI	0
20	Miss. State	0
2	Duke	10
6	Alabama	12
13	Florida	6
13	George Washington	0
33	Mississippi	6
33	Vanderbilt	6
27	Kentucky	0
0	LSU	7

1934

32	Centre	0
19	North Carolina	7
27	Mississippi	0
6	Alabama	13
14	Duke	6
12	Fordham	13
14	Miss. State	0
13	Vanderbilt	6
19	Kentucky	0
19	LSU	13

1936

13	Chattanooga	0
6	North Carolina	14
0	Auburn	6
0	Alabama	0
15	Duke	13
46	Georgia	0
34	Maryville	0
26	Vanderbilt	13
7	Kentucky	6
0	Mississippi	0

1937

32	Wake Forest	0
27	VPI	0
0	Duke	0
32	Sewanee	0
7	Alabama	14
32	Georgia	0
7	Auburn	20
13	Kentucky	0
7	Vanderbilt	13
32	Mississippi	0

1938

26	Sewanee	3
20	Clemson	7
7	Auburn	0
13	Alabama	0
44	Citadel	0
14	LSU	6
45	Chattanooga	0
46	Kentucky	0
14	Vanderbilt	0
47	Mississippi	0

1939

13	N. C. State	0
40	Sewanee	0
28	Chattanooga	0
21	Alabama	0
17	Mercer	0
20	LSU	0
34	Citadel	0
13	Vanderbilt	0
19	Kentucky	0
7	Auburn	0

1940

49	Mercer	0
13	Duke	0
53	Chattanooga	0
27	Alabama	12
14	Florida	0
28	LSU	0
41	Southwestern	0
41	Virginia	14
33	Kentucky	0
20	Vanderbilt	0

1946

13	Georgia Tech	9
12	Duke	7
47	Chattanooga	7
12	Alabama	0
6	Wake Forest	19
20	North Carolina	14
33	Boston College	13
18	Mississippi	14
7	Kentucky	0
7	Vanderbilt	6

1947

0	Georgia Tech	27
6	Duke	19
27	Chattanooga	7
0	Alabama	10
49	Tennessee Tech	0
6	North Carolina	20
13	Mississippi	43
38	Boston College	13
13	Kentucky	6
12	Vanderbilt	7

1948

6	Miss. State	21
7	Duke	7
26	Chattanooga	0
21	Alabama	6
41	Tennessee Tech	0
7	North Carolina	14
13	Georgia Tech	6
13	Mississippi	16
0	Kentucky	0
6	Vanderbilt	28

1949

10	Miss. State	0
7	Duke	21
39	Chattanooga	7
7	Alabama	7
36	Tennessee Tech	6
35	North Carolina	6
13	Georgia Tech	30
35	Mississippi	7
6	Kentucky	0
26	Vanderbilt	20

1950

56	Miss. Southern	0
0	Miss. State	7
28	Duke	7
41	Chattanooga	0
14	Alabama	9
27	Wash. & Lee	20
16	North Carolina	0
48	Tennessee Tech	14
35	Mississippi	0
7	Kentucky	0
43	Vanderbilt	0

1951

14	Miss. State	0
26	Duke	0
42	Chattanooga	13
27	Alabama	13
68	TPI	0
27	North Carolina	0
60	Wash. & Lee	14
46	Mississippi	21
28	Kentucky	0
35	Vanderbilt	27

1952

14	Miss. State	7
0	Duke	7
26	Chattanooga	6
20	Alabama	0
50	Wofford	0
41	North Carolina	14
22	LSU	3
26	Florida	12
14	Kentucky	14
46	Vanderbilt	0

HOMER NORTON

Record: 140–70–22
Hall of Fame 1971

CENTENARY 1920–21, 1926–33

1920–21

(Scores not available.)

1926

47	Union	7
0	Southern Methodist	37
14	Texas Christian	24
28	Mississippi College	14
0	Arkansas	33
14	Edmond	10
7	Louisiana Tech	0
34	Millsaps	0
56	Oglethorpe	7

1927

46	Wisconsin Mines	0
0	Detroit	58
14	De Paul	14
0	St. Viator	6
13	LaCrosse	13
6	Regis	7
0	St. Thomas	0
19	Luther	0

1928

46	Sam Houston	0
46	Southwestern La. Inst.	0
20	Daniel Baker	12
6	Texas A. & M.	0
6	Baylor	27
14	Chattanooga	21
0	Birmingham-Southern	0
6	Mississippi Aggies	6
66	Louisiana Tech	2
6	Loyola (New Orleans)	23
19	Lombard (Ill.)	7

1929

63	Commerce Tech	0
0	Texas	20
0	Texas Christian	28
35	Sam Houston	0
27	Baylor	12
0	Henderson	0
2	Arkansas	13
9	Oklahoma Teachers	0
20	Louisiana Tech	0
6	Loyola (New Orleans)	0

1930

27	Hendrix-Henderson	0
0	Texas	0
19	Iowa	12
9	Stetson	0
7	Baylor	2
6	Texas A. & M.	7
9	Edmond	0
20	Henderson	6
13	Louisiana Tech	0
7	Arkansas	6

1931

23	Louisiana Normal	2
46	Durant	0
24	Baylor	13
27	Stetson	0
0	Southern Methodist	19

0 Texas A. & M. 7
6 Purdue 49
19 Union 0
0 Texas 6
0 Arkansas 6

1932

47 Henderson 0
13 Texas 6
41 Louisiana 7
13 Mississippi 6
18 Southern Methodist 7
7 Texas A. & M. 0
47 Durant Teachers 0
6 Louisiana 0
0 Arkansas 0

1933

18 Louisiana 0
27 Henderson 0
19 Baylor 0
0 Louisiana 0
0 Texas 0
0 Texas Christian 0
20 Texas A. & M. 0
47 Union 0
7 Southern Methodist 0
7 Mississippi 6
28 Loyola (New Orleans) 12
7 Arkansas 7

TEXAS A. & M. 1934–47

1934

28 Sam Houston 0
14 Texas A. & I. 14
6 Temple 40
0 Centenary 13
0 TCU 13
10 Baylor 7
7 Arkansas 7
0 SMU 28
6 Rice 25
0 Texas 13
13 Michigan State 26

1935

37 Austin 6
25 Sam Houston 0
0 Temple 14
6 Centenary 7
14 TCU 19
6 Baylor 14
7 Arkansas 14
10 Rice 17
20 Texas 6
0 SMU 24

1936

39 Sam Houston 6
3 Hardin-Simmons 0
3 Rice 0
18 TCU 7
0 Baylor 0
0 Arkansas 18
22 SMU 6
38 San Francisco 14
20 Utah 7
0 Centenary 3
0 Texas 7
13 Manhattan 6

1937

14 Manhattan 7
14 Miss. State 0
7 TCU 7
0 Baylor 13
13 Arkansas 26
14 SMU 0
6 Rice 6
7 Texas 6
42 San Francisco 0

1938

52 Texas A. & I. 0
20 Tulsa 0
0 Santa Clara 7
6 TCU 34
6 Baylor 6
13 Arkansas 7
7 SMU 10
6 Texas 7
27 Rice 0

1939

32 Oklahoma A. & M. 0
14 Centenary 0
7 Santa Clara 3
33 Villanova 7
20 TCU 6
20 Baylor 0
27 Arkansas 0
6 SMU 2
19 Rice 0
20 Texas 0

1940

26 Texas A. & I. 0
41 Tulsa 6
7 UCLA 0
21 TCU 7
14 Baylor 7
17 Arkansas 0
19 SMU 7
25 Rice 0
0 Texas 7

1941

54 Sam Houston 0
41 Texas A. & I. 0
49 NYU 7
14 TCU 0
48 Baylor 0
7 Arkansas 0
21 SMU 10
19 Rice 6
0 Texas 23
7 Washington State 0

1942

7 LSU 16
19 Texas Tech 0
7 Corpus Christi NAS 18
2 TCU 7
0 Baylor 6
41 Arkansas 0
27 SMU 20
0 Rice 0
6 Texas 12
21 Washington State 0

1943

48 Bryan AFB 6
13 Texas Tech 0
28 LSU 13
13 TCU 0

0 North Texas AC (Arlington) 0
13 Arkansas 0
22 SMU 0
20 Rice 0
13 Texas 27

1944

39 Bryan AFB 0
27 Texas Tech 14
14 Oklahoma 21
7 TCU 13
7 LSU 0
61 North Texas AC (Arlington) 0
6 Arkansas 7
39 SMU 6
19 Rice 6
0 Texas 6
70 Miami 14

1945

54 Ellington Field 0
16 Texas Tech 6
19 Oklahoma 14
12 LSU 31
12 TCU 13
19 Baylor 13
34 Arkansas 0
3 SMU 0
0 Rice 6
10 Texas 20

1946

47 North Texas State 0
0 Texas Tech 0
7 Oklahoma 10
9 LSU 33
14 TCU 0
17 Baylor 0
0 Arkansas 7
14 SMU 0
10 Rice 27
7 Texas 24

1947

48 Southwestern 0
29 Texas Tech 7
14 Oklahoma 26
13 LSU 19
0 TCU 26
24 Baylor 0
21 Arkansas 21
0 SMU 13
7 Rice 41
13 Texas 32

KNUTE ROCKNE

Record: 104–12–5
Hall of Fame 1951

NOTRE DAME 1918–30

1918

26 Case Tech 6
67 Wabash 7
7 Great Lakes 7
7 Michigan State 13
26 Purdue 6
0 Nebraska 0

1919

14	Kalamazoo	0
60	Mount Union	7
14	Nebraska	9
53	Western State	0
16	Indiana	3
12	Army	9
13	Michigan State	0
33	Purdue	13
14	Morningside	6

1920

39	Kalamazoo	0
42	Western State	0
16	Nebraska	7
28	Valparaiso	3
27	Army	17
28	Purdue	0
13	Indiana	10
33	Northwestern	7
25	Michigan State	0

1921

56	Kalamazoo	0
57	DePauw	10
7	Iowa	10
33	Purdue	0
7	Nebraska	0
28	Indiana	7
28	Army	0
48	Rutgers	0
42	Haskell	7
21	Marquette	7
48	Michigan State	0

1922

46	Kalamazoo	0
26	St. Louis	0
20	Purdue	0
34	DePauw	7
13	Georgia Tech	3
27	Indiana	0
0	Army	0
31	Butler	3
19	Carnegie Tech	0
6	Nebraska	14

1923

74	Kalamazoo	0
14	Lombard	0
13	Army	0
25	Princeton	2
35	Georgia Tech	7
34	Purdue	7
7	Nebraska	14
34	Butler	7
26	Carnegie Tech	0
13	St. Louis	0

1924

40	Lombard	0
34	Wabash	0
13	Army	7
12	Princeton	0
34	Georgia Tech	3
38	Wisconsin	3
34	Nebraska	6
13	Northwestern	6
40	Carnegie Tech	19

1925

41	Baylor	0
69	Lombard	0
19	Beloit	3

0	Army	27
19	Minnesota	7
13	Georgia Tech	0
0	Penn State	0
26	Carnegie Tech	0
13	Northwestern	10
0	Nebraska	17

1926

77	Beloit	0
20	Minnesota	7
28	Penn State	0
6	Northwestern	0
12	Georgia Tech	0
26	Indiana	0
7	Army	0
21	Drake	0
0	Carnegie Tech	19
13	Southern Cal	12

1927

28	Coe	7
20	Detroit	0
19	Navy	6
19	Indiana	6
26	Georgia Tech	7
7	Minnesota	7
0	Army	18
32	Drake	0
7	Southern Cal	6

1928

12	Loyola	6
6	Wisconsin	22
7	Navy	0
0	Georgia Tech	13
32	Drake	6
9	Penn State	0
12	Army	6
7	Carnegie Tech	27
14	Southern Cal	27

1929

14	Indiana	0
14	Navy	7
19	Wisconsin	0
7	Carnegie Tech	0
26	Georgia Tech	6
19	Drake	7
13	Southern Cal	12
26	Northwestern	6
7	Army	0

1930

20	SMU	14
26	Navy	2
21	Carnegie Tech	6
35	Pittsburgh	19
27	Indiana	0
60	Pennsylvania	20
28	Drake	7
14	Northwestern	0
7	Army	6
27	Southern Cal	0

BILL ROPER

Record: 112–37–18
Hall of Fame 1951

VMI 1903–04

1903

24	Old Point College	0
6	North Carolina A. & M.	0
0	North Carolina	28

1904

0	North Carolina A. & M.	5
0	Navy	12
26	Officers of Marines	6
0	Virginia	17
12	St. John's	6
6	Davidson	0
5	Virginia Tech	17

PRINCETON 1906–08

1906

24	Villanova	0
22	Stevens	0
6	Wash. & Jeff.	0
52	Lehigh	0
5	Navy	0
32	Bucknell	4
14	Cornell	5
42	Dartmouth	0
8	Army	0
0	Yale	0

1907

47	Stevens	0
53	Wesleyan	0
52	Bucknell	0
45	Villanova	5
40	Wash. & Jeff.	0
5	Cornell	6
16	Carlisle	0
14	Amherst	0
10	Yale	12

1908

18	Springfield	0
21	Stevens	0
0	Lafayette	0
6	Villanova	0
10	Virginia Tech	4
17	Fordham	0
0	Syracuse	0
0	Army	0
6	Dartmouth	10
6	Yale	11

MISSOURI 1909

5	Washington (Mo.)	0
12	Kansas	6
13	Iowa	12
6	Iowa State	6
22	Drake	6
13	Missouri Mines	0
12	Monmouth	6
3	Kansas State	0

PRINCETON 1910–11

1910

18	Stevens	0
36	Villanova	0
12	NYU	0
13	Lafayette	0
6	Carlisle	0
6	Dartmouth	0
17	Holy Cross	0
3	Yale	5

FRANCIS SCHMIDT

Record: 159–56–11
Hall of Fame 1971

TULSA 1919–21

1911

37	Stevens	0
37	Rutgers	0
31	Villanova	0
6	Lehigh	6
31	Colgate	0
0	Navy	0
20	Holy Cross	0
8	Harvard	6
3	Dartmouth	0
6	Yale	3

SWARTHMORE 1915–16

1915

42	Dickinson	0
3	Bucknell	0
14	Ursinus	6
7	Franklin & Marshall	21
21	Johns Hopkins	12
0	Lafayette	17
0	Villanova	19
7	Haverford	2

1916

10	Lafayette	6
6	Pennsylvania	0
6	Franklin & Marshall	0
13	Ursinus	3
14	Johns Hopkins	6
18	Columbia	0
20	Dickinson	20
7	Haverford	10

PRINCETON 1919–30

1919

28	Trinity	0
9	Lafayette	6
34	Rochester	0
0	Colgate	7
0	West Virginia	25
10	Harvard	10
13	Yale	6

1920

17	Swarthmore	6
35	Maryland	0
34	Wash. & Lee	0
14	Navy	0
10	West Virginia	3
14	Harvard	14
20	Yale	0

1921

21	Swarthmore	7
19	Colgate	0
0	Navy	13
0	Chicago	9
34	Virginia	0
10	Harvard	3
7	Yale	13

1922

30	Johns Hopkins	0
5	Virginia	0
10	Colgate	0
26	Maryland	0
21	Chicago	18
22	Swarthmore	13
10	Harvard	3
3	Yale	0

1923

16	Johns Hopkins	7
17	Georgetown	0
2	Notre Dame	25
3	Navy	3
35	Swarthmore	6
0	Harvard	5
0	Yale	27

1924

40	Amherst	6
0	Lehigh	0
17	Navy	14
0	Notre Dame	12
21	Swarthmore	6
34	Harvard	0
0	Yale	10

1925

20	Amherst	0
15	Wash. & Lee	6
10	Navy	10
0	Colgate	9
19	Swarthmore	7
36	Harvard	0
25	Yale	12

1926

14	Amherst	7
7	Wash. & Lee	7
13	Navy	27
7	Lehigh	6
27	Swarthmore	0
12	Harvard	0
10	Yale	7

1927

14	Amherst	0
42	Lehigh	0
13	Wash. & Lee	0
21	Cornell	10
35	William & Mary	7
20	Ohio State	0
6	Yale	14

1928

50	Vermont	0
0	Virginia	0
47	Lehigh	0
3	Cornell	0
6	Ohio State	6
25	Wash. & Lee	12
12	Yale	2
0	Navy	9

1929

7	Amherst	0
12	Brown	13
7	Cornell	13
13	Navy	13
7	Chicago	15
20	Lehigh	0
0	Yale	13

1930

23	Amherst	0
0	Brown	7
7	Cornell	12
0	Navy	31
0	Chicago	0
9	Lehigh	13
7	Yale	10

1919

152	Oklahoma Baptist	0
60	Southwestern Okla.	0
27	Oklahoma	0
75	Northwestern Okla.	0
63	Arkansas	7
70	Trinity	0
71	Camp Burlson	7
7	Oklahoma A.&M.	7
67	Central Oklahoma	6

1920

121	Shawnee Catholic U.	0
151	Okla. Mines	0
88	Chilocco Indians	0
20	Oklahoma A.&M.	14
10	East Central Oklahoma	0
3	Central Oklahoma	0
81	Oklahoma Baptist	7
14	Northwestern Okla.	7
89	Kingfisher	0
0	Phillips University	0
45	Mo. Mines	0

1921

92	East Central Oklahoma	0
75	Chilocco Indians	13
17	Northwestern Oklahoma	7
0	Texas Christian	16
0	Haskell	21
0	Central Oklahoma	21
28	Oklahoma Baptist	0
24	Kingfisher	7
21	Phillips University	0

ARKANSAS 1922–28

1922

39	Hendrix	0
22	Drury	0
7	Ouachita	13
40	LSU	6
*1	Tulsa	0
0	Oklahoma A. & M.	13
7	Rice	31
9	SMU	0
13	Baylor	6

* Forfeited

1923

32	State Normal	0
26	Drury	0
26	LSU	13
0	Ouachita	0
32	Phillips	0
12	Oklahoma A. & M.	0
23	Rice	0
0	Baylor	14
6	SMU	13

1924

54	Northeastern Teachers	6
47	Missouri Teachers	0
34	Hendrix	3
20	Mississippi	0
10	LSU	7

Continued on next page

28 Phillips	6	
0 Oklahoma A. & M.	20	
0 Baylor	13	
14 SMU	14	
20 Texas Christian	0	

1925

0 Iowa	26
0 Baptist	6
45 Phillips	0
12 LSU	0
9 Oklahoma A. & M.	7
20 Tulsa	7
9 Rice	13
0 SMU	0
0 Texas Christian	3

1926

60 Arkansas Teachers	0
21 Mississippi	6
6 Oklahoma	13
14 Hendrix	7
33 Centenary	6
7 Kansas A. & M.	16
0 LSU	14
24 Oklahoma A. & M.	2
7 Tulsa	14
7 Texas Christian	10

1927

32 College of Ozarks	0
34 Missouri Mines	0
28 LSU	0
32 Oklahoma A. & M.	20
42 Austin College	0
20 Hendrix	7
13 Baylor	6
6 Texas A. & M.	40
10 Texas Christian	3

1928

0 Mississippi	25
21 College of Ozarks	0
7 LSU	0
45 Missouri Mines	6
57 Oklahoma Baptist	0
73 Southwestern	0
14 Baylor	0
7 Texas	20
27 Texas A. & M.	12

Texas Christian 1929–33

1929

61 Daniel Baker	0
20 Hardin-Simmons	0
28 Centenary	0
13 Texas A. & M.	7
22 Texas Tech	0
25 North Texas State	0
24 Rice	0
15 Texas	12
34 Baylor	7
7 SMU	7

1930

47 North Texas State	0
40 East Texas State	0
33 Austin College	7
0 Hardin-Simmons	0
40 Arkansas	

3 Texas A. & M.	0
26 Texas Tech	0
62 Abilene Christian	0
20 Rice	0
0 Texas	7
14 Baylor	35
13 SMU	0

1931

40 Texas Military	0
33 North Texas State	6
3 LSU	0
0 Tulsa	13
38 Austin College	0
6 Texas A. & M.	0
6 Hardin-Simmons	0
7 Arkansas	0
7 Rice	6
0 Texas	10
19 Baylor	6
0 SMU	0

1932

14 North Texas State	2
3 LSU	3
55 Daniel Baker	0
34 Arkansas	12
17 Texas A. & M.	0
68 Austin College	0
27 Baylor	0
27 Hardin-Simmons	0
14 Texas	0
16 Rice	6
8 SMU	0

1933

33 Austin College	0
28 Daniel Baker	6
13 North Texas State	0
0 Arkansas	13
20 Hardin-Simmons	0
13 Texas A. & M.	7
0 Centenary	0
0 Baylor	7
19 North Dakota	7
30 Texas	0
26 Rice	3
26 SMU	6

Ohio State 1934–40

1934

33 Indiana	0
13 Illinois	14
10 Colgate	7
28 Northwestern	6
76 Western Reserve	0
33 Chicago	0
34 Michigan	0
40 Iowa	7

1935

19 Kentucky	6
85 Drake	7
28 Northwestern	7
28 Indiana	6
13 Notre Dame	18
20 Chicago	13
6 Illinois	0
38 Michigan	0

1936

60 NYU	0
0 Pittsburgh	6
13 Northwestern	14
7 Indiana	0
2 Notre Dame	7
44 Chicago	0
13 Illinois	0
21 Michigan	0

1937

14 Texas Christian	0
13 Purdue	0
12 Southern Cal	13
7 Northwestern	0
39 Chicago	0
0 Indiana	10
19 Illinois	0
21 Michigan	0

1938

6 Indiana	0
7 Southern Cal	14
0 Northwestern	0
42 Chicago	7
32 NYU	0
0 Purdue	12
32 Illinois	14
0 Michigan	18

1939

19 Missouri	0
13 Northwestern	0
23 Minnesota	20
14 Cornell	23
24 Indiana	0
61 Chicago	0
21 Illinois	0
14 Michigan	21

1940

30 Pittsburgh	7
17 Purdue	14
3 Northwestern	6
7 Minnesota	13
7 Cornell	21
21 Indiana	6
14 Illinois	6
0 Michigan	40

Idaho 1941–42

1941

7 Utah	26
7 Oregon	21
21 Gonzaga	7
16 Utah State	0
33 Willamette	0
0 Oregon State	33
0 Washington State	26
0 Montana	16
39 Montana State	0

1942

0 Oregon State	33
0 Second Air Force	14
28 East Washington	7
7 Stanford	54
0 Oregon	28
21 Montana	0
0 Washington State	7
21 Portland	14
7 Utah	13
13 UCLA	40

ANDY SMITH
Record: 114–33–12
Hall of Fame 1951

PENNSYLVANIA 1909–12

1909
17	Cornell	6
6	Lafayette	6
3	Penn State	3
22	Ursinus	0
12	West Virginia	0
18	Dickinson	0
20	Gettysburg	0
29	Carlisle	6
13	Brown	5
6	Michigan	12

1910
12	Cornell	6
18	Lafayette	0
17	Franklin & Marshall	0
10	Penn State	0
5	Ursinus	8
38	West Virginia	0
18	Dickinson	0
29	Gettysburg	0
17	Carlisle	5
20	Brown	0
0	Michigan	0

1911
21	Cornell	9
23	Lafayette	6
14	Franklin & Marshall	0
6	Penn State	22
9	Ursinus	0
22	Villanova	0
22	Dickinson	10
5	Gettysburg	3
0	Carlisle	16
0	Brown	6
0	Michigan	11

1912
7	Cornell	2
3	Swarthmore	6
3	Lafayette	7
35	Franklin & Marshall	0
0	Penn State	14
34	Ursinus	0
16	Dickinson	0
35	Gettysburg	0
34	Carlisle	26
7	Brown	30
7	Michigan	21

PURDUE 1913–15

1913
26	Wabash	0
34	Northwestern	0
7	Wisconsin	7
0	Chicago	6
62	Rose Poly.	0
0	Illinois	0
42	Indiana	7

1914
27	Wabash	3
26	Western Reserve	0
7	Wisconsin	14
0	Chicago	21
40	Kentucky	6
34	Northwestern	6
23	Indiana	13

1915
7	Wabash	7
26	Beloit	0
3	Wisconsin	28
0	Chicago	7
19	Iowa	13
0	Kentucky State	7
7	Indiana	0

CALIFORNIA 1916–25

1916
23	Olympic Club	0
23	Originals	0
0	Olympic Club	0
13	Originals	0
21	Whittier	17
14	Oregon	39
13	Occidental	14
27	Southern Cal	0
48	St. Mary's	6
3	Washington	13
7	Washington	14

1917
0	Mare Island Marines	27
2	Olympic Club	6
0	Mare Island Marines	26
40	Olympic Club	0
33	Navy Hospital Corps	7
20	Occidental	0
14	Oregon Aggies	3
27	Washington	0
13	St. Mary's	14
0	Oregon	21
0	Southern Cal	0

1918
7	Fort MacDowell	21
13	S. F. Presidio	7
1	Fort Scott	0
40	St. Mary's	14
0	Mather Field	13
6	Oregon	0
67	Stanford	0
20	San Pedro Navy	0
33	Southern Cal	7

1919
12	Olympic Club	0
6	Olympic Club	6
19	St. Mary's	0
61	Occidental	0
0	Washington State	14
21	Oregon Aggies	14
14	Southern Cal	13
14	Stanford	10
0	Washington	7

1920
21	Olympic Club	0
88	Mare Island Marines	0
127	St. Mary's	0
79	Nevada	7
63	Utah	0
17	Oregon Aggies	7
49	Washington State	0
38	Stanford	0

1921
21	St. Mary's	0
14	Olympic Club	0
51	Nevada	6
21	Pacific Fleet	10
39	Oregon	0
14	Washington State	0
38	Southern Cal	7
72	Washington	3
42	Stanford	7

1922
45	Santa Clara	14
80	Mare Island Marines	0
41	St. Mary's	0
25	Olympic Club	0
12	Southern Cal	0
61	Washington State	0
45	Washington	7
61	Nevada	13
28	Stanford	0

1923
3	Alumni All-Stars	0
49	St. Mary's	0
48	Santa Clara	0
16	Olympic Club	0
26	Oregon Aggies	0
9	Washington State	0
0	Nevada	0
13	Southern Cal	7
9	Washington	0
9	Stanford	0

1924
13	Santa Clara	7
17	St. Mary's	7
28	Pomona	0
9	Olympic Club	3
20	Washington State	7
7	Southern Cal	0
7	Washington	7
27	Nevada	0
20	Stanford	20
14	Pennsylvania	0

1925
28	Santa Clara	0
54	Nevada	0
0	Olympic Club	15
6	St. Mary's	0
28	Oregon	0
27	Pomona	0
35	Washington State	0
0	Washington	7
14	Stanford	27

CARL SNAVELY
Record: 180–93–16
Hall of Fame 1965

BUCKNELL 1927–33

1927
43	Susquehanna	7
0	Geneva	0
13	Penn State	7
28	Villanova	12
34	Gettysburg	0
0	Army	34
20	Lehigh	6
3	Wash. & Jeff.	19
13	Temple	19
46	Dickinson	0

1928

7	Schuylkill	0
13	Geneva	7
6	Penn State	0
0	Lafayette	0
12	Gettysburg	14
6	Villanova	20
40	Lehigh	0
0	Wash. & Jeff.	0
33	Dickinson	0
7	Temple	7

1929

31	St. Thomas	0
33	Albright	0
6	Wash. & Jeff.	14
6	Lafayette	3
33	Gettysburg	0
13	Temple	0
9	Villanova	0
27	Penn State	6
0	Fordham	14
78	Dickinson	0

1930

46	Geneva	6
26	Albright	0
6	Temple	7
14	St. Thomas	0
26	Gettysburg	6
19	Penn State	7
20	Villanova	14
6	Wash. & Jeff.	7
0	Fordham	12

1931

34	St. Thomas	7
14	Geneva	14
23	Albright	7
0	Temple	0
46	Gettysburg	0
0	Villanova	0
7	Georgetown	0
10	Wash. & Jeff.	6
14	Fordham	13

1932

35	St. Thomas	0
13	Albright	6
0	Fordham	30
0	Temple	12
14	Lafayette	6
0	Villanova	13
14	Western Maryland	13
0	Wash. & Jeff.	14
6	Georgetown	6

1933

46	Waynesburg	7
34	Lebanon Valley	0
0	Duquesne	6
19	Villanova	17
21	Lafayette	0
20	Temple	7
13	Western Maryland	14
14	Furman	0
38	Wash. & Jeff.	6

NORTH CAROLINA 1934–35

1934

21	Wake Forest	0
7	Tennessee	19
14	Georgia	0

6	Kentucky	0
7	N.C. State	7
26	Georgia Tech	0
12	Davidson	2
7	Duke	0
25	Virginia	6

1935

14	Wake Forest	0
38	Tennessee	13
33	Maryland	0
19	Georgia Tech	0
35	N.C. State	6
14	Davidson	0
56	VMI	0
0	Duke	25
61	Virginia	0

CORNELL 1936–44

1936

74	Alfred	0
0	Yale	23
20	Syracuse	7
13	Penn State	7
13	Columbia	20
13	Princeton	41
6	Dartmouth	20
6	Pennsylvania	14

1937

26	Penn State	19
40	Colgate	7
20	Princeton	7
6	Syracuse	14
0	Yale	9
14	Columbia	0
6	Dartmouth	6
34	Pennsylvania	20

1938

15	Colgate	6
20	Harvard	0
17	Syracuse	19
21	Penn State	6
23	Columbia	7
14	Dartmouth	7
0	Pennsylvania	0

1939

19	Syracuse	6
20	Princeton	7
47	Penn State	0
23	Ohio State	14
13	Columbia	7
14	Colgate	12
35	Dartmouth	6
26	Pennsylvania	0

1940

34	Colgate	0
45	Army	0
33	Syracuse	6
21	Ohio State	7
27	Columbia	0
21	Yale	0
0	Dartmouth	3
20	Pennsylvania	22

1941

6	Syracuse	0
7	Harvard	0
0	Navy	14
21	Colgate	2

0	Columbia	7
21	Yale	7
33	Dartmouth	19
0	Pennsylvania	16

1942

20	Lafayette	16
6	Colgate	18
8	Army	28
0	Penn State	0
7	Syracuse	12
13	Columbia	14
13	Yale	7
21	Dartmouth	19
7	Pennsylvania	34

1943

7	Bucknell	6
27	Sampson NTS	13
7	Navy	46
30	Princeton	0
20	Holy Cross	7
7	Colgate	20
33	Columbia	6
13	Penn State	0
0	Dartmouth	20
14	Pennsylvania	20

1944

39	Syracuse	6
26	Bucknell	0
7	Yale	16
7	Colgate	14
13	Sampson NTS	6
23	Columbia	7
0	Navy	48
14	Dartmouth	13
0	Pennsylvania	20

NORTH CAROLINA 1945–52

1945

6	Camp Lee	0
14	Georgia Tech	20
14	VPI	0
0	Pennsylvania	49
20	Cherry Pt. M	14
6	Tennessee	20
6	W&M	0
13	Wake Forest	14
7	Duke	14
27	Virginia	18

1946

14	VPI	14
21	Miami	0
33	Maryland	0
21	Navy	14
40	Florida	19
14	Tennessee	20
21	W&M	7
26	Wake Forest	14
22	Duke	7
49	Virginia	14

1947

14	Georgia	7
0	Texas	34
7	Wake Forest	19
13	W&M	7
35	Florida	7
20	Tennessee	6
41	N.C. State	6

19 Maryland 0
21 Duke 0
40 Virginia 7

1948

34 Texas 7
21 Georgia 14
28 Wake Forest 6
14 N.C. State 0
34 LSU 7
14 Tennessee 7
7 W&M 7
49 Maryland 20
20 Duke 0
34 Virginia 12

1949

26 N.C. State 6
21 Georgia 14
28 South Carolina 13
28 Wake Forest 14
7 LSU 13
6 Tennessee 35
20 W&M 14
6 Notre Dame 42
21 Duke 20
14 Virginia 7

1950

13 N.C. State 7
7 Notre Dame 14
0 Georgia 0
7 Wake Forest 13
40 W&M 7
0 Tennessee 16
7 Maryland 7
14 South Carolina 7
0 Duke 7
13 Virginia 44

1951

21 N.C. State 0
16 Georgia 28
20 Texas 45
21 South Carolina 6
7 Maryland 14
7 Wake Forest 39
0 Tennessee 27
14 Virginia 34
7 Notre Dame 12
7 Duke 19

1952

7 Texas 28
7 Wake Forest 9
14 Notre Dame 34
14 Tennessee 41
7 Virginia 34
27 South Carolina 19
0 Duke 34
34 Miami 7

WASHINGTON (MO.) 1953–58

1953

26 Missouri Mines 7
40 Sewanee 20
13 Wayne 33
54 Illinois Wesleyan 6
18 Western Michigan 7
14 Western Reserve 20
27 Butler 14
28 Southern Illinois 6
34 Evansville 13

1954

58 Missouri Mines 14
52 Illinois Wesleyan 7
0 Wayne 27
33 Western Reserve 6
6 Western Michigan 7
42 Evansville 7
25 Butler 6
25 Southern Illinois 14
19 Bradley 20

1955

13 Missouri Mines 20
20 Wabash 14
19 Drake 39
6 Western Reserve 9
26 Western Michigan 14
27 Wash. & Lee 0
32 Southern Illinois 13
41 Butler 20
20 Bradley 27

1956

14 Missouri Mines 13
7 Wabash 27
6 Drake 14
13 Western Michigan 7
27 South Dakota 7
26 Southern Illinois 0
27 Bradley 33
21 Butler 20
40 Wash. & Lee 19

1957

14 Missouri Mines 7
21 Wabash 13
7 Drake 19
25 South Dakota 19
33 Omaha 6
13 Bradley 26
13 Butler 41
47 Wash. & Lee 0

1958

19 Missouri Mines 13
14 Wabash 13
0 Bradley 7
2 Western Michigan 34
12 Wash. & Lee 6
28 Omaha 6
21 Drake 28
12 Butler 20

BILL SPAULDING

Record: 145–83–15

WESTERN MICHIGAN 1907–21

1907

9 Grand Rapids HS 0
0 Albion 5
0 Olivet 3
27 Central Michigan 0
6 Michigan Normal 0
0 Ferris 0

1908

20 MacFadden's School of Physical
    Culture 0
0 Michigan State 35
0 Olivet 34
0 Albion 24
11 Central Michigan 5
2 Kalamazoo 0

1909

61 Otsego Independents 0
6 Albion 0
15 Battle Creek HS 0
47 Dowagiac HS 0
28 Benton Harbor Business College 3
26 Kalamazoo 5
11 Central Michigan 0

1910

3 Hillsdale 3
0 Albion 6
22 Culver Military Academy 5
16 Central Michigan 6
6 Hope 0
28 Kalamazoo 0

1911

6 Hillsdale 14
5 Albion 12
3 Culver Military Academy 27
62 Battle Creek Training School 6
34 Hope 0

1912

19 Culver Military Academy 13
6 Albion 3
0 Michigan State 20
54 Hope 0
7 Hillsdale 7
0 Michigan State Normal 6

1913

20 Albion 3
13 Culver Military Academy 6
14 Hope 0
12 Michigan State Normal 6

1914

28 Battle Creek Training School 0
3 Olivet 0
43 Albion 0
68 Ferris 0
28 Hillsdale 7
10 Michigan State Normal 0

1915

16 Hillsdale 20
54 Albion 7
79 Alma 0
40 Olivet 0
19 Michigan State Normal 0
83 Culver Military Academy 16

1916

93 Grand Rapids Veterinary 0
37 Albion 0
94 Indiana (Pa.) 6
77 Michigan State Frosh 3
6 Notre Dame Frosh 10
82 Ohio Northern 19

1917

26 Albion 6
13 Michigan 17
83 Notre Dame Frosh 0
14 Michigan State 0
61 Camp Custer Soldiers 7
6 Detroit 35
0 Indiana (Pa.) 40

1918

12	Albion	14
7	Michigan State	16
103	Hillsdale	0
62	Hope	0
39	Notre Dame Frosh	0

1919

88	Wayne State	0
21	Michigan State	18
27	Wabash	13
0	Notre Dame	53
20	Albion	7

1920

47	Olivet	7
0	Notre Dame	41
6	Chicago YMCA	10
7	Marquette	46
46	Hope	0
6	Earlham	0
7	Wabash	27

1921

49	Ferris	0
20	Albion	9
7	Notre Dame Frosh	0
3	Chicago YMCA	7
14	Michigan State	17
42	Earlham	7
65	Hope	0
62	Milwaukee Engineers	0

MINNESOTA 1922–24

1922

22	North Dakota	0
20	Indiana	0
7	Northwestern	7
9	Ohio State	0
0	Wisconsin	14
14	Iowa	28
7	Michigan	16

1923

20	Iowa State	17
13	Haskell	12
27	North Dakota	0
0	Wisconsin	0
34	Northwestern	14
20	Iowa	7
0	Michigan	10

1924

14	North Dakota	0
20	Haskell	0
7	Wisconsin	7
0	Iowa	13
0	Michigan	13
7	Iowa State	7
20	Illinois	7
0	Vanderbilt	16

UCLA 1925–38

1925

7	San Diego State	0
16	La Verne	3
26	Pomona	0
0	Whittier	7
9	Occidental	0
0	St. Mary's	28
23	Redlands	0
0	Stanford	82
10	Caltech	10

1926

25	Santa Barbara State	0
42	San Diego State	7
6	Whittier	16
27	Pomona	7
24	Occidental	7
26	Redlands	3
3	Caltech	7
0	Iowa State	20

1927

25	Whittier	6
8	Occidental	0
32	Redlands	0
7	Pomona	7
13	Caltech	0
33	Santa Barbara State	0
7	Fresno State	0
13	Arizona	16
6	Drake	25

1928

19	Santa Barbara State	0
7	Arizona	7
32	Caltech	0
7	Stanford	45
29	Pomona	0
6	Idaho	20
0	Washington State	38
65	La Verne	0
6	Oregon	26

1929

0	Southern Cal	76
56	Fresno State	6
0	Stanford	57
20	Pomona	0
31	Caltech	0
0	St. Mary's	24
0	Oregon	27
14	Montana	0

1930

0	Southern Cal	52
21	Pomona	0
6	St. Mary's	21
30	Caltech	0
0	Stanford	20
0	Oregon	7
0	Oregon State	19
20	Idaho	6

1931

0	Occidental	0
0	Washington State	13
0	Northwestern	19
46	Pomona	0
6	Stanford	12
12	St. Mary's	0
6	Oregon	13
13	Florida	0

1932

26	Calif. Aggies	0
6	Idaho	0
12	Oregon	7
51	Caltech	0
13	Stanford	6
7	St. Mary's	14
32	Montana	0
0	Washington State	3
0	Washington	19
2	Florida	12

1933

34	Los Angeles JC	0
13	San Diego State	0
0	Stanford	3
22	Utah	0
20	Loyola	7
0	Oregon	7
0	California	0
14	San Diego Marines	13
0	Washington	10
14	St. Mary's	22
7	Washington State	0

1934

14	Pomona	0
20	San Diego State	0
3	Oregon	26
16	Montana	0
0	California	3
49	Calif. Aggies	0
0	Stanford	27
6	St. Mary's	0
25	Oregon State	7
13	Loyola	6

1935

39	Utah State	0
20	Oregon State	7
7	Stanford	6
33	Oregon	6
2	California	14
0	SMU	21
19	Hawaii	6
14	Loyola	6
13	Idaho	6
13	St. Mary's	7

1936

21	Occidental	0
26	Pomona	0
30	Montana	0
0	Washington	14
17	California	6
22	Oregon State	13
6	Stanford	19
7	Oregon	0
7	Washington State	32
7	Southern Cal	7

1937

26	Oregon	13
7	Stanford	12
7	Oregon State	7
0	Washington State	3
14	California	27
0	Washington	26
13	SMU	26
13	Missouri	0
13	Southern Cal	19

1938

27	Iowa	3
12	Oregon	14
13	Washington	0
7	California	20
33	Idaho	0
6	Stanford	0
21	Washington State	0
7	Wisconsin	14
7	Southern Cal	42
6	Oregon State	6
46	Honolulu Town Team	0
32	Hawaii	7

FAT SPEARS

Record: 135–78–13

DARTMOUTH 1917–20

1917

14	Springfield	0
32	Middlebury	6
6	West Virginia	2
21	N.H. State	6
10	Penn State	7
0	Pennsylvania	7
0	Tufts	27
0	Brown	13

1918

20	Norwich	0
6	Syracuse	34
26	U.S. Marines	0
26	Middlebury	0
0	Brown	28
0	Pennsylvania	21

1919

40	Springfield	0
13	Norwich	0
27	MAC	7
19	Penn State	13
9	Cornell	0
7	Colgate	7
20	Pennsylvania	19
6	Brown	7

1920

31	Norwich	0
7	Penn State	14
27	Holy Cross	14
0	Syracuse	10
34	Tufts	7
14	Cornell	3
44	Pennsylvania	7
14	Brown	6
28	Washington	7

WEST VIRGINIA 1921–24

1921

34	W. Va. Wesleyan	3
50	Cincinnati	0
13	Pittsburgh	21
7	Ohio	0
0	Bucknell	0
12	Lehigh	21
28	Washington & Lee	7
7	Virginia	0
7	Rutgers	17
0	Wash. & Jeff.	13

1922

20	W. Va. Wesleyan	0
55	Marietta	0
9	Pittsburgh	6
12	Washington & Lee	12
28	Rutgers	0
33	Indiana	0
34	Cincinnati	0
13	Virginia	0
28	Ohio	0
14	Wash. & Jeff.	0
21	Gonzaga	13

1923

21	W. Va. Wesleyan	7
28	Allegheny	0
13	Pittsburgh	7
81	Marshall	0
13	Penn State	13
27	Rutgers	7
63	Washington & Lee	0
49	St. Louis	0
2	Wash. & Jeff.	7

1924

21	W. Va. Wesleyan	6
35	Allegheny	6
7	Pittsburgh	14
55	Geneva	0
13	Centre	6
71	Bethany	6
34	Colgate	2
6	Washington & Lee	0
40	Wash. & Jeff.	7

MINNESOTA 1925–29

1925

25	North Dakota	6
34	Grinnell	6
32	Wabash	6
7	Notre Dame	19
12	Wisconsin	12
33	Butler	7
33	Iowa	0
0	Michigan	35

1926

51	North Dakota	0
7	Notre Dame	20
0	Michigan	20
67	Wabash	7
16	Wisconsin	10
41	Iowa	0
81	Butler	0
6	Michigan	7

1927

57	North Dakota	10
40	Oklahoma A. & M.	0
14	Indiana	14
38	Iowa	0
13	Wisconsin	7
7	Notre Dame	7
27	Drake	6
13	Michigan	7

1928

40	Creighton	0
15	Purdue	0
33	Chicago	7
6	Iowa	7
9	Northwestern	10
20	Indiana	12
52	Haskell	0
6	Wisconsin	0

1929

39	Coe	0
15	Vanderbilt	6
26	Northwestern	14
54	Ripon	0
19	Indiana	0
7	Iowa	9
6	Michigan	7
13	Wisconsin	12

OREGON 1930–31

1930

20	Pacific	0
51	Willamette	0
6	Linfield	0
14	Drake	7
7	Washington	0
20	Idaho	6
7	UCLA	0
0	Oregon State	15
6	St. Mary's	7

1931

21	Pacific	6
20	Willamette	0
9	Idaho	0
13	Washington	0
0	Southern Cal	53
0	North Dakota	0
14	NYU	6
0	Oregon State	0
13	UCLA	6
0	St. Mary's	16

WISCONSIN 1932–35

1932

7	Marquette	2
34	Iowa	0
6	Purdue	7
39	Coe	7
7	Ohio State	7
20	Illinois	12
20	Minnesota	13
18	Chicago	7

1933

19	Marquette	0
0	Illinois	21
7	Iowa	26
0	Purdue	14
0	Chicago	0
25	West Virginia	6
0	Ohio State	6
3	Minnesota	6

1934

3	Marquette	0
28	South Dakota State	7
0	Purdue	14
0	Notre Dame	19
0	Northwestern	7
10	Michigan	0
7	Illinois	3
0	Minnesota	34

1935

6	South Dakota	13
0	Marquette	3
0	Notre Dame	27
12	Michigan	20
7	Chicago	13
8	Purdue	0
13	Northwestern	13
7	Minnesota	33

TOLEDO 1936–42

1936

32	Findlay	6
0	Boston U.	6
6	Denison	9

Continued on next page

0 Western Reserve	14
6 Wayne	9
0 Miami (Ohio)	13
0 Heidelberg	7
50 Otterbein	0

1937

26 Bluffton	0
19 Georgetown	0
6 Ohio Wesleyan	0
7 Akron	21
13 Miami (Ohio)	7
39 Wayne	19
12 Dayton	7
0 West Virginia	34
6 Xavier	8

1938

13 West Liberty	0
26 St. Joseph's	0
26 Ohio Wesleyan	0
13 Dayton	17
13 Marshall	7
39 Wayne	20
6 John Carroll	6
0 Xavier	13
7 Akron	13
13 St. Mary's (Texas)	7

1939

39 Valparaiso	0
19 Detroit Tech	6
20 St. Mary's	12
26 North Dakota	7
6 Scranton	7
6 Western Michigan	0
20 John Carroll	0
12 Marshall	14
12 Long Island	13
20 Xavier	0

1940

21 Detroit Tech	3
34 Davis & Elkins	12
7 Marshall	6
0 Scranton	6
12 Western Michigan	0
33 John Carroll	12
12 Baldwin-Wallace	14
20 Butler	6
7 Long Island	19

1941

0 St. Joseph's	3
55 Detroit Tech	0
7 Marshall	33
20 John Carroll	0
0 Western Michigan	34
9 Illinois Wesleyan	0
39 Camp Shelby	0
2 Butler	18
27 Baldwin-Wallace	7
14 Bradley	6
22 Jefferson Barracks	21

1942

26 Kent State	14
26 Illinois Wesleyan	0
0 Western Michigan	13
6 John Carroll	5
6 Marshall	0
0 U.S. Coast Guard	26
0 Butler	13
12 Youngstown	39
14 Bradley	13

MARYLAND 1943–44

1943

7 Curtis B. CG	13
13 Wake Forest	7
19 Rich. AAB	6
2 West Virginia	6
0 Penn State	45
43 Greenville AAB	18
0 Virginia	39
0 Bainbridge	46
21 VMI	14

1944

0 Hampden-Sydney	12
0 Wake Forest	39
6 West Virginia	6
0 Michigan State	8
6 Florida	14
7 Virginia	18
0 Michigan State	33
19 Penn State	34
8 VMI	6

AMOS ALONZO STAGG

Record: 314–197–35
Hall of Fame 1951

SPRINGFIELD COLLEGE (MASS.)
1890–91

(Scores not available.)

CHICAGO 1892–1932

1892

12 HPHS	0
12 Englewood HS	6
16 HPHS	10
18 YMCA	4
26 HPHS	0
18 YMCA	12
0 Northwestern	0
4 Northwestern	6
18 Lake Forest	18
10 Michigan	18
10 Illinois	4
0 Purdue	38
12 Illinois	28

1893

0 Lake Forest	10
12 Northwestern	6
10 Michigan	6
10 Purdue	20
28 Cincinnati	0
12 Oberlin	33
18 Armour	6
6 Northwestern	6
14 Lake Forest	14
10 Michigan	28
22 Northwestern	14
8 Notre Dame	0
52 "The Reserves"	0

1894

32 EHS	0
22 EHS	0
46 Manual Training	0
4 Chicago AA	12
46 Northwestern	0
14 Rush	6
16 Beloit	0
20 Chicago AA "Seconds"	0

0 Wisconsin	30
0 Chicago AA	30
18 Iowa	18
26 Prairie AC	0
0 Purdue	10
4 Englewood YMCA	0
28 Lake Forest	0
36 Northwestern	0
4 Michigan	6
24 Stanford	4
0 Stanford	12
0 Reliance AC	6
52 Salt Lake YMCA	0

1895

28 Englewood HS	0
42 Englewood YMCA	6
24 HPHS	0
28 Eureka	0
8 CAA	0
52 Lake Forest	0
6 Northwestern	22
24 Armour	4
6 Minnesota	10
22 Wisconsin	12
16 Western Reserve	0
6 Northwestern	0
0 Michigan	12

1896

24 Englewood HS	0
24 HPHS	0
12 Englewood HS	0
43 Wheaton	0
48 Eureka	0
43 Monmouth	0
34 Hahneman Med.	0
0 Iowa	0
18 Notre Dame	0
30 Oberlin	0
36 Armour	0
6 Northwestern	46
12 Illinois	0
0 Wisconsin	24
0 Lake Forest	0
18 Northwestern	6
7 Michigan	6

1897

22 HPHS	0
11 HPHS	0
21 Englewood HS	0
31 Monmouth	4
71 Lake Forest	0
24 Armour	0
39 Beloit	6
21 Northwestern	6
18 Illinois	12
34 Notre Dame	5
8 Wisconsin	23
21 Michigan	12

1898

22 Knox	0
8 Rush	0
24 Monmouth	0
22 P. & Surg.	0
38 Iowa	0
21 Beloit	0
34 Northwestern	5
11 Pennsylvania	23
17 Purdue	0
6 Wisconsin	0
11 Michigan	12

1899

40	Knox	0
12	P. & Surg.	0
23	Notre Dame	6
5	Iowa	5
29	Dixon	0
17	Cornell	6
58	Oberlin	0
5	Pennsylvania	5
44	Purdue	0
76	Northwestern	0
35	Beloit	0
29	Minnesota	0
17	Brown	6
17	Wisconsin	0

1900

24	Lombard	0
29	Monmouth	0
16	Knox	0
23	Dixon	5
17	Purdue	5
40	Rush	0
6	Minnesota	6
6	Brown	11
0	Pennsylvania	41
0	Iowa	17
0	Northwestern	5
5	Wisconsin	39
15	Michigan	6

1901

38	Lombard	0
23	Monmouth	0
12	Milwaukee Med.	0
6	Knox	0
22	Illinois Wesleyan	0
5	Purdue	5
0	Illinois	24
0	Pennsylvania	11
17	Beloit	17
5	Northwestern	6
0	Michigan	22
0	Wisconsin	35

1902

27	Lombard	6
24	Monmouth	0
53	Fort Sheridan	0
5	Knox	0
21	Cornell Coll.	0
33	Purdue	0
12	Northwestern	0
6	Illinois	0
18	Beloit	0
39	Indiana	0
0	Michigan	21
11	Wisconsin	0

1903

34	Lombard	0
23	Lawrence	0
108	Monmouth	0
34	Indiana	0
23	Cornell Coll.	0
22	Purdue	0
40	Rush	0
0	Northwestern	0
18	Illinois	6
15	Wisconsin	6
17	Haskell	11
6	Army	10
0	Michigan	28

1904

19	Lawrence	0
40	Lombard	5
56	Indiana	0
20	Purdue	0
39	Iowa	0
32	Northwestern	0
6	Illinois	6
68	Texas	0
12	Michigan	22
18	Wisconsin	11

1905

15	Wabash	0
38	Beloit	0
42	Iowa	0
16	Indiana	5
4	Wisconsin	0
32	Northwestern	0
19	Purdue	0
44	Illinois	0
2	Michigan	0

1906

39	Purdue	0
33	Indiana	8
2	Minnesota	4
63	Illinois	0
38	Nebraska	5

1907

27	Indiana	6
42	Illinois	6
18	Minnesota	12
56	Purdue	0
4	Carlisle	18

1908

39	Purdue	0
29	Indiana	6
11	Illinois	6
29	Minnesota	0
6	Cornell Coll.	6
18	Wisconsin	12

1909

40	Purdue	0
21	Indiana	0
14	Illinois	8
6	Minnesota	20
34	Northwestern	0
6	Cornell Coll.	6
6	Wisconsin	6

1910

0	Indiana	6
0	Illinois	3
10	Northwestern	0
0	Minnesota	24
14	Purdue	5
0	Cornell Coll.	18
0	Wisconsin	0

1911

23	Indiana	6
11	Purdue	3
24	Illinois	0
0	Minnesota	30
9	Northwestern	3
6	Cornell Coll.	0
5	Wisconsin	0

1912

13	Indiana	0
34	Iowa	14
7	Purdue	0
12	Wisconsin	30
3	Northwestern	0
10	Illinois	0
7	Minnesota	0

1913

21	Indiana	7
23	Iowa	6
6	Purdue	0
28	Illinois	7
14	Northwestern	0
13	Minnesota	7
19	Wisconsin	0

1914

34	Indiana	0
28	Northwestern	0
7	Iowa	0
21	Purdue	0
0	Wisconsin	0
7	Illinois	21
7	Minnesota	13

1915

7	Northwestern	0
13	Indiana	7
7	Purdue	0
14	Wisconsin	13
35	Haskell	0
7	Minnesota	20
0	Illinois	10

1916

0	Carleton	7
22	Indiana	0
0	Northwestern	10
7	Wisconsin	30
16	Purdue	7
20	Illinois	7
0	Minnesota	49

1917

48	Vanderbilt	0
27	Purdue	0
7	Northwestern	0
0	Minnesota	33
0	Wisconsin	18

1918

7	Naval Reserve	14
3	Purdue	7
0	Michigan	13
6	Northwestern	21
0	Illinois	29
0	Minnesota	7

1919

123	Great Lakes	0
16	Purdue	0
41	Northwestern	0
0	Illinois	10
13	Michigan	0
9	Iowa	6
3	Wisconsin	10

1920

20	Purdue	0
41	Wabash	0
10	Iowa	0

Continued on next page

6 Ohio State 7
0 Illinois 3
0 Michigan 14
0 Wisconsin 3

1921

41 Northwestern 0
9 Purdue 0
9 Princeton 0
35 Colorado 0
0 Ohio State 7
14 Illinois 6
3 Wisconsin 0

1922

20 Georgia 0
15 Northwestern 7
12 Purdue 0
18 Princeton 21
14 Ohio State 9
9 Illinois 0
0 Wisconsin 0

1923

34 Michigan Aggies 0
10 Colorado Aggies 0
13 Northwestern 0
20 Purdue 6
0 Illinois 7
27 Indiana 0
17 Ohio State 3
13 Wisconsin 6

1924

0 Missouri 3
3 Ohio State 3
19 Brown 7
23 Indiana 0
19 Purdue 6
0 Wisconsin 0
21 Illinois 21
3 Northwestern 0

1925

7 Dartmouth 33
9 Kentucky 0
3 Ohio State 3
0 Pennsylvania 7
6 Purdue 0
7 Wisconsin 20
6 Illinois 13
6 Northwestern 0

1926

21 Maryland 0
12 Florida 6
0 Ohio State 18
0 Pennsylvania 27
0 Purdue 6
7 Wisconsin 14
0 Illinois 7
7 Northwestern 38

1927

7 Oklahoma 13
13 Indiana 0
7 Purdue 6
13 Pennsylvania 7
7 Ohio 13
0 Michigan 14
6 Illinois 15
12 Wisconsin 0

1928

0 South Carolina 6
0 Ripon Reserves 12
47 Wyoming 0
3 Lake Forest 0
0 Iowa 13
7 Minnesota 33
0 Purdue 40
13 Pennsylvania 20
0 Wisconsin 25
0 Illinois 40

1929

27 Beloit 0
9 Lake Forest 6
13 Indiana 7
10 Ripon 0
18 Terre Haute 0
0 Purdue 26
15 Princeton 7
6 Wisconsin 20
6 Illinois 20
26 Washington 6

1930

19 Ripon 0
7 Hillsdale Reserves 6
0 Wisconsin 34
0 Florida 19
0 Mississippi 0
0 Princeton 0
7 Purdue 26
0 Illinois 28
0 Michigan 16

1931

12 Cornell Coll. 0
0 Hillsdale Reserves 7
7 Michigan 13
0 Yale 27
6 Indiana 32
6 Purdue 14
13 Arkansas 13
13 Illinois 6
7 Wisconsin 12
7 Iowa 0
0 Indiana 6

1932

41 Monmouth 0
7 Yale 7
29 Knox 0
13 Indiana 7
7 Illinois 13
0 Purdue 37
0 Michigan 12
7 Wisconsin 18

COLLEGE OF THE PACIFIC 1933–46

1933

0 Nevada 7
13 California Aggies 7
12 Fresno State 0
14 Chico State 0
6 San Jose State 12
26 Modesto JC 0
0 St. Mary's 7
7 Loyola 14
0 Monmouth (Oreg.) 12
3 California Ramblers 0

1934

14 Nevada 0
6 Fresno State 7
7 Chico State 6
0 San Jose State 13
21 San Diego Marines 7
6 California Ramblers 0
0 Southern Cal 6
6 California 7
7 Arizona 31

1935

7 Nevada 6
26 California Aggies 0
7 Fresno State 20
20 Chico State 0
0 San Jose State 0
0 St. Mary's 33
20 San Diego Marines 0
7 Southern Cal 19
0 California 39
19 San Diego State 7

1936

25 Nevada 0
13 California Aggies 0
17 Fresno State 0
20 Chico State 0
0 San Jose State 6
0 St. Mary's 34
6 Loyola 7
0 San Diego Marines 0
26 California Ramblers 0
0 California 14

1937

7 Nevada 3
13 California Aggies 6
0 Fresno State 20
13 Chico State 0
7 San Jose State 12
0 St. Mary's 0
14 San Diego Marines 14
4 California Ramblers 7
0 Southern Cal 40
0 California 20

1938

51 Nevada 0
34 California Aggies 6
18 Fresno State 13
20 Chico State 13
6 San Jose State 19
0 Loyola 7
14 San Diego Marines 0
28 California Ramblers 0
0 California 39
32 Chicago 0

1939

0 Nevada 6
21 California Aggies 12
0 Fresno State 7
31 Chico State 6
3 San Jose State 13
13 Loyola 13
0 San Diego Marines 14
32 California Ramblers 7
6 California 0
7 Arizona 12
6 South Dakota 0
19 Hawaii 6
7 Heakanis 18

1940

24	Nevada	6
7	California Aggies	6
0	Fresno State	3
27	Chico State	0
7	San Jose State	28
0	Loyola	20
3	San Diego Marines	6
6	California Ramblers	0
7	Notre Dame	25

1941

7	California Aggies	0
0	Fresno State	13
6	Chico State	0
0	San Jose State	7
20	California Ramblers	0
6	San Diego State	12
0	Hawaii	14
19	Humboldt State	0
0	SMU	34
6	Santa Barbara State	7
7	Pacific Lutheran	13

1942

15	California Aggies	7
0	Fresno State	13
27	Chico State	6
0	San Jose State	29
0	California Ramblers	0
9	St. Mary's Pre-Flight	38
0	Washington	27
7	Alameda Coast Guard	13
0	San Diego Navy	14

1943

19	St. Mary's	7
0	Southern Cal	6
12	California	6
13	St. Mary's Pre-Flight	7
14	Alameda Coast Guard	7
19	UCLA	7
16	Del Monte Pre-Flight	7
43	Yuma AAB	0
0	March Field	19

1944

14	Fresno State	6
0	Sacramento JC	6
6	Southern Cal	18
0	California	14
14	St. Mary's Pre-Flight	6
0	Alameda Coast Guard	19
7	UCLA	54
6	Fleet City	7
25	Fairfield AAB	0
0	San Francisco Coast Guard	13
2	Camp Beale	6

1945

0	Fresno State	13
0	Fresno State	16
0	St. Mary's	61
0	Southern Cal	52
0	St. Mary's Pre-Flight	69
0	UCLA	50
7	Camp Beale	13
6	Stockton AAF	12
7	Santa Barbara AB	7

1946

6	Oregon	7
12	El Toro Marines	0
31	Williams Field	0

21	Santa Barbara	0
13	Arizona	47
13	Northwestern	26
13	Hawaii	19
0	San Jose State	32
12	Fresno State	13
31	California Aggies	6
19	San Diego State	13
13	West Texas State	14

MAL STEVENS

Record: 54–45–10

YALE 1928–32

1928

27	Maine	0
21	Georgia	6
32	Brown	14
6	Army	18
18	Dartmouth	0
0	Maryland	6
2	Princeton	12
0	Harvard	17

1929

89	Vermont	0
0	Georgia	15
14	Brown	6
21	Army	13
16	Dartmouth	12
13	Maryland	13
13	Princeton	0
6	Harvard	10

1930

38	Maine	0
40	Maryland	13
14	Georgia	18
21	Brown	0
7	Army	7
0	Dartmouth	0
66	Alfred	0
10	Princeton	7
0	Harvard	13

1931

19	Maine	0
7	Georgia	26
27	Chicago	0
6	Army	6
33	Dartmouth	33
52	St. John's (Annapolis)	0
3	Harvard	0
51	Princeton	14

1932

0	Bates	0
7	Chicago	7
2	Brown	7
0	Army	20
6	Dartmouth	0
7	Princeton	7
19	Harvard	0

NEW YORK UNIVERSITY 1934–41

1934

32	Johns Hopkins	0
3	W. Va. Wesleyan	21
12	Lafayette	7
0	Georgetown	0
0	Carnegie Tech	6

38	CCNY	13
7	Rutgers	22
13	Fordham	39

1935

34	Bates	7
25	Carnegie Tech	6
33	Penn Military	7
7	Georgetown	6
14	Bucknell	0
45	CCNY	0
48	Rutgers	0
0	Fordham	21

1936

0	Ohio State	60
26	Penn Military	0
13	North Carolina	14
7	Georgetown	7
46	Lafayette	0
6	Carnegie Tech	14
46	Rutgers	0
25	CCNY	7
7	Fordham	6

1937

37	Penn Military	6
18	Carnegie Tech	13
6	North Carolina	19
59	St. John's	0
0	Lafayette	13
14	Colgate	7
13	Lehigh	0
0	Georgetown	6
7	Fordham	20

1938

19	Maine	0
25	Rutgers	6
0	North Carolina	7
6	Lafayette	7
0	Ohio State	32
45	Lehigh	0
13	Colgate	7
0	Fordham	25

1939

7	Colgate	6
43	Penn Military	0
7	North Carolina	14
6	Carnegie Tech	0
14	Georgia	13
14	Lafayette	0
7	Missouri	20
0	Georgetown	14
7	Fordham	18

1940

32	Penn Military	6
7	Lafayette	9
13	Syracuse	47
7	Holy Cross	13
0	Georgetown	26
0	Missouri	33
12	Franklin & Marshall	0
0	Penn State	25
0	Fordham	26

1941

25	Penn Military	7
6	Lafayette	0
7	Texas A. & M.	49
0	Syracuse	31

Continued on next page

0 Holy Cross 13
0 Penn State 42
0 Missouri 26
0 Tulane 45
9 Fordham 30

JOCK SUTHERLAND

Record: 143–25–14
Hall of Fame 1951

LAFAYETTE 1919–23

1919

13 Muhlenberg 0
6 Princeton 9
41 Haverford 0
0 Pennsylvania 23
21 Cornell 2
48 Dickinson 0
35 Trinity 0
10 Lehigh 6

1920

20 Muhlenberg 0
7 Navy 12
0 Pennsylvania 7
84 Catholic U. 0
0 Pittsburgh 14
10 Bucknell 7
34 Villanova 0
27 Lehigh 7

1921

48 Muhlenberg 0
6 Pittsburgh 0
27 Dickinson 0
20 Bucknell 7
28 Fordham 7
35 Rutgers 0
38 Pennsylvania 6
44 Delaware 0
28 Lehigh 6

1922

34 Richmond 0
7 Pittsburgh 0
62 Muhlenberg 0
28 Bucknell 7
12 Boston College 0
13 Washington & Jefferson 14
33 Rutgers 6
3 Lehigh 0
7 Georgetown 13

1923

20 Muhlenberg 0
0 Pittsburgh 7
33 Franklin & Marshall 0
21 Springfield 0
6 Rutgers 6
6 Washington & Jefferson 6
8 Pennsylvania 6
45 Dayton 0
13 Lehigh 3

PITTSBURGH 1924–38

1924

14 Grove City 0
13 Geneva 0
26 Johns Hopkins 0
0 Carnegie Tech 6
0 Lafayette 10
7 Syracuse 7

0 Wash. & Jeff. 10
14 West Virginia 7
24 Penn State 3

1925

28 Washington & Lee 0
9 Lafayette 20
13 Gettysburg 0
15 West Virginia 7
12 Carnegie Tech 0
6 Wash. & Jeff. 0
14 Pennsylvania 0
23 Penn State 7
31 Johns Hopkins 0

1926

9 Allegheny 7
6 Georgetown 6
7 Lafayette 17
19 Colgate 16
0 Carnegie Tech 14
88 Westminster 0
17 West Virginia 7
0 Wash. & Jeff. 0
24 Penn State 6

1927

42 Thiel 0
33 Grove City 0
40 West Virginia 0
32 Drake 0
23 Carnegie Tech 7
62 Allegheny 0
0 Wash. & Jeff. 0
21 Nebraska 13
30 Penn State 0

1928

20 Thiel 0
53 Bethany 0
6 West Virginia 9
29 Allegheny 0
0 Carnegie Tech 6
18 Syracuse 0
25 Wash. & Jeff. 0
0 Nebraska 0
26 Penn State 0

1929

53 Waynesburg 0
52 Duke 7
27 West Virginia 7
12 Nebraska 7
40 Allegheny 0
18 Ohio State 2
21 Wash. & Jeff. 0
20 Penn State 7
34 Carnegie Tech 13

1930

52 Waynesburg 0
16 West Virginia 0
52 Western Reserve 0
14 Syracuse 0
19 Notre Dame 35
0 Nebraska 0
7 Carnegie Tech 6
7 Ohio State 16
19 Penn State 12

1931

61 Miami 0
20 Iowa 0
34 West Virginia 0

32 Western Reserve 0
12 Notre Dame 25
41 Penn State 6
14 Carnegie Tech 6
26 Army 0
40 Nebraska 0

1932

47 Ohio Northern 0
40 West Virginia 0
33 Duquesne 0
18 Army 13
0 Ohio State 0
12 Notre Dame 0
19 Pennsylvania 12
0 Nebraska 0
6 Carnegie Tech 0
7 Stanford 0

1933

9 Wash. & Jeff. 0
21 West Virginia 0
37 Centre 0
34 Navy 6
3 Minnesota 7
14 Notre Dame 0
7 Duquesne 0
6 Nebraska 0
16 Carnegie Tech 0

1934

26 Wash. & Jeff. 6
27 West Virginia 6
20 Southern Cal 6
7 Minnesota 13
30 Westminster 0
19 Notre Dame 0
25 Nebraska 6
31 Navy 7
20 Carnegie Tech 0

1935

14 Waynesburg 0
35 Wash. & Jeff. 0
24 West Virginia 6
6 Notre Dame 9
9 Penn State 0
0 Fordham 0
29 Army 6
6 Nebraska 0
0 Carnegie Tech 0
12 Southern Cal 7

1936

53 Ohio Wesleyan 0
34 West Virginia 0
6 Ohio State 0
0 Duquesne 7
26 Notre Dame 0
0 Fordham 0
34 Penn State 7
19 Nebraska 6
31 Carnegie Tech 14

1937

59 Ohio Wesleyan 0
20 West Virginia 0
6 Duquesne 0
0 Fordham 0
21 Wisconsin 0
25 Carnegie Tech 14
21 Notre Dame 6
13 Nebraska 7
28 Penn State 7
10 Duke 0

1938

19	West Virginia	0
28	Temple	6
27	Duquesne	0
26	Wisconsin	6
34	SMU	7
24	Fordham	13
10	Carnegie Tech	20
19	Nebraska	0
26	Penn State	0
0	Duke	7

FRANK THOMAS

Record: 137–31–9
Hall of Fame 1951

CHATTANOOGA 1925–28

1925

40	Jacksonville	0
12	Cumberland	6
0	Howard	3
13	Mercer	7
7	Georgetown	0
0	Sewanee	28
0	Birmingham	6
2	Oglethorpe	6

1926

6	Auburn	15
72	Jacksonville	3
6	Citadel	3
14	Oglethorpe	14
7	Birmingham	7
60	Emory and Henry	0
23	Howard	0
61	Georgetown	0
24	Union	0
6	William & Mary	9

1927

18	Vanderbilt	44
44	Kentucky Normal	6
31	Citadel	6
38	Wofford	7
12	Birmingham	8
14	Virginia Tech	13
12	William & Mary	7
52	Southern Florida	6
19	Oglethorpe	0

1928

0	Vanderbilt	19
15	Furman	0
12	Birmingham	6
70	Louisville	0
21	Centenary	14
79	Southwestern	0
14	Howard	0
19	Miss. College	20
35	Oglethorpe	19
19	Southern Florida	0

ALABAMA 1931–42, 1944–46

1931

42	Howard	6
55	Mississippi	6
53	Miss. State	0
0	Tennessee	25
33	Sewanee	0
9	Kentucky	7
41	Florida	0

74	Clemson	7
14	Vanderbilt	6
49	Chattanooga	0

1932

45	Southwestern	6
53	Miss. State	0
28	George Washington	6
3	Tennessee	7
24	Mississippi	13
12	Kentucky	7
9	VPI	6
0	Georgia Tech	6
20	Vanderbilt	0
6	St. Mary's	0

1933

34	Oglethorpe	0
0	Mississippi	0
18	Miss. State	0
12	Tennessee	6
0	Fordham	2
20	Kentucky	0
27	VPI	0
12	Georgia Tech	9
7	Vanderbilt	0

1934

24	Howard	0
35	Sewanee	6
41	Miss. State	0
13	Tennessee	6
26	Georgia	6
34	Kentucky	14
40	Clemson	0
40	Georgia Tech	0
34	Vanderbilt	0

1935

7	Howard	7
39	George Washington	0
7	Miss. State	20
25	Tennessee	0
17	Georgia	7
13	Kentucky	0
33	Clemson	0
38	Georgia Tech	7
6	Vanderbilt	14

1936

34	Howard	0
32	Clemson	0
7	Miss. State	0
0	Tennessee	0
13	Loyola (New Orleans)	6
14	Kentucky	0
34	Tulane	7
20	Georgia Tech	16
14	Vanderbilt	6

1937

41	Howard	0
65	Sewanee	0
20	South Carolina	0
14	Tennessee	7
19	George Wash.	0
41	Kentucky	0
9	Tulane	6
7	Georgia Tech	0
9	Vanderbilt	7

1938

19	Southern Cal	7
34	Howard	0
14	N. C. State	0
0	Tennessee	13
32	Sewanee	0
26	Kentucky	6
3	Tulane	0
14	Georgia Tech	14
7	Vanderbilt	0

1939

21	Howard	0
7	Fordham	6
20	Mercer	0
0	Tennessee	21
7	Miss. State	0
7	Kentucky	7
0	Tulane	13
0	Georgia Tech	6
39	Vanderbilt	0

1940

26	Spring Hill	0
20	Mercer	0
31	Howard	0
12	Tennessee	27
25	Kentucky	0
13	Tulane	6
14	Georgia Tech	13
25	Vanderbilt	21
0	Miss. State	13

1941

47	Southwestern La. Inst.	6
0	Miss. State	14
61	Howard	0
9	Tennessee	2
27	Georgia	14
30	Kentucky	0
19	Tulane	14
20	Georgia Tech	0
0	Vanderbilt	7
21	Miami (Fla.)	7

1942

54	Southwestern La. Inst.	0
21	Miss. State	6
27	Pensacola NAS	0
8	Tennessee	0
14	Kentucky	0
10	Georgia	21
29	South Carolina	0
0	Georgia Tech	7
27	Vanderbilt	7
19	Georgia N. Pre-Flight	35

1944

27	LSU	27
63	Howard	7
55	Millsaps	0
0	Tennessee	0
41	Kentucky	0
7	Georgia	14
34	Mississippi	6
19	Miss. State	0

1945

21	Keesler AAF	0
26	LSU	7
55	South Carolina	0
25	Tennessee	7
28	Georgia	14

Continued on next page

60 Kentucky 19
71 Vanderbilt 0
55 Pensacola NAS 6
55 Miss. State 13

1946

26 Furman 7
7 Tulane 6
14 South Carolina 6
54 Southwestern La. Inst. 0
0 Tennessee 12
21 Kentucky 7
0 Georgia 14
21 LSU 31
12 Vanderbilt 7
7 Boston College 13
24 Miss. State 7

WALLACE WADE

Record: 169–47–9
Hall of Fame 1955

ALABAMA 1923–30

1923

12 Union 0
56 Mississippi 0
0 Syracuse 23
7 Sewanee 0
59 Spring Hill 0
0 Georgia Tech. 0
16 Kentucky 8
30 LSU 3
36 Georgia 0
6 Florida 16

1924

55 Union 0
20 Furman 0
51 Miss. Coll. 0
14 Sewanee 0
14 Georgia Tech. 0
61 Mississippi 0
42 Kentucky 7
0 Centre 17
33 Georgia 0

1925

53 Union 0
50 Birmingham Southern 7
42 LSU 0
27 Sewanee 0
7 Georgia Tech 0
6 Miss. State 0
31 Kentucky 0
34 Florida 0
27 Georgia 0

1926

54 Millsaps 0
19 Vanderbilt 7
26 Miss. State 7
21 Georgia Tech. 0
2 Sewanee 0
24 LSU 0
14 Kentucky 0
49 Florida 0
33 Georgia 6

1927

46 Millsaps 0
31 So. Pres. U. 0
0 LSU 0
0 Georgia Tech 13

24 Sewanee 0
13 Miss. State 7
21 Kentucky 6
6 Florida 13
6 Georgia 20
7 Vanderbilt 14

1928

27 Mississippi 0
46 Miss. State 0
13 Tennessee 15
42 Sewanee 12
0 Wisconsin 15
14 Kentucky 0
13 Georgia Tech 33
19 Georgia 0
13 LSU 0

1929

55 Miss. Coll. 0
22 Mississippi 7
46 Chattanooga 0
0 Tennessee 6
35 Sewanee 7
0 Vanderbilt 13
24 Kentucky 13
14 Georgia Tech 0
0 Georgia 12

1930

43 Howard 0
64 Mississippi 0
25 Sewanee 0
18 Tennessee 6
12 Vanderbilt 7
19 Kentucky 0
20 Florida 0
33 LSU 0
13 Georgia 0

DUKE 1931–41, 1946–50

1931

0 South Carolina 7
13 VMI 0
18 Villanova 0
0 Davidson 0
28 Wake Forest 0
2 Tennessee 25
7 Kentucky 0
0 N. C. State 14
0 North Carolina 0
6 Wash. & Lee 0

1932

13 Davidson 0
44 VMI 0
7 Auburn 18
34 Maryland 0
9 Wake Forest 0
13 Tennessee 16
13 Kentucky 0
0 N. C. State 6
7 North Carolina 0
13 Wash. & Lee 0

1933

37 VMI 6
22 Wake Forest 0
10 Tennessee 2
19 Davidson 7
14 Kentucky 7
13 Auburn 7
38 Maryland 7

21 North Carolina 0
7 N. C. State 0
0 Georgia Tech 6

1934

46 VMI 0
20 Clemson 6
20 Georgia Tech. 0
20 Davidson 0
6 Tennessee 14
13 Auburn 6
28 Wake Forest 7
0 North Carolina 7
32 N. C. State 0

1935

26 Wake Forest 7
47 South Carolina 0
26 Wash. & Lee 0
38 Clemson 12
0 Georgia Tech 6
0 Auburn 7
19 Tennessee 6
26 Davidson 7
25 North Carolina 0
7 N. C. State 0

1936

13 Davidson 0
6 Colgate 0
21 South Carolina 0
25 Clemson 0
19 Georgia Tech. 6
13 Tennessee 15
51 Wash. & Lee 0
20 Wake Forest 0
27 North Carolina 7
13 N. C. State 0

1937

25 VPI 0
34 Davidson 6
0 Tennessee 0
20 Georgia Tech 19
13 Colgate 0
43 Wash. & Lee 0
67 Wake Forest 0
6 North Carolina 14
20 N. C. State 7
0 Pittsburgh 10

1938

18 VPI 0
27 Davidson 0
7 Colgate 0
6 Georgia Tech. 0
7 Wake Forest 0
14 North Carolina 0
21 Syracuse 0
7 N. C. State 0
7 Pittsburgh 0

1939

26 Davidson 6
37 Colgate 0
13 Pittsburgh 14
33 Syracuse 6
6 Wake Forest 0
7 Georgia Tech 6
20 VMI 7
13 North Carolina 3
28 N. C. State 0

1940

23	VMI	0
0	Tennessee	13
13	Colgate	0
23	Wake Forest	0
41	Georgia Tech	7
46	Davidson	13
3	North Carolina	6
42	N. C. State	6
12	Pittsburgh	7

1941

43	Wake Forest	14
19	Tennessee	0
50	Maryland	0
27	Colgate	14
27	Pittsburgh	7
14	Georgia Tech	0
56	Davidson	0
20	North Carolina	0
55	N. C. State	6

1946

6	N. C. State	13
7	Tennessee	12
21	Navy	6
41	Richmond	0
0	Army	19
0	Georgia Tech	14
13	Wake Forest	0
39	South Carolina	0
7	North Carolina	22

1947

7	N. C. State	0
19	Tennessee	7
14	Navy	14
19	Maryland	7
13	Wake Forest	6
0	Georgia Tech	7
7	Missouri	28
0	South Carolina	0
0	North Carolina	21

1948

0	N. C. State	0
7	Tennessee	7
28	Navy	7
13	Maryland	12
7	Virginia Tech	0
7	Georgia Tech	19
20	Wake Forest	27
62	George Washington	0
0	North Carolina	20

1949

67	Richmond	0
21	Tennessee	7
14	Navy	28
14	N. C. State	13
55	Virginia Tech	7
27	Georgia Tech	14
7	Wake Forest	27
35	George Washington	0
20	North Carolina	21

1950

14	South Carolina	0
28	Pittsburgh	14
7	Tennessee	28
7	N. C. State	0
41	Richmond	0
14	Maryland	26
30	Georgia Tech	21

7	Wake Forest	13
47	Virginia Tech	6
7	North Carolina	0

POP WARNER

Record: 312–104–31
Hall of Fame 1951

GEORGIA 1895–96

1895

34	Wofford	0
0	North Carolina	6
6	North Carolina	10
30	Alabama	6
22	Sewanee	0
0	Vanderbilt	6
6	Auburn	16

1896

34	Wofford	0
24	North Carolina	16
26	Sewanee	0
12	Auburn	6

CORNELL 1897–98

1897

6	Colgate	0
16	Syracuse	0
15	Tufts	0
4	Lafayette	4
0	Princeton	10
5	Harvard	24
45	Penn State	0
42	Williams	0
0	Pennsylvania	4

1898

28	Syracuse	0
29	Colgate	5
41	Hamilton	0
47	Trinity	0
30	Syracuse	0
23	Carlisle	6
27	Buffalo	0
0	Princeton	6
6	Oberlin	0
12	Williams	0
47	Lafayette	0
6	Pennsylvania	12

CARLISLE 1899–1903

1899

16	Dickinson	5
16	Pennsylvania	5
10	Harvard	22
0	Princeton	12
36	Susquehanna	0
45	Columbia	0
2	California	0
81	Oberlin	0
32	Hamilton	0

1900

21	Dickinson	0
45	Gettysburg	0
6	Pennsylvania	16
0	Yale	35
5	Harvard	17
46	Susquehanna	0
6	Columbia	17

5	Wash. & Jeff.	5
17	Virginia	2
34	Lebanon Valley	0
27	Maryland	0

1901

18	Dickinson	11
6	Bucknell	5
5	Navy	16
4	Gettysburg	6
14	Pennsylvania	16
0	Harvard	29
0	Cornell	17
12	Columbia	40
0	Wash. & Jeff.	0
28	Lebanon Valley	0
29	Haverford	0
0	Michigan	22
19	Gallaudet	6

1902

0	Bucknell	16
5	Pennsylvania	0
0	Harvard	23
24	Susquehanna	0
5	Virginia	6
48	Lebanon Valley	0
21	Georgetown	0
24	Swarthmore	0
23	Reliance AC	0

1903

30	Franklin & Marshall	0
12	Bucknell	0
46	Gettysburg	0
16	Pennsylvania	6
11	Harvard	12
0	Princeton	11
6	Virginia	6
28	Lebanon Valley	0
28	Georgetown	6
12	Swarthmore	5
22	Utah	0
29	Northwestern	0

CORNELL 1904–06

1904

17	Colgate	0
29	Rochester	6
24	Hobart	0
34	Hamilton	0
24	Bucknell	12
36	Franklin & Marshall	5
6	Princeton	18
50	Lehigh	5
6	Columbia	12
0	Pennsylvania	34

1905

5	Hamilton	0
12	Colgate	11
28	Hobart	0
24	Bucknell	0
30	Pittsburgh	0
57	Haverford	0
0	Swarthmore	14
6	Princeton	16
6	Columbia	12
17	Penn Frosh	0
5	Pennsylvania	6

1906

0	Colgate	0
21	Hamilton	0
25	Oberlin	5
23	Niagara	6
24	Bucknell	6
29	Starkey	0
72	Bowdoin	0
5	Princeton	14
23	Pittsburgh	0
0	Penn Frosh	12
16	Holy Cross	6
28	Swarthmore	0
0	Penn Frosh	8
0	Pennsylvania	0

CARLISLE 1907–14

1907

15	Bucknell	0
26	Pennsylvania	6
18	Penn State	5
23	Harvard	15
0	Princeton	16
91	Susquehanna	0
40	Lebanon Valley	0
10	Villanova	0
14	Syracuse	6
12	Minnesota	10
18	Chicago	4

1908

16	Navy	6
6	Pennsylvania	6
12	Penn State	5
0	Harvard	17
39	Lebanon Valley	0
10	Villanova	0
6	Pittsburgh	0
12	Syracuse	0
6	Minnesota	11
53	Conway Hall	0
17	St. Louis	0
37	Nebraska	6
8	Denver	4

1909

48	Bucknell	6
35	Gettysburg	0
6	Pennsylvania	29
8	Penn State	8
8	Brown	21
36	Lebanon Valley	0
9	Villanova	0
3	Pittsburgh	14
14	Syracuse	11
32	St. Louis	0
35	East End AC	0
9	George Washington	5

1910

24	Dickinson	0
39	Bucknell	0
0	Navy	6
29	Gettysburg	3
5	Pennsylvania	17
6	Brown	15
0	Princeton	6
22	Virginia	5
53	Lebanon Valley	0
6	Villanova	0
0	Syracuse	14
39	Muhlenberg	0
12	Johns Hopkins	0
0	Harvard Law School	3

1911

17	Dickinson	0
16	Pennsylvania	0
12	Brown	6
18	Harvard	15
53	Lebanon Valley	0
28	Georgetown	5
17	Pittsburgh	0
11	Syracuse	12
32	Muhlenberg	0
29	Johns Hopkins	6
19	Lafayette	0
46	Mt. St. Mary's	5

1912

35	Dickinson	0
36	Lehigh	14
26	Pennsylvania	34
32	Brown	0
0	Wash. & Jeff.	0
45	Lebanon Valley	0
34	Georgetown	20
50	Albright	7
65	Villanova	0
27	Army	6
45	Pittsburgh	8
33	Syracuse	0
49	Toronto All-Stars	7
30	Springfield	24

1913

21	Lehigh	7
7	Pennsylvania	7
13	Brown	0
34	Dartmouth	10
7	Cornell	0
26	Lebanon Valley	0
34	Georgetown	0
25	Albright	0
6	Pittsburgh	12
35	Syracuse	27
61	Johns Hopkins	0
25	West Virginia	0
6	W. Va. Wesleyan	0
0	Delaware	33

1914

34	Dickinson	0
6	Lehigh	21
0	Pennsylvania	7
14	Brown	20
0	Cornell	21
0	Susquehanna	33
7	Lebanon Valley	0
20	Albright	0
3	Pittsburgh	10
3	Syracuse	24

(Scores incomplete.)

PITTSBURGH 1915–23

1915

32	Westminster	0
47	Navy	12
45	Carlisle	0
14	Penn	7
42	Allegheny	0
19	Wash. & Jeff.	0
28	Carnegie Tech	0
20	Penn State	0

1916

57	Westminster	0
20	Navy	19
30	Syracuse	0
20	Penn	0
14	Carnegie Tech	6
46	Allegheny	0
37	Wash. & Jeff.	0
31	Penn State	0

1917

14	West Virginia	9
40	Bethany	0
41	Lehigh	0
28	Syracuse	0
14	Penn	6
25	Westminster	0
13	Wash. & Jeff.	0
27	Carnegie Tech	0
28	Penn State	6

1918

34	Wash. & Jeff.	0
37	Penn	0
32	Georgia Tech	0
28	Penn State	6

1919

33	Geneva	0
26	West Virginia	0
3	Syracuse	24
16	Georgia Tech	6
14	Lehigh	0
7	Wash. & Jeff.	6
3	Penn	3
17	Carnegie Tech	7
0	Penn State	20

1920

47	Geneva	0
34	West Virginia	13
7	Syracuse	7
10	Georgia Tech	3
14	Lafayette	0
27	Penn	21
7	Wash. & Jeff.	0
0	Penn State	0

1921

28	Geneva	0
0	Lafayette	6
21	West Virginia	14
21	Cincinnati	14
35	Syracuse	0
28	Penn	0
0	Nebraska	10
0	Wash. & Jeff.	7
0	Penn State	0

1922

38	Cincinnati	0
0	Lafayette	7
6	West Virginia	9
21	Syracuse	14
7	Bucknell	0
7	Penn	6
62	Geneva	0
19	Wash. & Jeff.	0
14	Penn State	0
16	Stanford	7

1923

21	Bucknell	0
13	Grove City	7
7	Lafayette	0
7	West Virginia	13
0	Syracuse	3
0	Penn	6
13	Wash. & Jeff.	6
2	Carnegie Tech	7
20	Penn State	3

STANFORD 1924–32

1924

20	Occidental	6
7	Olympic Club	0
28	Oregon	13
3	Idaho	0
20	Santa Clara	0
30	Utah	0
41	Montana	3
20	California	20

1925

0	Olympic Club	9
20	Santa Clara	3
28	Occidental	0
13	Southern Cal	9
26	Oregon State	10
35	Oregon	13
0	Washington	13
82	UCLA	0
27	California	14

1926

44	Fresno State	7
13	Calif. Tech	6
19	Occidental	0
7	Olympic Club	3
33	Nevada	9
29	Oregon	12
13	Southern Cal	12
33	Santa Clara	14
29	Washington	10
41	California	6

1927

33	Fresno State	0
7	Olympic Club	6
0	St. Mary's	16
20	Nevada	2
13	Southern Cal	13
20	Oregon State	6
19	Oregon	0
13	Washington	7
6	Santa Clara	13
13	California	6

1928

0	YMI	7
21	West Coast Army	8
6	Olympic Club	12
26	Oregon	12
45	UCLA	7
47	Idaho	0
47	Fresno State	0
0	Southern Cal	10
31	Santa Clara	0
12	Washington	0
13	California	13
26	Army	0

1929

45	West Coast Army	0
6	Olympic Club	0

33	Oregon	7
57	UCLA	0
40	Oregon State	7
0	Southern Cal	7
39	Calif. Tech	0
6	Washington	0
7	Santa Clara	13
21	California	6
34	Army	13

1930

32	West Coast Army	0
18	Olympic Club	0
20	Santa Clara	0
0	Minnesota	0
13	Oregon State	7
12	Southern Cal	41
20	UCLA	0
25	Washington	7
57	Calif. Tech	7
41	California	0
14	Dartmouth	7

1931

46	West Coast Army	0
0	Olympic Club	0
6	Santa Clara	0
13	Minnesota	0
25	Oregon State	7
0	Washington	0
12	UCLA	6
0	Southern Cal	19
26	Nevada	0
0	California	6
32	Dartmouth	6

1932

6	Olympic Club	0
20	San Francisco	7
27	Oregon State	0
14	Santa Clara	0
26	West Coast Army	0
0	Southern Cal	13
6	UCLA	13
13	Washington	18
59	Calif. Aggies	0
0	California	0
0	Pittsburgh	7

TEMPLE 1933–38

1933

26	South Carolina	6
0	Carnegie Tech	25
31	Haskell	0
13	West Virginia	7
7	Bucknell	20
20	Drake	14
13	Wash. & Jeff.	0
0	Villanova	24

1934

34	Virginia Tech	0
40	Texas A. & M.	6
6	Indiana	6
28	West Virginia	13
28	Marquette	6
14	Holy Cross	0
34	Carnegie Tech	6
22	Villanova	0
0	Bucknell	0

1935

51	St. Joseph's	0
25	Centre	13
14	Texas A. & M.	0
6	Vanderbilt	3
13	Carnegie Tech	0
19	West Virginia	6
7	Michigan State	12
26	Marquette	6
14	Villanova	21
6	Bucknell	7

1936

18	St. Joseph's	0
50	Centre	7
12	Mississippi	7
14	Boston College	0
0	Carnegie Tech	7
3	Holy Cross	0
7	Michigan State	7
6	Villanova	0
0	Iowa	25
0	Bucknell	0
7	St Mary's (Calif.)	13

1937

18	VMI	7
0	Mississippi	6
7	Florida	0
0	Boston College	0
7	Carnegie Tech	0
0	Holy Cross	0
6	Michigan State	13
0	Bucknell	0
0	Villanova	33

1938

6	Albright	0
6	Pittsburgh	28
6	Texas Christian	28
26	Bucknell	0
26	Boston College	26
0	Georgetown	13
0	Holy Cross	33
7	Villanova	20
0	Michigan State	10
20	Florida	12

FIELDING YOST

Record: 197–38–13
Hall of Fame 1951

OHIO WESLEYAN 1897

10	OMU	0
33	Colorado Barracks	0
0	Michigan	0
5	Oberlin	14
6	Marietta	0
10	Western Reserve	6
46	Wittenberg	0
28	Colorado Mutes	12
6	Ohio State	0

NEBRASKA 1898

47	Missouri	6
18	Kansas	6
23	Ames	10
76	Hastings	0
0	William Jewell	24
11	Denver AC	10
12	Colorado	10
24	Tarkio	0
5	Drake	6
5	Iowa	6

Kansas 1899

12	Haskell	0
35	Washburn	0
29	Ottawa	0
29	Drake	0
18	Haskell	0
9	Ottawa	0
35	Emporia	0
35	Nebraska	20
25	Washburn	0
34	Missouri	6

San Jose State 1900

0	Stanford	35
0	Stanford	24
0	Nevada	0
6	California "B"	0
0	California	5
5	Chico Normal	0

Stanford 1900

6	Reliance AC	0
35	San Jose	0
6	Reliance A C	0
24	San Jose	0
0	Alumni	14
44	Reliance AC	0
34	Oregon	0
0	Nevada	6
5	California	0

Michigan 1901–23, 1925–26

1901

50	Albion	0
57	Case	0
33	Indiana	0
29	Northwestern	0
128	Buffalo	0
22	Carlisle	0
21	OSU	0
22	Chicago	0
89	Beloit	0
50	Iowa	0

1902

88	Albion	0
48	Case	6
119	MAC	0
60	Indiana	0
23	Notre Dame	0
86	OSU	0
6	Wisconsin	0
107	Iowa	0
21	Chicago	0
63	Oberlin	0
23	Minnesota	6

1903

31	Case	0
79	Beloit	0
65	Ohio Northern	0
51	Indiana	0
88	Ferris Institute	0
47	Drake	0
76	Albion	0
6	Minnesota	6
36	OSU	0
16	Wisconsin	0
42	Oberlin	0
28	Chicago	0

1904

33	Case	0
48	Ohio Northern	0
95	Kalamazoo	0
72	P. & S.	0
31	OSU	6
72	Am. Col. M. & S.	0
130	West Virginia	0
28	Wisconsin	0
36	Drake	4
22	Chicago	12

1905

65	Ohio Wesleyan	0
44	Kalamazoo	0
36	Case	0
23	Ohio Northern	0
18	Vanderbilt	0
31	Nebraska	0
70	Albion	0
48	Drake	0
33	Illinois	0
40	OSU	0
12	Wisconsin	0
75	Oberlin	0
0	Chicago	2

1906

28	Case	0
6	OSU	0
28	Illinois	9
10	Vanderbilt	4
0	Pennsylvania	17
0	Varsity Alumni	0

1907

9	Case	0
46	MAC	0
22	Wabash	0
22	OSU	0
8	Vanderbilt	0
0	Pennsylvania	6

1908

16	Case	6
0	MAC	6
12	Notre Dame	6
10	OSU	6
24	Vanderbilt	6
62	Kentucky	0
0	Pennsylvania	29
4	Syracuse	28

1909

3	Case	0
33	OSU	6
6	Marquette	5
44	Syracuse	0
3	Notre Dame	11
12	Pennsylvania	6
15	Minnesota	6

1910

3	Case	3
6	MAC	3
3	OSU	3
11	Syracuse	0
0	Pennsylvania	0
6	Minnesota	0

1911

24	Case	0
15	MAC	3
19	OSU	0

9	Vanderbilt	8
6	Syracuse	6
0	Cornell	6
11	Pennsylvania	9
6	Nebraska	6

1912

34	Case	0
55	MAC	7
14	OSU	0
7	Syracuse	18
7	South Dakota	6
21	Pennsylvania	27
20	Cornell	7

1913

48	Case	0
14	Mount Union	0
7	MAC	12
33	Vanderbilt	2
43	Syracuse	7
17	Cornell	0
13	Pennsylvania	0

1914

58	DePauw	0
69	Case	0
27	Mount Union	7
23	Vanderbilt	3
3	MAC	0
6	Syracuse	20
0	Harvard	7
34	Pennsylvania	3
13	Cornell	28

1915

39	Lawrence	0
35	Mt. Union	0
28	Marietta	6
14	Case	3
0	MAC	24
7	Syracuse	14
7	Cornell	34
0	Pennsylvania	0

1916

30	Marietta	0
19	Case	3
54	Carroll	0
26	Mt. Union	0
9	MAC	0
14	Syracuse	13
66	Washington	7
20	Cornell	23
7	Pennsylvania	10

1917

41	Case	0
17	Western State	13
69	Mt. Union	0
14	Detroit	3
27	MAC	0
20	Nebraska	0
62	Kalamazoo	0
42	Cornell	0
0	Pennsylvania	16
12	Northwestern	21

1918

33	Case	0
13	Chicago	0
15	Syracuse	0
21	MAC	6
14	Ohio State	0

1919

34 Case		0
26 MAC		0
3 Ohio State		13
16 Northwestern		13
0 Chicago		13
7 Illinois		29
7 Minnesota		34

1920

35 Case		0
35 MAC		0
6 Illinois		7
21 Tulane		0
7 Ohio State		14
14 Chicago		0
3 Minnesota		0

1921

44 Mount Union		0
65 Case		0
30 MAC		0
0 Ohio State		14
3 Illinois		0
7 Wisconsin		7
38 Minnesota		0

1922

48 Case		0
0 Vanderbilt		0
19 Ohio State		0
24 Illinois		0
63 MAC		0
13 Wisconsin		6
16 Minnesota		7

1923

36 Case		0
3 Vanderbilt		0
23 Ohio State		0
37 MAC		0
9 Iowa		3
26 Quantico Marines		6
6 Wisconsin		3
10 Minnesota		0

1925

39 MAC		0
63 Indiana		0
21 Wisconsin		0
3 Illinois		0
54 Navy		0
2 Northwestern		3
10 Ohio State		0
35 Minnesota		0

1926

47 Oklahoma A. & M.		3
55 MAC		3
20 Minnesota		0
13 Illinois		0
0 Navy		10
37 Wisconsin		0
17 Ohio State		16
7 Minnesota		6

BOB ZUPPKE

Record: 131–81–12
Hall of Fame 1951

ILLINOIS 1913–41

1913

21 Kentucky		0
24 Missouri		7
37 Northwestern		0
10 Indiana		0
7 Chicago		28
0 Purdue		0
9 Minnesota		19

1914

37 Christian Bros.		0
51 Indiana		0
37 Ohio State		0
33 Northwestern		0
21 Minnesota		6
21 Chicago		7
24 Wisconsin		9

1915

36 Haskell		0
75 Rolla Mines		7
3 Ohio State		3
36 Northwestern		6
6 Minnesota		6
17 Wisconsin		3
10 Chicago		0

1916

30 Kansas		0
3 Colgate		15
6 Ohio State		7
14 Purdue		7
14 Minnesota		9
7 Chicago		20
0 Wisconsin		0

1917

22 Kansas		0
44 Oklahoma		0
7 Wisconsin		0
27 Purdue		0
0 Chicago		0
0 Ohio State		13
6 Minnesota		27
28 Camp Funston, Kans.		0

1918

3 Chanute Field		0
0 Great Lakes		7
0 Municipal Pier		7
19 Iowa		0
22 Wisconsin		0
13 Ohio State		0
29 Chicago		0

1919

14 Purdue		7
9 Iowa		7
10 Wisconsin		14
10 Chicago		0
10 Minnesota		6
29 Michigan		7
9 Ohio State		7

1920

41 Drake		0
20 Iowa		3
7 Michigan		6
17 Minnesota		7
3 Chicago		0
9 Wisconsin		14
0 Ohio State		7

1921

52 South Dakota		0
2 Iowa		14
0 Wisconsin		20
0 Michigan		3
21 DePauw		0
6 Chicago		14
7 Ohio State		0

1922

7 Butler		10
7 Iowa		8
0 Michigan		24
6 Northwestern		3
3 Wisconsin		0
0 Chicago		9
3 Ohio State		6

1923

24 Nebraska		7
21 Butler		7
9 Iowa		6
29 Northwestern		0
7 Chicago		0
10 Wisconsin		0
27 Miss. A. & M.		0
9 Ohio State		0

1924

7 Nebraska		6
40 Butler		10
39 Michigan		14
45 DePauw		0
36 Iowa		0
21 Chicago		21
7 Minnesota		20
7 Ohio State		0

1925

0 Nebraska		14
16 Butler		13
10 Iowa		12
0 Michigan		3
24 Pennsylvania		2
13 Chicago		6
21 Wabash		0
14 Ohio State		9

1926

27 Coe		0
38 Butler		7
13 Iowa		6
0 Michigan		13
3 Pennsylvania		0
7 Chicago		0
27 Wabash		13
6 Ohio State		7

1927

19 Bradley		0
58 Butler		0
12 Iowa State		12
7 Northwestern		6
14 Michigan		0
14 Iowa		0
15 Chicago		6
13 Ohio State		0

1928

33 Bradley		6
31 Coe		0
13 Indiana		7
6 Northwestern		0

Continued on next page

0	Michigan	3
14	Butler	0
40	Chicago	0
8	Ohio State	0

1929

25	Kansas	0
45	Bradley	0
7	Iowa	7
14	Michigan	0
0	Northwestern	7
17	Army	7
20	Chicago	6
27	Ohio State	0

1930

7	Iowa State	0
27	Butler	0
0	Northwestern	32
7	Michigan	15
0	Purdue	25
0	Army	13
28	Chicago	0
9	Ohio State	12

1931

20	St. Louis	6
0	Purdue	7
20	Bradley	0
0	Michigan	35
6	Northwestern	32
6	Wisconsin	7
6	Chicago	13
0	Ohio State	40

1932

20	Miami (Ohio)	7
13	Coe	0
20	Bradley	0
0	Northwestern	26
0	Michigan	32
13	Chicago	7
12	Wisconsin	20
18	Indiana	6
0	Ohio State	3

1933

13	Drake	6
21	Washington (Mo.)	6
21	Wisconsin	0
0	Army	6
6	Michigan	7
3	Northwestern	0
7	Chicago	0
6	Ohio State	7

1934

40	Bradley	7
12	Washington (Mo.)	7
14	Ohio State	13
7	Michigan	6
7	Army	0
14	Northwestern	3
3	Wisconsin	7
6	Chicago	0

1935

0	Ohio	6
28	Washington (Mo.)	6
19	Southern Cal	0
0	Iowa	19
3	Northwestern	10
3	Michigan	0
0	Ohio State	6
6	Chicago	7

1936

9	De Paul	6
13	Washington (Mo.)	7
6	Southern Cal	24
0	Iowa	0
2	Northwestern	13
9	Michigan	6
0	Ohio State	13
18	Chicago	7

1937

20	Ohio	6
0	De Paul	0
6	Notre Dame	6
6	Indiana	13

6	Michigan	7
6	Northwestern	0
0	Ohio State	19
21	Chicago	0

1938

0	Ohio	6
44	De Paul	7
12	Indiana	2
6	Notre Dame	14
0	Northwestern	13
0	Michigan	14
14	Ohio State	32
34	Chicago	0

1939

0	Bradley	0
0	Southern Cal	26
6	Indiana	7
0	Northwestern	13
16	Michigan	7
7	Wisconsin	0
0	Ohio State	21
46	Chicago	0

1940

31	Bradley	0
7	Southern Cal	13
0	Michigan	28
0	Notre Dame	26
6	Wisconsin	13
14	Northwestern	32
6	Ohio State	14
7	Iowa	18

1941

45	Miami (Ohio)	0
6	Minnesota	34
40	Drake	0
14	Notre Dame	49
0	Michigan	20
0	Iowa	21
7	Ohio State	12
0	Northwestern	27

Appendix II

WHO'S WHO AMONG OTHER COLLEGE COACHES IN THE TWENTIES AND THIRTIES

First of all there are several honorables who deserve a salute but who were not included because most or the most important parts of their coaching careers properly belong before the twenties or in the forties: Enoch Bagshaw, Michael Donahue, Don Faurot, Percy Haughton, John Heisman, Frank Leahy, Jess Neely, Frank O'Neil, Bennie Owen, George Sanford, Clark Shaughnessy, John Wilce, and Henry Williams.

Others, not profiled, are worthy of an honorable mention, at least. So following is a list of those notables and their records, along with alma mater (in parenthesis), colleges, and year of election to the National Football Hall of Fame (if such is the case):

	YEARS	W	L	T	PCT.
CHARLES B. (CHARLIE) MORAN (Tennessee)	18	122	33	12	.766
Texas A. & M. 1909–14					
Centre 1919–23					
Bucknell 1924–26					
Catawba 1930–33					
ELMER C. (GUS) HENDERSON (Oberlin)	20	126	42	7	.740
Southern Cal 1919–24					
Tulsa 1925–35					
Occidental 1940–42					
JOHN J. MCEWAN (Army '17)	10	59	23	6	.705
Army 1923–25					
Oregon 1926–29					
Holy Cross 1930–32					
IKE J. ARMSTRONG (Drake '23)	25	140	55	15	.702
Utah 1925–49					
Hall of Fame 1957					
JESSE B. HAWLEY (Dartmouth '09)	12	63	28	4	.684
Iowa 1910–15					
Dartmouth 1923–28					
WARREN B. WOODSON (Baylor '24)	37	239	110	20	.675
Texarkana 1927–34					
Conway St. 1935–40					
Hardin-Simmons 1941–42, 1946–51					
Arizona 1952–56					
New Mexico St. 1958–67					
CHARLES E. (GUS) DORAIS (Notre Dame '14)	27	149	70	12	.671
Loras 1914–17					
Gonzaga 1920–24					
Detroit 1925–42					
Hall of Fame 1954					

	YEARS	W	L	T	PCT.
CLEO A. O'DONNELL (Holy Cross '08) Purdue 1916-17 Holy Cross 1919-29	13	74	35	7	.668
EDWARD P. (SLIP) MADIGAN (Notre Dame '20) Portland 1920 St. Mary's (Calif.) 1921-39 Iowa 1943-44	22	125	59	14	.667
MYRON E. WITHAM (Dartmouth '04) Purdue 1906 Colorado 1920-31	13	63	31	7	.658
MORLEY JENNINGS (Mississippi St. '12) Ouachita 1912-25 Baylor 1926-40	29	155	77	18	.656
BRANCH BOCOCK (Georgetown '07) Georgia 1908 Virginia Tech 1909-10 North Carolina 1911 Virginia Tech 1912-15 Louisiana St. 1920-21 South Carolina 1925-26 William & Mary 1928-30, 1936-37	17	95	48	9	.655
LAWRENCE T. (BUCK) SHAW (Notre Dame '22) North Carolina St. 1924 Nevada 1926 Santa Clara 1936-42 California 1945 Air Force 1956-57	12	66	33	9	.653
PETE W. CAWTHON (Southwestern [Texas] '18) Austin 1923-27 Texas Tech 1930-40	16	98	51	10	.648
BERNIE H. MOORE (Carson-Newman '17) Mercer 1925-27 Louisiana St. 1935-47 *Hall of Fame 1954*	16	95	51	8	.643
WILLIAM A. (BILL) INGRAM (Navy '19) William & Mary 1922 Indiana 1923-25 Navy 1926-30 California 1931-34	13	75	42	9	.631
ORIN E. (BABE) HOLLINGBERY (no college) Washington St. 1926-42	17	93	53	14	.625
FRANCIS J. (FRANK) MURRAY (Tufts '08) Marquette 1922-36 Virginia 1937-45 Marquette 1946-49	28	145	89	11	.614
WILLIAM H. (LONE STAR) DIETZ (Carlisle) Washington St. 1915-17 Purdue 1921 Louisiana Tech 1922-23 Wyoming 1924-26 Haskell 1929-32 Albright 1937-42	19	97	60	6	.613

	YEARS	W	L	T	PCT.
GLENN F. THISTLETHWAITE (Earlham '09)	24	114	71	14	.608

Earlham 1909-12
Northwestern 1922-26
Wisconsin 1927-31
Carroll (Wis.) 1932-33
Richmond 1934-41

JAMES M. (JIMMY) PHELAN (Notre Dame '19)	28	136	87	14	.603

Missouri 1920-21
Purdue 1922-29
Washington 1930-41
St. Mary's (Calif.) 1942-47

ALBERT A. EXENDINE (Carlisle '08)	20	93	60	15	.598

Otterbein 1909-11
Georgetown 1914-22
Washington St. 1923-25
Occidental 1926-27
Northeastern Oklahoma 1928
Oklahoma St. 1934-35

ANDY GUSTAFSON (Pittsburgh '26)	20	115	78	4	.594

Virginia Tech 1926-29
Miami (Fla.) 1948-63

ALONZO L. (LON) STINER	14	74	49	17	.589

Oregon St. 1933-42, 1945-48

HARRY C. (CURLY) BYRD (Maryland '08)	24	119	82	15	.586

Maryland 1911-34

MAURICE J. (CLIPPER) SMITH (Notre Dame '21)	22	108	76	12	.582

Gonzaga 1925-28
Santa Clara 1929-35
Villanova 1936-42
San Francisco 1946
Lafayette 1949-51

A. EARL (GREASY) NEALE (W. Va. Wesleyan '14)	16	78	55	11	.580

Muskingum 1915
W. Va. Wesleyan 1916-17
Marietta 1919-20
Washington & Jefferson 1921-22
Virginia 1923-28
West Virginia 1931-33
Hall of Fame 1967

HARRY W. HUGHES (Oklahoma '08)	31	125	89	18	.578

Colorado St. 1911-41

ERNEST L. (DICK) ROMNEY (Utah '17)	29	128	92	15	.577

Utah St. 1919-42, 1944-48
Hall of Fame 1954

OSCAR M. (OSSIE) SOLEM (Minnesota '15)	38	162	117	20	.575

Luther 1920
Drake 1921-31
Iowa 1932-36
Syracuse 1937-45
Springfield 1946-57

DOUGLAS C. (PEAHEAD) WALKER (Howard Co. '22)	25	129	94	10	.575

Atlantic Christian 1926
Elon 1927-36
Wake Forest 1937-50

	YEARS	W	L	T	PCT.
HARVEY J. HARMAN (Pittsburgh '22)	30	140	104	7	.572

Haverford 1922-29
Sewanee 1930
Pennsylvania 1931-37
Rutgers 1938-41, 1946-55

HARRY STUHLDREHER (Notre Dame '25)	24	110	87	15	.554

Villanova 1925-35
Wisconsin 1936-48

LEONARD B. (STUB) ALLISON (Carleton '17)	16	79	66	5	.543

Washington 1920
South Dakota 1922-26
California 1935-44

JOHN F. (JACK) MEAGHER (Notre Dame '17)	19	96	83	14	.534

St. Edward's 1924-28
Rice 1929-33
Auburn 1934-42

FRANK M. DOBSON (Princeton)	30	118	117	25	.502

Georgia 1909
Clemson 1910-12
Richmond 1913-17
South Carolina 1918
Richmond 1919-33
Maryland 1935-39

GWINN HENRY (Howard Payne)	21	105	107	8	.495

Howard Payne 1913-14
Emporia St. 1920-22
Missouri 1923-31
New Mexico 1934-36
Kansas 1939-42

INDEX